S0-FJP-808

Confederate States *of* America

Catalog and Handbook
of Stamps and Postal History

---

by
Patricia A. Kaufmann
Francis J. Crown, Jr.
and
Jerry S. Palazolo

Confederate Stamp Alliance, Inc.
www.csalliance.org
2012

DEDICATION

To Erin R. Gunter, Warren H. Sanders and Hubert C. Skinner whose research, studies and publications advanced our knowledge and understanding of Confederate philately.

ISBN 978-0-9818893-1-3
Library of Congress Control Number: 2012917018

Prepared and printed in the United States of America

Table of Contents

Table of Contents by Subject

Preface

August Dietz, Sr. published *The Postal Service of the Confederate States of America* in 1929. This monumental endeavor remains the most definitive work on Confederate Stamps and postal history to this day. This was followed in 1931 with the publication of his first catalog of Confederate stamps (*Dietz Specialized Catalog of the Postage Stamps of the Confederate States of America*). It was augmented with a supplement in 1932 and followed by subsequent editions of the Dietz Catalog in 1937, 1945, 1959 and 1986. In October 2006, the Confederate Stamp Alliance announced acquisition of the rights to *The New Dietz Confederate States Catalog and Handbook*, which was published in 1986. Immediately, work began on a new catalog for the 21st century.

This 21st century catalog takes advantage of all of the advances in technology that have occurred in the past quarter century, including publication in color. It is by no means a simple revision of prior catalogs. Much of the material in this catalog can be found in no other catalog or publication. It is a result of a major effort to build a new catalog from the ground up. A guiding principal of the editors was that items in the new catalog had to be confirmed by an image of the item. Information was derived from original period documents where possible, rather than repeated from the often conflicting statements of prior publications.

The CSA Catalog is the labor of dozens of learned contributors and not just the editorial board who organized and choreographed the submissions, as well as adding a great deal of substantive content. The editorial trio all individually made major contributions to the 1986 edition of the New Dietz Catalog and stress that this type of project cannot be done without the assistance of many. It would likely not exist without the efforts of the section editors and contributors, to whom we are most grateful.

Special recognition is extended to Steven M. Roth who selflessly served as Special Assistant to the Editors. Steve promptly took on virtually whatever project we provided him and his discerning eye often caused us to reconsider specific wording, approach or presentation in some sections.

Extensive input and assistance in their areas of specialty were provided by: John Birkinbine II; Larry Baum; Conrad L. Bush; Deane R. Briggs, MD; Richard L. Calhoun; Tony L. Crumbley; Charles W. Deaton; Donald F. Garrett; Brian M. Green; Louis E. Hannen; Galen D. Harrison; Leonard H. Hartmann; W. Wilson Hulme; Stefan T Jaronski, PhD; William H. Johnston; Earl Kaplan; John L. Kimbrough, MD; Thomas Lera; A. Eugene Lightfoot; Richard F. Murphy; Michael C. O'Reilly; William S. Parks; Peter W. W. Powell; Bruce Roberts, PhD; Steven M. Roth; Harvey S. Teal; Scott R. Trepel; and Steven C. Walske.

We also appreciate the cooperation of the Scott Publishing Company and, in particular, thanks are extended to Editor Jim Kloetzel, a long time CSA member.

Our sincere thanks go to efficient layout artists Anne Read (Cambridge, Massachusetts) and Merritt Engel (Kansas City, Missouri) who worked with us to ensure a cohesive end product. They endured seemingly endless versions of sections as we endeavored to correct content and format problems. Thanks also go to Rich Parsons of Parsons Graphics, Inc. and the Walsworth Print Group, Inc. (Missouri).

We owe a large debt to our spouses, Darryl Boyer, Judy Crown and Sandra Palazolo, who have offered a constant source of encouragement, support and tolerance during the six years while we worked literally thousands of hours on this catalog project, often at serious cost of family time.

The CSA Catalog Editorial Board
Patricia A. Kaufmann, Editor-in-Chief
Francis J. Crown, Jr.
Jerry S. Palazolo

September 2012

Contributors

The following alphabetical list acknowledges the many individuals and organizations who contributed to this catalog in some way, whether large or small. We offer our apologies to any contributors or volunteers whose efforts we may have unintentionally overlooked. Please know that, none the less, we are most appreciative.

Richard Andersen
McCary Ballard
Matthew Bennett International
Bernard Biales
John Birkinbine II
Larry Baum
Buck Boshwit
Ralph F. Brandon, MD
Deane R. Briggs, MD
Harry G. Brittain, PhD
Conrad L. Bush
Richard L. Calhoun
J. Bruce Campbell
James C. Cate
Roland H. Cipolla II
Thomas A. Cox
William T. Crowe
Tony L. Crumbley
William C. Davis
Charles W. Deaton
James P. Doolin
Bill Elliott
Bruce E. Engstler
Wayne Farley
Rex H. Felton
Cheryl R. Ganz, PhD
Donald F. Garrett
Richard B. Graham
Downey M. Gray
Alexander Lee Green
Brian M. Green
Maria P. Green
F. Terry Hambrecht, PhD
Louis E. Hannen
H. R. Harmer, Inc.
Galen D. Harrison
Leonard H. Hartmann
Joseph T. Holleman
Susan T. Hulme
W. Wilson Hulme
Thomas H. Jackson
Stefan T. Jaronski, PhD
William H. Johnston
Edward R. Joyce
Earl Kaplan
Richard Kaplan
John W. Kaufmann, Inc.
Robert J. Karrer
Lincoln F. Kilbourne II
John L. Kimbrough, MD
Vince King
James E. Kloetzel
Van Koppersmith
Andrew Kupersmit
Thomas Lera
A. Eugene Lightfoot
Robert Lisbeth
Menachim Max Mayo
A. Hudson McDonald
James W. Milgram, MD
Howard Mishoulam, MD
Nyle C. Monday
James L. D. Monroe
Richard F. Murphy
Randolph L. Neil
J.V. Nielsen
Sherrell Nunnelley
Anders Olason
Roger H. Oswald
Al Ottens
Michael C. O'Reilly
William S. Parks
Peter W. W. Powell
Joel Rind
Bruce Roberts, PhD
Steven M. Roth
D. Thomas Royster, Jr.
Marie V. Sanders
Scott Publishing Company
Schuyler J. Rumsey Auction Galleries, Inc.
Robert A. Siegel Auction Galleries, Inc.
William A. Shulleeta
Smithsonian National Postal Museum
Harvey S. Teal
James G. Thayer
Renate W. Thayer
Thomas K. Todsen
Scott R. Trepel
Shelby County Archives
Steven C. Walske
C. Scott Ward
Daniel C. Warren, MD
Richard S. Warren
Peter Wiksne
Richard F. Winter
Chris Winters, MD

Introduction

Each revised edition of the Dietz Catalog since its first publication over eighty years ago has seen many new listings. With the 1931 edition, the basic format was set and remained the same through the final 1986 edition. This new catalog takes a different approach, incorporating many of the features of the old Dietz Catalog and adding more. In the process some of the format was retained, but much was changed to increase the coverage contained in individual sections. Finally, an abbreviated subject index was added after the Table of Contents to aid the user.

To accomplish this task, the editors began with the listings contained in the 1986 Dietz Catalog and searched for any new listings. They also mandated that every listing in the new catalog be verified by an image of the item. In cases where no image could be found, the listing was retained as a legacy listing and indicated by an asterisk.

In comparing prior published works and catalogs, one invariably finds conflicting information. One of the most noticeable examples of this is in the section of Independent State and Confederate Use of US Postage. In order to ascertain the actual dates of secession and admission for each state, the editors re-examined the secession and admission processes of each state from original period documents. Where the results are subject to more than one interpretation or vary from previously accepted dates, the editors have set forth their explanation for the change in notes.

One of the new sections in the catalog is Confederate Postage Rates. The rates are detailed in text and tables. This much needed section covers all the rates set by Confederate law. It also includes some of the lesser known rates that were continued in force from US Postal Laws. Explanations are also given for the more confusing and misinterpreted rates.

In past catalogs, the Stampless Markings section was titled "Handstamped Paids" and, more recently, "Handstamped Provisionals and Other Markings." The latter title was somewhat misleading in that it applied the term "provisional" to all handstamped markings. This was counter to the generally accepted meaning of the term. The new title "Stampless Markings" covers those markings applied at the time of mailing to indicate the postage paid or due or other services. Stampless markings include not only those markings used to indicate the prepayment of postage or the amount of postage due but all other markings applied to indicate a type of mail or service. These include free, way, steam, ship, forwarded, missent, and advertised. Every attempt was made to illustrate all individual markings or combinations of markings representing a rate or service. When illustrations were not available, tracings from *The New Dietz Confederate States Catalog and Handbook* were used. In a few cases, no illustration of a marking could be found that was suitable for publication and these are so indicated. The Stampless Markings section is more than twice the size of the previous catalog edition.

One particularly useful tool for the user of this catalog is that Scott Catalogue numbers are listed in parentheses after the *Confederate States of America Catalog* and *Handbook of Stamps and Postal History* (CSA Catalog) numbers in the listings for Postmasters' Provisionals and General Issues. Stated values are CSA Catalog values and not Scott Catalogue values.

The General Issues numbering system used in this catalog is an extension of the Dietz and Scott numbers. The first number is the traditional one. This is followed by letters and numbers to indicate a major variety. These varieties have long been recognized, but were never given a formal designation.

Confederate lithograph student Leonard H. Hartmann has shared his in-depth study of the Misplaced and Shifted Lithograph Transfers in the General Issues section, something found in no other philatelic catalog. A misplaced transfer is an image that is on a printing stone in a position that differs from that on the transfer stone. They were first discovered in the 1920s by Edward S. Knapp and others. The shifted transfers are given catalog status as they are definitely constant varieties; up to six examples of some positions are known.

The new Perforated and Rouletted Stamps section was created from the files of the late Wilson Hulme, which the family graciously allowed us to use. This little understood area is now presented with detailed explanations of the officially perforated stamps as well as the accepted privately rouletted stamps.

The Postmasters' Provisionals section is far more detailed than in prior editions, over four times the size of the last edition, and includes information such as the earliest recorded dates of use and uses from other towns.

The government imprint section has been completely revamped with a new intuitive numbering system and separated into three sections: Official, Semi-Official and State Government. Although most Confederate semi-official imprints include the branch of government, it is not always easy to determine to which Department they belong. This is further confused by state semi-official imprints prepared by branches of state governments that mirrored the same branches of the Confederate Government. Some of these imprints bear no indication of either Confederate or state origin. The editors have made every effort to list the semi-official imprints under the proper department, bureau, service, district, division or army of the Confederate and state governments.

New catalog sections include Confederate Mail Carrier Services, Way Mail, Indian Nations, Covert Mail, Generals' Mail, a guide to Advertising Covers and a Glossary. Other sections, while presented in brief in former catalogs, have been expanded to such a degree that they can almost be considered new sections as well. For example, the Confederate Railroad Markings section, which fully explains the role of railroads in handling the mails, the role of the station agent and the route agent's markings, as well as the revised listings themselves.

Completely new revelations are offered regarding the Arizona Territory and the proper designation of New Mexico therein.

There are two recognized types of flag of truce mail: prisoner of war and civilian. These are presented together in the section entitled Flag of Truce Mail and Censor Markings. Major exchange points are detailed and listings are offered for mail with manuscript and handstamped censor markings, as well as Parole Camp Mail and Civilian Flag of Truce. Lists of prisons with mail recorded to or from prisoners are presented for Confederate prisons, Union prisons, Federal parole camps and temporary sites.

Private Express Company Mail is divided into two different categories: private across the lines express service and mail handled by express companies within the Confederate States. Suspension of Mail across the Lines includes some of the rarest and least understood mail as postal service in the seceded states was interrupted by the US Post Office Department. Trans-Mississippi Mails presents both official and private mail services, some of which are completely new listings such as Captain Bernos' Express, J.M. Barksdale's Express, E.W. Black's Express, and I.W. Sturdivant's Express, which join the more well-known listings of Arthur H. Edey's 5th Texas Regiment Express and E.H. Cushing's Express. Considerable additional information on these topics may be found in *Special Mail Routes of the American Civil War: A Guide to Across-the-Lines Postal History* by Steven C. Walske and Scott R. Trepel, published by the Confederate Stamp Alliance.

The Fakes and Facsimiles section has been completely redone to include examples most commonly encountered by collectors, along with brief biographies of those who produced them. The Confederate Stamp Alliance anticipates publishing a more in-depth book on this subject in the near future.

Scientific Testing and the Future of Confederate Philately

For decades visual characteristics such as the detail in the design, color of the ink, color of the paper, and the gum have been used to identify a steel plate 10¢ Archer & Daly print from a Keatinge & Ball print. In the several years this catalog has been in preparation, the reliability of these visual characteristics has come into question.

The problem first came to light when some imprint blocks or strips showed visual characteristics contrary to those associated with the printer. Stamps in blocks and strips with Archer & Daly imprints were a dark blue color with poor detail in the design, which are classic characteristics of Keatinge & Ball printings. Stamps with Keatinge & Ball imprints were a light blue color with excellent detail, classic characteristics of Archer & Daly printings.

Visual characteristics may soon be replaced by scientific tests using X-ray powder diffraction and infrared spectroscopy. These non-destructive tests penetrate the surface layers that provide the visual characteristics, and provide information regarding the subsurface layers that retain the original chemical characteristics of the ink and paper. Preliminary tests have revealed differences in both the ink and the paper used by Archer & Daly and Keatinge & Ball. At the moment, these are preliminary test results, and much more testing must be conducted before conclusive results are available.

The example given above details how scientific testing can impact the way we identify steel plate Archer & Daly and Keatinge & Ball printings. It can also change the way we identify London from Richmond printings of the 5¢ typographed issue. Users should be aware that the advances in scientific testing may materially change the way these and other stamps are identified in the future.

Whether the conclusions drawn from this sort of scientific testing will be practical for use by the average collector, dealer or even authentication groups, remains to be seen. The equipment is exceptionally expensive and specialized scientific knowledge is needed to interpret the findings.

The treatment of the 10¢ steel plate stamps in this catalog is based on the traditional visual characteristics.

Diamond Anniversary Campaign Donors

This catalog was made possible through donations to the Diamond Anniversary Campaign of the Confederate Stamp Alliance, Inc. The following donors are recognized for their contributions.

Platinum Underwriter
Philip V. Warman

Gold Underwriter
Edward B. Cantey

Vermeil Underwriter
Deane R. Briggs, MD
Tony L. Crumbley
Rex H. Felton
Robert L. Frailey
Alexander Hall
John L. Kimbrough, MD
James L. D. Monroe
Stanley M. Piller
Peter and Ethel Powell
Donald A. Robbins
James F. Taff
Scott R. Trepel
Steven C. Walske

Silver Underwriter
Harry L. Albert, Jr.
Maurice M. Bursey
Richard L. Calhoun
Francis J. Crown, Jr.
Wolfgang Jakubek
Patricia A. Kaufmann
Lincoln F. Kilbourne II
Van Koppersmith
Donald P. Lade, PhD
James E. Lee
Lewis Leigh, Jr.
A. Thomas Mickler
Jack E. Molesworth
Randy L. Neil
Sherrell Nunnelley
Michael C. O'Reilly
Jerry S. Palazolo
Peter A. Robertson
D. Thomas Royster, Jr.
Schuyler J. Rumsey
Christopher Rupp
Betty R. Scott
Randolph Smith
Donald Sundman
Michael L. Talton
Richard S. Warren

Benefactor
Albert N. Balzano
Charles F. Batchelder, III
Larry Baum
Robert W. Bauswell
James Bennitt
Robert J. Bourque
Ralph F. Brandon, MD
Conrad L. Bush
Richard H. Byne
J. Bruce Campbell
Patrick Campbell
David Canestro
Anthony G. Chila
John L. Church
Roland H. Cipolla
Richard M. Clack
Charles V. Covell, PhD
Thomas A. Cox
W. Newton Crouch, Jr.
William T. Crowe
Michael Daley
Joseph S. Dossen
T. J. Emison, Jr.
Wayne Farley
Michael D. Feinstein
Steve Feller
Gerald J. Gallagher
James M. Gobberdiel
Downey M. Gray III
F. Terry Hambrecht, MD
Louis E. Hannen
Charles F. Hanselmann
Michael P. Hardy
Richard E. Heiser
Ronnie Hicks
Edward R. Joyce
Robert G. W. Kappel
Robert J. Karrer, Jr.
Harold Katz
Michael A. Kent
Charles E. Kilbourne, III
Vince King
Thomas A. Lee
Thomas M. Lera
Duke R. Ligon
George Linardos
Corey B. Long
Bernard F. Losekamp
Thomas A. Lucid
A. Hudson McDonald
Stephen James McGrath
David McNamee
Howard Mishoulam, MD
James E. Montich
Harry Muldrow, Jr.
Richard F. Murphy
Thomas R. Nealeigh, MD
Richard A. Nowak
Roger H. Oswald
Fields Luther Parks, III
Ronald Lee Perdue
Earl T. Reeder
Michael Rice
James H. Richards
Thomas J. Richards
David Ridiman
Bruce Roberts, PhD
Lee J. Romanczyk
Thomas P. Ross
Gary M. Roush
Richard M. Rutter, Jr.
Kenneth Schopp
William A. Shulleeta
Thomas H. Smith
Henry C. Spalding, Jr.
Frank J. Stanley, III
Clive Stevens
James Stillman
Richard C. Stone, Jr.
James R. Stultz
Ralph Swap
Harvey S. Teal
James G. Thayer
Renate W. Thayer
Carl W. Thorsell, Jr.
Donald Tocher
Chester M. Tyminski
Duane P. Ulrich
John H. Walker
C. Scott Ward
Philip V. Warman, III
S. R. Whitehead
Peter Wiksne
Samuel H. Williams, Jr.
Richard F. Winter
Benjamin P. Wishnietsky
Lee Ann Wrisley

Sponsor
McCary Ballard
W. Bryson Bateman, Jr.
William J. Benjamin, Jr.
Richard A. Champagne
Charles W. Deaton
Harry G. Dow
Norman G. Gibson
Samuel D. Hatcher
Richard J. Hosking
Alfred S. Lippman
Robert G. Metcalf
Joe W. Overstreet
Arnold Selengut
Harton S. Semple, Jr.
James Shearon
Rev. Paul Sparling
Ian Tickell

Contributor
Paul M. Benson, MD
James B. Black
Steven Boyd
James G. Boyles
Robert A. Brown
David H. Cason
Raymond L. Chaon
David C. Collyer
William C. Davis
Dr. Mitchell C. Feinman
Tom E. Goodwin
Christian S. Knaur
H. Nellis Kraft, II
Kenneth M. Lemley
Gerald W. Lueckfeld
Garland E. Martin
George W. O'Kelley
S. Lee Pake
T. H. Pearce
Wallace L. Rueckel
Michael B. Sanford
Eugene Setwyn
David Swann
Jack Thomson
Richard B. Walsh, Jr.
William R. Welch
Arleigh R. Williams
Ryan Lee Williams
Reginald R. Wright

The CSA was formed in 1935 for the study of Confederate stamps and postal history, the exchange of relevant data, and dissemination of acquired knowledge. The founding principles of fraternity, research and cooperation are hallmarks of the society to this day. The CSA is open to anyone interested in membership. See the Alliance website at www.csalliance.org for details and application.

Condition Statement

General Considerations

Confederate stamps and many covers were produced under wartime conditions. The ravages of war; the limited availability of quality ink, paper, gum; and the Southern climate adversely affected the condition of much of the Confederate material extant today.

Condition and Evaluation of Stamps

Condition is a major consideration in valuing any stamp, provisional or general issue. An item in average condition may be valued at a fraction of the same item in very fine condition. Repaired stamps and those with creases, tears, stains, or missing parts are considerably less desirable.

Provisional stamps vary widely in condition. Many times the normal condition standards are irrelevant due to the scarcity and demand for issues from some towns. The more common examples are priced for stamps in very fine condition without gum. Scarcer issues are priced according to the condition of known examples

Gum is a very controversial subject. Some collectors put a high value on a stamp with original gum and a lower value for a stamp with original gum that has been hinged. For the lithographed general issues, the prices for unused stamps in this catalog are for examples in very fine condition without gum. Unused examples of the scarcer engraved issues, the T-E-N and the Frame Line, are also priced without gum. Prices for all the other general issues are for stamps with original gum. Stamps with original gum that show problems such as brown spots, paper cracks caused by gum, or other evidence of deterioration or interaction with the paper, are considered average to defective. For preservation, in recent years gum has been deliberately removed from many scarce to rare stamps.

Stamp colors can exhibit a wide range of shades due to the lack of consistent supplies of pigment and the daily hand mixing of inks. Major color variations are listed, but other shades exist for most issues.

Pricing

Prices in this catalog are for stamps in very fine condition. Superb examples sell for more. Those in less than very fine condition sell for less. Defective stamps sell for significantly less.

Condition

Superb: a very fine stamp with one or more special attributes such as an excellent color, wide margins, fresh paper or a clear and attractive cancellation.

Very Fine: a stamp without defects: no tears, creases or stains; no repairs; margins well clear of the design on all sides; and fresh color and paper. If used, it has a clear cancellation.

Fine: a stamp having an acceptable appearance, but may have light creases, narrow margins, or a shallow thin.

Average: a stamp that has several defects such as creases, cut into design, poor color, tears, stains, or dirty appearance.

Defective: a stamp with a bad crease, large tear, bad stain, extremely heavy cancellation or missing portions of the design.

Condition and Evaluation of Covers

It is extremely difficult to assign a specific catalog value to Confederate covers of any type because many represent unusual or unique uses or exhibit a balance between a superb envelope and an average stamp or marking. Other factors such as the town cancellation, the clarity of the markings, the address, rate, or historic connections can have significant impact on the desirability and price of a specific cover. A pen cancel is less valuable off cover because there is no indication of the town of origin, while manuscript cancels on cover from seldom-seen small towns often demand a premium. The current popularity of a given stamp, usage, state or town can influence market value.

Valuing covers is a very complex. Some special uses, such as patriotic covers or illustrated covers, are valued with the most commonly found franking, but no catalog can completely cover all variations. Legal and oversize covers generally sell for less. For historic use, rare towns, etc., the valuation is at the discretion of the buyer.

The absence of a listing for a specific marking or type of cover in this catalog does not imply unusual scarcity or high value.

Pricing

Prices in this catalog are for covers in very fine condition with the normal usage listed. Superb examples sell for more. Those in less than very fine condition sell for less. Defective covers sell for significantly less.

Condition

Superb: a cover that is fresh and complete with no defects. Any stamps must be in at least very fine condition, and postal markings and address must be clear and distinct.

Very Fine: a cover that is fresh. Any stamps must be in at least fine condition, and postal markings must be clear. The cover may have a closed tear that is not readily visible or a small replacement not affecting the stamp, markings or address. Most of the cover back must be present.

Fine: a cover that is not fresh, but presentable. Any stamp must be in at least average condition. The cover may have a visible closed tear and the postal markings and address may be indistinct. Portions of the envelope may be missing or replaced.

Defective: a cover not meeting the aforementioned criteria with major discoloration, tears and missing portions, a badly defective stamp, illegible markings or portions of the envelope missing or replaced.

Restoration, Repairs and Alteration

Stamps and covers have been repaired for over a century and it is an accepted practice when properly done. A cover restored in an archival manner such as to lightly clean, deacidify and remove stains or toning is acceptable.

It is fraud to change the nature of an item. The intent of such action is to deceive, but even if not, it is unacceptable. Examples of fraudulent practices include turning an unused patriotic into a used one, adding stamps or markings, changing an address to create a rare or unusual item, and replacing stamps with better copies. Such altered items have only a reference value.

Abbreviations and Symbols Key

[*]	symbol used after an item description to mean an unsupported listing
[–]	symbol used in place of value to mean insufficient information to assign a price
[?]	symbol used to mean unknown measurement, date or color
[italic]	value typeface indicating the item is difficult to price accurately
A&D	Archer & Daly
C	circle
CDS	circular date stamp
CS	Confederate States
CSA	Confederate States of America
DC	double circle
DLC	double [outer] line circle
DLO	Dead Letter Office
FL	folded letter
hsp	handstamp(ed)
H&L	Hoyer & Ludwig
IH	used in place of listing value when the item is held by an institution
K&B	Keatinge & Ball
mkg	marking
ms	manuscript
NA	used in place of a listing value when no examples are known to exist
NOR	no outer rim
NR	used in place of value when no examples have been recorded
OG	original gum
OV	oval
pk	cover bearing a postmark but no indication of rate
pl	plate
pmk	postmark
POD	Post Office Department
pos	position
SC	segmented circle
SFL	stampless folded letter
SL	straightline
US	United States
YD	year date

Independent State and Confederate Use of US Postage

The date traditionally accepted in both philatelic and academic circles as the founding date of the Confederate States of America is February 4, 1861. This is one of many significant dates in the founding of the Confederacy. The process began with South Carolina's secession on December 20, 1860, and proceeded step-by-step through February 8 when the assembly of delegates from the six seceded states approved a Provisional Constitution.

Beginning on February 4, 1861 and continuing through March 11, 1861, the founding delegates, among other matters, adopted a Provisional Constitution, elected a provisional President and Vice President, created a Post Office Department, confirmed John H. Reagan as the Postmaster General, and adopted a Permanent Constitution.

The principal dates in the formation of the Confederate States and the creation of its Post Office Department were:

December 20, 1860 South Carolina secedes.

February 4, 1861 Delegates from the six seceded states assemble and declare themselves a Provisional Congress in Montgomery, Alabama and present credentials pursuant to state secession ordinances or resolutions.

February 8, 1861 Confederate States of America formally established when Delegates sign the Provisional Constitution.

February 9, 1861 Jefferson Davis and Alexander H. Stephens elected provisional President and Vice President, respectively.

Committee appointed to draft a permanent constitution and to present the document to Congress.

Congress adopts all laws of the United States that were in effect on November 1, 1860, provided such laws do not conflict with the Provisional Constitution of the Confederate States.

February 20, 1861 Congress creates the Confederate Post Office Department as part of the Executive Department and creates the office of Postmaster General.

March 6, 1861 John H. Reagan confirmed as Postmaster General.

March 11, 1861 Congress adopts Permanent Constitution.

Congress votes to constitute itself as a permanent Congress under the Permanent Constitution.

Secession from the United States and Admission to the Confederate States

The first step required for the creation of the Confederate States of America was the secession of states from the United States, followed by the coming together of the then independent and sovereign seceded states to form a new government on February 4, 1861. This process began with South Carolina's secession in December 1860. It initially ended on February 8 with the formal adoption of a provisional constitution by the first six states to secede (Alabama, Florida, Georgia, Louisiana, Mississippi, and South Carolina). Four other states (Arkansas, North Carolina, Texas, and Virginia) were admitted prior to June 1, 1861.

In 1860, there was no precedent in United States history or jurisprudence to guide a state if it wanted to secede from the Union. Consequently, each state and territory which eventually comprised the Confederate States of America [CSA] created its own procedures to bring about secession from the United States and to effectuate its application for admission into the CSA. Nevertheless, the several processes fashioned among the states were remarkably similar in concept: the legislature would enact an ordinance decreeing or authorizing secession; that ordinance might or might not refer the matter to the state's voting citizens for approval; and, the matter might or might not be presented to the governor for his approval.

Beyond these familiar legislative steps, the states moved in uncharted waters. Because the process of secession was novel and often fueled by political and emotional catalysts, not all states adhered to their own legally mandated prerequisites to achieve secession: some states strictly followed their own procedures; some states skipped one or more prescribed steps; and, some states followed the required steps, but not in the stated order. In the end, however, each state implicitly concluded that it had sufficiently complied with its own legal requirements to have achieved secession.

In order to ascertain the actual dates of secession and admission for each state, the editors re-examined the secession and admission processes of each state. The results are listed below. Where the results are subject to more than one interpretation or vary from previously accepted dates, the editors have set forth their explanation for the change in the notes.

State or Territory	Date of Secession	Date of Admission
Alabama	January 11, 1861	February 4, 1861
Arizona Territory	March 16, 1861[1]	February 14, 1862
Arkansas	May 6, 1861	May 18, 1861
Florida	January 11, 1861[2]	February 4, 1861
Georgia	January 19, 1861	February 4, 1861
Indian Nations	Not Applicable[3]	March 15, 1861[4]
Kentucky	November 20, 1861[5]	December 10, 1862
Louisiana	January 26, 1861	February 4, 1861
Mississippi	January 9, 1861	February 4, 1861
Missouri	October 31, 1861[6]	November 28, 1861
New Mexico Territory	NA[7]	NA
North Carolina	May 20, 1861[8]	May 27, 1861
South Carolina	December 20, 1860	February 4, 1861
Tennessee	June 8, 1861[9]	July 2, 1861[10]
Texas	March 2, 1861[11]	March 5, 1861[12]
Virginia	April 17, 1861[13]	May 7, 1861

[1]**Arizona Territory**. The Mesilla convention voted secession by ordinance adopted on March 16, 1861 [Mesilla Ordinance]. This affected the area east of 109 degrees west longitude. On March 23, pursuant to the seventh resolution of the Mesilla Ordinance (which invited the citizens in the western part of Arizona to join in secession), a convention was held at Tucson which adopted the Mesilla proceedings with respect to the area west of 109 degrees west longitude. The March 23 action, as a ratification action which did not itself specify an effective date, automatically, as a matter of statutory construction, related back to the Mesilla Ordinance, and therefore was effective as of March 16, 1861. Both actions [March 16 and March 23] were subsequently ratified by popular vote held April 8, 1861, but since this referendum was not required by the secession statutes, it was not necessary and therefore had no legal effect on the date of secession. Lt. General John Robert Baylor declared Arizona a Confederate Territory on August 1, 1861. This declaration, too, had no legal effect. On January 13, 1862, the Provisional Confederate Congress passed legislation recognizing Arizona Territory. President Davis approved this legislation on February 14.

[2] **Florida**. The Florida secession process was a three step procedure under its 1838 Constitution (which remained in effect until the adoption of Florida's 1861 Constitution after secession). The process was: (1) passage of an ordinance of secession by the legislature; (2) presentation of the ordinance to the governor for approval; and, (3) approval of the ordinance by the governor. No signatures by legislators were required.

The governor could indicate his approval by signing the bill within five days of receiving it or by doing nothing for five days. In the latter instance, the bill would be deemed approved at the end of five days (Sunday excepted) and would relate back to the date the legislature presented the ordinance to the governor for approval [Florida Constitution 1838, Sections 116 and 117]. The Florida secession chronology was as follows: January 10, 1861 – legislature passed a secession ordinance; January 11, 1861 – ordinance presented to the governor for approval; January 16, 1861 – five days passed. (There is no record whether governor approved the ordinance on or before the expiration of five days or if he allowed to approval to occur by not acting). Under the terms of statutory construction described in Note 1, the expiration of the period for the governor to approve or disapprove the statute [January 16], related back to January 11 when he failed to act or, if he approved the statute, when he so approved it.

[3] **Indian Nations**. The Indian Nations, comprised of five sovereign nations [Cherokee, Chickasaw, Choctaw, Creek and Seminole], was not part of the United States. Therefore, it did not have to secede (and could not have seceded) from the United States. The Indian Nations could, however, affiliate with or become a part of the CSA in some capacity acceptable to it and to the CSA. This it did informally when it sent to the CSA Messrs. Elias Cornelius Boudinot [Cherokee], Robert McDonald Jones [Choctaw] and Samuel Benton Callahan [Creek & Seminole] as the Territorial Representatives of the Indian Nations. The tribes also entered into agreements with the CSA. These agreements were: (1) Articles of Confederation, dated July 1, 1861, among the Creek and Muscogee, Seminoles, Choctaws, Chickasaws and the CSA; (2) Declaration of Causes, dated October 28, 1861, between the Cherokee Nation and the CSA; and, (3) Resolutions of the Choctaw Nation, dated February 7, 1861.

[4] **Indian Nations**. On March 16, 1861, The Provisional Congress of the CSA reported that the President, the day before, had signed the Act to Establish a Bureau of Indian Affairs, which Act had previously been enacted by Congress. [*Jour-*

nal of the Congress of the Confederate States of America, Vol. 1, Senate, page 151, March 16, 1861]. This action by the president was tantamount to recognition that each of the nations comprising the Indian Nations had adopted a resolution pursuant to which it both loosely affiliated itself with the CSA and also expressed its wish to be more formally affiliated with the CSA.

[5] **Kentucky**. The effective date of secession, taken from the secession statute, is November 20, 1861. The secession session of the legislature likely started on November 18, and continued to November 20 when the secession statute, by its terms, became effective.

[6] **Missouri**. Ordinance of Secession passed by the Senate on October 28, 1861. Passed by the House on October 30, 1861. Signed into law by Governor Claiborne Fox Jackson on October 31, 1861.

[7] **New Mexico Territory**. New Mexico never seceded from the United States and never entered the CSA either as a territory or as a state.

[8] **North Carolina**. It has been argued that the legislature, which met late in the day on May 20, 1861, continued its meeting late enough into the night so that the secession ordinance actually passed in the early morning hours of May 21. It is clear, however, that the State of North Carolina treats May 20, 1861 as the official date of secession, and has so indicated on its state flag. Furthermore, the Ordinance of Secession dates itself as May 20, 1861 so that the editors believe this is the correct date regardless of whatever else might have occurred in the early morning hours of May 21.

[9] **North Carolina**. Dietz took the position that North Carolina's admission to the CSA occurred on the same day as the secession ordinance [i.e., May 20]. Dietz, A., *The Postal Service of the Confederate States of America* (1929), p. 34. It is clear, however, that North Carolina was admitted to the CSA on May 27, based on the following chronology: Secession ordinance passed on May 20, 1861; On May 27, the CSA Secretary of State [R. Toombs] sent a letter to Welden N. Edwards, the President of the secession convention, expressing his and President Jefferson Davis' pleasure with North Carolina's actions and conveying Davis' Executive Proclamation, dated May 27, 1861, accepting North Carolina as a state in the CSA. So while North Carolina might have expressed a desire on May 20 to be admitted to the CSA, the act of admission occurred on May 27.

[10] **Tennessee**. The legislature passed the Ordinance of Secession on May 6, 1861. The Ordinance required that the question thereafter be submitted to a popular referendum. This occurred on June 8, 1861, when the Ordinance was approved by a vote of 104,913 to 47, 238. All actions (other than the mandated referendum) related to secession after the passage of the Ordinance (such as the governor issuing his freedom proclamation on May 24) were superfluous and had no legal effect.

[11] **Texas**. The secession convention convened on January 28, 1861. The Ordinance of Secession passed at the Convention on February 1, 1861, by a vote of 166 to 8. Under Section 2 of the Ordinance, the issue had to be put to a popular referendum to be held on February 23. Under the terms of Section 2, if the popular referendum approved the Ordinance, it became effective on March 2, 1861, the date stipulated in the Ordinance. The referendum approved the Ordinance by a vote of 46,153 to 14,747. No further action to approve or to render the Ordinance effective was required.

[12] **Texas**. On March 2, 1861, the Provisional Congress of the CSA enacted a statute to admit Texas into the CSA. [Chapter XXIV "An Act to Admit Texas as a Member of the Confederate States of America]. By its terms, this Act was effective March 2, 1861. On March 5, 1861, the Texas Convention accepted the CSA invitation to join [Section 5 — An Ordinance in Relation to a Union of the State of Texas with the Confederate States of America]. The secession ordinance and the admission ordinance are silent as to whether formal acceptance by the Texas convention was required.

[13] **Virginia**. The commonwealth's procedure for seceding from the United States required that an ordinance of secession be passed by the legislature; that the ordinance then be ratified by popular vote; and expressly provided that upon ratification, secession would be deemed to have occurred as of the date the legislature passed the ordinance. Under this process, the following occurred: April 17, 1861: Ordinance of Secession passed by the legislature; May 7, 1861: Virginia accepted as a state into the CSA; and, May 23, 1861: popular referendum held throughout state; secession approved by referendum. Under the terms of the Ordinance of Secession, the date of secession related back to the date the ordinance passed [April 17].

The Establishment of the Confederate Post Office Department

The Confederate Post Office Department evolved from laws, regulations, practices and procedures, bookkeeping and accounting systems, and official forms that had existed and been used by the United States Post Office Department prior to the creation of the Confederacy.

Until June 1, 1861, when the Confederate Post Office Department took control of its own postal operations, the US Post Office Department provided postal services in the seceded states and, thereafter, the Confederate States. In doing so, US Postmaster General Blair imposed one condition on approximately 1,200 postmasters in the seceded states. These postmasters were required to agree, in writing, to be personally responsible for all stamps and stamped envelopes shipped to them. Adding to the turmoil in the spring of 1861 shortfalls in the appropriations from the previous year resulted in payments to many mail contractors in the South being six months behind. The resulting demoralization among contractors also spread among postmasters who could no longer depend on regular mail deliveries.

Finally, on May 13, 1861, Postmaster General Reagan issued a proclamation announcing 1 June as the date the Confederate Post Office Department would take over all postal operations in the Confederate States. He requested all postmasters remain in their positions and report their names and the name of their office to Richmond so new commissions could be issued. He also urged all postmasters to settle their financial accounts with Washington.

Continued US Postal Operations in the Confederate States. PMG Blair continued the services of the US Post Office Department in the seceded states and the Confederacy until May 31, 1861. By doing so, the United States Government hoped to entice the seceded states back into the Union by demonstrating good will and at the same time protect the interests of northern businesses owed money by southern customers.

Confederacy Allowed US Postal Operations within Its Territory. When the Provisional Congress authorized the creation of the Confederate Post Office Department, the administrative apparatus to independently perform postal services was not yet in place. It would take Postmaster General Reagan almost three months before he felt ready to take control of postal operations. In order to avoid the suspension of mail service in the Confederacy, and to maintain public confidence in the new government, Reagan cooperated with the US Post Office Department and encouraged its operations in the South while he implemented a new postal system.

The Independent Statehood Period and the Confederate States Period

The period during which United States stamps were lawfully used in the seceded states is divided into two periods: The Independent Statehood period (except in the case of Tennessee, as described below) ran from the date the state seceded through the day before it joined the Confederacy and the Confederate States period commenced the day the state joined the Confederacy and ran through May 31, 1861. To determine the date ranges of each period by state, refer to the Table of Dates of Secession from the United States and Admission to the Confederate States of America.

The Anomalous Circumstances of Tennessee. During the period preceding Tennessee's admission to the Confederacy, postal operations in Tennessee, especially in the eastern part of the state, were complex and confused. They reflected an erratic blend of US and Confederate postal services, and, occasionally, an attempt to amalgamate both.

Postmaster General Blair's May 27, 1861 order suspending Federal mail service beginning May 31 in the ten states then part of the Confederacy did not apply to Tennessee which, as of June 1, had not yet passed an ordinance of secession. The process of secession was finalized on June 8 with a referendum approving Tennessee's ordinance of secession.

On June 10, Blair responded to Tennessee's secession by formally suspending US mail operations in Middle and Western Tennessee which were strongly sympathetic to secession. Blair's order excepted Eastern Tennessee which opposed secession. On June 17, a notice appeared in Memphis newspapers stating that the Confederacy had taken control of the mails in Tennessee. Tennessee officially became part of the Confederacy on July 2.

During the period beginning when the Confederacy took over its own postal operations (June 1) and the date Tennessee formally entered the Confederacy (July 2), the mail situation in the state was very confused and, sometimes deliberately in violation of official regulations. This situation is illustrated by covers that demonstrate the puzzling and often contradictory situation existing in all parts of the state. There are covers which show: (1) United States postal rates paid with US stamps; (2) Confederate postal rates paid in cash or by postmaster's provisional stamps; (3) both US stamps and Confederate postage on the same cover; and (4) a choice of using either US or Confederate postage, determined not by the nature of the originating Tennessee post office, but by the destination of the cover.

The Use of United States Stamps and Stamped Envelopes after Secession

US postal rates and the use of US postage stamps continued in the Independent, Seceded and Confederate States until June 1, 1861. On this date, the Confederate Post Office Department took over its own operations and US stamps were no longer valid for postage in the Confederacy.

The listings for Independent State Use and Confederate Use of US postage are keyed to the legal status of states on the dates listed in the table above. The editors recognize that these dates may not coincide with all collectors' interests, particularly those who collect Florida and Texas. The detailed references for each state provide other dates that may be of interest to collectors of Confederate material before June 1, 1861.

Evaluation of Covers

Valuing covers in this section is complex. Uses on the date of secession from the United States and the date of admission to the Confederate States, as well as other key historical dates, greatly affect prices. Unusual and scarce frankings of US stamps are important pricing factors. This is especially true of covers addressed to foreign destinations. In all instances, valuations are for the most common type of US stamp or envelope for the issue. Scarcer varieties of the issue command a premium. The absence of a listing for a specific town or franking in this section does not imply unusual scarcity or high value.

Alabama

On December 6, 1860, Alabama Governor Andrew Barry Moore called for the election of delegates to a Secession Convention. On December 24, there was an election of delegates. The Secession Convention convened in Montgomery on January 7, 1861 and an Ordinance of Secession was adopted on January 11. Alabama was admitted to the Confederacy on February 4.

Independent State Use of US Postage
(January 11 through February 3, 1861)

Stamps and Stamped Envelopes

Abbeville	
3¢ 1860-61 envelope	500.
Athens	
3¢ 1857-60 stamp	500.
Autaugaville	
3¢ 1860-61 envelope	500.
Bellefonte	
3¢ 1853-55 envelope	500.
Chulafinnee	
3¢ 1860-61 envelope	500.
Columbiana	
3¢ 1860-61 envelope	500.
Fairfield	
3¢ 1857-60 stamp	500.
Greenville	
3¢ 1860-61 envelope	550.
Grove Hill	
3¢ 1860-61 envelope	500.
Huntsville	
3¢ 1860-61 envelope	500.
Kingston	
3¢ 1860-61 envelope	500.
Livingston	
3¢ 1860-61 envelope	500.
Maysville	
3¢ 1860-61 envelope	500.
Mobile	
1¢ 1857-60 stamp	750.
Same, strip of 3	500.
Same, with STEAMBOAT (hdsp)	1,500.
3¢ 1857-60 stamp	400.
3¢ 1853-55 envelope	400.
3¢ 1860-61 envelope	400.
Montevallo	
3¢ 1860-61 envelope	500.
Montgomery	
1¢ 1857-60 stamp	750.
Same, strip of 3	500.
3¢ 1857-60 stamp	400.
3¢ 1853-55 envelope	400.
3¢ 1860-61 envelope	400.
Prattville	
3¢ 1860-61 envelope	500.
Selma	
3¢ 1853-55 envelope	500.
Stows Ferry	
3¢ 1860-61 envelope	500.
Talladega	
12¢ 1857-60 stamp	1,500.
Tuscaloosa	
3¢ 1857-60 stamp	500.
12¢ 1857-60 stamp	1,500.
3¢ 1860-61 envelope	500.
Tuscumbia	
3¢ 1860-61 envelope	500.
Uniontown	
3¢ 1860-61 envelope	500.
Wetumpka	
3¢ 1857-60 stamp	500.
Same, with "Registered" (ms)	750.

Stampless Markings

MOBILE / Ala. (30; 1861; black)	
MOBILE / ALA (26 DC; 1861; black)	
30 [foreign destination]	1,500.
STEAMBOAT	1,000.
MONTGOMERY / Ala. (32 YD; 1861; black)	
STEAMBOAT with 6 (box)	1,500.
Wind Creek (ms; 1861; black)	
Ms Paid 3	500.

Confederate State Use of US Postage
(February 4 through May 31, 1861)

Stamps and Stamped Envelopes

Abbeville	
3¢ 1857-60 stamp	300.
Ala & Tenn River RR	
3¢ 1860-61 envelope	1500.
Argus	
3¢ 1857-60 stamp	350.
Arkadelphia	
3¢ 1860-61 envelope	350.
Athens	
3¢ 1860-61 envelope	300.
Autaugaville	
3¢ 1860-61 envelope	300.
Bowden	
3¢ 1857-60 stamp	350.
3¢ 1860-61 envelope	350.
Brooklyn	
3¢ 1860-61 envelope	350.
Burnsville	
3¢ 1860-61 envelope	300.
Cahaba	
3¢ 1860-61 envelope	300.
Calhoun	
3¢ 1853-55 envelope	300.
Central Institute	
3¢ 1860-61 envelope	750.
Columbia	
3¢ 1860-61 envelope	300.
Courtland	
3¢ 1860-61 envelope	300.
Decatur	
3¢ 1857-60 stamp	300.
3¢ 1860-61 envelope	300.

Florence
3¢ 1857-60 stamp 300.
Gainsville
1¢ 1857-60 stamp 600.
3¢ 1857-60 stamp 300.
3¢ 1860-61 envelope 300.
Greensborough
3¢ 1857-60 stamp 300.
3¢ 1853-55 envelope 300.
3¢ 1860-61 envelope 300.
Greenville
3¢ 1860-61 envelope 300.
Grove Hill
3¢ 1857-60 stamp 300.
3¢ 1860-61 envelope 300.
Hamburgh
3¢ 1860-61 envelope 350.
Hayneville
3¢ 1857-60 stamp 300.
3¢ 1860-61 envelope 300.
Huntsville
1¢ 1857-60 stamp 600.
3¢ 1857-60 stamp 250.
3¢ 1853-55 envelope 250.
3¢ 1860-61 envelope 250.
Jacksonville
3¢ 1860-61 envelope 300.
Larkinsville
3¢ 1860-61 envelope 300.
Manningham
3¢ 1860-61 envelope 300.
Marion
3¢ 1860-61 envelope 300.
Millville
3¢ 1860-61 envelope 300.
Mobile
1¢ 1857-60 stamp 600.
Same, pair 750.
Same, strip of 3 400.
3¢ 1857-60 stamp 300.
Same, with STEAMBOAT (hdsp) 1,000.
10¢ 1857-60 stamp 1,500.
24¢ 1857-60 stamp 2,500.
30¢ 1857-60 stamp 3,000.
3¢ 1860-61 envelope 250.
Same, with STEAMBOAT (hdsp) 1,000.
Montevallo
3¢ 1860-61 envelope 300.
Montgomery
1¢ 1857-60 stamp 600.
Same, pair 750.
Same, strip of 3 400.
3¢ 1857-60 stamp 250.
12¢ 1857-60 stamp 1,000.
3¢ 1853-55 envelope 250.
3¢ 1860-61 envelope 250.
Mount Pleasant
3¢ 1860-61 envelope 350.
Northport
3¢ 1860-61 envelope 300.
Pickensville
3¢ 1860-61 envelope 300.
Pine Apple
3¢ 1857-60 stamp 300.
Pine Level
3¢ 1857-60 stamp 350.
3¢ 1860-61 envelope 350.
Red Level
3¢ 1853-55 envelope 350.
Russellville
3¢ 1857-60 stamp 300.
Selma
1¢ 1857-60 stamp 600.
3¢ 1860-61 envelope 250.
Shiloh
1¢ 1857-60 stamp NR
Same, strip of 3 400.
Summerfield
3¢ 1860-61 envelope 300.
Talladega
3¢ 1857-60 stamp 300.
Tuscaloosa
1¢ 1857-60 stamp 600.
3¢ 1857-60 stamp 250.
12¢ 1857-60 stamp 2000.
3¢ 1853-55 envelope 300.
Tuscumbia
3¢ 1857-60 stamp 350.
3¢ 1860-61 envelope 350.
Tuskegee
3¢ 1857-60 stamp 300.
3¢ 1853-55 envelope 300.
3¢ 1860-61 envelope 300.
Union Springs
3¢ 1857-60 stamp 350.
3¢ 1860-61 envelope 350.
Uniontown
3¢ 1857-60 stamp 300.
3¢ 1853-55 envelope 300.
3¢ 1860-61 envelope 300.
Wetumpka
3¢ 1857-60 stamp 350.

Stampless Markings

BUTLER / ALA (37; 1861; black)
Ms Paid 3 350.
CHAMBERS C.H. / Ala. (34; 1861; black)
Ms Paid 9 500.
Clintonville (ms; 1861; black)
Ms Paid 3 350.
Houston (ms; 1861; black)
Ms Paid 3 350.
HUNTSVILLE / ALA (26 DC YD; 1861; blue)
No rate [drop letter] 500.
Mill Town (ms; 1861; black)
Ms Paid (no rate) 250.
MOBILE / ALA (26 DC; 1861; black)
30 [foreign destination] 1,250.
DROP / 1 ct (c) 750.

Steam / 6 (oval) [no town mark] 1,000.
MONTGOMERY / Ala. (32 YD; 1861; black)
PAID (no rate) 350.
PAID with "Paid 3" (ms) 350.
DROP / 1 ct (c) 750.
FREE 500.
Woodville (ms; 1861; black)
Ms Paid 3 350.

Arkansas

On December 24, 1860, Governor Henry M. Rector called for the General Assembly to authorize a Secession Convention. Voters approved the convention on February 18, 1861, but elected a majority of delegates who opposed secession. On March 4 the delegates convened, but adjourned after the motion to secede failed. The delegates reconvened again on May 6 and this time adopted an Ordinance of Secession. Arkansas was admitted to the Confederacy on May 18.

Independent State Use of US Postage
(May 6 through May 17, 1861)

Stamps and Stamped Envelopes

Batesville
3¢ 1860-61 envelope 1,000.
El Dorado
3¢ 1860-61 envelope 1,000.
Fort Smith
3¢ 1857-60 stamp 1,250.
Helena
3¢ 1857-60 stamp 1,000.
Little Rock
3¢ 1857-60 stamp 1,000.
3¢ 1860-61 envelope 1,000.
Mound City
3¢ 1857-60 stamp 1,250.
North Creek
3¢ 1860-61 envelope 1,250.
Princeton
3¢ 1857-60 stamp 1,000.
3¢ 1860-61 envelope 1,000.
Searcy
3¢ 1860-61 envelope 1,000.
Van Buren
3¢ 1860-61 envelope 1,000.
Washington
3¢ 1857-60 stamp 1,000.

Confederate State Use of US Postage
(May 18 through May 31, 1861)

Stamps and Stamped Envelopes

Atlanta
3¢ 1860-61 envelope 800.
Camden
3¢ 1860-61 envelope 750.
Hot Springs
3¢ 1860-61 envelope 800.
Little Rock
3¢ 1860-61 envelope 750.
Pine Bluff
3¢ 1853-55 envelope 750.
Princeton
3¢ 1857-60 stamp 800.
Searcy
3¢ 1857-60 stamp 800.
3¢ 1860-61 envelope 750.
Van Buren
3¢ 1860-61 envelope 750.
Washington
3¢ 1857-60 stamp 750.

Florida

On November 30, 1860, Governor Madison Perry signed a bill calling for a Secession Convention. On January 3, 1861, the delegates convened in Tallahassee and adopted an Ordinance of Secession on January 10. On January 11, 1861, the Ordinance was presented to the Governor for his approval under terms of the State Constitution. Florida was admitted to the Confederacy on February 4.

Independent State Use of US Postage
(January 11 through February 3, 1861)

Stamps and Stamped Envelopes

Apalachicola
1¢ 1857-60 stamp 2,000.
Bailey's Mill
3¢ 1857-60 stamp 1,500.
Houston
3¢ 1860-61 envelope 1,500.
Jacksonville
3¢ 1857-60 stamp 1,500.
Saint Augustine
3¢ 1857-60 stamp 1,500.
Tampa
3¢ 1857-60 stamp 1,500.

Confederate State Use of US Postage
(February 4 through May 31, 1861)

Stamps and Stamped Envelopes

Apalachicola
1¢ 1857-60 stamp 1000.
3¢ 1857-60 stamp 500.
Ellisville
3¢ 1857-60 stamp 500.
Enterprise
3¢ 1857-60 stamp 500.
Fernandina
3¢ 1857-60 stamp 500.
Jacksonville
1¢ 1857-60 stamp NR
Same, strip of 3 750.

3¢ 1857-60 stamp	500.
3¢ 1860-61 envelope	500.
Jasper	
3¢ 1857-60 stamp	500.
Key West	
3¢ 1853-55 envelope	500.
Lake City	
3¢ 1860-61 envelope	500.
Little River	
3¢ 1860-61 envelope	500.
Madison Court House	
3¢ 1860-61 envelope	500.
Mariana	
3¢ 1860-61 envelope	500.
Mellonville	
3¢ 1857-60 stamp	500.
Miccosukee	
3¢ 1857-60 stamp	500.
3¢ 1860-61 envelope	500.
Middleburg	
3¢ 1857-60 stamp	500.
Newport	
3¢ 1853-55 envelope	500.
Orange Lake	
3¢ 1857-60 stamp	500.
Pilatka	
3¢ 1860-61 envelope	500.
Quincy	
3¢ 1857-60 stamp	500.
Saint Augustine	
3¢ 1857-60 stamp	500.
3¢ 1853-55 envelope	500.
Same, with "for'd 3" (ms)	750.
Tallahassee	
3¢ 1857-60 stamp	300.
Waldo	
3¢ 1853-55 envelope	500.
Warrington	
3¢ 1857-60 stamp	500.
3¢ 1860-61 envelope	500.

Stampless Markings

Gainesville (ms; 1861; black)	
Ms Paid 3	500.
Houston (ms; 1861; black)	
Ms Paid 3	500.
NEWNANSVILLE / FLA (26; 1861; black)	
PAID / 3 (arc)	500.
Providence (ms; 1861; black)	
Ms Pd 3	500.

Georgia

On November 24, 1860, Governor Joseph Emerson Brown signed a bill authorizing an election of delegates to a Secession Convention. On January 16, 1861, delegates convened in Milledgeville and on January 19 adopted an Ordinance of Secession. Georgia was admitted to the Confederacy on February 4.

Independent State Use of US Postage
(January 19 through February 3, 1861)

Stamps and Stamped Envelopes

Athens	
3¢ 1860-61 envelope	300.
Atlanta	
3¢ 1857-60 stamp	300.
Augusta	
3¢ 1853-55 envelope	300.
Bainbridge	
3¢ 1860-61 envelope	300.
Blairsville	
3¢ 1860-61 envelope	300.
Calhoun	
3¢ 1857-60 stamp	300.
Cardsville	
3¢ 1860-61 envelope	300.
Craftsville	
3¢ 1860-61 envelope	300.
Crawfordsville (Crawfordville)	
3¢ 1857-60 stamp	300.
Same, with "ford 3" (ms)	300.
Dalton	
3¢ 1857-60 stamp	300.
Dawson	
3¢ 1860-61 envelope	300.
Fayetteville	
3¢ 1860-61 envelope	300.
Graysville	
3¢ 1860-61 envelope	300.
Griffin	
3¢ 1860-61 envelope	300.
Homer	
3¢ 1857-60 stamp	300.
Houston	
3¢ 1860-61 envelope	300.
Maxeys (Maxey)	
3¢ 1860-61 envelope	300.
McDonough	
3¢ 1857-60 stamp	300.
Milledgeville	
3¢ 1857-60 stamp	300.
Same, with "ford 3" (ms)	300.
3¢ 1860-61 envelope	300.
Penfield	
3¢ 1857-60 stamp	300.
Ringgold	
3¢ 1860-61 envelope	300.
Rome	
3¢ 1857-60 stamp	300.
Rutledge	
3¢ 1857-60 stamp	300.
Savannah	
1¢ 1857-60 stamp	750.
Same, strip of 3	500.
3¢ 1857-60 stamp	300.
Same, with STEAM BOAT (hdsp)	1,500.
3¢ 1860-61 envelope	300.

Same, with STEAM BOAT (hdsp) 1,500.

Caution: Excellent counterfeits of the STEAMBOAT marking exist.

Talbotton
3¢ 1853-55 envelope 300.

Stampless Markings

SAVANNAH Ga. (32; 1861; black)
10 [cross border foreign destination] 1,500.

Confederate State Use of US Postage
(February 4 through May 31, 1861)

Stamps and Stamped Envelopes

Albany
3¢ 1857-60 stamp 200.
3¢ 1860-61 envelope 200.
Same, with "Due 3" (ms) 300.
Alpharetta
3¢ 1860-61 envelope 200.
Americus
3¢ 1853-55 envelope 200.
Athens
3¢ 1857-60 stamp 200.
3¢ 1853-55 envelope 200.
3¢ 1860-61 envelope 200.

Atlanta
1¢ 1857-60 stamp 500.
Same, strip of 3 300.
3¢ 1857-60 stamp 200.
5¢ 1857-60 stamp 1,500.
30¢ 1857-60 stamp 2,500.
3¢ 1853-55 envelope 200.
1¢ 1860-61 envelope 1.500.
3¢ 1860-61 envelope 200.
Augusta
1¢ 1857-60 stamp NR
Same, strip of 3 300.
3¢ 1857-60 stamp 200.
3¢ 1853-55 envelope 200.
1¢ 1860-61 envelope 1,500.
3¢ 1860-61 envelope 200.
Bethany
3¢ 1853-55 envelope 200.
Blairsville
3¢ 1853-55 envelope 200.
3¢ 1860-61 envelope 200.
Bloomfield
3¢ 1853-55 envelope 200.
3¢ 1860-61 envelope 200.
Brunswick
3¢ 1853-55 envelope 200.
Calhoun
3¢ 1857-60 stamp 200.
3¢ 1860-61 envelope 200.
Campbellton
3¢ 1860-61 envelope 200.
Canton
3¢ 1857-60 stamp 200.
3¢ 1860-61 envelope 200.
Cassville
3¢ 1857-60 stamp 200.
3¢ 1860-61 envelope 200.
Cedartown
3¢ 1857-60 stamp 200.
Clayton
3¢ 1857-60 stamp 200.
3¢ 1860-61 envelope 200.
Columbus
3¢ 1857-60 stamp 200.
3¢ 1860-61 envelope 200.
Conyers
3¢ 1857-60 stamp 200.
Cottage Mills
1¢ 1857-60 stamp 500.
Covington
3¢ 1857-60 stamp 200.
Crawford
3¢ 1860-61 envelope 200.
Crawfordsville (Crawfordville)
3¢ 1857-60 stamp 200.
3¢ 1860-61 envelope 200.
Cuthbert
3¢ 1857-60 stamp 200.
Dahlonega
3¢ 1860-61 envelope 200.
Dalton
3¢ 1857-60 stamp 200.
3¢ 1853-55 envelope 200.
3¢ 1860-61 envelope 200.
Danville
3¢ 1853-55 envelope 200.
Dawson
3¢ 1857-60 stamp 200.
3¢ 1860-61 envelope 200.
Decatur
3¢ 1857-60 stamp 200.
3¢ 1860-61 envelope 200.
Double Wells
3¢ 1857-60 stamp 200.
Eatonton
3¢ 1853-55 envelope 200.
3¢ 1860-61 envelope 200.

Fort Gaines
3¢ 1860-61 envelope 200.
Fort Valley
3¢ 1853-55 envelope 200.
Gainesville
3¢ 1860-61 envelope 200.
Georgetown
3¢ 1860-61 envelope 200.
Gillsville
3¢ 1860-61 envelope 200.
Graysville
3¢ 1860-61 envelope 200.
Greensborough
3¢ 1857-60 stamp 200.
3¢ 1853-55 envelope 200.
3¢ 1860-61 envelope 200.
Greenville
3¢ 1860-61 envelope 200.
Griffin
3¢ 1857-60 stamp 200.
3¢ 1860-61 envelope 200.
Griswoldville
3¢ 1860-61 envelope 200.
Hillsboro
3¢ 1857-60 stamp 200.
3¢ 1860-61 envelope 200.
Homer
3¢ 1857-60 stamp 200.
Irwinton
3¢ 1857-60 stamp 200.
Jasper
3¢ 1860-61 envelope 200.
Jonesborough
3¢ 1860-61 envelope 200.
Kingston
3¢ 1857-60 stamp 200.
3¢ 1860-61 envelope 200.
Lafayette
3¢ 1857-60 stamp 200.
Lawrenceville
1¢ 1857-60 stamp NR
Same, strip of 3 300.
3¢ 1853-55 envelope 200.
Lexington
3¢ 1857-60 stamp 200.
3¢ 1860-61 envelope 200.
Linton
3¢ 1860-61 envelope 200.
Long Cane
1¢ 1857-60 stamp NR
Same, with 3¢ 1857-60 stamp 750.
3¢ 1857-60 stamp NR
Same, with 1¢ 1857-60 stamp 750.
Louisville
3¢ 1860-61 envelope 200.
Macon
1¢ 1857-60 stamp NR
Same, strip of 3 300.
3¢ 1857-60 stamp 200.
3¢ 1860-61 envelope 200.
Madison
3¢ 1857-60 stamp 200.
Marietta
3¢ 1857-60 stamp 200.
3¢ 1853-55 envelope 200.
3¢ 1860-61 envelope 200.
Marshallville
3¢ 1860-61 envelope 200.
Maxeys (Maxey)
3¢ 1860-61 envelope 200.
Milledgeville
3¢ 1857-60 stamp 200.
12¢ 1857-60 stamp 1,500.
3¢ 1860-61 envelope 200.
Mill Town (Milltown)
3¢ 1857-60 stamp 200.
Monroe
3¢ 1860-61 envelope 200.
Morven
3¢ 1857-60 stamp 200.
Mt Yonah
3¢ 1860-61 envelope 200.
Newnan
3¢ 1857-60 stamp 200.
3¢ 1853-55 envelope 200.
3¢ 1860-61 envelope 200.
Newton
3¢ 1857-60 stamp 200.
3¢ 1860-61 envelope 200.
Newton Factory
3¢ 1860-61 envelope 200.
Omega
3¢ 1857-60 stamp 200.
Penfield
3¢ 1857-60 stamp 200.
Perry
3¢ 1860-61 envelope 200.
Raysville
3¢ 1860-61 envelope 200.
Red Post Spring
3¢ 1857-60 stamp 200.
Rehoboth
3¢ 1857-60 stamp 200.
Resaca
3¢ 1860-61 envelope 200.
Richland
3¢ 1857-60 stamp 200.
3¢ 1860-61 envelope 200.
Ringgold
3¢ 1860-61 envelope 200.
Rome
3¢ 1857-60 stamp 200.
3¢ 1853-55 envelope 200.
3¢ 1860-61 envelope 200.
Roswell
3¢ 1857-60 stamp 200.
3¢ 1853-55 envelope 200.
3¢ 1860-61 envelope 200.
Savannah
1¢ 1857-60 stamp 750.

Same, pair 500.
Same, strip of 3 300.
3¢ 1857-60 stamp 200.
Same, with STEAM BOAT (hdsp) 1,000.
3¢ 1853-55 envelope 200.
3¢ 1860-61 envelope 200.
Same, with STEAM BOAT (hdsp) 1,000.
Caution: Excellent counterfeits of the STEAM BOAT marking exist

Sharon
3¢ 1853-55 envelope 200.

Social Circle
3¢ 1857-60 stamp 200.

So N Port (South Newport)
3¢ 1857-60 stamp 200.

Sparta
3¢ 1853-55 envelope 200.

Speirs Turn Out
1¢ 1857-60 stamp NR
Same, strip of 3 300.
3¢ 1857-60 stamp 200.

Starkville
3¢ 1857-60 stamp 200.
3¢ 1860-61 envelope 200.

Talbotton
3¢ 1857-60 stamp 200.
Same, with FORWARDED (box) (hdsp) 300.

Talmage
3¢ 1857-60 stamp 200.
3¢ 1860-61 envelope 200.

Thomson (Thompson)
3¢ 1860-61 envelope 200.

Thomaston
3¢ 1860-61 envelope 200.

Thomasville
3¢ 1857-60 stamp 200.
3¢ 1860-61 envelope 200.

Upper Kings Bridge
3¢ 1857-60 stamp 200.
3¢ 1860-61 envelope 200.

Valdosta
3¢ 1860-61 envelope 200.

Walnut Grove
3¢ 1857-60 stamp 200.

Warrenton
3¢ 1857-60 stamp 200.
3¢ 1860-61 envelope 200.

Washington
3¢ 1857-60 stamp 200.

Watkinsville
3¢ 1860-61 envelope 200.

Webster Place
3¢ 1857-60 stamp 200.

West Point
3¢ 1857-60 stamp 200.
3¢ 1860-61 envelope 200.

Woodstock
3¢ 1857-60 stamp 200.

Stampless Markings

AUGUSTA / GA (26 DC YD; 1861; black)
Ms Due 24 [foreign destination] 1,500.

Carnesville (ms; 1861; black)
Ms Free 350.

COLUMBUS / GA. ("A" high) (31; 1861; black)
PAID / 3 (c) 300.
PAID/ 3 (arc) 300.

ETOWAH / Ga. (34; 1861; blue)
Ms Free 300.

FORT VALLEY / GA. (32; 1861; black)
PAID / 3 (arc) 300.

FRANKLIN / GEO. (31 YD; 1861; black)
Ms Paid 6 cts 350.

Hog Mountain (ms; 1861; black)
Ms Free 300.

JEFFERSON / Ga. (37; 1861; black)
No rate 200.

KINGSTON / GA. "A" high (32; 1861; black)
PAID / 3 (c) 300.

LAWRENCEVILLE / Ga. (31; 1861; black)
PAID 10 [foreign destination] 2,500.

McBeen (ms; 1861/ black)
Ms Paid 3 cts 300.

MACON / GA (26 DC; 1861; black)
DUE 1 750.

MILLEDGEVILLE / Ga. "a." high (30; 1861; black)
PAID [circular rate implied] 500.

MILL TOWN / GEO. (32; 1861; black)
Ms Paid 3 300.

Mobley Pond (ms; 1861; black)
Ms Free 300.

NACOOCHEE / GA. "A" high" (27; 1861; black)
Ms Free 300.

Point Peter (ms; 1861; black)
Ms Free 300.

SAVANNAH / *GEO* (26; 1861; black)

SAVANNAH Ga. (32; 1861; black)
24 (c) [foreign destination] 1,500.
FREE 300.
STEAM BOAT 1,000.
Caution: Excellent counterfeits of the STEAM BOAT marking exist

STONE MOUNTAIN (35; 1861; black)
No rate [drop rate] 500.

Van Zants Store (ms; 1861; black)
Ms Paid in Money 3cts 500.

WEST POINT / Ga. (34; 1861; black)
PAID (box), "9" (ms) 300.

Louisiana

On December 10, 1860, Governor Thomas O. Moore called for a special session of the legislature. The legislature authorized a Secession Convention on December 20. The convention assembled in Baton Rouge on January 23, 1861, and adopted an Ordinance of Secession on January 26. Louisiana was admitted to the Confederacy on February 4.

Independent State Use of US Postage
(January 26 through February 3, 1861)

Stamps and Stamped Envelopes

Alexandria
3¢ 1860-61 envelope 500.
Bonner
3¢ 1860-61 envelope 500.
La Fayette City
3¢ 1857-60 stamp 500.
12¢ 1857-60 stamp 2,500.
Laurel Hill
5¢ 1857-60 stamp 750.
New Orleans
1¢ 1857-60 stamp 500.
Same, pair 750.
3¢ 1857-60 stamp 300.
Same, with WAY (hdsp) 750.
5¢ 1857-60 stamp 850.
10¢ 1857-60 stamp 1,250.
12¢ 1857-60 stamp 2,500.
24¢ 1857-60 stamp 3,500.
30¢ 1857-60 stamp 6,000.
3¢ 1853-55 envelope 300.
Same, with WAY (hdsp) 750.
3¢ 1860-61 envelope 300.
Same, with WAY (hdsp) 750.
Pecan Grove
3¢ 1857-60 stamp 500.
Shreveport
12¢ 1857-60 stamp 2,500.
3¢ 1853-55 envelope 500.
Taylor
3¢ 1857-60 stamp 500.
Water Proof
3¢ 1860-61 envelope 500.

Stampless Markings

NEW ORLEANS / LA. (32; 1861; black)
STEAMSHIP (c), 22 (ms) 1,500.
STEAMSHIP / 10 (c) [no town cancel] 750.
West Fork PO (ms; 1861; black)
Ms Paid [foreign destination] 750.

Confederate State Use of US Postage
(February 4 through May 31, 1861)

Stamps and Stamped Envelopes

Abbeville
3¢ 1860-61 envelope 300.
Alexandria
3¢ 1857-60 stamp 300.
10¢ 1857-60 stamp 1,000.
3¢ 1860-61 envelope 300.
Amite City
3¢ 1860-61 envelope 300.
Arcadia
1¢ 1857-60 stamp NR
Same, strip of 3 500.
Baton Rouge
3¢ 1857-60 stamp 300.
3¢ 1860-61 envelope 300.
Bethany
3¢ 1853-55 envelope 300.
Bonner
3¢ 1860-61 envelope 300.
Centreville
3¢ 1857-60 stamp 300.
Clinton
3¢ 1857-60 stamp 300.
3¢ 1860-61 envelope 300.
Collinsville
3¢ 1860-61 envelope 300.
Columbia
3¢ 1860-61 envelope 300.
Cotile
1¢ 1857-60 stamp NR
Same, strip of 3 500.
3¢ 1860-61 envelope 300.
Cotton Valley
3¢ 1853-55 envelope 300.
Dallas
3¢ 1857-60 stamp 300.
Delhi
3¢ 1857-60 stamp 300.
Donaldsonville
3¢ 1857-60 stamp 300.
5¢ 1857-60 stamp 750.
10¢ 1857-60 stamp 1,000.
12¢ 1857-60 stamp 2,000.
3¢ 1860-61 envelope 300.
Edgard
3¢ 1857-60 stamp 300.
Farmerville
3¢ 1860-61 envelope 300.
Franklin
3¢ 1860-61 envelope 300.
Jackson
3¢ 1860-61 envelope 300.
Keachie
3¢ 1860-61 envelope 300.
Kirk's Ferry
3¢ 1860-61 envelope 300.
Lamothe
3¢ 1860-61 envelope 300.
Lisbon
3¢ 1860-61 envelope 300.
Madisonville
3¢ 1860-61 envelope 300.
Millikens Bend
3¢ 1860-61 envelope 300.
Minden
3¢ 1860-61 envelope 300.
Monroe
3¢ 1857-60 stamp 300.
3¢ 1860-61 envelope 300.
Mount Lebanon
3¢ 1857-60 stamp 300,

3¢ 1860-61 envelope 300.
Natchitoches
3¢ 1860-61 envelope 300.
New Iberia
5¢ 1857-60 stamp 750.
10¢ 1857-60 stamp 1000.
New Orleans
1¢ 1857-60 stamp 500.
Same, pair 500.
Same, strip of 3 300.
3¢ 1857-60 stamp 250.
5¢ 1857-60 stamp 750.
10¢ 1857-60 stamp 1,000.
12¢ 1857-60 stamp 2,000.
24¢ 1857-60 stamp 3,000.
30¢ 1857-60 stamp 5,000.
3¢ 1853-55 envelope 250.
Same, with WAY (hdsp) 1,000.
3¢ 1860-61 envelope 250.
Same, with WAY (hdsp) 1,000.
Markings on incoming mail
ADV.1. (box) +200.
DUE 3 +100.
Opelousas
3¢ 1860-61 envelope 300.
Pecan Grove
3¢ 1857-60 stamp 300.
Red River Landing
3¢ 1860-61 envelope 300.
St. Francisville
3¢ 1860-61 envelope 300.
Saint Gabriel
3¢ 1857-60 stamp 300.
St. Martinsville
3¢ 1853-55 envelope 300.
Shreveport
3¢ 1857-60 stamp 300.
12¢ 1857-60 stamp 2,000.
3¢ 1853-55 envelope 300.
3¢ 1860-61 envelope 300.
Simmsport (Simmesport)
3¢ 1857-60 stamp 300.
3¢ 1860-61 envelope 300.
Spearsville
3¢ 1853-55 envelope 300.
Taylor
3¢ 1857-60 stamp 300.
Thibodeaux
1¢ 1857-60 stamp NR
Same, strip of 3 500.
Tigerville
3¢ 1857-60 stamp 300.
Vermillionville
3¢ 1860-61 envelope 300.
Warsaw
3¢ 1860-61 envelope 300.
Water Proof
3¢ 1857-60 stamp 300.
3¢ 1860-61 envelope 300.
Wheeling
3¢ 1860-61 envelope 300.

Stampless Markings

ARCADIA / LA (26; 1861; black)
PAID (no rate) 300.
KEACHIE / LA (26; 1861; black)
PAID (no rate) 300.
LAKE PROVIDENCE / La. (32; 1861; black)
PAID / 3 (c) 500.
PAID, "18¢" (ms) 750.
NEW ORLEANS / LA. (sans serif) (32; 1861; black)
NEW ORLEANS / LA. (serif) (32; 1861; black)
NEW ORLEANS / LA (26 DC; 1861; black)
DROP / 1 ct. (c) 1,500.
30 [foreign destination] 3,000.
SHIP [transit marking, no town mark] 1,000.
SHIP, 5 (ms) 2,500.
SHIP / 6 3,000.
STEAM / 6 1,500.
STEAMSHIP / 10 (c) 1,500.
STEAMSHIP (c), 26 3,500.
POINTE COUPEE / La. (29; 1861; red)
PAID, 3 (ms) 300.
ROSEDALE / LA. (32; 1861; black)
PAID, 3 (ms) 300.
SAINT GABRIEL / La. (36; 1861; black)
PAID (no rate) 250.
ST. MARTAINSVILLE / LA. (33; 1861; black)
PAID / 3 300.

Mississippi

On November 13, 1860, Governor John J. Pettus issued a proclamation calling for a special session of the legislature. The legislature convened on November 26 and passed a bill on November 28 calling for an election of delegates to a Secession Convention. The delegates convened in Jackson on January 7, 1861, and adopted an Ordinance of Secession on January 9. Mississippi was admitted to the Confederacy on February 4.

Independent State Use of US Postage
(January 9 through February 3, 1861)

Stamps and Stamped Envelopes

Aberdeen
3¢ 1857-60 stamp 300.
3¢ 1860-61 envelope 300.
Augusta
3¢ 1857-60 stamp 500.
Brandon
3¢ 1853-55 envelope 300.
Canton
3¢ 1857-60 stamp 300.
3¢ 1853-55 envelope 300.
Carrollton
3¢ 1857-60 stamp 300.
3¢ 1853-55 envelope 300.

3¢ 1860-61 envelope	300.
Centreville	
3¢ 1860-61 envelope	500.
Clinton	
3¢ 1860-61 envelope	300.
Coffeeville	
3¢ 1860-61 envelope	300.
Columbus	
3¢ 1860-61 envelope	300.
Crystal Springs	
3¢ 1860-61 envelope	300.
Dunbarton	
3¢ 1853-55 envelope	500.
Friar's Point	
3¢ 1860-61 envelope	300.
Garner's Station	
3¢ 1853-55 envelope	500.
Greenville	
3¢ 1860-61 envelope	500.
Grenada	
3¢ 1860-61 envelope	500.
Herbert	
3¢ 1860-61 envelope	500.
Holly Springs	
3¢ 1857-60 stamp	300.
3¢ 1853-55 envelope	300.
3¢ 1860-61 envelope	300.
Hopson's	
3¢ 1857-60 stamp	500.
Jackson	
3¢ 1857-60 stamp	300.
3¢ 1860-61 envelope	300.
Lauderdale Station	
3¢ 1857-60 stamp	300.
Lexington	
3¢ 1860-61 envelope	300.
Long Branch	
3¢ 1853-55 envelope	500.
Louisville	
3¢ 1860-61 envelope	300.
Macon	
3¢ 1860-61 envelope	300.
Natchez	
1¢ 1857-60 stamp	750.
3¢ 1857-60 stamp	300.
Same, with STEAM (hdsp)	1,500.
3¢ 1853-55 envelope	300.
3¢ 1860-61 envelope	300.
Oakland College	
3¢ 1857-60 stamp	750.
Oxford	
3¢ 1860-61 envelope	500.
Pass Christian	
3¢ 1853-55 envelope	500.
Percy's Creek	
3¢ 1853-55 envelope	500.
Philadelphia	
3¢ 1857-60 stamp	500.
Pine Ridge	
3¢ 1860-61 envelope	500.
Pittsborough	
3¢ 1860-61 envelope	500.
Tacaluche	
3¢ 1860-61 envelope	500.
Torrance	
3¢ 1860-61 envelope	300.
Vaiden	
3¢ 1857-60 stamp	300.
3¢ 1860-61 envelope	300.
Vernon	
3¢ 1860-61 envelope	300.
Vicksburgh	
3¢ 1860-61 envelope	300.
Winona	
3¢ 1857-60 stamp	300.
3¢ 1860-61 envelope	300.
Yazoo City	
1¢ 1857-60 stamp	NR
Same, strip of 3	750.
3¢ 1857-60 stamp	500.

Stampless Markings

CANTON / Miss. (31 YD; 1861; black)	
PAID, 3 (box)	500.
WILLIAMSBURG / MISS (32; 1861; black)	
PAID / 3 (c)	500.

Confederate State Use of US Postage
(February 4 through May 31, 1861)

Stamps and Stamped Envelopes

Aberdeen	
3¢ 1857-60 stamp	250.
3¢ 1860-61 envelope	250.
Ashfordville	
3¢ 1860-61 envelope	300.
Bankston	
3¢ 1860-61 envelope	300.
Brandon	
3¢ 1857-60 stamp	250.
3¢ 1860-61 envelope	250.
Byhalia	
1¢ 1857-60 stamp	NR
Same, strip of 3	500.
1860-61 envelope	300.
Campbellton	
3¢ 1860-61 envelope	300.
Canton	
1¢ 1857-60 stamp	750.
Same, strip of 3	500.
3¢ 1857-60 stamp	250.
3¢ 1853-55 envelope	250.
3¢ 1860-61 envelope	250.
Carrollton	
3¢ 1857-60 stamp	250.
3¢ 1853-55 envelope	250.
3¢ 1860-61 envelope	250.

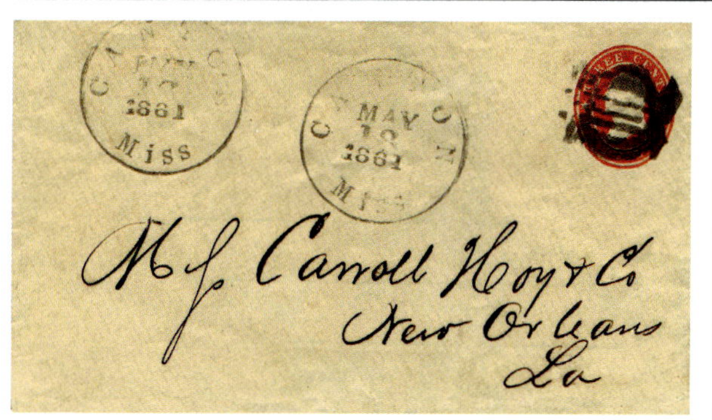

Central Academy	
3¢ 1860-61 envelope	300.
Cherry Hill	
3¢ 1857-60 stamp*	300.
Clinton	
3¢ 1860-61 envelope	250.
Coffeeville	
3¢ 1857-60 stamp	250.
3¢ 1860-61 envelope	250.
College Hill	
3¢ 1857-60 stamp	300.
3¢ 1860-61 envelope	300.
Columbus	
3¢ 1857-60 stamp	250.
3¢ 1853-55 envelope	250.
3¢ 1860-61 envelope	250.
Corinth	
1¢ 1857-60 stamp	NR
Same, strip of 3	500.
3¢ 1857-60 stamp	300.
3¢ 1860-61 envelope	300.
Dunbarton	
3¢ 1860-61 envelope	300.
Early Grove	
3¢ 1857-60 stamp	300.
Same, with “5 cts” (ms) [Registry fee]	500.
Edinburgh	
3¢ 1860-61 envelope	300.
Elm Grove	
3¢ 1857-60 stamp	300.
Enterprise	
1¢ 1857-60 stamp	NR
Same, strip of 3	500.
3¢ 1853-55 envelope	250.
3¢ 1860-61 envelope	250.
Friar’s Point	
3¢ 1857-60 stamp	250.
3¢ 1860-61 envelope	250.
Garlandsville	
3¢ 1860-61 envelope	250.
Garner’s Station	
3¢ 1860-61 envelope	300.
Goodman	
3¢ 1860-61 envelope	250.
Greenville	
3¢ 1860-61 envelope	300.
Greenwood	
3¢ 1860-61 envelope	250.
Grenada	
3¢ 1857-60 stamp	250.
3¢ 1860-61 envelope	250.
Hernando	
3¢ 1853-55 envelope	300.
Holly Springs	
1¢ 1857-60 stamp	NR
Same, strip of 3	500.
3¢ 1857-60 stamp	250.
3¢ 1860-61 envelope	250.
Hopson	
3¢ 1860-61 envelope	300.
Horn Lake	
3¢ 1857-60 stamp	250.
Jackson	
1¢ 1857-60 stamp	NR
Same, strip of 3	500.
3¢ 1857-60 stamp	250.
3¢ 1853-55 envelope	250.
3¢ 1860-61 envelope	250.
Kirkwood	
3¢ 1860-61 envelope	250.
Knoxville	
3¢ 1857-60 stamp	300.
Kosciusko	
3¢ 1860-61 envelope	300.
Lauderdale Station	
3¢ 1857-60 stamp	250.
3¢ 1853-55 envelope	250.
Lexington	
3¢ 1853-55 envelope	250.
3¢ 1860-61 envelope	250.
Livingston	
3¢ 1853-55 envelope	250.
Louisville	
3¢ 1857-60 stamp	250.
Macon	
3¢ 1860-61 envelope	250.
Madison Station	
3¢ 1860-61 envelope	250.
Middleton	
3¢ 1860-61 envelope	300.
Mitchell’s X Roads	
3¢ 1857-60 stamp	300.
Morton	
3¢ 1860-61 envelope	250.
Natchez	
1¢ 1857-60 stamp	NR
Same, strip of 3	500.
3¢ 1857-60 stamp	300.
Same, with STEAM (hdsp)	1,500.
3¢ 1853-55 envelope	300.
Okolona	
3¢ 1857-60 stamp	250.
Oxford (dateless town mark)	
3¢ 1860-61 envelope	300.
Palo Alto	
3¢ 1857-60 stamp	300.
Panola	
3¢ 1857-60 stamp	300.
3¢ 1860-61 envelope	300.

Paulding
3¢ 1857-60 stamp 300.
3¢ 1860-61 envelope 300.
Pickens Station
3¢ 1857-60 stamp 250.
Pigeon Roost
3¢ 1860-61 envelope 300.
Pittsboro
3¢ 1860-61 envelope 300.
Pontotoc
3¢ 1857-60 stamp 250.
Port Gibson
3¢ 1857-60 stamp 250.
3¢ 1853-55 envelope 250.
Raymond
3¢ 1860-61 envelope 250.
Ripley
3¢ 1857-60 stamp 300.
Sharon
3¢ 1860-61 envelope 250.
Shell Mound
3¢ 1853-55 envelope 250.
Shieldsborough
3¢ 1857-60 stamp 250.
Sidon
3¢ 1860-61 envelope 300.
Starkville
3¢ 1860-61 envelope 300.
Steelville
3¢ 1860-61 envelope 300.
Steam Mill
3¢ 1857-60 stamp 300.
Sucarnochee
3¢ 1860-61 envelope 300.
Tacaluche
3¢ 1860-61 envelope 300.
Taylor Depot (Taylor's Depot)
3¢ 1860-61 envelope 300.
Terry
3¢ 1860-61 envelope 250.
Torrance
3¢ 1860-61 envelope 250.
Vaiden
3¢ 1860-61 envelope 250.
Valley Hill
3¢ 1860-61 envelope 300.
Vernon
3¢ 1860-61 envelope* 250.
Vicksburg
3¢ 1857-60 stamp 250.
3¢ 1860-61 envelope 250.
Water Valley
3¢ 1860-61 envelope 300.
Winona
3¢ 1860-61 envelope 250.
Same, with PAID (box) (hdsp) 300.
Woodville
3¢ 1857-60 stamp 250.
Yazoo City
3¢ 1857-60 stamp 250.
3¢ 1853-55 envelope 250.
3¢ 1860-61 envelope 250.

Stampless Markings

Batesville Miss (ms; 1861; black)
Ms Paid 3 300.
BRANDON / MISS (32 YD; 1861; black)
PAID, 3 (ms) 300.
Central Academy Miss (ms; 1861; black)
Ms Paid 3 300.
COMO DEPOT / MISS (25; 1861; black)
PAID (oval box) No rate 300.
CORINTH / MISS (37; 1861; black)
PAID 300.
PAID, 3 (ms) 300.
Ms Paid 3 cts 300.
FRIARS POINT / MISS (32; 1861; black)
PAID / 3 (c) 300.
Fair River Miss (ms; 1861; black)
Ms Paid (no rate) 300.
GREENVILLE / MISS (26 DC YD; 1861; blue)
Ms Paid 3 300.
Ms Paid 6 500.
GRENADA / MISS. (32; 1861; black)
Ms Paid 3 300.
HAZLEHURST / MISS (25; 1861; black)
PAID (oval box) (no rate) 300.
HERNANDO / Miss. (32; 1861; black)
PAID (no rate) 300.
PAID, 3 (ms) 300.
JACKSON / MISS (32; 1861; black)
PAID / 3 / Cts. (c) 500.
LAUDERDALE STATION / MISS (26; 1861; black)
Ms Paid 3 300.
LIBERTY / MISS (35; 1861; black)
Ms Paid 3 300.
McNutt Miss (ms; 1861; black)
Ms Paid 3 300.
NATCHEZ / Miss. / 1 (32; 1861; black) 1,500.
OXFORD / MISS (26; 1861; black)
PAID / 3 (arc) 300.
POPLAR CREEK / MISS. (26; 1861; black)
Ms Free 300.
Prentiss Miss (ms; 1861; black)
Ms Paid 300.
Ms Paid 3 300.
Preston Miss (ms; 1861; black)
Ms Paid 3 300.
Queens Hill (ms; 1861; black)
Ms Free 300.
QUITMAN / MISS (25; 1861; black)
Ms Paid 3 300.
SHOOBOTA / MISS. (25; 1861; black)
PAID 3c. 300.
SUMMIT / MISS (36; 1861; black)
PAID (no rate) 300.
PAID, 9 (ms) 500.
Vinton Miss (ms; 1861; black)
Ms Paid 300.

WINONA / MISS (26; 1861; black)	
PAID (box), "3c" (ms)	300.
Same, (no rate)	250.
WOODVILLE / Mi. (32; 1861; black)	
PAID / 3 (oval)	500.

North Carolina

On January 29, 1861, the General Assembly voted to put the question of a Secession Convention to the people in an election to be held on February28 at which time the measure was defeated. Governor John Willis Ellis called for a special session of the legislature on May 1, 1861. The legislature authorized the election of delegates to an unrestricted convention. The delegates assembled in Raleigh on May 20 and adopted an Ordinance of Secession. North Carolina was admitted to the Confederacy on May 27.

Independent State Use of US Postage
(May 20 through May 26, 1861)

Stamps and Stamped Envelopes

Alexandria	
3¢ 1860-61 envelope	500.
Company Shops	
3¢ 1857-60 stamp	500.
Happy Home	
3¢ 1860-61 envelope	500.
Jefferson	
3¢ 1860-61 envelope	500.
Magnolia	
3¢ 1860-61 envelope	500.
Newbern	
3¢ 1857-60 stamp	500.
Raleigh	
3¢ 1857-60 stamp	500.
3¢ 1853-55 envelope	500.
Scuppernong	
3¢ 1853-55 envelope	500.
3¢ 1860-61 envelope	500.
Wilmington	
3¢ 1857-60 stamp	500.
3¢ 1860-61 envelope	500.

Confederate State Use of US Postage
(May 27 through May 31, 1861)

Stamps and Stamped Envelopes

Ashville	
3¢ 1860-61 envelope	500.
Beaufort	
3¢ 1860-61 envelope	500.
Franklin	
3¢ 1857-60 stamp	500.
3¢ 1860-61 envelope	500.
Enola	
3¢ 1860-61 envelope	500.
Gold Hill	
3¢ 1857-60 stamp	500.
Greensborough	
3¢ 1857-60 stamp	500.
3¢ 1860-61 envelope	500.
Hamptonsville	
3¢ 1857-60 stamp	500.
Jerusalem	
3¢ 1860-61 envelope	500.
Louisburgh	
3¢ 1857-60 stamp	500.
Morgantown	
3¢ 1857-60 stamp	500.
3¢ 1860-61 envelope	500.
Pittsboro	
3¢ 1857-60 stamp	500.
Plymouth	
3¢ 1857-60 stamp	500.
Raleigh	
3¢ 1857-60 stamp	500.
Salem	
3¢ 1860-61 envelope	500.
Scuppernong	
3¢ 1860-61 envelope	500.
Shelby	
3¢ 1860-61 envelope	500.
Summerville	
3¢ 1860-61 envelope	500.
Trinity College	
3¢ 1857-60 stamp	500.
Wentworth	
3¢ 1860-61 envelope	500.
Wilmington	
3¢ 1860-61 envelope	500.

Stampless Markings

Turkey Cove (ms; 1861; black)	
Ms Paid 3	500.

South Carolina

On November 5, 1860, Governor William Henry Gist requested the legislature call a Secession Convention. The delegates assembled in Columbia on December 17, but adjourned to Charleston where they adopted an Ordinance of Secession on December 20. South Carolina was admitted to the Confederacy on February 4, 1861.

Independent State Use of US Postage
(December 20, 1860 through February 3, 1861)

Stamps and Stamped Envelopes

Aiken	
3¢ 1857-60 stamp	300.
Beaufort	
3¢ 1857-60 stamp	300.
Bennettsville	
3¢ 1853-55 envelope	300.
Camden	
3¢ 1857-60 stamp	300.
Charleston	
1¢ 1857-60 stamp	500.
Same, strip of 3	300.
3¢ 1857-60 stamp	200.
24¢ 1857-60 stamp	2,500.
30¢ 1857-60 stamp	3,000.
3¢ 1853-55 envelope	200.
6¢ 1853-55 envelope	750.
3¢ 1860-61 envelope	200.
Cheraw	
3¢ 1860-61 envelope	300.
Chester Court House	
3¢ 1853-55 envelope	300.
Clinton	
3¢ 1857-60 stamp	300.
Columbia	
1¢ 1857-60 stamp	500.
Same, strip of 3	300.
3¢ 1857-60 stamp	300.
10¢ 1857-60 stamp	750.
3¢ 1853-55 envelope	300.
3¢ 1860-61 envelope	300.
Georgetown	
3¢ 1857-60 stamp	300.
3¢ 1860-61 envelope	300.
Greenville Court House	
3¢ 1857-60 stamp	300.
Guthriesville	
3¢ 1857-60 stamp	300.
Hamburgh	
3¢ 1860-61 envelope	300.
Same, with PAID (hdsp)	300.
Hodges	
3¢ 1857-60 stamp	300.
Johnsonville	
3¢ 1857-60 stamp	300.
Laurens Court House	
3¢ 1853-55 envelope	300.
Marion Court House	
3¢ 1857-60 stamp	300.
Midway	
3¢ 1857-60 stamp	300.
Monticello	
3¢ 1857-60 stamp	300.
Newberry Court House	
3¢ 1860-61 envelope	300.
Sandover	
3¢ 1857-60 stamp	300.
Spartanburg Court House	
3¢ 1857-60 stamp	300.
Sumter	
3¢ 1853-55 envelope	300.
Unionville	
3¢ 1853-55 envelope	300.

Stampless Markings

CHARLESTON S.C. / 24 (32 YD; 1861; black)	1,500.
COLUMBIA / S.C. (32; 1861; blue)	
[free] (addressed to postmaster)	500.
LANCASTER / S.C. (26 DC; 1861; black)	
Ms Pd 3	500.
TIMMONSVILLE / S.C. (30; 1861; black)	
PAID, "3" (ms)	500.
Twelve Mile [12 Mile] (ms; 1861; black)	
Ms Free	500.

Confederate State Use of US Postage
(February 4 through May 31, 1861)

Stamps and Stamped Envelopes

Abbeville CH	
1¢ 1857-60 stamp	500.
3¢ 1857-60 stamp	200.
3¢ 1860-61 envelope	200.
Adams Run	
3¢ 1857-60 stamp	200.
Aiken	
3¢ 1860-61 envelope	200.
Ashepoo Ferry	
3¢ 1857-60 stamp	300.
Bachelors Retreat	
3¢ 1860-61 envelope	300.
Beaufort	
3¢ 1857-60 stamp	200.
3¢ 1860-61 envelope	200.
Belleview	
3¢ 1857-60 stamp	300.
Bennettsville	
3¢ 1860-61 envelope	300.
Bradford Springs	
3¢ 1857-60 stamp	300.
Brushy Creek	
3¢ 1857-60 stamp	300.

Camden
- 3¢ 1857-60 stamp 200.
- 3¢ 1860-61 envelope 200.

Charleston
- 1¢ 1857-60 stamp 500.
  - Same, strip of 3 300.
- 3¢ 1857-60 stamp 175.
  - Same, with "3" (ms) 500.
  - Same, with "Registered" (ms)* 1,500.
  - Same, with "Way 1" (ms) 1,000.
- 24¢ 1857-60 stamp 2,500.
- 30¢ 1857-60 stamp 3,500.
- 3¢ 1853-55 envelope 175.
- 3¢ 1860-61 envelope 175.
  - Same, with ADVERTISED / ONE CENT (box) (hdsp) 750.
  - Same, with "for 3" (pencil) 500.

Cheraw
- 3¢ 1857-60 stamp 200.
- 3¢ 1860-61 envelope 200.

Chester CH
- 3¢ 1853-55 envelope 200.
- 3¢ 1860-61 envelope 200.

Clinton
- 3¢ 1857-60 stamp 200.

Cokesbury
- 3¢ 1857-60 stamp 200.
- 3¢ 1860-61 envelope 200.

Columbia
- 1¢ 1857-60 stamp 500.
  - Same, strip of 3 300.
  - Same, block of 4 with "Due 2" (ms) 1,000.
- 3¢ 1857-60 stamp 200.
- 3¢ 1860-61 envelope 200.

Darlington CH
- 3¢ 1860-61 envelope 200.

Due West Corner
- 3¢ 1860-61 envelope 300.

Ebenezer (Ebenezerville)
- 3¢ 1857-60 stamp 300.

Friendship
- 3¢ 1860-61 envelope 300.

Georgetown
- 1¢ 1857-1860 stamp NR
  - Same, strip of 3 300.
- 3¢ 1857-60 stamp 300.
- 24¢ 1857-60 stamp* 2,000.
- 3¢ 1853-55 envelope 300.
- 3¢ 1860-61 envelope 300.

Glenn Springs
- 3¢ 1857-60 stamp 200.
- 3¢ 1853-55 envelope 200.

Grahamville
- 3¢ 1857-60 200.

Greenville C.H.
- 3¢ 1857-60 stamp 200.
- 3¢ 1860-61 envelope 200.

Guthrieville
- 3¢ 1857-60 stamp 300.

Johnson
- 3¢ 1857-60 stamp 300.

Limestone Springs
- 3¢ 1860-61 envelope 300.

Manning
- 3¢ 1857-60 stamp 300.

Marion CH
- 3¢ 1860-61 envelope 300.

Midway
- 3¢ 1853-55 envelope 300.

Monticello
- 3¢ 1857-60 stamp 300.

Mt. Carmel
- 3¢ 1857-60 stamp 300.

Mount Pleasant
- 3¢ 1857-60 stamp 300.

Newberry C.H
- 3¢ 1857-60 stamp 300.
- 3¢ 1853-55 envelope 300.
- 3¢ 1860-61 envelope 300.

New Market
- 3¢ 1860-61 envelope 300.

Pendleton
- 3¢ 1857-60 stamp 300.
- 3¢ 1853-55 envelope 300.

Pocotalico
- 3¢ 1857-60 stamp 300.

Rock Hill
- 3¢ 1860-61 envelope 300.

Society Hill
- 3¢ 1860-61 envelope 300.

Spartanburg
- 3¢ 1857-60 stamp 300.
- 12¢ 1857-60 stamp 2,000.
- 3¢ 1853-55 envelope 300.

Sumter
- 1¢ 1857-60 stamp NR
  - Same, strip of 3 300.
- 3¢ 1857-60 stamp 200.
- 3¢ 1853-55 envelope 200.

Thomas's X Roads
- 3¢ 1857-60 stamp 300.

Timmonsville
- 3¢ 1860-61 envelope 300.

Unionville
- 3¢ 1857-60 stamp 300.

Yorkville
- 3¢ 1860-61 envelope 300.

Stampless Markings

ADAMS RUN / S.C. (32; 1861; black)
- Ms Paid 3 500.

AIKEN / S.C. (26 DC; 1861; black)
- PAID 3 500.

BEAUFORT / S.C. (32 YD; 1861; black)
- PAID / 3 (c) 500.

Cartersville (ms; 1861; black)
- Ms Paid 3 300.

CHARLESTON / S.C. (26 DC; 1861; black)

CHARLESTON / S.C. (32 YD; 1861; black)

CHARLESTON S.C. / Paid (32 YD; 1861; black)
CHARLESTON S.C. / 15 (32 YD; 1861; black)
CHARLESTON S.C. / 24 (32 YD; 1861; black)
CHARLESTON S.C. / 30 (32 YD; 1861; black)

24	1,500.
FREE	500.

Dacusville (ms; 1861; black)

Ms Paid 3	300.

DARLINGTON C.H. / S.C. (32; 1861; black)

PAID (box), 3	500.

Fair Play (ms; 1861; black)

Ms Paid (no rate)	300.

GEORGETOWN / S.C. (32 YD; 1861; black)

No rate	300.
PAID / 1 (c)	500.
PAID (c) no rate	300.

GRANITEVILLE / S.C. (36; 1861; black)

PAID / 3 (arc)	500.

HAMBURGH S.C / PAID (32; 1861; black)

3*	500.
(no rate) [unsealed circular]	500.

Lancaster (ms; 1861; black)

Ms Paid 3*	300.

Level Land (ms; 1861; black)

Ms Paid 3	300.

MANNING / SC (26; 1861; black)

Ms Paid 3	300.

Monticello (ms; 1861; black)

Ms Paid 3	300.

POMARIA / --- S.C. --- (27; 1861; red)

FREE (with postmaster's signature)	500.

Privateer (ms; 1861; black)

Ms Paid 3	300.

Sandy Grove (ms; 1861; black)

Ms Free	300.

UNIONVILLE / S.C. (25; 1861; black)

PAID / 3 (arc)	500.

[Whetstone] no town mark

Ms Free	200.

YORKVILLE / S.C. (31; 1861; black)

PAID, 3	500.

Tennessee

On January 7, 1861, Governor Isham Harris asked the legislature to adopt a resolution to be put to the citizens in an election calling for a Secession Convention. On February 9 the voters rejected secession. On May 6, the General Assembly adopted an Ordinance of Secession subject to the approval of the voters in a referendum. On May 7, Governor Harris negotiated a Military League with the Confederate government which was subsequently ratified by the legislature. On June 8, 1861, the voters overwhelmingly approved secession. Tennessee was admitted to the Confederacy on July 2.

Independent State Use of US Postage
(June 8 through July 1, 1861)

In the wake of the June 8 Referendum, the US Post Office Department began to suspend mail operations throughout Tennessee. In order to prevent disruption of service, the Confederate Post Office Department announced on June 17 that it would assume the operation of the postal service in the state. However, that action was not immediately implemented in all parts of Tennessee. Thus, both US and Confederate rates can be found on mail posted between June 8 and July 2.

Stamps and Stamped Envelopes

Beans Station	
3¢ 1857-60 stamp	500.
Ducktown	
3¢ 1860-61 envelope	500.
Hazel Flat	
3¢ 1857-60 stamp	500.
Henderson's Mills	
1¢ 1857-60 stamp	NR
Same, strip of 3	750.
Jackson	
3¢ 1860-61 envelope	500.
Lenoir's	
3¢ 1860-61 envelope	500.
Kimsey's Store	
3¢ 1853-54 envelope	500.
Knoxville	
3¢ 1857-60 stamp	500.
Madisonville	
3¢ 1860-61 envelope	500.
Memphis	
3¢ 1857-60 stamp	500.
Mt. Pleasant	
3¢ 1860-61 envelope	500.
Nashville	
3¢ 1857-60 stamp	500.
Pulaski	
3¢ 1857-60 stamp	500.
3¢ 1860-61 envelope	500.
Randolph	
3¢ 1857-60 stamp	500.
Richland Sta (Richland Station)	
3¢ 1860-61 envelope	500.
Sale Creek	
3¢ 1860-61 envelope	500.
Sulphur Springs	
3¢ 1860-61 envelope	500.
Tullahoma	
3¢ 1857-60 stamp	500.

Stampless Markings

Barren Plain (ms; 1861; black)

Ms Paid 5	500.

CHARLESTON / TENN (30; 1861; black)

Ms Due 5	500.

CHATTANOOGA / Ten. (33 YD; 1861; black)

PAID 5 (c)	500.

DRESDEN / TEN (26; 1861; black)

PAID, 10 (ms)	500.

HUNTINGDON / Te. "e" high (30; 1861; black)

PAID, 3 (ms)	600.

JACKSBOROGH / TEN (25; 1861; black)
Ms Due 3* 500.
JACKSON / TEN. (31; 1861; black)
PAID (arc), 10 (ms) 500.
Ms Paid 5 500.
Lenoir's (ms; 1861; black)
Ms Due 5 500.
MEMPHIS / Ten. (31 YD; 1861; black)
PAID, 5 500.
PAID, 10 750.
Montvale Springs (ms; 1861; black)
Ms 5¢ pd 500.
NASHVILLE / Ten. (32 YD; 1861; blue)
PAID, 5 (large) 500.
PAID, 5 (small) 500.
Same, with "Due 3" (ms) [applied at Athens, Tennessee] 750.
PAID, 10 500.
PAID, 20 (ms) 750.
Richland Station
Paid 5 (ms) 500.
Paid 10 (ms)* 500.
RIPLEY / TENN. (30; 1861; black)
PAID / 3 (c) 750.
SPRING HILL / TEN (33; 1861 ;black)
PAID 5 500.
Union City (ms; 1861; black)
Pd 5 (ms) 500.

Confederate State Use of US Postage

The Confederate use of US postage does not apply in Tennessee.

TEXAS

On January 8, 1861, Texans elected delegates to a state convention to consider secession. The convention convened in Austin on January 28 and adopted an ordinance of secession on February 1 to be put to the voters in a popular referendum on February 23. The measure won overwhelming approval of the voters and became effective on March 2, 1861, as stipulated in the ordinance. On March 2 the Confederate Congress enacted a statute to admit Texas to the Confederacy and the Texas convention accepted the invitation on March 5.

Independent State Use of US Postage
(March 2 through March 4, 1861)

Stamps and Stamped Envelopes

Austin
3¢ 1857-60 stamp 750.
Bagdad
3¢ 1857-60 stamp 750.
Centreville (Centerville)
3¢ 1857-60 stamp 750.
Chapel Hill
3¢ 1857-60 stamp 750.
Clinton
3¢ 1860-61 envelope 750.
Cypress Top
3¢ 1853-55 envelope 750.
Decatur
3¢ 1860-61 envelope 750.
Elysian Fields
3¢ 1860-61 envelope 750.
Fort Davis
3¢ 1860-61 envelope 750.
Jefferson
3¢ 1860-61 envelope 750.
Paris
3¢ 1857-60 stamp 750.
Richmond
3¢ 1860-61 envelope 750.

Confederate Use of US Postage
(March 5 through May 31, 1861)

Stamps and Stamped Envelopes

Alta Springs
3¢ 1853-55 envelope 500.
Anderson
3¢ 1857-60 stamp 500.
Athens
3¢ 1857-60 stamp 500.
Austin
3¢ 1857-60 stamp 500.
Bastrop
3¢ 1857-60 stamp 500.
Belleville
3¢ 1857-60 stamp 500.
Birdsville
3¢ 1860-61 envelope 500.
Bonham
3¢ 1860-61 envelope 500.
Brenham
3¢ 1857-60 stamp 500.
3¢ 1860-61 envelope 500.
Brownsville
3¢ 1857-60 stamp 500.
Burnet
3¢ 1860-61 envelope 500.
Camanche Peak
3¢ 1857-60 stamp 500.
Camp Hudson
3¢ 1857-60 stamp 500.
Capt's Mills
3¢ 1860-61 envelope 500.
Castroville
3¢ 1853-55 envelope 500.
Centreville (Centerville)
3¢ 1860-61 envelope 500.
Chapel Hill
3¢ 1857-60 stamp 500.
Chireno (Cherino)
3¢ 1860-61 envelope 500.
Clarksville
3¢ 1860-61 envelope 500.

Clinton
3¢ 1860-61 envelope 500.
Colita
3¢ 1857-60 stamp 500.
Columbia
3¢ 1857-60 stamp 500.
Corpus Christi
3¢ 1857-60 stamp 500.
3¢ 1853-55 envelope 500.
Cunningham's
3¢ 1860-61 envelope 500.
Cypress Top
3¢ 1853-55 envelope 500.
Daingerfield
3¢ 1860-61 envelope 500.
Dallas
3¢ 1860-61 envelope 500.
Danville
3¢ 1860-61 envelope 500.
Decatur
3¢ 1853-55 envelope 500.
Denton
3¢ 1860-61 envelope 500.
Eagle Lake
3¢ 1860-61 envelope 500.
Egypt
3¢ 1860-61 envelope 500.
Elysian Fields
3¢ 1860-61 envelope 500.
Fairfield
3¢ 1860-61 envelope 500.
Fayetteville
3¢ 1860-61 envelope 500.
Fort Davis
3¢ 1860-61 envelope 500.
Fort Teran (Fort Turan)
3¢ 1857-60 stamp 750.
Fort Worth
3¢ 1860-61 envelope 500.
Gainesville
3¢ 1860-61 envelope 500.
Galveston
3¢ 1857-60 stamp 300.
3¢ 1860-61 envelope 300.
Gilleland Creek
3¢ 1853-55 envelope 500.
Gonzales
3¢ 1857-60 stamp 500.
Graham's Mills
3¢ 1860-61 envelope 500.
Greenville
3¢ 1860-61 envelope 500.
Hempstead
3¢ 1857-60 stamp 500.
3¢ 1853-55 envelope 500.
Herrington
3¢ 1853-55 envelope 500.
Hollandale
3¢ 1860-61 envelope 500.
Honey Grove
3¢ 1857-60 stamp 500.
3¢ 1860-61 envelope 500.
Hope
3¢ 1860-61 envelope 500.
Houston
3¢ 1857-60 stamp 300.
3¢ 1860-61 envelope 300.
Huntsville
3¢ 1857-60 stamp 500.
3¢ 1860-61 envelope 500.
Independance (Independence)
3¢ 1857-60 stamp 500.
Jefferson
3¢ 1857-60 stamp 500.
3¢ 1860-61 envelope 500.
Jonesville
3¢ 1860-61 envelope 500.
Kaufman
3¢ 1857-60 stamp 500.
Ladonia
3¢ 1860-61 envelope 500.
LaGrange
3¢ 1857-60 stamp 500.
3¢ 1853-55 envelope 500.
3¢ 1860-61 envelope 500.
Lampasas
3¢ 1857-60 stamp 500.
Liberty
3¢ 1857-60 stamp 500.
Linden
3¢ 1860-61 envelope 500.
Livingston
3¢ 1860-61 envelope 500.
Marshall
3¢ 1857-60 stamp 500.
McKinney
3¢ 1860-61 envelope 500.
Milford
3¢ 1857-60 stamp 500.
Morganville
3¢ 1860-61 envelope 500.
Moscow
3¢ 1857-60 stamp* 500.
Mount Enterprise
3¢ 1860-61 envelope 500.
Mount Pleasant
3¢ 1860-61 envelope 500.
Muskete
3¢ 1860-61 envelope 500.
Nacogdoches
3¢ 1857-60 stamp 500.
New Braunfels
3¢ 1857-60 stamp 500.
3¢ 1853-55 envelope 500.
Oso
3¢ 1860-61 envelope 500.
Palestine
3¢ 1860-61 envelope 500.
Paris
3¢ 1860-61 envelope 500.

Petersburg
3¢ 1860-61 envelope 500.
Pleasanton
3¢ 1857-60 stamp 500.
Port Lavaca
3¢ 1857-60 stamp 500.
3¢ 1853-55 envelope 500.
Port Sullivan
3¢ 1860-61 envelope 500.
Prairie Plains
3¢ 1860-61 envelope 500.
Prairieville
3¢ 1857-60 stamp 500.
Richmond
3¢ 1857-60 stamp 500.
3¢ 1860-61 envelope 500.
Ridge
3¢ 1860-61 envelope 500.
Sabine Pass
3¢ 1857-60 stamp 500.
San Antonio
3¢ 1857-60 stamp 500.
San Felipe
3¢ 1860-61 envelope 500.
Sherman
1¢ 1857-60 stamp NR
Same, strip of 3 750.
3¢ 1860-61 envelope 500.
Sutherland Springs
3¢ 1857-60 stamp 500.
Texana
3¢ 1860-61 envelope 500.
Same, with Due 3 (ms) 500.
Trinity Mills
3¢ 1860-61 envelope 500.
Twin Sisters
3¢ 1857-60 stamp 500.
Tyler
3¢ 1860-61 envelope 500.
Unionville
3¢ 1860-61 envelope 500.
Victoria
3¢ 1860-61 envelope 500.
Waco Village
3¢ 1860-61 envelope 500.
Wallisville
3¢ 1857-60 stamp 500.
Washington
3¢ 1860-61 envelope 500.
Waxahatchie (Waxahachie)
3¢ 1857-60 stamp 500.
Wheeling
3¢ 1860-61 envelope 500.
Wheelock
3¢ 1857-60 stamp 500.

Stampless Markings

Athens (ms; 1861; black)
Ms Paid 3 500.
Ms Paid 36 750.
BOSTON / TXS (31; 1861; black)
PAID / 3 (c) 500.
BRENHAM / TEX (32; 1861; black)
Ms Paid 3 500.
CARTHAGE / TEX (32; 1861; black)
PAID, 20 (ms) [double domestic rate to California)] 750.
El Paso (ms; 1861; black)
Ms Paid (no rate) 500.
HOLLANDALE / TEX (25; 1861; black)
PAID (oval box), 12cts (ms) 500.
LANCASTER / TEX (26; 1861; black)
PAID (oval box) (no rate) 500.
Leon Springs (ms; 1861; black)
Ms Free H.A.P.M. 500.
PALESTINE / Tex. (36; 1861; black)
Ms Free 500.
PARIS / TEXAS. (31; 1861; black)
PAID, 3 500.
TYLER / TEXAS. (32; 1861; black)
PAID, "9" (ms) 750.
VICTORIA / TEX. (34; 1861; black)
PAID, 21 (ms) 750.
WACO VILLAGE / TEX. (34; 1861; black)
PAID / 3 (c)* 500.

VIRGINIA

On November 15, 1860, Governor John Letcher called for a Special Session of the General Assembly to consider secession. On January 7, 1861, the legislature authorized a Secession Convention to convene on February 13 in Richmond. On April 17, the convention adopted an Ordinance of Secession on condition of ratification by a statewide referendum. The voters overwhelmingly approved the measure on May 23 thus ratifying the terms stipulating the effective date of secession as of April 17, 1861. Virginia was admitted to the Confederacy on May 7.

Independent Use of US Postage
(April 17 through May 6, 1861)

Stamps and Stamped Envelopes

Abingdon
3¢ 1857-60 stamp 300.
Alexandria
3¢ 1857-60 stamp 300.
3¢ 1860-61 envelope 300.
Amherst C. H.
3¢ 1857-60 stamp 300.
Arrington
3¢ 1857-60 stamp 300.
Ayletts
3¢ 1857-60 stamp 300.
Balcony Falls
3¢ 1857-60 stamp 300.
Bealeton
3¢ 1857-60 stamp 300.

Belington
  1¢ 1857-60 stamp — NR
    Same, strip of 3 — 750.
Beverly
  3¢ 1860-61 envelope — 500.
Blue Sulphur Springs
  3¢ 1857-60 stamp — 500.
Buckingham C.H.
  3¢ 1860-61 envelope — 300.
Catlett
  3¢ 1857-60 stamp — 300.
Charlotte C.H
  3¢ 1857-60 stamp — 300.
Charlottesville
  3¢ 1857-60 stamp — 300.
Christiansburg
  3¢ 1860-61 envelope — 300.
Chula Depot
  3¢ 1860-61 envelope — 300.
Clear Branch
  3¢ 1860-61 envelope — 300.
Covington
  3¢ 1857-60 stamp — 300.
Craigsville
  3¢ 1860-61 envelope — 300.
Culpepper C.H.
  3¢ 1857-60 stamp — 300.
Cumberland C.H.
  3¢ 1857-60 stamp — 300.
Draper's Valley
  3¢ 1857-60 stamp — 300.
Dublin
  3¢ 1860-61 envelope — 300.
Emory
  1¢ 1857-60 stamp — 500.
Falmouth
  3¢ 1857-60 stamp — 500.
Farmville
  3¢ 1853-55 envelope — 300.
Fincastle
  3¢ 1860-61 envelope — 300.
Fishersville
  3¢ 1857-60 stamp — 300.
Ford's Depot
  3¢ 1857-60 stamp — 300.
Fredericksburg
  3¢ 1860-61 envelope — 300.
Fredericks Hall [Frederickshall]
  3¢ 1860-61 envelope — 300.
Front Royal
  3¢ 1860-61 envelope — 300.
Gold Hill
  3¢ 1857-60 stamp — 300.
Gordonsville
  3¢ 1857-60 stamp — 300.
Harper's Ferry
  3¢ 1857-60 stamp — 500.
    Same, with "Ford 3" (ms) — 500.
  3¢ 1860-61 envelope — 500.
Head Waters
  3¢ 1860-61 envelope — 300.
Junction
  3¢ 1857-60 stamp — 300.
Leesville
  3¢ 1860-61 envelope — 300.
Lexington
  3¢ 1857-60 stamp — 300.
  3¢ 1860-61 envelope — 300.
Liberty
  3¢ 1857-60 stamp — 300.
Lynchburg
  3¢ 1857-60 stamp — 300.
  3¢ 1860-61 envelope — 300.
Martinsburg
  3¢ 1860-61 envelope — 500.
Moorefield
  3¢ 1860-61 envelope — 300.
New Interest
  3¢ 1857-60 stamp — 300.
New Plymouth
  3¢ 1860-61 envelope — 300.
News Ferry
  3¢ 1857-60 stamp — 300.
Norfolk
  3¢ 1857-60 stamp — 300.
  3¢ 1860-61 envelope — 300.
Old Point Comfort
  3¢ 1860-61 envelope — 300.
Orange C.H.
  3¢ 1857-60 stamp — 300.
Otter Bridge
  3¢ 1857-60 stamp — 300.
Owl Run
  3¢ 1860-61 envelope — 300.
Palmyra
  3¢ 1860-61 envelope — 300.
Pattonsburg
  3¢ 1857-60 stamp — 300.
  3¢ 1860-61 envelope — 300.
Petersburg
  1¢ 1857-60 stamp — NR
    Same, strip of 3 — 500.
  3¢ 1857-60 stamp — 300.
  3¢ 1860-61 envelope — 300.
Piedmont
  3¢ 1857-60 stamp — 300.
Pittsylvania Court House
  3¢ 1857-60 stamp — 300.

Port Conway
3¢ 1860-61 envelope 300.
Portsmouth
3¢ 1857-60 stamp 300.
Randolph Macon College
3¢ 1857-60 stamp 500.
Richmond
1¢ 1857-60 stamp 750.
Same, pair 500.
3¢ 1857-60 stamp 250.
3¢ 1853-55 envelope 250.
3¢ 1860-61 envelope 250.
Roaring Run
3¢ 1857-60 stamp 300.
Romney
3¢ 1857-60 stamp 500.
Salem
3¢ 1857-60 stamp 300.
Scottsville
1¢ 1857-60 stamp NR
Same, strip of 3 500.
Stanardsville
3¢ 1853-55 envelope 300.
Staunton
1¢ 1857-60 stamp NR
Same, strip of 3 500.
3¢ 1857-60 stamp 300.
Same, with DUE 3 (hdsp) 500.
Stony Point
3¢ 1860-61 envelope 300.
Theo Seminary (Theological Seminary)
3¢ 1857-60 stamp 500.
Timberville
3¢ 1857-60 stamp 300.
Tudor Hall
3¢ 1860-61 envelope 300.
Union Mills
3¢ 1860-61 envelope 300.
University of Virginia
3¢ 1860-61 envelope 500.
3¢ 1857-60 stamp 500.
Upperville
3¢ 1860-61 envelope 300.
Washington
3¢ 1853-55 envelope 300.
Williamsville
3¢ 1857-60 stamp 300.
Wilson's Depot
3¢ 1857-60 stamp 300.
Winchester
3¢ 1857-60 stamp 300.
3¢ 1860-61 envelope 300.
Woods X Roads
3¢ 1857-60 stamp 300.

Stampless Markings

FREDERICKSBURG VA / 3 PAID ("URG" AND "A" small caps raised) (32; 1861; black) 500.
FREDERICKSBURG / VA. ("A" raised) (32; 1861; black)
FREE 500.
Leatherwood
Ms Free B.F. Gravely P.M. 500.
Mt. Carmel (ms; 1861; black)
Ms Paid 3 500.
NORFOLK / Va. (YD; 32; 1861; blue)
FREE 500.
PATTONSBURG / Va. (34; 1861; blue)
Ms Free 500.
PIEDMONT STATION / VA (26; 1861; black)
FREE 500.
RICHMOND / Va. (32; 1861; black)
POST OFFICE BUSINESS / FREE (c) 750.
(no rate) [addressed to a postmaster] 500.
Vernon Hill (ms; 1861; black)
Ms Free 500.

Confederate Use of US Postage
(May 7 through May 31, 1861)

Stamps and Stamped Envelopes

Alexandria
3¢ 1857-60 stamp 250.
3¢ 1860-61 envelope 250.
Amherst C. H.
3¢ 1857-60 stamp 250.
Arrington
3¢ 1857-60 stamp 250.
Ashland
3¢ 1857-60 stamp 250.
Ayletts
3¢ 1857-60 stamp 250.
Belmead Mills
3¢ 1857-60 stamp 250.
3¢ 1853-54 envelope 250.
3¢ 1860-61 envelope 250.
Berryville
3¢ 1857-60 stamp 250.
Body Camp
3¢ 1857-60 stamp 250.
Bowling Green
3¢ 1857-60 stamp NR
Same, with "3 fwd" (ms) 250.
Boydton
3¢ 1860-61 envelope 250.
Ca Ira
3¢ 1857-60 stamp 300.
Chamblissburg
3¢ 1857-60 stamp 250.
Chantilly
3¢ 1857-60 stamp 250.
Charlotte C.H.
3¢ 1860-61 envelope 250.
Charlottesville
3¢ 1857-60 stamp 250.
Same, with FORWARDED (box) (hdsp) 500.
3¢ 1853-54 envelope 250.
3¢ 1860-61 envelope 250.

Chester	
3¢ 1857-60 stamp	250.
Christianburg	
3¢ 1857-60 stamp	250.
3¢ 1860-61 envelope	250.
Christianville	
3¢ 1857-60 stamp	250.
Clarksville	
1¢ 1857-60 stamp	250.
Same, with "Due 2" (ms)	500.
Cowpasture Bridge	
3¢ 1857-60 stamp	250.
Culpepper C.H.	
3¢ 1860-61 envelope	250.
3¢ 1857-60 stamp	250.
Dinwiddie C. H.	
3¢ 1860-61 envelope	250.
F Hall (Fredrickshall)	
3¢ 1857-60 stamp	250.
3¢ 1860-61 envelope	250.
Fairmont	
3¢ 1860-61 envelope	250.
Falmouth	
3¢ 1860-61 envelope	250.
Farmville	
3¢ 1853-55 envelope	250.
3¢ 1860-61 envelope	250.
Fincastle	
3¢ 1857-60 stamp	250.
Fords [Fords Depot]	
3¢ 1857-60 stamp	250.
Franklin Depot	
3¢ 1860-61 envelope	250.
Fredericksburg	
3¢ 1860-61 envelope	250.
Gainesville	
3¢ 1857-60 stamp	250.
Grayson C. H.	
3¢ 1857-60 stamp	250.
Greenville	
3¢ 1857-60 stamp	250.
Hague	
3¢ 1857-60 stamp	250.
Halifax [Halifax C.H.]	
1¢ 1857-60 stamp	NR
Same, strip of 3	500.
Hamp Sidney College (Hampden Sidney College)	
3¢ 1860-61 envelope	300.
Harmony	
3¢ 1857-60 stamp	250.
Harpers Ferry	
3¢ 1857-60 stamp	500.
3¢ 1853-54 envelope	500.
3¢ 1860-61 envelope	500.
Heathsville	
3¢ 1857-60 stamp	250.
Indian Valley	
3¢ 1857-60 stamp	250.
Keswick Depot	
3¢ 1860-61 envelope	250.
Leesburg	
3¢ 1857-60 stamp	250.
Lexington	
1¢ 1857-60 stamp	750.
Same, strip of 3	500.
3¢ 1857-60 stamp	250.
1¢ 1860-61 envelope	NR
Same, with pair 1¢ 1857-60 stamp	1,000.
3¢ 1860-61 envelope	250.
Loretto	
3¢ 1860-61 envelope	250.
Lynchburg	
3¢ 1857-60 stamp	250.
3¢ 1860-61 envelope	250.
Marion	
3¢ 1860-61 envelope	250.
Martinsburg	
3¢ 1860-61 envelope	500.
McGaheysville	
3¢ 1857-60 stamp	250.
Morgantown	
3¢ 1857-60 stamp	300.
Mount Sydney	
3¢ 1860-61 envelope	250.
Norfolk	
3¢ 1857-60 stamp	250.
3¢ 1860-61 envelope	250.
Oakville	
3¢ 1857-60 stamp	250.
Old Church	
3¢ 1857-60 stamp	250.
3¢ 1860-61 envelope	250.
Same, with "Way 1" (ms)	750.
Orange Court House	
3¢ 1857-60 stamp	250.
3¢ 1860-61 envelope	250.
Parkersburg	
3¢ 1857-60 stamp	250.
Petersburg	
3¢ 1857-60 stamp	250.
3¢ 1860-61 envelope	250.
Piedmont	
3¢ 1857-60 stamp	250.
Pittsylvania C.H.	
3¢ 1860-61 envelope	250.
Point Pleasant	
3¢ 1860-61 envelope	250.
Portsmouth	
3¢ 1857-60 stamp	250.
3¢ 1860-61 envelope	250.
Providence	
3¢ 1857-60 stamp	250.
Richmond	
1¢ 1857-60 stamp	750.
Same, strip of 3	500.
3¢ 1857-60 stamp	200.
3¢ 1853-54 envelope	200.
3¢ 1860-61 envelope	200.
Romney	
3¢ 1860-61 envelope	500.

Rose Mills	
3¢ 1860-61 envelope	250.
Salem	
3¢ 1857-60 stamp	250.
Shacklefords	
3¢ 1857-60 stamp	250.
Shrewsbury	
3¢ 1853-54 envelope	250.
Spotsylvania C.H.	
3¢ 1860-61 envelope	250.
Staunton	
3¢ 1857-60 stamp	250.
3¢ 1860-61 envelope	250.
Stony Point	
3¢ 1860-61 envelope	250.
Sunny Side	
3¢ 1860-61 envelope	250.
Tenth Legion	
3¢ 1860-61 envelope	250.
Tudor Hall	
3¢ 1860-61 envelope	250.
Tunstalls	
1¢ 1857-60 stamp	NR
Same, strip of 3	500.
University of Virginia	
3¢ 1857-60 stamp	300.
3¢ 1860-61 envelope	300.
Upperville	
3¢ 1860-61 envelope	250.
VA C. R.R./Cobham	
3¢ 1857-60 stamp	1,000.
Wheeling	
3¢ 1860-61 envelope	500.
Whittle's Mills	
3¢ 1853-55 envelope	250.
Williamsburg	
3¢ 1857-60 stamp	250.
Wilson's Depot	
3¢ 1857-60 stamp	250.
Winchester	
3¢ 1857-60 stamp	250.
3¢ 1860-61 envelope	250.
Woodville	
1¢ 1857-60 stamp	NR
Same, strip of 3	500.
Wytheville	
1¢ 1857-60 stamp	NR
Same, strip of 3	500.

Stampless Markings

ALEXANDRIA / VA (26 DCDS; black; 1861	
FREE	500.
Floyd C.H. (ms; 1861; black)	
Ms Paid 3c	500.
FREDERICKSHALL / VA. (29; 1861; black)	
PAID 3 (C)	500.
NORFOLK / Va. (32 YD; 1861; blue)	
FREE	500.
Pedlar's Mills (ms; 1861; black)	
Ms 3 with additional "Paid 3" (ms)	500.
RICHMOND / Va. (30 YD; 1861; black)	
FORWARDED 3	750.
STONY POINT / VA (32; 1861)	
Ms Free	500.
WINCHESTER / VA. (26 YD DC; 1861; black)	
PAID / 3	500.

Confederate State Use of US 30¢ 1860 issue to France

US Star Die envelope used from Charleston, S.C. on December 20, 1860, which is the day South Carolina seceded from the Union.

US 3¢ 1857 issue used from Montgomery, Alabama on February 4, 1861—the day delegates from the six seceded states assembled in Montgomery and declared themselves a Provisional Congress.

Confederate Postage Rates

The adoption of a Constitution by the Confederate Provisional Congress on February 8, 1861 was the first step in the process that led to the establishment of postal rates in the new Confederacy. The next day the Congress adopted the Act of February 9, 1861. This Act continued all laws of the United States in force and in use as of November 1, 1860 which were not inconsistent with the Constitution of the Confederate States. This included all laws governing the Post Office Department and its operation that were in effect under the United States Government on November 1, 1860. The Post Office Department's October 1, 1861 *Instructions to Postmasters* expanded on this by stating that all laws and regulations embraced in the *Postal Laws and Regulations* issued by the United States Post Office Department on May 15, 1859 (1859 *PL&R*) and not conflicting with the laws of the Confederacy were continued in force by the Act of February 9, 1861.

In effect the Act of February 9, 1861 established the Confederate postage rates and services as those in effect in the United States on November 1, 1860. Any changes to these rates and services had to be specifically addressed in new Confederate legislation.

The first legislation addressing postal rates was the Act of February 23, 1861. This Act established new postage rates, required the prepayment of postage, limited the franking privilege and eliminated the registration system. Before the rates could go into effect, the Act of May 13, 1861 made changes in the rates for packages, newspapers and periodicals. In addition the Act extended the franking privilege for official mail to specific bureau chiefs of the Post Office Department and the Auditor of the Treasury Department for the Post Office Department.

Subsequent laws made relatively minor changes to postal rates with the exception of the Act of July 29, 1861 that provided specific exemptions to the prepayment requirement and the Act of April 19, 1862 that established a uniform letter rate.

Between February 8 and May 31, 1861, several Acts were passed setting postage rates. Some sections of these Acts were superseded by new Acts and the rates in the original Acts were never effective. References to Acts containing sections that were never effective.are not included in the references given with the various rates.

The rates established in the Act of February 23, and as amended by the Act of May 13, 1861, were to be effective on a day to be set by Postmaster General Reagan for the takeover of postal operations in the Confederate States. The Act of May 9, 1861 authorized the Postmaster General to set a date for the takeover of mail service in the Confederacy. On May 13, 1861 Postmaster General Reagan issued a proclamation setting June 1, 1861 as the day the Confederate Post Office Department would assume all postal operations in the Confederate States.

The following paragraphs address the postage rates set by the Confederate Government and the rates that remained in effect in the Confederacy under the 1859 *PL&R*. This section does not address rates contained in the 1859 *PL&R* for specialized types of mail for which there are few or no examples extant.

The rates are arranged as follows:

Basic Postage Rates
- Letter Postage
- Waterway Mail
- International Letter Mail
- Books
- Circulars, Handbills and Pamphlets
- Newspapers and Periodicals
- Packages
- Treasury Notes and Bonds
- Conveyance of Mail Matter by Private Expresses

Prepayment and Exemptions
- Prepayment of Postage
- Prepayment Exemptions

Additional Services
- Advertised Mail
- Forwarded Mail
- Way Letters
- Trans-Mississippi Mail

Free Mail
- Franking Privilege
- Free Mail

Basic Postage Rates

Letter Postage *(Acts of February 23, 1861 and April, 19 1862)*

There were two types of letter postage: Regular letters (those for delivery beyond the office of mailing) and drop letters (letters for delivery at the mailing office).

Regular letter postage was determined by weight and, initially, by distance (Table 1).

Drop letter postage was charged by the letter without regard to weight (Table 1).

In all but a few cases, letter postage was required by law to be prepaid. In practice unpaid letters were accepted and marked with the postage due by some postmasters throughout the war.

Exemptions to the prepayment requirement are addressed in the "Prepayment of Postage and Exemptions" section that follows.

Inland Waterway Mail (*1859 PL&R*)

Inland waterway mail was not specifically addressed in Confederate legislation. Consequently the 1859 *PL&R* governed the rates of postage for such mail.

Postage rates for a letter carried on an inland waterway vessel were dependent on the type of vessel carrying the letter (contract or non contract) and whether the letter was prepaid or unpaid (due). Mail carried by a contract vessel in closed mailbags was treated as if it was transported overland. Such mail received no special markings and cannot be distinguished from bagged mail that was transported entirely overland.

Both contract and non-contract vessels picked up loose mail. This mail was either collected by the vessel captain or, in the case of a contract vessel, by the route agent if one was aboard. The captain or route agent was required to turn over all loose mail to the postmaster at the first port-of-call with a post office. If prepaid there was no additional charge. If unpaid the letters were rated as "Ship Letters." These rates were the same as unpaid letters listed in Table 2. Depending on the type of letter and type of vessel the letter was to be marked "Steam" or "Steamboat", "Ship" or "Way." In practice these markings were not always applied and some markings were used in lieu of others. See the **Inland Waterway Mail** and **Way Mail** sections for information on these markings.

Contrary to the provisions of the 1859 *PL&R,* the New Orleans postmaster charged 7¢ for unpaid and prepaid letters received from vessels for delivery at New Orleans.

Inland waterway rates listed in Table 2 make reference to "letter postage." These are the regular letter rates listed in Table 1. For a more detailed treatment of inland waterway mail see the **Inland Waterway Mail** section of this Catalog.

International Letter Mail *(Acts of February 23, 1861, March 1, 1861 and* 1859 *PL&R)*

The Acts of February 23 and March 1, 1861 authorized the Postmaster General to make arrangements of for the exchange of mails with foreign governments. The Union blockade of Southern ports and the failure of foreign governments to recognize the Confederate States prevented any effort to enter into mail arrangements with a foreign government.

Although there were no formal postal arrangements, international mail was carried to and received from foreign nations. Such mail was carried either by a blockade runner, an express company or as a favor by an individual. The domestic postage was required to be paid on all incoming and outgoing international mail.

Incoming mail carried by ship from foreign countries was to be delivered by the ship captain to the port post office. For this captains of domestic vessels were entitled to a fee of 2¢ per letter, captains of foreign vessels were not. A fee of 2¢ was to be added to all letters addressed beyond the port-of-entry regardless of whether the 2¢ captain's fee was paid or not. In practice this added 2¢ fee was not always charged. All incoming mail from a foreign port was also to be annotated "Ship," but this was not always done either.

In practice some incoming mail was illegally carried by passengers who posted the letters at the port post office. No additional fee was applied to such letters because they were presented as regular mail.

The postmaster at a seaport of departure was entitled to receive 1¢ for each letter left in his office for delivery by a transient vessel to a foreign port. There is no evidence this fee was charged to the sender as additional postage.
In practice most outgoing mail was delivered to a forwarding agent at a port, who in turn entrusted the captain of a blockade runner to deliver the mail to a foreign port. Othertimes a passenger would carry letters secretly and illegally for posting in a foreign port. Outgoing mail can only be identified as originating in the Confederacy by the enclosure or in some cases the docketing on the cover.

Table 1
Letter Postage Rates

Distance	Effective June 1, 1861 (per half ounce)	Effective July 1, 1862 (per half ounce)
Regular letters		
Not more than 500 miles	5¢	
More than 500 miles	10¢	
All distances		10¢
Drop letters	2¢[1]	2¢[1]

1. The drop rate was by letter, not weight.

Table 2
Inland Waterway Rates for Loose Mail
(Effective June 1, 1861)

Vessel Type / Postage	Postage for Delivery at Port-of-Entry	Postage for Delivery Beyond Port-of-Entry
Non-Contract Vessel		
Prepaid	Letter postage[1]	Letter postage[1]
Unpaid	6¢	Letter postage + 2¢[2]
Contract Vessel		
Prepaid	Letter postage	Letter postage
Unpaid	6¢	Letter postage + 2¢[2]

1. Postage calculated from point where the letter was placed aboard the vessel to the destination post office.
2. Postage calculated from port post office at which the vessel delivered the letter to the destination post office.

Table 3
International Mail
(Domestic Rates Only)

Means of Conveyance	Effective June 1, 1861
By Sea	
Incoming ("Ship Letters")	
Delivery at port-of-entry	6¢
Delivery beyond the port-of-entry	Letter rate + 2¢
Outgoing	Letter rate[1]
By Land	Letter rate[2]

1. There was no international rate for outgoing mail. Domestic rates applied from the point of mailing to the port-of-departure.
2. Letter rate from border port-of-entry to destination office or point of mailing to border port-of-departure.

Books *(Acts of May 13, 1861* and *April 29, 1863)*

Books published in the Confederacy and not weighing over four pounds were mailable. The postage rate was 2¢ per ounce for any distance. For books published outside the Confederacy the rate was double. This rate was effective June 1, 1861.

Circulars, Handbills and Pamphlets *(Acts of May 13, 1861* and *April 29, 1863)*

Postage on circulars (not sealed), handbills and pamphlets was based on weight and the place of publication. See Table 4.

Newspapers and Periodicals *(Acts of May 13, 1861* and *April 29, 1863)*

There were two different rate structures for newspapers and periodicals: one was for subscribers and one for non-subscribers.

Postage rates for subscribers were initially based on quarterly subscriptions. In 1863 the rates were simplified by charging postage on a per issue basis. In both cases the postage was required to be paid quarterly in advance. See Tables 5, and 6.

Postage rates for non-subscribers were on a per issue basis. These rates were the same as for circulars, handbills and pamphlets. See Table 4.

Packages *(Act of May 13, 1861)*

Postage rates for packages (including money packages) were the same as for letters (see Table 1). This rate was effective June 1, 1861

Treasury Notes and Bonds *(Act of May 1, 1863)*

The Act of May 1, 1863 declared Treasury notes and bonds packed in boxes mailable matter. These boxes were restricted to transport by railroad. The postage rates on such shipments were to be fixed by agreement between the Postmaster General and the Secretary of the Treasury. No information on the rate set for these shipments has been found.

Conveyance of Mail Matter by Private Expresses (*Acts of March 15, 1861, April 19, 1862,* and *1859 PL&R)*

Effective June 1, 1861 express companies were authorized to carry all mailable matter provided the Confederate postage was paid from the point of receipt to the point of delivery. The Act of April 19, 1862 rescinded all laws regarding the carriage of mailable matter by express companies and reinstated the provisions of the 1859 *PL&R* effective June 1, 1862.

The provisions of the 1859 *PL&R* allowed express companies to carry letters over post roads provided they were in sealed stamped envelopes (postal stationary). Letters prepaid by stamps were prohibited. The Confederate Post Office Department never issued stamped envelopes so technically this prohibited private expresses from carrying letters. This was actually how the law was implemented as confirmed in Postmaster Reagan's Report to the President dated May 2, 1864. This prohibition was specifically aimed at the Southern Express Company which continually violated the law regarding the transportation of mail. It was also used to shut down the Cushing Express in September 1864.

The 1859 *PL&R* permitted the carriage of newspapers and periodicals by private expresses provided the appropriate postage for this type of mail was prepaid.

Table 4
Domestic Circular, Handbill, Pamphlet, and Non-Subscriber Newspaper Rates[1]

	Effective June 1, 1861		Effective July 1, 1863	
Type	**First 3 ounces**	**Each additional ounce**	**First ounce**	**Each additional ounce**
Newspapers, circulars, etc.	2¢	2¢	1¢	1¢
Drop (delivery at mailing office)[2]	1¢	—	1¢	—

1. Foreign publications charged double the domestic rate.
2. Rate was per item, not weight. Double rates for foreign publications did not apply to drop publications.

Table 5
Subscriber Rates for Domestic Newspapers[1]
(Rate per Quarter Prepaid)

	Effective June 1, 1861		Effective July 1, 1863	
Type Subscription	**First 3 Ounces**	**Each additional Ounce**	**First 3 Ounces**	**Each Additional Ounce**
Daily	70¢	35¢		
Six times a week	60¢	30¢		
Tri-weekly	30¢	15¢		
Semi-weekly	20¢	10¢		
Weekly	10¢	5¢		
All subscriptions[2]			1¢	½¢

1. Foreign newspapers charged double the domestic rate.
2. Rate per issue prepaid quarterly.

Table 6
Subscriber Rates for Domestic Periodicals[1]
(Rate per Quarter Prepaid)

	Effective June 1, 1861		Effective July 1, 1863	
Type Subscription	**Rate/Weight**	**Each additional ounce**	**Rate/Weight**	**Each additional ounce**
More than semi-monthly[2]	Charged as Newspaper[3]	—		
Semi-monthly	5¢[4] First 1½ ounces	5¢		
Monthly	2½¢[4] First 1½ ounces	2½¢		
Quarterly or bi-monthly	2¢[4] First ounce	2¢		
Any subscription			1¢[4] First ounce	1¢

1. Foreign periodicals charged double the domestic rate.
2. The Act states "bi-monthly" but the intent was "semi-monthly." The Post Office Department's October 1, 1861 Instructions to Postmasters states "semi-monthly."
3. See Table 5 for subscriber newspaper rates.
4. Rate per issue prepaid quarterly.

Prepayment of Postage and Exemptions

Prepayment of Postage *(Acts of February 23, 1861, May 13, 1861* and *April 29, 1863)*

The postage on all mail was required to be prepaid with very few exceptions (see next paragraph). Any unpaid letters received at a post office were to be sent to the Dead Letter Office. In practice unpaid letters were accepted by some postmasters throughout the war.

The same requirement for prepayment should have superseded the provision for the acceptance of unpaid ship and steamboat letters under the provisions of the 1859 *PL&R*. Examples of such mail show that they continued to be accepted by at least some port postmasters.

Prepayment Exemptions *(Acts of July 29, 1861, August 29, 1861* and *August 31, 1861)*

Several types of mail were granted exemptions from the prepayment requirement. In all cases the recipient was required to pay the postage.

Soldier's Letters and other Mailable Matter. The Act of July 29, 1861 permitted any officer, musician or private of the army, engaged in the actual service of the Confederate States, to send all types of mailable matter without the prepayment of postage. The postage was to be collected on delivery from the recipient. Postage rates were the same as if the letters and other mailable matter were sent prepaid. All such mail was to be endorsed with the name and unit of the soldier. In the case of officers they were to also include their title. In practice soldiers of all ranks normally included their name, rank and unit. It is assumed this Act was effective July 29, 1861, as the legislation did not include an effective date.

This Act specifically states the exemption is for members of the "army engaged in the actual service of the Confederate States." In practice members of the Navy and Marine Corps also used the exemption.

The soldier's prepayment exemption did not apply to Trans-Mississippi Express Mail. This was a special service and required prepayment.

The soldier's prepayment exemption did not apply to members of state militias that were under state control.

Congressional Letters. Congressmen were permitted to send letters without the prepayment of postage. The postage was to be paid on delivery by the recipient. All such letters were to be endorsed with the signature of the congressman. It is doubtful this privilege was widely used as congressmen were probably reluctant to have their constituents pay to receive their letters. It is assumed this Act was effective July 29, 1861 as the legislation did not include an effective date.

State Officials. The Act approved August 29, 1861 provided that all mailable matter addressed to officers of the several states could be sent without the prepayment of postage. The postage was to be collected from the state government at the office of delivery. Such mail had to be endorsed by the sender with his title and the nature of the matter mailed. This exemption was primarily intended for official mail from county and city officials to the various departments of the state government. It is assumed this Act was effective August 29, 1861 as it did not include an effective date.

Dealers in Newspapers and Periodicals. The Act of August 31, 1861 allowed persons engaged as dealers in newspapers and periodicals to order and receive by mail any quantity of newspapers or periodicals without prepayment of the postage. Postage was due at the place of delivery at the same rate as charged subscribers. It is assumed this Act was effective August 31, 1861 as it did not include an effective date.

Additional Services

Advertised Mail (*Act of February 23, 1861* and *1859 PL&R)*

Letters that remained unclaimed in a post office beyond a specific period of time were advertised in the local newspaper. The frequency of such advertisements depended on the quarterly gross receipts of an office. The period ranged from once each week at the largest offices to once in six weeks at the smallest offices. Such mail was charged an additional fee of two cents to be paid by the recipient. The regulations regarding advertised mail were effective June 1, 1861.

Refused letters, drop letters, circulars and free packets containing printed matter were not to be advertised.

Forwarded Mail *(1859 PL&R)*

Forwarded Letters. Confederate postal legislation did not address forwarding mail. Therefore the 1859 *PL&R* applied. This regulation stated, "it is proper to forward a letter when duly requested." The regulations further stated a forwarded letter "must be charged with additional postage according to distance . . . which additional postage may be paid at either the forwarding office or at the office of delivery." Rules applying to forwarded mail were effective June 1, 1861.

Although the Confederate Post Office Department required the prepayment of postage, most forwarded mail was sent postage due as was the practice under the former US postal system.

Missent Letters. Some Confederate covers bear a "Missent" marking. This marking meant the letter was misdirected by a postmaster. There was no additional charge on a missent letter. Sometimes both a "Missent" and "Forwarded" marking appear on a cover. The use of a "Forwarded" marking on missent letters was not required and did not result in an additional charge.

Soldiers Letters. The Act of July 29, 1861 provided for the forwarding of mail directed to officers, musicians or privates in the army free of additional postage when they were lawfully moved to a new location. In practice this was applied to unit movements and individual movements. It is assumed this Act was effective July 29, 1861, as the legislation did not include an effective date.

Way Letters *(1859 PL&R)*

Confederate postal legislation did not address way mail. Therefore the 1859 *PL&R* applied. Way letters were those letters received by a mail carrier on his way between two post offices. The mail carrier was to deliver the letters to the next post office on his route. There, if he demanded, he could receive 1¢ for each letter delivered. If paid, the 1¢ was added to the postage on the letter. The postmaster was required to annotate such letters with the word "Way" next to the rate. Rules applying to way mail were effective June 1, 1861.

Prepaid loose mail picked up by route agents on railroads and steamboats between stations or landings with post offices was also classified as way mail but normally not marked as such. Unpaid loose letters picked up by non-contract steamboats were handled as "ship mail." See **Inland Waterway Mail** section for these rates.

Trans-Mississippi Mail *(Acts of October 6, 1862, April 16, 1863* and *May 1, 1863)*

The first effort to establish a speedy mail service across the Mississippi River was the Act of October 6, 1862. This Act authorized the Postmaster General to employ special agents to "secure the speedy and certain transportation of mails across the Mississippi River." Apparently this Act did not result in the desired improvement in service and the next year two new mail services were authorized: Preferred Mail and the Trans-Mississippi Express Mail.

Preferred Mail. The Act of April 16, 1863 authorized the Postmaster General "to establish a mail route for the more speedy transmission of letters and dispatches, only, between the States lying east and those lying west of the Mississippi River." The rate of postage was set at fifty cents per half ounce or fraction thereof.

The name "preferred mail" comes from the title of the Act that authorized it, "An Act to establish a preferred mail across the Mississippi River."

There is no evidence Postmaster General Reagan used this authorization to establish a preferred mail service. Post Office records indicate all his efforts were focused on establishing a Trans-Mississippi Express mail that was authorized two weeks later.

Several Trans-Mississippi covers exist that bear 50¢ in postage. There is no evidence these were carried as "Preferred Mail." Some of the covers bear the same routing notations as found on Trans-Mississippi Express mail indicating they were carried as Trans-Mississippi Express Mail. One explanation for the covers bearing 50¢ in postage is a purported newspaper notice about the Trans-Mississippi Express Mail that erroneously stated the rate was 50¢.

Trans-Mississippi Express Mail. The Act of May 1, 1863 authorized the Postmaster General "to establish express mails for the conveyance of letters and government dispatches only." The Act set a maximum rate of $1.00 per half ounce or fraction thereof for any distance not exceeding 500 miles and double the rate for distances over 500 miles. The Postmaster General set the rate at 40¢ per half ounce or fraction thereof and ignored the two tier distance rate structure required by the legislation.

There is no effective date for the Trans-Mississippi Express Mail as it was left to the Postmaster General to establish the service. The earliest recorded Trans-Mississippi Express covers are dated in October 1863.

The Trans-Mississippi Express Mail was a premium service. It did not replace the regular letter rate of 10¢ for letters directed across the Mississippi. Soldier's due letters were not authorized to be carried in the Trans-Mississippi Express Mail.

Free Mail

Franking Privilege *(Acts of February 23, 1861, May 13, 1861* and *May 23, 1864)*

Post Office Department Officials. The Acts of February 23 and May 13, 1861 authorized specific members of the Post Office and Treasury Departments to use the franking privilege for mail that was sent on official business. An Act of May 23, 1864 extended the franking privilege to the Agent for the Trans-Mississippi Agency and the Auditor of the Trans-Mississippi Department. This Act was more restrictive allowing the Trans-Mississippi officials the franking privilege only "upon all matter connected with the adjustment and settlement of postal accounts."

Franked mail matter was to be endorsed on the back of the letter or package "Official Business" over the signature of the authorized official. In practice the endorsements were normally on the front of letters. Officials authorized the franking privilege and the effective dates are listed below:

- Postmaster General and chief clerks (effective June 1, 1861)
- Agent for the Trans-Mississippi Agency (effective May 23, 1864)
- Auditor of the Treasury for the Post Office Department (effective June 1, 1861)
- Auditor of the Trans-Mississippi Department (effective May 23, 1864)
- Chief of Appointment Bureau (effective June 1, 1861)
- Chief of Contract Bureau (effective June 1, 1861)
- Chief of Finance Bureau (effective June 1, 1861)

Postmasters. Postmasters were permitted to send free of postage letters and packages that related exclusively to the business of their office or to the business of the Post Office Department. Postmasters sending such mail were to endorse on the letter or package over their signature the words, "Post Office Business." In practice postmasters used various forms of the endorsement or merely the word "Free." This privilege was effective June 1, 1861.

Post office business included letters and packages between postmasters and the Post Office Department in Richmond, between individual postmasters and between postmasters and publishers of newspapers and periodicals. The latter was to inform publishers that a subscriber had moved, died or was not taking delivery of a publication.

Free Mail *(Acts approved May 13, 1861, August 31, 1861, May 23, 1864 and January 30, 1865)*

Publishers. Publishers of newspapers and periodicals were authorized to exchange one copy of their publication with other publishers free of postage. This was effective June 1, 1861.

Newspapers to Soldiers. On December 7, 1864 Senate Bill 130 was introduced authorizing newspapers to be mailed to soldiers free of postage. The bill was passed by both the Senate and House of Representatives but was vetoed by President Davis on January 25, 1865. On January 28 the Senate voted to override the veto and the House followed on January 30. This was late in the war and it is not known if or when the Act was implemented.

THE DAILY TIMES.

City Official Journal.

Confederate States Postage.

Envelopes properly stamped will be furnished at the Post Office until Government stamps can be procured.

The postage on all single letters not exceeding 500 miles will be 5 cents; over 500 miles 10 cents.

All single letters mailed at this office for Virginia, North Carolina, Arkansas, Texas, Louisiana (except New Orleans,) Memphis, Tenn., North and West Mississippi, will pay 10 cents.

Single letters are such as weigh not exceeding half an ounce, every additional half ounce or fraction of an ounce will double the postage.

All drop letters will pay 2 cents.

Business men will do well to preserve this list for reference, as all letters must be prepaid in full.

May 31—d2t H. M. JETER, P. M.

From *The* [Columbus, Georgia] *Daily Times* of May 31, 1861.

LITTLE ROCK
10

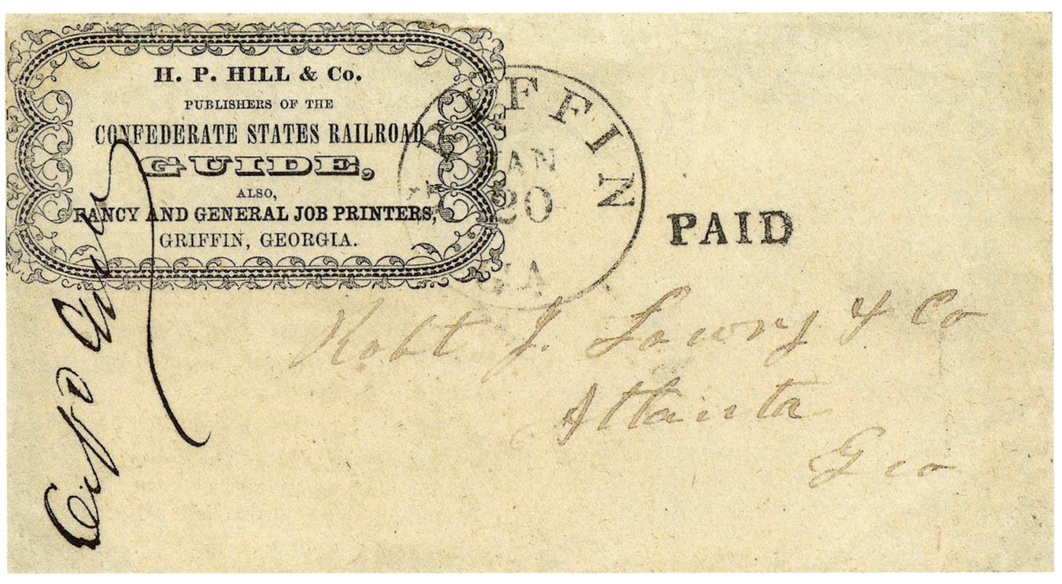
H. P. HILL & Co.
PUBLISHERS OF THE
CONFEDERATE STATES RAILROAD
GUIDE,
ALSO,
FANCY AND GENERAL JOB PRINTERS,
GRIFFIN, GEORGIA.
PAID

STAMPLESS MARKINGS

In past catalogs, this section was titled "Handstamped Paids" and more recently "Handstamped Provisionals and Other Markings." The latter title was somewhat misleading in that it applied the term "provisional" to all handstamped markings. This was counter to the generally accepted meaning of the term. The new title "Stampless Markings" covers those markings applied at the time of mailing to indicate the postage paid or due or other services.

When the Confederate postal system went into operation on June 1, 1861, there were no stamps available to prepay postage on letters. Each postmaster was left to his own devices to come up with a way to indicate the postage paid or due on letters. Postmasters at many offices had a supply of handstamping devices left over from the late 1840s and early 1850s. These included "PAID," "DUE," "5," and "10" markings that met the requirements for the new postage rates. Postmasters of smaller offices, which never had any handstamping devices, resorted to marking letters with manuscript rates. Other postmasters had markings prepared for their use or even prepared their own.

As noted above, stampless markings include not only those markings used to indicate the prepayment of postage or the amount of postage due but all other markings applied to indicate a type of mail or service. These include free, way, steam, ship, forwarded, missent, and advertised. All such markings are included in this section.

The handstamped markings are listed by state and alphabetically by town within a state. Markings for each town are listed by paid rates, due rates, and auxiliary markings. Each individual marking or combination of markings is assigned a type letter. If there are varieties of a type, they are listed under the type letter without further designation. All manuscript markings are listed under the single type "Ms." They are arranged in the same manner as the handstamped markings. Some town listings have the type "Pk." This type is used to designate covers with a postmark but no other markings to indicate the rate or postal service rendered. Some may have been drop letters and others oversights. Markings followed by an asterisk indicate that the listing was carried forward from the 1986 *New Dietz Confederate States Catalog and Handbook* but has not been confirmed by a copy of the marking.

Prepayment of postage was required in almost all cases except soldier's letters after the end of July 1861. The existence of covers with only a numeral rate marking without the requisite soldier's endorsement indicates this policy was not strictly followed. While these may appear to be prepaid letters, in almost all instances it was not the case. Accounting procedures at the time required a postmaster to separately account for all paid and unpaid letters on a post bill. The paid and due letters had to match the tally on the post bill. Unless the word "paid" was handstamped or written on a letter with a rate marking, there was no way to tell if a letter was paid or due. Furthermore, postmasters received a commission based on the net proceeds of their office. A due letter sent from their office did not count toward their net proceeds. Instead it accrued at the office of delivery. Consequently postmasters had a monetary incentive to make sure all paid letters were properly marked as "paid." Admittedly postal regulations required unpaid letters (except for soldier's letters and a few others) to be forwarded to the Dead Letter Office. The relatively large number of civilian letters with only a numeral marking indicates many were not forwarded to the Dead Letter office. For these reasons, the editors have classified them as due or collect letters.

Every attempt was made to illustrate all individual markings or combinations of markings representing a rate or service. When illustrations were not available, tracings from the 1986 *New Dietz* were used. In a few cases, no illustration of a marking could be found and these are so indicated. Illustrations of actual markings are approximately 80% of actual size. Tracings are not reduced.

The absence of a marking or combination of markings in the listings included in this section does not imply scarcity.

ABBREVIATIONS AND SYMBOLS KEY—STAMPLESS

[*]	symbol used after an item description to mean an unsupported listing
[–]	symbol used in place of value to mean insufficient information to assign a price
[?]	symbol used to mean unknown measurement, date or color
[*italic*]	value typeface indicating the item is difficult to price accurately
DC	double circle
DLC	double [outer] line circle
IH	used in place of listing value when the item is held by an institution
mkg	marking
ms	manuscript
NA	used in place of a listing value when no examples are known to exist
NOR	no outer rim
NR	used in place of value when no examples have been recorded
OV	Oval
Pk	cover bearing a postmark but no indication of rate
pmk	postmark
SC	segmented circle
SL	straightline
YD	year date

Folded letter dated May 29, 1861 franked with US 3¢ 1857 stamp postmarked Troy, Ala. June 1 [1861], the first day Confederate rates took effect. The Confederate postmaster did not recognize the US 3¢ stamp for payment of postage and handstamped the letter PAID 5 to show the proper Confederate postage was paid.

Mobile, Alabama July 6, 1861 use on all-over grocer advertising cover franked with PAID 2 revalued by PAID 5.

ALABAMA

Abbeville

A

ABBEVILLE / ALA. (32; 1861; black)

A	PAID 5, revalued 10 (ms)	300.
Ms	Paid 10*	150.

Alexandria

PAID

A

ALEXANDRIA / ALA (37; 1861; black)

A	PAID, 5 (ms)*	175.

Andalusia

Andalusia Ala (ms; 1861; black)

A	PAID, 25 (ms) [not illustrated]	300.

Arbor Vitae

Arbor vitae Ala (ms; 1861; black)

Ms	Miss Sent and Foured [Missent and Forwarded]	300.

Athens

PAID 5

A B

Athens Ala (ms; 1862; black)

ATHENS / ALª ("N" reversed) (31; 1861; black)

A	PAID 5	200.
B	PAID X	300.
	Same (blue)*	500.
Ms	Paid 5*	175.
	10 [due]*	150.

Auburn

PAID 5

PAID 10

A B

AUBURN / Ala. (32; 1861; blue-green)

A	PAID 5 (blue-green)	300.
B	PAID 10 (blue-green)	300.

Autaugaville

A

AUTAUGAVILLE / ALA (26; 1861-62; black)

A	PAID 5	200.

Bashi

Bashi Ala (ms; 186-; black)

Ms	Paid 10	150.

Bellefonte

A

Bellefonte Ala (ms; 1861; black)

BELLAFONTE / ALª (?; 1861; black)

A	PAID 5	150.
Ms	Paid 5*	175.

Benton

PAID

PAID

A B

PAID 5

PAID 10

C D

BENTON / ALA. (26; 186-; black)

BENTON / Ala. (31; 186-; black)

A	PAID, 40 (ms)*	300.
B	PAID 5 (altered rate)*	200.
C	PAID 5	200.
D	PAID 10	200.

Bladon Springs

Paid 10 CTS

A B

BLADON SPRINGS / Ala. (32; 1861-64; black)

A	Paid, 5 (ms) CTS	300.
B	Paid, 10 (ms) CTS	300.

Ms Paid 10 150.
10 [due]* 150.
Paid 30 200.

Blakely

B

BLAKELY / ALA. (30 YD; 1862; black)
A PAID [no rate] [not illustrated]* 200.
B PAID 10* 200.
Ms Paid 10* 150.

Blountsville

Blountsville Ala (ms; 186-; black)
Ms Due 10* 150.

Blue Mountain

Blue Mt Ala (ms; 1864; black)
Ms Paid 10 cts 150.
Due 10 150.

Blue Pond

Blue pond (ms; 1861; black)
Ms Paid 5 175.

Bridgeville

A

BRIDGEVILLE / ALA (26; 1861; black)
A PAID 5 200.

Buford

Bufford Al (ms; 1862; black)
Ms Due / 10 150.

Burnt Corn

Burnt Corn Ala (ms; 1861; black)
Ms Pd 20* 200.

Butler

A

B

BUTLER / ALA (37; 1861; black)
A PAID 5 200.
B PAID 10* 200.

Buycksville

Buycksville Ala (ms; 186-; black)
Ms Paid 10 150.

Cahaba

A B

C

D

CAHABA / AL[a] (31; 1861; black)
CAHABA / Ala. (34; 186-; black)
A PAID 5* 200.
B PAID 10 200.
C FORWARDED 5 500.
D STEAMBOAT 10* 1,000.

Camden

A B

CAMDEN / Ala (35; 1861; black)
A PAID 5* 200.
B PAID 10* 200.

Canton

Canton Ala (ms; 186-; black)
Ms 10 [due]* 150.

Carlowsville

A

CARLOWSVILLE / ALA (30; 1863; black)
A PAID 10 200.

Carthage

Carthage, Ala (ms; 1861; black)

Ms	Paid / 10	150.

Cedar Bluff

PAID (5)

A

Cedar Bluff Ala (ms; 1862; black)

A	PAID 5*	200.

Central Institute

PAID

A

CENTRAL INSTITUTE / ALA. (37; 186-; black)

A	PAID, 5 (ms)*	200.

Centre

PAID (5) PAID (10)

A  B

CENTRE / ALA. (31; 1861; black)

A	PAID 5	200.
B	PAID 10*	200.

Centreville

PAID 5 PAID 5

A  B

Centreville Ala (ms; 1861; black)
CENTREVILLE / Ala. (30; 1861; black)

A	PAID 5	200.
B	PAID 5*	200.
Ms	Pd 5	175.

Chambers Court House

PAID 5 PAID 10

A  B

10

a

CHAMBERS C. H. / Ala. (34; 1861; black, blue)

A	PAID 5*	200.
	Same (blue)*	250.
	Same (blue), revalued 10 (type *a*) (blue)	500.
B	PAID 10 (blue)	200.

Chanahatchee

Chanahatchee Ala (ms; 1861, black)

Ms	Pd 10*	150.

Childersburg

Childersburg ala (ms; 186-; black)

Ms	Paid 10	150.

Chunenuggee

PAID PAID (5)

A  B

CHUNENUGGE / Ala (31; 186-; black)

A	PAID, 5 (ms)*	200.
B	PAID 5*	200.

Citronelle

PAID 5

A

Citronelle Ala (ms; 1861; black)

A	PAID 5	200.

Claiborne

PAID

A

CLAIBORNE / Ala. (30; 1861; black)

A	PAID, 15 (ms)*	300.
B	PAID 10 [not illustrated]	200.

Clayton

A  B

C

CLAYTON / Ala. (30; 1864; black)

A	PAID, 5 (ms)	200.
	Same, 40 (ms)*	300.
B	PAID 5	200.
C	PAID 10*	200.

Clinton

A

CLINTON / AL. (30; 1861; orange)

A	PAID 5 (orange)*	500.

Coleta

Coleta (ms; 1863; black)

Ms	pd 10*	150.

Columbia

COLUMBIA / ALA (31; 1861; black)

A	PAID 5, revalued 10 (ms)* [not illustrated]	250.

Columbiana

A

COLUMBIANA / Ala (27; 1861; black)

A	PAID 5	200.

Courtland

COURTLAND / Ala. (?; 186-; blue)

Ms	10 [due]	150.

Cowikee

Cowikee Ala (ms; 1861; black)

Ms	Paid 10c	150.

Crawford

Postmark unknown

Ms	Paid 5*	175.

Cross Keys

A

CROSS KEYS / ALA (31; 186-; blue)

A	PAID 5 (blue)	300.

Cusseta

A  B

CUSSETA / Ala. (34; 186-; black)

A	PAID [no rate]*	200.
B	PAID [no rate]	200.
	Same, 10 (ms)*	200.

Dadeville

A  B

D

DADEVILLE / Ala (32; 1862; black)

A	PAID 5	200.
B	PAID 5	200.
C	PAID 5 (red) [not illustrated]*	300.
D	PAID 10	200.

Dayton

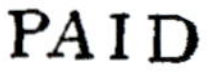

A  B

C  D

DAYTON / Ala. (30; 1862; black)

A	PAID, 5 (ms)*	200.
B	PAID 5*	200.

C	PAID 10*	200.
D	PAID 10	200.

DECATUR

A B

C

DECATUR / Ala. (30; 1861-62; black)

A	PAID 5*	200.
B	PAID 5*	200.
C	PAID 10*	200.

DEMOPOLIS

A B

DEMOPOLIS / Ala. (31; 1861-64; black)

A	PAID [no rate]	200.
	Same, 10 (ms)*	200.
B	PAID 5	200.
Ms	Paid 5*	175.
	Paid 10	150.
	Due 10	150.
	Due 30*	200.

DESOTO

Desoto Ala (ms; 1861; black)

Ms	Paid 5*	175.

ELYTON

Elyton ala (ms; 1861; black)
ELYTON / Al. (?; 1862; black)

Ms	Paid / 5	175.
	Paid / 5c	175.

EUFAULA

A B C

D E

F

EUFAULA / Ala. (30; 1861-64; black)

A	C. S. Paid. [no rate]*	500.
B	PAID [no rate]	200.
C	PAID 2*	500.
D	PAID 5	200.
	Same, struck twice	300.
E	PAID 10	200.
	Same, struck twice	300.
F	10 [due]	150.
Ms	Due 10 cts*	150.

EUTAW

A B C

D E

F G

EUTAW / ALA (25 DC YD; 1861-64; black)

A	PAID [no rate]*	200.
B	PAID 5	200.
C	PAID 5	200.
D	PAID 10	200.
E	PAID 10	300.
F	10 [due]	200.
G	DUE 5	250.

EVERGREEN

EVERGREEN / ALA (30; 186-; black)

Ms	Paid 5*	175.

Fauns Dale

Fauns Dale ala (ms; 1864; black)

Ms	Paid 10	150.

Fayetteville

Fayetteville Ala (ms; 1861; black)

Ms	Paid*	150.

Florence

PAID — A
PAID 5 — B 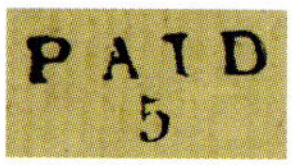

FLORENCE / ALA (26 DC YD; 1861; black)
FLORENCE / Ala. (29; 1861; black)

A	PAID, 5 (ms)	200.
B	PAID 5	200.

Forkland

FORKLAND / ALA (30; 1861; black)

Ms	PD 5	175.
	Pd 10	150.

Fort Deposit

PAID — A

FORT DEPOSIT / ALA. (32; 1861; black)

A	PAID, 5 (ms)	200.
	Same, 10 (ms)	200.
Ms	5*	175.
	10*	150.

Gainesville

PAID — A
PAID — B 
PAID 5 — C 
PAID 10 — D  
MISSENT — E

GAINESVILLE / Ala. (32; 1861-64; black)

A	PAID, 30 (ms)	300.
	Same, 35 (ms)	300.
B	PAID, 10 (ms)*	200.
C	PAID 5	200.
D	PAID 10*	200.
E	MISSENT	500.
Ms	Paid 10*	150.
	Missent 5	200.

Gaston

GASTON / Ala. (30; 1861; red)

Ms	Paid 10	150.

Georgiana

PAID 10 — A

GEORGIANA / ALA (32; 186-; ?)

A	PAID 10	200.

Glennville

Glennville / Ala. (?; 1861; black)

Ms	Paid 10	150.

Green Hill

Green Hill / Ala (ms; 1861; black)

Ms	Paid 5	175.

Greensborough

PAID 5 — A
PAID 5 — B  
PAID 10 — C
PAID 10 — D 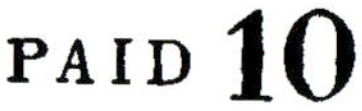 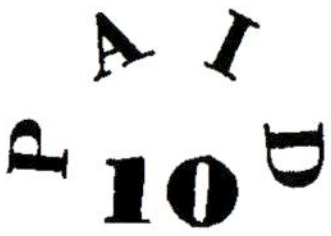
PAID 10 — E
PAID 20 — F 
10 — G 

GREENSBOROUGH / Ala. (32; 1861-63; black)

A	PAID 5	200.
B	PAID 5*	200.
C	PAID 10	200.
D	PAID 10	200.
E	PAID 10	200.
F	PAID 20	300.
G	10 [due]	150.
Ms	Missent & Forwd	150.
	P. Office [free]	150.

GREENVILLE

A B C D

GREENVILLE / Ala. (34; 1861-62; black)

A	PAID, 5 (ms)*	200.
B	PAID 5*	200.
C	PAID 5	200.
D	PAID 10	200.
Ms	Paid 10	150.

GROVE HILL

A B

GROVE HILL / ALA (24; 1861; black)

A	PAID, 5 (ms)	200.
B	PAID 5	200.
Ms	Due 10*	150.
	Paid 10	150.

GUNTERSVILLE

Guntersville Ala (ms; 186-; black)

Ms	Paid 5 cts	175.

HAMDEN

Hamden Ala (ms; 1861; black)

Ms	Paid 5*	175.

HARDAWAY

Hardaway Ala (ms; 186-; black)

Ms	Pd 10*	150.

HATCHECHUBBEE

A

HATCHECHUBBEE / ALA (40 x 9 SL; 1861; black, brown)

A	PAID 10*	200.
	Same (brown)	300.

HAVANNA

A B C D

HAVANNA / ALA. (27; 186-; blue)
HAVANNA / ALA. (32; 1861; black, blue)

A	PAID (blue) [no rate]	200.
	Same, 10 (ms)*	200.
B	PAID 5 (blue)	300.
C	PAID 5*	200.
D	PAID 10 (blue)	300.
Ms	Ford / Due 10	150.

HAW RIDGE

A

Haw Ridge Ala (ms; 186-; black)
HAW RIDGE / ALA. (30; 186-; black)

A	PAID 10	200.
Ms	Paid 10	150.

HAYNEVILLE

A B

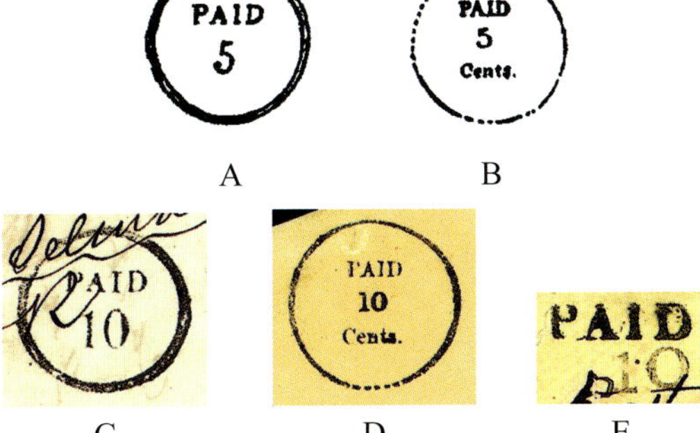

C D E

HAYNEVILLE / Ala. (33; 1861-62; black)

A	PAID 5	200.
B	PAID 5 Cents.	500.
C	PAID 10	200.
D	PAID 10 Cents	500.
E	PAID 10*	200.
	Same, revalued 5 cts (ms)	300.

Hickory Grove

A

HICKORY GROVE / ALA (32; 1862; black)

A	PAID 5	200.

Hillabee

Hillabee (ms; 186-; black)

Pk	No rate or paid markings	150.

Huntsville

A B C D

E F G

H I

J K

L M N

HUNTSVILLE / ALA (26 DC YD; 1861-62; blue)
HUNTSVILLE / Ala (32 YD; 1861; black, blue)

A	PAID (blue), 5 (ms)	200.
B	PAID 5 (blue)	200.
	Same (blue), revalued 10 (Type F)	300.
C	PAID 5 (blue)	200.
D	PAID 5 (blue)	200.
E	PAID 5 (blue)	200.
F	PAID 10 (blue)	200.
G	PAID 10 (blue)	200.
	Same (blue), revalued 5 (type D)*	300.
H	PAID 10 (blue)	200.
I	PAID 10 (blue)	200.
J	PAID 10 (blue)*	200.
K	PAID 10 (blue)	200.
L	DUE 5 (red)	200.
M	DUE 5 (blue)	200.
N	DUE 10 (blue)	200.

Indian Creek

Indian Creek Ala (ms; 186-; black)

Ms	Paid / 10 cts	150.

Jamestown

James Town Ala (ms; 186-; black)

Ms	Paid / 10	150.

Jasper

Jasper Ala (ms; 186-; black)

Ms	Paid 10*	150.
	Due 10*	150.

Jefferson

A

JEFFERSON / Ala. (30; 1861; brown)

A	PAID 5 (brown)	300.

Kingston

A

KINGSTON / ALA (26; 1861; black)

A	PAID 5*	200.

LaGrange

Postmark unknown

A	PAID 10 [not illustrated]*	200.

Leighton

Leighton / ALA. (33; 1861; black)

Ms	Paid 5¢	175.

Lime Kilns

Lime Kilns Ala (ms; 186-; black)

Ms	Paid 10	150.

Livingston

A B

LIVINGSTON / Ala. (33; 1861-62; black)

A PAID 5 200.
B PAID 10 200.
Ms Paid 5* 175.

Loachapoka

A B

C

LOACHAPOKA / ALA (26; 186-; black)

A	PAID [no rate]	200.
B	PAID 5*	200.
C	PAID 10*	200.
Ms	Due 10	150.

Louina

A

LOUINA / ALA (32; 1862; black)

A	PAID, 5 (ms)	200.

Louisville

A

LOUISVILLE / AL[a] (30; 1861; black)

A	PAID 10	200.

Lower Peach Tree

LOWER PEACH TREE / ALA (25; 1861; black)

Ms	Paid 5	175.

Lowndesborough

A B

LOWNDESBOROUGH / ALA. (32; 186-; black)

A	PAID 10	200.
B	5, Paid (ms) with PM initials*	175.

Note: The Type B marking initialed by the postmaster suggests it was prepared in advance as a provisional. At this time there is insufficient information to make this conclusion.

Macon

Macon Ala (ms; 1863; black)

Ms	Paid 10 cts	150.

Manningham

MANNINGHAM. / ALA. (27; 1861-62; black)

A	PAID 10 [not illustrated]*	200.
Ms	Paid 5*	175.
	Paid 10	150.

Marion

A B

C

MARION / Ala. (30; 1861-62; black)

A	PAID 5	200.
B	PAID 10	200.
C	5 [due]	200.
D	PAID 10 (10 circled) [not illustrated]	150.

Maysville

A

MAYSVILLE / ALA. (26; 1861; black)

A	PAID, 5 cts (ms)	200.

McKinley

A B C

M[c]KINLEY / Ala (32; 1861; black)

A	PAID [no rate]	200.
B	PAID 5	200.
C	5, Paid (ms)	200.
Ms	Paid 5*	175.

Memphis

Memphis Ala (ms; 1861; black)

Ms	Paid 5*	175.

Mill Town

Mill Town Ala (ms; 186-; black)

Ms	Paid 10*	150.

Mobile

A B C

D E F

G H I

J K

MOBILE / ALA (25 DC YD; 1861-64; black)

A	PAID 2*	500.
	Same, revalued 5 (Type B)	750.
B	PAID 5	200.
	Same, revalued 10 (Type C)	300.
C	PAID 10	200.
	Same, struck twice [20¢]	300.
D	2 [due]	500.
E	5 [due]	200.
	Same, Due (ms)*	200.
F	10 [due]	200.
	Same, revalued Due 5 (ms)*	300.
G	20 [due]	300.
H	DUE 10*	200.
I	ADV. 2	500.
J	MISSENT	500.
K	SHIP, 12 (pencil)	10,000.

Note: There is only one recorded example of the Type K ship marking.

Montevallo

PAID

A

MONTEVALLO / Ala. (33; 1861-62; black)

A	PAID [no rate]	200.
	Same, 5 (ms)	200.
	Same, 10 (blue, ms)	200.
Ms	Due 10*	150.

Montgomery

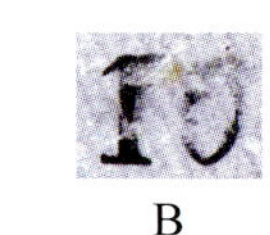

A B C

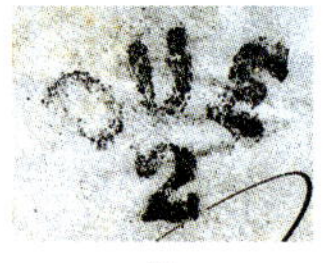

D E

F

G

H

MONTGOMERY / Ala. (32 YD; 1861-62; black)

A	PAID (blue), 2 (ms)	500.
B	10 [due]	200.
C	10 [due]	200.
D	DUE 2	500.
E	DUE. 5.	200.
F	DUE 10	200.
G	FORWARDED 10	500.
H	STEAMBOAT (blue)	750.
Ms	Ford 5	200.
	Ford 10	200.
Pk	No rate or paid marking	200.

Moulton

PAID

A

MOULTON / AL[a] (32; 1862; black)

A	PAID, 10 (ms)	200.

Mount Hope

PAID

A

MOUNT HOPE / ALA. (32; 1861; black)

A	PAID, 5 (ms)	200.
Ms	Paid 5*	175.

Mount Vernon

PAID

A

MOUNT VERNON / ALA. (34; 186-; black)

A	PAID, 5 (ms)	200.
Ms	Due 5c*	175.

Mount Willing

Mt Willing (ms; 186-; black)

Ms	Paid 40	300.

Mulberry

Mulberry ala (ms; 186-; black)

Ms	Paid / 10	150.

Nanafalia

Nanafalia Ala (ms; 1862; black)

Ms	Due 5c	150.

New Market

PAID

A

NEW MARKET / ALA (25; 1861; black)

A	PAID, 5 (ms)	200.

New Providence

New Providence Ala (ms; 186-; black)

Ms	Paid 10	150.

New Salem

New Salem / ALA (32; 1861; black)

Ms	Paid 10*	150.

Northport

PAID 5 PAID 10

A B

NORTHPORT / ALA (32; 1862-64; black)

A	PAID 5	200.
B	PAID 10	200.
Ms	Paid 10*	150.

Oak Bowery

PAID 5 PAID 10

A B

OAK BOWERY / Ala. (32; 1862; black)

A	PAID 5*	200.
B	PAID 10	200.

Oak Grove

Oak Grove Ala (ms; 1862; black)

Ms	Paid 10	150.

Oakley

Oakley Ala (ms; 1861; black)

Ms	Paid 5	175.

Oaky Streak

Oaky Streak Ala. (ms; 1861; black)

Ms	Paid 5*	175.

Opelika

PAID 5 5

A B D

OPELIKA / ALA (25; 1861-64; red, blue, brown)

A	PAID (brown) [no rate]	200.
B	PAID 5 (red)	300.
C	PAID 10 (red) [not illustrated]*	300.
D	5 (blue) [due]	200.
Ms	Due 10	150.

Open Pond

PAID 5

A

OPEN POND / Ala. (30; 1861; blue)

A	PAID 5 (blue)	200.

Orrville

PAID 5

A

ORRVILLE / ALA (32; 1861; black)

A	PAID 5	200.

Oxford

PAID

A

Oxford Ala (ms; 1862; black)

OXFORD / ALA (32; 1861-64; black)

A	PAID [no rate]	200.

	Same, 10 (ms)*	200.
Ms	Pd 5*	175.
	Due 10	150.
	Due 20	200.

Perote

PAID

A

PEROTE / ALA (37; 1861; black)
PEROTE / ALA. (29 YD; 1863; black)

A	PAID [no rate]*	200.
	Same, 40 (ms)	500.
Ms	Paid 5	175.

Perryville

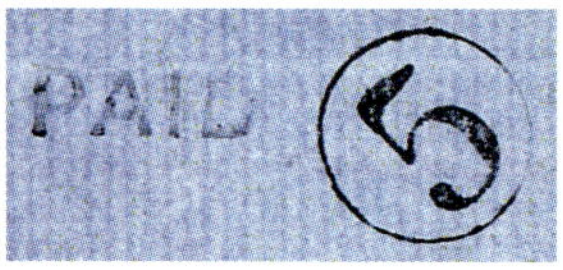

A  a

PERRYVILLE /ALA (30; 1861; black)

A	PAID 5	200.
	Same, revalued 10 (Type *a*)	300.

Pickensville

A  B  C

PICKENSVILLE / ALA (26; 1861-63; black)

A	PAID [no rate]*	200.
	Same, 5 (ms)*	200.
	Same, 10 (ms)*	200.
B	PAID 5	200.
C	5, Paid (ms)*	200.
	Same [due]	200.
Ms	Paid 5*	175.

Pine Hill

Pine Hill (ms; 1861; black)
PINE HILL / ALA. (?; 1861; black)

Ms	pd 10 cts	150.
	Missent & Forwarded	300.

[–]	symbol used in place of value to mean insufficient information to assign a price
NR	used in place of value when no examples have been recorded

Pine Level

A

PINE LEVEL / 5 / ALA / PAID (24; 1862; black)

A	5 PAID	750.

Plantersville

Plantersville Ala (ms; 1864; blue)

Ms	Pd 10*	150.

Pollard

PAID 10

A 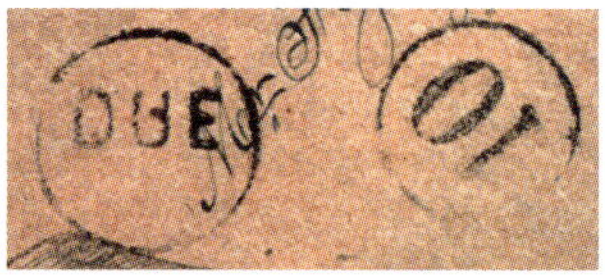 B

C

POLLARD / ALA. (? YD; 1862; black)

A	PAID 10	200.
B	DUE 10	200.
C	10 [due]*	200.

Prattville

5 PAID PAID 10

A  B

PRATTVILLE / Ala. (33; 1861-62; black)

A	PAID 5	200.
B	PAID 10	200.

Rehoboth

REHOBOTH / ALA (31; 1861; blue)

Ms	Paid / 5	175.

Rockville

Rockville Ala (ms; 1861; black)

Ms	Paid 5	175.

Rocky Head

Rocky Head Ala (ms; 186-; black)

Ms	Pd /10	150.

Russelville

A B

RUSSELVILLE / ALA (25; 1861-62; black, red)

A	PAID 5	200.
	Same (red)*	300.
	Same (brown)	300.
B	PAID 10 (black)*	300.
	Same (red)*	

Salem

SALEM / ALA (32; 1861; black)

Ms	Paid 10*	150.

Scottsville

SCOTTSVILLE / Ala (?; 1861; black)

Ms	P 5	175.

Seales Station

Seales Station Ala (ms; 186-; black)

Ms	Paid 10*	150.

Selma

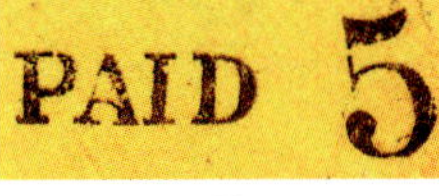

A B

C D E

SELMA / Ala (32; 1861-62; black)

A	PAID, 10 (ms)*	200.
B	PAID 5	200.
	Same, revalued 10 (ms)	300.
C	PAID 10	200.
D	5 [due]	175.
E	10 [due]*	175.
Ms	Due 10*	150.
	10 [due]*	150.

Shelby Springs

Shelby Springs Ala (ms; 1861-62; black)

Ms	Paid 5	175.
	Paid 10*	150.
	Due 5	175.
	Due 10*	150.

Society Hill

SOCIETY HILL / ALA (32; 1862; black)

Ms	Paid 10*	150.

Somerville

PAID

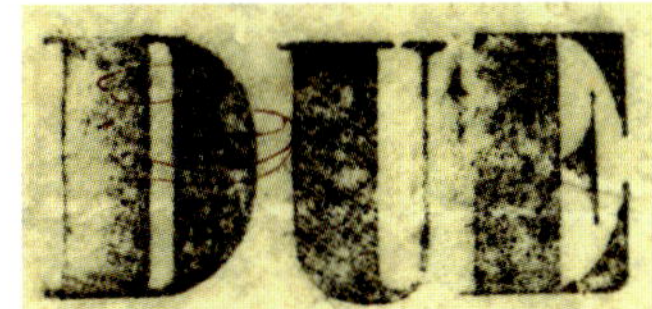

A B

SOMERVILLE / ALA (26; 1862-63; black)

A	PAID, 5 (ms)*	200.
	Same, 10 (ms)*	200.
B	DUE	200.

South Florence

PAID

A

SOUTH FLORENCE / ALA. (32; 186-; black)

A	PAID, 5 revalued 10 (ms)	200.
	Same, 10 (ms)*	200.

Sparta

Sparta Ala (ms; 186-; black)

A	PAID 10 (red) [not illustrated] *	300.
Ms	Paid 10*	150.

Springville

Springville Ala (ms; 1863; black)

Ms	Paid 10	150.

Stevenson

Stevenson Ala (ms; 1861; black)

Ms	Paid 5*	175.

Suggsville

Suggsville Ala (ms; 1862; black)

Ms	Paid 10	150.

Summerfield

A

SUMMERFIELD / Ala. (30; 1861-65; black)

A	PAID 5	200.
	Same, struck twice	300.
B	PAID 10 [not illustrated]*	200.
Ms	Paid 10	150.

Sylacauga

A

B

Sylacauga Ala (ms; 1861-62; black)

A	PAID 5	200.
B	PAID 10 (brown)	200.
Ms	Paid 10*	150.

Talladega

PAID

A

B

C

PAID 10

D

E

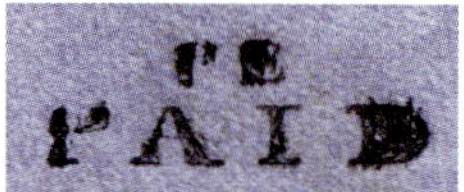
F

G

TALLADEGA / Al. (30; 1861-65; black)

A	PAID, 10 (ms)*	200.
	Same, 20 cts*	300.
B	PAID 5	200.
C	I E / PAID 5	200.
D	PAID 10*	200.
E	I E / PAID 10	200.
F	I E / PAID, 20 cts (ms)	200.
G	10 [due]	175.

Note: When postally unused, Types C and E are considered provisionals (see Provisional section).

Tallassee

Tallassee ala (ms; 186-; black)

Ms	Paid 10	150.

Tensaw

Tensaw Ala (ms; 1864; black)
TENSAW / ALA (?; 186-; black)

Ms	Paid 10c	150.
Ms	Missent & Forwarded	175.

Tompkinsville

A

TOMPKINSVILLE / Ala. (34; 1861; brown)

A	PAID 5 (brown)	200.
Ms	Paid 10*	150.

Triana

Triana Ala (ms; 1861; black)

Ms	Paid 5	175.

Trinity

Postmark unknown

Ms	Paid 5*	175.

Troy

A

PAID (5)

B

C

TROY / Ala. (34; 1861; black)
TROY / ALABAMA (30 YD; 1862-63; black)

A	PAID 5	200.
B	PAID 5*	200.
C	PAID 10	200.
Ms	Missent & ford (pencil)	150.

Tuscaloosa

A B

C

D

E

G H I

TUSCALOOSA / Al. (30; 1861-62; black)
TUSKALOOSA / ALA (31 YD; 1862; black)

A	PAID, 15c (ms)	300.
	Same, 20 (ms)*	300.
	Same, 30c (ms)	300.
B	PAID 5	200.
C	PAID 5	200.
	Same, revalued 10 (type G)*	300.
D	PAID 10	200.
E	PAID 20 [not illustrated]	300.
F	DUE 10	200.
G	10 [due]*	175.
H	FORWARDED	500.
I	MISSENT	500.

Note: An "X" marking is found on some covers from Tuscaloosa (see illustration below). It is theorized the marking was used on due mail.

Tuscaloosa "X" marking

Tuscumbia

PAID

A

TUSCUMBIA / ALA. (31; 1861-62; black)

A	PAID, 20c (ms)*	300.

Tuskegee

A

B

TUSKEGEE / ALA. (26 DC YD; 1861-62; blue-green)

A	PAID 5 (blue-green)	200.
B	PAID 10 (blue-green)	200.

Uchee

Postmark unknown

A	PAID / 5 (C) (blue) [not illustrated]*	200.

Union

PAID 5

A

UNION / ALA (?, 1861; black)

A	PAID / 5	200.

Union Springs

PAID 10

A

UNION SPRINGS / A^{LA} (32; 1864; black)

A	PAID 10	200.

Uniontown

A

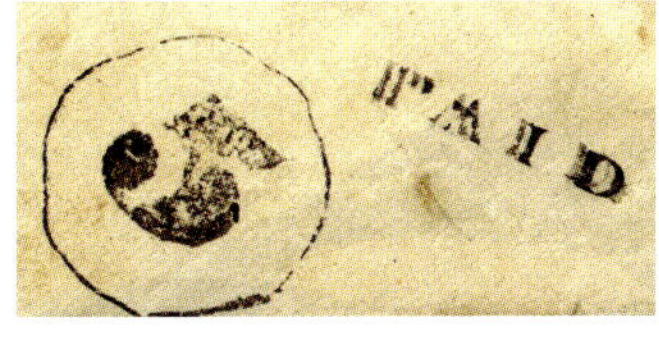

B

C

D

E

UNIONTOWN / Ala. (30; 1862; black)

A	PAID 5	200.
B	PAID 5	200.
C	10 PAID	200.
D	10 PAID	200.
E	5 [due]*	175.
Ms	Paid 5*	175.

Valley Head

Valley Head Ala (ms; 186-; black)

Ms	Paid 10*	150.

Van Buren

Van Buren Ala (ms; 1861; black)

Ms	Paid 5*	175.
	10 / Paid	150.

Vienna

Vienna Ala (ms; 1861; black)

Ms	5 (due)	175.

Villula

A B

VILLULA / Ala (31; 1861; blue)

A	PAID (blue) [no rate]*	200.
B	PAID 5	200.

Warrenton

Warrenton Ala (ms; 1863; black)

Ms	Paid 10*	150.

Warsaw

Warsaw (ms; 1865; pencil)

Ms	Paid [10]	150.

Wedowee

A

WEDOWEE / ALA (24; 186-; red)

A	PAID 10 (red)	300.

Wetumpka

A

B

WETUMPKA / ALA (26 DC YD; 1861-63; black, blue)

A	PAID 5	200.
	Same (blue)*	300.
	Same, revalued 10 (Type B) (blue)*	300.
B	PAID 10	200.
	Same (blue)	300.

White Plains

A

WHITE PLAINS / ALA (25; 186-; black)

A	PAID [no rate]	200.

Wilsonville

A

Wilsonville Ala (ms; 1861; ?)

WILSONVILLE / ALA. (31; 186-; black)

A	DUE 10*	200.
Ms	PD 5	150.

Wolf Creek

Wolf Creek Ala (ms; 186-; black)

Ms	Paid 10*	150.

Woodville

Woodville Ala (ms; 1861; black)

Ms	Paid / 5	150.

Younguesborough

Yongesboro Ala (ms; 1863; black)

Ms	Paid 10*	150.

ARKANSAS

Alder Brook
Alder Brook Ark. (ms; 1861; black)

Ms	Paid 5	350.
	Paid 10*	350.

Arkadelphia
A B

ARKADELPHIA / Ark. (32; 1862; black)

A	PAID 5	500.
B	PAID 10	400.

Askew
Askew ark (ms; 186-; black)

Ms	Paid 5 cents	350.

Auburn
Auburn Ark (ms; 1863; black)

Ms	Due 10 cts	300.

Augusta
AUGUSTA / * ARK. * (36 YD; 1861; black)

A	PAID, 5 (ms) [not illustrated]	400.

Austin
AUSTIN / ARK (25; 186-; black)

Ms	Paid / 10	350.
	Due / 10	300.

Barkada
Barkada Ark (ms; 186-; black)

Ms	Paid 10	350.

Batesville
A B C

BATESVILLE / Ark. (1861-2; 30; black)

A	PAID 5*	500.
	Same, revalued 10 (ms)	600.
B	PAID 10*	500.
C	PAID 10	500.

Benton
B

BENTON / Ark (35; 1862; black)

A	PAID 5 altered 3c handstamp [not illustrated]*	500.
B	PAID, 10 (ms)	350.

Black's Ferry
Black's Ferry Ark. C.S.A. (ms; 1862; black)

Ms	Paid / 5¢	350.

Boonsboro
BOONSBORO / ARK (33; 1861; black)

Ms	Paid 5	350.

Brownsville
A

BROWNSVILLE / ARK (33; 1861; black)

A	paid 5	500.

Buchanan
Buchanan Ark (ms; 1864; black)

Ms	Due 10	300.

Buckhorn
A B

C *a*

BUCKHORN / ARK. (31; 1861; black)

A	PAID 5	750.
B	PAID 10	750.
C	5, revalued 10 (Type *a*), Due (ms)	1,000.

Camden

A B

C

D

CAMDEN / ARK (25 DC; 1861; black)
CAMDEN / Ark. (35; 1862-64; black)

A	PAID [no rate]	400.
B	PAID 10	500.
C	PAID 10	500.
D	DUE 10	400.
Ms	Forwarded / Due 5 cts	300.
	Due 10	300.

Carrollton

Carrollton ark (ms; 186-; black)

Ms	Paid 10*	350.

Cat Island

Cat Island Ark (ms; 1861; black)

Ms	Paid 10	350.

Centre Point

CENTRE POINT / Ark. (27 NOR; 1861; black)

A	Paid 3, revalued 5 (ms) [not illustrated]	1,000.

Chalybeate Springs

Chalybeate spg (ms; 1862; black)

Ms	Paid 5	350.

Champagnolle

Champagnolle Ark (ms; 1862; black)

Ms	Due 10	300.

Charleston

Charleston Arks (ms; 1862; black)

Ms	Paid 10*	350.

Clarksville

No Postmark (1862)
CLARKSVILLE / ARK (27; 1862; black)

A	PAID, 10 (ms) [not illustrated]	400.
Ms	Paid 10	350.

Columbia

PAID

A

PAID 5

B

C

COLUMBIA / ARK (31; 1861-2; black)

A	PAID, 5 (ms)	500.
B	PAID 5	500.
C	PAID 5, revalued 10 (ms)	600.

Cummins

Cummins, Ark. Co. Ark. (ms; 1861; black)

Ms	Paid 5 cts / C.S.A.	500.

Cut Off

Cut off (ms; 186-; black)

Ms	Due 10	300.

Dardanelle

PAID (5)

A

PAID (10)

B

Dardanelle Ark (ms; 186-; black)
DARDANELLE / ARK (31; 186-; black)

A	PAID 5	500.
B	PAID 10	500.

Des Arc

DES ARC / ARK (26; 1861-62; black)

Ms	Paid 5	350.
	Paid 10	350.
	Due 10	300.

Dover

Dover Ark (ms; 1861; black)

Ms	Paid 5	350.

El Dorado

EL DORADO Ark. (33; 1861-62; black)

Ms	Paid 10 cts	350.
	Due 10	300.

Eudora

Eudora ark (ms; 1861; black)

Ms	Paid 5	350.

Eunice

(PAID)

A

Eunice Ark (ms; 1861; black)

A	PAID (red), 10 (ms)	600.
B	PAID 5 (red)* [not illustrated]	750.

Fair Play

A

FAIR PLAY / ARK (?; 1861; black)

A	PAID, 5 blue (ms)	400.

Fayetteville

FAYETTEVILLE / Ark. (36; 186-; black)

Ms	Due 10	300.

Flat Bayou

Flat Bayou Aks (ms; 1861-62; black)

Ms	Paid 10	350.

Florence

A

FLORENCE / Ark. (32; 1861; black)

A	PAID, 10 (ms)	500.

Fort Smith

A

FORT SMITH / ARK (26 DC; 1861-63; black)

A	PAID, 5 (ms)	400.
	Same, 10 (ms)	400.
Ms	Due 10	300.

Genoa

Genoa Ark (ms; 186-; black)

Ms	P. O. Business Free	IH

Grand Glaze

A

Postmark Unknown

A	PAID 5*	400.

Greensboro

Greensboro ak (ms; 1861; black)

Ms	Paid 5	350.

Hamburg

A

HAMBURG / ARK (27; 1861; black)

A	PAID, 5 (ms)	350.
	Same, 10 (ms)	350.
Ms	Due 10	300.

Hampton

Hampton ark (ms; 1862; black)

Ms	Paid 10	350.

Harrisburg

Harrisburg ark (ms; 1862; black)

Ms	Paid 5	350.

Helena

A B

HELENA / ARK. (26 DC; 1861-62; black)

A	PAID, 10 (ms)	400.
B	PAID 5	500.
	Same, revalued 10 (ms)	500.
Ms	5 Paid (5 struck out)	400.

Hibernia

Hibernia Aks (ms; 186-; black)

Ms	Paid 10	350.

Hillsboro

A B

HILLSBORO / ARK. (31; 1862; black)

A	PAID 5	600.
B	PAID 10	600.

Hix's Ferry

A

Hix's Ferry Ark (ms; 1861; black)

A	PAID, 5 (ms)	400.

Hot Springs

HOT SPRINGS / ARK. (34; 1861; black)

Ms	Paid 5	350.

Jacksonport

PAID

A

JACKSONPORT / ARK (33 NOR; 1861; black)

A	PAID, 5 (ms)	400.
Ms	Paid 5	350.

Laconia

PAID

A

LACONIA / * Ark * (27; 186-; black)

A	PAID, 5 (ms)*	400.
	Same, [no rate], revalued Due 5 (ms)	500.

Lake Village

PAID 5 CENTS

A

LAKE VILLAGE / Ark. (32; 1861-62; black)

A	PAID / 5 CENTS	1,000.
	Same, revalued 10 (ms)	1,250.

Leaton

Leaton Ark (ms; 186-, black)
LEATON / ARK (29; 1861; black)

Ms	Pd 5	350.
	Paid 10	350.

Lewisburg

PAID

A

LEWISBURG / ARK (26; 186-; black)

A	PAID, 5 ct (ms)	400.

Lewisville

PAID

A

Lewisville Arks (ms; 1864; black)
LEWISVILLE / ARK (36; 1861-62; black)

A	PAID [no rate]	400.
	Same, 10 (ms)	500.
Ms	Due 10	300.

Lisbon

Lisbon Ark (ms; 1862; black)

Ms	Paid 10c	350.

Little Rock

PAID 5 PAID

A B

PAID 10 DUE 10c. 10

C D E

LITTLE ROCK / ARK (26 DC YD; 1861-63; black)
LITTLE ROCK / ARK (26 DC; 1862; black)

A	PAID [no rate]*	400.
B	PAID 5	500.
	Same, revalued 10 cts (ms)	600.
C	PAID 10	400.
D	DUE 10c.	500.
E	10 [due]	400.
	Same, Due (ms)	400.
	Same, rerated PAID 10 (Type B)*	500.
Ms	Paid 25	500.
	Due 5	300.
	Due 10	300.
	Due 20	300.
	forwd 10	400.

Long View

Long View Ark (ms; 1861; black)

Ms	Paid 5 cts*	350.

Luda

Luda Ark (ms; 1861; black)

Ms	Paid / 10	350.

Madison

PAID 10

A

MADISON / ARK (26 DC; 1861; black)

A	PAID 10	500.
	Same (brown)	600.
	Same (violet)*	750.

Magnolia

A

MAGNOLIA / Ark (37; 1861-64; black)

A	PAID, 5 (ms)	400.
	Same, 10 (ms)*	400.
Ms	Paid 5	350.
	Paid / 10¢	350.

Marion

Marion Arks (ms; 1861; black)

Ms	Paid 5	350.

Monticello

A

B

C

MONTICELLO / Ark (32; 1861-64; black)

A	PAID 5	500.
B	PAID 10	500.
C	10 [due]	400.
Ms	Due 5	300.

Mount Holly

Mt Holly Arks (ms; 1861; black)

Ms	Paid 5	350.

Napoleon

A

B

a

Napoleon Ark (ms; 1862; black)
NAPOLEON / ARK (26 DC YD; 1861; black)

A	PAID 5	500.
	Same, revalued 10 (Type *a*)	600.
	Same, with Due 5 (ms)	600.
B	PAID 10*	500.
Ms	Paid 5	350.

Norristown

NORRISTOWN / ARK. (33 DLC; 1861; black)

Ms	Paid 5	350.

Old Town

Old Town Ark (ms; 1861; black)

Ms	Paid 5	350.

Osceola

Osceola Ark (ms; 1861-62; black)

Ms	Paid 5	350.
	Paid 5¢	400.
	Paid 10*	350.
	Paid 10, revalued 5 (ms)	400.

Paraclifta

PARACLIFTA / ARK (26; 1863; black)

Ms	Paid 10 cts	350.

Parkersburg

Parkersburg / Ark (ms; 1861; black)

Ms	Paid / 5	350.

Perryville

Perryville Arks (ms; 1861; black)

Ms	Paid 20 cts	500.

Pine Bluff

A B

C

D

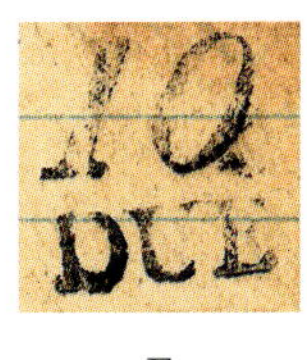

E

PINE BLUFF / ARK (26 DC YD; 1861-63; black)

A	PAID, 20 (ms)	500.
	Same, 80 (ms)	1,000.
B	PAID 5	500.
C	PAID 10	500.
D	5 DUE	400.
E	10 DUE	400.
	Same (blue)	750.
Ms	Due 5	300.

Pocahontas

A B

POCAHONTAS / ARK (33; 1861; black)

A	Paid 5	500.
B	Paid 10	400.

Post Oak

Post Oak Ark (ms; 1864; brown)

Ms	Due 10	300.

Princeton

A

Princeton Ark (ms; 1861; black)
PRINCETON / Ark. (34; 1861-62; black, green)

A	PAID 10 (brown)	500.
	Same (green)	1,500.
Ms	Due 10	300.

Richmond

Richmond Arks (ms; 186-; black)

Ms	Paid 10	350.

Rob Roy

Rob Roy Ark (ms; 1861; black)

Ms	Paid / 10	350.

Rockport

Rockport Arks (ms; 1861; black)

Ms	Due 10 cts*	300.

Russellville

Russellville Ark (ms; 186–; black)

Ms	Paid 10	350.

Scotland

Scotland Aks (ms; 1861; black)

Ms	Paid / 10	350.

Searcy

A

B

SEARCY / ARK (26; 1861-62; black)

A	PAID 5	500.
B	PAID 10	500.
Ms	Pd 5 cts	350.

South Bend

South Bend Ark (ms; 1862-63; black)
SOUTH BEND / ARK (33; 1862-64; black)

Ms	Due 10	300.
	Due 15	400.

Spring Bank

Spring Bank Ark (ms; 1862; black)

Ms	Due 10 cts	300.

Spring Hill

Spring Hill ark (ms; 1863; black)

Ms 10 [due]	300.

Taylor's Creek

PAID

A

TAYLOR'S CREEK / ARK (33; 1861; black)

A	PAID, 10 (ms)	400.

Three Creeks

3 Creeks Ark (ms; 186-; black)

Ms	Paid 10	350.

Tulip

TULIP / ARK. (26; 1861; black)

Ms	Paid 10	350.

Van Buren

PAID 10

A B

VAN BUREN / Ark (27; 1864; black)
VAN BUREN / Ark. (33; 1861-63; black)

A	PAID [no rate]	400.
	Same, 5 (ms)	400.
	Same, 10 (ms)	400.
B	PAID 10	500.
Ms	Due 10	300.

Walnut Bend

Walnut Bend Ark (ms; 1861; black)

Ms	Paid 5c	350.

Washington

PAID PAID 5

A B C

WASHINGTON / Ark. (30; 1861-64; black)

A	PAID, 10 (ms)*	400.
B	PAID 5	600.
C	DUE 10 [not illustrated]	400.
D	10 [due]	400.
Ms	5 [due]	300.
	10 [due]	300.

FLORIDA

Adamsville

A

B

ADAMSVILLE / Fla. (30; 1861; black)

A	PAID 5	750.
B	5 [due]	500.

Apalachicola

A

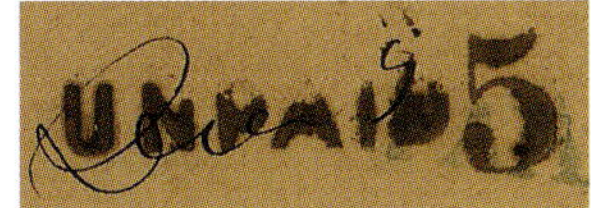
B

APALACHICOLA / FLA (26 DC YD; 1861-62; black)
No postmark

A	PAID 10	750.
B	UNPAID 5	—

Archer

Archer (ms; 1863; black)

Ms	Pd 10	IH

Aspalaga

Aspalaga Fla (ms; 186-; black)

Ms	Due 10 changed to Paid (ms)	750.

Atsena Otie

A

ATSEENA OTIE / FLA (31; 1861; black)

A	PAID 5	1,500.

Austinville

Austinville Fla (ms, 186-; black)

Ms	Paid 10	750.

Baldwin

Baldwin Fla (ms; 1864; black)

Ms	Paid 10	500.
	Due 10	500.

Bay Port

A

Bayport Fla (ms; 186-; black)
BAY PORT / Fla. (32; 1861-63; black)

A	PAID, 5c (ms)	1,000.
Ms	Paid 10¢	1,000.

Brooksville

Brooksville Fla (ms; 1861-64; black)

Ms	Pd 5 cts	500.
	Paid 10	500.
	Pd 10	750.

Campbellton

CAMPBELLTON / FLA (32; 186-; black)

Ms	Paid 10	1,000.

Cedar Tree

Cedar Tree (ms; 1861; black)

Ms	Paid 5 cts	1,000.

Cerro Gordo

Cerro Gordo Flo (ms; 1862; black)

Ms	Pd / 10	IH

Chattahoochee

CHATTAHOOCHEE/ FLO (30; 1862; black)

Ms	Pd 5	1,000.

Columbus

Columbus Fla (ms; 1862; brown)

Ms	Paid / 5 (brown)	IH

Cork

Cork Flo (ms; 1862; brown)

Ms	Pd 10 (brown)	IH

Cuyler

Cuyler Fla (ms; 1862; brown)

Ms	Pd / 5 (brown)	IH

Etoniah

Etoniah Fla (ms; 1862; black)

Ms	Paid 5	IH
	Paid 10	750.

Fayettevllle

FayetteVille Fla (ms; 1862; black)

Ms	paid 5	IH

Fernandina

A

PAID 5

B

PAID 10

C

Fernandina (ms; 1862; black)
FERNANDINA / Flª (32 YD; 1861-62; black)
FERNANDINA / FLA. (33; 1861; black)

A	PAID 5	1,500.
B	PAID 5	500.
C	PAID 10	500.
Ms	Paid / 5	500.
	Due 10	500.

Flemington

A

FLEMINGTON / FLA. (32 YD; 1864; black)

A	PAID 10	750.
Pk	No rate or paid marking	500.

Fort Dade

Ft Dade Fla (ms; 1862; brown)

Ms	Paid 5	IH

Fort Taylor

Fort Taylor (ms; 1864; black)

Ms	Paid 10	750.

Gainesville

A

GAINESVILLE / FLA (25; 1862-64; black; blue)

A	PAID [no rate]	350.
	Same, 10 (ms)	500.
	Same (blue), 10 (ms)	500.
Ms	Pd 10	350.

IH	used in place of listing value when the item is held by an institution
NR	used in place of value when no examples have been recorded

Greenwood

A

GREENWOOD / FLA (25; 1861; black)

A	PAID 5	1,000.

Hawkinsville

Hawkinsville Fl (ms; 1861; brown)

Ms	Paid 5 (brown)	IH

Homosassa

Homosassa Fla (ms; 1862; black)

Ms Paid 5	750.

Houston

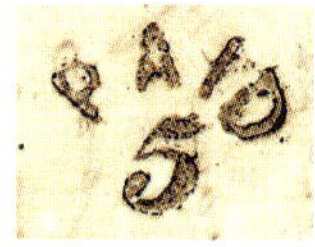

A

PAID 10

B

Houston Fla. (ms; 1861-62; black)
HOUSTON / FLA (31 YD; 1862-63; black)

A	PAID 5	750.
B	PAID 10	750.
Ms	Paid 5	500.
	Paid 10	IH

Iola

Iola Fla (ms; 1862; black)

Ms	Paid 10	IH

Jacksonville

A

B

10

a

JACKSONVILLE / FLA (26 DC YD; 1861; black)
JACKSONVILLE / Flor. (34; 1861-62; black)

A	PAID 5	750.
	Same, struck twice	1,000.
	Same, revalued 10 (type *a*)	1,250.
B	PAID 10	500.
	Same, 10 struck twice	750.

Jasper

A B

JASPER/ ***FLA*** (28; 186-; black)
JASPER / FLA. (32 YD; 1862; black)

A	PAID, 10 (ms)	1,000.
B	PAID 10	1,000.

Jennings

Jennings Fla (ms; 186-; black)

Ms	Pd 10	IH

Lake Butler

Lake Butler Fla (ms; 1861; blue, brown)

Ms	Paid / 5 (blue)	IH
	Paid / 5 cts (brown)	IH

Lake City

A B

C D

E F

LAKE CITY / FLA. (sans serif) (32; 1862-65; black)
LAKE CITY / FLA (serif) (32; 1863-64; black)

A	PAID, 20 (ms)	500.
B	PAID 5	500.
C	PAID 10	500.
D	PAID 10	250.
E	PAID 10	500.
	Same, no postmark	350.
F	DUE 10	350.

Little River

Little River Fla (ms; 1861-62; black)

Ms	Paid in money 5c	2,500.
	Paid 10	IH

Live Oak

Live Oak Fla (ms; 1862; Brown)

Ms	Paid 5 (brown)	IH

Long Pond

Long Pond F (ms; 1863; brown)
Long Pond Fla (ms; 1863; brown)

Ms	Paid 10¢	1,000.

Madison Court House

A B

C D *a*

Madison (ms; 1863; brown)
Madison Fla (ms; 1863; black)
MADISON / FLO (25; 1861-62; black)
MADISON / Flo (32; 1862; black)
MADISON C. H. / FLA (31; 1864; black)

A	PAID 5	750.
	Same, revalued 10 (Type *a*)	1,250.
B	PAID 10	350.
C	PAID 10	350.
	Same, struck twice	750.
D	DUE 10	350.
Ms	Paid 10	500.
	Paid / 10	500.
	Due 10 (brown)	1,500.

Mariana

A B

C D

MARIANA / FLA. (32; 1861-63; black)

A	PAID [no rate]	350.
B	PAID 5	750.
C	PAID 10	750.
D	PAID 10	750.
Ms	Forwd 5c	350.

Mellonville

Mellonville Fl (ms; 1861; black)

Ms	Paid 5c	IH

Micanopy

A

MICANOPY / FLO (27; 1862; black)

A	PAID 5	NR

Note: The only recorded example of this marking used on a stampless cover was lost in a fire. A second example of the marking is recorded on a provisional envelope.

Miccosukee

A

MICCOSUKEE / FLA (33; 1861; black)

A	PAID 5	1,000.

Middleburg

Middleburg (ms; 1862-64; brown)
Middleburg F (ms; 1862; brown)

Ms	Paid / 10c	500.
	Pd / 10	500.

Monticello

A

B

C

MONTICELLO / Flor. (34; 1861-64; black)

A	PAID 5	750.
B	PAID 10	500.
C	PAID 10	500.
Ms	Due 10 (pencil)	500.

Mount Pleasant

Mt. Pleasant Flo (ms; 1864; brown)

Ms	Paid 10	1,000.

New Smyrna

PAID 10

A

NEW SMYRNA FLA (32 NOR; 1861; black)

A	PAID 10	3,000.

Newnansville

A

NEWNANSVILLE / FLA (25; 1861-62; black)
NEWNANSVILLE / FLA. (33; 1863; black)

A	PAID, 5 (ms)	750.
	Same, 10 (ms)	750.
Ms	Paid 10	500.

Oakland

Oakland Fla (ms; 1862; brown)

Ms	Paid / 10	750.

Ocala

A

B

C

D

OCALA / Fla. (34; 1861-65; black)

A	PAID, 20 (ms)	350.
B	PAID 5	1,000.
C	PAID 10	2,500.
D	Paid 10	500.
Ms	Pd 10	350.

Orange Springs

Orange Spring Fl (ms; 1861; black, blue)

Ms	Paid 5	IH
	Pd 5 (blue)	750.

Orlando

Orlando Fla (ms; 1862; brown)

Ms	Paid 10c (brown)	IH

Patrick

Patrick Fla (ms; 1863; black)

Pk	No rate or paid marking	1,000.

Pensacola

A B

C D

E F G

H I

J K *a*

PENSACOLA / Flor. (30; 1861; black)
PENSACOLA / Fla (32; 1861-62; black)

A	PAID [no rate]*	500.
	Same, 5 (ms)	350.
	Same, 10 (ms)	350.
	Same, 20 (ms)	500.
B	PAID, 5 (ms)	300.
	Same, 10 (ms)	300.
C	PAID 5	750.
D	PAID 5	350.
	Same, revalued 10 (type *a*)	2,000.
E	PAID 5	350.
	Same, 5 struck twice	750.
F	PAID 5	250.
G	PAID 5	350.
H	PAID 10	500.
I	PAID 10	500.
J	PAID 10	350.
K	5, plus Due 5 (ms)	350.
Ms	Due 10	350.

Pilatka

A

B

PILATKA / FLA (26; 1861-62; black)

A	PAID 5	750.
B	PAID 5	750.
C	PAID 10 [not illustrated]	500.

Providence

Providence F (ms; 1862; black, brown)

Ms	Paid / 5¢	IH
	Pd / 10	IH

Quincy

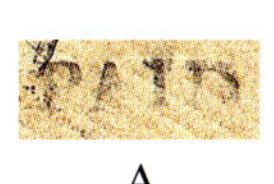
A

B

C

D

QUINCY / Flor. (31; 1861-63; black)

A	PAID [no rate]	500.
B	PAID 5	500.
C	PAID 10	500.
D	DUE 10	750.
Ms	10 Paid	500.
	Due 10	500.

ms	manuscript
YD	year date
NR	used in place of value when no examples have been recorded
IH	used in place of listing value when the item is held by an institution
[*]	symbol used after an item description to mean an unsupported listing

Saint Augustine

A

B a

SAINT AUGUSTINE / Fla. (32; 1861-62; black)

A	PAID 5 (blue), revalued 10 (Type *a*)	1,500.
B	PAID 10	750.

Saint Marks

A B

C *a*

ST MARKS / FLA (31; 1863; black)

A	PAID [no rate]	500.
B	PAID 5, revalued 10 (Type *a*)	750.
C	PAID 10	500.

Sanderson

Sanderson Fla (ms; 1862; black)

Ms	Paid 5	IH

Sandy Ford

Sandy Ford Fla (ms; 1862; black)

Ms	Paid 5	350.

Southern Confederacy

Southern Confederacy (ms; 186-; black)

Ms	Paid 5	IH

Stark

Stark Fla (ms; 1862; black)

Ms	Paid [no rate]	IH
	Paid 10	500.

Sumpterville

Sumpterville Fla (ms; 1862; brown)

Ms	Pd 10c (brown)	IH

Suwannee Shoals

Suwannee Shoals Fla (ms; 1861; black)

Ms	Paid 5	750.

Tallahassee

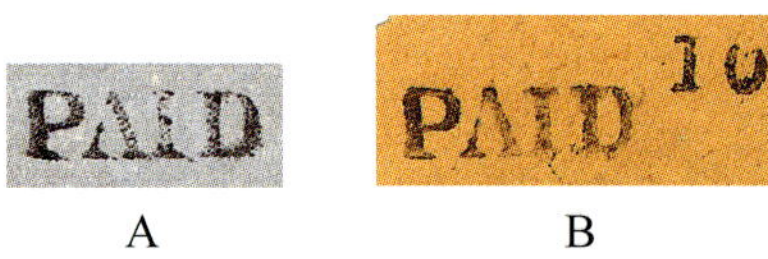

A B

C D

TALLAHASSEE / Fla (31; 1861-64; black)

A	PAID [no rate]	350.
	Same, 5 (ms)*	350.
	Same, 5 cts (pencil)	250.
	Same, 10 (ms)	250.
	Same, 20 (ms)	750.
B	PAID 10	500.
C	PAID 10	350.
D	10 [due]	350.
Ms	Due 10*	350.

Tampa

Tampa F (ms; 1864; brown)

Ms	60 cts Paid	750.

Vernon

Vernon Fla (ms; 1864; black)

Ms	Paid / 10	IH

Waldo

Waldo (ms; 1865; black)

Ms	Pd / 10	750.

Warrington

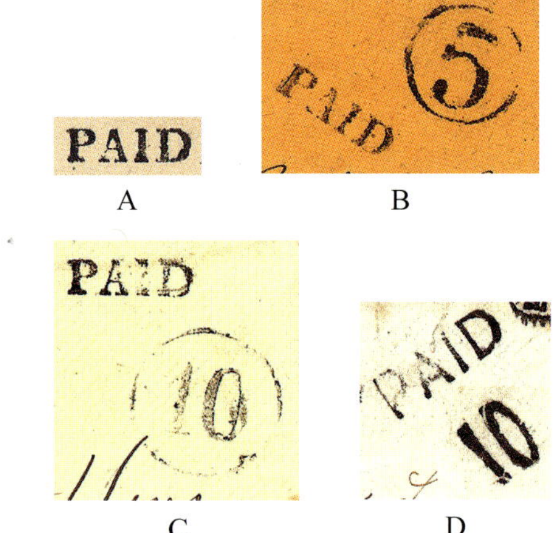

A B

C D

E

F

G

H

a

WARRINGTON / Fla. (33; 1861-62; black)
WARRINGTON / Fla. (30 YD; 1861; black)

A	PAID [no rate]	500.
	Same, Pd / 5 (ms)	500.
B	PAID 5	250.
C	PAID 10	350.
D	PAID 10	350.
E	DUE 5	350.
F	DUE 10	350.
G	POSTAGE DUE 5	750.
H	5, Paid (ms)	350.
	Same [due]	350.
	Same, revalued 10 (Type a)	350.

Waukeenah

A

Waukeenah Fl (ms; 1865; black)
WAUKEENAH / Fla. (30; 1861-62; brown)

A	PAID 5 (brown)	1,000.
Ms	Paid 10	500.

Welaka

A

B

WELAKA / FLA. (31 DC; 1861-62; black)

A	PAID, 5¢ (ms)	750.
	Same, 10¢ (ms)	750.
B	PAID 5	750.

White Springs

A

WHITE SPRINGS / Fla. (31; 1863; black)

A	PAID 10, 10 struck twice	1,000.

GEORGIA

Acworth

ACWORTH / GEO (32; 186-; black)

Ms	Paid / 10	150.

Adairsville

A

ADAIRSVILLE / Geo. (29; 186-; blue)

A	PAID 5 (blue)	200.

Albany

A

B

C

ALBANY / Ga (32 YD; 1861-64; black; blue, greenish-blue)

A	PAID 10 (blue)	300.
B	POST OFFICE BUSINESS FREE	500.
C	MISSENT AND FORWARDED (greenish-blue)	750.
Ms	Paid 25	200.

Allatoona

Allatoona (ms; 186-; black)

Ms	Paid 10	150.

Alpharetta

Alpharetta Ga (ms; 1862; black)

Ms	Paid 5*	175.
	Paid 10	150.

Americus

PAID

A

B

C

a

AMERICUS / Ga. (30; 1861; black)

A	PAID, 5 (ms)	200.
	Same, 10 (ms)	200.
B	PAID 5	200.
	Same, revalued 10 (Type *a*)*	300.
C	PAID 10	200.
Ms	Paid 5	175.
	Paid 10	150.

Andersonville

A

10

B

ANDERSONVILLE / GA (26; 186-; black)
ANDERSONVILLE / GA (33 DC; 186-; black)

A	PAID, 10 (ms)	500.
B	PAID 10	750.
Ms	Due 10	500.

Appling

Appling Ga (ms; 1861-62; black)

Ms	Paid / 5	175.
	Paid / 10	150.
	Free	300.

Athens

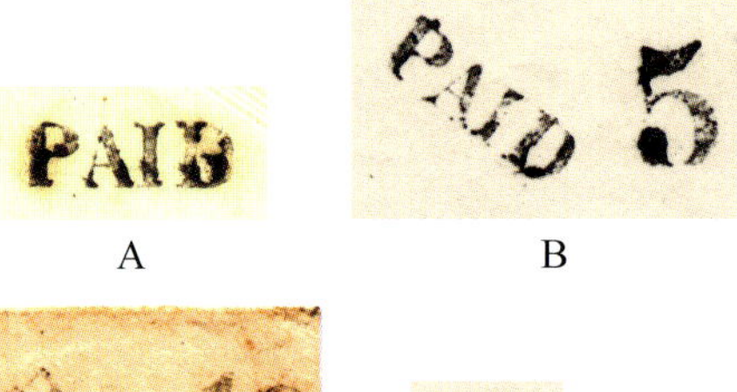

A B

C

a

b

ATHENS / Ga (31; 1861; black)
ATHENS GA / PAID (32; 1861-62; black)

A	PAID [no rate]*	200.
	Same, 10 (ms)	200.
B	PAID 5	200.
	Same, revalued 10 (Type *b*)	300.
	Same, plus 10 (Type *b*) struck twice*	300.

	Same, plus 10 (Type *b*) struck twice and 5 (Type *a*)	300.
C	PAID 10	200.
Ms	Due 10 (pencil)	150.
	10 [due]*	150.

ATLANTA

A B

C

ATLANTA / Ga. (32 YD; 1861-62; black)

A	PAID 10	750.
B	DUE 5	500.
C	DUE 10	500.
Pk	No rate or paid marking	300.

ATTAPULGUS

Attapulgus Ga (ms; 186-; blue)

Ms	Paid 10	150.

AUGUSTA

A B C

D E F

G H I

J

AUGUSTA / GA (26 DC; 1861-62; black)
AUGUSTA / Ga. (32; 186-; violet)

A	PAID, 2 (pencil)	200.
	Same, 20 (pencil)	300.
	Same, 30 cent (ms)	300.
B	PAID 5	200.
	Same, revalued 10 (Type J)	300.
	Same, revalued 10 cts (ms)	300.
C	PAID 5	200.
	Same, revalued 10 (Type J)	300.
D	PAID 5	200.
	Same, revalued 10 (Type J)	300.
	Same, plus Due 5 (ms)	300.
E	PAID 5	200.
F	PAID 5	200.
	Same, revalued 10 (Type J)	300.
	Same, plus Due 5 (ms)	300.
	Same, plus Due 5c (ms)	300.
G	PAID 10	200.
	Same, plus PAID 10 (Type I)	300.
H	PAID 10	200.
	Same, revalued 5 (ms)	300.
I	PAID 10	200.
	Same (violet)	300.
	Same, plus PAID 10 (Type G)*	300.
J	10 [due]*	175.
	Same (violet) [due]	300.
Ms	Due 10 ct, revalued 5 ct*	200.
	Forwarded	200.

BAINBRIDGE

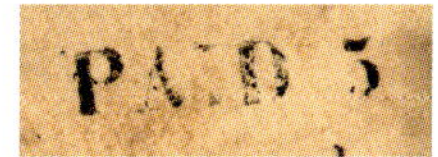

A B

C

BAINBRIDGE / Ga (32; 1861-62; black)

A	PAID 5	200.
B	PAID 5	200.
C	PAID 10*	200.

BAIRDSTOWN

A

Bairdston Ga (ms; 1861-62; black)

A	PAID, 5 (ms)	200.
Ms	Paid 10	150.

BARNESVILLE

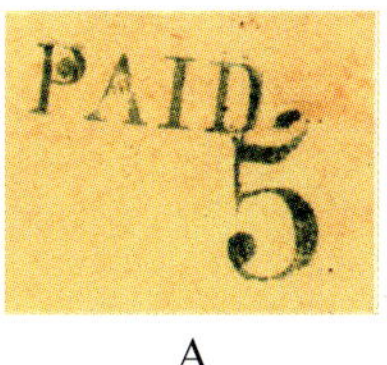

A B

BARNESVILLE / Ga. (32; 1861; black, blue)

A	PAID 5*	200.

	Same (blue)	300.
B	PAID 10	200.
	Same (blue), 10 struck twice	300.

Barnett

Barnett Ga (ms; 186-; black)

Ms	Pd 10c*	150.

Bartow

A B C

Bartow (ms; 1862; black)
Bartow Ga (ms; 186-; black)
BARTOW / G^{A} (32 YD; 1862-63; black)

A	PAID, 5 (ms)*	200.
B	PAID, 5 (ms)	200.
C	PAID 10	200.
Ms	Paid / 10	150.

Berzella

Berzelia (ms; 1861-62; black)
Berzelia Ga (ms; 186-; black)

Ms	Paid / 5	175.
	Paid 5, revalued 10 (ms)*	200.
	Paid / 10	150.

Big Creek

Big Creek Ga (ms; 186-; black)

Ms	Paid 20*	200.

Big Shantee [Big Shanty]

A B

Big Shantee (ms; 1861-63; brown)
BIG SHANTY / BIG SHANTY (26x11 SL month-day; 1862; black)

A	PAID [no rate]	300.
B	PAID 5	300.
Ms	Paid [no rate]	175.
	Paid / 5	200.
	Paid / 10	200.

Black Creek

Black Creek Ga (ms; 1861; black)

Ms	Paid 5 Cts	175.

Blackshear

BLACKSHEAR / GA (25; 186-; black)

Ms	Paid 10	150.

Blakely

A

BLAKELY / Ga. (30; 1862; black)

A	PAID [no rate]	200.
B	5 [due] [not illustrated]*	175.
Ms	Paid [no rate]*	150.
	Paid 5*	175.
	Paid 10 (pencil)	150.

Bloomfield

Bloomfield (ms; 1861; black)

Ms	Paid 5	175.

Boston

A

BOSTON / GEO (33; 186-; black)
BOSTON / G^{a} (32; 186-; black)

A	PAID 10	200.
Ms	Pd 10	150.

Bottsford

Bottsford Ga (ms; 1861; black)

Ms	Paid 10	150.

Bowdon

BOWDON / GA. (30; 1862; black)

A	PAID, 10 (pencil) [not illustrated]	200.
Ms	Paid 10*	150.

Box Spring

Box Spring Ga (ms; 1862; black)

Ms	Paid 5, revalued 10 (ms)	200.
	Paid 10*	150.

Brick Store

BRICK STORE / GA. (32; 186-; red)

Ms	Paid 10	150.

Broad River

Broad River Ga (ms; 186-; black)

Ms	Paid 10	150.

DC	double circle
DLC	double [outer] line circle
mkg	marking
ms	manuscript

Brunswick

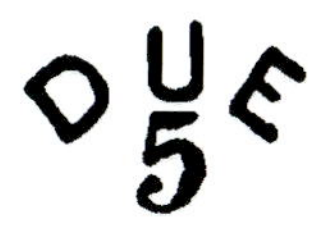

A B C

BRUNSWICK / Ga. (30; 1861-62; black)

A	PAID, 5 (ms)	200.
	Same, 10 (ms)	200.
B	PAID 5	200.
C	DUE 5	200.
Ms	Due 5	175.

Buck Eye

BUCK EYE / GEO. (33 DLC; 1861; red)

Ms	Paid 5cts	200.
	Pad 5 cts	200.

Buena Vista

A B

BUENA VISTA / Gª (32; 186-; red)

A	PAID (red) [no rate]*	300.
B	PAID 10 (red)	300.
Ms	Due 5 cts*	175.

Calhoun

A

B

C

Calhoun Ga (ms; 1862; black)

CALHOUN / Ga. (33; 1861-62; black)

A	PAID 5	200.
B	PAID 10	200.
C	10 [due]	175.
Ms	Paid / 5	175.

Campbellton

Campbellton Ga (ms; 186-; black)

Ms	Paid 10	150.

Canton

A B

CANTON / Ga. (30; 1861; black)

A	PAID [no rate]	200.
B	PAID 5	300.

Note: Prewar and Confederate uses of the Type B marking are indistinguishable. Confederate use must be determined from other aspects of a cover.

Carrollton

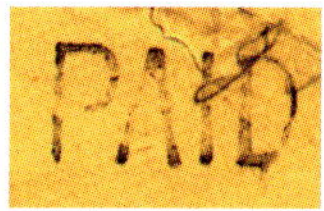

A

CARROLLTON / GA. (26; 1861; black)

A	PAID, 5 (ms)	200.
	Same, 10 (ms)*	200.
	Same, 15 (ms)*	300.

Cartersville

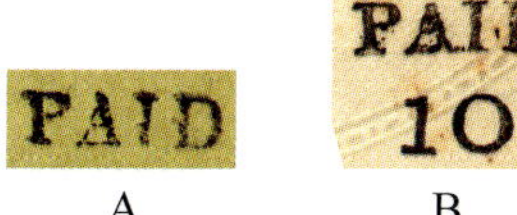

A B

CARTERSVILLE / Ga. (32; 1861-62; black, red)

A	PAID [no rate]	200.
	Same (red) [no rate]	300.
	Same (red), 10 (ms)	300.
B	PAID 10	200.

Cassville

A B

C

CASSVILLE / Ga. (30; 1861-62; blue)
A PAID (blue), 5 (ms) in black circle 300.
B PAID 5 (blue) 200.
C PAID 10 (blue) 200.

Catoosa Springs

Catoosa Springs Ga (ms; 1861; black)
Ms Paid 5 175.
Paid 5c 175.

Cave Springs

A

CAVE SPRING / G^{A} (32; 1861; black)
A PAID 5 200.

Cedar Town

Cedar Town Ga (ms; 1861-63; black)
Ms Paid 10 150.
Pd 10 150.

Chalybeate Springs

Chalybeate spg (ms; 1862; black)
Chalybeate Springs (ms; 1861; black)
Ms Paid 5 175.

Chickasawhatchie

A

Chickasawhatchie (ms; 186-; black)
CHICKASAWHATCHIE / Ga. (35; 1861; black)
A PAID 5 300.
Ms Paid 10 150.

Clarksville

A B

C D

Clarksville Habersahm Co. Geo. (ms; 1862; black)
CLARKSVILLE / G^{a} (30; 1861-63; black, blue, brown)
A PAID, 5 (ms)* 200.
Same (brown), 5 (ms) 300.
Same, 10 (ms) 200.
B PAID 5* 200.
Same (blue) 300.
C PAID 10* 200.
Same (blue)* 300.
D 10 (blue) [due]* 200.

Clay Hill

Clay Hill Ga (ms; 1861-62; black)
Ms Paid 10c 150.

Coal Mountain

COAL MOUNTAIN / GEO. (33; 1862; black)
Ms Paid 5 175.
Pd 5 175.

Cohuttah Springs

Cohuttah Springs Ga (ms; 1863; black)
Ms 10 / Paid 150.

Colaparchee

A

COLAPARCHEE / Ga. (30; 1861; black)
A PAID 5 200.

Columbia Mine

COLUMBIA MINE / GA. (?; 1862; black)
Pk drop letter [no rate]* 200.

Columbus

A B

C D E

COLUMBUS / G^{A} (31; 1861; black)
COLUMBUS GA (32; 1861-63; black)
A PAID 5 200.
Same, revalued 10 (Type B) 300.
B PAID 10 200.
C DUE 5 200.

D	DUE 10	175.
	Same, revalued PAID 10 (Type B)	500.
E	10 (red) [due]	200.

Conyers

Conyers Ga (ms; 1861-62; black)

Ms	Pai 10 ct	150.

Coosa

Coosa Ga (ms; 1863; black)

Ms	10 Paid	150.

Cornucopia

Cornucopia GA (ms; 1861; blue)

Ms	Paid / 10 / cts	150.

Cottage Mills

Cottage Mills Ga (ms; 1861; black)

Ms	Paid 5	175.

Covington

A B

C

COVINGTON / Ga. (30; 1861-62; black, blue-green)

A	PAID, 5 (ms)	200.
	Same (blue-green), 5 (ms)	300.
	Same, 10 (ms)	200.
	Same (blue-green), 10 (ms)	300.
	Same (blue-green), 20 (ms)	300.
B	PAID 5 cts (blue-green)	300.
C	PAID 5 (blue-green)	300.
	Same (blue-green) revalued 10 (ms)*	500.
Ms	P. O. B.	500.

Crawford

Crawford Ga (ms; 1861-62; black)

Ms	Paid 5	175.
	Paid 5, revalued 10 (ms)	175.
	Paid 10*	150.

Crawfordville

A

CRAWFORDSVILLE / GA. (25; 1861-62; black)

A	PAID, 5 (ms)	200.
	Same, 10 (ms)	200.
Ms	Paid 10	150.

Crosby

Crosby Ga (ms; 1862; black)

Ms	Paid / 5 cts	175.
	Paid / 10	150.

Cross Keys

Cross Keys Ga (ms; 1862; black)

Ms	Paid / 5 cts	175.

Culloden

A

CULLODEN / Ga. (30; 186-; blue, brown)

A	PAID 10 (blue)	300.
	Same (brown)	300.

Culverton

CULVERTON / GEO (32 DLC; 1862; blue)

Ms	Paid 10	200.

Cumming

A

CUMMING / Ga. (35; 1861-63; black)

A	PAID, 5 (ms)	200.
	Same, 10 (ms)	200.

Curtright

Curtright Ga (ms; 1865; black)

Ms	Paid / 10	150.

Cut Off

Cutoff Ga (ms; 186-; black)

Ms	Paid 5 cts	175.

Cuthbert

A B

C

CUTHBERT, / Ga. (30; 186-; black)
CUTHBERT / Ga. (33; 1861-63; black)

A	PAID [no rate]	200.
	Same, 5 (ms)*	200.
B	PAID 5	200.
C	PAID 10	200.

Dahlonega

PAID   PAID 10

A   B

Dahlonega Ga (ms; 186-; black, brown)
DAHLONEGA / Ga. (30; 1861; black, brown)

A	PAID, 5 (ms)*	200.
	Same (brown), 10 (ms)*	300.
B	PAID 10*	200.
Ms	Paid 5	175.
	Paid 5, revalued 10 (ms)*	200.
	Paid 10	150.

Dallas

Dallas Ga (ms; 186-; black)

Ms	Paid 10	150.

Dalton

B

C

D

DALTON / Ga. (31 YD; 1861-63; black)
DALTON / Ga. (31; 186-; black)

A	PAID 5 [not illustrated]*	200.
B	PAID 10*	200.
C	DUE 10	200.
D	MISSENT	500.

Danburg

Danburg Geo (ms; 186-; black)

Ms	Paid 10 cts	150.

Danville

A

Danville Ga (ms; 1861-62; black)

A	PAID, 5 (ms)	200.
Ms	Paid / 5	175.
	Paid / 10	150.

Darien

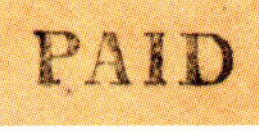

A

B

C

DARIEN / Ga. (29; 1861-62; black)

A	PAID, 5 (ms)	200.
	Same, 5¢ (ms)	200.
B	PAID 5	200.
C	PAID 10	200.

Dartsville

A

B

DARTSVILLE Ga (31x29 OV YD; 1862; black)

A	PAID 10	500.
B	PAID 10	750.

Davisboro

Davisboro (ms; 1862; black)

Ms	Paid / 10	150.

Dawson

PAID

A

DAWSON / G^A (33 YD; 186-; black)

A	PAID [no rate]	200.

Dawsonville

Dawsonville Ga (ms; 186-; black)

Ms	Paid 5	175.

Decatur

A B

C D E

DECATUR / Gª (30; 1861-62; black, blue, red, brown)

A	PAID [no rate]*	200.
	Same (brown) [no rate]	300.
	Same (red), 10 (ms)	300.
B	PAID 5	200.
	Same (blue)*	300.
	Same (red)	300.
	Same (brown)	300.
C	PAID 5*	200.
	Same (red)*	300.
D	PAID 10*	200.
	Same (brown)	300.
E	5 [due]*	150.

Dennis

Dennis Ga (ms; 1861; black)

Ms	Paid 10*	150.

Dirt Town

Dirt Town (ms; 186-; black)

Ms	Paid [no rate]*	150.
	Paid 5	175.

Doctor Town

Dr Town ga (ms; 1865; black)

Ms	Paid / 10	150.

Double Wells

Double Wells (ms; 1862; brown)
Double Wells Geo (ms; 1861; black)

Ms	Pad 10	150.
	Paid 10c	150.

Dover

DOVER / Ga. (?; 1861; red)

Ms	Paid 5	200.

Drayton

A

DRAYTON / Geo. (?; 1861; ?)

A	5 [due]	150.

Dublin

A

B

DUBLIN / Ga. (31; 1861; black, blue)

A	PAID [no rate]*	200.
	Same, 15 (ms)*	300.
B	PAID 5	200.
	Same (blue)*	300.

Ducanville

A

DUCANVILLE / GEO. (32; 1861; black)

A	PAID 5	200.

East Point

East Point Ga (ms; 186-; black)

Ms	Paid 10	150.

Eatonton

A B

C D

E

EATONTON / GA. (26 DC; 1861-65; black)

A	PAID [no rate]	200.
	Same [no rate], struck twice	300.
	Same, 10 (ms)*	200.
B	PAID 5*	200.
	Same, 5 stuck twice	300.
C	PAID 10	200.
D	5 [due]*	175.
E	10 [due]	175.

Edenfield

EDENFIELD / GA. (?; 1861; black)

A PAID 5 [not illustrated]* 200.

Egypt

Egypt Ga (ms; 186-; black)

Ms Paid 5* 175.
Paid 10* 150.

Elberton

A

ELBERTON / GA (23; 1861; black)

A PAID, 10 (ms) 200.
Ms Paid 5 175.
Paid 10 150.

Ellaville

A C

ELLAVILLE / GA. (25; 1862-63; blue)

A PAID (blue) [no rate] 300.
Same (blue), 5 (ms)* 300.
B PAID 5 (blue) [not illustrated]* 300.
C PAID 10 (blue) 300.
Ms Pd 10 150.

Etowah

ETOWAH / Ga. (34; 1861; blue)

Ms Paid 5 200.
Paid 10 200.

Eubanks

Eubanks Ga (ms; 1862; brown)

Ms Paid 5* 175.
Paid 10 150.

Flat Pond

Flat Pond Ga. (ms; 1863; black, brown)

Ms Paid 10 150.
Paid / 10 150.

Forsyth

A B

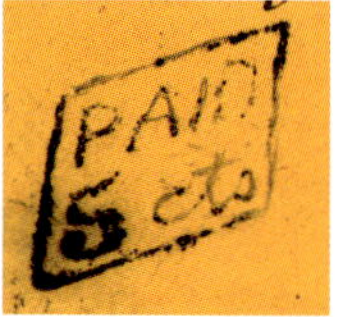
C

D

E

FORSYTH / GEO. (32; 1861-64; black)

A PAID 5 500.
B PAID 5 300.
C PAID 5 300.
D PAID 10 300.
E DUE 10 300.
Ms Paid / 5 cts 175.

Note: Some Forsyth covers addressed to Miss Yerby have a small handstamped "10." This marking is not of Confederate origin. See LaGrange for more information.

Fort Gaines

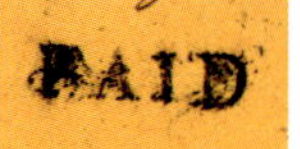

A

FORT GAINES / Ga. (31; 1862; black)

A PAID [no rate] 200.

Fort Valley

B

10

C

FORT VALLEY / GA. (32; 186-; black)

A PAID 5, revalued 10 [not illustrated]* 300.
B PAID 10 200.
C 10 [due]* 175.
Ms Paid 10* 150.

Franklin

A

FRANKLIN / GEO. (31 YD; 1861-62; black)

A PAID, 5 (ms) 200.
Same, 10 (ms) 200.

Gainesville

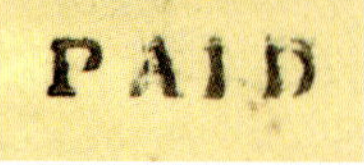

A

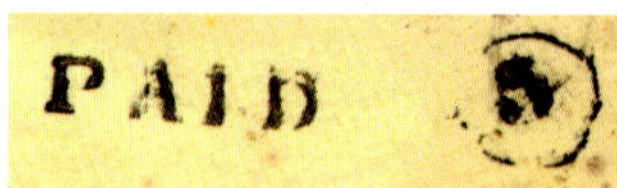

B

C

GAINESVILLE / G^{A} (30; 1861-62; black)

A	PAID [no rate]*	200.
B	PAID 5	200.
C	PAID 10	200.

Geneva

A

GENEVA / GA (25; 1862; black)

A	PAID, 5 (ms)	200.
	Same, 10 (ms)*	200.
Ms	Pd / 5	175.
	PAID 10	150.
	10 [due]	150.

Georgetown

A

GEORGETOWN / GA (26; 186-; black)

A	PAID 10	200.

Georgian

Georgian Ga (ms; 1861-62; black, brown)

Ms	Paid 5	175.
	Paid 10*	150.

Gillsville

Gillsville Ga (ms; 1861; black)

Ms	Free	300.

Gordon

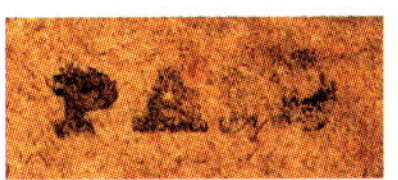

A

Gordon Ga (ms; 1861; black)
GORDON / GEO. (32 DLC; 186-; black)

A	PAID [no rate]	200.
Ms	Paid 10	150.

Pk	cover bearing a postmark but no indication of rate
pmk	postmark
SC	segmented circle

Grantville

A

GRANTVILLE / GA (25; 1862; black)

A	PAID 10	200.

Green Cut

GREEN CUT / Ga. (37; 1861; green)

Ms	Paid / 10	300.

Greensborough

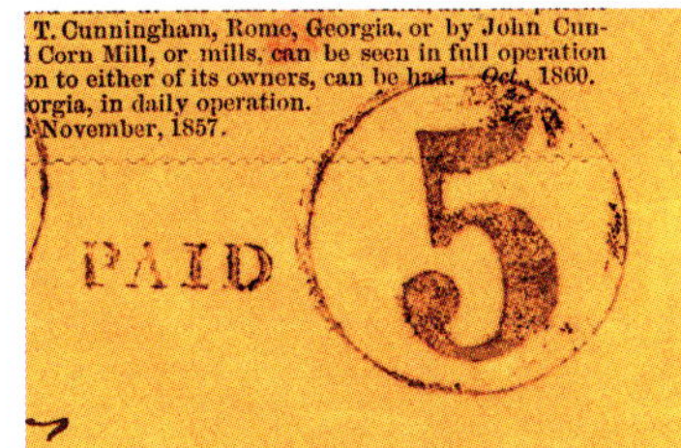

A B

C D

GREENSBOROUGH / Ga. (30; 1861-62; black)

A	PAID, 10 (ms)*	200.
	Same, 15 (ms)	300.
	Same, 20 (ms)*	300.
	Same, 80 (ms)	500.
B	PAID 5	300.
C	PAID 10	300.
D	10, Due (ms)*	175.

Greenville

A

B

C

GREENVILLE / GA (26; 1861; black)

A	PAID 5	200.
B	PAID 10	200.
C	PAID 10	200.

GRIFFIN

A

B

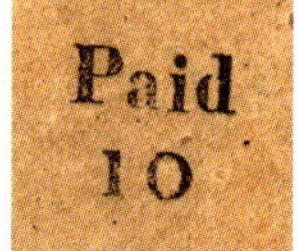

C

D

E

F

a

GRIFFIN / G^{A} (32; 1861-64; black)

A	PAID [no rate]	200.
B	PAID 5	200.
	Same, revalued 10 (Type F)	300.
	Same, revalued 10 (Type *a*)*	300.
	Same, revalued 10 (ms)*	300.
C	PAID 10	200.
D	PAID 10*	200.
E	PAID 10	200.
F	10 [due]	175.

GRISWOLDVILLE

PAID

A

Postmark unknown

A	PAID, 5 (ms)*	200.

GROOVERVILLE

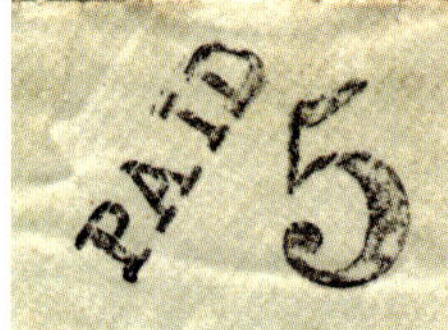

A

PAID 10

B

GROVERVILLE / GEO (33; 1862; black)

A	PAID 5	200.
B	PAID 10	200.

GUYTON

A

Guyton Ga (ms; 1862; black)
•GUYTON• Ga. (32; 1862; black)

A	PAID 5	200.

HALCYONDALE

A

HALCYONDALE / G^{a} (31 YD; 1863; black)

A	PAID 10	200.

HAMILTON

PAID

A

PAID 5

B

HAMILTON / Ga. (30; 1862; black)

A	PAID, 10 (ms)	200.
B	PAID 5*	200.

HARALSON

Haralson Ga (ms; 1861; black)

Ms	Paid 10*	150.

HARTWELL

HARTWELL / GA. (32; 1861; black)

Ms	Paid / 5 c	175.
	Paid 10*	150.

HAWKINSVILLE

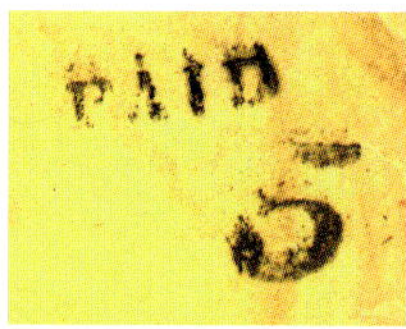

A

PAID *10*

B

C

HAWKINSVILLE / Ga. (34; 1861-62; black)
HAWKINSVILLE / GA (? (YD); 1863, black)

A	PAID 5	200.
B	PAID 10*	200.
C	PAID 10	200.

Henderson

Henderson Ga (ms; 186-; black)

Ms	Paid 10	150.

Hillsborough

Hillsboro Ga (ms; 1861-64; brown)

Ms	Paid 5	175.
	Paid 10	150.
	Paid 10 ct	150.

Hoganville

Hogansville Ga. (ms; 1861; black)

Ms	Paid 10	150.

Holcombe

PAID (5)

A

HOLCOMBE / Geo. (30; 1861; black)

A	PAID 5*	200.
	Same, 5 struck twice	300.

Hollingsworth

Hollingsworth Ga (ms; 1861; black)

Ms	Paid 5 cts	175.

Homer

Homer Ga (ms; 1863; black)

Ms	Paid 10	150.

Houston

PAID 5

A

HOUSTON / GEO. (30; 1861; black)

A	PAID 5	200.
Ms	Paid 10*	150.

Howard

Howard Ga (ms; 186-; brown)

Ms	Paid 10	150.

Indian Spring

A

B

INDIAN = SPRING / G^{a} (31; 186-; black)

A	PAID 5	300.
B	PAID 10	300.
Ms	Paid 5	200.
	Due 10*	175.

Irwinton

IRWINTON / Ga. (36; 186-; black)

A	PAID, 5 (ms)*	200.
Ms	Paid 10	150.

Jasper

A

JASPER / Ga (32; 1862; black)

A	PAID 5	200.

Jefferson

JEFFERSON / Ga (37; 1862; black)

Ms	Paid / 5	175.

Johnston's Station

Johnston Station Ga (ms; 1863; black)

Ms	Pd 10	150.

Jonesborough

A

B

JONESBOROUGH / GA (33; 1861; black)

A	PAID [no rate]	200.
	Same, 10 (ms)	200.
B	PAID 5	200.

Kingston

A B

C D

E *a* *b*

KINGSTON / G^{A} (32; 1861-63; black)
KINGSTON / G^{a} (?; 1862; black)

A	PAID 5	200.
	Same, revalued 10 (Type *b*)	300.
B	PAID 5 CENTS	300.
C	PAID 10	200.
D	PAID 10	200.
	Same, revalued 20 by 2 (Type *a*)	500.
E	DUE 10	200.

Knoxville

KNOXVILLE / Ga. (?; 186-; black)

Ms	Paid 10	175.

LaFayette

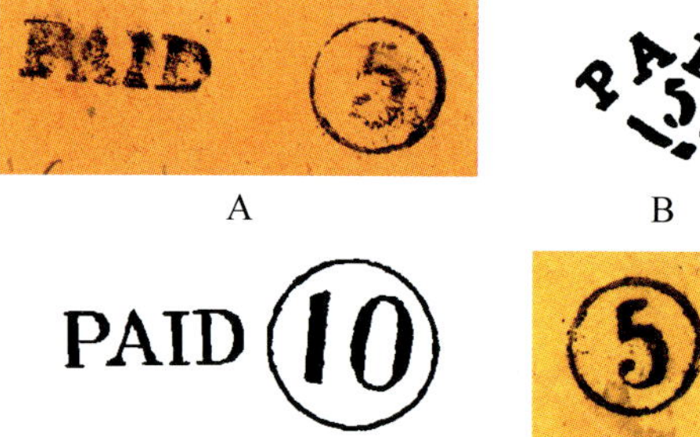

A B

C D

Lafayette / PO Ga (ms; 186-; brown)
LAFAYETTE / Ga. (31; 1861-62; black)
LAFAYETTE / GEO. (33; 1863; black)

A	PAID 5	200.
	Same, 5 struck twice	300.
B	PAID 5	300.
C	PAID 10*	200.
D	5	175.
Ms	Paid 10	150.
	Due 10*	150.

LaGrange

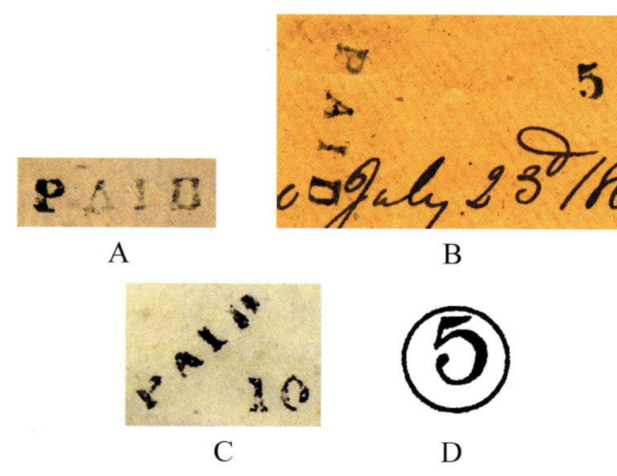

A B

C D

LAGRANGE / G^{a} (30; 1861-62; black, blue)

A	PAID [no rate]*	200.
	Same, 10 (ms)	200.
B	PAID 5	200.
	Same (blue)*	300.
C	PAID 10	200.
D	5 [due]*	175.
Ms	Paid 10*	150.
	Paid 20*	200.

Note: Many LaGrange covers addressed to a Miss Yerby have a small handstamped "10" (see illustration below) in addition to one of the LaGrange markings illustrated here. This marking is not of Confederate origin and was added at a later date.

Bogus "10" Marking

Lawrenceville

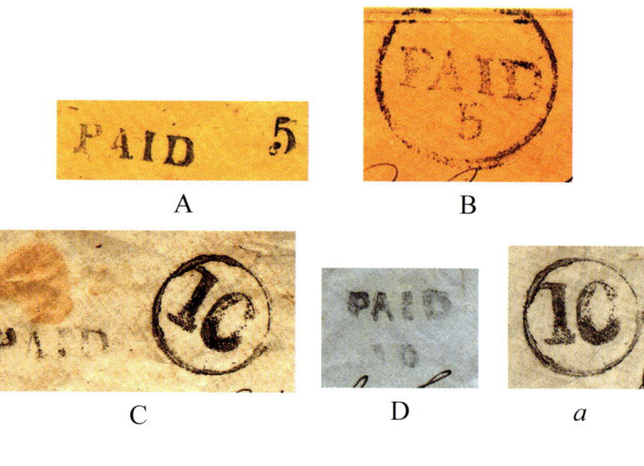

A B

C D *a*

LAWRENCE VILLE / Ga. (31; 1861; black)

A	PAID 5	200.
	Same, revalued 10 (Type *a*)	300.
B	PAID 5	200.
C	PAID 10	200.
D	PAID 10	200.

Leathersville

Leathersville (ms; 1862; black)

Ms	Paid 10	150.

Lester's District

Lesters Dist Ga (ms; 1862; black)

Ms	Pd 10	150.

Lexington

A  B

C 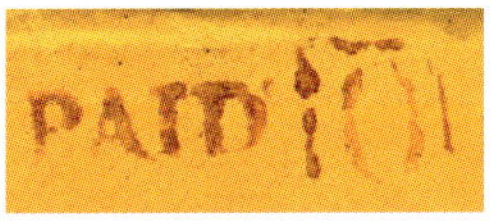 D

E

LEXINGTON / GA (33; 1861-62; red)
LEXINGTON GA / 3 PAID (32; 1861; red)

A	PAID (red), 5 (ms)	300.
	Same (red), 20 (ms)	500.
B	PAID 5 (red)	300.
	Same (red), revalued 10 (Type E)	500.
C	PAID 10 (red)	300.
D	PAID 10 (red)	300.
E	10 (red), Due (ms)	200.

Lincolnton

Lincolnton Ga (ms; 1861; black)

Ms	Paid / 5 cts	175.

Linton

A  B

Linton (ms; 1861; brown)
LINTON / GA. (31 YD; 1862; black, red)

A	PAID 5 (red)	300.
B	PAID 5*	200.
	Same (red)	300.

Linwood

LINWOOD / Ga. (?; 1862; black)

A	PAID 10 [not illustrated]*	200.

Lombardy

Lombardy (ms; 1862; black)

Ms	Paid / 10	150.

Louisville

PAID 5

A  B

10

a

LOUISVILLE / Geo. (33; 186-; blue)

A	PAID 5 revalued 10 (type *a*) (blue)	200.
B	PAID 10 (blue)	300.
	Same (blue), 10 struck twice	500.
Ms	Paid 5*	175.

Lumpkin

A

PAID 5

B  C

LUMPKIN / Ga. (30; 1861; black)

A	PAID, 5 (ms)	200.
	Same, 10 (ms)	200.
B	PAID 5*	200.
C	PAID 10	200.
Ms	Paid 10	150.

Macon

A

B  C

D  E

PAID
10

F

G

MACON / GA (26 DC; 1861-63; black)
MACON, GEO. (31; 1861; black)

A	PAID [no rate]	150.
	Same, 5 (ms)*	150.
	Same, 10 (ms)*	150.
	Same, 15 (ms)*	200.
B	PAID 5	200.
C	PAID 5	200.
	Same, struck twice*	300.
D	PAID 5	200.
	Same, revalued 2 (Types A and *a*)*	300.
	Same, struck twice	300.
	Same, revalued 10 (Type K)	300.
E	PAID 10	200.
	Same, stuck twice	300.
F	PAID 10*	200.
G	PAID 10	200.

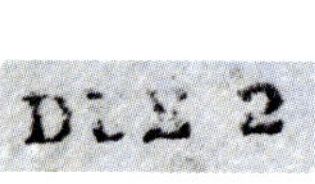

H

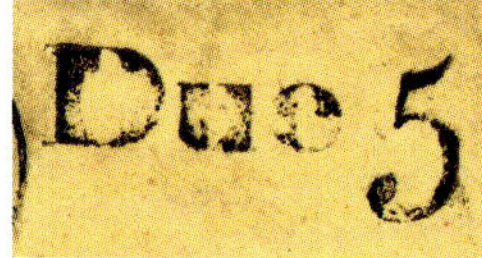

I

J

K

L

M

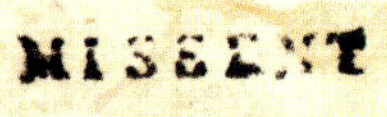

N

a

H	DUE 2	500.
I	Due 5	200.
J	Due 10	200.
K	10 [due]	175.
L	ADVERTISED	500.
M	FORWARDED*	500.
N	MISSENT	500.
Ms	Fowd 10 c	200.

Madison

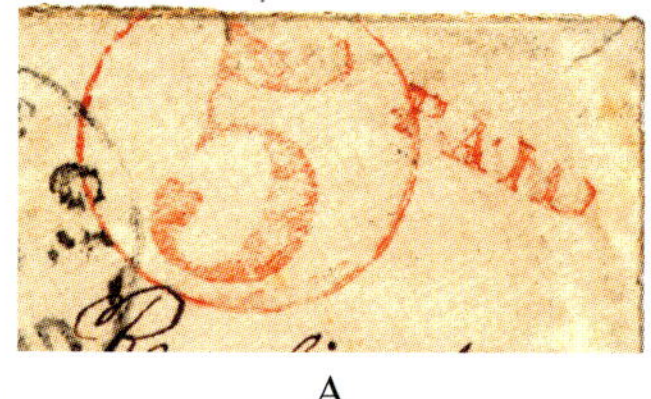

A

B

a

MADISON / Ga. (30; 1861; red)

A	PAID 5 (red)	300.
	Same, revalued 10 (red) (Type *a*)	500.
B	PAID 10 (red)*	300.

Manassas

A

MANASSAS / GA (31 YD; 1862-63; blue)

A	PAID 10 (blue)	300.

Marietta

A B

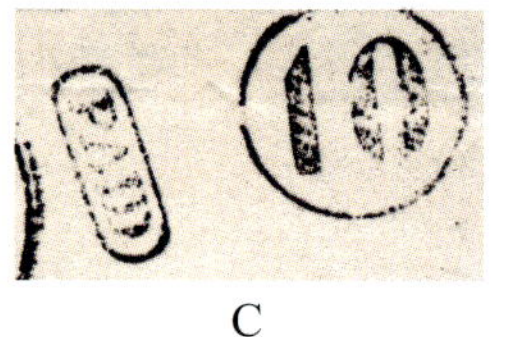

C

D

MARIETTA / GEO. (31; 1861-63; black, red)

A	PAID, 20 (ms)*	200.
B	PAID 5	200.
C	PAID 10	200.
D	5	175.
Ms	Due 10*	150.
	Ford 10	150.

MARION

A

Postmark unknown

A	PAID 5*	200.

MARSHALLVILLE

A B

MARSHALLVILLE / GA. (25; 186-; black)

A	PAID 5*	200.
B	PAID 10*	200.

MAYFIELD

A

Postmark unknown

A	PAID 5*	200.

McDONOUGH

A B

McDonough / Ga. (30; 1862; black)
M^{c}DONOUGH / Ga. (?; 1862; black)

A	PAID 5	200.
B	PAID 10	200.

McGUIRE'S STORE

McGuire Store Ga (ms; 1861; black)

Ms	Paid 5 (pencil)	175.

McINTOSH

McIntosh (ms; 1862; black)

Ms	Paid 10	150.

MILLARD

Millard Ga (ms; 186-; black)

Pk	No paid or rate marking	150.

MILLEDGEVILLE

A B

C D

E F

G *a* *b*

MILLEDGEVILLE / G^{a} (30; 1861-64; black)

A	PAID [no rate]*	175.
	Same [no rate or postmark]	200.
	Same, 20 (pencil)	300.
	Same, 50 (pencil)	300.
B	PAID [no rate or postmark]	175.
	Same, 20 (pencil)	300.
C	PAID 5	200.
	Same, revalued 10 (Type *b*)*	300.
D	PAID 5	200.
E	PAID 10	200.
F	PAID 10*	200.
	Same, revalued 5 (Type *a*)*	300.
G	10 [due]	200.
	Same, Due (ms)	200.
Ms	Due 10*	150.

MILLEN

Millen Ga (ms; 186-; black)

Ms	Paid 10	150.

MILLSTONE

Millstone Ga (ms; 186-; black)

Ms	Paid 10 cts	150.

[*]	symbol used after an item description to mean an unsupported listing
[–]	symbol used in place of value to mean insufficient information to assign a price
[?]	symbol used to mean unknown measurement, date or color

Milltown

A

MILL TOWN / GEO. (32; 1862; black)

A	PAID 5	200.
Ms	Paid 10*	150.

Millwood

Millwood Ga (ms; 1864; black)

Ms	Paid 10	150.

Minton

Minton Ga (ms; 1861; black)

Ms	Paid 5 cts	175.

Missionary Station

A

MISSIONARY STATION / Ga. (30; 1861; black)

A	PAID 5	300.

Note: Prewar and Confederate Type A markings are indistinguishable. Confederate usage must be determined from other aspects of a cover.

Mobley Pond

Mobley Pond (ms; 1862; black)

Ms	Paid / 5	175.
	Paid 10	150.

Monroe

A

B

C

MONROE / Gª (31; 1861-62; black, blue-green)

A	PAID 5	200.
B	PAID 10	200.
	Same (blue-green)	300.
	Same, 10 struck three times	500.
C	5 [due]*	175.

Montezuma

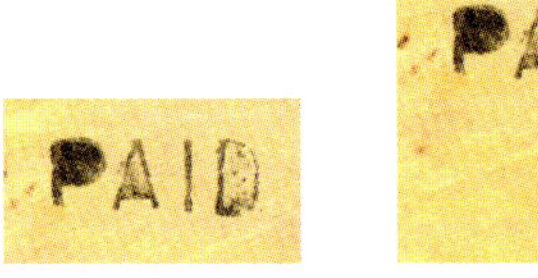

A

B

C

MONTEZUMA / Ga. (30; 1862; black)

A	PAID [no rate]	200.
B	PAID 5	200.
C	PAID 10	200.
Ms	Misent & ford	200.

Monticello

A

PAID 10

B

MONTICELLO / Gª (32; 1861-62; green)

A	PAID 5 (green)	300.
B	PAID 10 (green)	300.
Ms	Due 10	150.

Montpelier

Montpelier Ga (ms; 1864; black)

Ms	Paid 10 cts*	150.

Morgan

A

MORGAN / GA (26; 186-; black)

A PAID [no rate] 200.

Moultrie

Moultrie Ga (ms; 1861; black)

Ms Paid 10* 150.

Mount Vernon

Mt. Vernon Ga (ms; 186-; black)

Ms Paid 10 150.

Mount Zion

MOUNT ZION / GA. (33; 1862; black)

Ms Paid 5 200.

Mulberry

MULBERRY / GEO. (33; 1862; black)

Ms Paid 10 200.

Nails Creek

Nails Creek Ga (ms; 186-; black)

Ms Paid 5 175.

New Bridge

New Bridge Ga (ms; 186-; black)

Ms Paid 10c* 150.

Newnan

A B

C D

NEWNAN / Ga. (35; 1861-65; black)

A PAID 5 200.

Same, revalued 10 (Type D) 300.

B PAID 5 200.

Same, revalued 10 (Type D) 300.

C PAID 10 200.

D 10 [due] 150.

Newton

A

NEWTON / Ga. (37; 1861; black)

A PAID, 5 (ms) 200.

Same, 10 (ms) 200.

Ms Pd 10 150.

Oak Hill

Oak Hill Ga (ms; 1861; black)

Ms Paid 5 175.

Odchodkee

Odchodkee Ga (ms; 186-; brown)

Ms Paid 10 150.

Ogeechee

Ogeeche (ms; 1861; black)

Ms Paid 10 150.

Oglethorpe

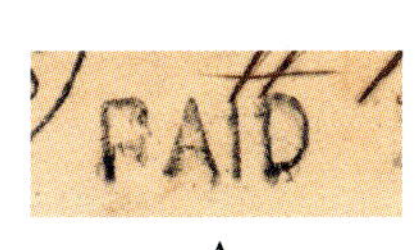

A B

C

OGLETHORPE / GA. (32; 1861; black)

OGLETHORPE / Ga. (30; 186-; black)

A PAID [no rate] 200.

Same, 5 (ms)* 200.

Same, 10 (ms)* 200.

Same, 15 (ms)* 300.

B PAID 5 200.

C PAID 10 200.

Okapilco

Okapilco Geo (ms; 1862; black)

Ms Paid 10 150.

Oxford

A 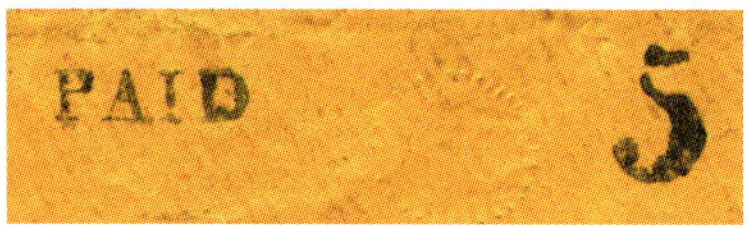 B

OXFORD / Ga. (29; 1861-62; black, blue)

A	PAID, 5 (ms)*	200.
	Same (blue), 10 (ms)*	300.
B	PAID 5	200.
	Same (blue)*	300.

Palmetto

A  B

PALMETTO / Ga (37; 186-; black)

A	PAID 5	200.
B	PAID 10	200.

Penfield

A

PENFIELD / Ga. (30; 1861; black)

A	PAID 10	200.

Perry

PAID

A

PERRY / GEO. (32; 186-; black)

A	PAID [no rate]	200.

Philomath

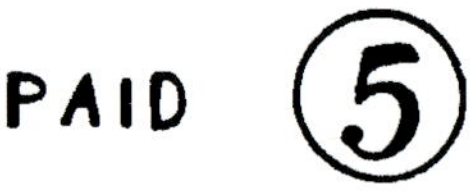

A

PHILOMATH / Ga. (30; 1861; red)

A	PAID 5 (red)	300.

Pine Hill

Pine Hill Ga (ms; 1862; black)

Ms	Paid 5	175.

Pine Log

Pine Log Ga (ms; 186-; black)

Ms	Paid 10	150.

Plains of Dura

A  B

C  D

PLAINS OF DURA / GA (26; 1861-62; black)

A	PAID, 5 (ms)	200.
	Same (struck twice), 5 (ms)	300.
	Same, 10 (ms)*	200.
B	PAID 5	200.
C	PAID 10	200.
D	PAID 10	200.

Point Peter

Point Peter Ga (ms; 1861; black)

Ms	Paid / 5	175.

Powder Springs

A

Powder Springs Ga (ms; 1862; black)
POWDER SPRINGS / Geo. (29; 1861; black)

A	PAID 5	200.
Ms	Paid / 5	175.

Powelton

Powelton Ga (ms; 1861; brown)

Ms	Paid 10	150.

Powers

Powers Ga (ms; 1862; black)

Ms	Paid 10*	150.

Prince Edward

Prince Edward Ga (ms; 1861; black)

Ms	paid / 5	175.

Quitman

A

B

No postmark

A	PAD, 5 (ms) [inside postmark]	200.
	PAD, 10 (ms) [inside postmark]	200.
B	PAD 5 (brown)	300.
	PAD 5, P 10 (ms) [outside postmark]	200.

Note: The Quitman postmaster converted a postmark to a rate handstamp. The "PAID" portion of the postmark is characterized by the missing cross bar in the letter "A" and the missing letter "I." The marking doubled as the town postmark. The date (month and day) were written in manuscript outside the postmark.

Red Clay

A

B

C

RED CLAY / Ga. (32; 1861-62; black)

A	PAID [no rate]*	200.
B	PAID 5	200.
C	PAID 10*	200.
Ms	Paid 10	150.
	Paid / 10	150.
	Due 10	150.

Renwick

A

RENWICK / GA (26; 186-; blue)

A	PAID (blue) [no rate]	200.
Ms	Paid 10, revalued 20 (ms)	200.
	due 2 (pencil) [no postmark]	300.

Reynolds

Reynolds Ga (ms; 186-; black)

Ms	Paid 10	150.

Riceborough

A

RICEBORO – Ga. – (28 DC; 1861; black, brown)

A	PAID, 5 (ms)	200.
	Same (brown), 5 (ms)	300.
	Same, 5 (ms) revalued 10 (ms)	300.
	Same, 10 (ms)	200.
	Same (brown), 10 (ms)	300.

Richland

Richland Ga (ms; 1864; black)

Ms	Paid / 10	150.

Richmond Factory

Richmond Factory (ms; 1863; black)

Ms	X [10]	200.

Ringgold

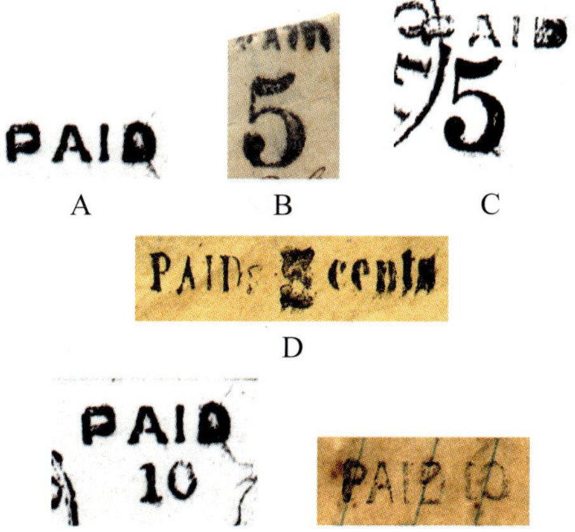
A B C D E F

Ringold Ga (ms; 1862; black)

RINGGOLD / GEO. (32; 1861-63; black, blue-black)

A	PAID, 10 (ms)*	200.
	Same (blue-black), 10 (ms)	300.
B	PAID 5	200.
	Same (blue-black)	300.
C	PAID 5	200.
D	PAID 5 cents	300.
E	PAID 10	200.
F	PAID 10 (blue-black)	300.
Ms	Paid 10*	150.
	5	175.
	Due 10	150.
	Due / 10	150.

Rock Bridge

A

ROCK BRIDGE / Ga. (30 ; 1863; black)

A	PAID 10	200.

Rocky Mount

Rocky Mt Ga (ms; 186-; black)

Ms	Paid / 10	150.
	Paid cts /10	150.

Rome

A

B

C

a

ROME / Ga. (32; 1861-62; black)

A	PAID [no rate]	200.
	Same, 5 (ms)*	200.
	Same, 10 (ms)	200.
B	PAID 5	200.
	Same, revalued 10 (Type *a*)	300.
C	PAID 10	200.

Note: The Type B PAID 5 marking is indistinguishable from prewar usages. Confederate use must be determined by other aspects of the cover.

Roswell

A

B

C

ROSWELL / Ga. (31; 1861-62; black, blue, green, blue-green, violet)

A	PAID (blue-green), 5 cts (ms)	200.
	Same (blue), 5 (pencil)	200.
	Same (green), 5 (pencil)	200.
	Same (blue), 10 (ms)*	200.
B	PAID 5 (blue)	200.
	Same (green)	500.
	Same (violet)	300.
	Same, revalued 10 (Type C) (blue-green)	300.
C	PAID 10 (blue)	200.
	Same, revalued 5 (blue) (Type B)	300.
	Same (violet)*	300.

Ruckersville

Ruckersville Ga (ms; 1861; black)

Ms	Paid 10*	150.

Rutledge

Rutledge (ms; 186-; black)

Ms	Paid 10*	150.

Saint Mary's

PAID 5

A

Postmark unknown

A	PAID 5*	200.

Salt Spring

Salt Spring (ms; 1862; black)

Ms	Pd 10 ct	150.

Sandtown

Sand Town Ga (ms; 1861; black)

Ms	Pd 5	175.

Sandersville

A

B

PAID *10*

C

a

SANDERSVILLE / Ga. (31; 1861-62; black, blue)

A	PAID 5*	200.
	Same (blue)	300.
	Same (blue) struck twice	500.
	Same, revalued 10 (Type *a*)*	300.
B	PAID 10 (blue)	200.
	Same (blue), "10" struck twice	500.

C	PAID 10*	200.
	Same (blue)*	300.
	Same, with PAID 5 (Type A)*	300.

Savannah

A B

C D

F

G H

I J

SAVANNAH / *GEO* (26; 1861-63; black, red)
SAVANNAH / Ga. (32 YD; 1861-62; black)
SAVANNAH / Ga. (33; 186-; black)
SAVANNAH Ga. / Paid (32 YD; 1861-62; black)
SAVANNAH GEO / PAID (31; 1861-62; black)
SAVANNAH GEO / 5 PAID (31; 1861; black)

A	PAID [no rate]*	175.
	Same, p 2 (pencil)	250.
	Same, 15 (ms)*	300.
	Same, 50 (pencil)	300.
B	Paid (integral postmark), no rate	200.
	Same, 2 (ms)	500.
	Same, 10 (Type N)	300.
C	PAID 2	500.
D	PAID 5*	200.
E	PAID 5 [not illustrated]	200.
F	PAID 5	200.
	Same, revalued with PAID (Type A) and 2 (pencil)	500.
	Same, revalued 10 (Type H)	300.
G	PAID 10*	200.
H	PAID 10	200.
I	PAID 60	500.
J	DUE 5 (red)	300.

K

L

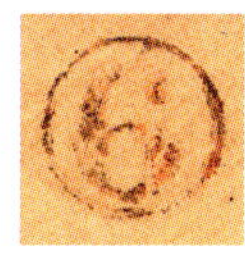
M

N

O P

Q

R

S

T

U

K	2, Due (ms)*	500.
L	5 [due]	200.
M	6 [due] (red)	750.
N	10 [due]	200.
O	20 [due]*	300.
P	FORWARDED*	500.
Q	FORWARDED 10 (10 red)	500.
R	FORWARDED 20	750.
S	P. O. BUSINESS FREE	1,000.
T	SHIP, with 7 (ms) (red)	4,000.
U	STEAM BOAT*	750.
	Same, with DUE 5 (red) (Type J)	1,000.

Scarborough

A

SCARBOROUGH / GA (26; 186-; black)

A	PAID, 10 (ms)	200.

Screven

Screven Ga (ms; 1861; brown)
Ms Paid / 5 175.

Scull Shoals

A

SCULL SHOALS / Geo (29; 1861-62; black)
A PAID 5, revalued 10 (ms) 200.

Shady Dale

Shady Dale (ms; 1862; brown)
Ms Paid 10 150.

Sharon

Sharon Geo (ms; 1862; black, brown)
Ms Paid 10 150.
Pd 10 150.

Snapping Shoals

A

SNAPPING SHOALS / GEO (31; 1861; black)
A PAID 5 200.

Sneed

Sneeds Ga (ms; 186-; black)
Ms Paid 5 175.

Social Circle

A

B

SOCIAL CIRCLE / Geo. (32; 186-; red)
A PAID [no rate] (red) 200.
B PAID 10 (red) 300.

Sparta

A

B

C

D

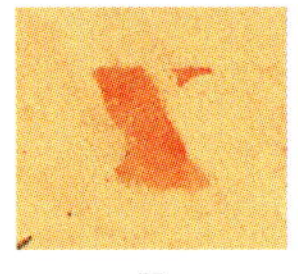

E

a

b

SPARTA / Ga. (35; 1861-65; black, red, green)
A PAID 5 (red)* 300.
Same (red), "5" struck twice 500.
Same revalued 10 (Type *b*) (red)* 500.
B PAID 5 (red)* 300.
C PAID 10 (red)* 300.
Same (red) revalued 5 (Type *a*) 500.
Same (green) 500.
D PAID 10 (red) 300.
E X (red) [due] 300.
Ms Paid / 10 150.

Speir's Turn Out

A

SPEIRS TURN OUT / GA (26; 1861; black)
A PAID, 5 (ms) 200.
Ms Paid 5 175.

Spring Place

A

PAID 10
B

SPRING PLACE / Ga. (33; 1862; black)
A PAID 5 200.
B PAID 10 200.

Starkville

PAID
A

B

C

STARKVILLE / Ga. (34; 1861-62; black)
A PAID, 5 (ms)* 200.

B	PAID 5	200.
C	PAID 10	200.
Ms	Paid [no rate]	150.

Stockton

Stockton Ga (ms; 1863; black)

Ms	Pd 10	150.

Stone Mountain

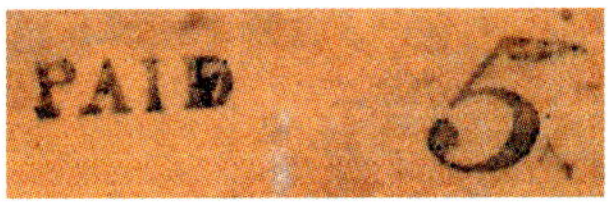

A  B

STONE MOUNTAIN / Ga. (35; 1861; black)

A	PAID 5	200.
B	PAID 10	200.
Ms	Paid 10¢	150.
Pk	No rate [drop letter]	250.

Sulphur Springs

Sulphur SprinGa (ms; 1861; brown)

Ms	Paid 10	150.

Summerville

A

SUMMERVILLE / GA (26; 1861; black)

A	PAID 5	200.

Swainesborough

Swainsesboro Ga (ms; 1861; black)

Ms	Paid 5	175.

Sylvania

Sylvania Ga (ms; 1861; black)

Ms	Paid 5 cts	175.

Talbotton

PAID PAID 10

A  B

TALBOTTON / Ga (32; 186-; black)
TALBOTTON / GA (26 DC YD; 1861-64; black)

A	PAID [no rate]	200.
B	PAID 10*	200.
	Same, with 10 struck twice	300.

Tebeauville

A

Tebeauville Ga (ms; 1861-63; black)
TEBEAUVILLE / GA. (29 YD; 1863; black)

A	PAID 10	300.
Ms	Paid 5	175.
	Pd 10	150.

Tennville

A  B

TENNVILLE / GA (26; 186-; black)

A	PAID, 10 (ms)	200.
B	PAID [no rate]	200.
	Same, 10 (ms)*	200.
Ms	Due 10	150.

The Rock

THE ROCK / Geo. (30; 186-; black)

Ms	Due 10	200.

Thomaston

A  B

C  D

PAID 10

E

THOMASTON / Ga. (31; 1861-62; black)

A	PAID, 2 (ms)	500.
	Same, 5 (ms)*	200.
B	PAID 5	200.
C	PAID 5	200.
D	PAID 10	200.
E	PAID 10	200.
Ms	Paid 10	150.

Thomasville

A

B

C

THOMASVILLE / Ga (29; 1861; black)
THOMASVILLE / Ga. (33; 1862; black)

A	PAID 5	200.
B	PAID 10	200.
C	10 [due]*	150.

Thompson

A

B

C

D

Thomson Ga (ms; 1863; black)
THOMPSON / GA (26; 1861-62; black)

A	PAID [no rate]	200.
	Same, 5 (ms)*	200.
	Same, 5 (ms), revalued 10 (ms)	300.
	Same, 10 (ms)*	200.
B	PAID 5*	200.
	Same, revalued 10 (ms)*	300.
C	PAID 5	200.
D	PAID 10	200.
Ms	Paid / 10	150.

Tilton

Tilton Geo (ms; 1861; black)

Ms	Paid 5	175.
	Due [no rate]	150.

Toomsboro

Toombboro Ga (ms; 1862; brown)

Ms	Due / 10	150.

Troup Factory

TROUP FACTORY / GEO. (31; 1862; blue)

Ms	Paid 5	200.
	Paid 10	175.
	Pd 10	175.

Tunnel Hill

A

B

TUNNEL HILL / Ga. (32; 1861-62; red)

A	PAID 5 (red)	300.
B	PAID 10 (red)	300.

Union Point

A

Union Point (ms; 186- black)
Union Point Ga (ms; 186-; brown)
UNION POINT / Ga. (32; 1861; black, ochre)

A	PAID 10 (ochre)	500.
Ms	Paid 10	150.
	Paid / 10	150.

Upper Kings Bridge

Upper Kings Bridge Ga (ms; 1863; black)

Ms	Paid 10	150.

Valdosta

A

B

C

D

E

F

VALDOSTA / GA (26; 1862; black)
VALDOSTA / GA. (31 YD; 1862-63; black)

A	PAID, 10 (ms)*	200.
B	PAID 5	200.
	Same, revalued 10 (ms)	300.
C	PAID 5*	200.
D	PAID 5*	200.
E	PAID 10	200.
F	DUE 10	175.
Ms	Paid 20*	200.

Vienna

VIENNA / GA (27; 1861; black)

Ms	Paid 5*	175.

Villa Rica

A

VILLA RICA / Ga. (32; 1861-64; black)

A	PAID 5	200.
Ms	Pd 10 (pencil)	150.

Villanow

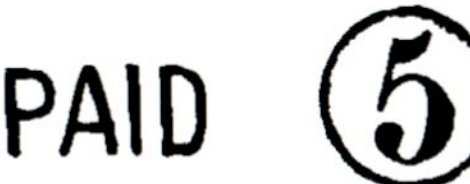

A

VILLANOW / GEO (31; 186-; black)

A	PAID 5*	200.

Wallace

Wallace Ga (ms; black; 1861)

Ms	Paid 10	150.

Walthourville

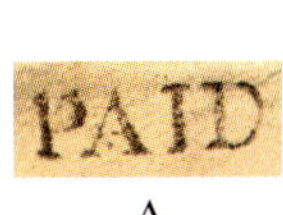

A

B

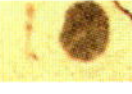
a

WALTHOURVILLE / GEO. (28; 1861; black, red)

A	PAID (red), 10 (ms)	300.
B	PAID 5	200.
	Same, revalued 10 (Type *a*)	300.

Walton's Ford

Waltonsford Ga (ms; 1861; black)

Ms	Paid 5	175.

Waresborough

Waresboro (ms; 1861; black)

Ms	Paid / 5	175.

Warrenton

A

B

C

WARRENTON / Geo. (31; 1861; black)

A	PAID [no rate]*	200.
	Same, 5 (ms) revalued 20 (ms)	300.
	Same, 20 (ms)*	300.
B	PAID 5	200.
	Same, revalued 10 (ms)	300.
C	10 [due]	150.

Warthen's Store

Warthen's Store Ga (ms; 186-; black)

Ms	Pd / 10	150.

Washington

A

B

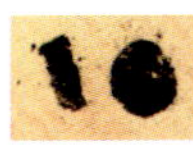

a

WASHINGTON / Ga. (32; 1861; black)
WASHINGTON / Ga. (32 YD; 1861-62; black)

A	PAID, 10 (ms)	200.
B	PAID 5	200.
	Same, revalued 10 (ms)*	300.
	Same, revalued 10 (Type a)	300.
C	PAID 10	200.

Watkinsville

A

WATKINSVILLE / Ga. (37; 1861; blue)

A	PAID 5 (blue)	300.

Waverly Hall

Waverly Hall Ga (ms; 1863; black)

A	PAID 10 [not illustrated]*	200.
Ms	Paid 10	150.

Waynesborough

A

WAYNESBOROUGH / Ga. (33; 186-; black)

A	PAID [no rate]	200.

Waynesville

A  B

Waynesville Ga (ms; 1861; blue)
WAYNESVILLE / GA (31; 186-; black)

A	PAID 5	200.
B	PAID 10	200.
Ms	pd 10 (blue)	150.

Way's Station

Ways Station / Geo (ms; 1861; black)

Ms	Paid 5	175.

West Point

A

WEST POINT / Ga. (34; 1861-62; black)

A	PAID, 5 (ms)	200.
	Same, 10 (ms)	200.
Ms	Paid 5*	175.
	Due 10	150.

Weston

Weston Ga (ms; 186-; black)

Pk	No rate or paid marking	200.

White Oak

White Oak Ga (ms; 1861; black)

Ms	Paid 5*	175.

Whitesville

WHITESVILLE / Ga. (30; 1865; black, red)

Ms	Paid 10	175.
	Due 10*	175.

Winfield

Winfield Ga. (ms; 186-; black)

Ms	Paid	150.

Woodville

PAID PAID 5

A 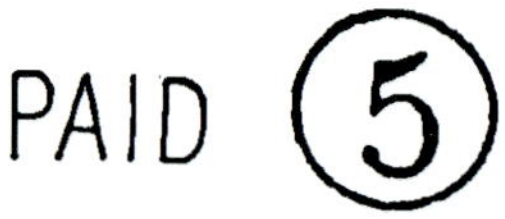 B

WOODVILLE / Geo. (31; 1861; black, red)

A	PAID, 10 (ms)*	200.
	Same (red), 10 (ms)*	300.
B	PAID 5 (red)	300.

Yarborough

YARBOROUGH / Ga. (32; 1864; black)

Ms	10 cts Paid	175.

KENTUCKY

Bowling Green

PAID

A

B

C

BOWLING GREEN / K.Y. (30; 1861-62; black, blue)
Bowling Green (ms; 1861; black)

A	PAID 5	1,000.
B	PAID 10	750.
C	5 [due]	750.
Ms	Pd 5	500.
	Paid 5	500.
	Pd 10	500.
	Paid 10	500.
	Due 5	500.
	D 5 [Due 5]	500.
	Due 10	500.
	10 [due]	500.

Cave City

Cave City Ky (ms; 1861; black)

Ms	Paid 5	1,500.
	Paid 10	1,500.

Columbus

A

COLUMBUS / KY (26; 1861-62; black)

A	PAID, 5 (ms)	750.
	Same, 10 (ms)	750.
	Same, 20 (ms)	1,000.
Ms	Due / 5	500.

Cumberland Ford

Cumberland Ford (ms; 1862; black)

Ms	Paid 5cts	1,500.

Elizabethtown

ELIZABETHTOWN / KY. (32; 1861; black)

Ms	Due 10*	—

Glasgow

PAID

A

GLASGOW / Ky. (30; 1862; black)

A	PAID, 5 (ms)*	—

Hickman

HICKMAN / KY (26 DC YD; 1861-62; black)

Ms	Pd 5	1,000.

Hopkinsville

A

B

HOPKINSVILLE / KY (26 DC YD; 1861-62; black)

A	PAID 5	1,500.
B	PAID 10	1,500.
Ms	Due 5	1,500.

Moscow

Moscow Ky (ms; 186-; black)

Ms	Paid 10	500.

Oakland

Oakland Ky (ms; 1861; black)

Ms	pd 10	1,500.

Russellville

A

RUSSELLVILLE / K^{Y} (32; 1861-62; black)

A	10, Due (ms)	1,500.
Ms	Due 10	1,500.

Woodbury

A

WOODBURY / Ky. (32; 1861; black)

A	5 [due]	750.

Zollicoffer's Brigade

Zollicoffers Brigade Ky (ms; 1861-62; black)

Ms	Paid 5	2,000.

[*] symbol used after an item description to mean an unsupported listing

[–] symbol used in place of value to mean insufficient information to assign a price

DC double circle

LOUISIANA

Abbeville

A

B

ABBEVILLE / La. (37; 1861; black)
- A PAID, 5 (ms)* 250.
- B PAID 5 300.

Alexandria

A

B

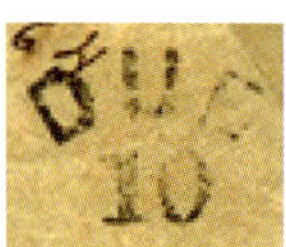
C

ALEXANDRIA / L^A (32; 1861-64; red, black)
- A PAID 5 (red) 300.
- B PAID 10 (red) 300.
- C DUE 10 250.
- Ms Due 5* 200.

Algiers

A

ALGIERS / LA (26; 1861; black)
- A PAID, 10 (ms) 300.

Amite City

A

AMITE CITY / La. (39; 1861; black)
- A PAID (brown) [no rate] 300.
- Same, 5 (ms) 300.
- Same, 10 (ms)* 300.
- Same, 20 (ms) 500.

Arcadia

A

Arcadia La (ms; 1862; black)
ARCADIA / LA (27; 1861; black, blue)
- A PAID [no rate] 300.
- Same, 5 (ms)* 300.
- Same, Paid 5 cts (ms) 300.
- Ms Paid 5 200.

Arnaudville

Arnaudville (ms; 1861; brown)
ARNAUDVILLE / LA (26; 1861-62; black)
- Ms Paid 5 300.
- Paid 5c* 300.

Ashwood

Ashwood (ms; 1861; black)
- Ms Paid 5¢ 200.

Bastrop

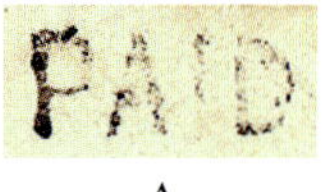

A

BASTROP / LA (?; 186-; black)
- A PAID [no rate] 300.

Baton Rouge

A

PAID 5
B

C

D

PAID. 10
E

5
F

G

BATON ROUGE / La. (34 YD; 1861; black)
- A PAID, 10 (ms)* 300.
- B PAID 5 300.
- C PAID. 5 300.
- D PAID 10 500.
- E PAID. 10* 500.
- F 5 [due] 250.
- G 10 [due] 250.
- Ms 2 (drop) [due] 750.

Bayou Goula

A

B

a

BAYOU GOULA / LA (26; 1861; black)
BAYOU GOULA / La. (32; 1861; black)

A	PAID 5	300.
	Same, revalued "10" (Type *a*)	500.
B	PAID 10	300.
Ms	Paid 5¢ revalued "PAID 10" (Type B)	300.
	Paid 10¢*	250.

Bayou Sara

PAID 5

A

BAYOU SARA / LA (27; 1861; black)

A	PAID 5	300.

Bellevue

PAID 5

A

BELLEVUE / LA (26; 1861; black)

A	PAID 5*	300.

Berwick City

BERWICK CITY. / LA. (fleuron at bottom)
(32 DC; 1861; black)

Ms	Paid 5	300.
	Pd 5	300.
	Paid 10*	300.

Bonner

Bonner La (ms; 1861; black)

Ms	Paid 5	200.

Brashear

A

B

BRASHEAR, LA. (fleuron at bottom)
(32 DC; 1861; black, brown)

A	PAID, 10 cs (ms)*	300.
B	PAID 5	300.
	Same (brown)	300.

Campti

CAMPTI / La (26; 1861; brown)

A	DUE 10 (c) [not illustrated]*	250.
Ms	Paid 5	250.

Carrollton

A

CARROLLTON / L^A (32; 1861; blue)

A	5, Due (pencil)	250.
Ms	Paid 5*	250.

Ceneterville

CENTERVILLE / La. (37; 186-; black)

Ms	Pd 5*	300.

Cheneyville

A

CHENEYVILLE / La. (30; 1861; black, red)

A	PAID, 5¢ (ms)	300.
	Same (red) 5 (ms)*	300.
Ms	Due 5*	250.
	Due 10	250.

Chicot Pass

CHICOT PASS / La (38; 1861; ?)

Ms	Paid / 5	300.

Clinton

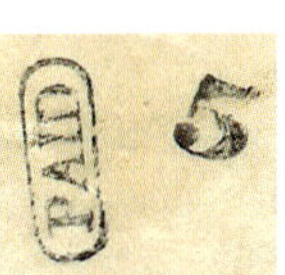
A

B

CLINTON / LA (26 DC YD; 1861; black)

A	PAID 5	300.
B	PAID 5	300.

Collinsburgh

A

COLLINSBURGH / LA (26; 1861; black)

A	PAID, 10 (ms)	300.
Ms	Due 5	250.

Cooke's Store

Cooke's Store La (ms; 1861; black)

Ms	5 (due)*	200.

Copenhagen

Copenhagen, La (ms; 1861; black)

Ms	Paid 5 cts	200.

Cotile

A

COTILE / LA (26; 1861; blue, black)
Cotile (ms; 186-; black)

A	PAID, 5 (ms)*	300.
	Same (blue), 5 (ms)	300.
Ms	5 Paid	250.
	Paid 10*	250.
	Due 10*	250.

Coushatee Chute

Coushatee Chute / LA (31; 1861; black)

Ms	Paid 5*	200.
	Paid 10	200.

Covington

A

COVINGTON / L^{a} (?; 1862; black)

A	PAID, 5 (ms)	300.

Dallas

Dallas La (ms; 1861; black)

Ms	Paid 5c	200.

Darlington

Darlington (ms; 1861; black)

Ms	Paid 5 cents*	200.

Delhi

Delhi La (ms; 186-; black)

Ms	Paid 5	200.
	Due 10	200.

Donaldsonville

A

DONALDSONVILLE / La. (29; 1861; black)

A	PAID 5	300.

Evergreen

A B

EVERGREEN / La (38; 1861; red)

A	PAID (red) [no rate]	300.
	Same (red), 5 (ms)	300.
B	PAID 5*	300.

Farmerville

A

FARMERVILLE / La. (30; 1861; black)

A	PAID, 10 (ms)*	300.

Fillmore

A B

C D

FILLMORE / LA (26; 1861; black, blue)

A	PAID 5 (blue)*	300.
	Same revalued 10 (Type D)	500.
B	PAID 5	300.
C	PAID 10 (blue)*	300.
D	10 (blue) [due]*	250.

Flat Lick

Flat Lick La (ms; 186-; black)

Ms	Paid 10	200.

Franklin

A

FRANKLIN / La. (34; 186-; black)

A	PAID, 5 (ms)	300.
	Same, 10 (ms)	300.
Ms	10 (due)	200.
	Due 10*	250.

French Settlement

French Settlement La. (ms; 1863; blue)

Ms	Paid 10¢	200.

Greensburg

A

GREENSBURG / LA. (31; 1862; black)

A	PAID 5	300.

Greenwood

Greenwood (ms; 1861; black)

Ms	Paid 10	200.

Gum Springs

Gum Springs La (ms; 1864; black)

Ms	Paid 10*	200.

Harrisonburg

A

HARRISONBURG / La. (30; 1861; black)

A	PAID, 5 cents (ms)	300.

Hermitage

A

HERMITAGE / LA (26; 1861; red)
HERMITAGE / La. (29; 1861; red)

A	PAID (red) , 5 (ms)	300.

Homer

A B

HOMER. C.H. / L^{A} (33; 1861; black)

A	PAID 3 revalued 5*	500.
B	PAID 10 (inverted 10)	300.
Ms	Paid 5	250.
	Pd 5	250.
	Paid 10*	250.
	Due 5*	250.
	5 [due]	250.

Houma

A B C

HOUMA / L^{A} (31; 1861; black)
HOUMA / LA (25; 1861; black)

A	PAID 5	300.
B	PAID 5	300.
C	PAID 10	300.
Ms	Paid 10*	250.

Jackson

A

JACKSON / L^{A} (33; 1861; black)

A	PAID, 5 (ms)*	300.
Ms	Paid 5	300.

Jeaneretts

A

JEANERETTS / La. (30; 1861; black)

A	PAID 5	300.
	Same revalued 10 (ms)	300.
Ms	Paid 5*	250.

Keachie

A B C

KEACHIE / LA (26; 1861; black)

A	PAID [no rate]	300.
	Same, 5 (ms)*	300.
B	PAID, 10 (ms)*	300.
C	PAID 5	300.
D	PAID (boxed), 10 [not illustrated]	300.

Lake Charles

LAKE CHARLES / La (31; 186-; black)

Ms	Due 10	250.

Lake Providence

A B

LAKE PROVIDENCE / La. (34; 1861; black)
LAKE PROVIDENCE / LA. (32 YD; 1861; black)

A	PAID/5 (altered 3)	300.
B	PAID 5	300.

Laurel Hill

PAID

A

LAUREL HILL / LA (31; 1861; brown)

A	PAID (brown) [no rate]*	300.
	Same (brown), 5 (ms)	300.

Lecomte

A

LECOMTE / LA (30; 1861; black)

A	PAID 10	300.

Live Oak

A

LIVE OAK / La (30; 186-; brown)

A	PAID 5 (brown)	300.

Livonia

PAID
5

A

LIVONIA / LA. (33 YD; 1862; black)

A	PAID 5	300.

Lobdell's Store

A

B

LOBDELL'S STORE / LA. (31; 1861; black)

A	PAID 5	300.
B	PAID 10	500.

Mansfield

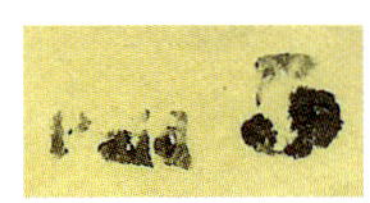

A

B

Paid 10

C

MANSFIELD / La. (32; 1861; black)

A	Paid 5	300.
	Same revalued 10*	500.
B	PAID 5	300.
C	Paid, 10*	500.
	Same revalued 5*	500.
Ms	Paid 10	250.

Mansura

Mansura La (ms; 1861; black)

Ms	Paid 10 cts	200.

Marksville

PAID

A

MARKSVILLE / La. (38; 1861; black)

A	PAID, 5 (ms)	300.
Ms	Due 10*	250.

Milikens Bend

A

MILIKENS BEND / La. (29; 1861; blue)

A	PAID (blue), 5¢ (ms)	300.

Minden

A

B

PAID 10

C

MINDEN / La. (30; 1861; black)

A	PAID 3 revalued 5 (ms)*	500.
B	PAID 5	300.
C	PAID, 10	300.
Ms	Paid 5	250.
	Paid 10*	250.

Monroe

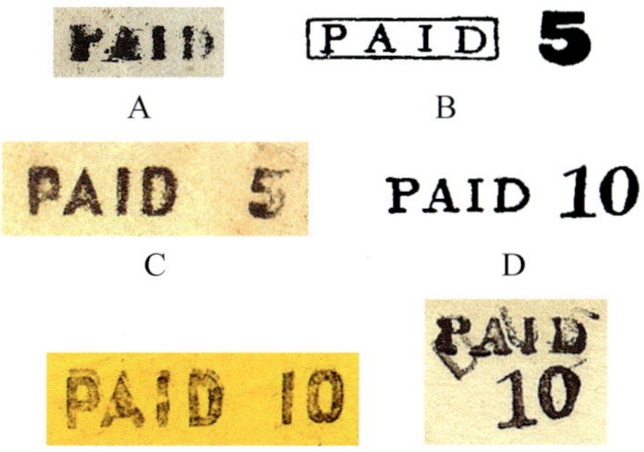

A B C D E F

MONROE / La. (33; 1861-64; black)

A	PAID [no rate]	300.
B	PAID 5*	300.
C	PAID 5	300.
D	PAID 10*	300.
E	PAID 10*	300.
F	DUE revalued PAID 10 (Type D)	500.
Ms	Due 10	250.
	Due 10c	250.
	5 [due]*	250.
	10 [due]*	250.
Pk	No paid or rate marking	150.

Montgomery

Montgomery La (ms; 1863; black)

Ms	Paid [no rate]	200.
	Paid 10*	200.

Monticello

A

MONTICELLO / La (36; 1861; black)

A	PAID, 5 (ms)	300.
	Same, 10c (ms)	300.

Mount Lebanon

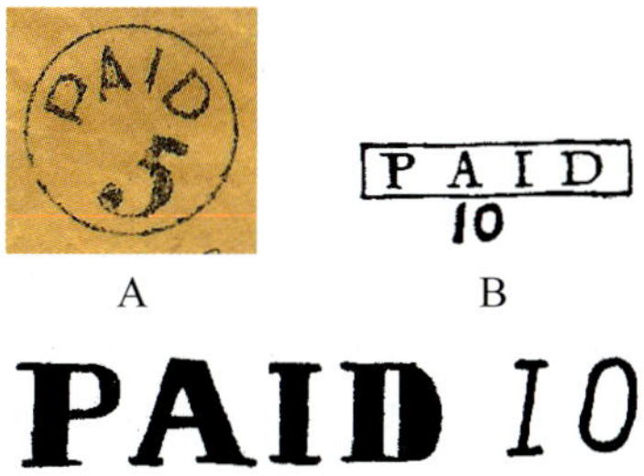

A B C

MOUNT LEBANON / La. (36; 1861; black)
Mount Lebanon La. (ms; 1861; black)

A	PAID 5 (altered 3)	300.
B	PAID 10 *	300.
C	PAID 10	300.
Ms	Paid 10	250.
	Due 10	250.

Natchitoches

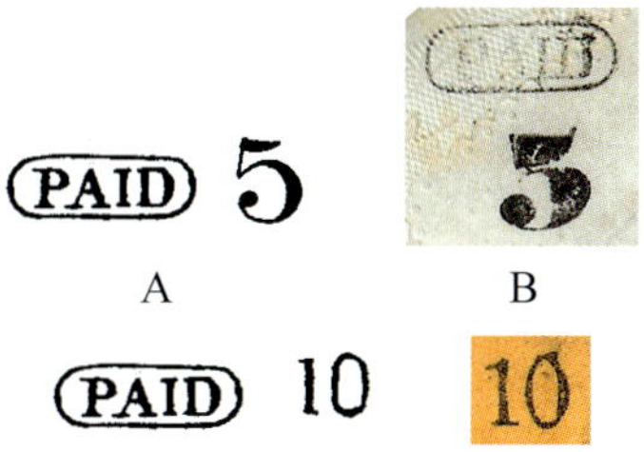

A B C D

NATCHITOCHES / LA (26 DC; 1861; black)
NATCHITOCHES / LA (26 DC YD; 1861; black)

A	PAID 5	300.
B	PAID 5	300.
C	PAID 10*	300.
D	10 [due]	250.
	Same, Due (ms)	250.
Ms	Pd 10*	

New Carthage

NEW CARTHAGE / L^A (33; 1861; black)

Ms	Paid 10	300.

New Iberia

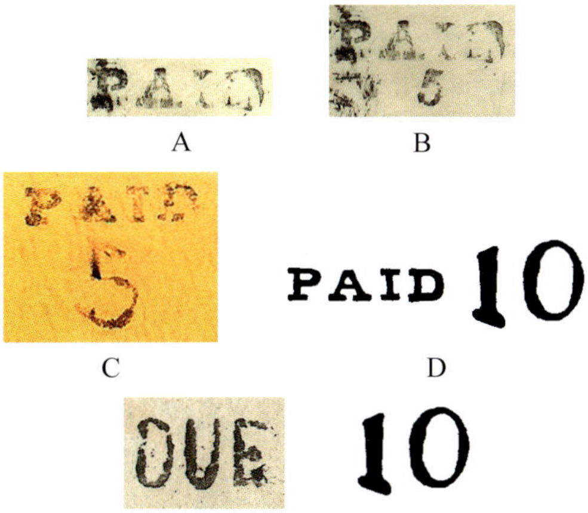

A B C D E G

NEW IBERIA / LA (25; 1861; black)

A	PAID [no rate]	250.
	Same, 5 (ms)	300.
B	PAID 5	300.
	Same revalued 10 (Type a)*	500.
C	PAID 5	300.
D	PAID 10*	300.
E	DUE [no rate]	200.
F	5 [due] [not illustrated]*	250.
G	10 [due]*	250.
	Same, Due (ms)*	250.

New Orleans

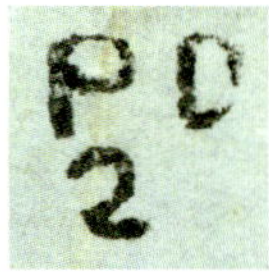

A

B

C

D

due 20

E

F

G

H

NEW ORLEANS / LA. (25 YD; 1861-62; black, red)
NEW ORLEANS / LA. (32; 1861; black)

A	PD 2	1,000.
B	PD 2 CTS N.O.P.O.	5,000.
C	due 5	300.
D	due 10	500.
E	due 20	750.
F	ADV. .	500.
G	P. O. BUSINESS FREE	1,000.
H	Steam 7 [due]	2.000.
Ms	Paid 10 (blue crayon)*	250.
	10 [due]	250.
	10 (red crayon) [due]*	250.
	10 (pencil) [due]	250.
	15c / Pd / J.L.R. / P.M.	750.
	15 [due]*	500.
	Free / POB	500.

Opelousas

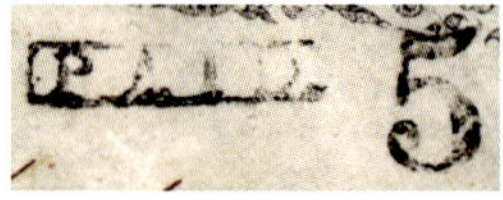

A

B

OPELOUSAS / La (34; 1861; black)

A	PAID 5	300.
B	PAID 10	300.

Ouachita City

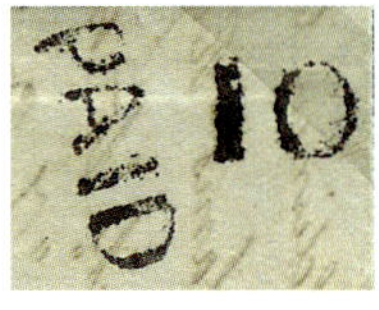

A

Ouachita City La. (ms; 1861; black)

A	PAID 10	300.

Paincourtville

A

PAINCOURTVILLE / La. (30; 1861; black)

A	5, paid 5cts (ms)	300.
	Same, paid 5c (ms)	300.

Pattersonville

PAID

A

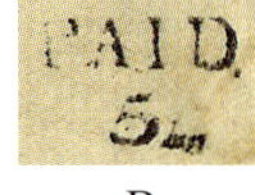

B

PAID
10

C

PATTERSONVILLE / La. (30; 1861; black)

A	PAID [no rate]	300.
B	PAID 5	300.
C	PAID 10*	300.
	Same revalued 20 (ms)	500.

Plainville

Plainville La (ms; 1861; black)

Ms	Paid 5cts	200.

Plaquemine

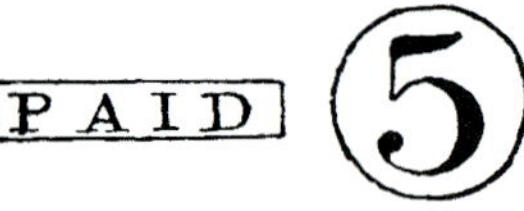

A

PLAQUEMINE / La. (32 YD; 1861; black)

A	PAID 5*	300.

Pleasant Hill

A

PLEASANT HILL / LA. (26; 1861; black)

A	PAID [no rate]	300.

	Same, 5 (ms)	300.
Ms	Paid 5*	250.

Point Jefferson

Pt. Jefferson La (ms; 1861; black)

Ms	Paid 5c	200.

Ponchatoula

A

PONCHATOULA / La (36; 1862; red)

A	DUE 5	300.
Ms	Due 10*	250.

Port Hudson

A C

PORT HUDSON / LA (25; 1861-63; black)

A	PAID [no rate]	300.
	Same, 10 (ms)*	300.
B	PAID (arc in circle), Paid 10cts (ms) [not illustrated]*	300.
C	10 [due]	250.
Ms	Due 10	200.

Port Jefferson

Port Jefferson La (ms; 1861; black)

Ms	Paid / 5	200.

Raceland

Race Land (ms; 1861; black)

Ms	Paid 5¢	200.

Red River Landing

PAID 5 PAID 10

A B

RED RIVER LANDING / LA (32; 1861; red)

A	PAID, 5 (red)	300.
B	PAID, 10 (red)*	300.

Ringgold

Ringgold La (ms; 1862; black)

Ms	Paid / 5	200.

Saint Francisville

A B C

St. FRANCISVILLE / La. (30; 1861; black)

A	PAID 5	300.
B	PAID 5	300.
C	5 [Due]	250.

Saint Gabriel

PAID 5 C.S.A.

A B

SAINT GABRIEL / La. (36; 1861; black)

A	PAID 5	300.
	Same, struck twice*	500.
B	PAID 5 C.S.A.*	750.
	Same revalued 10 (ms)*	750.

Note: Rate markings known without the CDS

Saint Joseph

PAID 5

A

ST. JOSEPH / LA. (32; 1861; blue)

A	PAID 5*	300.
Ms	Paid 5	250.

Saint Martainsville

PAID 5 10

A B *a*

ST. MARTAINSVILLE / LA. (32; 1861; black, blue)

A	PAID 5 (blue)*	300.
	Same revalued 10 (Type *a*)*	500.
B	PAID 10	300.

Shreveport

A  B

C  E  F

G

SHREVEPORT / LA. (26 DC YD; 1861-64; black)

A	PAID [no rate]	250.
	Same, 15 (ms)	500.
	Same, 40 (ms)	500.
B	PAID 5	300.
C	PAID 10	300.
D	PAID / 10 (arc) [not illustrated]	300.
E	DUE, 10 (ms)*	250.
F	DUE 5*`	250.
G	DUE 10	250.
Ms	Paid 20*	300.
	Due 20	300.
	20 [due]	300.

Spearsville

Spearsville La. (ms; 1862; black)

Ms	Paid 10	200.

Tangapaho (Tanapiho)

A  B

TANGIPAHO / LA. (31; 1861; black)
TANGAPAHO / LA (25; 1861; black)

A	PAID, 5 (ms)	200.
B	PAID 5	250.
Ms	Due 5*	200.
	Due 10	200.

Thibodeaux

A  B

THIBODEAUX / La (32 YD; 1861-62; black)

A	PAID 5	300.
B	PAID 10	300.

Tigerville

TIGERVILLE / LA (26; 1861; black)

Ms	Paid 10	300.

Trenton

Trenton La (ms; 1862; black)

Ms	Paid 5	200.

Trintity

TRINITY / LA (26; 1861; black)

Ms	Paid 5c	300.
	10 [due]	300.

Vermillionville

A

VERMILLIONVILLE / La. (30 SC; 1863; black)

A	PAID [no rate]	300.
Ms	Due 10	250.

Vienna

Vienna (ms; 1862; black)

Ms	Paid 10c	200.
	Due 10*	200.
	10 [due]	200.

Washington

Washington / La. (30; 186-; black)

Ms	Paid 5*	200.

Water Proof

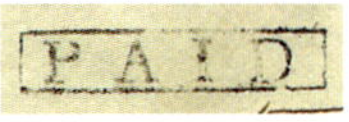

A

WATER.PROOF / LA. (32; 1861; black)

A	PAID, 5 (ms)	300.

Waterloo

A

WATERLOO / L^{A} (26; 1861; red)

A	PAID 5 (red)	300.

Winnfield

A

WINNFIELD / La. (32; 1861; black)

A	PAID, 5 cts (ms)*	300.

MISSISSIPPI

ABERDEEN

A  B

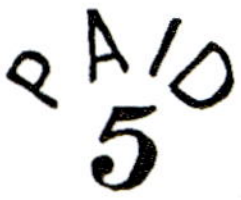

C  D  E

ABERDEEN / MISS. (32; 1861-62; black)

A	PAID [no rate]	200.
	Same, 10 (ms)	200.
B	PAID 5	300.
C	PAID 5	300.
D	PAID 10*	300.
E	DUE 10	250.
Ms	2 [due]	750.

ARCABUTLA

Arcabutla Miss (ms; 186-; black)

Ms	Paid 10	200.

ATTALAVILLE

Attalaville Miss (ms; 1861; black)

Ms	Paid 5	200.

AUGUSTA

Augusta Mi (ms; 1862; black)

Ms	Paid 10	200.

AUSTIN

A

AUSTIN / MISS (1862; 30; black)

A	PAID 5	300.

AUSTRALIA

Australia Miss (ms; 1861; black)

Ms	Paid 5	200.
	Pd 10	200.

BALDWIN

A

BALDWIN / MISS (26; 1861-62; black)

A	PAID [no rate]	250.
	Same, 5 (ms)	250.

BANKSTON

Bankston Miss (ms; 1864; black)

Ms	Paid 10	200.

BATESVILLE

A

Batesville Miss (ms; 1861; black)

A	PAID (brown), 5 (ms)	300.
Ms	Paid 5	300.

BENTON

A

BENTON / MISS (?; 186-; black)

A	PAID 10	300.
Ms	10 [due]	200.

BILOXI

Biloxi (ms; 1861; black)

Ms	Paid 5	250.

BLUFF SPRINGS

Bluff Springs Mi (ms; 1861; black)

Ms	Pd 5	200.

BOLIVAR

A

BOLIVAR / MISS. (30; 1861; black)

A	PAID [no rate]	250.
	Same, 10 (ms)	300.

BOLTON'S DEPOT

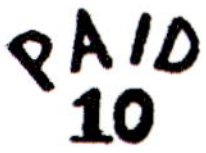

A

BOLTONS DEPOT / MISS (32; 1863; red)
Boltons Depot Mis (ms; 1861-62; black)

A	PAID 10 (red)	300.
Ms	Paid / 5	200.
	Paid / 10	200.

BOONEVILLE

Booneville Miss (ms; 1861; black)

Ms	5 Paid	200.

Brandon

A

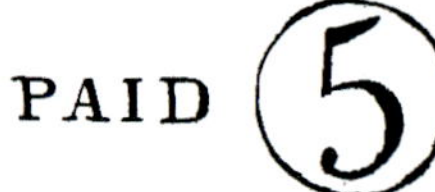

B

C

D

BRANDON / Miss. (32 YD; 1861-62; black)

A	PAID 5	300.
B	PAID 5	300.
C	PAID 5	500.
D	PAID 10	300.

Brookhaven

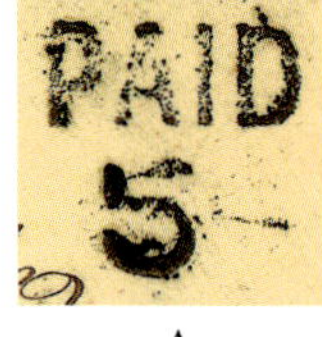

A

B

C

BROOKHAVEN / MISS. (32; 1861-62; black, blue)

A	PAID 5	300.
B	PAID 10	300.
	Same, revalued 20 (ms)	500.
C	DUE 5*	250.
	Same (blue)	250.
D	DUE 10 (blue) [not illustrated]	250.

Brookville

A

BROOKVILLE / MISS. (32; 1861-62; black)

A	PAID 5	300.
	Same, revalued 10 (ms)	300.

Buena Vista

Buena Vista Miss (ms; 1862; black)

Ms	Due 10	200.

Burnsville

BURNSVILLE / MISS. (30 YD; 1862; black)

Ms	Due 5c	200.

Burtonia

Burtonia Miss (ms; 1861; black)

Ms	Paid 10	200.

Byhalia

A

BYHALIA / MISS (32; 186-; black)

A	PAID, 20 (ms)*	300.
Ms	paid 5	250.
	Free	500.

Byram

Byram Miss (ms; 1861; black)

Ms	Paid 5	200.

Calhoun

Calhoun Miss (ms; 1861; black)

Ms	Paid 5 cts	200.

Camden

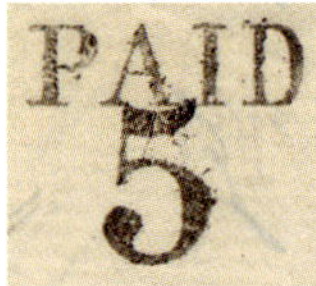

A

B

CAMDEN / MISS. (32; 1862; black)

A	PAID 5	300.
B	PAID 10	300.
Ms	Due [no rate]*	200.

Canton

A

B

C

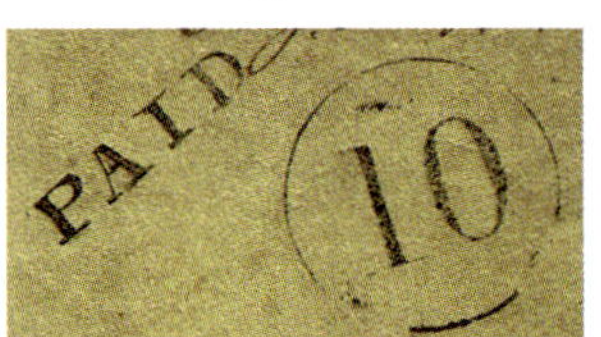

D

E

F

G

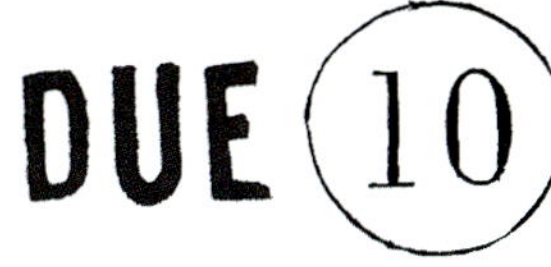
H

I

J

a

CANTON / Mi. (32; 1861; black)
CANTON / Miss. (32 YD; 1861; black)
CANTON / Miss (33; 186-; black)

A	PAID 2	750.
B	PAID 5	200.
C	PAID 5	500.
	Same, revalued 2 (Type A)	750.
D	PAID 10	300.
E	PAID★10	500.
F	10 [due]	200.
	Same, Due (ms)*	200.
	Same, plus 5 (Type a)*	250.
G	DUE [no rate]*	150.
	Same, 10 (ms)	150.
H	DUE 10	200.
I	AD, 2 (pencil)	500.
	Same, 2 (ms) plus 10 (Type F)	750.
J	AD 2	750.
	Same, Due 10 (ms)	750.
Ms	Due 10	150.

Note: Three letter month handstamps are frequently found on Canton advertised letters.

Carrollton

A

CARROLLTON / MISS (32; 1861-62; black)
CARROLLTON / Miss (32 YD; 1861-62; black)

A	PAID 5	200.
B	PAID 10 (PAID (c)) [not illustrated]	250.
Ms	Paid 5	150.
	Same (pencil)	150.

Note: Year date in above sometimes replaced with slug.

Cartersville

Cartersville Ms (ms; 1862; black)

Ms	Due 5	200.

Carthage

A

CARTHAGE / MISS. (36; 1861; black)

A	PAID 5 (altered 3)	300.

Cato

Cato Miss (ms; 1861; black)

Ms	Paid 5	200.

Centreville

CENTERVILLE / MISS[1]
(29; 1862; brown)

Ms	Due 10 and ford	250.

Charleston

CHARLESTON / MISS (25; 1861-62; black)
Charleston Miss (ms; 186-; black)

Ms	Paid 5	300.
	Due 10	200.

China Grove

China Grove Miss (ms; 1861; black)

Ms	Paid 5	200.

Choctaw Agency

Choctaw Agency (ms; 1861; black)

Ms	Paid 10cts*	500.

Chulahoma

CHULAHOMA / Mi (30; 1861; black)

Ms	Due 5	250.

Church Hill

Churchill Miss (ms; 1861; black)

Ms	paid 5¢	200.
	paid 10¢	200.

Claiborne

Claiborne Mi (ms; 186-; black)

A	PAID 10 [not illustrated]	250.
Ms	Paid (no rate)	200.

Clinton

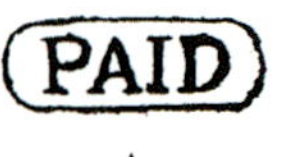

A

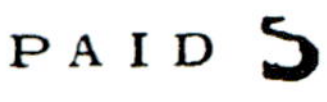

B

C

D

E

F

CLINTON / MISS (25; 1861-62; black)
Clinton Miss (ms; 1864; black)

A	PAID [no rate]	200.
B	PAID 5	300.
C	PAID 5	300.
D	PAID 5	300.
E	PAID 5	300.
F	PAID 10	300.
Ms	Paid 10¢	200.
	Due 10	200.

Coffeeville

A

B

C

COFFEEVILLE / MISS (25; 1861; black)
COFFEEVILLE / Miss (32; 1861-63; black)
Coffeeville Miss (ms; 1864; black)

A	PAID, 5 (ms)	250.
B	PAID 5*	300.
C	PAID 5	300.
Ms	Pd 10	200.
	Paid / 20	500.

Columbus

A

B

C

COLUMBUS / MISS. (32; 1861-62; black)

A	PAID (drop) [no rate]	500.
	Same [no rate]	200.
	Same, 5 (pencil)	250.
B	PAID 10	300.
C	10 [due]	200.
Ms	Paid*	200.

Como Depot

A

B

C

COMO DEPOT / MISS (25; 1862; black)

A	PAID 5*	300.
B	PAID 10	300.
C	5, Paid (ms)	250.

Coonewar

A

Postmark unknown

A	PAID 5*	300.

Corinth

A

B

C

a

CORINTH / MISS (37; 1861-62; black)
CORINTH / MISS. (29 DLC; 1861-62; black)

A	PAID 3, revalued 5 (ms)	500.
B	PAID [no rate]	300.
	Same, 5 (ms)*	300.
C	PAID 5	300.
	Same (brown)*	300.
	Same, revalued 10 (Type *a*)*	500.
Ms	Paid 5	200.
	Due 5	200.
	10 (pencil) [due]	200.
Pk	Postmark - no paid or rate markings	200.

Crawfordville

CRAWFORDVILLE / Miss. (33; 186-; red)

Ms	Paid 5	300.
	Due 5	250.

Cross Roads

Cross Roads Mi (ms; 186-; black)

Ms	Paid / 10	200.

Crystal Springs

CRYSTAL SPRINGS / MISS (26; 1862; black)
C. Springs Miss (ms; 186-; black)

A	PAID [no rate] [not illustrated]	250.
B	PAID 5 [not illustrated]	300.

Daleville

Daleville Miss (ms; 1863-64; black)

Ms	Paid 10*	200.

Danville

Danville Miss (ms; 1861; black)

Ms	Paid 5	200.
	Paid 5cts	200.

Decatur

Decatur Miss (ms; 1861; black)

Ms	Paid 5*	200.

Deer Creek

Deercreek Mi (ms; 1861; black)

Ms	5 [due]	200.

De Kalb

PAID

A

DE KALB / Mi. (32; 1861-63; black)

A	PAID, 5 (ms)	300.
	Same, 10 (ms)	300.

Dry Grove

Dry Grove Miss (ms; 1861; black)

Ms	Paid 5¢	200.

Duck Hill

DUCK HILL / MISS (25; 1862; black)

Ms	Paid 5	250.

Durant

DURANT / MISS (26; 1862; black)

Ms	Paid 5*	250.

Ebenezer

Ebenezer Miss (ms; 1861; black)

Ms	Paid 5	200.

Edwards Depot

Edwards Depot Miss (ms; 1862-63; black)

Ms	Pd 5*	200.
	Paid 10¢	200.
	Due 10 cts*	200.

Ellisville

Ellisville Miss (ms; 1861; black)

Ms	Paid 5	200.

Elm Grove

Elm Grove Miss (ms; 1861; black)

Ms	Paid 10	200.

Emory

Emory Miss (ms; 1862; black)

Ms	Paid 10	200.

Enterprise

PAID

A

PAID 5

B

PAID 5

C

PAID 10

D

10

E

Enterprise / MISS (25; 1861; black)

A	PAID [no rate]	200.
B	PAID 5	300.
C	PAID 5	500.
	Same, struck twice	500.
	Same, revalued 10 (Type E)	500.
D	PAID10	300.
E	10 [due]	200.
F	DUE 10 [not illustrated]	200.

Fannin

Fannin Miss (ms; 1862; black)

Ms	Due 10 cents*	200.

Fayette

PAID 5

A

PAID 10

B

10

C

FAYETTE / Miss. (34; 1861; blue)

A	PAID 5 (blue)	300.
B	PAID 10 (blue)	300.
C	10 (blue), Due (ms)	250.
Ms	Due 10*	200.

Forest

Forest Miss (ms; 186-; black)

Ms	Paid 10	200.
	Due 10	200.

Fort Adams

A

FORT ADAMS / MISS (30; 1861; black)

A	PAID 5	300.

Friars Point

A B

C

FRIARS POINT / MISS (32; 1861-62; black)

A	PAID, 10 (ms)	300.
	Same, 10 (pencil)	250.
B	PAID 5 (altered 3)	300.
C	PAID 5	300.

Fulton

A B

FULTON / MISS (33; 186-; black)

A	PAID 5	300.
B	PAID 10*	300.

Gainesville Junction

Gainesville Junction Miss (ms; 1865; black)

Ms	Paid 10cts*	200.

Garlandsville

A

GARLANDSVILLE / MISS (25; 1861; black)
Garlandsville (ms; 1861; black)

A	PAID, 10 (ms)	300.
Ms	Paid 5	250.
	Paid 5c	250.

Goodman

A

GOODMAN / MISS (25; 1861; black)

A	PAID, 5 (ms)	300.
	Same, 10 (ms)*	300.
Ms	Paid 10	250.
	Due 10	250.

Grand Gulf

A

GRAND GULF / MISS (25; 186-; black)

A	PAID, 5¢ (ms)	300.

Green Leaf

Green Leaf Miss (ms; 1861; black)

Ms	Paid 5	200.

Greensboro

Greensboro Miss (ms; 186-; black)

Ms	Paid 5*	200.
	Paid 10	200.

Greenville

GREENVILLE / MISS (34; 1861; blue)

Ms	Paid 5*	300.
	Paid 10	300.
	Due 5	250.

Greenwood

A B

GREENWOOD / Miss. (32; 1861-62; blue)

A	PAID (blue) [no rate]	300.
	Same, 5 (ms)*	300.
	Same, 10 (ms)*	300.
B	PAID 10 (blue)	300.
Ms	Due 10	250.

Grenada

A

GRENADA / Mi (30; 1861; black)
GRENADA / MISS. (32; 1861; black)
Grenada Miss (ms; 1861; black)

A	10. [due]	300.
Ms	Paid 5	300.
	Pd 5	300.
	Paid 10	300.
	Due 5	250.
	Due 20*	300.
	10 (pencil) [due]	200.

Hamilton

PAID 5

A

HAMILTON. / MISS. (26; 186-; red, black)

A	PAID 5 (red)	300.
B	DUE 10 [not illustrated]*	300.

Handsboro

PAID

A

PAID 5

B

HANDSBORO / MISS (26; 1861; black)

A	PAID [no rate]	250.
	Same, 5 (ms)	300.
	Same, 10 (ms)*	300.
B	PAID 3, revalued 5 (ms)	500.
Ms	Due 10	200.

Hardy's Station

Hardys Station Mis (ms; 1862; black)

Ms	Paid 5	200.

Hazle Hurst

PAID

A

PAID 5

B

HAZLE HURST /MISS (25; 1861-62; black)
HAZLEHURST / Miss (31 YD; 1863; black)

A	PAID, 5 (ms)	300.
	Same, 10 (ms)*	300.
	Same revalued Due 5 (ms)	300.
B	PAID 5	300.
Ms	Due 5*	250.

ms	manuscript
SL	straightline
YD	year date

Hernando

A

HERNANDO / Miss. (32; 1861; black)

A	PAID 5	300.

Hickory

Hickory Miss (ms; 1861; black)

Ms	Paid 5c	200.

Hohenlinden

Hohenlinden Miss (ms; 1861; black)

Ms	Paid 5*	200.

Holly Springs

PAID

A

HOLLY SPRINGS / Miss (32 YD; 1861-63; black)
HOLLY SPRINGS / Miss (32; 1862; black)

A	PAID [no rate]*	250.
	Same, 5 (ms)	300.
	Same, 10 (ms)	300.
Ms	Due 5	250.
	Due 10	250.
	Due 10 (pencil)	200.
	10 (pencil) [due]	200.

Note: Some examples of this postmark have an error date of 1860.

Horn Lake

A

PAID 5

B

HORN LAKE / MISS (32; 1861-62; black)

A	PAID, 5 (ms)	300.
	Same, 10 (ms)	300.
B	PAID 5	300.

Houston

A

PAID 5

B

HOUSTON / Miss. (33; 1861-63; black)

A	PAID [no rate]	250.
	Same, 5 (ms)*	300.
B	PAID 5*	300.
Ms	paid / 5	250.

Iuka

A

IUKA. / Miss. (30 YD; 1861; black)
IUKA / MISS (32; 1861; black)

A	PAID, 5 (ms)	300.
	Same, 10 (ms)*	300.
Ms	Paid 5	250.
	Due 5	250.

Jackson

A  B  C

E

F  G  H

JACKSON (34 x 7 SL; 1863; black)
JACKSON Miss (32; 1861-62; black)
JACKSON / MISS. (31; 1863-65; black)

A	DROP 2 CENTS	750.
B	PAID [no rate]	300.
C	PAID	300.
D	PAID 20 [not illustrated]*	500.
E	DUE 5*	250.
F	DUE 10	250.
	Same (struck twice)	500.
	Same, revalued DUE 5 (Type E)*	300.
G	5 [due]	250.
H	10 [due]	250.
	Same with straight line postmark	750.
Ms	Due 10	200.
	10 [due]*	200.
	Miss & fwd	200.

Note: A "CHARGED TO BOX" marking in a shield is sometimes found on due letters addressed to Jackson.

Jonesborough

Jonesborough Miss (ms; 1861; black)

Ms	Paid 5*	200.

Kilmichael

Kilmichael Miss (ms; 1862; black)

Ms	Paid 5 cts	200.
	Paid / 10	200.

Kirkwood

Kirkwood Miss (ms; 1862; black)

Ms	Paid 5	200.
	Paid 10	200.

Lake

Lake Mi (ms; 186–; black)

Ms	Paid 5 cts	200.
	Paid 10 cts	200.

Lauderdale Station

LAUDERDALE STATION / MISS (25; 1861; black)

Ms	Paid 5	250.
	Pd 5	250.
	Paid 10	250.

Lexington

A  B

C  D

LEXINGTON / Miss. (34; 1861; black)
LEXINGTON / MISS (25; 1862; black)

A	PAID, 5 (ms)*	250.
B	PAID 5	300.
C	PAID 5*	300.
D	PAID 10	300.
E	DUE 10 [not illustrated]	250.
Ms	Due 10	200.

Liberty

LIBERTY / Miss. (35; 186-; black)

Ms	Paid 5c	250.
	Paid 10 cts	250.
	Due 2c	500.

Livingston

A

LIVINGSTON / MISS (25; 1861-62; black)

A	PAID, 5 (ms)	300.
Ms	Paid 5	250.
	5 [due]	200.

Louisville

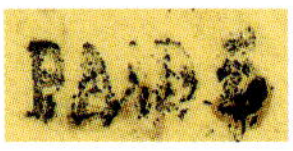

A

LOUISVILLE / MISS (32 YD; 1861; black)
LOUISVILLE / Mi. (33; 1861-62; black)

A	PAID 5	300.
	Same, revalued 5 (ms)	300.

Macon

A B

MACON / MISS (25 DC; 1861-62; black)

A	PAID [no rate]	200.
B	PAID 5	300.
	Same, revalued 10 (ms)	300.
Ms	Paid 10	250.
	Due 10	200.

Magnolia

A

MAGNOLIA / MISS. (32; 1862; black)

A	PAID 10	300.
B	PAID 20 [not illustrated]	500.

Marion

A

MARION / Mi. (30; 186-; black)

A	PAID, 5 (ms)*	300.

Marion Station

A B C D

MARION STATION / MISS (25; 1861; black, brown)

A	PAID (brown), 5 (ms)	250.
B	PAID, 5 (ms)	250.
C	PAID 5	300.
	Same (brown)	300.
D	PAID 5 (brown)	300.
E	PAID 5 revalued 10 (ms) [not illustrated]*	300.
Ms	Due 5*	250.

Mark Well

Mark Well Miss (ms; 1864; black)
Markwell Miss (ms; 186-; black)

Ms	Due 10	250.

Mayhew

A

MAYHEW / MISS (28; 186-; black)

A	PAID 10	300.

McLaurins

McLaurins Miss (ms; 1864; black)

Ms	Paid 10*	200.

Meadville

A B

MEADVILLE / MIS (30; 1861-62; black)
Meadville (ms; 186-; black)

A	PAID [no rate]*	250.
	Same, 5 (ms)	300.
B	PAID 10	300.
Ms	10 (due)*	250.

Meridian

A

MERIDIAN MISS (45x4 SL; 1861; black)
MERIDIAN / MISS. (31 YD; 186-; black)
Meridian Miss (ms; 1862; black)

A	PAID 5*	300.
	Same with straight line postmark	1,000.
Ms	Paid 5*	250.
	Paid 10*	250.

Middleton

A

MIDDLETON / Miss. (33; 1861; red)

A	PAID (red) [no rate]	300.

Mississippi City (Miss City)

A B

MISS CITY / MISS (25; 1861; black)

A	PAID 5	300.
B	5 [due]*	250.

Monticello

A

MONTICELLO / Mi. (33; 1862; black)

A	PAID 10	300.

Morton

A

MORTON / MISS (33; 186-, black, red)
Morton Miss (ms; 1864; black)

A	DUE [no rate]	250.
	Same (red) [no rate]*	300.
	Same, 10 (ms)*	300.
	Same, Due 20 (ms)	500.
B	DUE 10 [not illustrated]	300.
Ms	Paid 10 cts*	200.

Natchez

A

PAID 5

B

C

PAID 10

D

E

F

G

NATCHEZ / Miss. (32 YD; 1861-62; black)
NATCHEZ / MIss. (32 YD; 1862; black)

A	PAID, 2 (red pencil)	750.
B	PAID 5	300.
C	Paid 5	300.
D	PAID 10	300.
E	Paid 10	300.
F	STEAM, Due 6 (ms)	750.
G	STEAM 6	1,000.

Note: A damaged version of the second listed town cancel was used during the reoccupation of the city in 1862.

New Albany

NEW ALBANY / MISS (31; 186-; red)

Ms	Paid 5¢	250.
	Paid 10	250.

New Prospect

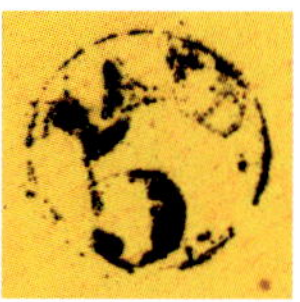

A

NEW PROSPECT / —MISS— (30; 186-; black)

A	PAID 5	300.

Newton

Newton Miss (ms; 1863; black)

Ms	Due 10*	200.

Newton Station

Newton Station Miss (ms; 1862; black)

Ms	Paid 10 cts*	200.

Newtonia

PAID

A

Postmark unknown

A	PAID 5*	300.

North Mt. Pleasant

A

NORTH Mt PLEASANT / Mi (34; 1861; blue)

A	PAID 10 (blue)	300.

Oakland

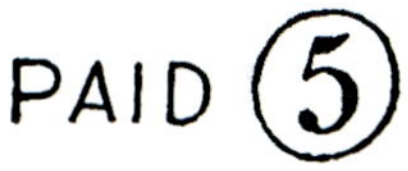

A

OAKLAND / MISS (30; 186-; black)
Oakland Mi (ms; 1861; black)

A	PAID 5	300.
Ms	Paid 5 Cents	250.

Oakland College

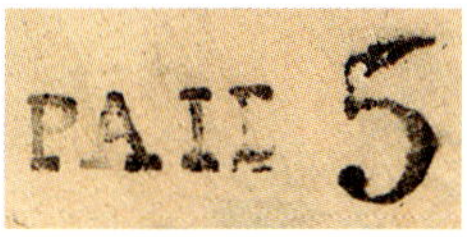

A

OAKLAND COLLEGE / Miss (30; 1861; black)

A	PAID 5	500.

Ocean Springs

OCEAN SPRINGS/MISS (28; 1861; black)

A	5 [due] [not illustrated]*	250.

Okolona

A  B  C

D

E  G

OKOLONA / MISS (25; 1861; black)

A	PAID, 10 (ms)	250.
B	PAID 5	300.
C	PAID 5	300.
	Same 10 (ms)*	300.
D	PAID 10	300.
E	DUE 5	250.
F	DUE (no box) [not illustrated]	200.
G	DUE 10	300.
Ms	Paid 20	300.
	Due 5*	200.
	Due 10*	200.

Olive Branch

Olive Branch Miss (ms; 1861-62; black)

Ms	Paid 5	250.
	Paid 10	250.

Osyka

A

Osyka, Miss (ms; 1865; black)
OSYKA / MISS. (32; 1861-62; black, brown)

A	PAID, 5 Cents (ms)	300.
	Same (brown), 5 Cts	300.
	Same, 10 Cts (ms)	300.
Ms	Paid 5 cents	250.
	Paid 20	300.

Oxford

A  B

C  D

OXFORD / MISS (30; 1861; black)

A	PAID, 2 (ms)*	750.
B	PAID 5	300.
	Same, revalued 10*	300.
C	PAID 10	300.
D	10, Due (ms)	250.
Ms	Due [no rate]*	200.

Pascagoula

PASCAGOULA / MISS (25; 186-; black)

Ms	due 10	300.

Pass Christian

A  B

PASS CHRISTIAN / MISS. (33; 1861; black)

A	PAID 5	300.
B	FORWARDED 5	750.

Paulding

PAULDING / Miss (32; 1862-64; black)

A	PAID [no rate] [not illustrated]	300.
Ms	Paid 10	250.

Pensacola

Pensacola Miss (ms; 1861; black)

Ms	Paid / 5 cts	200.

Philadelphia

PHILADELPHIA / MISS (36; 1862; black)

Ms	Paid 5	250.

Pickens Station

Pickens Station (ms; 1862; black)

Ms	Paid 5	200.

Polkville

POLKVILLE / MISS (24 x36 rimless arc; 1862; black)
Polkville Miss (ms; 1861; black)

Ms	Paid / 5	250.
	Pd 10 with rimless arc postmark	500.

Pontotoc

A B

PONTOTOC / Miss. (33; 1861; black)

A	PAID 5	300.
	Same, revalued 10 (ms)	300.
B	PAID 10	300.
	Same, revalued 5	300.
Ms	Paid 5 cts	250.
	Paid 10c	250.

Popes Depot

Popes Miss (ms; 186-; black)

Ms	Paid 10	200.

Poplar Creek

POPLAR CREEK / MISS (26; 186-; black)

Ms	Paid 10 ct	250.

Poplar Springs

Poplar Springs Miss (ms; 186-; black)

Ms	Due 5cts	200.

Port Gibson

PAID A PAID 5 B PAID 5 C

PAID 10 E

PORT GIBSON / Miss. (30 YD; 1861-62; black)

A	PAID, 10 (ms)*	300.
B	PAID 5	300.
C	PAID 5	300.
D	PAID 10 (sans serif) [not illustrated]	300.
E	PAID 10	300.
Ms	Ford 10	300.

Preston

PAID A

PRESTON / MISS (26; 1861; black)
Preston, Miss (ms; 1862; black)

A	PAID, 5 (ms)	300.
Ms	Paid 5	250.

Quitman

PAID 5 A

QUITMAN / MISS (25; 1861-62; black)
QUITMAN / MISS. (30; 1862; black)

A	PAID 5	300.
Ms	Paid 10	300.

Raleigh

RALEIGH / Mi. (32; 186-; black)

Ms	Paid / 10	250.

Raymond

PAID 5 A

RAYMOND / MISS. (32; 1861; black)

A	PAID 5	300.
Ms	Paid 10*	250.

Red Bluff

Red Bluff Miss (ms; 1864; black)

Ms	Paid / 10	200.

Richland

PAID 5 A

RICHLAND / MISS (32; 1861-62; black)

A	PAID 5	300.
B	PAID10 [not illustrated]	300.

Richmond

A

Postmark unknown

A	PAID (green), 10 (ms)	500.

Rienzi

A

RIENZI / MISS. (30; 1861-62; black)

A	PAID 5	300.

Ripley

A B

C D

RIPLEY / MISS. (32; 1861-62; black)

A	PAID 5	300.
B	PAID 5	300.
C	PAID 10	300.
D	PAID 10	300.
E	PAID 10 (small PAID) [not illustrated]	300.
Ms	Due 5*	250.
	Due 10	250.

Rodney

A

RODNEY / Miss. (32; 1861-62; black)

A	PAID 5	300.

Sardis

Sardis Miss (ms; 1861; black)

Ms	Paid [no rate]*	200.
	Paid 5	200.
	Paid 10	200.
	Due 10	200.

Sarepta

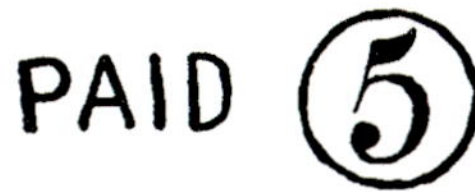

A

SAREPTA / MISS (31; 186-; black)

A	PAID 5	300.

Satartia

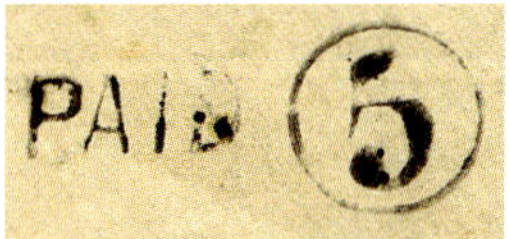

A

SATARTIA / MISS (31; 1861; black)

A	PAID 5	300.

Scooba

A B

SCOOBA / Miss. (31; 1861; black)

A	PAID [no rate]	250.
B	PAID 5	300.
Ms	Ford Due 10	300.

Senatahoba

A

SENATAHOBA / MISS (23; 186-; black)

A	PAID, 10 (ms)	300.

Sharon

Sharon Mis (ms; 186-; black)

Ms	Paid / 5	200.

Shell Mound

Shell Mound Miss (ms; 1862; black)

Ms	Paid 5	200.

Shieldsborough

SHIELDSBOROUGH Miss. (37; 1861; black)
SHIELDSBORO / MISS (26; 186-; black)

Ms	Paid 5*	300.
	Due 5	250.

Shoobota

A

SHOOBOTA / MISS (25; 1861; black)

A	PAID 5	300.
B	PAID 10 (box) [not illustrated]	300.
Ms	Paid 10	250.

Shufordville

Shufordville Miss (ms; 1861; black)

Ms	Paid 5	200.

Shuqualak

SHUQUALAK / MIS. (30; 1861; black)

Ms	Paid 5*	250.

Siloam

SILOAM / MISS (32; 1861; brown)

Ms	Paid 5¢	250.

Skipwith's Landing

Skipwiths Ldg Mi (ms; 1861; black)

Ms	Paid 5	200.

Spring Ridge

A

SPRING RIDGE / MIS (30; 1864; black)

A	PAID 10	300.

Stateland

A B

a

STATELAND / MISS (32; 1861; black)

A	PAID 5	300.
	Same, revalued 10 (Type *a*)	300.
B	PAID 10*	300.

Sulphur Springs

Sulphur Springs Miss (ms; 1862; black)

Ms	Paid / 10	200.

Summit

A B

SUMMIT / MISS. (36; 1862-64; black)

A	PAID [no rate]	250.
B	PAID 5	300.
Ms	due 5	250.
	due 10c	250.

Swan Lake

Swan Lake Miss (ms; 1861; black)

Ms	Paid 10*	250.

Tardyville

Tardyville Miss (ms; 1861; black)

Ms	Due 5	200.

Tchula

A

Tchula Mi (ms; 1862; black)

A	PAID 5	300.

Terry

A B

C

TERRY / MISS (32; 1861-62; red)

A	PAID (red) [no rate]	250.
	Same (red), 10 (ms)*	300.
B	PAID 5 (red)	300.
C	PAID 10 (red)*	300.
Ms	Due 5*	250.

Toccopola

Toccopola Miss (ms; 186-; black)

Ms	Paid 10	200.

Torrance

Torrance Miss (ms; 1861; black)

Ms	Paid 5	200.

Tupelo

A B C

TUPELO / MISS (30 YD; 1862; black)

A	PAID10*	300.
B	DUE 5	250.
C	DUE10	300.
Ms	Paid 10	250.

Turnerville

Turnerville Miss (ms; 1861; black)

Ms	Paid 5*	200.

Union Church

A

UNION CHURCH / MISS (25; 1861; black)

A	PAID, 10 (ms)	300.

Vaiden

A B

VAIDEN / MISS (25; 1861-63; black, blue)

A	PAID, 5 (ms)*	300.
B	PAID 5	300.
Ms	Paid 5	250.
	Pd 5	250.
	P 5	250.
	Paid 10*	250.
	Due [no rate]*	200.

Vernal

Vernal Miss (ms; 1861; black)

Ms	Paid 5	200.

Vernon

A

VERNON / Mi (30; 1861; black)

A	PAID, 5 (ms) plus Due 5 (ms)	500.

Verona

A

VERONA/Miss. (30 YD; 1862; black)
Verona Miss (ms; 1865; black)

A	PAID 10	300.
Ms	Due / 10	250.
	10 [due]*	250.

Vicksburg

A

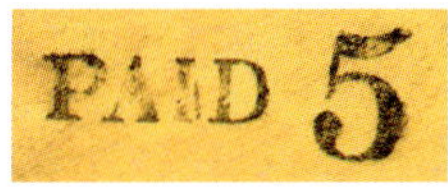

B

C

D

E

F

VICKSBURG / MISS (25 DC YD; 1861; black)
VICKSBURG / MISS (25 DC; 1861-62; black)
VICKSBURGH / Miss. (32; 1862; black)
VICKSBURG / MISS. (30; 1863; black)

A	PAID [no rate]	250.
	Same, 5 (ms)*	300.
	Same, 10 (ms)*	300.
B	PAID 5	250.
C	PAID 10	300.
D	DUE 10	250.
E	5, revalued 10 (ms)	250.
F	10 [due]	250.
	Same, Due (ms)*	200.
Ms	Paid 5	250.
	Due 10*	250.

Warrenton [Warrentown]

A

WARRENTOWN / MISS (26; 1861; black)

A	PAID 5	300.

Washington

A

WASHINGTON / MISS (32; 1861; red)

A	PAID 5 (red)*	300.

Water Valley

A 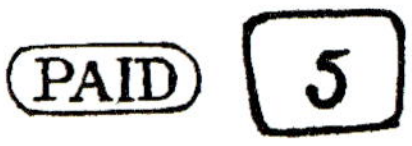 B

WATER VALLEY / MISS (25; 1861-62; black)

A	PAID, 10 (ms)*	300.
B	PAID 5	300.
Ms	Due 10	250.

Waynesboro

Waynesboro Miss (ms; 1863; black)

Ms	Paid 10	200.

West Point

A  B  C

D  E

F  G

WEST POINT / Miss. (30; 1861-62; black, brown)

A	PAID (brown), 10 (ms)*	250.
B	PAID 5	300.
C	PAID 10	300.
D	PAID 10	300.
	Same, "10" struck twice	500.
E	PAID 10*	300.
F	DUE 5*	300.
G	DUE 10*	500.

West's Station (Wests)

Wests Miss (ms; 1862; black)

Ms	Paid 10	200.

Williamsburg

WILLIAMSBURG / MIS. (32; 1862; black)

Ms	Due 5	250.

Winona

A

WINONA / MISS (25; 1861; black)

A	PAID [no rate]	250.
	Same, PAID struck twice [no rate]	250.
	Same, 5 (ms)	300.
	Same, 5c (ms)	300.
Ms	Paid [no rate]*	200.
	Paid 5	250.
Pk	No paid or rate marking	200.

Woodville

A  B  C

WOODVILLE / Mi. (32; 1861-62; black)

A	PAID 5	300.
B	PAID 10	300.
C	10 [due]	250.

Yazoo City

A  B  C

D

YAZOO CITY / MISS (32 YD; 1861-63; black)
YAZOO CITY / Miss. (32 YD; 1863; black)

A	PAID [no rate]	250.
B	PAID 5*	300.
C	PAID10	300.
D	DUE 10	300.
Ms	Paid [no rate]*	200.
	Due 5*	250.
	Due 10*	250.

NORTH CAROLINA

Abbott's Creek

Abbotts Creek (ms; 186-; black)

Ms Paid 10 175.

Albemarle

No postmark

Ms Paid 10 175.

Allensville

ALLENSVILLE / N C (31; 186-; black)

Ms Forwarded to Oxford N C from Allensville 175.

Anderson's Store

Andersons Store nc (ms; 1862; black)

Ms Paid 10 250.

Aquone

Aquone N C (ms; 186-; black)

Ms 10 / pd IH

Argyle

Argyle N. C. (ms; 1861; black)

Argyle (ms; 1862; black)

Ms Paid 150.

Paid 5 150.

Ashboro

A

B

C

D

E

ASHBORO / N. C. (26; 1861; black, blue)

A	PAID [no rate]*	150.
B	PAID 5 (blue)	200.
C	PAID 5 (blue)*	200.
D	PAID 10 (blue)	200.
E	5, Paid (ms)*	200.
Ms	Pd 10	200.
	Way	500.

Ashville

A

B

C

D

E

F

G

ASHVILLE / N. C. (31 YD; 1862-65; black)

ASHVILLE / N. C. (31; 1864-65; black)

A	PAID [no rate]*	150.
	Same, 5 (ms)	150.
	Same, 10 (ms)*	150.
	Same, 20 (ms)	250.
B	PAID 5	200.
C	PAID 10	200.
D	PAID 10	200.
E	PAID 10	200.
F	5 [due]*	150.
G	10, Due (ms)	150.
Ms	Due 10	150.

Ashland

Ashland NC (ms; 186-; black)

Ms Paid / 10 250.

Averysboro

A

AVERYSBORO / N. C. (25; 186-; black)

A	PAID, 5 (ms)	250.
	Same, 10 (ms)	250.

Ayersville

Ayersville N. C (ms; 186-; black)

Ms Paid / 10 175.

Bath

Bath N. C (ms; 1861; black)

Bath N. Ca. (ms; 1862; black)

Ms Paid 250.
Paid 5 150.
Pd 5 250.

Battleboro
Battleboro N C (ms; 1862; black)
Ms Paid 5 IH

Bay River
Bay River N C (ms; 1861; black)
Ms Paid 5 175.

Beaufort
A B

BEAUFORT / N. C. (33; 1861-62; black)
A PAID, 5 (ms)* 250.
B PAID 5 250.

Beaver Dam
Beaver Dam N. C (ms; 1862; black)
Ms Paid 10* 175.

Berea
Berea N. C. (ms; 1861; black)
Ms Paid 5¢ 250.

Bethania
A

Bethania N. C. (ms; 186-; black)
BETHANIA / N. C. (25; 1865; black)
A PAID, 10 (ms) 250.
Ms Paid / 10 250.

Big Falls
Big Falls (ms; 1862; black)
Ms Paid 5 175.

Blackman's Mills
Blackman's Mills N. C. (ms; 1863; black)
Ms Paid / 10 175.

Bloomington
A

BLOOMINGTON / N. C. (32; 186-; black)
A PAID 250.

Boone
Boone N C (ms; 186-; black)
Ms Paid 10 IH

Branch's Store
Branches N. C (ms; 186-; black)
Ms Paid 10 175.

Brick Church
Brick Church (ms; 186-; black)
Ms Pd 10 250.

Bridge Water
Bridge Water (ms; 1861; black)
Ms Paid 5* 250.

Broad Run Station
Broad Run Station (ms; 1861; black)
Ms Paid / 5 175.

Brower's Mills
Brower's Mills / N. C. (31; 186-; black)
Ms 10 / Paid 250.

Brownsville
A

Brownsville N. C. (ms; 1861; black)
BROWNSVILLE / N. C. (31; 186-; blue)
A PAID 10 (blue) 250.
Ms Paid 5 175.
Paid 10 175.

Buck Shoals
Buck Shoals N C (ms; 186-; black)
Ms Paid 10 IH

Burgaw
Burgaw N. C. (ms; 186-; black)
Ms Due 10 175.

Burnsville
A B

BURNSVILLE / —N. C.— (36; 1862; black)
A PAID 5 250.
B PAID 10 250.

Bushy Fork
Bushy Fork N C (ms; 1865; black)
Ms Paid 10 250.

Byrdsville

Byrdsville N C (ms; 1861; black)

Ms	Paid / 5	IH

Caldwell

Caldwell N C (ms; 186-; black)

Ms	Paid 10*	250.

Carbonton

Carbonton N C (ms; 1861; black)

Ms	Paid 10 cts	175.

Carolina City

A

B

C

Carolina City (ms; 1861; black)
C. City (ms; 1861; black)
CAROLINA CITY / N. C. (32 YD; 1862; black)

A	5. Paid	250.
B	Paid 5.	250.
C	PAID 5*	250.
Ms	Paid 5	250.
	Pd / 5	250.

Note: The Type A and B markings served as both postmarks and rate markings. There is no separate postmark on covers bearing these markings.

Carthage

A

CARTHAGE / N. C. (25; 1861; black)

A	PAID [no rate]	250.
Ms	Paid / 5	250.
	Paid 10	250.

Castalia

Castalia N C (ms; 186-; black)

Ms	Paid 5	IH

Castania Grove

Castania Grove (ms; 1861; black)

Ms	Paid 5	250.
	Paid / 10	250.

Catawba Station

A

B

CATAWBA STATION / N. C. (33; 1861; black)

A	PAID 10	250.
B	PAID 10	250.
Ms	Paid 5*	250.
	Paid 10*	250.
	Due 10	150.

Cedar Grove

Cedar Grove N C. (ms; 186-; black)

Ms	Paid 10	175.

Chapel Hill

A

PAID 5

B

CHAPEL-HILL / N. C. (31; 1861-62; black)

A	PAID [no rate]*	200.
	Same, 5 (ms)	250.
	Same, 10 (ms)	250.
B	PAID 5*	250.
Ms	Missent to Chapel Hill N C	250.

Charlotte

A

B

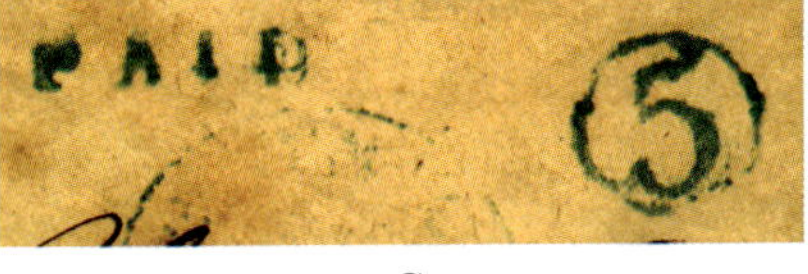

C

D

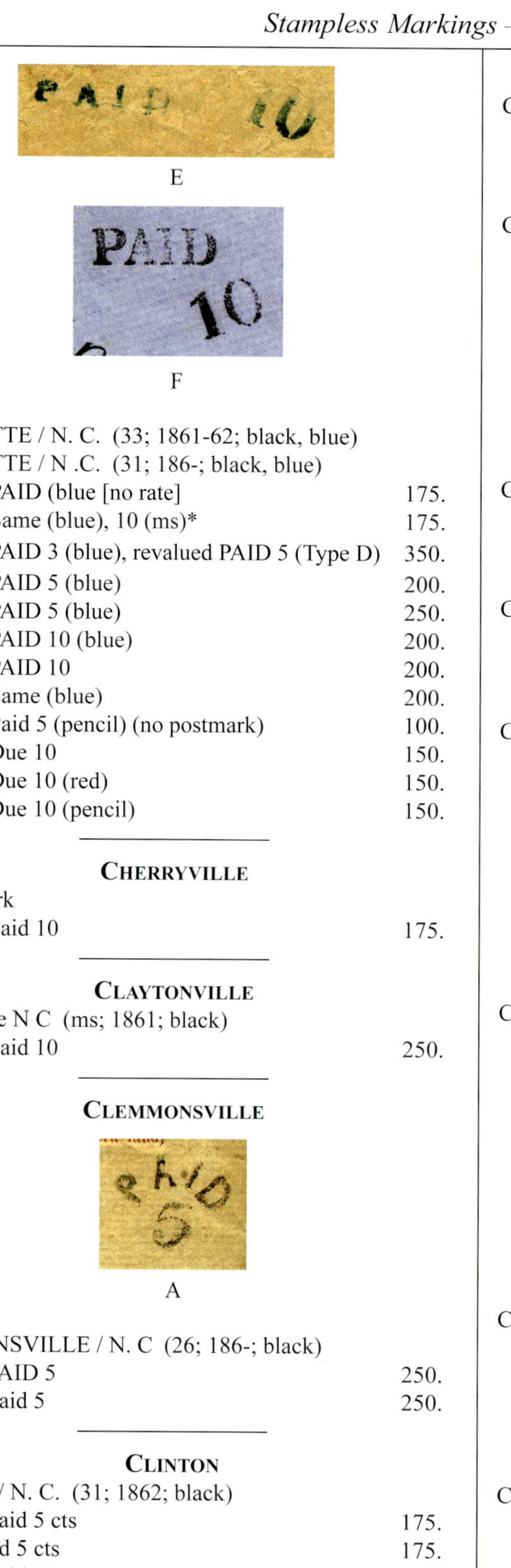

E

F

CHARLOTTE / N. C. (33; 1861-62; black, blue)
CHARLOTTE / N .C. (31; 186-; black, blue)

A	PAID (blue [no rate]	175.
	Same (blue), 10 (ms)*	175.
B	PAID 3 (blue), revalued PAID 5 (Type D)	350.
C	PAID 5 (blue)	200.
D	PAID 5 (blue)	250.
E	PAID 10 (blue)	200.
F	PAID 10	200.
	Same (blue)	200.
Ms	Paid 5 (pencil) (no postmark)	100.
	Due 10	150.
	Due 10 (red)	150.
	Due 10 (pencil)	150.

Cherryville

No Postmark

Ms	Paid 10	175.

Claytonville

Claytonville N C (ms; 1861; black)

Ms	Paid 10	250.

Clemmonsville

A

CLEMMONSVILLE / N. C (26; 186-; black)

A	PAID 5	250.
Ms	Paid 5	250.

Clinton

CLINTON / N. C. (31; 1862; black)

Ms	Paid 5 cts	175.
	Pd 5 cts	175.
	Paid 10cs	IH
	Paid / 10 cts	IH

Coleman's

Coleman's P. O. (ms; 186-; black)

Ms	Paid 10*	175.

Colerain

COLERAIN / N C (?; 1861; black)

Ms	Pd / 5	150.

Colesville

Colesville N C (ms; 186- ; black)

Ms	P 10	150.

Columbia

A

COLUMBIA / N. C. (27; 186-; red)

A	PAID (red), 5 (ms)	250.

Columbus

Columbus N. C. (ms; 1862; black)

Ms	Pd 5	IH

Comfort

Comfort N C (ms; 1863; black)

Ms	Pd 10	250.
	Due 10	175.

Company Shops

PAID 5

A

COMPANY SHOPS. / N. C. (34; 1861; black)

A	PAID 5*	250.
Ms	Paid 5	250.
	Paid 10*	250.

Concord

A

CONCORD / N. C. (26; 1862; blue)

A	PAID (blue), 5 (ms)	200.
	Same (blue), 10 (ms)	200.
Ms	Paid 10	200.

Cool Springs

Cool Springs N C (ms; 186-; black)

Ms	Paid 10	175.

Cottage Home

Cottage Home N C (ms; 1864; black)

Ms	Paid 10	175.

Cotton Grove

Cotton Grove N. C. (ms; 1863; black)

Ms	Paid 10	175.

County Line

Couny Line NC (ms; 1861-63; black)

Ms	5 / Paid	175.
	10 Paid	175.

Cowan's Ford

Cowans ford (ms; 186-; black)

Ms	Paid 10	175.

Crabtree

Crabtree N C (ms; 1861; black)

Ms	Paid 5	250.

Creaghead [Craighead]

Craighead N C (ms; 186-; black)

Ms	Paid / 10	250.

Crooked Creek

Crooked Creek N C (ms; 1861; black)

Ms	Paid / 5	IH

Crowder's Creek

Crowders Creek N. C (ms; 1861; black)

Ms	5 cts	175.

Currituck C H

A

CURRITUCK C H / N C (32; 186-; black)

A	Paid	350.

Curtis' Mills

Curtis Mills (ms; 186-; black)

Ms	Paid 10	175.

Dallas

A

DALLAS / N. C. (31; 1862; black)

A	PAID 5, struck twice	IH

Danbury

No postmark

Ms	5 Paid	IH
	Paid 10	IH

Davidson College

PAID 5

A

PAID 10

B

DAVIDSON COLLEGE / N. C. (32; 1861-64; black)

A	PAID 5	500.
B	PAID 10	500.

Davidson's River

Davidson's River (ms; 186-; black)

Ms	Due 10	250.

Dundarrack

Dundarrack N C (ms; 1862; black)

Ms	Paid / 5	250.
	Paid 10 cts	250.

Dunn's Rock

PAID 5

A

PAID 10

B

DUNN'S – ROCK / N. C. (33 YD; 186-; black)
DUNN'S ROCK / N. C. (33 YD; 1861; red)
DUNN'S ROCK / N. C. (33; 1861; red)

A	PAID 5 (red)*	350.
B	PAID 10	250.
Ms	Paid 5	250.

Durham's

Durhams N. C. (ms; 1861; black)

Ms	Paid 5	250.
	Pd 5	250.

Edenton

A

B

Edenton N C (ms; 1862; black)
EDENTON / N. C. (33; 1861; black)

A	PAID 5	250.
B	5 [due]	250.
Ms	Paid / 10	200.
	Due [no rate]*	150.

IH used in place of listing value when the item is held by an institution

Elizabeth City

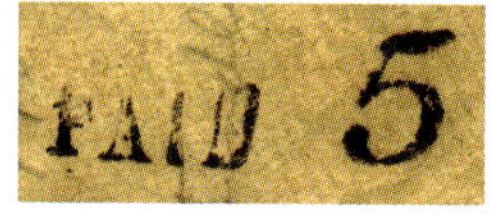
A

B

ELIZABETH CITY / N. C. (32; 1861; black)

A	PAID 5	200.
B	5 [due]*	150.
	Same, Forward due (ms)	200.

Elizabethtown

A

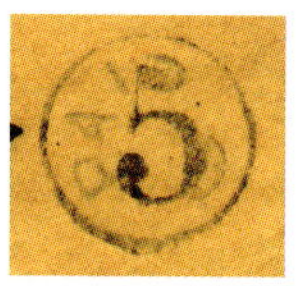
B

C

D

a

ELIZABETHTOWN / N. C. (31; 1862-64; black)

A	PAID, 10 (ms)	IH
B	PAID 3, revalued 5 (Type *a*)	350.
C	PAID 5	200.
D	PAID 5	200.
	Same, struck twice	300.

Elkin

A

ELKIN / N. C. (34, hollow letters; 186-; black)

A	PAID 10	1,500.

Elkville

A

B

Elkville N C (ms; 186-; black)
Elkville N. C. (ms; 186-; black)
ELKVILLE / N C (29; 1861; red)

A	PAID 5	250.
B	PAID 10	IH
Ms	Paid [no rate]	IH
	Paid 10	IH

Enfield

A

ENFIELD / N. C. (37; 186-; blue)

A	PAID (blue) [no rate]	250.
Ms	Paid 5*	200.

Fair Grove

Fair Grove N C (ms; 186-; black)

Ms	Paid / 10	250.

Fair Haven

Fair Haven N C (ms; 1862; black)

Ms	Paid 5	175.

Fall Creek

Fall Creek (ms; 186-; black)

Ms	Paid 10	175.

Farmington

A

FARMINGTON / N. C. (32; 1861; black)

A	Paid 5	200.

Fayetteville

A

B

C

D

FAYETTEVILLE / N. C. (26 DC YD; 1861-62; black)

FAYETTEVILLE / N. C. (32 YD; 1863; black)

A	PAID 5	200.
B	PAID 10	200.
C	PAID 10	200.
	Same, revalued 5 (Type A)	350.
D	FREE	500.
Ms	Missent to, & Ford	250.

Flat Branch

Flat Branches N. C (ms; 186-; black)

Ms	Paid 10 cts	175.

Flat Rock

A B

C D *a*

FLAT ROCK / N. C. (31; 1862; black)

A	PAID, 10 (ms)	200.
	Same, 20 (ms)	300.
B	PAID 5	200.
C	PAID 10	200.
D	PAID 10	200.
	Same, with added 10 (Type a)	350.
Ms	ford / Due 10	150.

Flat Shoal

Flat Shoal N C (ms; 1861; black)

Ms	Paid 10	250.

Forestsville

PAID

A

Forestville N C (ms; 186-; black)

A	PAID, 10 (ms)*	250.

Fort Defiance

Fort Defiance N. C. (ms; 1862; black)

Ms	Paid 5	150.

Fort Hembree

Fort Hembree (ms; 186-; black)

Ms	Paid / 10 (pencil)	250.

Francisco

Francisco N C (ms; 1862; black)

Ms	Paid / 5	250.

Franklin

A

FRANKLIN / N. C. (31; 1861-64; black)

A	FRANKLIN N. C. 5	750.
	Same, with added Paid / 10cts (ms)	200.
Ms	Paid 5	200.
	Paid 10	200.
	Paid 20	200.
	Paid 30	600.

Franklinton

PAID

A B

PAID 10

C

FRANKLINTON / N. C. (26; 1861-62; black)

A	PAID, 10 (ms)*	200.
B	PAID 5	200.
C	PAID 10*	200.
Ms	Paid 5*	200.
	Pd 5	200.
	Paid 10*	200.
	10 [due] with PAID (Type A) lined out	150.

Franklinville

Franklinville N. C. (ms; 186-; black)
Franklinsville N C (ms; 186-; black)

Ms	Paid / 10	250.

French Broad

French Broad (ms; 186-, black)

Ms	Paid 5	250.

Fulton

Fulton N. C. (ms; 1862; black)

Pk	No rate or paid marking	IH

Gardners Ford

Gardners Ford N C (ms; 186-; black)

Ms	Paid 10*	175.

Garysburg

A

Garysburg N C (ms; 1861-62; black)

A	PAID 10*	250.
Ms	Paid 5	200.
	Paid 10	200.
	Due 5	150.
	Due 10	150.

Gaston

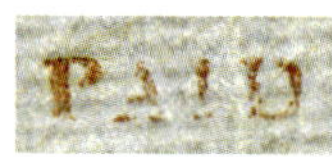

A

GASTON / N. C. (30; 186-; black, red)

A	PAID (red)	250.
Ms	Due 10c	150.

Gatesville

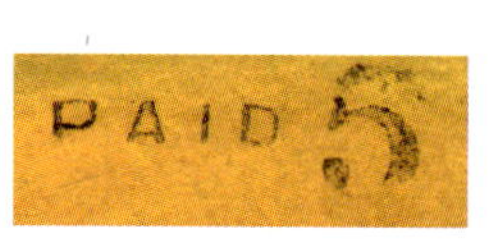

A B

Gatesville N C (ms; 186-; black)
GATESVILLE / N C (30; 1861; black)

A	PAID 5	200.
B	PAID 10	300.
Ms	P 10	200.

Germanton

A

Postmark unknown

A	PAID 10 (blue)	200.

Gibsonville

Gibsonville N C (ms; 1862; black)
Gibville N C (ms; 1864; black)

Ms	Paid / 5	175.
	Paid 10 cts	175.

Gilmore's Store

Gilmore's Store N. C. (ms; 1861; black)

Ms	Paid 5	250.

Gilopolis

PAID

A B

GILOPOLIS / N. C. (37; 186-; black)

A	PAID, 10 (ms)*	250.
B	PAID 10	250.

Globe

Globe N C (ms; 186-; black)

Ms	Paid / 10	250.

Gold Hill

PAID 

A B C

GOLD HILL / N. C (31; 186-; black)

A	PAID [no rate]	200.
B	PAID 5*	300.
C	PAID 10	300.

Goldsborough

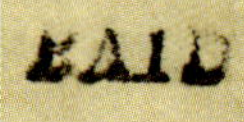

PAID 10

A B

C D

E

GOLDSBOROUGH / N. C. (32; 1862-63; black, blue)

A	PAID [no rate]	150.
	Same, 5 (ms)*	200.
	Same, 5 (ms) with Due 5 (ms)	250.
	Same, 10 (ms)*	200.
B	PAID 10*	250.
C	PAID 10	200.
	Same (blue)	200.
D	DUE [no rate]	150.
E	DUE 10	150.
	Same, revalued "PAID" (Type A)*	350.
Ms	Due 5	150.
	Due 10*	150.

Graham

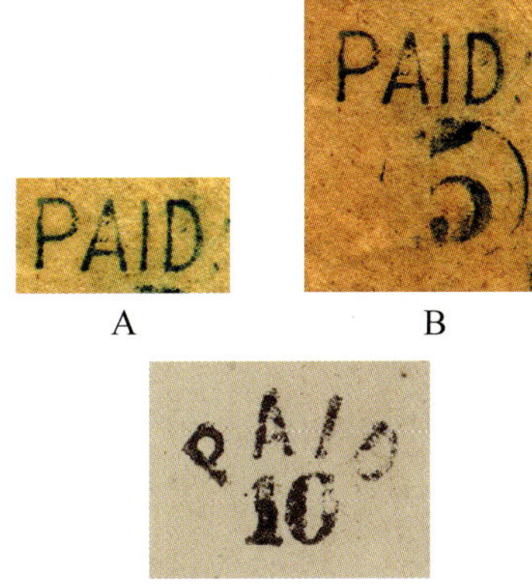

A B

C

GRAHAM / N. C. (36 SC; 1861; black, blue)
GRAHAM / N. C. (30; 1862; black)

A	PAID [no rate]	150.
	Same (blue) [no rate]	150.
	Same (blue), 5 (ms)*	200.
	Same (blue), 10 (ms)	IH
B	PAID 5 (blue)	200.
C	PAID 10	200.
Ms	Paid 5	200.
	Due 10	150.

Granite Hill

Granite Hill N. C. (ms; 186-; black)

Ms	Paid / 5	175.
	Paid 10*	175.

Gray's Creek

Grays Creek N C (ms; 186-; black)

Ms	Paid / 10	250.

Greensborough

A

B

PAID 10

C

D

E

GREENSBOROUGH / N. C. (32; 1861-62; blue, red)

A	PAID (blue), 10 (ms)	200.
B	PAID 5 (blue)	200.
	Same (blue), 5 struck twice	250.
C	PAID 10 (red)*	200.
D	PAID 10. (blue)	200.
	Same (red)	200.
E	DUE 10 (red)	200.
Ms	Paid 2	500.
	Due 2	350.
	Due 10	150.
	Missent (pencil)	150.

Greenville

A

B

GREENVILLE / N. C. (30; 1863; black)

A	PAID, 5 (ms)	IH
B	DUE 10	175.
Ms	Paid [no rate]	175.
	Paid 5*	200.
	Paid 10	200.
	Due 10	150.

Halifax Court House

A

B

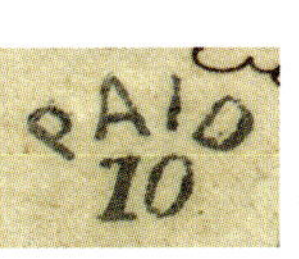

C

D

F

G

HALIFAX / N. C. (29; 186-; black)
HALIFAX / N. C. (30 YD; 1863; black, blue)

A	PAID 5	200.
B	PAID 5	200.
C	PAID 10	200.
	Same, struck three times*	300.
D	PAID, 10 (ms)	200.
E	5 [due] [not illustrated]*	150.
F	10 [due]	150.
G	FORWARDED, Due 5 cts (ms)	750.

Hamilton

HAMILTON / N C (32; 186-; black)

A	PAID 10	175.
Ms	Due 10	175.

Hamptonville

Hamptonville N C (ms; 1861-63; black)
HAMPTONVILLE / N. C. (31; 186-; black, red)

Ms	Pd 5	IH
	Paid / 5 cts	300.
	Paid / 5 cts (pencil)	IH
	Paid / 5¢, revalued 10 (ms)	300.
	Paid 10	200.
	Pd 10	200.
	Pd / 10	200.

Hannersville

Hannersville / N C. (ms; 186-; black)

Ms	Paid 10	175.

Happy Home

Happy Home (ms; 1861; black)
Happy Home N. C (ms; 186-; black)

Ms	P 5	250.
	Paid 10	250.

Harrells Store

Harrells Store N. C (ms; 1861; black)

Ms	Paid 5 cts	250.

Harrellsville

A

Harrellsville / N C (ms; 186-; black)
HARRELLSVILLE / N. C. (31; 1861; red)

A	PAID 5	250.
Ms	due 10	150.

Harrington

A

HARRINGTON / N. C. (29; 186-; black)

A	PAID 10	200.
	Same, struck three times	300.
Ms	Paid 5	150.

Harrisville

Harrisville NC (ms; 186-; black)

Ms	Paid 10	IH

Haw Branch

Haw Branch N C (ms; 1861; black)

Ms	Paid / 5cts	175.

Haw River

Haw River N C (ms; 1861; black)

Ms	cents / Paid 5	175.
	Paid 10*	175.

Haywood

Haywood N. C. (ms; 1862; black)

Ms	Paid 10	250.

Henderson

A B

HENDERSON / N. C. (30; 1862; black)

A	PAID, 10 (ms)	250.
B	PAID 5	250.
Ms	Paid 5*	200.
	Paid 10*	200.

Hendersonville

A

B

HENDERSONVLLE / N. C. (31; 186-; black)

A	PAID [no rate]*	175.
	Same, 10 (ms)*	200.
B	PAID 10	IH

Ms	Paid 5	200.
	Pd 5*	200.
	Paid 10	200.

Hertford

A

HERTFORD / N. C. (33; 1862; red)

A	PAID 5 (red)	250.

Hickory Tavern (Hickory Station)

PAID

A

Hickory Station (ms; 1862; black)
H. TAVERN. (33 NOR; 1862; black)

A	PAID [no rate]*	500.
Ms	Paid 5 cts	250.

Hicksville

Hicksville N C (ms; 186-; black)

Ms	Paid 10	175.

High Point

A

HIGH POINT / N. C. (37; 1861; black)

A	PAID [no rate]	175.
	Same, 5 (ms)	250.
Ms	Due 5 (pencil)	150.

Hilliardston

Hilliardston / NC (ms; 186-; black)

Ms	Paid 10	250.

Hills Store

Hills Store N C (ms; 186-; black)

Ms	Paid 10	250.

Hillsboro

A B

C D

Hillsboro N. C. (ms; 1862; black, blue)
HILLSBORO / N. C. (26 DC YD; 1861; black, blue)
HILLSBORO / N. C. (26 DC; 1863; blue)

A	PAID 5 (blue)	200.
	Same (blue), 5 struck twice	500.
B	PAID 5 (blue)	200.
C	PAID 10 (blue)	200.
D	5 [due]	150.
Ms	Paid	175.
	Due 10*	150.

Hillsdale

Hillsdale N. C (ms; 186-; black)

Ms	Paid / 10	175.

Hogans Creek

Hogans Creek N C (ms; 1862; black)

Ms	Paid / 5 cts (pencil)	IH
	Paid / 10	175.

Holtsburg

Holtsburg (ms; 1864; black)

Ms	Pd / 10	175.

Holt's Store

Holts Store N C (ms; 1862; black)

Ms	Paid 5	175.
	Paid 10	175.

Hookerstown

Hookerton N. C. (ms; 1863; black)

Ms	Due 10¢	175.

Huntsville

A

Huntsville N C (ms; 1862-64; black)
HUNTSVILLE / N. C. (31; 186-; black)

A	PAID 5	500.
Ms	Paid 10	250.
	Paid 10 cts	250.
	forwarded from Huntsville N. C.	200.

Hurdles Mills

Hurdles Mills N C (ms; 1861; black)

Ms	Paid 5 ¢	250.

Jackson

A

JACKSON / N. C. (30; 1861-64; black)

A	5, Paid (ms)	250.
Ms	Paid [no rate]	250.
	Paid 10*	250.
	Paid 15c	300.

Jacksons Creek

Jacksons Creek (ms; 1861; black)

Ms	Paid 10*	250.

Jamestown

A

JAMESTOWN / N. C. (36 SC; 1862; black)

A	PAID [no rate]	250.
Ms	Paid 5 (pencil)	IH

Jefferson

Jefferson (ms; 1864; black)
Jefferson N C (ms; 1861; black)

Ms	Paid / 5	IH
	Paid / 10	250.

Jerusalem

Jerusalem N C (ms; 1861; black)

A	PAID (blue) [not illustrated]*	300.
Ms	Pd 5	300.

Jonesville

A

Jonesville N C (ms; 186-; black)
JONESVILLE / N. C. (37; 186-; black)

A	PAID, 10 (ms)	300.
Ms	Paid / 10	200.

Joyner's Depot

Joyners N C (ms; 186-; black)

Ms	Pd / 10	175.

Judesville

Judesville N. C. (ms; 1862; black)

Ms	Paid / 10	250.

Kenansville

KENANSVILLE / N. C. (32; 186-; blue)
KENANSVILLE / N. C. (32 DC; 1861; black)

Ms	Paid / 5	IH
	Pd / 10	200.
	Due 10	150.

Killian's Mills

Killians Mills N C (ms; 1861; black)

Ms	Pd 5	175.

King's Creek

King's Creek N. C. (ms; 186-; black)

Ms	10 / Paid	175.

Kinston

A B

C

KINSTON, N. C. (26; 1861-63; black)

A	PAID [no rate]	175.
	Same, 5 (ms)	200.
	Same, 10 (ms)	200.
	Same, 20 (ms)	300.
B	DUE 10	150.
C	MISSENT	500.
Ms	Paid 5	200.
	Due 5	150.
	Due 10	150.

Kittrell

Kittrell N C (ms; 1862-63; black)

Ms	Paid / 5	175.
	Paid / 10	175.
	Fwd 20	300.

Lake Comfort

Lake Comfort N C (ms; 1861; black)

Ms	Pd / 5	250.

Lanes Creek

Lanes Creek (ms; 186-; black)

Ms	Paid 5*	250.

Laurinburgh

Laurinburgh (ms; 1861; black)

Ms	Paid / 5	175.
	Paid 10*	175.

Leaksville

Leaksville N C (ms; 186-; black)

Ms	Paid 10	175.
	5 [due]	175.

Leasburg

Leasburg N C (ms; 186-; ?)

Ms	5 [due]*	175.

Lenoir

A  B

C  D

E  F

LENOIR / N. C. (26; 1861-62; black, blue)

A	PAID (blue), 10 (ms)	175.
B	PAID 5*	200.
	Same (blue)	200.
C	PAID 5 (blue)	200.
	Same (blue), revalued 10 (ms)	250.
D	PAID 10*	200.
	Same (blue)	200.
E	5 (blue), [Due]	200.
F	10 (blue), Paid (ms)*	200.
Ms	Paid 5	200.
	Due 10	150.

Lenox Castle

Lenox Castle N C (ms; 1864; black)

Ms	Paid 10	250.

Lexington

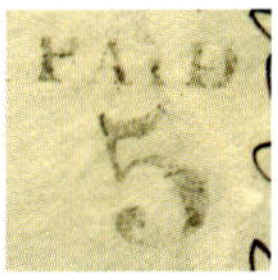

A  B

C

LEXINGTON / N. C. (26; 1861; black, brown)

A	PAID 5	250.
B	FORWARDED (brown)	500.
C	MISSENT (brown)	500.

Lilesville

Lilesville N C (ms; 186-; black)

Ms	Pd 10	175.

Lincolnton

A  B

C

LINCOLNTON / N. C. (30; 1862; black, red)

A	PAID [no rate]	200.
	Same, 10 (ms)*	200.
	Same, 15 (ms)	250.
B	PAID 5	200.
C	PAID 10	200.

Linton

Linton (ms; 186-; black)

Ms	Paid / 10	175.

Linville River

Linville River N C (ms; 1861; black)

MS	Pd 5	250.

Little Rock Fish

LITTLE ROCK FISH / N. C. (31; 186-; black)

Ms	Paid 5 + 5 / 10	250.
	Paid 10	250.

Little's Mills

Little's Mills N. C. (ms; 1862-63; black)

Ms	Paid 5	250.
	Paid 10	250.
	Paid 10 cts	250.
	5 [due]	200.

Littleton

Littleton N. C (ms; 1862; black)

Littleton N. Ca (ms; 1862; black)

Ms	Paid / 5	IH
	Paid 10	IH

Long's Mills

Longs Mills N C (ms; 186- ; black)

Ms	Paid 10	175.

Louisburg

A

PAID 5

B

C

D

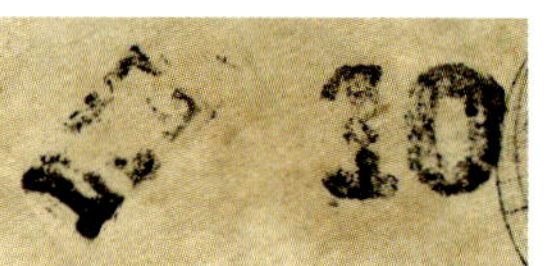

E

LOUISBURG / N. C. (33; 1861; black)

A	PAID [no rate]	175.
	Same, 2 (pencil)	IH
	Same, 10 (ms)*	200.
B	PAID 5*	250.
C	PAID 10	250.
D	DUE 10	IH
E	DUE 10	200.
Ms	Paid 5	200.
	10 Paid	200.
	Missent	200.

Lovelace

Lovelace N. C. (ms; 186-; blue)

Ms	Paid / 10 cts	IH

Lumberton

PAID

A

LUMBERTON / N C (26; 1861; black)

A	PAID, 5 (ms)	200.

Mackey's Ferry

PAID 

A

MACKEY'S FERRY / N C (28; 1861; black)

A	PAID 5	300.

Macon Depot

Macon Depot N C (ms; 1861-64; black)

Ms	5 / Paid	175.
	Due 10	175.

Madison

A

B

MADISON / N. C. (37; 1861-63; black, red, brown)

A	PAID (red), 10 (ms)	250.
B	PAID 5	250.
	Same (brown)	300.
Ms	Due 10	150.

Magnolia

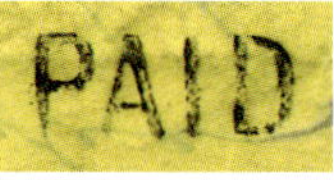

A

MAGNOLIA / N. C. (33; 1863; black)

A	PAID, 10 (ms)	200.
B	PAID 5 [not illustrated]*	200.
Ms	Due 10 (pencil)	150.

Manchester

Manchester N C (ms; 1862; black)

Ms	Paid 5*	250.

Mangum

Mangum N. C. (ms; 1861; black)

Ms	Paid 10	250.

Manson

Manson N. C. (ms; 1862; black)

Ms	Paid / 5	250.
	Paid 10*	250.

Marion

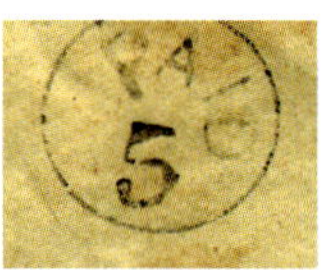

A

MARION / N. C. (29; 1861-62; black)

A	PAID 5	200.
Ms	Paid 5	200.
	Paid 10*	200.
	Due 5	150.

Marley's Mills

Marleys Mills, N. C. (ms; 186-; black)

Ms	Paid 10	250.

Martindale

A

Martindale N. C. (ms; 1861-65; black)
Martindale, N. C. (? SL; 1861; black)

A	PAID V	300.
Ms	Paid 5	250.
	Same (used with SL postmark)	2,000.
	Paid 10	250.

McCray's Store

M Crays Store N C (ms; 186-; black)

Ms	Paid 10	250.

McLeansville

McLeansville N C (ms; 1862; black)

Ms	Paid 5	175.

Mebaneville

A  B

Mebaneville N. C (ms; 1862; black)
MEBANEVILLE / N. C. (25; 1861; black)

A	PAID 5	500.
B	10 [due]*	150.
Ms	Paid 5	200.
	Paid /10	200.

Melville

A

MELVILLE / N. C. (26; 1861; black)

A	PAID, 5 (ms)	200.
Ms	P 10*	200.

Middletown

A  B

Incomplete postmark (?; 1861; black)

A	PAID 5*	200.
B	5, Paid (ms)	200.

Mill River

Mill River (ms; 186-; black)

Ms	Pd 10	IH

Milton

A

MILTON / N. C. (32; 1861; black)

A	PAID, 5 (ms)*	200.
Ms	Paid 5	200.

Minersville

Minersville N C (ms; 1861; black)

Ms	Paid 5 cts	250.

Mocksville

A  B

C  D

E  F

MOCKSVILLE / N. C. (32; 1861-63; black)

A	PAID, 5 (ms)	250.
B	PAID, 40 (ms)	300.
C	PAID 5	200.
D	PAID 5	200.
E	PAID 10	200.
F	PAID 10	200.
Ms	Pd 5	200.
	Due 5	150.

Monroe

A

MONROE / - N. C. - (28; 1863; red)

A	PAID (red), 10 (ms)	250.
Ms	Due 10	150.

Monroeton

Monroeton N C (ms; 186-; black)

Ms	Paid 5c plus 5c general issue	250.

Montpelier

Montpelier N. C. (ms; 186-; black)

Ms	Paid 5 cts*	200.
	Paid 10	175.

Morehead City

A

MOREHEAD CITY / N. C. (27; 1861; black)

A	PAID [no rate]	175.
Ms	Paid 5*	200.

Morgantown

A B

C D

E

MORGANTOWN / N. C. (33; 1861-62; blue)

A	PAID (blue), 5 (ms)*	200.
B	PAID 5 (blue)	200.
C	PAID 5 (blue)*	200.
D	PAID 10 (blue)	200.
E	10 (blue), Paid (ms)	200.
Ms	Paid 5	200.
	Due 10	150.
	Due 10 (pencil)	150.

Morrisville

Morrisville N. C (ms; 1861; ?)

Ms	5*	175.

Morven

Morven N C (ms; 1864; black)

Ms	Paid 10	175.
	Paid / 10	175.

Mount Airy

Mt. Airy N C (ms; 1862; black)

Ms	Pd. 10	250.

Mount Mourne

A

MOUNT MOURNE / N. C. (31; 186-; black, red)

B	PAID 10	250.

Mount Olive

A B

MOUNT OLIVE / N .C. (30; 1863-64; black)

A	PAID 10	300.
B	DUE 10	200.
Ms	Due 5¢ / forwarded	200.

Mount Pleasant

A

MOUNT PLEASANT / N. C. (26; 1861; black)

A	PAID 5	200.

Mountain Island

Mountain Island N. C. (ms; 1862; black)

Ms	Pd 5	250.

Murfreesborough

A B

C

MURFREESBOROUGH / N. C. (37; 1861-62; black)

A	PAID 5	200.
B	PAID 10*	200.
C	5 [due]	150.

MURPHEY

A

B

Murphy N C (ms; 186-; black)
MURPHEY / N C (37; 1861-62; black)

A	PAID, 10 (ms)*	250.
B	PAID 5	300.
Ms	Paid 10	250.

NASHVILLE

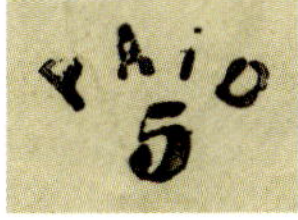

A

B

NASHVILLE / N C (31 YD; 1862; black)

A	PAID 5	200.
B	PAID 10	200.

NEW PORT

New Port N C (ms; 1862; black)

Ms	Paid 5cts	175.

NEWBERN

A

B

NEWBERN / N. C. (33; 1861-62; blue)

A	PAID 5 (blue)*	300.
B	5 PAID [integral postmark]*	300.
	Same (blue)	300.
	Same (blue) , revalued 15 (ms)	350.

NEWTON

A

Newton N C (ms; 1861; black)

A	PAID, 5 (ms)*	250.
Ms	Pd 5	200.

NEWTON GROVE

Postmark unknown

Ms	Paid 10*	250.

NORMAL COLLEGE

A

Normal College N C (ms; 1863; black)

A	10, Paid (ms)	350.

OAK GROVE

Oak Grove N C (ms; 1861; black)

Ms	Paid 5	175.

OAK HILL

Oak Hill N C (ms; 1862; black)

Ms	Paid 5	250.

OAK RIDGE

Oak Ridge N C (ms; 186-; black)

Ms	Paid 10	250.

OAKS

A

B

Oaks N C (ms; 1861; black)
OAKS / N C (32; 1861-62; black)

A	PAID [no rate]	175.
	Same, 5 (ms)	250.
	Same, 10 (ms)	250.
B	PAID 5	250.
Ms	Paid / 5	250.
	Pd 5	250.

OLIN

Olin N C (ms; 1864; black)

Ms	Paid 10 cts	250.

Onslow Court House

A

Onslow C H (ms; 1863; black)
ONSLOW C. H. /. N C (30; 186-; black)

A	PAID 10	300.
Ms	Paid 10	300.

Orange Factory

Orange Factory N. C. (ms; 1861; black)

Ms	Paid / 5¢	250.

Owenville

A

Owenville, N C (ms; 186-; red)
OWENVILLE / N. C. (31; 186-; black)

A	PAID 5	200.
Ms	Paid 10	200.

Oxford

A  B  C

D  E

OXFORD / N. C. (33; 1861; black)

A	PAID [no rate]	200.
B	PAID 5	200.
C	PAID 5	250.
D	PAID 10	250.
E	10 [due]	200.
Ms	Paid 10	200.

Pacific

Pacific N C (ms; 1862-64; black)

Ms	5 / Paid	200.
	10 / Paid	250.

Pactolus

Pactolus N. C. (ms; 1862; black)

Ms	Paid 5¢	250.
	Paid 10¢	250.

Palmyra

Palmyra N C (ms; 186-; black)

Ms	10 Paid	250.

Panther Creek

Panther Creek N C (ms; 1863; black)

Ms	Paid 10	250.

Patterson

A  B

C

PATTERSON / N. C. (31; 186-; black)

A	PAID [no rate]	250.
	Same, 10 (ms)*	250.
B	PAID 5*	500.
C	PAID 10	500.

Patton's Home

Pattons Home N. C. (ms; 186-; black)

Ms	Paid 10	200.

Pedlars Hill

Pedlars Hill N. C (ms; 1861; black)

Ms	Paid 5	175.

Perkinsville

Perkinsville N. C. (ms; 1861; black)

Ms	Paid 5	175.

Philadelphus

Philadelphus N C (ms; 186-; black)

Pk	No rate	175.

Pilot Mountain

Pilot Mt (ms; 1861; black)

Ms	Paid 10	175.

Pine Level
Pine Level N C (ms; 1864; black)
Ms Paid 10 250.

Pink Hill
A

PINK HILL / N. C. (29; 1861; black)
A PAID 5 500.

Pioneer Mills
Pioneer Mills N C (ms; 1861; black)
Ms Paid 5 250.

Pittsboro
A  B

PITTSBORO / N C (25; 1861; black)
A PAID [no rate] 175.
B PAID 5 200.
C PAID 10 [not illustrated]* 200.
Ms Due 5 cts 150.

Pleasant Hill
A

P. Hill. N. C. (ms; 1864; black)
P. HILL / N. C. (NOR; 186-; brown)
A DUE 10 (brown) 750.
Ms Paid 10c 250.

Pleasant Retreat
Pleasant Retreat N. C (ms; 1861; black)
Ms Paid / 5 250.

Plymouth
A  B

PLYMOUTH / N. C. (33 YD; 1861-62; red)
A PAID (red), 15 (ms) 250.
B PAID 5 (red) 250.

Pocket
Pocket N. C (ms; 186-; black)
Ms 10 250.

Poplar Bridge
Poplar Bridge N. C (ms; 1862; black)
Ms Paid / 5 250.

Prospect Hill
Prospect Hill (ms; 1864; black)
Ms Paid 10 250.

Quallatown
Qualla Town N C (ms; 186-; black)
Ms Paid 250.

Queensdale
Queensdale N C (ms; 1861; black)
Ms Paid / 5 175.

Raleigh
A B  C

D  E

F  G

H  I

J  K

Raleigh (ms; 1862; black)
RALEIGH / N. C. (26 DC YD; 1861-64; black, blue, red, orange)
RALEIGH / N. C. (31; 186-; blue)
A PAID [no rate] 150.
Same (blue) [no rate] 150.
Same (red) [no rate]* 150.
Same (red), 2 (ms) 350.

	Same (blue), 5 (ms)	200.
	Same (red), 5 (ms)	200.
B	PAID [no rate]	150.
	Same (blue) [no rate]	150.
	Same (red) [no rate]*	150.
	Same (red), 5 (ms)*	200.
	Same (red), 10 (ms)*	200.
C	PAID 5 (blue)	200.
	Same 5 (red)	200.
D	PAID 10 (red)	200.
E	PAID 10 (blue)	200.
	Same (green)	350.
F	PAID 10 (blue)	200.
G	DUE 5 (blue)	150.
H	DUE 10 (blue)	150.
	Same (orange)	300.
I	ADVERTISED (blue)	500.
J	FORWARDED (blue)	500.
	Same (blue), 5 (ms)	500.
	Same (red), with DUE 10 (red) (Type H)	500.
K	MISSENT (blue), with PAID 5 (red) (Type C)	400.
Ms	Paid 5	175.
	Due 2*	250.
	Due 30	350.
	Due 50*	350.

Ransom's Bridge

Ransoms Bridge (ms; 186-; black)

Ms	Paid 5	IH
	Pd 5	IH
	5 [due]	IH

Reed Creek

Reed Creek N C (ms; 1864; black)

Ms	Pd 10	250.

Reidsville

Reidsville N. C. (ms; 1861; black)

Ms	Paid / 5	250.

Richlands

Richlands N C (ms; 1862; black)

Ms	Paid 10	250.

Richmond Hill

Richmond Hill N C (ms; 1861; black)

Ms	Paid 5*	250.
	Paid / 10	250.

Ridgeway

A B C D

RIDGEWAY / N. C. (25; 1861-63; black)

A	PAID 5	250.
B	PAID 5	300.
C	PAID 10*	250.
D	10, Due (ms)	150.
Ms	Paid 5*	200.
	Paid 10*	200.

Rocky Mount

A B C

ROCKY MOUNT / N. C. (32; 1861; black)

A	PAID [no rate]	175.
	Same, 10 (ms)	200.
B	PAID 5	200.
C	5 [due]*	150.
Ms	Paid 5	200.
	Paid 10	200.
	Paid 20	200.

Rogers Store

Rogers Store (ms; 186-; black)

Ms	Paid 10*	250.

Round Hill

Round Hill (ms; 1861; black)

Ms	Paid / 5	250.

Roxboro

A

Roxboro N C (ms; 1862; black)

A	PAID 10	200.
Ms	Paid 5	200.
	Paid 10	200.

Rush's Mills

Rush's Mills N C (ms; 1864; black)

Ms	Paid / 10	250.

Rutherfordton

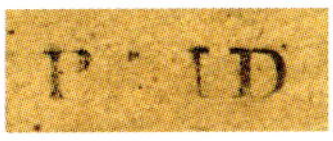

A

RUTHERFORDTON / N. C. (32; 186-; black)

A	PAID, 5 (ms)	300.
Ms	Paid 10*	300.

Saint Charles

Saint Charles N C (ms; 186- black)

Ms	Paid 10	175.

Saint Lawrence

Saint Lawrence NC (ms; 1861; ?)

Ms	Paid 10	250.

Saint Paul's

St. Pauls N C (ms; 186-; black)

Ms	Paid 10*	250.

Salem

A  B

C  D

E

SALEM / N. C. (32; 186-; black)

A	PAID 5	250.
	Same, revalued 2	400.
B	PAID 10	250.
C	DUE 5	150.
D	ADVERTISED	500.
E	FORWARDED 5	500.
Ms	Due 10	150.

Salem Chapel

Salem Chapel N. C. (ms; 1861; black)

Ms	Paid 5	250.

Salem Church

Salem Church N C (ms; 186-; black)

Ms	Paid 10	250.

Salisbury

A  B

PAID
10

C

SALISBURY / N. C. (32 YD; 1861-65; black)

A	PAID [no rate]	150.
	Same, 5 (ms)	200.
	Same, 10 (ms)	200.
B	PAID 5	200.
	Same, with ms "2" to make "25"	350.
C	PAID 10*	200.
Ms	Pid 10	200.
	Du 10	150.

Sandy Creek

A

SANDY CREEK / N. C. (30; 1862; black)

A	PAID 5	250.

Sandy Mush

Sandy Mush N C (ms; 1861; black)

Ms	Paid / 5	250.
	Paid 10	250.

Saxapahaw

A

B

Saxapahaw N C (ms; 1862; black)

A	PAID 5	300.
B	PAID 10	300.

Scuppernong

A B

SCUPPERNONG / N. C. (30; 1861; black, brown)

A	PAID 5	200.
	Same, revalued 10 (ms)*	250.
B	5 [due]	150.

Shelby

A B

C D

SHELBY / N. C. (30 DLC; 1862; black)

A	PAID, 50 (ms)*	300.
B	PAID 5	250.
C	PAID 5	250.
D	PAID 10	250.

Shepardsville

Shepardsville N C (ms; 1861; black)

Ms	Paid / 5 cts	250.

Silver Hill

Silver Hill (ms; 186-; black)

Ms	Paid 10	250.

Smith Grove

Smith Grove N C (ms; 1863; black)

Ms	Pd 10	250.

Smithfield

A B

C

SMITHFIELD / N. C.. (30; 186-; black)

A	PAID [no rate]	150.
B	PAID 5*	200.
C	PAID 10	200.
Ms	Paid 10	200.

Smithville

A

Smithville N. C. (ms; 1861; black)

A	PAID 5 (over 3 handstamp)	300.
Ms	Paid 10	IH

Snow Camp

Snow Camp N C (ms; 186-; black)

Ms	Paid 5*	250.

Snow Hill

SNOW HILL / N. C. (29; 1864; black)

Ms	Paid 5	250.
	Paid 10	IH

Spencer

Spencer N C (ms; 1862; black)

Ms	Paid 10	250.

Spring Creek

Spring Creek N C (ms; 1861; black)

Ms	5 [due]	250.

Staceyville

A

STACEYVILLE / N. C. (26; 186-; black, red)

A	PAID 5 (red)	250.

Stanhope

Stanhope N C (ms; 1862; black)

Ms	paid 5*	250.

Statesville

A

B

STATESVILLE / N. C. (30; 1862; black)

A	PAID 10	200.
B	PAID 10	200.
Ms	Forwarded 10 Due	250.

Stephens

Stephens N C (ms; 186-; black)

Ms	Paid 10	250.

Summerfield

Summerfield N C (ms; 1862; black)

Ms	Paid 5	250.

Swannano

Swannano N C (ms; 1864; black)

Ms	Pai 10	250.

Tawboro

A B

C D E

Tarboro, N. C. (ms; 186-; black)
TARBORO / N. C. (31; 186-; black)
TAWBORO / N. C. (35; 1863; black)

A	PAID, 10 (ms)*	200.
B	PAID 5	200.
C	PAID 10	200.
D	10, Paid (ms)*	200.
E	10, du (ms)	150.
Ms	Paid 5*	200.
	Paid 10	200.
	10 [due]*	150.
	Due 10	150.

Taylorsville

A B

C D

TAYLORSVILLE / N. C. (30; 1861; black, blue)

A	PAID, 10 (ms)	150.
B	PAID 5	200.
C	PAID 5 (blue)	200.
D	PAID 10 (blue)	200.
Ms	Paid 10*	200.

Thomasville

A B

THOMASVILLE / N. C. (28; 186-; black)
THOMASVILLE / N. C. (33; 186-; black)

A	PAID [no rate]	175.
	Same, 5 (ms)*	200.
B	PAID, 10 (ms)	200.
Ms	Paid 5	200.

Townesville

Townesville N C (ms; 1861; black)

Ms	Paid 5	250.

Trap Hill

Trap Hill N. C (ms; 1861; black)

Ms	Paid 5	250.

Trenton

Trenton N. C. (ms; 1861; black)

Ms	Paid 5 cts	250.

Trinity College

A B

TRINITY COLLEGE / N. C. (26; 1861; black)

A	PAID [no rate]*	500.
	Same, 5 (ms)	750.
	Same, 10 (ms)*	750.
B	PAID 5*	750.

Troy

Troy No Ca (ms; 1862-64; black)

Ms	Paid 10 cts	250.
	Paid 30	350.

Troy's Store

Troy's Store N. C. (ms; 1864; black)

Pk	No rate or paid marking	150.

Turkey Cove

Turkey Cove N C (ms; 1862; black)

Ms	Paid / 5	250.

Wadesborough

A B

WADESBORO / N. C. (30; 1861-62; black)

A	PAID, 10 (ms)	200.
B	Paid 5	200.
C	MISSENT [not illustrated]*	500.
Ms	Paid 5	200.
	Due 5	150.

Walnut Cove

A

Walnut Cove N. C. (ms; 1861; black)

A	PAID 10*	250.
Ms	Pd 5 cts	250.

Walnut Grove

Walnut Grove (ms; 1865; black)

Ms	Paid 10	250.

Walnut Lane

Walnut Lane N. C. (ms; 1862; black)

Ms	Paid 10c	250.

Warren Plains

Warren Plains N C (ms; 1865; black)

Ms	Due 10	250.

Warrenton

A B C

D E F

a

WARRENTON / N. C. (33; 1861-64; black)

A	PAID, 20 (ms)	250.
B	PAID 5*	250.
C	PAID 5	200.
D	PAID 5	200.
	Same, revalued 10 (type *a*)	250.
E	PAID 10	200.
F	PAID 10	200.
Ms	Due 5	150.

Warsaw

A B

WARSAW / N. C. (30; 1861-62; black)

A	PAID [no rate]*	175.
	Same, 5 (ms)	200.
B	PAID 10	200.

Washington

A B

a

WASHINGTON / N. C. (30; 1861; black)

A	PAID 5	200.
	Same, revalued 10 (type *a*)	350.
B	PAID 10	200.
C	DUE (arc) / 5 [not illustrated]*	150.
Ms	Unpaid 5	200.
	Missent	150.

Weldon

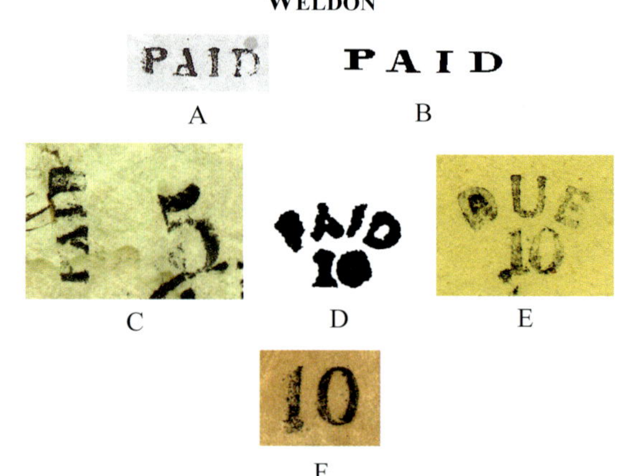

A B C D E F

WELDON / N. C. (32 YD; 1862-63; black)

A	PAID [no rate]	175.
	Same, 5 (ms)*	200.
	Same, 10 (ms)	200.
B	PAID, 5 (ms)*	200.
C	PAID 5	200.
D	PAID 10	200.
E	DUE 10	150.
F	10 [due]	150.
Ms	Due 10	250.

Wentworth

A  B

Wentworth N. C. (ms; 1862; black)
WENTWORTH / N. C. (25; 186-; black)

A	PAID 5*	250.
B	PAID 10	250.
Ms	Paid 5	200.

West Point

West Pont N C (ms; 186-; black)

Ms	Pd 10	250.

White Hall

White Hall N C (ms; 1861; black)

Ms	Paid 10	250.

White Sulphur Springs

N C W S Springs (ms; 186-; ?)

Ms	Paid 10*	250.

Whites Creek

Whites Creek N C (ms; 1862; black)

Ms	Paid 10	250.

Whitesville

A  B

WHITEVILLE / N. C. (31; 1865; black)

A	PAID 5*	200.
B	PAID 10	200.

Why Not

Why Not N. C. (ms; 1862; black)

Ms	Paid 10	250.

Wilkesborough

A  B

C  D

E

WILKESBORO / N. C. (25; 1861; black)
WILKESBOROUGH / N. C. (38; 1862; black)

A	PAID [no rate]	175.
B	PAID 5	200.
	Same, revalued 10 (Type C)	200.
C	PAID 10	200.
D	10 [due]	150.
E	WAY	IH

Williamsborough

WmsBoro N. C (ms; 1862-65; black)

Ms	Paid 5	250.
	Paid 10	250.

Williamston

A  B

C  D

WILLIAMSTON / N. C. (31; 186-; black)
WILLIAMSTON / N. C. (32; 1862; black)

A	PAID 5	200.
B	PAID 5	200.
C	PAID 10	200.
D	PAID 10*	200.
	PAID 10, struck four times	350.

Wilmington

A B

C D

E F

G H

I J

K

WILMINGTON N. C. (31; 186-; black)
WILMINGTON / N. C. (31; 1861-63; black)

A	PAID 5	200.
B	PAID 5*	200.
	Same, revalued 10*	250.
C	PAID 5*	200.
D	PAID 5*	200.
E	5 PAID (integral postmark)	250.
	Same, 32 (ms)*	4,500.
F	PAID 5 (integral postmark)	250.
	Same, 12 (ms)*	4,000.
	Same, revalued 10*	400.
G	PAID 10	200.
H	5 [due]	150.
I	10 [due]	150.
J	MISSENT	400.
K	SHIP, 2 (ms)	4,000.
	Same, 6 (ms)*	3,000.
	Same, 12 (ms)	3,000.
	Same, 22 (ms)	4,500.
	Same, 32 (ms)*	4,500.
	Same, 52 (ms)	4,500.
	Same with DUE 10, revalued 40 (ms)*	4,000.
	Same with 10¢ General Issue	5,000.
	Same, Due 2 (ms) with 10¢ General Issue	6,000.
	Same, Due 22 (ms)	5,000.
L	WAY [not illustrated]	500.
Ms	12 [due]	1,000.
	22 [due]	1,500.
	32 [due]	1,500.
	42 [due]	2,000.
	Due 10*	150.
	Due 12	150.
	Missent	150.

Note: Many letters bearing the Wilmington Type J "MISSENT" marking do not bear a Wilmington forwarding postmark.

Wilson

WILSON / N. C. (31; 1863; black)

Ms	Paid 2	1,000.

Windsor

A

WINDSOR / N. C. (30; 1861-64; black)

A	PAID 10	250.
Ms	Paid 5*	200.
	Paid 10	200.
	Due 5	150.

Winston

Winston N C (ms; 1862-63; black)

Ms	Paid 5	250.
	Paid 10	250.

Woodlawn

Woodlawn N C (ms; 186-; black)

Ms	Paid / 5	250.

Yadkinville

Yadkinville N. C. (ms; 1862; black)

Ms	Paid [no rate]	IH
	Paid 5	IH
	Paid 10 cs	IH

Yanceyville

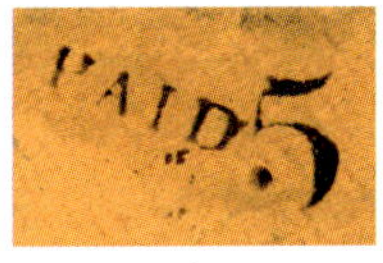
A

B

C

YANCEYVILLE / N. C. (31 YD; 1862; black, red)

A	PAID 5	200.
B	PAID 10*	200.
	Same (red)	200.
C	PAID 10 (red)	250.

York Collegiate Institute

York Coll. Inst NC (ms; 1862; black)

Ms	Paid 10	500.

Abbreviations and Symbols Key—Stampless

[*]	symbol used after an item description to mean an unsupported listing
[–]	symbol used in place of value to mean insufficient information to assign a price
[?]	symbol used to mean unknown measurement, date or color
[*italic*]	value typeface indicating the item is difficult to price accurately
DC	double circle
DLC	double [outer] line circle
IH	used in place of listing value when the item is held by an institution
mkg	marking
ms	manuscript
NA	used in place of a listing value when no examples are known to exist
NOR	no outer rim
NR	used in place of value when no examples have been recorded
OV	Oval
Pk	cover bearing a postmark but no indication of rate
pmk	postmark
SC	segmented circle
SL	straightline
YD	year date

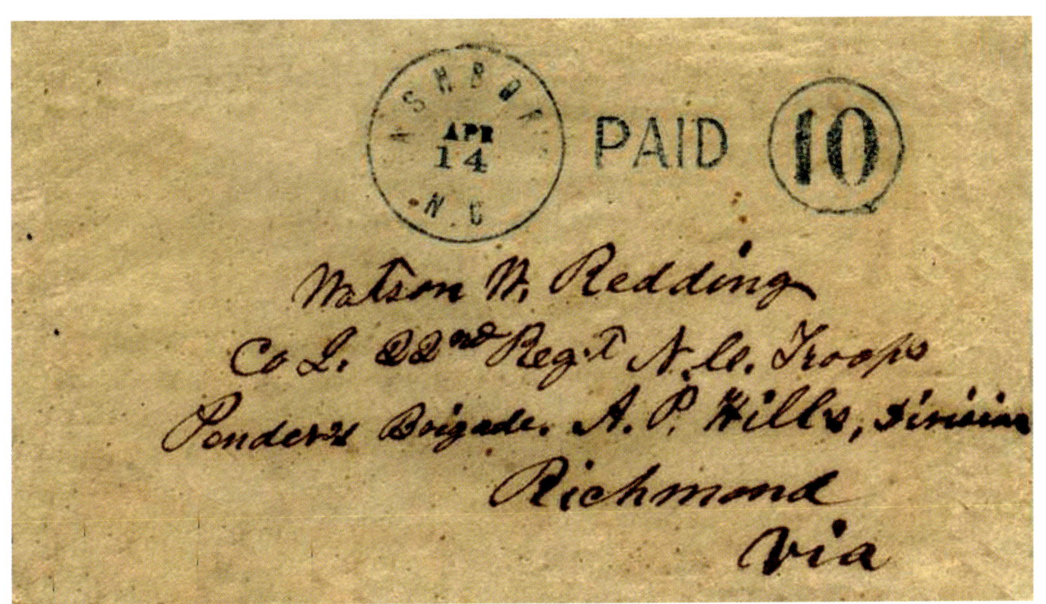

SOUTH CAROLINA

Abbeville

A B

ABBEVILLE C. H. / S. C. (30; 186-; black, red)
ABBEVILLE C. H. / S. C. (32; 1861; black)

A	PAID 5	200.
B	PAID 10	250.
	Same (red)*	250.
	Same (red), struck three times	300.

Adams' Run

A B

Adams Run S C (ms; 1862; black)
ADAMS RUN / S C (32; 186-; black)

A	PAID [no rate]	150.
	Same, 10 (ms)*	150.
B	PAID [no rate]	250.
Ms	Paid*	125.
	Paid 5	125.
	Due*	100.
	Due 10	125.

Aiken

A B

AIKEN / S. C. (25 DC; 1861; black)
AIKEN / S. C. (32; 1861; black)

A	PAID 5	200.
	Same, with "excess 5 due" (ms)	250.
B	PAID 10	250.
Ms	Due 10	200.

Allendale

Allendale S C (ms; 1861; black)
Allendale S. C. (ms; 186-; black)

Ms	Paid 5	200.
	Paid 10	200.

[*]	symbol used after an item description to mean an unsupported listing
DC	double circle
ms	manuscript
YD	year date

Alston

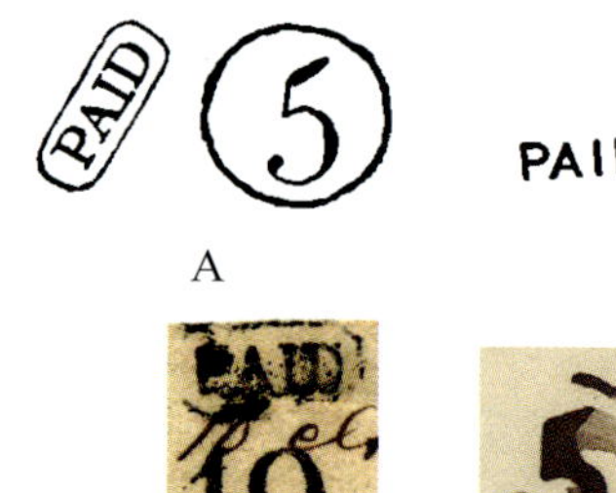

A B

C D

ALSTON / S. C. (25; 1861; black)

A	PAID 5*	250.
B	PAID 10*	250.
C	PAID 10	250.
D	5 [due]	250.

Anderson Court House

PAID 5

A B

C

ANDERSON C. H. / S. C. (32; 186-; black)
ANDERSON C. H. / S. C. (33; 186-; black)

A	PAID [no rate]	125.
	Same, 5 (ms)*	150.
	Same, 10 (ms)	175.
B	PAID 5*	200.
C	PAID 5	200.
Ms	Paid 5	150.
	Due 10 (pencil)	150.

Anderson's Mills

Anderson Mills / S C (ms; 1861; black)

Ms	Paid 5	250.

Antioch

Antioch S C (ms; 1865; black)

Ms	Paid 10	250.

Arnolds Mills

Arnold Mills, SC (ms; 186-; black)

Ms	P 10*	200.

Ashepoo Ferry

Ashepoo Ferry S C (ms; 1862; black)

Ms	Paid [no rate]*	150.
	Paid 5	175.

Bachelor's Retreat

B. Ret (ms; 1865; black)
B Retreat S C (ms; 186-; black)

Ms	Paid*	250.
	Paid 5*	250.
	Paid / 10	150.
	Pd 10	250.

Bamburg

A B

C

BAMBERG / S. C. (25; 186-; black)

A	PAID 5	250.
B	PAID 10*	250.
C	PAID 10	250.

Beaufort

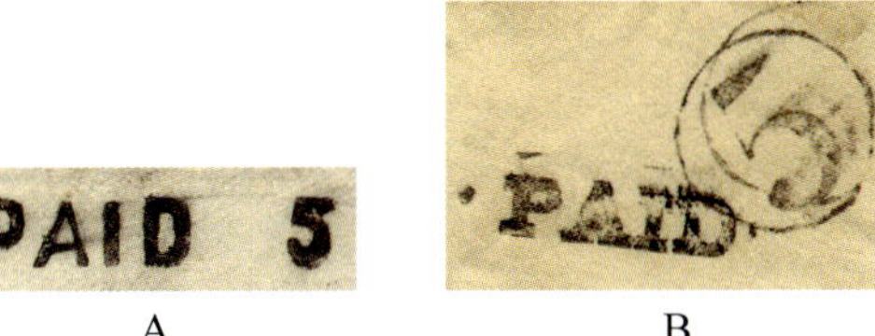

A B

C D

BEAUFORT / S. C. (32 YD; 1861; black)

A	PAID 5	300.
B	PAID 5	250.
C	PAID 5	300.
D	5 [due]*	200.

Beaver Pond

Beaver Pond S. C. (ms; 1862; black)

Ms	Paid 5	250.

Belton

Belton S C (ms; 1861-64; black)

Ms	Paid 5	200.
	Paid 10*	200.
	Due 10	150.

Bennettsville

A

B

BENNETTSVILLE / S. C. (34; 1864; black)

A	PAID [no rate]	200.
	Same, 10 (ms)	200.
B	PAID 10	200.
Pk	No rate	200.

Beth Eden

Beth Eden S. C. (ms; 1861; black)

Ms	Paid 5	250.

Bishopville

Bishopville S C (ms; 1861-64; black)

Ms	Paid 5	200.
	Paid 10	200.

Bivingsville

Bivingsville S C (ms; 1861-64; black)

Ms	Paid 5 c	200.
	Paid 10	250.

Black Mingo

A

BLACK MINGO / S C (37; 186-; black, brown)

A	PAID [no rate]	350.
	Same, 5 (ms)*	250.

Black Oak

Black Oak S C (ms; 1861; black)

Ms	Paid*	200.

Blackstocks

Blackstocks (ms; 1862-65; black)

Ms	Paid 10	200.

[–] symbol used in place of value to mean insufficient information to assign a price
[?] symbol used to mean unknown measurement, date or color

Blackville

A  B

BLACKVILLE / S. C. (32; 186-; black)

A	PAID 5*	200.
B	PAID 10	200.
	Same, revalued 20 (ms)	300.

Blairsville

Blairsville (ms; 186-; black)

Ms	Paid 10	250.

Blue House

Blue House (ms; 1864; black)
Blue House So. Ca. (ms; 1864; black)

Ms	Paid 10	250.
	Due / 10	250.

Bluffton

A

BLUFFTON / S. C. (28; 1861; black)

A	PAID 5	250.

Boydton

Boydton S C (ms; 1861; black)

Ms	Pd / 5	250.

Branch Island

Branch Island (ms; 1864; black)

Ms	Paid 10*	200.

Branchville

A

BRANCHVILLE / S. C. (36; 1861-64; black)

A	PAID [no rate]	200.
	Same, 10 (ms)*	200.
	Same, Paid 20 (ms)	250.
Ms	Due 10	200.

Brighton

Brighton S C (ms; 186-; black)

Ms	Paid / 10	250.

Broxton's Bridge

Broxtons Bridge S C (ms; 1862; black)

Ms	Paid / 5	250.

Bucksville

Bucksville / S C (ms; 1861; black)

Ms	Pd 5	250.

Buena Vista

Buena Vista S. C. (ms; 186-; black)

Ms	Paid 5*	250.
	Paid 10*	250.
	Pd / 10	250.

Bufford's Bridge

BUFFORD'S BRIDGE / S C (32; 186-; black)

Ms	10 Paid	200.

Cairo

Cairo S C (ms; 1861; black)

Ms	Paid 5*	250.
	5 [due]	250.

Calhoun's Mills

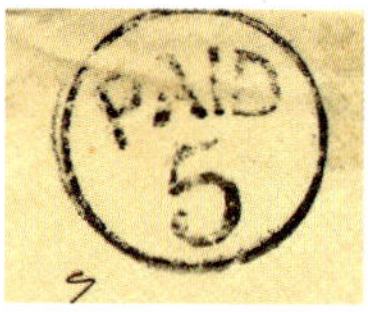

A  C

CALHOUN'S MILLS / S. C. (31; 1861; black)
CALHOUN'S MILLS / S. C. (32; 1861; black)

A	PAID 5	200.
B	PAID 10 (in circle) [not illustrated]*	250.
C	PAID 10	250.

Camden

A  B  C

D  E

F

CAMDEN / S. C. (26 DC; 1861; black, red)
CAMDEN / S. C. (30; 1863; black)
CAMDEN / S. C. (32; 186-; black)

A	PAID (red) [no rate]	200.
	Same, 20 (ms)	250.
B	PAID 5	150.
	Same (red)*	175.
C	PAID 5	200.
	Same (red)*	200.
D	PAID 10	175.
E	PAID 10	250.
F	10 [due]	200.
Ms	Paid 10	125.
	Due 2	350.

Note: The "PAID" and "10" in the Type E marking are not in fixed positions.

Cedar Hill

Cedar Hill S C (ms; 1863; black)

Ms	Pd 10	250.

Cedar Shoal

Cedar Shoal S C (ms; 1861; black)

Ms	Paid 5 cts	250.

Cedar Springs

Cedar Spring S C (ms; 1862; black)

Ms	5 Paid	250.
	10 Pd	250.

Chappell's Bridge

Chappells S C (ms; 186-; black)

Ms	Paid 5	200.

Charleston

A B

C D

E F

G

H I J K

L M

N

O

Pk

CHARLESTON / S. C. (26 DC YD; 1861-64; black)
CHARLESTON / S. C. (29; 186-; black)
CHARLESTON / S. C. (32 YD; 1861-64; black)
CHARLESTON S. C. / Paid (32 YD; 1861; black)

A	PAID [no rate]*	200.
	Same, 10 (ms)*	200.
	Same, 15 (red pencil)	300.
	Same, 20 (pencil)	300.
	Same, 70¢ (ms)	400.
B	PAID 2	1,000.
C	PAID 2	500.
	Same, revalued 5 (Type E)	750.
	Same, revalued 10 (Type G)*	750.
D	PAID 5	250.
E	PAID 5	150.
	Same, struck twice*	300.
	Same, revalued 10 (Type G)	750.

F	PAID 10	1,000.
G	PAID 10	150.
	Same, struck twice	250.
	Same, revalued 2 (Type C)	750.
	Same with 10 (Type L)	250.
H	2 [due]	500.
	Same, revalued PAID 2 (Type C)	500.
	Same [due], care Penny Post	3,500.
I	5 [due]	125.
	Same, due (pencil)	125.
J	6 [due - blockade]	2,500.
	Same, revalued 12 (pencil) [due]	2,500.
K	10 [due]	75.
	Same, Due (ms)	125.
	Same, due (blue) (ms)	200.
	Same, revalued 2 (Type H)	750.
L	HELD FOR POSTAGE	750.
M	SHIP, 12 (ms)*	4,000.
	Same, 22 (ms)	5,000.
	Same, 32 (ms)*	5,000.
N	STEAM-SHIP [no rate]	4,000.
	Same, 12 (pencil)	4,000.
	Same, 22 (pencil)	4,000.
	Same, 32 (pencil)	5,000.
O	STEAM-SHIP 22	7,500.
Pk	Integral "Paid" postmark, no rate, on newspaper	300.
Ms	Due 5 (red pencil)	150.
	Due (red pencil), 12 (blue pencil)	2,000.
	Due 20	200.
	Due 40 (pencil)	200.
	for 5 (red pencil)	200.
	Ford / 20¢	200.

Cheraw

A B

C D E

F H

CHERAW / S. C. (26 DC; 1861-64; black)

A	PAID [no rate - circular]	250.
	Same, 2 (ms)*	200.
B	PAID 5	175.
C	PAID 5	150.
D	PAID 10	150.
E	PAID 10	150.
F	PAID 10*	200.
G	DUE 5 [not illustrated]*	150.
H	15 [due]*	350.

Cherokee Iron Works

Cherokee Iron Works / S. C. (ms; 1861; black)

Ms	Pd 5	250.

Chester Court House

A B

C D

E F G

CHESTER C. H. / S. C. (26; 186-; blue)

CHESTER C. H. / S. C. (26 DC YD; 1861; black, red, blue)

A	PAID [no rate]	150.
	Same, 5 (ms)*	125.
	Same, 10 (ms)	125.
B	PAID 5*	200.
C	PAID 5	200.
D	PAID 10	200.
	Same (red)	200.
E	DUE, 20 (ms)	250.
F	DUE 10	200.
	Same (red)	200.
	Same (blue)	200.
G	10 (blue) [due]*	200.

Clayton's Mills

Clayton Mills S. C (ms; 186-; black)

Ms	10 Paid	250.

Clinton

CLINTON / S. C. (36 YD; 1861; black)

Ms	Paid 5	200.

Cokesbury

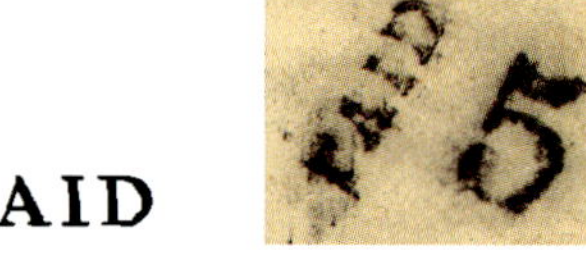

A B

C

COKESBURY / S. C. (25; 186-; black)
COKESBURY / S. C. (32; 186-; black)

A	PAID [no rate]*	200.
	Same, Out of Stamps (ms)*	500.
B	PAID 5	200.
C	PAID X*	300.
Ms	Pd 10 (blue pencil)	200.

Cold Spring

Cold Spring S C (ms; 186-; black)

Ms	Paid 10	250.

Columbia

A

B

C

D

E

F

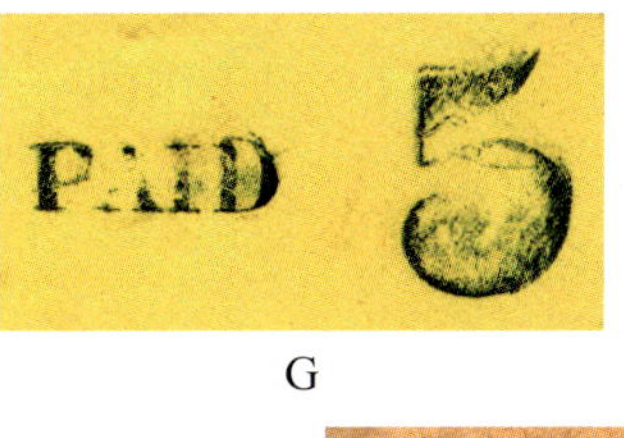

G

H

I

J

K

L

M

N

O

P

Q

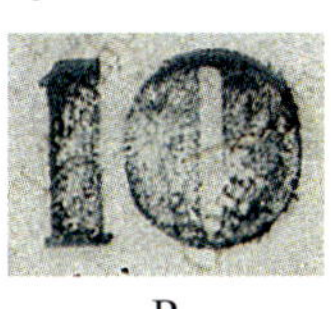

R

No postmark
COLUMBIA / S. C. (26 DC; 186-; blue)
COLUMBIA / S. C. (32; 1861-64; blue)
COLUMBIA / S. C. (33; 186-; blue)
COLUMBIA, S. C. / 5 cts. (30; 1861-62; blue)

A	PAID (blue) [no rate]	150.
	Same (blue), 5c Paid (pencil)	150.
	Same (blue), 10 (blue pencil)	150.
	Same (blue), 20 (red ms)	200.
	Same (blue), 30 (ms)*	500.
B	PAID (blue) [no rate]	150.
	Same (blue), 20 (ms)	250.
	Same (blue), 50 (blue pencil)	500.
C	PAID 2 (blue)	750.
D	2 PAID (blue) (integral postmark with altered rate)	1,000.
E	PAID 5 (blue)	200.
F	PAID 5 (blue)	200.
G	PAID 5 (blue)	250.
	Same (blue), with added 5 (blue) (Type *a*)	350.
H	PAID 5 (blue)	500.
I	PAID 5 (blue)	750.
J	PAID 10 (blue)	150.
K	PAID 10 (blue)	200.
	Same (blue), 10 struck twice	750.
L	PAID 10 (blue)	300.
M	PAID 10 (blue)	200.
N	5 (blue) [due]	150.
O	5 cts (blue) (integral postmark), with PAID (Type A)	250.
P	10 (blue) [due]	350.
Q	10 (blue) [due]	300.
R	10 (blue) [due]	250.
	Same (blue), Due (ms)*	200.
	Same (blue), Ford 10 (ms)	250.

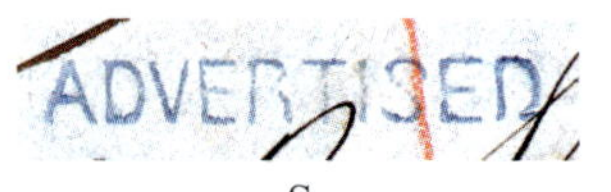

S

T

a

S	ADVERTISED (blue)	500.
T	MISSENT (blue)	500.
Ms	Due (red pencil) [no rate]	150.
	Due 5 (red pencil)	150.
	Due 20 (red pencil)	250.
	Fwrd 5	250.
	P O B / Free	250.

Conwayborough

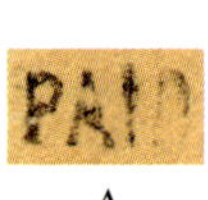
A

B

C

D

CONWAYBORO / S. C. (26; 186-; black)
CONWAYBOROUGH / S. C. (34; 186-; black)
CONWAYBOROUGH / S. C. (37; 1862; black)

A	PAID [no rate]	200.
	Same, 5 (ms)*	200.
B	PAID 5	250.
C	PAID 10	250.
D	10 [due]	250.

Coosawhatchie

Coosawhatchie (ms; 1861-62; black)

Ms	Pd 10	200.
	Due 5	200.
	Due 10	250.

Cowpen Branch

Cowpen Branch (ms; 1861; black)

Ms	Paid 10	200.

Cross Hill

Cross Hill (ms; 186-; black)
Cross Hill S C (ms; 1861; black)

Ms	Paid 5	200.
	Paid / 10	200.

Dacusville

Dacusville S C (ms; 1861; black)

Ms	Paid 5	250.
	Paid 10	250.

Darlington Court House

A

B

C

DARLINGTON C. H. / S. C. (34; 1861-64; black)

A	PAID, 10 (ms)*	200.
B	PAID 5	200.
C	PAID 10	250.

Donaldsville

Donnalsville S C (ms; 186-; black)

Ms	Pd 5	250.

Dorn's Gold Mines

A

DORN'S GOLD MINES / S. C. (?; 1863; black)

A	PAID 10	1,250.

Dorn's Mill

Dorn's Mill S C (ms; 186-; black)

Ms	PaId 10c	200.

Double Branches

Double Branches, S.C. (ms; 1863; black)

Ms	paid 10 cts*	200.

Due West Corner

Due West (ms; 186-; black)

Ms	Paid 10	200.

Ebenezerville

Ebenezerville, S C (ms; 1861; black)

Ms	Paid 5	250.

Echaw

Echaw S. C (ms; 1861; black)

Ms	Pd 5 cts	250.

Edgefield Court House

A  B

C

D  E

F

H

EDGEFIELD C. H. / S. C. (30; 186-; black)
EDGEFIELD C. H. / S. C. (33 DLC; 186-; black)

A	PAID, 10 (ms)	200.
B	PAID 2	500.
C	PAID 5	200.
D	PAID 10	250.
E	PAID 10	250.
F	PAID 15	500.
G	10 [due] [not illustrated]*	200.
H	ADVERTISED, 2 (ms)	500.
Ms	For 5	200.
	For 10	200.

Edisto Island

Edisto Island S C (ms; 186-; black)

Ms	5 [due]*	200.

Effingham

Effingham S C (ms; 186-; black)

Ms	Paid 10	200.

Ella's Grove

Ella's Grove (ms; 1864; black)

Ms	Paid 10	300.

Elton

Elton S. C. (ms; 186-; black)

Ms	Paid 10	250.

Equality

Equality S C (ms; 1861; black)

Ms	Pd 5	250.

Fair Forest

Fair Forest S C (ms; 186-; black)

Ms	Paid 10*	200.

Fair Play

Fair Play (ms; 1861; black)
Fair Play S C (ms; 186-; black)

Ms	Pai 5	250.
	Pd / 10	250.

Feasterville

Feasterville (ms; 186-; black)

Ms	Paid 10	250.

Five Forks

5 Forks (ms; 186-; black)

Ms	Paid 10	500.

Five Mile

A

FIVE MILE S C // PAID (27; 1861-63; black)

A	Postmark with integral PAID [no rate]	500.
Ms	Paid 10*	250.
	Due 10*	200.

Flat Shoals

Flat Shoals (ms; 1861; black)

Ms	Paid 5	250.

Flintville

Flintville S. C (ms; 1862; black)

Ms	Paid 5	250.
	Paid 10 cts	200.

Florence

A  B

FLORENCE / S. C. (25; 186-; black)

A	PAID [no rate]	250.
	Same, 5 (ms)*	250.
	Same, 10 (ms)*	250.
B	PAID 10	250.
Ms	Paid 10*	200.
	Due 10	150.

Floydsville

Floydsville S C (ms; 1862; black)

Ms	Pd / 5	200.

Fort Mill

Fort Mill (ms; 1862; black)
Fort Mill S C (ms; 1861-62; blue)

Ms	Paid 5	200.
	Paid / 5 (blue)	200.
	Pd / 10	200.

Fort Motte

Fort Motte S C (ms; 1861; black)

Ms	5 [due]	200.

Friendship

Friendship S. C. (ms; 1861-62; black)

Ms	Paid / 5 cts	200.
	Paid / 10	250.
	Due 5	200.

Frog Level

PAID 5

A

FROG LEVEL / S. C. (?; 1862; black)

A	PAID 5	250.

Fulton

Fulton S. C. (ms; 1862; black)

Ms	Paid 5	200.
	10 Paid	200.

Georgetown

A  B  C  D  E  F  G  H  I

GEORGETOWN / S. C. (32 YD; 1861-64; black)

A	PAID [no rate - drop letter]	350.
	Same, 10 (ms)*	200.
	Same, 25 (ms, blue)	500.
	Same, 40 (ms, blue)	500.
B	PAID [no rate]	350.
C	PAID 2	500.
D	PAID 5	250.
E	PAID 5	200.
	Same, revalued 10 (type H)	250.
F	PAID 10	250.
G	5 [due]	250.
H	10 [due]	150.
I	FORWARDED 10 [due]	250.
Ms	Due 5	200.

Gilchrist's Bridge

Gilchrist Bridge S C (ms; 1862; black)

Ms	Paid / 5	250.

Gillisonville

A

Gillsonville / S. C. (31; 186-; black)

A	PAID, 10 (ms)	300.
Pk	No rate marking	200.

Gladden's Grove

Gladdens Grove S C (ms; 186-; black)

Ms	Paid 10	250.

Glenn Springs

A

GLENN SPRINGS / S. C. (26; 1861; red)

A	PAID 5 (red)	200.

Golden Spring

Golden Spring S C (ms; 1861; black)

Ms	Paid / 5	250.

Gourdin

Gourdin S C (ms; 186-; black)

Pk	No rate [due]	250.

Gowensville

Gowensville S. C. (ms; 186-; black)

Ms	Paid 10	200.

Graham's Turn Out

B

C

GRAHAM'S TURN OUT / S. C. (31; 186-; black)

A	PAID 5 [not illustrated]*	200.
B	PAID 10	200.
	Same (blue)*	200.
C	PAID 10	200.
	Same (blue)*	200.

Grahamville

A

B

C

GRAHAMVILLE / S. C. (30; 1861-63; black)

A	PAID [no rate]	200.
	Same, 5 (ms)*	200.
	Same, struck twice, 5 (ms)	250.
	Same, 10 (ms)*	200.
B	PAID 2	500.
C	PAID 5	200.
D	PAID 10 [not illustrated]*	200.
Ms	Paid 5*	200.
	Due 5	150.
	Due 5 (pencil)	150.
	Due 10	150.
	Due 20*	200.

Graniteville

A

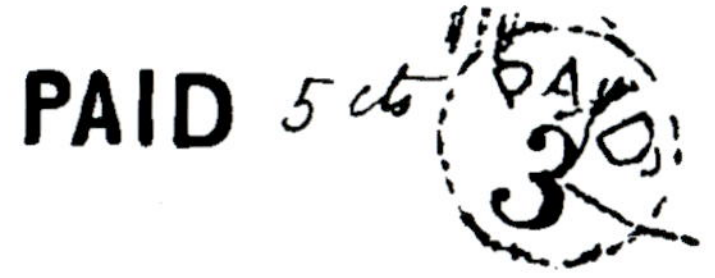

B

GRANITEVILLE / S. C. (36; 1861; black)

A	PAID, 5 (ms)	200.
	Same, 5 cts (ms)	200.
	Same, 10 (ms)*	200.
B	PAID, 5 cts (ms) over PAID 3 marking*	500.

Green Pond

Green Pond S. C. (ms; 1863-64; black)

Ms	Paid 10	150.
	Paid 10¢	150.
	Paid / 10¢	150.
	Due 10	125.

Greenville Court House

A

B

C

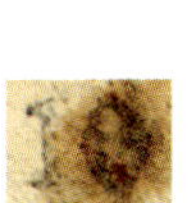

D

E

GREENVILLE C. H. / S. C. (26 DC; 186-; black)
GREENVILLE C. H. / S. C. (30; 186-; black)
GREENVILLE C. H. / S. C. (32; 1864; black)

A	PAID [no rate]	200.
B	PAID 5	200.
C	PAID 10	200.
	Same, revalued 20 (ms)	300.
D	10, Paid to P. M. (ms)	250.
E	10 [due]	250.
Ms	Paid 2	750.
	Due 2	500.
	10 Due*	200.
	forwd 10	200.

Greenwood

A

GREENWOOD / S. C. (30 YD; 1862; black, blue)

A	PAID 10 (blue)	250.
Pk	No rate	200.

Grove Station

Grove Station S C (ms; 186-; black)

Ms	Paid 10	250.

Guthriesville

Guthriesville (ms; 1861-62; black)

Ms	Pd 5	200.
	Pd 10	200.

Hamburgh

A

B

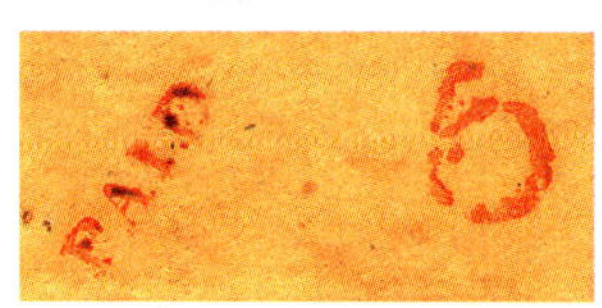

C

PAID 10

D

E

Hamburgh S C (ms; 1864; black)
HAMBURG / S. C. (30; 1861; black, red)
HAMBURG, S. C. / PAID (32; 186- black, red)

A	PAID [no rate] (on circular)	1.250.
	Same (red) [no rate] (on circular)	1,250.
B	PAID, 5	300.
C	PAID 5 (red)	300.
D	PAID 10 (red)*	250.
E	5 [due]	300.
Ms	Paid / 10	200.
	Drop Due 2	750.

[*]	symbol used after an item description to mean an unsupported listing
[–]	symbol used in place of value to mean insufficient information to assign a price

Hardeeville

A

B

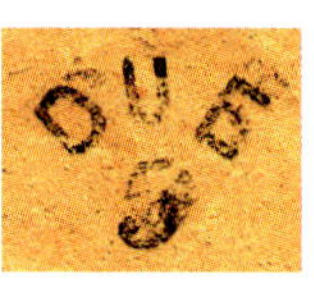

C

Hardeeville (ms; 1861-62; black)
Hardeeville So Ca (ms; 1861; black)
HARDEEVILLE / S. C. (32 YD; 1862-63; black)

A	PAID 5	200.
B	PAID 10	250.
C	DUE 5	200.
D	DUE 10 [not illustrated]*	200.
Ms	Pd 5	200.
	Due 5	200.

Hartsville

Hartsville S. C (ms; 186-; black)

Ms	Pd 10	250.

Hazlewood

Hazlewood (ms; 186-; black)
Hazelwood S C (ms; 186-; black)

Ms	Paid 10	250.

Hebron

Hebron S C (ms; 186-; black)

Ms	Paid*	250.

Highland Home

Highland Home S C. (ms; 186-; black)

Ms	10 cents paid	250.

Hodges

A

B

a

Hodges (ms; 1861; blue)
HODGES / S. C. (32 DLC; 1861; black)

A	PAID 5	250.
	Same, revalued 10 (Type *a*)	250.
B	PAID 10	250.
C	DUE (arc) / 5 [not illustrated]*	200.
Ms	Paid 5	250.

Honea Path

Honea Path S C (ms; 1861-; black)

Ms	Paid 10	200.

Hope Station

Hope Station S. C (ms; 1864; black)

Ms	Paid / 10 cts	250.

Horse Shoe

Horse Shoe S C (ms; 186-; black)

Ms	Paid 20 cts	250.

Jacksonborough Depot

Jacksonboro depot (ms; 1861; black)

Ms	Paid*	250.
	Pd 5¢	250.

Jackson's Creek

Jacksons Creek S C (ms; 1862; black)

Ms	Paid / 10	250.

Jefferson

Jefferson S C (ms; 186-; black)

Ms	Paid 10	250.

Jeffrey's Creek

A

Jeffries Creek S. C. (ms; 1862; black)

A	PAID 10	250.

Johnson

JOHNSON (SL in oval; 1861; black)

Ms	Due 5	250.

Johnsonville

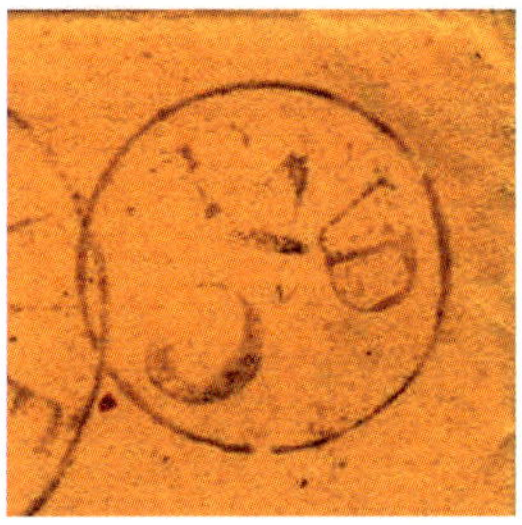

A

JOHNSONVILLE / S. C. (30; 1862; black)

A	PAID 5	250.

Jonesville

Jonesville S C (ms; 186-; black)

Ms	Paid 5	250.

Kingstree

Kingstree S C (ms; 186-; black)
KINGSTREE / S. C. (32; 186-; black)

A	PAID [not illustrated]*	250.
Ms	Paid / 5	200.
	Paid 10	200.
	Paid / 10	200.

Kirksey's Cross Roads

Kirkseys X Roads S. C. (ms; 1862; black)

Ms	Paid / 5	250.

Lancaster Court House

LANCASTER C. H. / S. C. (31; 186-; black)

Ms	Paid 2*	500.
	Paid 5*	200.
	Paid 10*	200.

Laurens Court House

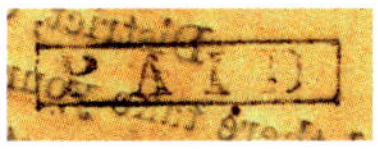

A  B

C

E

LAURENS C. H. / S. C. (25; 1862; black)
LAURENS C. H. / S. C. (32; 1861; black)

A	PAID, 10 (ms)	200.
	Same, 90 (ms)	750.
B	PAID 5	200.
C	PAID 5	200.
D	PAID 10 [not illustrated]*	200.
E	PAID X	350.

Lawtonville

Lawtonville S C (ms; 1863; black)
Lawtonville So Ca (ms; 1861; black)

Ms	Paid 10	200.
	5 [due]	150.

Leavenworth

A

LEAVENWORTH / S. C. (25; 186-; black)

A	PAID 10	250.

Leesville
Leesville S. C. (ms; 186-; black)

Ms	Paid 10	250.

Lenude's Ferry
Lenud's Ferry S C (ms; 186-; black)

Ms	Paid 5*	200.

Level Land
Level Land S C (ms; 186-; black)

Ms	Paid 5	250.

Lewisville
Lewisville S. C (ms; 186-; black)

Ms	Paid 10	250.

Lexington Court House

A

LEXINGTON / S. C. (30; 186-; black)

A	PAID [no rate]	250.
	Same, 5 (ms)	250.

Liberty Hill

A B

LIBERTY HILL / S. C. (31; 186–; black, brown)

A	PAID 5 (brown)	250.
B	PAID 10	250.
Ms	P 5*	200.

Lightwood Creek
Lightwood Creek S. C. (ms; 1864; black)

Ms	Paid 10 cts	200.

Lima
Lima, SC (ms; 1862; black)

Ms	Paid 10*	200.

Lott's
Lotts S. C (ms; 1861; black)

Ms	Paid 10	250.

Lowndesville
Lowndesville S C. (ms; 1861; black)

Ms	Paid 5*	200.

Lowrysville
Lowryville S. C. (ms; 186-; black)

Ms	Paid 5*	200.

Lynchburg
Lynchburg S C (ms; 186-; black)

Ms	Paid 10	200.

Manchester
Manchester (ms; 1861; black)
Manchester S C (ms; 186-; black)
Manchester S C (ms; 186-; black)

A	PAID, 10 (ms) [not illustrated]	200.
Ms	Paid / 5	200.
	Paid / 10	200.
	Due 5	150.

Manning

A

MANNING / S. C. (26; 1861; black)

A	PAID.10	250.
Ms	Pd 5	150.
	Pd / 5c	150.
	Ford 5c	200.
	Forwarded Due 5c	200.
Pk	No rate	200.

Marion Court House

A

B C

No postmark
MARION C. H. / S. C. (32; 1861; black, blue)

A	PAID [drop letter]	200.
B	PAID 5	250.
	Same (blue)	250.
C	PAID 10	350.
Ms	Farad 5 [Forwarded 5]	200.

Mars Bluff

A

MARS BLUFF / S C (36; 1861-62; black)

A	PAID 5	200.

Martin's Depot

Martins Depot (ms; 1862; black)

Ms	Paid 5	200.
	Paid 10	200.

Mayesville

Mayesville S C (ms; 1861; black)
MAYSVILLE / S. C. (34; 1865; black)

A	PAID (no rate) [not illustrated]	200.
Ms	Paid / 10	200.
	5 [due]	200.

McConnellsville

McConnellsville (ms; 1862; blue)

Ms	Paid 5 (blue)	250.

Merrittsville

Merrittsville S. C. (ms; 186-; black)

Ms	Paid 5*	250.

Midway

Midway S C (ms; 1861; black)

Ms	Paid 5	200.
	Paid 10	200.

Note: The single recorded example of the Paid 5 manuscript marking has the signature of the postmaster, John L. Sease, below it. The signature may have been intended as a control mark on a postmaster's provisional envelope. At this time there is insufficient information to support this conclusion.

Monticello

Monticello (ms; 1861; black)
Monticello S C (ms; 186-; black)

Ms	Paid 5	200.
	Paid 10	250.

Mount Carmel

A

MT. CARMEL / S. C. (?; 1862; black)

A	PAID 10	750.

Mush Creek

Mush Creek S C (ms; 1861; black)

Ms	Paid 5	250.
	Due 10	200.

New Centre

New Centre (ms; 186-; black)

Pk	No rate	200.

New Market

New Market S C (ms; 1863; black)

Ms	Paid 10	250.

Newberry Court House

A  B

C  D

E

NEWBERRY C. H. / S. C. (26 DC YD; 1862-64; black, red)
NEWBERRY C. H. / S. C. (30; 186-; red)

A	PAID, 10 (ms)	150.
	Same, 10 (pencil)	125.
B	PAID 5 (red)	200.
C	PAID 10	175.
D	PAID X	200.
	Same (red)	200.
E	MISSENT	250.
Ms	Paid 10*	150.

Ninety-Six

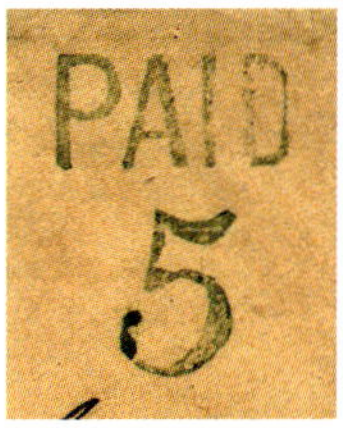

A

96 S C (ms; 186-; black)
Ninety 6 S C (ms; 186-; black)
NINETY SIX / S. C. (32; 1861; green)

A	PAID 5 (green)	250.
Ms	Paid 5*	150.
	Paid 10	150.
	Due 10*	150.
	5 [due]	150.

Oaklawn

Oaklawn S C (ms; 186-; black)

Ms	Paid 5*	200.

Oakway

Oakway S C (ms; 186-; black, blue)

Ms	Paid 5 (blue)	250.
	Paid 10	250.

Oconee Station

Oconee Station S. C. (ms; 1861; black)

Ms	Paid / 5	250.

Orangeburg Court House

A

ORANGEBURG / S. C. (26 DC YD; 1861; black)

A	PAID [no rate]	200.
Ms	2 [due] (drop letter)	500.

Packsville

Packsville S C (ms; 186-; black)

Ms	Paid / 10	250.

Pendleton

A B C D

PENDLETON / S. C. (26; 1861; blue, violet)
PENDLETON / S. C. (30; 1861; blue, violet)

A	PAID (blue), 2 (ms)	750.
	Same (blue), 10 (ms)	200.
B	PAID 5 (blue)*	200.
C	PAID 5 (blue)*	250.
	Same (violet)	250.
	Same (blue), revalued 10 (ms)	250.
D	PAID 10 (blue)	250.
	Same (violet)	250.
Ms	Due 5*	200.
	10 [paid (charge box marking)]	200.

Phoenix

Phoenix S C (ms; 1862; black)

Ms	Paid 5	200.
	Paid 10	200.

Pickens Court House

Pickens C H S C (ms; 1861; black)

Ms	Paid 5	250.

Pickensville

Pickensville S C (ms; 186-; black)

Ms	Pd 5	250.
	Paid 10	250.

Pineville

Pineville S C (ms; 1861; black)

Ms	Paid [no rate]	200.
	Paid 5	200.
	Paid 10	200.

Pleasant Hill

Pleasant Hill S C (ms; 186-; black)

Ms	Paid 5*	200.
	Paid 10	250.

Pleasant Mound

Pleasant Mound / S. C (ms; 1862; black)

Ms	Paid 5	250.

Plowden's Mills

Plowden's Mills S C (ms; 186-; black)

Ms	Paid 10	250.

Pocotaligo

A B C D E F

POCOTALIGO / S. C. (25; 186-; black)

A	PAID [no rate]	175.
	Same, 10 (ms)	175.
B	PAID 5	175.
C	PAID 10	200.
	Same, revalued 20 (ms)	350.
D	DUE 10	200.
	Same, revalued PAID 10 (Type C)*	250.
E	5 [due]	125.
F	10 [due]	150.
Ms	5 [due]	100.
	due 5 cts	100.

DC	double circle
YD	year date

POMARIA

A

B

Pomaria S C (ms; 186-; black)
POMARIA / – S. C. – (27; 1861-62; red)

A	PAID 5 (red)	250.
B	10, Paid (ms)	250.
Ms	Paid 10 (red pencil)	200.

POOLSVILLE

Poolsville P. O. (ms; 1862; black)

Ms	Paid 5	200.

RIDGE

Ridge S C (ms; 186-; black)

Ms	Paid 10	200.
Pk	No rate	200.

RIDGEWAY

A

RIDGEWAY / S. C. (32; 186-; black)

A	PAID 5	250.
Ms	Pd 5	200.
	Pd 10	200.

ROBERTVILLE

A

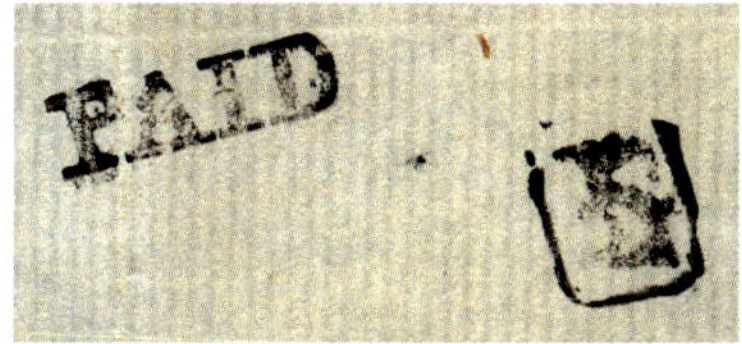

B

C

D

ROBERTVILLE / S. C. (29; 1862; black)

A	PAID, 5 (ms)	200.
	Same, 10 (red pencil)	200.
B	PAID 5	200.
C	PAID 10	250.
D	10 [due]	200.
Ms	Paid 2*	750.
	Drpt 2c	750.

ROCK HILL

A

Rock Hill (ms; 1862; black)
Rock Hill S C. (ms; 1862; black)
ROCK HILL / S. C. (25; 186-; black)

A	PAID [no rate]	200.
	Same, 5 (ms)	200.
	Same, 10 (ms)	250.
Ms	Paid 5*	200.
	Due 5 cts, missent & forwarded	200.

ROSSVILLE

Rossville / S C (ms; 1861; black)

Ms	Pd 5	250.

SAINT MATTHEWS

A

St MATTHEWS / S. C. (30; 1862; black, blue)

A	PAID, 5 (ms)	250.
Ms	5 [due]	200.

SAINT STEPHENS DEPOT

St. Stephens S C (ms; 186-; black)
St. Stephens Depot S C (ms; 186-; black)

Ms	Paid 10	250.

SALEM

Salem S C (ms; 1862; black)

Ms	Paid / 5	250.

SALUBRITY

Salubrity S C (ms; 1862; black)

Ms	Paid 5	250.

Sandersville

Sandersville S. C. (ms; 1861; black)

Ms	Paid 5	250.
	Paid 10*	250.

Sandover

Sandover S C (ms; 1861; black)

Ms	Paid [no rate]*	250.
	Pd 5	250.
	Pd 10	250.
Pk	No rate	200.

Sandy Flat

Sandy Flat S. C. (ms; 186-; black)

Ms	Paid [no rate]	200.
	Paid 5*	200.

Sandy Run

A

SANDY RUN / S. C. (32; 186-; black)

A	PAID 10	250.

Santuc

Santuc S. C. (ms; 1861; black)

Ms	Paid 5	250.

Selkirk

Selkirk S C (ms; 186-; black)

Ms	Paid 10	250.

Sawyer's Mills

Sawyer's Mills S C (ms; 1862; black)

Ms	Paid 5*	200.

Shallow Ford

Shallowford (ms; 1862; black)

Ms	Paid 5	250.

Shelton

Shelton (ms; 186-; black)

Ms	Paid / 10	250.

Silverton

Silverton S C (ms; 186-; black)

Ms	Ford Due 10	200.

Simpson's Mill

Simpsons Mills S C (ms; 186-; black)

Ms	Paid 10	250.

Simsville

Simsville S C (ms; 186-; black)

Ms	Paid 10	250.

Smith's Turn Out

Smith's T O S C (ms; 1864; black)

Ms	Paid 10	250.

Snow Creek

Snow Creek S C (ms; 1862; black)

Ms	Paid 5	250.

Society Hill

A

SOCIETY HILL / S. C. (30; 1861; black,)

A	PAID, 5 (ms)	200.
	Same, 10 (ms)	200.

Sparta

Sparta S C (ms; 1861-64; black)

Ms	Paid 5	250.
	Paid 10	250.

Spartanburg Court House

PAID

A

B

C

D

E

F

SPARTANBURG / S. C. (26 DC YD; 1862; black)
SPARTANBURG. C. H. / S. C. (32 YD; 1863; black)

A	PAID, 2 (ms)	750.
	Same, 10 (ms)*	200.
B	PAID 5	150.
	Same, struck twice	200.
C	PAID 5	150.
D	PAID 10	200.
E	PAID 10	200.
F	PAID 10	200.

Ms	Paid / 10 (blue)	200.
	due 10	200.

STATEBURGH

A  B

STATEBURGH / S. C. (26; 1861; black)

A	PAID 5	200.
B	PAID 10	250.

STOREVILLE

Storeville S C (ms; 186-; black)

Ms	Paid 10*	200.

STROTHER

Strother (ms; 1861; black)

Ms	Pd 5	250.

SUMMERVILLE

A

SUMMERVILLE / S. C. (32 YD; 1863; black)

A	PAID 10	250.

SUMTER

A  B

C  D

E  F

SUMTER / S. C. (32; 1864; black)
SUMTER / S. C. (32 YD; 1861-62; black)

A	PAID, 5 (ms)	200.
B	PAID 5	125.
C	PAID V*	250.
	Same, revalued 10 (type E)	300.
D	PAID 10	150.
	Same, revalued 2 (ms)	500.
E	PAID 10*	250.
F	10 [due]	250.
Ms	Due [10]	200.

SUNNY DALE

Sunnydale S. C (ms; 1861; black)

Ms	Paid 5	250.
Pk	No rate	250.

TABLE MOUNTAIN

Table Mtain S. C. (ms; 1863; black)

Ms	10 [due]*	200.

TAYLOR'S

Taylors S C (ms; 186-; black)

Ms	Paid / 10	200.

THOMASON'S CREEK

Thompson's Creek S C (ms; 1864; black)

Ms	Paid / 10	250.

TILLER'S FERRY

Tillers Ferry S C (ms; 1862; black)

Ms	Paid / 5	250.
	Paid / 10	250.

TIMMONSVILLE

A

TIMMONSVILLE / S. C. (30; 1861; black)

A	PAID 5	250.
Ms	Due 10 (blue pencil)	200.

TOWNVILLE

Townville S. C. (ms; 186-; black)

Ms	Paid 10	250.

TUCKERS POND

Tuckers Pond, S. C. (ms; 186-; black)

Ms	Paid 5 cts	250.

TUNNEL HILL

Tunnel Hill (ms; 1862; black)

Ms	Pd 10	250.

Twenty-Six

26 S. C. (ms; 186-; black)

Ms	Paid 10*	250.

Unionville

B  C  D

E  F

UNIONVILLE / S. C. (25; 1861; black)

A	5 over Paid 3 [not illustrated]*	200.
B	PAID, 5 (ms)*	150.
	Same, 10 (ms)	200.
C	PAID 5	250.
D	PAID 5	250.
E	PAID 10*	250.
F	PAID 10*	250.
Ms	Paid / 5	250.

Vance's Ferry

A

B

Vance's Ferry S.C. (ms; 186-; black)
VANCE'S FERRY / S. C. (30; 1861; black)

A	PAID 5	250.
B	PAID 10	200.
Ms	Paid*	200.
	5 [due]*	200.

Walhalla

A

Walhalla S C (ms; 186-; black)
Walhalla So Ca (ms; 186-; black)
WALHALLA / S. C. (25; 1861; black)

A	PAID, 5 (ms)	200.
	Same, 10 (ms)*	200.
Ms	Paid 10	150.
	Paid 20*	250.

Walkers

Walkers / S. C (ms; 1861; black)

Ms	Pd 5	250.

Walterborough

A  B

C  D

E

WALTERBOROUGH / S. C. (30; 1862; black, red-brown)

A	PAID, 20 (ms)	250.
B	PAID 5	250.
C	PAID 10*	250.
D	PAID 10	200.
E	10, Paid (ms)*	200.

Warrenton

Warrenton / S C (ms; 1861; black)

Ms	Paid 5 cts	250.

Warsaw

Warsaw S Ca (ms; 186-; black)

Ms	Paid 5	250.

Well Ridge

Well Ridge S C (ms; 1861; black)

Ms	Paid 5 ct	200.

Whetstone

Whetstone S C (ms; 1862; black)

Ms	5 Paid	250.

Whippy Swamp

Whippy Swamp S C (ms; 186-; black)

Ms	Paid*	250.
	Pd 5*	250.

White Hill

White hill S.C. (ms; 1863; black)

Ms	Paid 10*	250.

White Horse

White Hous S C (ms; 186-; black)

Ms	Paid / 10	250.

Wideman's

Wideman's S. C. (ms; 1861; black)

Ms	Paid 5 c	250.

Williamston

A B

WILLIAMSTON / S. C. (25; 1861-62; black)

A	PAID, 5 (ms)	250.
	Same, 10 (ms)	250.
B	PAID 5	250.
Ms	Pd 5*	200.

Willington

Willington S C (ms; 1861; black)
Willington So Car (ms; 1862; blue)

Ms	Paid / 5	200.
	Paid / 10	200.
	5 [due]	200.
	5 [due] (blue)	200.

Williston

A

WILLISTON / S. C. (25; 186-; black)

A	PAID 10	200.
Ms	Paid 10*	200.
	Due 10*	200.

Winnsborough

A B

C

D

E

WINNSBOROUGH / S. C. (33; 1861-63; black)

A	PAID 5	200.
B	PAID 10	250.
C	DUE 5	250.
D	DUE 5	250.
E	10, Due (ms)	175.

Wolf Creek

Wolf Creek, S. C. (ms; 186-; black)

Ms	Pd 10*	250.

Woodlawn

Woodlawn S. C. (ms; 186-; black)

Ms	Paid 10	250.

Wright's Bluff

Wrights Bluff (ms; 186-; black)

Ms	Paid / 5*	200.
	Paid 10	200.
	Due 10*	200.
Pk	No rate or paid marking	200.

Yonguesville

Yonguesville S C (ms; 186-; black)

Ms	Paid 10	200.

Yorkville

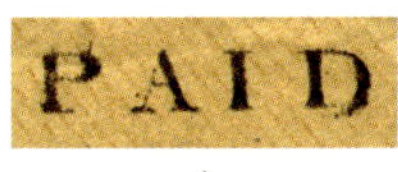

A

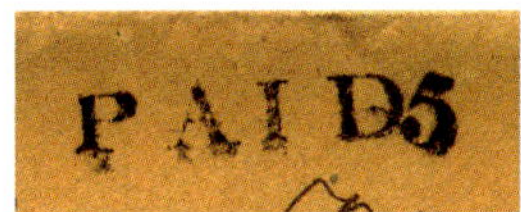

B

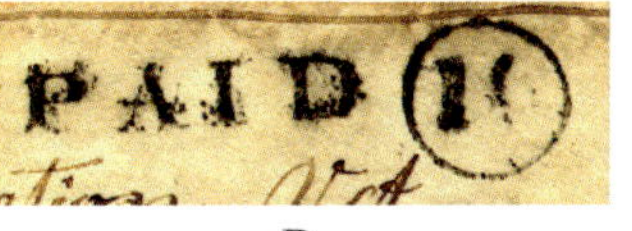
D

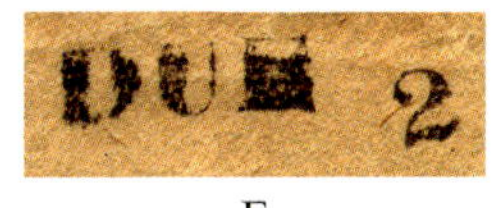

E

Yorkville S C (ms; 1862; black)
YORKVILLE / S. C. (31; 1862; black)

A	PAID [no rate]	150.
	Same, 10 (ms)*	150.
B	PAID 5	200.
C	PAID 5 (5 in circle) [not illustrated]*	250.
D	PAID 10	250.
E	DUE 2	500.
Ms	Paid 5	250.
	Paid 10	150.
	Paid 20	250.
	Due 10	125.

Young's Store

Youngs St (ms; 186-; black)
Young's Store S C (ms; 186-; black)

Ms	Pd 10	250.

Zeno

Zeno S C (ms; 186-; black)
Zeno S Car (ms; 1862; black)
Zeno So Ca (ms; 186-; black)

Ms	Paid 5	200.
	Paid 5 ct	200.
	Pd 5	200.
	Paid 10	200.
	Pd	200.

TENNESSEE

ADAMS' STATION

No postmark

Adams Station Ten (ms; 1861; black)

Ms	Paid 5	200.

ATHENS

A

B

C

ATHENS / TEN (26 DC YD; 1861-63; black)

A	PAID 5	300.
	Same, "5" struck twice*	500.
B	PAID 5 ★ C. S. A. ★*	500.
C	10 [Due]	250.
Ms	Due 5	250.

BARREN PLAIN

Barren Plain Ten (ms; 1861; black)

Ms	Paid 5*	200.

BEANS STATION

PAID 10

A

B

BEANS STATION / TEN. (26; 1862-63; black)

A	PAID 10	300.
B	DUE 10	300.
Ms	Due 10	250.

BEERSHEBA SPRINGS

BEERSHEBA / SPRINGS (32; 1861; black)

Ms	Paid 5	250.

BELFAST

Belfast Ten (ms; 1861; black)

Ms	10 Paid	200.

BELLSBURGH

Bellsburgh Tn (ms; 186-; black)

Ms	Paid 10	200.

BENTON

PAID 5

A

BENTON-TENN- (29; 1861; black)

A	PAID 5*	300.
B	PAID 10 [not illustrated]*	300.

BLOUNTSVILLE

PAID 
A

BLOUNTSVILLE / TENN. (33; 1861; black)

A	PAID 5	300.
Ms	Paid 5*	250.

BOLIVAR

A

B

BOLIVAR / Ten. (36; 1861-62; black, blue)

A	PAID 5*	300.
	Same (blue)	300.
B	PAID 10 (blue)	500.

BROWNSVILLE

A

BROWNSVILLE / Te. (34; 1861-62; black)

A	PAID 5	300.

BROYLESVILLE

A

BROYLESVILLE / TEN (26; 186-; brown)

A	PAID, 10 ms	300.

CALHOUN

Calhoun Ten (ms; 1863; black)

Ms	Due 10*	200.

CARTER'S CREEK

Carters Creek Ten (ms; 1861; black)

Ms	5 Paid	200.

Carter's Depot

CARTER'S DEPOT / TENN. (34; 1862; black)

Ms	Paid 5	300.
	Pd 5	300.
	Due 5*	250.
	Due 10	250.

Centre Point

Centre Point Tenn (ms; 1861; black)

Ms	Paid 5*	200.

Charleston

A

CHARLESTON / TENN. (30; 186-; black, brown)

A	10 (brown) [due]	300.
Ms	Due 10*	250.

Charlotte

CHARLOTTE / TEN. (36; 1861; blue, brown)

Ms	Paid 5*	250.
	Paid 10*	250.

Caution: The original postmarking device survived the war and has been used to make a number of excellent fakes.

Chattanooga

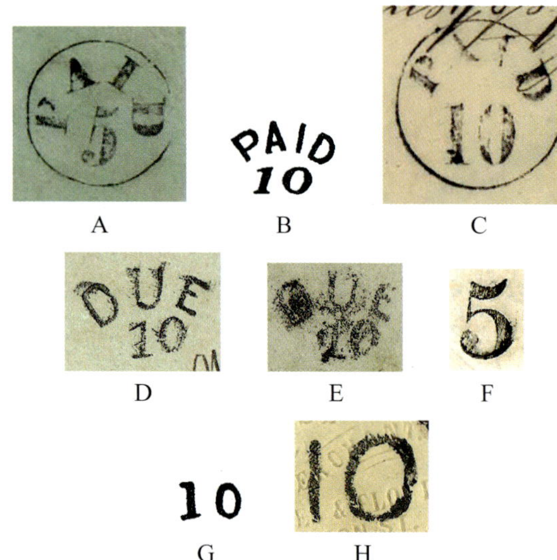

A B C D E F G H

CHATTANOOGA / Ten. (33 YD; 1861-62; black)
CHATTANOOGA / Ten. (33; 1862; black)
CHATTANOOGA / TENN. (32 YD; 1862; black)

A	PAID 5	300.
B	PAID 10*	300.
C	PAID 10	300.
D	DUE 10	250.
E	DUE 20 (altered 10)	500.
F	5 [due]	250.
	Same, Due (ms)*	500.
G	10 [due]	200.
H	10 [due]	200.
Ms	Due*	150.

Note: The rim of Type A marking was dented several times, resulting in an almost hexagonal shape as illustrated below.

Chewalla

A

CHEWALLA / Tenn. (31; 1861; brown)

A	DUE 5 (red brown)	300.

Chickamauga

Chickamauga Ten (ms; 1863; black)

Ms	Due 10	500.

Clarksville

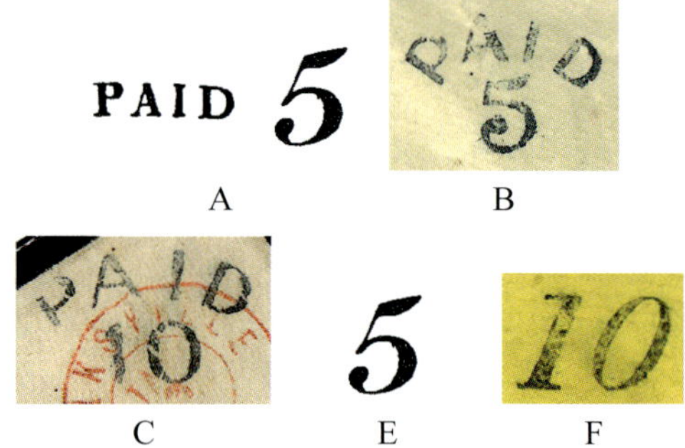

A B C E F

CLARKSVILLE / TEN (26 DC; 1861; red)
CLARKSVILLE / Ten. (32 YD; 1861; black, red, blue)

A	PAID 5*	300.
	Same (blue)*	300.
B	PAID 5 (blue)	300.
C	PAID 10 (blue)	500.
	Same (red)	500.
D	DUE 5 (red) [not illustrated]*	250.
E	5 (blue) [due]*	200.
F	10 [due]	250.

Cleveland

A

PAID 10

B

C

CLEVELAND / TEN (26; 1861; black)

A	Paid 5	300.
B	PAID 10	300.
C	Paid 10.	250.
Pk	No paid or rate marking	200.

Clinton

CLINTON / TEN (25; 186-; black)

Ms	Due 10	250.

Colliersville

A

COLLIERSVILLE / TEN (32; 1862; blue)

A	PAID 5 [altered 3]*	300.
	Same (blue), struck twice	500.
B	PAID, 5 (blue) [not illustrated]*	300.

Columbia

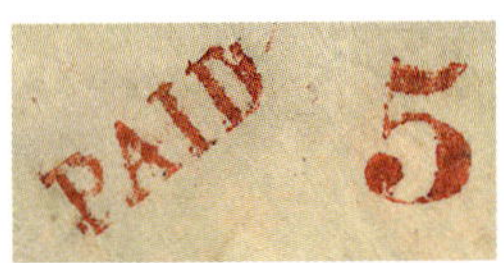

A

B

5

C

D

COLUMBIA / TEN (26 DC; 1861-62; black, red)
COLUMBIA / TEN (26 DC YD; 1862; black, red)

A	PAID 5	300.
	Same (red)	300.
B	PAID 10	300.
	Same (red)	500.
C	5 [due]*	250.
D	10, Paid (ms)	250.
	Same, [due]	250.
Ms	Due 10*	200.

Concord

CONCORD / TEN (36; 1862; black)
Ms Paid 5*

Cornersville

A

CORNERSVILLE / TEN (26; 1861; black)

A	PAID 5	500.
	Same, struck twice*	750.

Covington

COVINGTON / Te. (35; 1862; blue)

Ms	Due 5	300.
Pk	No paid or rate marking	250.

Cumberland Gap

C Gap Ten (ms; 1861; black)
Cumb Gap (ms; 1861; black)
Cumberland Gap (ms; 1862; black)

Ms	Paid 5	250.
	Paid 5 ct	200.
	Pd 5	250.

Cumberland Iron Works

CUMBERLAND IRON WORKS / TEN.
(32 DC; 186-; blue)

Ms	Paid 30¢	500.

Decherd

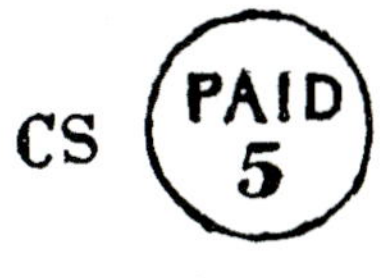

A

DECHERD / TEN (26; 1861; black)
Decherd Ten (ms; 1861-62; black)

A	PAID 5 with "CS"	500.
Ms	Paid 5*	200.

Dover

A

DOVER / TEN (32; 1861; black)

A	PAID 5	300.
	Same, without postmark	250.

Dresden

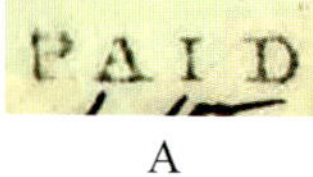

A

DRESDEN / TEN (26; 1861; black)

A PAID, 10 (ms) 300.

Ducktown

A B

DUCKTOWN / TENN. (32; 1861; black)

A PAID [no rate] 300.
B PAID 10* 300.
Ms Pd 5* 250.

Dyers Station

DYERS STATION / TENN. (29 DLC; 1861; black)

Ms Paid 5 300.
Paid 5 (pencil) 200.

Dyersburgh

A

DYERSBURGH / TENN. (30; 1862; black)

A PAID 5 500.

Elizabethton

A

ELIZABETHTON / TENN. (33 DLC; 1861-62; black)

A PAID 5 300.

Fayetteville

B

FAYETTEVILLE / Te. (33; 1861; black)

A PAID 5 [not illustrated] 300.
B 10 [due]* 250.
Ms Due 5* 200.

Florence

Florence Tenn (ms; 1861; black)

Ms Paid / 5 200.

Five Mile Branch

Five Mile Branch (ms; 1861; black)

Ms Paid 5* 200.

Franklin

A

FRANKLIN / TEN. (32; 1861; black)

A PAID 5 300.
Ms Due 5 250.
Due 10* 200.

Freedom

FREEDOM / TEN. (25; 186-; black)

Ms Paid 10 500.

Gallatin

A

B

GALLATIN / Ten. (33 YD; 1861-62; black)

A PAID 5 300.
B PAID 10 300.

Germantown

A

GERMANTOWN / TEN. (32; 186-; black)

A PAID, 5 cts (ms) 300.
Ms Paid 10* 300.

Goodlettsville

GOODLETTSVILLE / TEN. (?; 186-; black)

Ms Paid 5 300.

[*] symbol used after an item description to mean an unsupported listing

[–] symbol used in place of value to mean insufficient information to assign a price

Grand Junction

A B C

GRAND JUNCTION / TEN. (26; 1861; black)

A	PAID 5	300.
B	PAID 10	300.
C	5 [due]*	250.
Ms	Due 5	250.

Greenville

A C

GREENVILLE / Ten. (34; 1861-62; black)

A	PAID 5	300.
B	PAID 10 [not illustrated]*	300.
C	DUE 10	250.
Ms	Due 10	200.

Gum Grove

Gum Grove Tenn (ms; 1861; black)

Ms	Paid 5cts*	200.

Haynesville

Haynesville Tenn (ms; 186-; black)

Ms	Paid 5	200.
	Same (pencil)	150.
	Paid / 10	200.

Hickory Withe

HICKORY WITHE / TENN (36; 186-; black)

Ms	Pd 10	300.

Humboldt

Humboldt Tenn (ms; 1862; black)

Ms	Due 5	200.

Huntersville

Huntersville Tn (ms; 186-, black)

Ms	Due 10*	200.

Huntingdon

A

HUNTINGDON / Te. (30; 1861; black)

A	PAID 5	300.

Indian Mound

Indian Mound Tenn (ms; 1861; black)

Ms	Paid 10	200.

Jacksborough

A B

C

JACKSBOROUGH / TEN (25; 1861; black)

A	PAID, 5 (ms)	300.
B	DUE, 5 (ms)	300.
C	DUE 10	300.
Ms	Paid 10*	250.

Jackson

A B

C D

JACKSON / TEN. (31; 1861-62; black)

A	PAID, 10 (ms)	300.
B	PAID 5	300.
C	PAID 10	500.
D	5, Paid (pencil)	250.

Jessamine

Jessamine Ten (ms; 1861; black)

Ms	Paid 5, revalued 10 (ms)	300.

Jonesboro

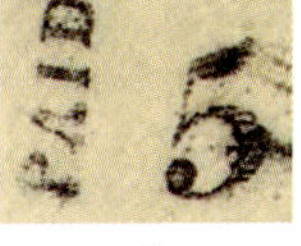

A B C

(PAID) 10 — D

PAID 10 — E

PAID 10 — F

JONESBORO / TEN (25; 1861-62; black, blue, brown)
JONESBORO / Te. (32; 1862-63; black, blue)
JONESBORO / Tenn (30; 186-; black)

A	PAID [no rate]	250.
B	PAID 5*	300.
C	PAID 5	300.
	Same (blue)	300.
D	PAID 10*	300.
E	PAID 10*	300.
F	PAID 10	300.
Ms	Due 3 (pencil)	300.
	Due 10	250.

Kingsport

A

KINGSPORT / TEN (26; 1862-63; red)

A	PAID (red), 10 (ms)	300.
Ms	Paid 10	250.

Kingston

A

KINGSTON / TEN (26; 1861-62; black, red)

A	PAID, 5 (ms)	300.
	Same, 10 (ms)	300.
Ms	Paid 5	250.
	Paid 10	250.
	Due 10	250.

Kinney's Store

Kinney's Store Tenn (ms; 1862; black)

Ms	Paid 10*	200.

Knoxville

A

PAID 5 — B

DC double circle
DLC double [outer] line circle
YD year date

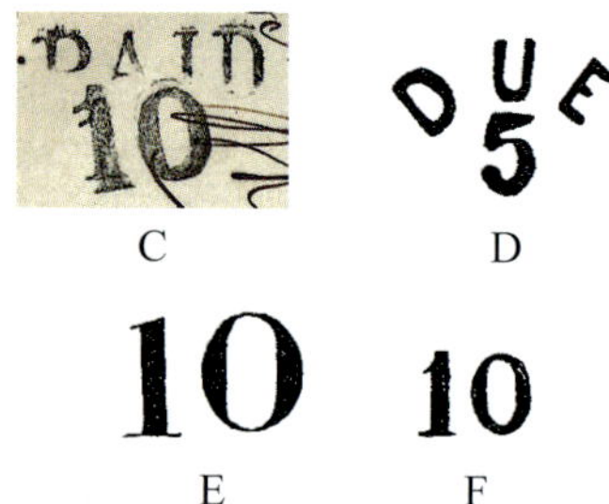

C D

10 — E

10 — F

KNOXVILLE / TEN (26 DC YD; 1861; black)

A	PAID 5	300.
B	PAID 5*	300.
C	PAID 10	300.
D	DUE 5	250.
E	10 [Due]*	200.
F	10 [Due]	200.
	Same, Due (ms)*	200.
Ms	Paid 5*	200.
	Paid 10*	200.
	Due 5	200.

Note: Some Knoxville markings are known on addressed covers without postmarks. Some postmarks do not have the year date.

Lebanon

PAID — A

PAID 5 — B

PAID 5 — C

PAID 10 — D

LEBANON / Ten. (32 YD; 1861-63; black)

A	PAID, 4 (ms)	1,000.
B	PAID 5	300.
C	PAID 5	300.
D	PAID 10*	300.
Ms	Due 5*	250.
	Due 10*	250.

Lenoir

Lenoir's Tenn (ms; 1861; black)

Ms	Paid 5	200.
	Due 5*	200.

Livingston

PAID 5 — A

PAID (5) — B

LIVINGSTON / Tenn. (31; 1862; black)

A	PAID 5*	300.
B	PAID 5*	300.
C	PAID 10* [not illustrated]	300.
Ms	Paid 5*	250.

Loudon

A

Loudon Tenn (ms; 186-; black)
LOUDON / TEN (26; 1862; black)

A	10 (Due)	250.
Ms	Paid 5*	250.
	Paid 10*	250.

Lynnville

A

LYNNVILLE / TEN (26; 1861; black)
LYNNVILLE / TENN (32; 186-; black)

A	PAID, 5 (ms)	300.
B	PAID 10*	300.

Madisonville

A B

MADISONVILLE / Te. (31; 1861-62; black)
Madisonville Te (ms; 186-; black)

A	PAID, 5 (ms)*	300.
B	PAID 5	300.
Ms	Paid 5	250.
	Paid 10	250.

Marble Hall

Marble Hall Tn (ms; 186-; black)

Ms	Paid 10	200.

Maryville

MARYSVILLE / TEN (26; 1862; black)

Ms	Paid 5	300.
	Due 10*	300.

Maynarsdville

Maynardville Tenn (ms; 186-; black)

Ms	Paid / 10	200.

McMinnville

A

MCMINNVILLE / Ten. (32; 1861-62; black)

A	PAID, 10 (pencil)	250.
B	Paid 5 [not illustrated]*	300.
Ms	Due 10	250.

Memphis

A B

C D

E F G

H I *a*

MEMPHIS / Ten. (31 YD; 1861-62; black)

A	PAID, 10 (ms)*	300.
B	PAID 5	300.
C	PAID 5	300.
D	PAID 10	500.
E	DUE [no rate]*	250.
F	DUE 2	1,500.
G	DUE 5	300.
	Same revalued "2" (Type *a*)*	1,000.
	Same revalued "DUE 10" (Type H)	500.
H	DUE 10	300.
I	20, Due (ms)	500.
Ms	Paid 10*	250.
	Due 2 c	750.
	Due*	200.

Note: The Type G and H markings were applied to much of the due mail that originated at other post offices but which passed through the Memphis post office enroute to its destination.

Montvale Springs

Montvale Springs Tenn (ms; 186-; black)

Ms	Pd 5*	200.
	5¢ Pd	200.

Morristown

MORRISTOWN / Ten. (31; 1861-62; black)

Ms	Paid 5	250.
	Paid 10*	300.
	Due 5*	250.
	Due 10	250.

Moscow

MOSCOW / TENN. (30; 1862; black)

Ms	Paid 10*	300.
	Due 5cts	250.

Mossy Creek

Mossy Creek T (ms; 1861; black)

Ms	Paid 5	IH

Mouth of Sandy

Mouth of Sandy Te (ms; 186-; black)

Ms	Paid 5*	200.

Murfreesboro

A B D

MURFREESBORO / Ten. (33 YD; 1861-62; black)
MURFREESBORO / TEN. (30 YD; 1862-63; black)

A	PAID, 5 (ms)	300.
	Same, 10 (ms)	300.
B	PAID [no rate]	250.
	Same, 5 (ms)	300.
	Same, 35 (ms)	500.
C	PAID 5 revalued 10 [not illustrated]*	300.
D	DUE10	250.
Ms	Paid 10*	250.

Nashville

A B

C D

F G *a*

NASHVILLE / Ten. (32 YD; 1861; blue)

A	PAID [no rate]	250.
	Same (blue), 4 (ms)	1,500.
	Same, 5 (ms)*	250.
	Same, 20 (ms)	500.
B	PAID 5 (blue)*	300.
C	PAID 5 (blue)	300.
	Same revalued "10" (Type *a*)	500.
D	PAID 5 (blue)	300.
E	PAID, 5 (C) (blue) [not illustrated]*	300.
F	PAID 10 (blue)	300.
	Same. "10" struck twice	500.
G	5 [due]	250.
	Same (blue), Due (ms)	300.
Ms	Due [no rate]*	200.
Pk	(No paid or rate marking)	200.

New Market

New Market Ten (ms; 1861; black)

Ms	Paid 5	200.

Nicojack

No postmark

Ms	Paid / 10	200.

Okolona [Ocolono]

A

OCOLONO / TENN (28 DC; 1861; black)

A	PAID 5	300.

Oregon

Oregon (ms; 186-; black)

Ms	Paid 10	200.

Panther Springs

Panther Springs Ten (ms; 1861; black)

Ms	Paid 5	200.

Paris

Paris Ten (ms; 1861; black)
PARIS / Ten. (33 YD; 1861; black)

Ms	Paid 5	300.
	Same (blue crayon)	300.

Philadelphia

Philadelphia Tenn (ms; 1862; black)
Phila Tenn (ms; 1862; black)

Ms	Paid 5	200.

Pulaski

A B C

PULASKI / Ten. (32; 1861-62; black)

A	PAID, 5 (ms)*	300.
	Same, 10 (pencil)	300.

B	PAID, 10 (ms)*	300.
C	PAID 5	300.
D	PAID 10 [not illustrated]*	300.
Ms	Due 5*	250.

Purdy

PURDY / TEN. (31; 1862; black)

Ms	Due 5*	300.

Riceville

Riceville Tenn (ms; 1861; black)

Ms	Paid 5	IH

Richland Station

Richland Sta / T (ms; 1861; black)
Richland Sta Ten (ms; 186-; black)

Ms	Paid 5	200.

Rockford

ROCKFORD / TEN (?; 1861; black)

Ms	Paid 5	250.

Rogersville

A 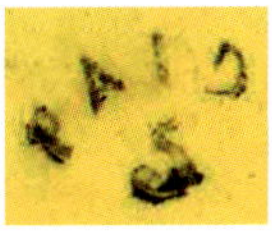 B 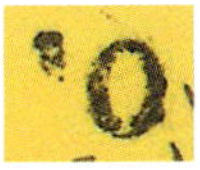 C

ROGERSVILLE / TEN. (32; 1861-62; black)

A	PAID 5	300.
B	PAID 5	300.
	Same struck twice	500.
C	10 (due)	250.

Rossville

Rossville Te (ms; 1861; black)

Ms	Paid 5*	250.

Russellville

A  B  C

RUSSELLVILLE / TENN (36; 1861-62; black)

A	PAID [no rate]	300.
B	PAID 10*	300.
C	10 [due]	250.
Ms	Due 10*	200.

Rutledge

Rutledge Tenn (ms; 1861; black)

Ms	Paid 5*	200.

Salisbury

Salisbury Tenn (ms; 186-; black)

Ms	Paid 5	250.

Savannah

SAVANNAH / TEN (25; 1861; black)

Ms	Paid 10	250.

Shelbyville

A  B  C

D 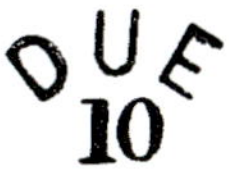 E

SHELBYVILLE / TEN (26 DC YD; 1862; black)
SHELBYVILLE / Te. (34; 1861-63; black)

A	PAID [no rate]	200.
B	PAID 5	250.
C	PAID 10	300.
D	DUE [no rate]	200.
	Same, Due 10 (ms)*	250.
	Same, 5 (ms)*	200.
E	DUE 10	250.
Ms	Due 10	200.

Showns Crossroads

Showns X Roads Ten (ms; 186-; black)

Ms	Paid 5	200.

Smyrna

A

SMYRNA / TENN (32; 186-; black)

A	PAID 5	300.

Somerville

A

SOMERVILLE / TEN (26 DC; 1861; black)

A	PAID, 10 (ms)	300.

Sparta

A

SPARTA / TEN. (36; 186-; black)

A	PAID 5*	300.
Ms	5 [due]*	250.
	10 [due]*	250.

Spring Creek

PAID

A

Spring Creek Ten (ms; 1861; black)

A	PAID, 5 (ms)	300.

State Line

State Line Ten (ms; 1861; black)

Ms	Due 10	200

Strawberry Plains

A

STRAWBERRY PLAINS / TEN (26; 1861; black)
STRAWBERRY PLAINS / Tenn. (30; 186-; black)

A	DUE 10	300.
Ms	Paid 5*	250.
	Pai[d] 5	250.
	Pd 5	250.

Sweet Water

SWEET WATER / TEN (25; 186-; black)

Ms	Due 10	250.

Sycamore

Sycamore (ms; 186-; black)

Ms	Due 10*	200.

Tazewell

PAID

A B

PAID 10

C D

TAZEWELL / TEN. (25; 1861-62; black)

A	PAID, 20 (ms)	500.
B	PAID 5	300.
C	PAID 10	300.
D	10 [due]	250.
Ms	Paid 10	250.

Trammel

Trammel Tenn (ms; 1862; black)

Ms	Due 5	200.

Triune

A

TRIUNE / TEN (30; 186-; brown)

A	PAID 10 (brown)	300.

Troy

TROY / TEN (25; 186-; black)

Ms	Paid 10	300.

Tullahoma

PAID

A B

C D

TULLAHOMA / Ten. (31 YD; 1862; black)
TULLAHOMA / TEN (36; 186-; black)

A	PAID, 20 (ms)	500.
B	PAID 10	300.
C	PAID 10	300.
D	DUE 10	300.
Ms	Due 10	250.

Tyner

Tyner Ten (ms; 1861; black)
TYNER [TENN] (? SL; 186-; black)

Ms	Paid / 5	200.
	Paid 10	IH
	Due 10	200.

DC	double circle
DLC	double [outer] line circle
IH	used in place of listing value when the item is held by an institution

Union City

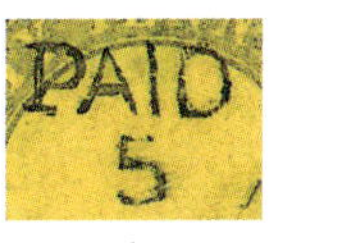
A

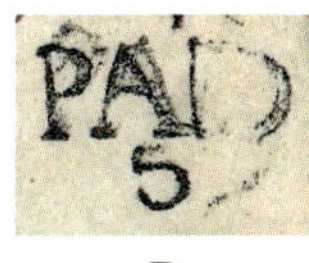
B

C

D

U City Ten (ms; 1861; black)
UNION CITY TENNESSEE (negative letters with starburst at bottom) (38; 1861-62; black)

A	PAID 5	500.
B	PAID 5	500.
C	PAID 5	500.
	Same revalued 10 (ms)	500.
D	5 [due]	300.
Ms	Paid [no rate]	300.
	Same (pencil) [no rate]	250.
	Pd / 5	300.
	Paid 10*	300.
	5 [due]	300.

Note: Some strikes of the Type A marking show a partial circle around the markings.

University Place

University Place Tenn (ms; 1861; black)

Ms	Paid 10*	200.

Vernon

Vernon Tenn (ms; 1861; black)

Ms	Paid 10	200.

Watertown

Watertown Ten (ms; 1861; black)

Ms	Forwd pd 5	200.

Waverly

A

WAVERLY / TENN (32; 186-; black)

A	PAID 5	IH

Whitesburg

WHITESBURG / Tenn. (34; 186-; black)

Ms	Paid 5*	300.

Winchester

A

WINCHESTER / Ten. (34; 1861; blue)

A	PAID 5 (blue)	300.
Ms	Due 10*	250.

Yellow Store

Yellow Store Tenn (ms; 1861; black)

Ms	Paid 5 cts	200.

Zollicoffer

A

Zollicoffer (ms; 186-; black)
ZOLLICOFFER / TENN (31; 1862; black)

A	DUE 10	300.
Ms	Paid 10	300.
	Due 10*	300.

TEXAS

Alleyton [Alleton]

A

B

C

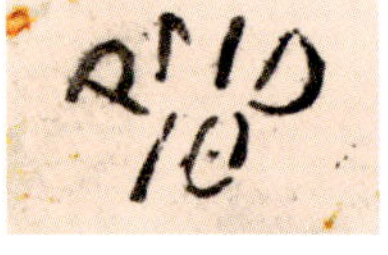
D

E

Alleton (ms; 1863; black)
ALLETON / TEX (25 DC; 1862-63; black)

A	PAID 5	400.
B	PAID 10	400.
C	PAID 10	500.
D	PAID 10	500.
E	DUE, 10 (ms)	400.
Ms	Paid 10	300.

Note: The "10" in the Type D marking is recorded at various angles in relation to the "PAID" but the top always slopes to the right.

Alto

A

ALTO / TEX (26; 1862-64; black)

A	PAID, 5 (ms)	500.
	Same, 10 (ms)*	500.
Ms	Due 5	400.
	Paid 10 (pencil)	400.
	Pd 10 (pencil)	500.
	Due 10	400.

Anderson

A

B

C

ANDERSON / Tex. (35; 1861-65; black)

A	PAID [no rate]	300.
	Same, 10 (ms)	300.
	Same, 20 (ms)*	750.
B	PAID [no rate]*	300.
C	PAID 5	300.
Ms	Paid [no rate] (pencil)	300.
	Paid 5*	300.
	Paid 10	300.
	Paid 10 (pencil)	300.
	Paid 20*	750.
	Due 10	300.

Athens

Athens Texas (ms; 1862-64; black)
Athens, Tex (ms; 1865; pencil)

Ms	Paid 5	IH
	Paid 10	IH
	Paid 10 (pencil)	300.
	Paid / 10	300.

Austin

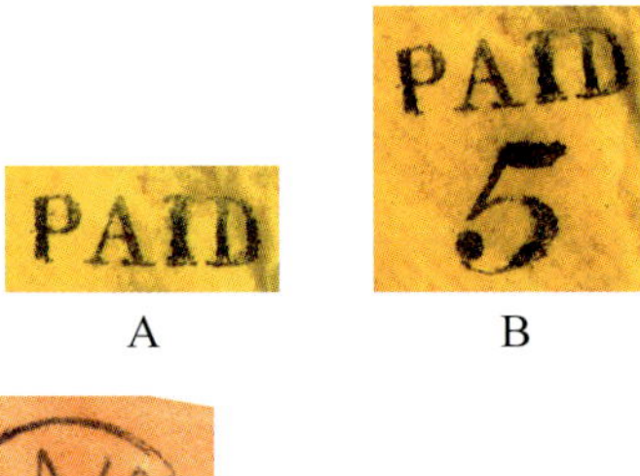
A B

C

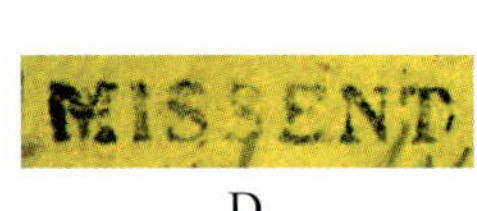
D

AUSTIN / TEX (26 DC YD; 1861-62; black)
AUSTIN / TEX (26 DC; 1861-64; black)

A	PAID [no rate]*	300.
	Same, 10 (ms)	300.
	Same, 20 (ms)*	750.
	Same, 40 (ms)	750.
B	PAID 5	300.
C	PAID 6 (triple rate circular)	750.
D	MISSENT	750.
Ms	Paid 10	300.
	Due 5	300.

Bandera

Bandera Tex (ms; 1861-64; black)

Ms	Paid 15	500.

Bastrop

A

B

C

BASTROP / TEXAS (32; 1861-64; black)

A	PAID 5	300.
B	PAID 10	300.
C	10, Due (ms)	300.

Beaumont

A

Beaumont Tex (ms; 1862-64; black)
BEAUMONT / TEX (28 NOR; 1862-63; black, red)

A	PAID [no rate]	300.
	Same, Way 10 (ms)	750.
Ms	Paid 10	300.
	Due 5	300.

Belleview

PAID

A

BELLEVIEW / TEX (37; 1861; brown)

A	PAID, 5 (ms)	300.

Belleville

PAID

A

BELLEVILLE / TEX (32; 1861-63; black)

A	PAID, 10 cts (ms)	300.

Belmont

Belmont Texas (ms; 1862; black)

Ms	Paid 5	300.
	Paid 10	300.

Belton

PAID PAID 5

A  B

PAID 10

C

Belton Texas (ms; 1861; black)
BELTON / TEX. (32; 1862-64; black)

A	PAID [no rate]	300.
B	PAID 5	300.
C	PAID 10	300.
Ms	Paid 10c	300.
	Due 10	300.

Black Oak

Black Oak Tex (ms; 1864; black)

Ms	Paid 10c	300.

Blanco

Blanco Tex (ms; 1861-62; black)

Ms	Paid 10	300.

Bonham

BONHAM / TEXAS. (30; 1861-64; black)

A	PAID [no rate] [not illustrated]	300.
	Same, Paid 10 (ms)	300.
B	10 (c) [due] [not illustrated]	300.
Ms	Paid 5	300.
	Paid 10 (pencil)	300.
	Paid 10¢	300.
	Paid 20*	500.
	Due 5	300.
	Due 10 (pencil)	300.
	20 [due]*	500.

Boston

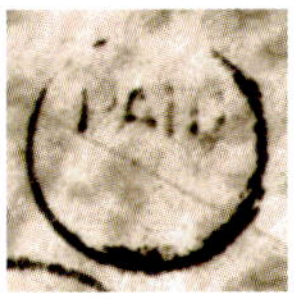

A  B

C  D 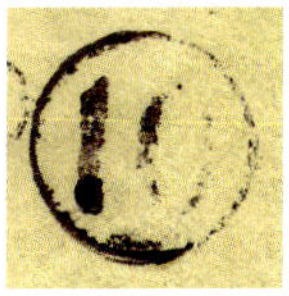 *a*

BOSTON / TXS (31; 1861-63; black)

A	PAID [no rate]	300.
B	PAID 5	400.
	Same, revalued “10” (Type a)*	500.
	Same, Due 5 (ms)	500.
C	PAID 10	400.
D	5 [due], revalued “Pd 10” (ms)	750.
Ms	Paid 10cts	300.

Brazoria

PAID

A  B

BRAZORIA / TEXAS (32; 1861-64; black)

A	PAID [no rate]	300.
	Same, 10 (ms)*	400.
B	PAID 10	500.
Ms	Paid 10*	300.

Brazos St. Jago

PAID 10

A

BRAZOS ST JAGO / TEXAS (28 DC; 186-; black, blue)

A	PAID 10	400.
	Same (blue)*	500.

Brenham

A

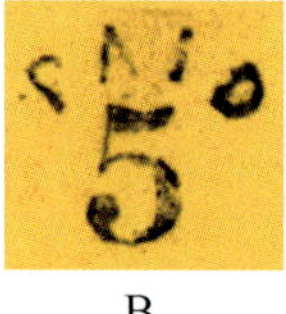

B

C

D

BRENHAM / Tex (32; 1861-62; black)
BRENHAM / TEXAS (32 YD; 1861-64; black)

A	PAID, 20 (ms)	750.
B	PAID 5	300.
C	PAID 10	300.
D	10 [due]	300.
Ms	Paid 10 (pencil)	300.

Note: The "PAID" and rate markings in the Type B and C markings are separate markings.

Bright Star

Bright Star Texas (ms; 1863; black)

Ms	5 Paid	300.
	10 Paid	IH

Brownsville

A

B

C

BROWNSVILLE / Tex. (29 NOR YD; 1861-65; black)
BROWNSVILLE / Tex. (29; 1861-63; black)
BROWNSVILLE / TXS. (33; 1861; black)

A	PAID 5	300.
B	PAID 10	300.
C	PAID 10	300.
Ms	Paid 5*	300.
	Paid 10*	300.
	Paid 30	500.

Bryants Station

Bryants Station Tx (ms; 1864; black)

Ms	Paid 10	300.

Burkeville

Burkeville (ms; 1861-64; black)

Ms	Paid 10	300.

Burnet [Burnett]

Burnet Tex (ms; 1862; black)
Burnett Texas (ms; 1864-65; black)

Ms	Paid [no rate]	300.
	Paid / 5	300.
	Paid 10	300.

Butler

Butler Texas (ms; 1861; black)

Ms	Due [no rate]	300.

Caldwell

PAID

A

B

PAID 10

C

CALDWELL / TEX. (33; 1862-64; black, blue)
CALDWELL / TXS (33 NOR; 186-; red)

A	PAID, 5 (ms)*	300.
B	PAID 5 (blue)	500.
C	PAID 10 (red)	500.
Ms	Paid 10	300.

Cameron

A

CAMERON / TEX (24; 1861; black)
CAMERON / TEX (30; 1864; black)

A	PAID 5 (altered PAID 3)	300.

Camp Stockton

A

CAMP STOCKTON / TEXAS (31; 1861; blue)

A	DUE 5 (blue)	500.

Caney

Caney Tex (ms; 1861; black)

Ms	Paid 5	300.

NOR	no outer rim
YD	year date

Capt's Mill

Capt's Mill Texas (ms; 1861-62; black)

Ms	Paid / 5	300.

Carthage

CARTHAGE / TEX (32; 1861-63; black)

Ms	Paid 10	300.

Castroville

PAID

A

CASTROVILLE / TEX. (36; 1861-62; green)

A	PAID (green) [no rate]*	500.
	Same (green), 10 (ms)	750.

Cedar Grove

5

A

CEDAR GROVE / Ts. (29; 1861-62; black)

A	5, Paid (ms)	300.
Ms	Paid 10	300.

Chapel Hill

PAID A; PAID B; PAID 5 C; PAID 5 D; PAID 10 E; PAID 10 F; PAID 10 G;  5 H

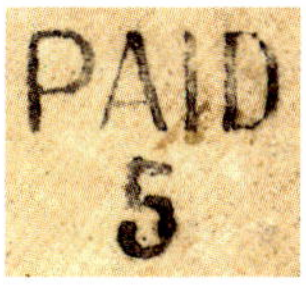

CHAPEL HILL / Tex (32; 1861-64; black)

A	PAID [no rate]*	300.
B	PAID, 10 (ms)	300.
C	PAID 5	500.
D	PAID 5	300.
E	PAID 10	500.
F	PAID 10	300.
G	PAID 10	300.
H	5 [due]	300.
	Same, Due 5 (ms)	300.

Charleston

Charleston Tex (ms; 1861; black)

Ms	Paid / 5 cts	300.

Cherino

Cherino Texas (ms; 1861-62; black)

Ms	Paid 10	300.

Clarksville

10 PAID B; PAID 10 C; 10 D; DUE 10 E

CLARKSVILLE / Tex. (34; 1861-64; black)

A	PAID 5 [not illustrated]*	NR
B	PAID 10	300.
	Same, struck twice	750.
C	PAID 10*	500.
D	10 [due]	300.
E	DUE 10	300.
Ms	Due 5	300.
	Due / 5	300.
	Due / 10	300.

Clinton

PAID A; PAID 5 B; PAID 10 C

CLINTON / TEX (32; 1861-62; black)
CLINTON / TEX. (*sans serif*) (31; 1863; black)

A	PAID, 10 (ms)	300.
B	PAID 5*	300.
C	PAID 10	300.
Ms	5 [due]	300.

Cold Spring

PAID PAID 10 

A B C

COLD SPRING / TEX (25; 1862-64; black)

A	PAID, 5 (ms)	500.
B	PAID 10	500.
C	DUE 10	300.

Colita

Colita Texas (ms; 1861-63; black)

Ms	Paid 5	300.

Columbia

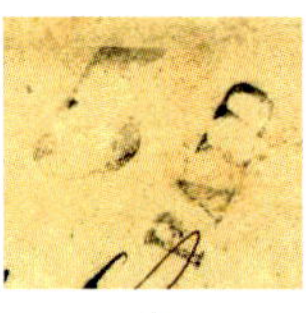

PAID 10 10

A B *a*

COLUMBIA / Tex. (35; 1862; black)

A	PAID 5	500.
	Same, revalued "10" (Type *a*)	750.
B	PAID 10	300.
Ms	10 [due]	250.

Columbus

A B

Columbus Texas (ms; 1861; black)
COLUMBUS / TEX (26 DC; 1861-63; black)
COLUMBUS / TEXAS (32; 1861-63; black)

A	PAID 10	300.
B	PAID 10	300.
Ms	Paid 10	300.

Comfort

A

COMFORT / TEX^{S} (31 YD; 1863-65; black)

A	PAID 10	500.

Concrete

CONCRETE / TEX (25; 1863-64; black, red)

Ms	Paid 10	300.

Corpus Christi

A B

CORPUS CHRISTI / TEX (25; 1861-65; black)

A	PAID, 5 (ms)	500.
	Same, 10 (ms)	500.
B	5 [due]	300.

Corsicana

CORSICANA / TEX (26; 1862; black)
CORSICANA / TEX. (36 SC; 1862-63; black)

Ms	Paid 10	500.

Cotton Gin

Cotton Gin Tex (ms; 1863; black)

Ms	Paid 10	300.

Courtney

A

COURTNEY / TEX. (32; 1862-63; black)

A	PAID [no rate]	300.
	Same, 5 (ms)*	500.
Ms	Paid [no rate]	500.
	Paid 10	500.

Covington

Covington Texas (ms; 1863; black)

Ms	Paid 10	300.

Coxville

Coxville (ms; 1862; black)
Coxville Texas (ms; 1862; black)

Ms	Paid / 5	500.
	Pd / 5	500.

Crimea

Crimea Tex (ms; 1863; black)

Ms	Paid 10	300.

Crockett

A B

Crockett Tex (ms; 1863-65; black)
CROCKETT / TEXAS (32; 1861-65; black)

A	PAID 5	500.
B	PAID 10	500.
Ms	Paid	IH

	Paid 10	300.
	Paid / 10	300.
	Due 5	300.

Cunningham's

Cunningham's Texas (ms; 1861-63; black)

Ms	5 [due]	500.

Daingerfield

A  B

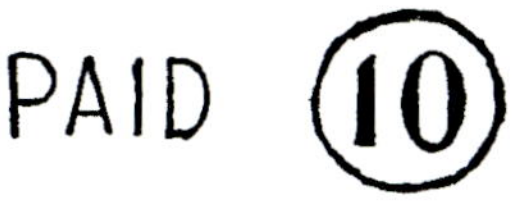

C

DAINGERFIELD / TEX (33; 1861-62; black)

A	PAID 5	300.
B	PAID 5	300.
C	PAID 10*	300.
Ms	Due 10*	250.

Dallas

Dallas Tex (ms; 1864-65; black)
Dallas Texas (ms; 1862; black)
DALLAS / TEX (25; 1861; black)

Ms	Paid 5*	400.
	Pd 5	400.
	Pd 10	400.
	Due 10	300.
	ford 5	300.

Dayton

Dayton Tex (ms; 1861; black)

Ms	Paid 5*	300.

Decatur

Decatur (ms; 1861; black)

Ms	Paid 5	300.

Dixie

Dixie (ms; 1863; black)

Ms	Paid 10*	300.

Douglass

Douglass Tx (ms; 1862-64; black)

Ms	Paid 5	IH
	Paid 10	IH
	Due 10	IH

Eagle Lake

Eagle Lake (ms; 1861-65; black)

Ms	Pad 10	300.
	P 10	300.

Eagle Pass

A  B

EAGLE PASS / TEX (30; 1862-65; black)

A	PAID [no rate]	500.
B	10 [due]*	500.
	Same, unpaid (ms)	500.
Ms	Paid 10	500.

El Paso

A

EL PASO / TEX (32; 1862-63; black)

A	PAID [no rate]	500.
	Same, 10 (ms)	750.
Ms	Due 10	750.

Elkhart

Elkhart Tex (ms; 1865; black)

Ms	Post Office Business / T W Daily P M	IH

Elysian Fields

Elysian Fields Tex (ms; 1861-62; black)

Ms	Due 10	300.

Eutaw

EUTAW / TEX (22; 1861; black)

A	PAID (box), 20¢ (ms) [not illustrated]	300.

Fairfield

A  B

a

Fairfield Tex (ms; 1862-64; black)
FAIRFIELD / TEX (26 YD; 1861-62; black)
FAIRFIELD / TEX (26; 1862; black)

A	PAID 5	500.
	Same plus "10" Type (a)	750.
B	PAID 10	500.
Ms	Paid 5	300.
	Paid 10	300.
	Paid / 10	300.

Farmersville

Farmersville Tex (ms; 1864; black)

Ms	Paid / 10	300.

Fincastle

Fincastle Tex (ms; 1861; black)

Ms	Paid 10	300.

Fort Clark

FORT CLARK / TEX (25; 1861-62; black)

Ms	Paid 5 cts	500.
	Paid 10	500.

Fort Davis

A B

FORT DAVIS / TEXAS (33 YD; 1861-62; black)

A	PAID 5	500.
B	DUE 10	500.

Fort Worth

FORT WORTH / TEX (32; 1861; black)

Ms	Pd 10	500.

Fredericksburg

A B

FREDERICKSBURG / TEX (30; 1861; black)
FREDERICKSBURGH / TEX (36; 1861-64; black)

A	PAID 5	300.
B	PAID 10	300.

Galveston

A

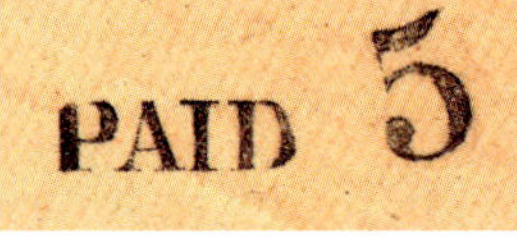

B

C D

E F G

GALVESTON / TEX (25 DC YD; 1861-64; black, blue) [YD replaced with slug in 1864]
GALVESTON / TEX (32; 1862; blue)

A	PAID blue [no rate]	300.
B	PAID 5	300.
C	PAID 10	300.
D	PAID 10*	500.
E	PAID 20*	750.
F	5 [due]	300.
	Same, revalued "10" (Type G), Due (ms)	500.
G	10 [due]	300.
	10 (blue) [due]*	500.
	Same, Due (ms)	300.

Georgetown

GEORGETOWN / Tex. (32; 1861-64; black)

Ms	Paid 10	300.
	Paid 25*	750.
	Paid 30	750.

Gillelands

Gillelands Creek Texas (ms; 1861; black)

Ms	Paid 10 cents	300.

Gilmer

A

GILMER / Tex (36; 1862-63; black)

A	PAID 10	500.
Ms	Due 5*	400.

Goliad

A B

GOLIAD / TEX (25; 1861; black)
GOLIAD / TEX (22 NOR; 1861; black, red)

A	PAID, 5 (ms)*	500.

B 5 [due] 500.
Same (red) 500.
Ms 15 [due] 500.

Golindo

Golindo Tex (ms; 1864; black)
Ms Paid 10 300.

Gonzales

PAID

A

GONZALES / TEX. (25 DC; 1861-65; black)
A PAID [no rate]* 500.
Same, 30 (ms) 750.
Ms P O. B / Free IH

Greenville

PAID

A

GREENVILLE / TEX. (36; 1861-63; black)
A PAID [no rate] 300.

Gulf Prairie

Gulf Prairie P.O. (ms; 1864; black)
Ms Due 10 300.
Due 10c 300.

Hackberry

Hackberry (ms; 1865; black)
Ms Post Office / Business IH

Hallettsville

A B

HALLETTSVILLE / TEX. (30; 1862-63; black)
A PAID [no rate] 500.
Same, 5 (ms) 500.
Same, 10 (ms)* 500.
Same, 20 (ms)* 750.
B DUE / 10 500.

IH	used in place of listing value when the item is held by an institution
SL	straightline

Hardeman

A

HARDEMAN TEX. (? SL; 1862; black)
A PAID 10 1,000.
Ms Paid 5* 300.

Harrisburgh

(PAID) 5

A B

HARRISBURGH / TEX (25; 1861-64; black)
A PAID [no rate] 300.
Same, 5 (ms)* 400.
B PAID 5* 500.

Helena

HELENA / TEX (25; 1862; black)
Ms Paid 5 300.
Paid 10* 300.

Hempstead

PAID
5

A B C

HEMPSTEAD / TEX (25; 1861-63; black, blue, red)
HEMPSTEAD / TEX. (36; 1861-63; black, blue, red)
A PAID 5 300.
Same (blue) 500.
B PAID 5* 300.
Same (blue) 500.
Same (blue) struck twice 750.
C PAID 10 (blue) 300.

Henderson

HENDERSON / TEXAS (29; 1861-64; black)
A PAID [no rate] [not illustrated] 500.
Ms Paid / 5 400.
Paid / 10 400.
Paid / 20 750.
Pk No rate 300.

Herringtons

Herringtons Tex (ms; 1862-63; black)
Herrington Tex (ms; 1863; black)
Ms Pad 5 IH

	10 Paid	IH
	Paid / 10	IH

High Hill

High Hill Tex (ms; 1863; black)

Ms	Paid 10c	300.

Hockley

PAID

A

HOCKLEY / TEX (25; 1862; black)

A	PAID [no rate]	300.

Hollandale

A B

HOLLANDALE / TEX (25; 1861-62; black)

A	PAID [no rate]	300.
	Same [no rate] (struck twice)	500.
B	PAID 5	500.

Homer

Homer Texas (ms; 1862; black)
Homer Tex (ms; 1863; black)

Ms	Paid 5	IH
	10 Paid	IH

Honey Grove

A

Honey Grove Texas (ms; 1861; black)
HONEY. GROVE / Texas (30; 1862-63; red)

A	PAID 10 (red)	500.
Ms	Paid 10	300.

Hopkinsville

HOPKINSVILLE / TEX (26 DC; 1863; black)

A	DUE / 10 [not illustrated]*	300.

Houston

PAID

A B

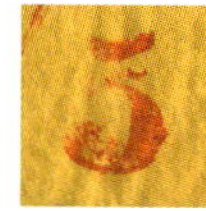

C D

HOUSTON / TEX. (34 YD; 1861-65; black)
HOUSTON / TEX. (34 YD; 1863-64; black)

A	PAID [no rate]	300.
	Same, 10 (ms)	400.
	Same, 20 (ms)	750.
	Same, 30 (ms)	750.
B	PAID 5*	500.
	Same (red), revalued 10 (ms)	500.
C	5 [due] struck twice	300.
	5 [due] (red)	500.
D	10 [due]	300.
	Same, Due (ms)	300.
Ms	Paid / 10	300.
	Due 5	300.
	Due 10	300.
	P O B / Free	750.

Huntsville

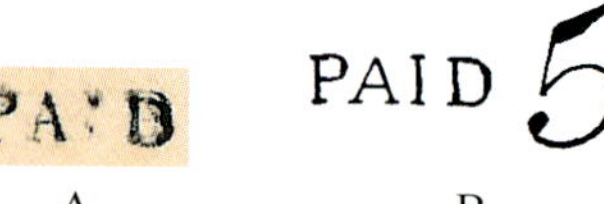

PAID 5

A B

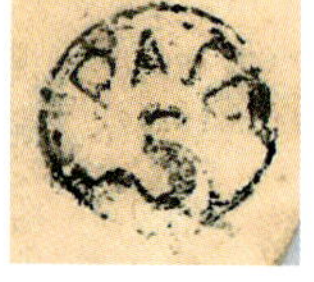

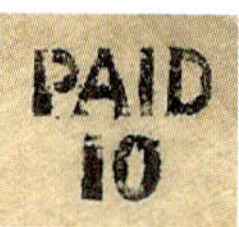

C D E

HUNTSVILLE / Tex. (34; 1861-65; black)

A	PAID [no rate]	500.
B	PAID 5	500.
C	PAID 5 (altered 3)	500.
D	PAID 10	500.
E	PAID 10	500.
Ms	2	750.
	Due 20	500.
	P.O.B. Free G.A.Ash A.P.M.	750.

Independence

PAID PAID 5

A B

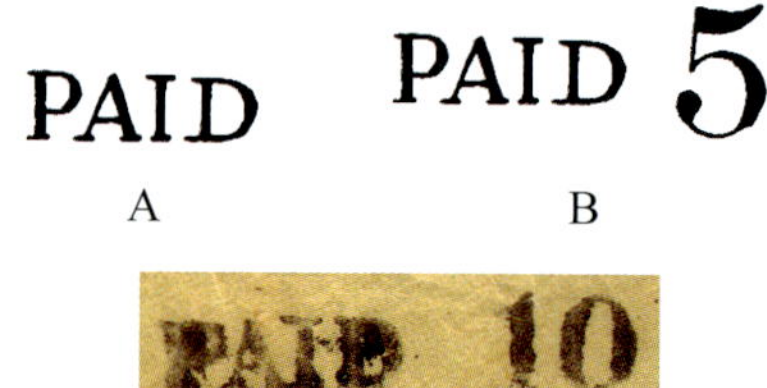

C

INDEPENDANCE / TEX (32; 1861-62; black)

A	PAID, 40 (ms)*	500.
B	PAID 5	300.
C	PAID 10	300.

INDIANOLA

PAID

A 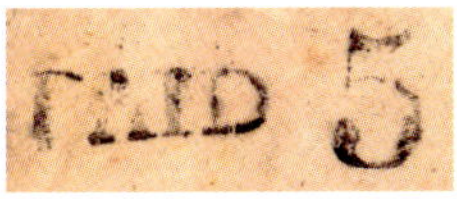 B

Indianola (ms; 186-; ?)
INDIANOLA / TEX (26 DC YD; 1861-63; black)

A	PAID, 10 (ms)	500.
B	PAID 5	500.
Ms	Paid 10	300.

JACKSBORO

Jacksboro Tex (ms; 1861; black)

Ms	Paid 5 cts	300.

JASPER

PAID 5 CENTS

A 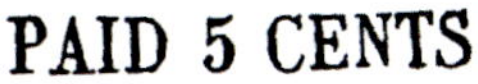 B

C  D

E

JASPER / TEX (26; 1861-64; black)

A	PAID 5	500.
B	PAID 5 CENTS*	500.
C	PAID 5 (ms) C T S	500.
D	PAID 10	500.
E	DUE 10	500.

JEFFERSON

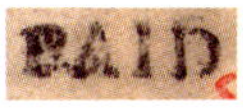

A  B

C  D

JEFFERSON / Tex. (34; 1862; black, red)

A	PAID [no rate]	300.
	Same, 5 (red) (ms)	500.
	Same, 10 (pencil)	500.
	Same, 10 (blue crayon)	500.
B	PAID 10	500.
C	DUE 10 (red)	500.
D	DUE 10 (black)	500.
Ms	Pa 10	300.
	Due 10	300.

KAUFMAN

A

KAUFMAN / TEXAS (30; 1862; black)

A	PAID [no rate]*	300.
	Same, 2 (ms) (circular rate)	1,500.
Ms	Paid 5*	300.

KERRSVILLE

Kerrsville Texas (ms; 1862-63; black)

Ms	Paid 10	300.

KICKAPOO

KICKAPOO / TEX (26; 1861; ?)

Ms	Paid 10	500.

KIMBALL

Kimball Tex (ms; 1861-63; black)
Kimball (ms; 1863; black)

Ms	Paid 5	300.
Ms	Paid 10	300.

KNOXVILLE

Knoxville Tex (ms; 1861; black)

Ms	Paid 5 (pencil)	IH

LA GRANGE

PAID

A

PAID V

B  C

PAID 10 PAID (10)

D  E

F G

H I J

LA GRANGE / TEX. (33 YD; 1861-63; black)
LA GRANGE / Txs. (?; 186-; black)

A	PAID, 10 (ms)*	300.
B	PAID V*	500.
C	PAID V	500.
D	PAID 10*	500.
E	PAID 10	500.
F	PAID X	500.
G	PAID X	500.
H	PAID X	500.
I	V, Due (ms)	300.
J	10 [due]	300.
Ms	Paid 50	500.

Lamar

Lamar Tex (ms; 1864; black)

Ms	Paid 10¢	400.

Lampasas

Lampasas (ms; 1861-65; black)

Ms	Paid 10	300.
	Pd 10	300.

Lancaster

A

LANCASTER / TEX (26; 1861-63; black)

A	PAID [no rate]	500.
Ms	Paid 10	300.

Larissa

Larissa Tex (ms; 1862-64; black)
LARISSA / TEX. (30; 1861-64; black)

Ms	Paid 5	IH
	Paid 10	300.

Lavernia

Lavernia Tex (ms; 1864; black)

Ms	Paid 10	300.

Leona

Leona (ms; 1863-64; black)

Ms	Pd 10	300.

Lexington

Lexington Texas (ms; 1861-62; black)

Ms	Paid 5	300.

Liberty

A B

LIBERTY / TEXAS (31; 1862-64; black)

A	PAID [no rate]	NR
B	PAID 5*	500.
	Same (5 struck twice)	750.
Ms	Paid 10	300.

Linden

A

Linden Tex (ms; 1863; black)
LINDEN / TEX (25; 1861; black)

A	PAID, 10 (ms)	500.
	Same, 10c (ms)	500.

Liverpool

Liverpool Texas (ms; 1861-62; black)

Ms	Paid / 10	300.

Livingston

Livingston (ms; 1861-63; black)

Ms	Due 10	300.

Lockhart

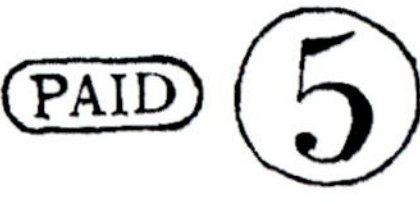

A B

LOCKHART / TEX. (26; 1861-65; black, blue)

A	PAID 5	300.
B	5 (blue) [due]*	300.
Ms	Paid / 5	300.
	Paid / 10	300.

London

London Tex (ms; 186-; black)

Ms	Paid 10	500.

IH	used in place of listing value when the item is held by an institution
ms	manuscript

Lone Star

A

LONE STAR / TEX (32; 1861-63; red)

A	PAID 5	300.

Note: The only recorded example is on a piece.

Long Point

Long Point Tex (ms; 1862-64; black)

Ms	Paid 10	300.

Lynchburg

LYNCHBURG / TEX (26; 1861; black)

Ms	Due 5	300.
	Due [no rate]*	300.
	Official Business / free	500.

Madisonville

Madisonville (ms; 1861; black)

Ms	Paid 5 cts	300.

Magnolia

A

Magnolia Texas (ms; 1863; black)
Circular postmark (?; 1862; black)

A	PAID 5	500.
Ms	Pd 10	IH

Magnolia Springs

Magnolia Springs Tex (ms; 1861; black)

Ms	Paid 5c	300.

Malakoff

Malakoff Tex (ms; 1861; black)

Ms	Paid 5	IH

Marlin

A

MARLIN / TEX (25; 1861-63; black)

A	PAID [no rate]	300.
B	5 (circled) [due] [not illustrated]	500.
Ms	Paid 10*	500.
	5 [due]*	300.

Marshall

A

B

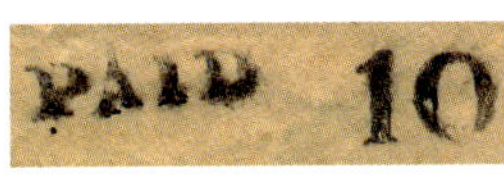

C

D

E

F

MARSHALL / TEX (32; 1861-65; black)
MARSHALL / TEX (25 DC YD; 1861-64; black)

A	PAID [no rate]*	300.
B	PAID 10 [narrow "0"]	500.
C	PAID 10 [wide "0"]	500.
D	PAID 10	750.
E	PAID 10 cents	300.
F	10 [due]	300.
Ms	Paid 20	500.
	Due 10	300.

Mason

Mason, Texas (ms; 1861; black)

Ms	Paid 5¢	300.

Matagorda

A B

MATAGORDA / TXS (33; 1861-64; black, brown)

A	PAID [no rate]	300.
B	PAID 5*	500.
	Same struck twice (10c rate)	500.
Ms	Paid 10	300.
	free	500.

McKinney

A

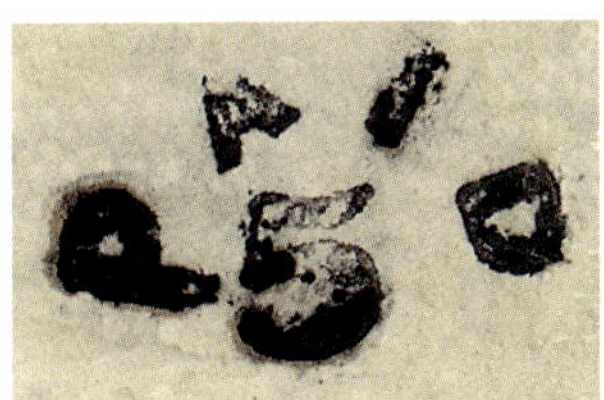

B

McKINNEY / Texas. (31; 1861-63; black)

A	PAID 10	500.
B	PAID 5	500.
Ms	Paid 10	500.

Melrose

MELROSE / TEX (26; 1861; black)

Ms	Paid 5c	300.

Meridian

A

MERIDIAN / TEX (26; 1861; black)

A	PAID 10	300.

Milam

Milam (ms; 1862; black)

Ms	Paid / 5	IH

Mill Creek

Mill Creek Tex (ms; 1862; black)

Ms	Paid 10 (pencil)	300.

Millican

A B

Millican Tx (ms; 1865; black)
MILLICAN / PAID (28 NOR; 1863-65; black)

A	PAID [no rate]	500.
	Same, Paid (ms)	500.
	Same, Paid 10 (pencil)	500.
B	DUE [no rate]	500.
Ms	Paid 10	300.

Note: There is no separate postmark used with Type A. The Type B marking is used with the Type A marking.

Montgomery

A B

C D

MONTGOMERY / TEX (25; 1861-65; black, red)

A	PAID [no rate]*	500.
B	PAID 10*	500.
C	V [due]	500.
D	10 [due]	300.

Moscow

MOSCOW / TEX. (32; 1861-64; black)

A	PAID [no rate] [not illustrated]	500.
Ms	Due 10*	300.

Mosquito Prairie

Mosquito Prairie Texas (ms; 1861-62; black)

Ms	Paid 10	300.

Mount Enterprise

A B

MOUNT ENTERPRISE / TEX. (26; 1861-64; black)

A	PAID 10	500.
B	PAID 10	500.

Mount Pleasant

A B

Mt Pleasant Tex (ms; 1862; black)
MT PLEASANT / TEXAS (32; 1861-62; black)

A	PAID, 5 (ms)	500.
B	PAID 5*	500.
	Same, 5 struck twice	500.
	Same, 5 struck four times	750.
Ms	Paid 5	300.
	Pd 5	300.
	Paid 10	300.

Nacogdoches

A B

C D

NACOGDOCHES / TEX. (32 YD; 1861-64; black)

A	PAID [no rate]*	350.
	Same, 2c (ms)	1,500.
B	PAID 5	400.
C	PAID 10	400.
D	10 [due]	350.

NAVASOTA

A

NAVASOTA / TEX. (32; 1863-64; black)

A	PAID [no rate]*	500.
	Same, 10 (ms)	500.
Pk	No rate	300.

Note: The Type A markings are struck inside an undated postmark.

NEW BRAUNFELS

A

NEW BRAUNFELS / Tex. (33; 1861-64; black)

A	PAID 10	400.
	Same, 20 (ms)*	

NEW DANVILLE

New Danville Tex (ms; 1861; black)
NEW DANVILLE / TEX (26; 1861; ?)

Ms	Paid 5 cts	350.
	Paid / 5	300.

NEW PORT

New Port Tx (ms; 1864; black)

Ms	Paid 10	300.

NEW SALEM

New Salem Tx (ms; 186-; black)
New Salem Tex (ms; 186-; black)
New Salem Texas (ms; 1861-62; black)

Ms	Paid 5	IH
	Paid 10	300.
	Pid 10	IH

OAKLAND

Oakland Texas (ms; 1863-64; black)

Ms	Paid 10	300.

ORANGE

PAID 5

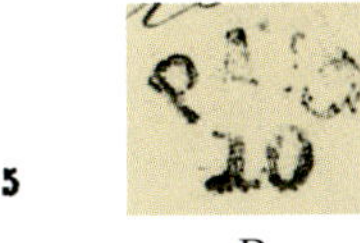

DUE 10

A B C

ORANGE / TEX (32; 1861-63; black)
ORANGE. / TEXAS (30 no date logos; 1862-63; black)

A	PAID 5*	500.
B	PAID 10	500.
C	DUE 10	300.
Ms	Paid 10	300.
	Paid / 10	300.

ORIZABA

Orizaba Tx (ms; 1862; black)

Ms	Paid 5	300.

OSAGE

Osage Tex (ms; 1864; black)

Ms	Paid 10	300.

OSO

OSO / TEX. (32; 1861; red, blue)

Ms	Paid 10	300.

OWENSVILLE

A

Owensville Tex (ms; 1861-62; black)
OWENSVILLE / TEX (32; 1861-63; black)

A	PAID [no rate]	300.
	Same, 5 (ms)*	500.
Ms	Paid 10	300.

PALESTINE

PAID 5 5

A B

PALESTINE / Tex. (36; 1861-64; black)

A	PAID 5	500.
B	5 [due]*	300.

PANNA MARIA

Panna Maria (ms; 1863; black)

Ms	Paid 10¢	300.

Paris

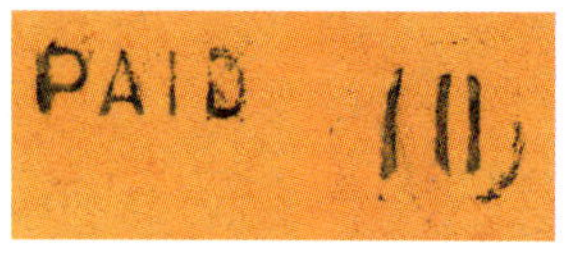
A

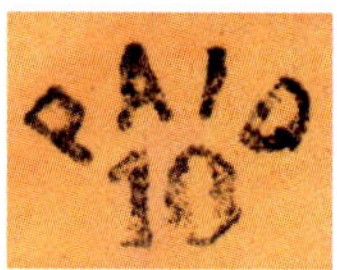
B

C

PARIS / TEXAS. (31; 1861-64; black, blue)

A	PAID 10	750.
	PAID 10 (blue)	1,000.
B	PAID 10	500.
	Same (blue)	750.
C	DUE 10	300.
Ms	Paid / 10	300.
	Due 10	300.

Pilot Grove

PILOT GROVE / TEX (?; 1862; black)

Ms	Due 10c	300.
	Due / 10	300.

Pilot Point

Pilot Point Tx (ms; 1861-62; black)

Ms	Paid 5	300.

Plano

Plano Texas (ms; 1861; black)

Ms	Paid / 5	300.
	Due 10	300.

Plenitude

Plenitude Tex (ms; 1861-62; black)

Ms	Paid 5	300.

Port Lavaca

A

B

PAID 10

C

PORT LAVACA / TEX. (32 YD; 1861-63; black)

A	PAID, 10 (ms)	300.
B	PAID 5	500.
C	PAID 10*	500.
	Same, revalued 20 (ms)	500.
Ms	due 10	300.

Post Oak Island

Post Oak Island Texas (ms; 1862; black)

Ms	Paid 10	300.

Prairie Plains

Prairie Plains (ms; 186-; black)
Prairie Plains Texas (ms; 1861-64; black)

Ms	Paid 10	300.

Prairieville

Prairieville Tex (ms; 1861; black)

Ms	Paid 10 cents	300.

Quitman

QUITMAN / TEX. (32; 1862-64; black)

A	PAID [no rate] [not illustrated]	500.
Ms	Paid / 10	300.

Rabbit Creek

Rabbit Creek (ms; 1862; black)

Ms	Paid 5	300.

Red Oak

Red Oak Texas (ms; 1862-64; black)

Ms	Paid 10	300.

Richmond

PAID 10

A

RICHMOND / TEX (30; 1861-64; red, blue)

A	PAID 10	300.
Ms	Due 10	300.

Rio Grande City

A

RIO GRANDE CITY / TEX (25; 1861-62; black)

A	PAID [no rate]	300.
Ms	Due 10c*	300.

Rock Wall

ROCK WALL / TEX. (26; 1862-63; black)

Ms	Paid 5	300.

Round Rock

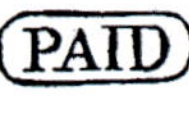
A

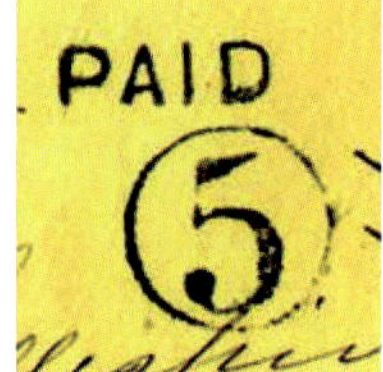
B

Round Rock (ms; 1863; black)
ROUND ROCK / TEXAS. (34 DLC; 1861; black)

A	PAID, 5c (ms)*	500.
	Same, 10 (ms)*	500.
B	PAID 5	500.

Round Top

A B

ROUND TOP / TEX (26; 1861-64; black)
ROUND TOP / TEX. (33; 1862-65; black)

A	PAID, 5 (ms)	500.
	Same, 10 (ms)	500.
B	PAID [no rate]	500.
	Same, 5 (ms)*	500.
	Same, 10 (ms)	500.
C	P.O.BUSINESS / FREE [not illustrated]	IH

Rusk

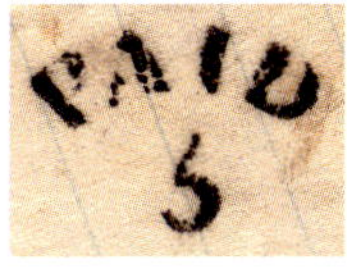

A B

Rusk Texas (ms; 1863; black)
Rusk / Texas (ms; 1863; black)
RUSK / TEXAS. (31; 1861-63; black)

A	PAID 5	300.
B	PAID 10	300.
C	DUE / 5 (in arc) [not illustrated]*	300.
Ms	Paid 10	300.
	Paid 10 cts	IH
	10 ct Paid	300.
	Paid 40	750.
	Due 10 (pencil)	IH
	forwd [no rate]	300.

Rutersville

Rutersville (ms; 186–; ?)

Ms	Paid 10	300.

Sabinetown

Sabinetown Tex (ms; 1862-64; black)
Sabinetown Texas (ms; 1864; black)

Ms	Paid 10	300.
	Paid 10 (pencil)	300.
	Due 10	IH

Salado

Salado (ms; 1862; black)

Ms	Paid 10	300.

San Antonio

A B C

D E F

G H I

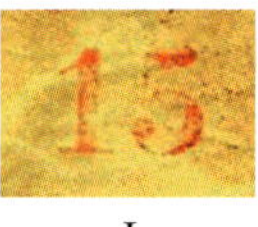

J K L

SAN ANTONIO / TEX. (31; 1861-65; black, blue, green)
SAN ANTONIO TEX (32 YD; 1864, black)*
SAN ANTONIO TEX (32; 1861-64; green)
SAN ANTONIO TEX / PAID (33; 1861-64; black; red, green)

A.	PAID [no rate]	500.
	Same (red), 10 (red pencil)	
	Same (red), 15 (ms)*	
	Same, 40 (blue pencil)	750.
B	PAID (integral postmark)	750.
C	PAID 5 (red)	750.
D	PAID 10 (red)	500.
E	PAID 10	500.
	Same (red)	750.
F	PAID 10 (red) (integral postmark)	750.
G	PAID 20	500.
H	10 [due]	300.
I	10, Due (blue crayon)	300.
J	15 (red) [due]	750.
K	DUE 5 (green)	750.
L	MISSENT (green)	1,000.
Ms	Due 10 (blue crayon)	300.

Note: The Type F marking was used as both a stampless and provisional marking. Each example must be considered on its own merits.

San Augustine

A

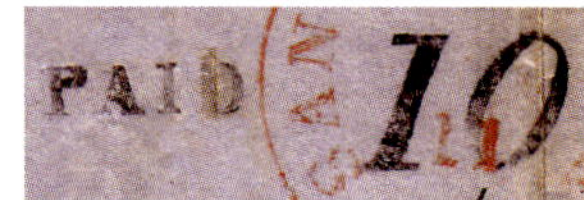

B

San Augustine (ms; 1863-64; black)
SAN AUGUSTINE / Tex. (34; 1861-63; black, red)

A	PAID 5*	500.
	Same (red)	500.
B	PAID 10	500.
	Same (red)	500.
Ms	Paid 10	300.
	10 [due]	300.

San Jacinto

SAN JACINTO / TXS (star in center) (24; 1861-63; black)

Ms	Paid 5cts	500.
	Due 10*	500.

San Marcos

A

San Marcos (ms; 1862-64; black)
SAN MARCOS / TEX (26; 1862-4; black)

A	PAID, 5 (ms)*	300.
Ms	Paid 5	300.
	Paid 10	300.
	Free / P. O. B	IH

San Patricio

San Patricio Texas (ms; 1861-63; black)

Ms	Paid 10	300.

Note: On the single recorded copy, part of the rate is torn off.

Sand Springs

Sand Springs Tex (ms; 1864; black)

Ms	Paid 10 cts	300.

Sandy Point

A

SANDY POINT / TEX. (33 DLC; 1861-62; black)

A	PAID [no rate]	500.
Ms	Pd 10	300.

Searsville

Searsville Texas (ms; 1861; black)

Ms	Paid 5*	300.

Seguin

A

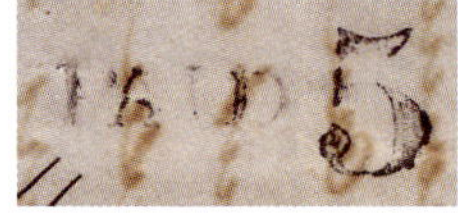

B

Seguin (ms; 1865; black)
SEGUIN / * TEXAS * (28; 1861-63; black)

A	PAID [no rate]	300.
	Same, 10 ms)	500.
	Same, 20 (ms)*	750.
B	PAID 5	500.
	Same, 5 struck twice*	750.
Ms	Paid (no rate)	750.

Selma

No postmark

Ms	under chgd 5 / due 10	300.

Shelbyville

SHELBYVILLE / TEXAS. (32; 1863; black)

Ms	Due 10	300.

Sherman

PAID 10

A

SHERMAN / TEX (25; 1861-65; black)
SHERMAN / TEX. (32; 1862-64; black)

A	PAID 10	300.

Smithfield

Smithfield (ms; 186-; black)

Ms	Paid 10	300.

Spencer

Spencer Texas (ms; 1861; black)

Ms	Paid 10	300.

Spring Hill

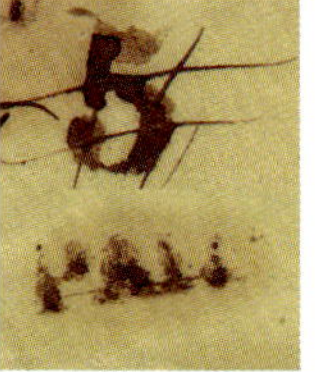

A

SPRING HILL / TEX. (30; 1861; brown)

A	PAID 5 (brown)	500.
	Same (brown), revalued Paid 10 cts (ms)	500.

Springfield

A

B

C

SPRINGFIELD / TEX. (32; 1861-63; black)

A	PAID 5	500.
B	5, Paid (ms)	500.
C	FREE	750.
Ms	Paid 5*	300.

Starrville

PAID

A

STARRVILLE / TEX (32; 1861-65; black)

A	PAID, 5 (ms)	500.

Stonewall

Stonewall Tex (ms; 1863-64; black)

Ms	Paid 10	300.

Sumpter

A

B

SUMPTER / TEX. (36; 1861-62; black)

A	PAID [no rate]	300.
	Same, 5 (ms)	500.
B	PAID 5	500.
Ms	Paid 5 cts*	300.

Sutherland Springs

PAID

A

Sutherland Springs (ms; 1861-63; black)

A	PAID, 10 (ms)*	500.
Ms	Paid 10	300.

Tarrant

PAID

A

TARRANT / TEX (37; 1862-63; black)

A	PAID [no rate]*	300.
	Same, 5 (ms)*	500.

Texana

PAID

A

B

C

D

10

E

TEXANA / TEX. (36; 1861-64; black)

A	PAID [no rate]	300.
B	PAID 10	500.
C	DUE 10	300.
	Same struck twice	750.
D	DUE [no rate]	500.
E	10 [due]*	500.

Thompsonville

Thompsonville (no pmk)

Ms	Missent to Thompsonville	300.

Town Bluff

Town Bluff (ms; 1863; black)

Ms	Paid 10	300.

Travis

A

TRAVIS / TEXAS. (29 YD; 1863-65; black)

A	PAID 10	500.

Trinity Mills

Trinity Mills / Tex (ms; 1861; black)

Ms	Paid 10 cts	500.

Turners Point

Turners Point Texas (ms; 1861; black)

Ms	No rate	300.

[*]	symbol used after an item description to mean an unsupported listing

Tyler

A

TYLER / TEX (26; 1863-65; black)
TYLER / TEXAS. (32; 1861-63; black)

A	PAID, 10 (ms)	300.
	Same, 30 (ms)*	500.
Ms	Due 10*	500.

Note: There is one Paid 10 marking recorded on cover with a "GEO. YARBROUGH" handstamp. Although Yarbrough was postmaster at Tyler, there is insufficient information to conclude this was intended as a postal marking or control.

Unionville

Unionville Tx (ms; 1861-64; black)

Ms	Paid [no rate]	300.
	Paid 10*	500.

Uvalde

A

UVALDE / TEX (26; 1862; black)

A	PAID [no rate]	500.

Velasco

B

C

D

VELASCO / TEX. (33; 1861-64; black)

A	PAID 5 (arc) [not illustrated]*	500.
B	PAID 10	500.
C	DUE 5	500.
D	DUE 10	500.
Ms	Paid 5*	300.
	Paid 5 ct*	300.
	Paid 10*	300.
	Due / 10	300.

Victoria

A

B

PAID 10

C

D

VICTORIA / TEX. (34; 1861-63; black, red, brown)

A	PAID [no rate]	300.
	Same, 20 (red pencil)	300.
	Same, 30 (ms)	500.
B	PAID 5 (red)	500.
	Same (brown)*	500.
C	PAID 10 (red)*	500.
	PAID 10 (brown)*	500.
D	10 [due]	300.
	10 [due] (red)	500.

Waco [Waco Village]

PAID

A

PAID 5

B

PAID 5

C

PAID 10

D

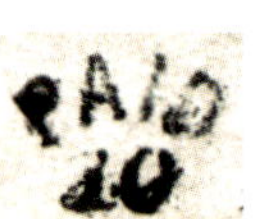

E

WACO VILLAGE / Tex. (34; 1861; black)
WACO VILLAGE / Tex. (34 YD; 1862 black)

A	PAID [no rate]*	500.
	Same, 10 (ms)*	500.
B	PAID 5	750.
C	PAID 5*	500.
D	PAID 10*	500.
E	PAID 10	500.

Wallers Store

Wallers Store Tex (ms; 1861-62; black)

Ms	Paid 10	300.

Warren

Warren Tex (ms; 1863; black)

Ms	Paid 10	300.

Washington

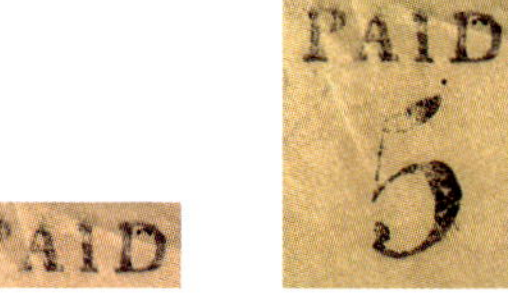

A B

C

WASHINGTON / Tex. (34; 1861-64; black)

A	PAID [no rate]*	300.
B	PAID 5	500.
C	PAID 10	500.

Waverley

A

WAVERLEY / TEX (26; 1862-63; black)

A	PAID [no rate]	500.
Ms	10 [due]	300.

Waxahachie

A

B

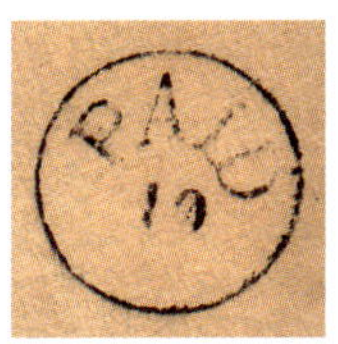

C

WAXAHACHIE / TEX. (32; 1861-64; black)

A	PAID 5	500.
B	PAID 10	500.
C	PAID 10	500.
Pk	No rate	300.

Weatherford

A

WEATHERFORD / TEX (26; 1861-64; black)

A	PAID, 5 (ms)*	500.
Ms	Paid 5	500.
	Paid 10*	500.

Webberville

WEBBERVILLE / TXS. (30; 1861-63; black)

Ms	Paid 10*	300.

Wharton

A

B

WHARTON / Tex. (31; 1861-62; black)

A	PAID 5	500.
B	PAID 10	500.

Wheelock

Wheelock Tex (ms; 1861-63; black)
WHEELOCK / ROBERTSON / TEXAS. (37; 1863; black)
WHEELOCK / TEXAS (32; 1864; black)

A	Paid 10 [not illustrated]*	300.
Ms	Paid [no rate]	300.
	Paid 5	300.
	Paid 10	300.
	Paid / 10	300.

Wiess Bluff

Wiess Bluff Tex (ms; 1861; black)

Ms	Paid 5¢	300.

Woodville

A

WOODVILLE / TEXAS (30; 1861; black)

A	PAID 5	300.

Yegua

Yegua Texas (ms; 1861; black)

Ms	Paid 10	300.

Yorktown

YORKTOWN / TEX (32; 1862; black)

Ms	Paid 5	300.
	Paid 5ct	300.

Youngs Settlement

Youngs Settlement (ms; 1863; black)

Ms	10 cts Paid	300.

VIRGINIA

Abingdon

A B

C D

E F G

ABINGDON / VA. (29; 186-; black)
ABINGDON / Va. (32 YD; 1861-62; black, red)

A	PAID, 5 (ms)	150.
B	PAID 5	250.
C	PAID 5*	175.
D	PAID 10*	250.
E	5 [due]*	175.
F	10 [due]*	175.
G	DUE 10	175.
	Same (red)	200.
Ms	Due 5	150.
	Due 10	150.

Academy [West Virginia]

Academy (ms; 1861; black)

Ms	Paid 5	300.

Accokeek

A

Accokeek Va (ms; 1861; black)
ACCOKEEK / V^{a} (31 YD; 1861-62; black)

A	PAID 5	175.
B	DUE 5 [not illustrated]*	150.
Ms	Paid 5*	150.
	10 / Paid	150.
	Due 5*	150.
	Due 10	150.

Afton

Afton Va. (ms; 1861-64; black)

Ms	Due 10*	150.

Aldie

A

ALDIE / Va. (33; 1861-62; black, red)

A	PAID 5*	150.
B	FREE [not illustrated]*	IH.

Alum Springs

A B

Alum Springs Va (ms; 1863; black)
ALUM SPRINGS / VA (33; 1861-65; black)

A	PAID, 10 (ms)	150.
B	PAID 5	175.
Ms	5 (pencil) [due]	250.
	Due 10	150.

Amelia Court House

AMELIA CH / Va (29; 1861-63; black)
AMELIA C H / Va (31; 1861; black)

Ms	Paid 5	150.
	Paid 10*	150.

Amherst Court House

A

AMHERST C. H. / VA (26; 1861-62; black, brown)

A	PAID [no rate]	150.
	Same (brown) [no rate]	200.
	Same, 5 (ms)*	175.
	Same, 10 (ms)*	175.
B	10 (C), Paid (ms) [not illustrated]*	250.
Ms	Paid 5*	150.

Arbor Hill

Arbor Hill (ms; 1861; black)
Arbor Hill Va (ms; 1861-63; black)

Ms	Paid 5	150.
	Paid 10	150.

[*]	symbol used after an item description to mean an unsupported listing
[–]	symbol used in place of value to mean insufficient information to assign a price
IH	used in place of listing value when the item is held by an institution

Arrington

A

Arrington (ms; 186-; black)
Arrington Va (ms; 1862-64; black)
ARRINGTON / VA (26; 1861; black)

A	PAID, 5 (ms)	175.
Ms	Paid 5	150.
	Paid / 10	150.
	Due 5*	150.

Ashland

A

ASHLAND / Va. (32 DLC; 1861-63; black)

A	PAID [no rate]	175.
	Same, 5 (ms)*	250.
B	DUE, 10 (ms) [not illustrated]*	175.
Ms	Due 10	150.

Austinville

Austinville, Vª (ms; 1862; black)

Ms	Paid 5	150.
	Paid 10	150.

Axton

Axton Va (ms; 1862; black)

Ms	Paid 5	150.

Back Creek Valley

B. C. Valley Va (ms; 1861-64; black)

Ms	Paid*	150.

Balcony Falls

PAID

PAID 10 C.S.

A B

BALCONY FALLS / Va. (33; 1861-64; blue)

A	PAID (blue), 5 (ms)*	175.
B	PAID 10 C. S. (blue)	500.
Ms	Paid 5*	150.

Ballsville

Ballsville Va (ms; 1861; black)

Ms	Paid 5*	150.

Barksdale

Barksdale Va (ms; 1861; black)

Ms	Free Official Business*	IH

Barter Brook

PAId5

A

Barter Brook Va (ms; 1861; black)

A	Paid 5	300.

Bath Alum

Bath Alum Va (ms; 1861; black)

Ms	Due 5	150.

Bath Court House

A

Bath C H Va (ms; 186-; black)
BATH C. H. / Va. (32; 1861-63; black)

A	PAID, 5 (ms)	175.
	Same, 10 (ms)*	175.
	Same, 12 (ms)*	200.
B	DUE, 10 (ms) [not illustrated]*	150.
Ms	Paid 10	150.
	Due 10*	150.

Beaver Dam Depot

Beaver Dam (ms; 1862; black)
B. D. Depot (ms; 1861-63; black)
Beaver Dam Depot (ms; 1861-63; black)

Ms	Paid 5	150.
	5 [due]	150.
	Due 10*	150.

Belfast Mills

Belfast Mills Vª (ms; 1861; black)

Ms	Paid 5c	150.

Belmead Mills

Belmead Mills (ms; 1862; black)
Belmead Mills Va (ms; 1861; black)

Ms	Paid 5	150.
	Paid 5 cts	150.

Bent Creek

Bent Creek (ms; 1863; black)

Ms	Paid 10 cts	150.

Bentivoglio

A

Bentivoglio Va (ms; 1861-64; brown)

A	PAID 5 (brown)	175.

Berger's Store

Bergers Store Va (ms; 186-; black)

Ms	Paid 5 cts*	IH

Berrys Ferry

Berrys Ferry Va (ms; 1861-62; black)

Ms	Paid 5	150.

Berryville

A

BERRYVILLE / Va. (30; 1861-62; black)
BERRYVILLE / V^A (30; 1862; black)

A	PAID [no rate]*	175.
	Same, 5 (ms)	175.
B	DUE 10 [not illustrated]*	150.
Ms	Due 10*	150.

Beverly [West Virginia]

Beverly Va (ms; 1861-62; black)
Beverly V^a (ms; 186-; black)

Ms	Paid 5	300.
	Paid 5 cts	300.
	Pd 5	300.
	Pd / 5	300.
	Paid 10	300.

Big Island

A

BIG ISLAND / VA. (25; 1862-63; black)

A	PAID [no rate]	175.
	Same, 5 (ms)*	150.

Big Lick

A

BIG LICK / V^A (32; 1861-62; black)

A	PAID 5	175.
Ms	Paid 10*	150.
	10¢ due	150.

Black Walnut

Black Walnut (ms; 1861-64; black)
BLACK WALNUT / VA. (32; 1861; black)

Ms	Paid 5*	150.

Blacksburg

Blacksburg Va (ms; 1861-64; black)
BLACKSBURG / VA (26; 1861-63; black)

Ms	Paid [no rate]	150.
	Paid 5*	150.
	Paid 10	150.
	P. O. B. Free*	IH

Blue Ridge

Blue Ridge Va (ms; 1861; black)

Ms	Paid 5	150.

Blue Stone

Blue Stone Va (ms; 1861-64; black)

Ms	Paid / 10	150.

Bonsack's

A B

Bonsack Va (ms; 1864-65; black)
BONSACK'S / Va (32; 1861; black)
BONSACK / VA (30; 1862-65; black)

A	PAID [no rate]*	175.
	Same, 5 (ms)	175.
	Same, struck twice, 5 (ms)	175.
B	PAID 10	250.
Ms	Paid 5	150.
	Paid 10*	150.

Boone's Mill

Boons Mills Va (ms; 1862; black)

Ms	Paid 5	150.

Botetourt Springs

A

BOTETOURT SPRINGS / Va (37; 1861-64; black)

A	Paid 5	500.
Ms	Paid 10	150.

Bothwick

Bothwick Va (ms; 1861; ?)

Ms	Free Official Business*	IH

Bowling Green

Bowling Green (ms; 1863-65; black)
BOWLING GREEN / VA (26; 1861-63; green, blue)

Ms	Due 10	175.

Boydton

A B

BOYDTON / V^a (30; 1861-64; black)

A	PAID 5*	175.
B	PAID 10	175.
Ms	Paid / 10	150.

Brandy Station

Brandy Station (ms; 186-; black)
BRANDY STATION / Va. (37; 1861; black)

Ms	Paid 5	150.
	Way	500.

Breckinridge

Breckinridge V^a (ms; 1862; black)

Ms	Paid 5	150.

Bremo Bluff

Bremo Bluff (ms; 1861-63; black)

Ms	5 / Paid	150.
	Due 10	150.

Brentsville

BRENTSVILLE / VA (32; 1861; black)

Ms	Due 10*	150.

Bridgewater

A

BRIDGEWATER / VA (29; 1861-63; black)

A	PAID 5*	200.

Bristoe Station

A C

BRISTOE STATION / VA. (25; 1861; black)

A	PAID [no rate]*	175.
	Same, 5 (ms)*	175.
	Same, 10 (ms)	175.
B	DUE 5 [not illustrated]*	200.
C	DUE 10	200.
Ms	Paid 5	200.
	Paid / 5	150.
	Pd 10	150.
	Due 5*	150.
	Due 10*	150.

Broad Run Station

Broad Run Station (ms; 1861; black)

Ms	Paid 5	150.
	Paid / 5	150.

Broadway Depot

Broadway Va (ms; 1861-64; black)

Ms	Paid 5*	150.
	Paid 10*	150.

Brooke's Station

A

Brooke's Station Va (ms; 1861; black)

A	PAID 5*	200.

Brownsburgh

A

BROWNSBURGH / Va (33; 1861-63; black)
BROWNSBURG / VA (33; 1862-63; black, brown)

A	PAID, 5 (ms)	200.
	Same, 10 (ms)*	200.
Ms	Paid 5	150.
	Paid 10	150.

Buckingham Court House

A

BUCKINGHAM C. H. / Va (31; 1861-64; red)

A	PAID (red), 5 (ms)*	200.
	Same (red), 10 (ms)	250.
Ms	Paid 10*	150.
	P. O. Business*	IH

Buckton

Buckton Va (ms; 1861; black)

Ms	Paid 10*	150.

Bunger's Mill [West Virginia]

Bungers Mill Va (ms; 1861-62; black)

Ms	Due 10	300.

Burkes Mills

Burkes Mill (ms; 186-; black)

Ms	Due 10*	150.

Burkesville

(PAID)

A

Burkesville (ms; 1862; black)
BURKESVILLE / VA (26; 1861; black)

A	PAID, 5 (ms)*	175.

Burnt Ordinary

PAID

A

Burnt Ordinary Va (ms; 1862; black)
BURNT ORDINARY / Va (32; 1861; brown)

A	PAID (brown) [no rate]	200.
	Same (brown), 5c (ms)	200.
Ms	Paid 5*	150.

Cady's Tunnel

PAID 10

B

Cadys Tunnel (ms; 1861-62; black)
CADYS TUNNEL / VA. (30 YD; 1861-64; black)

A	PAID (arc) / 5 [not illustrated]*	300.
B	PAID 10	200.
Ms	Pd 5	150.
	Paid 5*	150.

Camp Shenandoah

Camp Shenandoah Va (ms; 1862; black)
CAMP SHENANDOAH / Va (32; 1862; black)

Ms	Paid 10	300.

Campbell Court House

C Ct House Va (ms; 1861-63;black)
Campbell C H Va (ms; 1862; black)

Ms	Paid 5 cts (pencil)	150.

Cappahosic

Cappahosic Va (ms; 186-; black)

Ms	Paid 10c	150.

DC	double circle
DLC	double [outer] line circle
YD	year date

Carter's Bridge

PAID

A

Carters's Bridge Va (ms; 1861-64; black)
CARTER'S BRIDGE / Va (37; 1861-62; black)

A	PAID, 5 (ms)*	200.
Ms	Pd 5*	150.

Cartersville

Cartersville (ms; 1861-64; black)

Ms	Paid 10¢	150.

Cascade

Cascade V^{a} (ms; 1861-63; black)

Ms	Paid 5c	150.

Castle Craig

Castle Craig Va (ms; 1862; black)

Ms	5 Paid	175.

Catlett

(PAID) (10) (10)

A B

CATLETT / VA (26; 1861-62; black, blue)

A	PAID 10*	200.
	Same (blue)*	300.
B	10 (blue) [due]*	175.
Ms	Due 10*	150.

Cedar Grove Mills

C. G. Mills (ms; 1861-64; black)

Ms	Pd / 10	150.

Centreville

Centreville Va (ms; 1861-62; black)

Ms	Paid 5	150.
	Pade 5	150.
	Pd 5	150.
	Pd 5	150.
	P 5 (pencil)	150.
	Due 5*	150.
	Due 10	150.

Chalk Level

Chalk Level Va (ms; 1861-63; black)

Ms	Paid 10*	150.

Chantilly

Chantilly Va (ms; 1861; black)

Ms	Paid 5*	150.

CHARLEMONT

A

CHARLEMONT / Va. (31; 1861; black)

A	PAID 5	200.

CHARLESTOWN [WEST VIRGINIA]

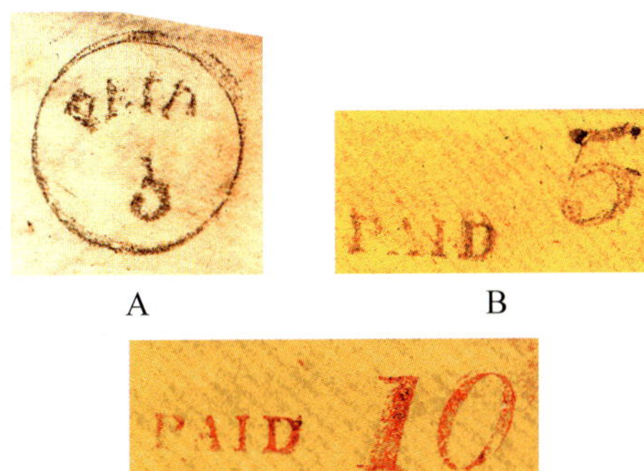

A B

C

CHARLESTOWN / Va. (31; 1861-63; black)

A	PAID 5	500.
B	PAID 5	400.
C	PAID 10 (red)	500.
D	DUE 10 [not illustrated]	400.
Ms	Due 5	300.

CHARLOTTE COURT HOUSE

A

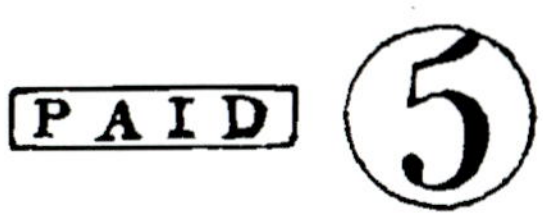

B

CHARLOTTE C. H. / Va. (34; 1861; black, blue, brown)

A	PAID 5	200.
	Same (brown)	300.
B	PAID 5*	200.
	Same (brown)	300.
	Same (blue), 5 struck twice	300.
	Same (brown), 5 struck twice*	500.
Ms	Official Business*	IH

CHARLOTTESVILLE

A B

C

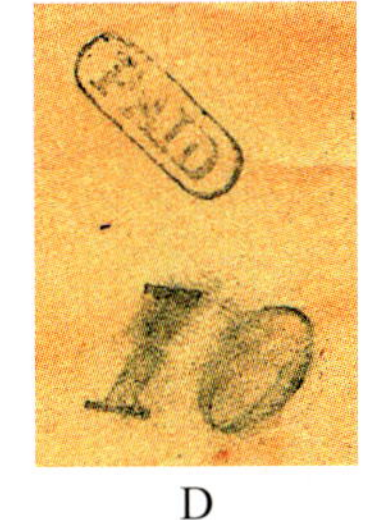

D E

F G

H I J

K

L M

CHARLOTTESVILLE / VA (26 DC YD; 1861-64; black, blue)

CHARLOTTEVILLE / VA (26 DC YD; 1864-65; black)

A	PAID (blue) [no rate]	300.

	Same (blue), struck twice [no rate]	500.
B	PAID 5 (blue)	300.
C	PAID 5 (blue)	300.
D	PAID 10 (blue)*	300.
	Same (blue) revalued 5 (Type I)	500.
E	PAID 10 (blue)	300.
	Same, revalued 20 (ms)	500.
F	DUE 2 (blue)	300.
G	DUE 5 (blue)	300.
H	DUE 10	200.
	Same (blue)	300.
I	5 [due]	175.
J	10 [due]	175.
	Same (blue) [due]	200.
	Same (blue), ford (ms)	200.
K	ADVERTISED	500.
L	FORWARDED, 10	500.
M	MISSENT (blue) and FORWARDED (blue), 5 (ms)	500.
Ms	Paid 5*	150.
	Due 10	150.
	Ford 10	150.
	Missent	150.

Childress Store

Childress Store Va (ms; 1862-63; black)

	Paid 10*	150.

Christiansville

Christiansville V[a] (ms; 1861-63; brown)

Ms	Pd 10 cts	150.

Chula Depot

PAID

A

CHULA DEPOT / VA (26; 1861-62; black)

A	PAID [no rate]	175.
	Same, 5 (ms)	150.

Churchland

PAID 5

A

PAID 10

B

PAID 10

C

PAID 10

D

10

E

CHURCHLAND / Va. (31; 1861-62; red)

A	PAID 5 (red)	200.
B	PAID 10 (red)*	200.
C	PAID 10 (red)	200.
D	PAID 10 (red)*	300.
E	10 (red) [due]	200.

Churchville

PAID

A

CHURCHVILLE / VA (25; 1861-64; black)

A	PAID, 5 (ms)*	175.
Ms	Paid 10	150.
	Due 10*	150.
	Drop 2 cts Due (no postmark)	200.

City Point

PAID 5

A

CITY POINT / Va (31; 1861-62; black)

A	PAID 5	200.
Ms	Paid 5 Cts	150.
	Pd 5	150.
	Due 5*	150.

Clarksville

PAID

A

PAID 5

B

PAID 5

C

PAID 10

D

CLARKSVILLE / Va. (33; 1861-63; black, red, blue, green)

A	PAID, 2 (ms)*	300.
B	PAID 5	200.
	Same (blue)*	300.
	Same (green)	500.
C	PAID 5	175.

	Same (red)	200.
D	PAID 10*	175.
	Same (blue)*	300.

Clifton

Clifton (ms; 1861; black)

Ms	P 5 cts*	150.

Clover Depot

A

Clover Depot V (ms; 1861-63; black)
CLOVER DEPOT / VA (26; 1861; black)

A	PAID, 5¢ (ms)	175.
Ms	Paid 5	150.

Cobham

A

COBHAM / V^a (28; 1861-62; black)

A	PAID, 5 (ms)	175.
B	PAID 10 [not illustrated]	200.

Cole's Ferry

A

Coles Ferry Va (ms; 1861; black)

A	PAID 5	200.
Ms	Paid 5	150.

Collerstown

COLLIERSTOWN / Va (34; 1861-64; blue)

Ms	Paid 5*	175.
	Paid 10	150.
	Due 10	150.

Columbia

Columbia Va (ms; 1861-63; black)

Ms	Paid 5	150.
	Paid 10*	150.

Conrads Store

Conrads Store Va (ms; 1863-64; black)
CONRADS STORE / Va. (30; 186-; black)

Ms	Due 10*	150.

Cool Well

Cool Well (ms; 1861; black)

Ms	Paid 5	150.

Coopers

Coopers Va (ms; 1861-62; black)

Ms	Paid 5	150.

Covesville

Covesville (ms; 1862-64; black)
COVESVILLE / VA (33; 1861-62; black, red)

A	PAID 5 [not illustrated]*	200.
Ms	Pd 5	150.
	Paid 5	150.
	Paid 10	150.

Covington

COVINGTON / VA (26; 1861-62; black)

Ms	Paid 5	150.
	Pd 5	150.
	Due 5	150.

Crows

Crows (ms; 1861; black)

Ms	Paid 5	150.

Culpepper Court House

PAID

A

B

C

CULPEPER C. H. / Va. (33 YD; 1861; black)
CULPEPER C. H. / Va. (32; 1862-63; black)

A	PAID [no rate]*	200.
	Same, 5 (ms)*	200.
	Same, 10 (ms)	200.
B	PAID 5	200.
C	DUE 10	200.
Ms	Paid 5*	150.
	Paid 10*	150.
	Due 10*	150.

Cumberland Court House

Cumberland C. H. Va (ms; 1861-65; black)

Ms	Due 10*	150.

Cypress Island

Cypress Island (ms; 1862; black)

Ms	Paid 5*	150.

[*]	symbol used after an item description to mean an unsupported listing
ms	manuscript

Danville

PAID A
PAID B  
PAID 5 C
PAID 5 D 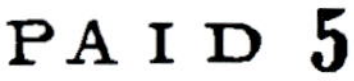
PAID 5 E 
PAID 5 F 
PAID 5 G 
PAID 10 H 
PAID 10 I 
PAID 10 J 
DUE 10 K 
DUE 10 L
FORWARDED N
FORWARDED 10 O 
FREE P
MISSENT Q
MISSENT R

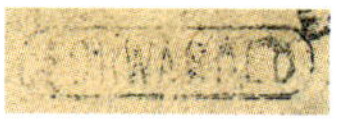

DANVILLE / V^{A} (31; 1861-65; black, blue)
DANVILLE / VA. (31 YD; 1863; black)

A	PAID, 5 (ms)*	175.
	Same, 10 (ms)*	175.
B	PAID, 5 (ms)*	200.
C	PAID 5	200.
D	PAID 5*	200.
E	PAID 5*	200.
F	PAID 5*	200.
G	PAID 5	200.
	Same (blue)*	300.
H	PAID 10*	200.
I	PAID 10*	200.
	Same (blue)	300.
J	PAID 10*	200.
K	DUE 10*	200.
L	DUE 10	200.
	Same (red)	300.
M	ADVERTISED (blue) [not illustrated]	500.
N	FORWARDED	300.
	Same, with DUE 10 (Type L)	500.
O	FORWARDED 10	500.
P	FREE with “Forward to” (ms)	500.
Q	MISSENT (blue)	500.
R	MISSENT (blue)	750.

Darlington Heights

Darlington Heights (ms; 1862; black)

Ms	Due 5*	150.

Dayton

Dayton Va (ms; 1862-64; black)

Ms	Paid 5*	150.
	Paid 10*	150.

Diamond Grove

Diamond Grove Va (ms; 1861; black)

Ms	Post Office Business Free*	IH

Dinwiddie Court House

Dinwiddie C. H. Va. (ms; 1861-63; black)

Ms	Paid 5¢	150.

Dover Mills

Dover Mills Va (ms; 1864; black)

Ms	Pd / 10	150.

Drake's Branch

PAID A
PAID 5 B 
PAID 10 C

DRAKE'S BRANCH / VA (31; 1861-65; blue)

A	PAID (blue) [no rate]*	300.
B	PAID 5 (blue)*	300.
C	PAID 10 (blue)	300.

Draper's Valley

Drapers Valley V^{a} (ms; 1861-63; black)

Ms	5 Paid	150.

Dublin

A

Dublin Vª (ms; 1861; black)
DUBLIN / VA (26; 1861-64; black, blue)

A	PAID [no rate]	200.
	Same (blue) [no rate]	300.
	Same, 5 (ms)*	200.
	Same, 10 (ms)*	200.
B	DUE (arc) / 10 [not illustrated]*	200.
C	FORWARDED [not illustrated]*	300.
D	MISSENT [not illustrated]*	300.
Ms	Paid 5	150.
	Paid / 5	150.
	Due 5¢	150.
	Due 10*	150.

Duffields [West Virginia]

Duffields Va (ms; 186-; black)

Ms	Due 30	500.

Dumfries

PAID

A

DUMFRIES / Va. (29; 1861-62; black)

A	PAID [no rate]*	200.

Dunmore [West Virginia]

Dunmore (ms; 186-; black)

Ms	Paid 10 cts	300.

Dupree's Old Store

Duprees Old Store Va (ms;1862; black)

Ms	Paid / 2 (pencil)	300.

Dyers Store

Dyers Store Va (ms; 186-; black)

Ms	Paid 10	150.

Eastville

PAID 5

A

EASTVILLE / Va. (30; 1862-65; black)
EASTVILLE / Va. (35; 1861; black)

A	PAID 5 (blue)	300.

Edenburgh

PAID 5

A

Edenburg Va (ms; 1861; black)
Edinburg Va (ms; 186-; black)
EDENBURGH / Va (36; 1861; black)

A	PAID 5*	200.
Ms	Paid 5*	150.
	Pd 10	150.

Edge Hill

Edge Hill (ms; 1862; black)

Ms	P 10	150.

Edmund's Store

Edmunds (ms; 1861-62; black)
Edmunds Store Vª (ms; 1861-63; black)

Ms	Paid 5*	150.
	Official Business / Free	IH

Edom

Edom Va (ms; 1861-63; black)

Ms	Paid 5	150.

Emaus

Emaus Va (ms; 1861; black)

Ms	Paid 5*	150.

Emory

PAID

A

PAID 5

B

PAID 5

C

D

DUE

E

EMORY / Va. (33; 1861; blue, red)

A	PAID 5 (blue)	300.
	Same (blue), struck twice	500.
B	PAID 5 (blue)*	300.
C	PAID 5 (red)*	300.
D	5 [due] (blue)	300.
	Same, [due], struck twice	500.
E	DUE (blue) [no rate]	300.

Estillville

Estillville Va (ms; 1861; black)

Ms	Paid 5*	150.
	Paid 10*	150.

Fabers Mills

Fabers Mills Va (ms; 1865; black)

Ms	Paid 10	150.

[*] symbol used after an item description to mean an unsupported listing

YD year date

Fairfax Court House

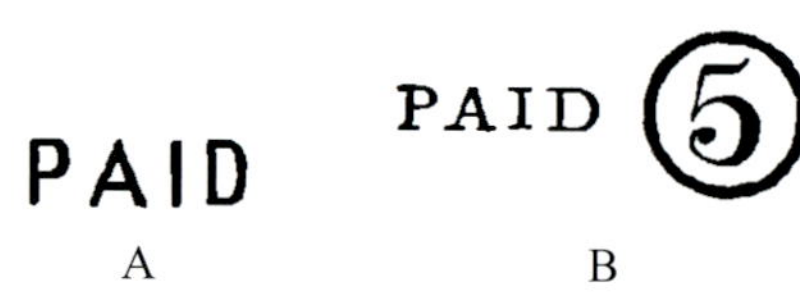

A B

C

D

E

Fairfax C H / Va (ms; 1861; black)
FAIRFAX C. H. / Va. (34; 1861; black)
FAIRFAX C. H. / Vª (34 YD; 1861; black)

A	PAID, 5 (ms)*	175.
B	PAID 5*	175.
C	PAID 5	175.
D	PAID 10	175.
E	DUE 5	200.
Ms	Paid 5	150.
	Pd 5	150.
	Pd /5	150.
	(Pd) 5	150.
	Paid 10	150.
	Due 5	150.
	Due 10	150.

Fairfax Station

A

B

Fairfax Sta (ms; 1861; black)
Fairfax Station (ms; 1861; black)
FAIRFAX STATION / Vª (31 YD; 1861; black)

A	PAID 5	150.
B	PAID 10*	150.
Ms	Paid 5	100.
	Paid 5 cts	100.
	Pd 5	100.
	Pd 5 (pencil)	100.
	Paid 10 cts	100.
	Due 5*	100.
	Due 10*	100.
	5 [due]	100.
	10 [due]	100.

Fairfield

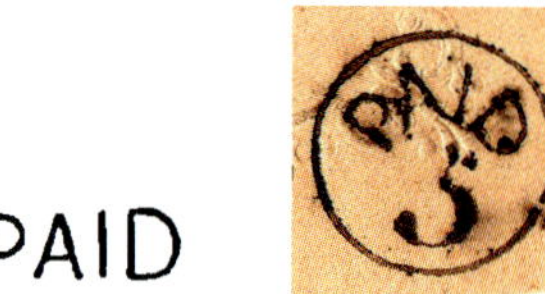

A B

Fairfield Va (ms; 1863; black)
FAIRFIELD / VA (25; 1862; black)
FAIRFIELD / Va. (30; 1861-62; black, brown)

A	PAID (brown), 5 (ms)	200.
	Same, 10 (ms)	200.
B	PAID 5	300.
Ms	Paid 5*	150.
	Due 10 cts*	150.
	Forwd 5	150.

Falmouth

Falmouth Va (ms; 1861; black)

Ms	Pd 5*	150.

Fancy Hill

A B

FANCY HILL / VA. (32; 1861-64; blue)

A	PAID (blue) [no rate]	300.
	Same (blue), 5 (ms)*	300.
	Same, 10 (ms)*	175.
	Same (blue), 10 (ms)*	300.
B	PAID 5 (blue)*	150.

Farmville

A B

FARMVILLE / VA (32; 1861-64; black, blue)

A	PAID, 5 (ms)*	175.
	Same, 5 (ms), revalued 10 (ms)*	200.
B	PAID, 5 (ms)	175.
	Same, 10 (ms)	175.
C	DUE / 10 [not illustrated]*	175.

Fayetteville [West Virginia]

A

Fayetteville / Va. (37; 1861; black, brown)

A	PAID [no rate]	300.
	Same (brown), 5 (ms)	500.

Fincastle

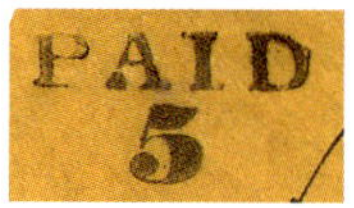

A

Fincastle Va. (ms; 1862; black)

FINCASTLE / VA. (26; 1861-65; black)

A	PAID 5	175.
B	FREE [not illustrated]*	IH
Ms	Paid 5*	150.
	Paid 10	150.
	Paid 20	200.

Fine Creek Mills

Fine Creek Mills (ms; 1861; black)

Ms	Paid 5 cts	150.

Finney Mills

Finney Mills Va. (ms; 1861; black)

Ms	Paid 5	150.

Fishersville

A

Fishersville Va (ms; 1865; black)
FISHERSVILLE / Va. (31; 1861; black)

A	PAID 5	175.
Ms	Paid 10*	150.

Fleetwood Academy

Fleetwood Academy Vª (ms; 1861; black)

Ms	Paid / 5	175.

Floyd Court House

Floyd C H (ms; 1861-62; black)

Ms	Paid / 5	150.
	Paid / 10	150.

Flukes

Flukes Va (ms; 1861-62; black)

Ms	Paid 5 cts	150.

Ford's Depot

Fords Va (ms; 1861-64; black)
Ford's Depot Va (ms; 1861; black)

A	PAID, 5 (ms) [not illustrated]*	175.
Ms	Pd 5	150.

Forest Depot

A B

C D

Forest Depot (ms; 1861-1862; black)
FOREST DEPOT / Va (31 NOR; 1861; black)
FOREST DEPOT / Va (36;1861-63; black)

A	PAID 5	300.
B	PAID 5 CENTS	500.
C	PAID 5 [altered "3"]	500.
D	PAID 5*	200.
E	PAID 10 [not illustrated]*	200.
F	10 [due] [not illustrated]*	200.
Ms	Paid 5*	150.
	Paid 10	150.
	Due 5	150.

Forkland

Forkland Vª (ms; 1861; black)

Ms	Paid 5	150.

Forksville

Forksville Va (ms; 1861; black)

Ms	P. O. B. E. J. Moseley, PM.*	IH

Fort Blackimore

Fort Blackimore (ms; 1861; black)

Ms	Paid 5	150.

Frankford [West Virginia]

Frankford Va (ms; 1861-62; black)

Ms	Due*	150.

Franklin [West Virginia]

FRANKLIN / VA (32; 1862; black)

Ms	Paid, 5 cts	150.

Franklin Depot

A B

FRANKLIN DEPOT / VA (25; 1861-63; blue)
FRANKLIN DEPOT / Vª (32; 1862-64; blue)

A	PAID 5 (blue)	300.
B	DUE 10 (blue)	300.
Ms	Due 10*	150.

Fredericksburg

A

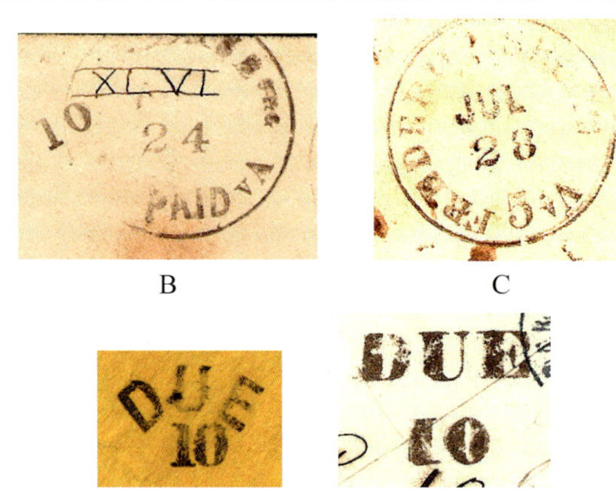

B C

E F

FREDERICKSBURG VA / 5 (32; 1861-62; black)
FREDERICKSBurg VA / PAID (32; 1862; black)
FREDERICKSBURG / VA (32; 1861-62; black)
FREDERICKSBURG / VA (34 YD; 1861-63; black)

A	5 (integral postmark) with PAID	300.
	Same, revalued 10 (ms)	300.
B	PAID (integral postmark) with 10	300.
C	5 (integral postmark) [due]	300.
D	DUE / 5 [not illustrated]*	200.
E	DUE 10	200.
F	DUE 10	200.
Ms	Paid 5*	150.
	Due 5*	150.
	Due 10*	150.

Frederickshall

PAID

A

F Hall (ms; 186-; black)
F Hall Va (ms; 1861-64; pencil)
FREDERICKSHALL / VA (29; 1861; black)

A	PAID, 5 (ms)*	200.
Ms	due 10	150.

Front Royal

A

FRONT ROYAL / Va. (33; 1861; black)

A	PAID, 5 (ms)	200.
	Same, 5 revalued 10 (ms)*	250.

Gainesville

Gainesville Va (ms; 1861; black)
GAINESVILLE / Va. (36; 1861-63; black)

Ms	Paid 5*	150.
	Paid 10*	150.
	Due 10*	150.

Garys Store

Garys Store Va (ms; 1863; black)

Ms	Pd 10c	150.

Garysville

Garysville (ms; 1862; black)

Ms	Paid 5	150.

Gauley Bridge [West Virginia]

Gauley Bridge Vª (ms; 1861; black)

Ms	Paid 5	150.

Gilboa

Gilboa Va (ms; 186-; black)

Ms	Paid / 10	150.

Gilmores Mills

Gilmores Mills (ms; 1861-64; black)

Ms	Paid 5*	150.
	Paid 10 cts*	150.

Gish's Mills

Gishs Mills Va (ms; 1862-64; black)

Ms	Due 10*	150.

Glade Spring Depot

GLADE SPRING DEPOT / VA (33; 1861-64; black, blue)

Ms	Paid [no rate]	150.
	5 Paid	150.
	Due 10*	150.

Gladesborough

Gladesboro Va. (ms; 1861-63; black)

Ms	5 cts Paid	100.
	Paid 10	100.
	Paid / 10 cts	150.
	10 cts Paid	100.

Glenwood

Glenwood Va (ms; 1861-63; black)

Ms	Paid 5	150.

Gold Hill

Gold Hill (ms; 1861; black)

Ms	Paid / 5	150.

Goochland Court House

Goochland C H V (ms; 1861; black)
Goochland C H Vª (ms; 1861-65; black)

Ms	Paid 5	150.
	Paid 10	100.

[–]	symbol used in place of value to mean insufficient information to assign a price
[?]	symbol used to mean unknown measurement, date or color
[*italic*]	value typeface indicating the item is difficult to price accurately

Goodson

A

B

C

GOODSON / Va. (34; 1861-64; black)
Goodson (28 x 5 SL; 186-; black)

A	PAID 5*	200.
B	PAID 5	200.
C	PAID 10*	200.
D	DUE / 10 [not illustrated]*	200.
Ms	Due 10	150.

Gordonsville

A

B

D

E

F

G

Gordonsville Va (ms; 1864; black)
GORDONSVILLE / VA (26; 1861-63; black)
GORDONSVILLE / Va. (31; 1861-64; black)
GORDONSVILLE / VA. (32 YD; 1862; black)

A	PAID [no rate]*	200.
	Same, 5 (ms)*	200.
B	PAID 5	250.
C	PAID 5 [not illustrated]*	200.
D	PAID 10	200.
E	PAID 10*	200.
F	DUE 5*	200.
	Same, revalued DUE 10 (Type G)*	250.
G	DUE 10	200.
	Same, revalued 20 (blue pencil)	300.
Ms	Due 10	150.
	20 cts [due]	200.

Goshen Bridge

Goshen Bridge Va (ms; 1861-64; black)

Ms	Paid 5*	150.
	Paid 10	150.

Graham's Forge

Grahams Forge Va (ms; 1862-63; black)

Ms	Paid 10	150.

Gravel Hill

Gravel Hill Va (ms; 1861-64; black)

Ms	Paid 5	150.
	Paid 10*	150.

Green Bay

Green Bay Va (ms; 1863; black)

Ms	Paid 10c*	150.

Green Hill

Green Hill (ms; 1864; black)

Ms	Paid 10 cents	150.

Greenville

A

Greenville Va (ms; 1862; black)
GREENVILLE / Va. (31; 1861-62; black)

A	PAID 5	200.
	Same, struck twice [10c]*	300.
Ms	Paid 20*	200.
	10 [due]	150.

Greenwood Depot

Greenwood Depot (ms; 1864; black)
GREENWOOD DEPOT / Va. (36; 1861-63; black)

Ms	Paid 10	150.
	Due 5	150.

Grove Landing

Grove Landing V[a] (ms; 1861-62; black)

Ms	Paid 5	150.
	Paid / 5	150.
	Paid 5, revalued 10 (ms)*	200.
	Paid / 10	150.
	Due 10*	150.

Groveton

Groveton Va (ms; 1862; black)

Ms	Paid 5	150.

Guiney's

Guineys Va (ms; 1862-64; black)
GUINEYS / VA (26; 1862; black)
GUINEYS / Va (31; 1862-64; black)

A	DUE 10 [not illustrated]*	200.
Ms	Paid 5*	150.
	10 cts due	150.
	Due / 10	150.
	10 due	100.

	due 10 (pencil)	150.
Pk	No rate or paid marking	150.

Hague

Hague Va (ms; 1861-62; black)

Ms	Due 10*	150.

Halifax Court House

PAID

A

Halifax C H / Va (ms; 1864; black)
HALIFAX C. H. / Va. (34; 1861-63; black)

A	PAID, 5 (ms)*	200.
Ms	Due 10*	150.
	Missent & Ford	100.

Hamilton

Hamilton Va (ms; 1861; black)

Ms	Paid 5*	150.

Hampden Sidney College

PAID

A

H S College (ms; 1861-63; black)
HAMPDEN SIDNEY COLLEGE / VA (26; 1861-63; black)

A	PAID, 5 (ms)*	200.
Ms	Paid 5*	150.

Hanging Rock [West Virginia]

Hanging Rock / V^a^ (ms; 1861; black)

Ms	Paid	300.

Hanover Court House

Hanover C H (ms; 1864; black)
HANOVER C H / Va (36; 1861-65; black)

Ms	Due 10	150.

Hardwicksville

Hardwicksville (ms; 1862-63; black)

Ms	paid 5 cts	150.
	Pd 5	150.
	Due 10 cts	150.

Harper's Ferry [West Virginia]

PAID

A B

C

Harpers Ferry Va (ms; 1861; black)
HARPERS FERRY / VA (26 DC YD; 1861; black)

A	PAID [no rate]	500.
	Same, 5 (ms)*	500.
B	PAID 5	300.
C	PAID 10	300.

Harrisonburg

A B

Due 10 10

E F

Harrisonburg (ms; 1864; black)
H Burg (ms; 1865; black)
HARRISONBURG / Va. (30; 1861-63; black)

A	PAID [no rate]	200.
B	PAID 5	200.
C	PAID 10 [not illustrated]*	200.
D	DUE 10	200.
E	DUE / 10 [not illustrated]*	200.
F	10 [due]*	175.
Ms	Paid 10	150.
	Due 2 cts*	150.
	Due 5	150.
	Due 10*	150.
	5 [due]	150.

Harveys Store

Harveys Store Va (ms; 1861-63; black)

Ms	Paid 5*	150.

Hay Market

HAY MARKET / VA (35; 1861; black)

A	PAID [not illustrated], 5 cts (ms)*	200.
Ms	Paid 5*	150.

Hayes' Store

Hayes' Store Va (ms; 1862; black)

Ms	Paid / 10	150.

Healing Springs

PAID 5

A B

HEALING SPRINGS / VA. (26; 1861-62; black)

A	PAID, 5 (ms)	200.
	Same, 10 (ms)*	200.
B	PAID 5*	200.
Ms	Due 5*	150.
	Ford 5	150.

HEATHSVILLE

Heathsville Va (ms; 1861-62; black)

Ms	Pd 5cts	150.

HERMITAGE

Hermitage Va (ms; 1861-62; black)

Ms	Pd 5	150.

HICKORY FORK

HICKORY FORK / Va (36; 1861-62; black)

A	PAID, 5 (ms) [not illustrated]*	200.
Ms	Paid 5	150.

HICKSFORD

PAID
A

PAID 5
B

PAID 10
C

10
D

HICKSFORD / Va (30; 1861-65; black, green)

A	PAID (green) [no rate]*	500.
	Same, 5 (ms)*	200.
	Same, 10 (ms)*	200.
	Same (green), 10 (ms)	500.
B	PAID 5*	200.
C	PAID 10*	200.
D	10 [due]*	200.
Ms	Due 10*	150.

HIGHTOWN

Hightown (ms; 1861-62; black)

Ms	Paid 5	150.
	Due 10	150.

HOPE MILLS

Hope Mills Va (ms; 1861; black)

Ms	Paid 5	150.

HORSE PASTURE

Horse Pasture Va (ms; 1863; black)
HORSE PASTURES / VA (26; 1861-63; black)

Ms	Paid 5	150.
	Pd 5	150.
	Paid 10	150.

HOWARDSVILLE

PAID
A

PAID 5
B

PAID 10
C

PAID 10
D

Howardsville Va (ms; 1861; black)
HOWARDSVILLE / VA (32; 1861-65; black, blue)

A	PAID, 10 (ms)*	200.
B	PAID 5 (blue)*	300.
C	PAID 10 (blue)	300.
D	PAID 10	200.
	Same (blue)*	300.

HUNTERSVILLE [WEST VIRGINIA]

DUE 5
A

Huntersville Va (ms; 1861-62; black)

A	DUE 5	400.
Ms	Paid 5	200.
	Pd 5	200.
	Paid 10*	200.
	Pd 10	200.
	10 / Paid	200.
	due 5	200.
	5 Due	200.
	due 10	200.
	Due /10	200.
	10 / Due	200.

HUTTONSVILLE [WEST VIRGINIA]

Huttonsville Va (ms; 1861; black)

Ms	Paid [no rate]	300.
	Paid 5	300.
	Free	500.

HYCO

Hyco Va (ms; 1864; black)

Ms	Pd 10	150.

IRISBURG

Irisburg Va (ms; 1861-64; black)

Ms	Paid 5	150.
	Paid 10	150.

IVY DEPOT

Ivy Depot Va (ms; 1861-65; black)
IVY DEPOT / VA (26; 1862; black)

Ms	5 Pd	150.
	10 [due]	150.

Jamestown

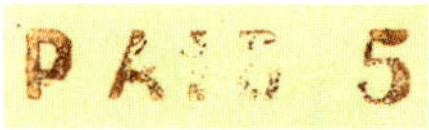

A  B

Jamestown V[a] (ms; 1861; black)
JAMESTOWN / Va (35; 1861-62; black)

A	PAID 5	200.
B	PAID 10*	200.
C	5 [due] [not illustrated]*	200.
Ms	Paid 5	150.

Jarratts

Jarratts V[a] (ms; 1862; black)
Jarretts Station Va (ms; 1864; black)

Ms	Paid 5	150.
	Paid 10*	150.

Jeffress' Store

Jeffress's Store Va (29; 1861; black)

Ms	Free Official Business*	IH

Jennings Gap

Jennings Gap Va (ms; 1863; black)

Ms	Paid 5*	150.
	Paid 10	150.

Jerusalem

Jerusalem V[a] (ms; 1861-63; black)

Ms	Paid 5	150.

Jetersville

Jetersville, Va (ms; 1864; black)
JETERSVILLE / VA (31; 1861; black)

Ms	Paid 5*	150.
	Paid 5, revalued 10 (ms)	150.
	Paid 10*	150.

Jonesville

A

Jonesville Va (ms; 1861-62; black)
JONESVILLE / VA (32; 1861-62; blue-green)
JONESVILLE / Va. (37; 1862; blue)

A	PAID 5 (blue-green)*	400.
	Same (blue)	500.

Jumping Branch [West Virginia]

Jumping Branch Va (ms; 1861; black)

Ms	pd 5 (pencil)	400.

Junction

Junction V[a] (ms; 1861-64; black)

Ms	Paid 5	150.
	Paid 10*	150.
	Due 10	150.

Kabletown [West Virginia]

Kabletown Va (ms; 1861; black)

Ms	Paid 5	300.

Kanawha Court House [West Virginia]

A  B

KANAWHA C. H. / Va. (30; 1861-62; black)

A	PAID [no rate]	500.
	Same, 5 (ms)	500.
B	PAID [no rate]*	500.
	Same, 5 (ms)	500.

Kennedys

Kennedys Va (ms; 1861-62; black)

Ms	Due 10	150.
	Official Business Free*	IH

Kerr's Creek

Kerr's Creek / V[A] (ms; 1861; black)

Ms	Paid 5	150.

Keswick Depot

A  B

KESWICK DEPOT / VA. (26; 1861-65; black)

A	PAID [no rate]	200.
	Same, 5 (ms)*	200.
B	PAID 5	300.

Keysville

A 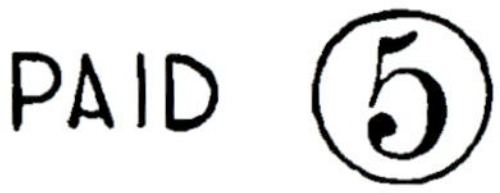 B

Keysville V (ms; 1863; black)
KEYSVILLE / VA. (26; 1861-64; black)

A	PAID 5	200.
B	PAID 5*	200.

Kirkwood

Kirkwood Va (ms; 1861-64; black)

Ms	Paid 5*	150.

Lacey Spring

Lacy Springs Va (ms; 186-; black)

Ms	Paid 5 cts	150.
	Paid 10*	150.

La Fayette Hill

La Fayette Hill Va (ms; 1861; black)

Ms	5 / Paid	150.

Lancaster Court House

A

LANCASTER C.H. / Va. (30; 1861; black)

A	5c. LAN. C.H., pd (ms)*	400.

Lawrenceville

A

Lawrence Va (ms; 186-; black)
LAWRENCEVILLE / Va. (30; 1861-62; blue)

A	PAID (blue) [no rate]*	300.
	Same (blue), 10 (ms)	300.
B	FREE [not illustrated]*	IH
Ms	Free Post Office Business*	IH
	Free P. Off. Business*	IH
	P. Off. Business. Free	IH
	P. O. B.*	IH

Leatherwood's Store

Leatherwood V[a] (ms; 1861-64; black)

Ms	Paid 5	150.
	Paid 10	150.
	Paid / 10	150.

Lebanon

A B

LEBANON / VA. (29; 1861-63; blue, green)

A	PAID 5 (blue)	300.
	Same (green)*	500.
B	PAID 10 (blue)*	300.
Ms	Paid 10*	150.

Leesburg

A

LEESBURG / VA (26 DC YD; 1861-62; black)
LEESBURG / Va. (29; 1861-62; black)

A	PAID [no rate]	200.
	Same, 5 (ms)	200.
	Same, 10 (ms)*	200.
Ms	Paid 5*	150.
	5 [due]*	150.

Leesville

A

Leesville Va (ms; 1861-63; black)
LEESVILLE / VA. (30; 1861-63; black)

A	PAID 5	200.
B	PAID 10 [(not illustrated]*	200.
Ms	Pd 10 cts*	150.

Lewis' Store

Lewis's Store Va (ms; 1861-62; black)

Ms	Due 10	150.

Lewisburgh [West Virginia]

5

A *a*

Lewisburg V[a] (ms; 1861-64; black)
LEWISBURG / VA. (26; 1861-65; black)
LEWISBURGH / V[A] (31; 1861-62; black)

A	PAID 5	300.
	Same, struck twice, 5 (ms)	500.
	Same, plus 5 (Type a)*	500.
Ms	Paid 5	200.
	Due 5*	200.
	10 Due	200.

[*]	symbol used after an item description to mean an unsupported listing
IH	used in place of listing value when the item is held by an institution

Lexington

PAID A  B  C 
PAID 10 D  E  F

LEXINGTON / Va. (32; 1861-65; black, blue)

A	PAID (blue), 5 (ms)*	300.
	Same (blue), 15 (ms)*	500.
B	PAID 5	200.
	Same (blue)	300.
	Same (blue), revalued 10 (Type a)*	500.
C	PAID 10	200.
D	PAID 10 (blue)	300.
E	5 (blue) [due]	300.
F	10 (blue) [due]	300.
Ms	Paid 5*	150.
	Due 10	150.

Note: Some strikes of the Type B and C markings show portions of a large outer circle.

Liberty

A

Liberty Va (ms; 1863; black)
LIBERTY / Va. (34; 1861-64; black)

A	PAID 5	200.
Ms	Paid 5¢	150.
	Pd 5c	150.
	Ford Due 5¢	150.

Lisbon

A

LISBON / VA. (32; 1861-63; black, brown)

A	PAID (brown), 5 (ms)	300.

Locust Bottom

Locust Bottom Va (ms; 1861-62; black)

Ms	Paid 5 cts	150.

Lombary Grove

Lombary Grove Va (ms; 1861-63, black)

Ms	Official business*	IH

Long Glade

Long Glade Va (ms; 186-; black)

Ms	Paid 10*	150.

Longwood

Longwood V[a] (ms; 1861-62; black)

Ms	Paid / 5	150.
	Paid 10*	150.

Loretto

Loretto Va (ms; 1861-64; black)

Ms	10 [due]*	150.

Louisa Court House

PAID 5

A

LOUISA C. H. / Va. (30; 1861-62; blue)

A	PAID 5 (blue)*	150.
B	DUE 10 (blue) [not illustrated]*	150.
Ms	Due 10*	150.

Lovingston

PAID 5 Paid 10

A 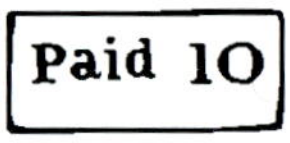 B

LOVINGSTON / Va (37; 1861-63; black)

A	PAID 5*	200.
B	Paid 10*	500.

Lowsville

Lowsville V[a] (ms; 1861-63; black)

Ms	Paid 10	150.

Lowry

Lowry Va (ms; 1861-63; black)

Ms	Paid 5	150.
	Paid 10¢	150.

Loyds

Loyds Va (ms; 1861-64; black)

Ms	Paid 5	150.
	Due 10*	150.

Lunenburg Court House

Lunenburg C H Va (ms; 1861; black)

Ms	Paid 5	200.

Luney's Creek [West Virginia]

Luneys Creek Va (ms; 1861; black)

Ms	Paid 5	150.
	Pd 5	150.

Luray

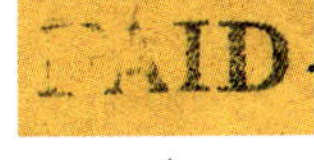

A

B

Luray Va (ms; 1863-65; black)
LURAY / V^{a} (30; 1861-63; black, blue)

A	PAID (blue) [no rate]	300.
B	PAID 5	200.
	Same (blue)	300.
Ms	Paid 5	150.
	Pd 5	150.
	Paid 10	150.
	Due 10*	150.

Lyells Store

Lyells Store (ms; 1861-62; black)

Ms	Paid 5 cts	150.

Lynchburg

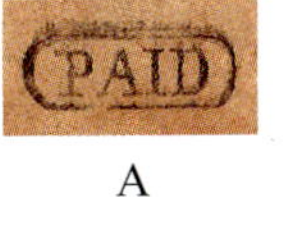

A

B

C

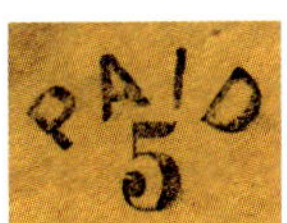

D

E

F

G

H

I

J

K

L

M

N

O

No Postmark
LYNCHBURG / Va. (32; 1861-64; black, blue, red, green, brown, violet)
LYNCHBURG / VA (32 YD; 1861-62; black, blue, red-brown)

A	PAID [no rate]	200.
B	PAID 2*	300.
	Same (blue)*	300.
C	PAID 5	200.
	Same, revalued 10 (Type E)	300.
D	PAID 5	200.
	Same (blue)*	300.
	Same (blue), revalued 10 (type J)*	300.
E	PAID 10	200.
F	PAID 10	200.
	Same (blue)*	300.
	Same (red-brown)*	300.
G	PAID 20*	300.
H	DUE 5	200.
	Same (blue)	500.
I	DUE 10 (blue)	300.
	Same (red-brown)	300.
J	10 [due]*	200.
K	ADVERTISED 2	500.
L	FORWARDED. (blue)	500.
	Same (blue) with FREE (blue) (Type N)	750.
M	FORWARDED 10 (blue), due (ms)	500.
N	FREE	300.
	Same (blue)	500.
O	MISSENT	400.
Ms	P. O. B.*	IH

Macon

Macon V^{a} (ms; 1861-65; black)

Ms	Paid 5	150.
	Paid 5 cts	150.
	Paid 10	150.

Madison Court House

A

B

C

D

MADISON C. H. / VA (26; 1861-63; black)
MADISON C. H. / VA. (30; 1863-65; black)

A	Paid 5	300.
B	PAID 5*	250.
C	PAID 5	200.
D	PAID 10*	200.
E	DUE (circle), 10 (circle) [not illustrated]*	200.
Ms	Due 10*	150.

Madison Mills

Madison Mills Va. (ms; 1861; black)

Ms	Paid 5 cts	150.

Malonesville

Malonesville / Va (ms; 1861-64; black)

Ms	Unpaid	175.

Manchester

Manchester Va (ms; 1861; black)
MANCHESTER / Va. (37; 1861; black)
MANCHESTER / VA (31 YD; 1861-63; black)

A	DUE (arc) / 10 [not illustrated]*	200.
Ms	Due 5*	150.
	Due 10*	150.

Maple Lawn [West Virginia]

Maple Lawn Va (ms; 1861; black)

Ms	Paid 5 cts	150.

Marion

A  B  C  D

MARION / VA (31; 1861-64; black)

A	PAID [no rate]	200.
B	PAID 5	200.
C	PAID 5*	200.
D	PAID 10	200.
Ms	Due 10*	150.

Martin's Mills

Martins Mills Va (ms; 1863; black)

Ms	Due 10¢	150.

Martinsburg [West Virginia]

A B

MARTINSBURG / Va. (32; 1861-62; black)

A	PAID [no rate]	300.
B	PAID 5	300.
Ms	Paid 5*	200.
	Due 5	200.

Martinsville

A  B  C

MARTINSVILLE / VA (26; 1861-63; black)
MARTINSVILLE / Va. (36; 1861; black)

A	PAID, 5 (ms)*	200.
B	PAID 5	300.
C	PAID 5	200.
D	FREE [not illustrated]*	IH
Ms	Official S. Pretzel PM*	IH

Marysville

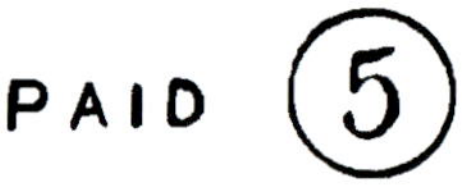

A

Marysville Va (ms; 1861-63; black)

A	PAID 5*	200.
Ms	Paid / 10	150.

Matamoras

MATAMORAS / VA (33; 1861; black)

Ms	Paid 5	100.

Max Meadows

Max Meadows Va (ms; 1861-62; black)

Ms	Paid 5	150.

Mayo Forge

Mayo Forge (ms; 186-; black)
Mayo Forge Va (ms; 1861-63; black)

Ms	Paid 5	150.
	Paid 10	150.

McDowell

McDowell V (ms; 1861-63; black)

Ms	Paid 5	150.
	Paid 10*	150.

McFarland's

Macfarlands Va (ms; 1861-64; black)
MacFarlands Va (ms; 186-; black)

Ms	Paid 5	150.
	Paid 5 cts	150.
	10 [due]	150.

McGaheysville

PAID ⑤

A B

McGaheysville Va (ms; 1862; black)
MCGAHEYSVILLE / VA (33; 1861-64; black)

A	PAID, 5 (ms)	200.
B	PAID 5*	200.
Ms	paid 10	150.

Meadow Dale

Meadow Dale (ms; 1861-62)

Ms	Pad 5	150.

Meadsville

Meadsville (ms; 1862; black)
MEADSVILLE / VA (37; 1861; black)

Ms	Paid [no rate]*	150.
	Paid 5*	150.
	10 [due]	150.

Mechum's River

PAID PAID 

A B

MECHUM'S RIVER / VA. (34; 1861-63; black)

A	PAID, 5 (ms)	200.
B	PAID 5	200.

Melrose

Melrose Va (ms; 1861; black)

Ms	Paid 5*	150.

Meyerhoeffer's Store

Meyerhoeffer's Store Va. (ms; 1862; black)

Ms	Paid 5¢	150.

Middle Mountain

Middle Mountain (ms; 1862; black)

Ms	Paid 5	150.

Middlebrook

Middlebrook / Va (ms; 1861-65; black)

Ms	Paid 10	150.

Middleburg

PAID

A

MIDDLEBURG / Va. (30; 1861-62; black)

A	PAID, 5 (ms)	200.

Middletown

Middletown Va (ms; 1861-64; black)

Ms	Due 10*	150.

Middleway [West Virginia]

A

Middleway Va (ms; 1861-62; black)
MIDDLEWAY / Va. (32; 1862; black)

A	PAID, 5 (ms)	200.
Ms	Paid 5*	150.

Midlothian

A

Midlothian Va (ms; 1862-64; black)
MIDLOTHIAN / V^A (32; 1861-63; black, brown)

A	PAID [no rate]*	200.
	Same (brown) [no rate]	300.

Milford

Milford Va (ms; 1861-64; black)

Ms	Due 10*	150.

Millboro Springs

Millboro Springs (ms; 1861-63; black)

Ms	Paid 10¢	150.
	Due 5*	150.

Millwood

A

MILLWOOD / Va. (33; 1861-62; black)

A	PAID, 5 (ms)	200.
	Same, 10 (ms)*	200.
B	PAID (serif), 5 (ms) [not illustrated]	200.

Mitchells Station

Mitchells Sta (ms; 1861-63; black)

Ms	Paid / 5	150.
	Paid 10*	150.

Moffatts Creek

Moffatts Creek V^a (ms; 1861-64; black)

Ms	Paid 10	150.

[*italic*]	value typeface indicating the item is difficult to price accurately
ms	manuscript

Monterey

A B

C  E

C D E

MONTEREY / Va. (30; 1861-62; black)

A	PAID 5*	200.
B	PAID 5	250.
	Same, struck twice	300.
C	PAID 10*	200.
D	5 [due]*	200.
	Same, due (ms)	175.
	Same, due (blue pencil)	200.
E	10 [due]	200.
Ms	Paid 10	150.
	Due 10*	150.
	10 [due]	150.

Montgomery Springs

A

MONTGOMERY SPRINGS / VA (26; 1861-63; black, blue)

A	PAID (blue), 5 (ms)*	200.
	Same (blue), 10 (ms)	200.
Ms	Paid / 10	150.

Montross

A

Montross V^a (ms; 1861; black)

A	PAID, 5 (ms)	200.
Ms	Paid 5*	150.
	10c [due]	150.

Moorefield [West Virginia]

PAID

A

MOOREFIELD / Va. (30; 1861; black)

A	PAID, 5 (ms)	200.

Moore's Ordinary

Moores Ordinary Va (ms; 1861-65; black)

Ms	Due 10*	150.

Morris

Morris Va (ms; 1861-64; black)

Ms	Paid 10*	150.

Mossingford

Mossingford Va (ms; 1861-63; black)
Mossingford V^a (ms; 1861; black)
MOSSINGFORD / VA (26; 1861; black)

Ms	Paid 5	150.

Mossy Creek

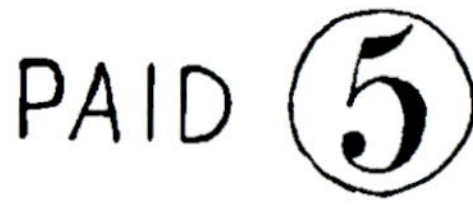

A

Mossy Creek Va (ms; 1861-63; black)
MOSSY CREEK / AUGUSTA CO / Va (37; 1861-63; black)

A	PAID 5	300.
B	PAID 10 [not illustrated]*	300.
Ms	Paid 5*	175.
	Paid 10	175.

Mount Airy

Mount Airy Va (ms; 1861-62; black)

Ms	Paid 5	150.

Mount Crawford

A

B

a

Mt. Crawford Va (ms; 186-; black)
MOUNT CRAWFORD / VA. (29; 1863; black)
MOUNT CRAWFORD / VA. (33; 1861-63; black)

A	PAID 5	200.
	Same, revalued 10 (Type *a*)*	200.
B	PAID 10*	200.
Ms	Due 10*	150.
	Due 20	150.
	10 [due]*	150.

Mount Jackson

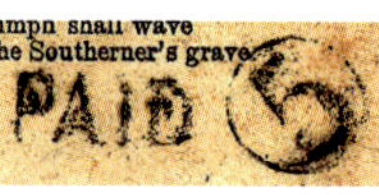

A

MOUNT JACKSON / Va. (32; 1861-64; black)

A	PAID 5	200.
	Same, struck twice	300.
Ms	Due 10*	150.
	10 [due]*	150.

Mount Laurel

PAID

A

Mt Laurel Va (ms; 1863; black)
MOUNT LAUREL / VA (26; 1861; black)

A	PAID [no rate]*	200.

Mount Meridian

PAID 5

A

Mt Meridian (ms; 1861; black)

A	PAID 5*	200.
Ms	Paid 5*	150.
	Due 10	150.

Mount Pleasant

Mount Pleasant Va (ms; 1861; black)

Ms	Paid 5	150.

Mount Sidney

PAID   PAID 5   10

A   B   *a*

M^T SIDNEY / Va. (31; 1861-64; black)

A	PAID, 10 (ms)*	200.
B	PAID 5	200.
	Same, revalued 10 (Type *a*)*	250.
	Same, revalued 10 (ms)	250.
C	PAID 10 [not illustrated]*	300.
Ms	Paid 10	150.

Mount Vinco

Mt Vinco (ms; 1861; black)

Ms	Paid 5	150.

Mouth of Wilson

Mouth Wilson Va (ms; 1863; black)

Ms	Paid / 10	150.

Naffs

Naffs V^a (ms; 1861; black)

Ms	Paid 5	150.

Natural Bridge

Natural Bridge Va (ms; 1861; black)
N(atural) Bridge Va (ms; 1865; black)
NATURAL BRIDGE / Va. (35; 1861; black)

A	5, Due (ms) [not illustrated]	200.

Nebraska

Nebraska Va (ms; 1861-64; black)

Ms	Paid 5*	150.
	Official WAJ PM*	IH

Nellys Ford

Nellys Ford (ms; 1863-64; black)

Ms	Paid 10	150.

Nelson Station

NELSON STATION / VA (26; 1861-65; black)

Ms	Paid 5*	150.
	Paid 10*	150.
	Due 10*	150.

New Canton

New Canton (ms; 1861-63; black)
NEW CANTON / VA (26; 1861-62; black)

Ms	Paid / 5 ct	150.

New Castle

New Castle Va (ms; 1861-64; black)

Ms	Paid 10 revalued Due 10 (ms)	150.

New Glasgow

New Glasgow (ms; 1863; black)
NEW GLASGOW / VA (26; 1861; black)
NEW GLASGOW / Va (30; 1861; black)

Ms	Paid 5*	150.

New Kent Court House

PAID

A

NEW KENT C. H. / VA. (26; 1861; black)

A	PAID, 5 (ms)	200.

New London

PAID   PAID 5

A   B

New London (ms; 1863; black)
NEW LONDON / Va. (36; 1861-63; black, red)

A	PAID, 10 (ms)*	250.
B	PAID 5	250.

New Market

A

B

NEW MARKET / VA. (33; 1861-64; black)

A	PAID, 5 (ms)*	200.
B	DUE 10	200.
Ms	Paid 5	150.
	Paid 10*	150.
	Due 5*	150.
	Due 10	150.
	Way	150.

Newbern

A

NEWBERN / Va. (31; 1862; black)
NEWBERN / VA. (25; 1862-64; black)

A	PAID [no rate]	200.
Ms	Due 10	150.

News Ferry

News' Ferry P. O. (ms; 1861; black)
News' Ferry Va (ms; 1861-65; black)

Ms	Paid / 5	150.

Newtown Stephensburgh

A

NEWTOWN STEPHENSBG / Va. (35; 1861-62; black)

A	PAID 5	200.
Ms	Paid 5*	150.
	Due 10*	150.

Norfolk

A

PAID 5

B

C

D

PAID 10 C.

E

PAID 10

F

20

G

Due 5

H

I

J

K

NORFOLK / VA (26 DC YD; 1861-62; blue)
NORFOLK / Va. (32 YD; 1861-62; blue)

A	PAID (blue) [no rate]	200.
B	PAID 5 (blue)*	300.
C	PAID 5 C. (blue)	200.
	Same (blue), revalued 10 (Type J)*	300.
D	PAID 5 (blue)	300.
E	PAID 10 C. (blue)	200.
	Same (blue), revalued 5 (Type I)*	300.
F	PAID 10 (blue)	300.
G	PAID 20 (blue)	500.
H	Due 5*	200.
I	5 (blue) [due]	200.
J	10 (blue) [due]	200.
	Same (blue), Due (pencil)	200.
K	FREE (blue)	300.
Ms	Due 2 (pencil)	150.

North Garden

North Garden Va (ms; 1861-65; black)

Ms	Paid 5	150.
	Due*	150.

North Mountain

N Mountain Va (ms; 1862-64; black)

Ms	5 [due]	150.

Nottoway Court House

Nottoway C H Va (ms; 1861; black)
NOTTOWAY CH / Va. (32; 1861-63; black)

Ms	Paid 5 cts	150.

Oak Forest

Oak Forest Va (ms; 1861-65; black)

Ms	Paid 10¢	150.

Oak Park

Oak Park Va (ms; 1861; black)

Ms	Paid 5	150.

Old Church

A

Old Church V^a (ms; 1861-64; black)
OLD CHURCH / Va. (31; 1861; black)

A	5, Paid (ms)	200.
Ms	Paid 5	150.

Orange Court House

A  B 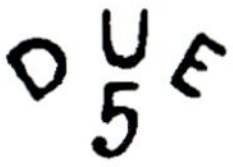 C  D

O C House (ms; 1862; black)
ORANGE – C. H. / V^a (30; 1861-63; black, brown, red)
ORANGE C. H. / VA. (30 YD; 1861-63; black, red)

A	PAID (brown), 5 (ms)*	300.
	Same (red), 5 (ms)	300.
	Same, 10 (ms)*	200.
	Same (red), 10 (ms)*	300.
B	PAID 10*	200.
C	DUE 5*	200.
D	DUE 10	200.
	Same (red)	300.
E	10 (red) [due] [not illustrated]*	300.
F	FORWARDED [not illustrated]	300.
Ms	5 [due]	150.
	Due 10*	150.
	Due / 10 (pencil)	150.

Otter Bridge

Otter Bridge Va (ms; 1861-63; black)

Ms	Paid 5*	150.

Paineville

Paineville Va (ms, 1861-62; black)

Ms	Paid 10 cts	150.

Palmyra

A  B

PALMYRA / Va. (32; 1861-64; black, brown)

A	PAID [no rate]*	100.
	Same (brown), [no rate]	300.
	Same (brown), struck twice [no rate]	300.
	Same, 5 (ms)*	200.
	Same (brown), 5 (ms)	300.
	Same, 10 (ms)*	200.
B	PAID 10*	200.

Paris

Paris, Va (ms; 1861; black)

Ms	Paid 5*	150.

Parnassus

Parnassus (ms; 1861-63; black)

Ms	Paid 10	150.

Partlows

Partlows Va (ms; 1861-64; black)

Ms	Paid 10 cts*	150.

Patrick Court House

A

Pat C H Va (ms; 1861; black)
Patrick C H Va (ms; 1861; black)
PATRICK C H / Va (38; 1861-64; black)

A	PAID [no rate]	200.
	Same, 5 (ms)*	200.
B	FREE [not illustrated]*	IH
C	POST OFFICE BUSINESS FREE [not illustrated]*	IH
Ms	Paid 5	150.
	Due 5*	150.
	Official Business L. G. Rucker P. M.*	IH

Patrick Springs

Patrick Springs V^a (ms; 1861; black)

Ms	Paid 5 cts	150.

Pattonsburg

A  B 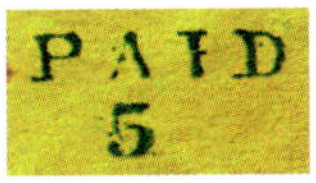 C  D  E  *a*

PATTONSBURG / Va. (34; 1861-65; black, blue)

A	PAID, Paid 10 (ms)*	200.
B	PAID 5 (blue)	300.
C	PAID 5 (blue)	300.
	Same (blue), revalued 10 (ms)	300.
D	PAID 10 (blue)*	300.
E	MISSENT (blue) with FORWARD 5¢ (blue) (Type *a*)	500.
Ms	Due 10*	150.

Pedlar's Mills

Pedlar Mills (ms; 1861-64; black)

Ms	Paid 5 cts	150.

Pemberton

Pemberton Va (ms; 1861-64; black)

Ms	Paid / 5 cts	150.
	Paid / 10 cts	150.

Penn's Store

A

PENN'S STORE / Va. (30; 1861-62; black)

A	PAID, 5 (ms)	200.

Penola

Penola Va (ms; 1861-63; black)

Ms	Paid 5*	150.

Petersburg

A B C D E F G H J K L

M N

a

PETERSBURG / Va. (30; 1861-65; black, blue, red)
PETERSBURG Va / 3 cts (30; 1861; blue)
PETERSBURG VA / 5 cts (30; 1861-65; blue)

A	PAID (blue), 2 (red pencil)	500.
	Same (blue), 5 (ms)*	300.
	Same (blue), with "5 cts" integral rate postmark (type a)	300.
B	PAID 5 (blue)	300.
C	PAID 5 (blue)	300.
D	PAID 10 (blue)	300.
E	PAID 10 (blue)	300.
F	PAID 10 (blue)	300.
G	PAID 10 (blue)	300.
H	DUE 5 (blue)	500.
I	DUE 10 (blue) [not illustrated]*	300.
J	5 (blue), Due (ms)*	300.
K	10 [due]	200.
L	10 (red) [due]	300.
	Same (blue), Due (ms)	300.
M	ADVERTISED	500.
N	MISSENT (blue)	500.
Ms	Due 5	150.
	Due 40	150.
	Ford 5	200.

Peterstown

Peterstown (ms; 186-; black)
PETERSTOWN / VA. (?; 1862; black)

Pk	No rate or paid marking	150.

Piedmont

Piedmont, Va (ms; 1861; black)

Ms	Paid 5	150.

Piedmont Station

PIEDMONT STATION / VA. (26; 1861-62; black)

A	PAID, 5 (ms) [not illustrated]*	200.
Ms	Paid 5*	150.
	Paid 10	150.

Pierceville

Pierceville (ms; 1861-63; black)

Ms	Paid 10	150.

Pigeon Run

Pigeon Run Va (ms; 1861-62; black)

Ms	P 5*	150.

Pittsylvania Court House

A B C

D E

F G

H I

Pitt^a C H (ms; 1865; black)
PITTSYLVANIA C. H. / Va. (34; 1861-65; black, red)

A	PAID, 5 (ms)*	200.
B	PAID, 10 (ms)*	200.
C	PAID 5	200.
D	PAID 5*	200.
E	PAID 5	200.
F	PAID 10	200.
G	PAID 10	200.
H	PAID 10*	200.
I	PAID 10*	200.
Ms	Paid 10*	150.
	Due 10	150.

Plantersville

Plantersville / V^a (ms; 1861-63; black)

A	FREE [not illustrated]*	IH
Ms	Pd 10	150.

Pleasant Gap

Pleasant Gap (ms; 1861-63; black)

Ms	Pd 5	150.

Pleasant Valley

Pleasant Valley Va (ms; 1861; black)

Ms	Paid 5*	150.

Port Conway

Port Conway V^a (ms; 1861-62; black)

Ms	Paid 5	150.

Port Republic

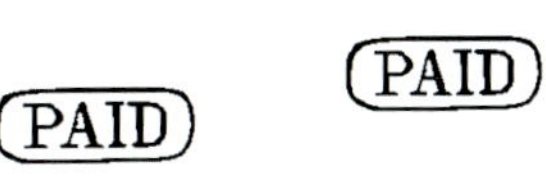

A B

C

PORT REPUBLIC / VA (26; 1861-63; black)

A	PAID, 5 (ms)*	200.
B	PAID 5*	200.
C	PAID 10*	200.

Port Royal

A

PORT ROYAL / Va. (30; 1861; black, blue)
PORT ROYAL / Va. (37; 1862; black)

A	PAID 5	200.

Portsmouth

A B

C D E

F G

PORTSMOUTH / VA (26 DC YD; 1861-62; blue)
PORTSMOUTH / Va (32; 1861; blue)
PORTSMOUTH Va / 10 Paid (32 YD; 1861; blue)

A	PAID 5 (blue)	300.
B	PAID 5 (blue)	300.
	Same (blue), revalued 10 (Type D)*	500.

	Same (blue) with “10 Paid” postmark*	500.
C	PAID 10 (blue)*	300.
D	10 Paid (blue) (integral postmark)	500.
E	10 (blue) [due]*	300.
F	FORWARDED (blue)	500.
G	FREE (blue)	500.
Ms	Pd 10	150.
	Due 10*	150.

Powhatan Court House

POWHATAN C. H. / VA (32; 1861-65; black)

Ms	Paid 5	150.
	Paid 10*	150.

Prince George Court House

Pr Geo CH (ms; 1862; black)
Prince George C. H. (ms; 1861; black)

Ms	Paid 10	150.

Princeton [West Virginia]

PRINCETON / VA. (32; 1862; black)

Ms	Paid 5	150.

Proctors Creek

Proctors Creek Va (ms; 1861-1862)
PROCTOR’S CREEK / V^{a} (32 YD; 1862-63; black)

A	DUE (arc) / 10 [not illustrated]*	200.
Ms	Due 10*	150.

Prospect

Prospect Va (ms; 1861-62; black)

Ms	Paid 5*	150.

Pruntys

Pruntys V^{a} (ms; 1862; black)

Ms	Paid 10	150.
	Free	150.

Racoon Ford

Racoon Ford Va (ms; 1862; black)

Ms	Paid 5*	150.

Raleigh Court House [West Virginia]

Raleigh C H V^{a} (ms; 1861; black)

Ms	Paid 5	150.

Randolph Macon College

A

RANDOLPH MACON COLLEGE / VA (26; 1861-62; black)

A	PAID 5 CSA	500.

Rapid Ann Station

A B

C

Rapid Ann St Va (ms; 1862; black)
RAPID ANN STATION / VA (26; 1861-63; black)

A	PAID 5	200.
B	PAID 10*	200.
C	DUE 10	200.

Ravens Nest

Ravens Nest Va (ms; 1861; black)

Ms	5c / Paid	150.

Red House

A B

RED HOUSE / Va. (33; 1861; red)
RED HOUSE / Va. (30x21 NOR Arc; 1862; red)

A	PAID (red), 5 (ms)*	300.
B	PAID 5 (red)*	300.

Rehoboth

Rehoboth Va (ms; 1862; black)

Ms	Paid / 5	150.

Retreat

Retreat Va (ms; 1861; black)

Ms	Due 5*	150.

Riceville

Riceville Va (ms; 1861; black)

Ms	Paid / 5c (pencil)*	IH

Richmond

A B C

D E

F

G  H

I  J  K

L

M  N  O

P  Q

R  S

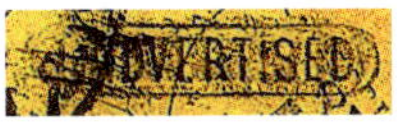

T  U

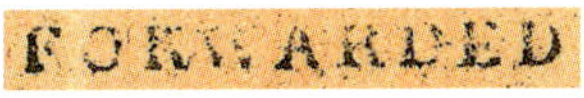

V

W

X  Y

Z  AA  BB

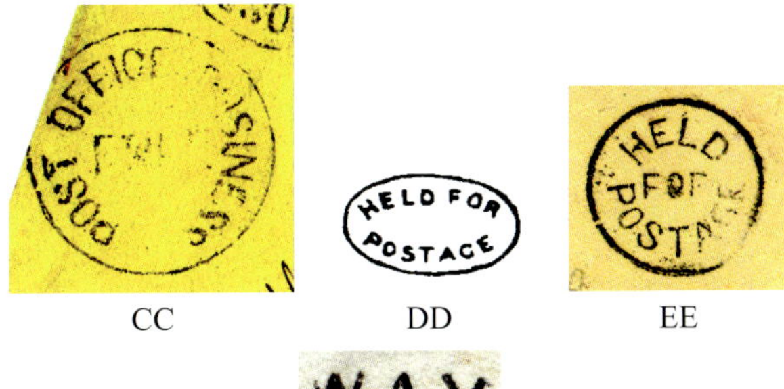

CC DD EE

FF

RICHMOND / Va. (31 YD; 1861; black)
RICHMOND / V^A (32.5 YD; 1861-62; black)
RICHMOND / Va. (31 YD; 1862-63; black, blue)
RICHMOND / VA. (30 YD; 1862-63; black)
RICHMOND / V^a (33; 1863-65; black)
RICHMOND / V^a (33; 1863-65; black, blue)
RICHMOND / VA. (32 YD; 1863-65; black, blue)
RICHMOND / VA. (32; 1863; black, blue)
RICHMOND / VA. (30.5; 1863; black)

A	PAID [no rate]	200.
	Same, 2 (pencil)	500.
	Same, 2 (crayon)	500.
	Same, 4 (crayon)	
	Same, 20 (ms)	500.
	Same, 20 (pencil)	500.
	Same, 30 (ms)*	500.
	Same, 50 (ms)*	500.
B	PAID 2	500.
C	PAID 2	750.
D	PAID 5	100.
	Same, revalued 10 (Type R)	200.
E	PAID 5	100.
	Same, revalued 10 (ms)*	200.
	Same, revalued 10 (Type H)	200.
F	PAID 5 Cts	100.
	Same, revalued 10 (ms)*	200.
	Same, revalued 10 (Type H)*	200.
	Same, struck three times	500.
G	PAID 10	100.
H	PAID 10	100.
I	PAID 15	500.
	Same, revalued 10 (Type H)	750.
J	PAID 20	500.
K	PAID 20	500.
L	PAID 30	750.
M	DUE 2	500.
N	DUE 2	500.
O	DUE 5	150.
	Same (blue)	
	Same, revalued 10 (ms)*	250.
P	DUE 10.	100.
	Same, rerated DUE 2 (Type M)	500.
Q	DUE 10	100.
	Same (blue)	
	Same, revalued DUE 5 (Type N)*	300.
	Same, plus 2 (ms)*	500.

	Same, plus Due 10 / 20 (ms)*	750.
R	10 [due]*	150.
S	20 [due]	200.
T	ADVERTISED	500.
U	ADVERTISED 2	500.
V	FORWARDED	500.
W	FORWARDED 5*	500.
X	FORWARDED 5	500.
Y	FORWARDED 5	500.
Z	FORWARDED 10	500.
	Same (blue)	1,000.
AA	FREE	500.
	Same (blue)	
BB	FREE*	500.
CC	POST OFFICE BUSINESS /FREE	750.
DD	HELD FOR POSTAGE*	750.
	Same, Due 2 (ms)*	1,000.
EE	HELD FOR POSTAGE	750.
	Same, with DUE 2 (Type N)	1,000.
FF	WAY	1,000.
Ms	Paid 5	150.
	Due 2 (pencil)	250.
	Due 5	150.
	Due 10*	150.

Ridgeway

Ridgeway Vª (ms; 1863; black)

Ms	Paid 10	150.

Rippon [West Virginia]

Rippon Va (ms; 1861; black)

Ms	Paid 5*	150.
	Paid 10	150.

Rochelle

Rochelle Va (ms; 1861-63; black)

Ms	Paid 5*	150.

Rockbridge Baths

Rockbridge Baths Va (ms; 1861-63; black)

Ms	Paid 5*	150.
	Due 10*	150.

Rock Fish

A

ROCK FISH / VA. (31; 1861-62; brown)

A	PAID, 5 (ms)	500.

Rockfish Depot

Rockfish Depot (ms; 1861-64; black)

Ms	Paid 5*	150.
	Paid 10	150.

Rocky Mount

No Postmark

Ms	Paid 5	150.
	Paid 10*	150.

Note: One example of the manuscript "Paid 5" marking includes the signature of the postmaster, Jno. D. Noble. This suggests that the marking may have been prepared in advance as a provisional. At this time there is insufficient information to make this conclusion.

Romney [West Virginia]

A B C

ROMNEY / VA (25; 1861-62; black)

A	PAID 5	500.
B	5 [due]*	400.
	Same, Due (ms)	500.
C	10 [due]	400.
	Same, Due (magenta) (ms)	500.

Rose Mills

Rose Mills Vª (ms; 1861-63; black)

Ms	Paid 10	150.

Round Hill

Round Hill Va (ms; 1861-62; black)

Ms	Paid 5*	150.

Rural Retreat

Rural Retreat (ms; 1861-63; black)

Ms	Paid 5*	150.
	Paid 10	150.

Salem

Salem (ms; 1861-64; black)

SALEM / Va. (34; 1861-62; black)

A	PAID, 5 (ms) [not illustrated]*	200.
Ms	Paid 5	150.
	Paid 5 c	150.
	Paid 5 (pencil)	150.
	Paid 10	150.
	Due 10 (pencil)	150.

Salem Fauquier

PAID

A

SALEM FAUQUIER / VA (36; 1861-62; black)

A	PAID, 5 (ms)*	200.
	Same, 10 (ms)	150.

Salt Sulphur Springs [West Virginia]

A

Salt Sulphur Springs Va (ms; 1862-65; black)
SALT SULPHUR SPRINGS / Va. (36; 1861; black)

A	PAID 10*	200.
Ms	Paid 10*	150.

Saltville

A B

Saltville (ms; 1863; black)
SALTVILLE / VA (26; 1862-63; black, blue)
SALTVILLE / VA (34; 1863; black; green)

A	PAID [no rate]	200.
	Same (blue) [no rate]	300.
	Same (green) [no rate]	500.
B	PAID, 5 (ms)*	200.
	Same (green), 5 (ms)*	500.
	Same, 10 (ms)*	200.
Ms	Paid*	150.
	Paid 10	150.
	Due 5*	150.

San Marino

San Marino (ms; 1863-65; black)

Ms	Paid 10¢	150.

Sandy Plains

Sandy Plains Va (ms; 186-; black)

Ms	Pd 10	150.

Sangerville

A

Sangerville Va (ms; 1864; black)
SANGERVILLE / V^A (31; 1862-64; black)

A	10, Paid (ms)	200.
Pk	No rate or paid marking	150.

Scottsburg

PAID 10

A B

Scottsburg Va (ms; 1861-63; black)
SCOTTSBURG / VA (26; 1861; black)

A	PAID [no rate]	200.
	Same, 5 (ms)	200.
B	PAID 10	200.
Ms	Paid 5	150.

Scottsville

Scottsville Va (ms; 1861-62; black)
SCOTTSVILLE / VA (32; 1861-63; black)

A	PAID (oval box) [no rate] [not illustrated]*	200.
B	PAID 10 [not illustrated]*	200.
C	10 [due] [not illustrated]	200.
Ms	Pd 5*	150.
	Paid 10*	150.

Selma

Selma V^a (ms; 1861-64; black)

Ms	Paid 5*	150.
	Paid 10	150.

Seven Mile Ford

7 Mile Ford Va (ms; 1862-64; black)

Ms	Paid*	150.
	Paid 5*	150.

Shady Grove

Shady Grove Va (ms; 1861; black)

Ms	Paid 5 Post Office Business*	IH

Shannon Hill

Shannon Hill (ms; 1862; black)

Ms	Due 10*	150.
	Forwarded from Shannon Hill*	300.

Shepherdstown [West Virginia]

PAID

A B

SHEPHERDSTOWN / VA. (31; 1861-62; black)

A	PAID, 10 (ms)*	300.
B	PAID 5	300.
Ms	Due 5	200.

Sherando

Sherando Va (ms; 1861-63; black)

Ms	Paid 10*	150.

Singers Glen

Singers Glen Va (ms; 1861; black)

Ms	5 Paid*	150.

Smithfield

PAID

A B

PAID X V X

C D *a*

SMITHFIELD / V^a (30; 1861-64; red, orange)

A	PAID (red) [no rate]*	300.
	Same (red), 15 (ms)*	500.
B	PAID V (red)	300.
	Same (red), revalued 10 (Type *a*)	500.
C	PAID X (red)*	300.
D	V [5] (red), Due (ms)	300.
Ms	Paid 10	150.

Somerville

Somerville Va (ms; 1861; black)

A	PAID (box), 10 (circle) [not illustrated]*	200.

Sparta

Sparta Va (ms; 1861-62; black)

Ms	Paid 5*	150.

Sperryville

SPERRYVILLE / Va. (37; 1861-63; black)

Ms	Paid 5 cts*	150.

Spottsylvania Court House

PAID 10

A

Spottsyla C. H. Va (ms; 1861; black)

A	PAID 10*	200.
Ms	Paid 5	150.

Stanardsville

Stanardsville Va (ms; 1861-63; black)

STANARDSVILLE / Va (37; 1862; black)

Ms	Pd 10*	150.

Staunton

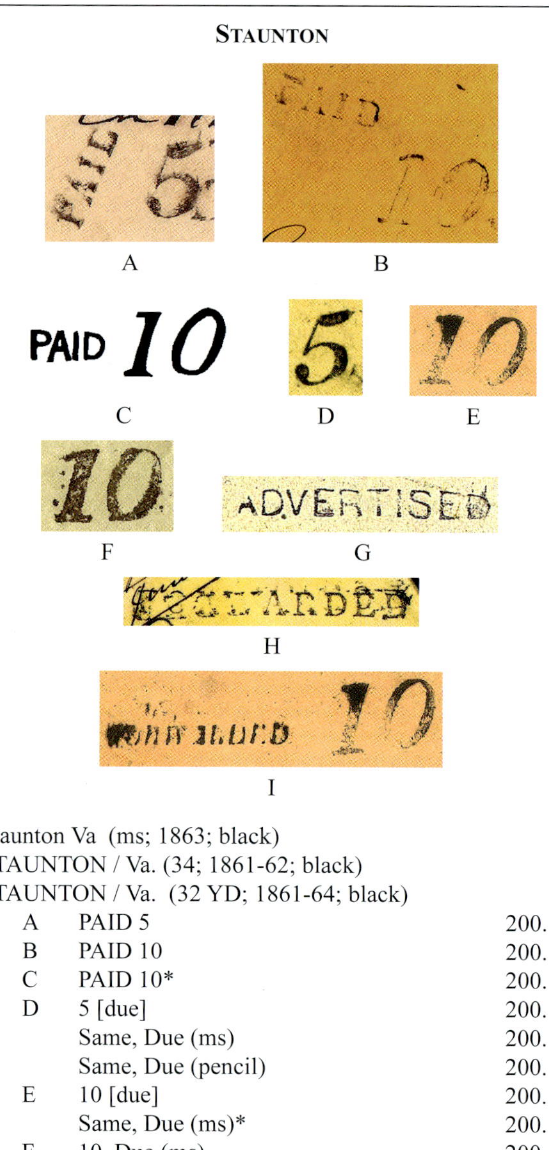

A B C D E F G H I

Staunton Va (ms; 1863; black)

STAUNTON / Va. (34; 1861-62; black)

STAUNTON / Va. (32 YD; 1861-64; black)

A	PAID 5	200.
B	PAID 10	200.
C	PAID 10*	200.
D	5 [due]	200.
	Same, Due (ms)	200.
	Same, Due (pencil)	200.
E	10 [due]	200.
	Same, Due (ms)*	200.
F	10, Due (ms)	200.
	Same, Ford (ms)	200.
G	ADVERTISED	300.
H	FORWARDED	300.
I	FORWARDED 10	300.
Ms	Due 40*	300.

Steele's Tavern

Steeles Tavern V^a (ms; 1861-64; black)

Ms	Paid 5	150.
	Pd 10*	150.

Stephenson's Depot

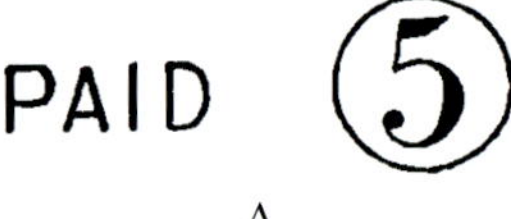

A

STEPHENSON'S DEPOT / VA (31; 186-; black)

A	PAID 5*	200.

Stevensville

Stevensville Va (ms; 1861-62; black)

Ms	Paid 10*	150.

Stony Creek Warehouse

Stony Creek W. H. Va (ms; 1861-63; black)
Stony Creek Va (ms; 1864-65; black)

Ms	Due 10*	150.

Stony Point

A

Stony Point (ms; 1862; black)
STONY POINT / VA (32; 1861-63; black, magenta)

A	PAID 5	200.
	Same (magenta)	500.
Ms	Paid 40c	150.

Stony Point Mills

Stony Pt Mills Va (ms; 1862-65; black)

Ms	Paid 40c	200.
	Due 10*	150.
	Due 40*	200.
	Free P. O. Business*	IH

Strait Creek

Strait Creek Va (ms; 1861; black)

Ms	Pd / 5	150.

Strasburg

A  B

C  D

Strasburg (ms; 1864; black)
STRASBURG / VA. (26; 1861; black)

A	PAID 5	200.
	Same, revalued 10 (type D)*	300.
B	PAID 10	200.
C	5 [due]*	200.
	Same, due (ms)	200.
D	10 [due]*	200.
Ms	Due 5*	150.
	Due 10*	150.

Stribling Springs

STRIBLING SPRINGS / VA (33; 1861-63; black)

A	PAID 10 [not illustrated]*	200.
Ms	Paid 10	150.

Sturgeonville

Sturgeonville (ms; 1861; black)

Ms	Paid 5	150.

Suffolk

A  B  C

D  E  F

SUFFOLK / Va. (34; 1861-62; black)

A	PAID, 5 (ms)*	200.
B	PAID 5	200.
C	PAID 5	200.
	Same, revalued 10 (type F)	300.
D	PAID 10*	200.
E	5 [due]	200.
	Same, Due (ms)*	200.
F	10 [due]	200.
Ms	Paid 5*	150.

Summers

A

SUMMERS / Va. (31; 1861; black; green)

A	5 [due]	200.
	Same (green) [due]*	500.

Summit Point

Summit Point (ms; 1861-62; black)

Ms	Paid 5	150.

Sunny Side

Sunny Side Va (ms; 1861-62; black)

Ms	Paid 5	150.
	Paid 5 cts	150.

Surry Court House

Surry C H V^a (ms; 1861-63; black)

Ms	Paid 5	150.
	Paid 5¢	150.
	Paid / 5¢	150.
	Paid 10	150.

Sutherland's

Sutherlands Va (ms; 1861-65; black)

Ms	Paid [no rate]	150.
	Paid 5	150.

Sweet Chalybeate

PAID

A

SWEET CHALYBEATE / VA (26; 1861-62; black)

A	PAID, 5 (ms)	200.
	Same, 10 (ms)*	200.

Sweet Springs [West Virginia]

PAID

A

Sweet Springs Va (ms; 1863; black)

SWEET SPRINGS / Va. (37; 1861; black)

A	PAID, 5 (ms)	200.

Tappahannock

Tappahannock (ms; 1862; black)

TAPPAHANNOCK / Va. (33; 1861-64; black)

A	PAID 5 [not illustrated]	200.
Ms	Pd / 5	150.

Taylor's Store

Taylors Store Va (ms; 1861-63; black)

Ms	Paid 10	150.

Taylorsville

PAID (5) (10)

A B

Taylorsville Va (ms; 186-; black)

TAYLORSVILLE / VA (25; 1861-63; black; red)

A	PAID 5	200.
	Same, 5 struck twice	300.
B	10 [due]*	200.
Ms	Due 10	150.

Tazewell Court House

PAID (5)

A

Tazewell CH Va (ms; 1863; black)

TAZEWELL C H / Va. (37; 1861-64; black, blue)

A	PAID 5	200.

Tenth Legion

Tenth Legion Va (ms; 1861-63; black)

Ms	Due 10*	150.

Thaxton's

Thaxtons Va (ms; 1861-65; black)

Ms	Due 10	150.

The Plains

The Plains (ms; 1861-62; black)

Ms	Paid 5*	150.
	Paid 10*	150.

Thoroughfare

Thoroughfare Va (ms; 1861-62; black)

Ms	Due 5*	150.

Timber Ridge

Timber Ridge V^a (ms; 1861-64; black)

Ms	Paid / 5	150.

Timberville

Timberville Va (ms; 1861-64; black)

Ms	Paid 10 cents*	150.

Travellers Repose [West Virginia]

Travellers Repose V. (ms; 1861-64; black)

Travellers Repose V^a (ms; 1861; black)

Travelers Repose V^a (ms; 1861; black)

Traveler's Repose Va (ms; 186-; black)

Travl Repose Va (ms; 186-; black)

Trav Repose (ms; 1861; black)

Trav Repose V^a (ms; 186-; black)

Trav Repose Va (ms; 1861; black)

Ms	Paid 5	300.
	Paid / 5	300.
	Pd / 5	300.
	Pd / 5¢	300.
	Paid 10	300.
	Pd / 10	300.
	Due / 5	300.
	Due 10	300.
	due 10	300.

Trevilian's Depot

A

Trevilians Va (ms; 1864-65; black)
TREVILIAN'S DEPOT / VA (30; 1861-63; black)

A	PAID 5	200.
Ms	Paid 10*	150.

Tudor Hall

PAID  

A B C

D E

F *a*

Tudor Hall Va (ms; 1861; black)
TUDOR HALL / Vª (30 YD; 1861-62; black)
TU DOR HALL / Vª (30 YD; 1862; black)
TUDOR HALL / VA. (30 YD; 1861-62; black)

A	PAID, 5 (ms)*	100.
	Same, 20 (ms)*	200.
B	PAID 5	100.
	Same, revalued 10 (type C)*	200.
C	PAID 10	150.
D	DUE 5	100.
E	DUE 10	100.
F	10, Due (ms)*	100.
	Same, revalued 20 (Type *a*), Due (ms)*	200.
	Same, [due]	150.
Ms	Paid 5*	100.
	Paid 10*	100.
	Due 5 (pencil)	100.
	Due 10*	100.
	Due 20*	100.
	5 (ms) [due]	100.
	10 (ms) [due]*	100.

Tye River Warehouse

A

Ty R Whouse (ms; 1862; black)
Tye River Warehouse (ms; 1861-64; black)

A	PAID 5 (over PAID 3 marking)*	500.
B	PAID 10 [not illustrated]*	200.
Ms	Paid 5	150.
	Paid / 5cts	150.
	Pd 5	150.
	Paid 10 cts*	150.

Union [West Virginia]

A

Union Vª (ms; 1861-64; black)
UNION / Va (30; 1861-62; black)

A	PAID, 5 (ms)	500.
Ms	Paid 5	300.

Union Furnace

Union Furnace Va (ms; 1864; black)
Union Furnace Vª (ms; 1861-64; black)

Ms	Paid 10	150.

Union Level

Union Level Va (ms; 1863; black)

Ms	Official Business*	IH

Union Mills

Union Mills (ms; 1861-64; black)

Ms	Paid 10	150.

University of Virginia

A B

PAID 5 5

C D

E F

UNIVERSITY OF VIRGINIA / VA (26 DC YD; 1861-64; black, blue)
UNIVERSITY of / Va. (32; 1864; black, blue)

A	PAID (blue) [no rate]	300.
B	PAID 5	200.
	Same (blue)	300.
C	PAID 5*	200.
D	5 [due]*	200.
E	FORWARDED (blue)	500.

F	FORWARDED 5 (blue)	500.
Ms	10 [due]	150.

Upperville

PAID 5

A

UPPERVILLE / Va. (30; 1861-62; black)

A	PAID 5 (altered 3c handstamp)*	300.

Verdierville

PAID 5

A

VERDIERSVILLE / Va. (32; 1861; black)

A	PAID 5	200.

Verdon

Verdon V[a] (ms; 1861-63; black)

Ms	Paid [no rate]	150.

Villa

Villa Va (ms; 186-; black)

Ms	Paid / 10	150.

Wakefield Station

Wakefield Station V[a] (ms; 1861-63; black)

Ms	Paid 5	150.

Warrenton

PAID 5 PAID 5 5

A B C

WARRENTON / Va. (29; 1861-62; black)

A	PAID 5*	200.
B	PAID 5*	200.
C	5 [due]*	175.
Ms	Paid / 5	150.
	Paid 10*	150.

Warrenton Springs

Warrenton Springs (ms; 1862; black)

WARRENTON SPRINGS / Va (32; 1861; black)

Ms	Pad / 5	150.

Washington

Washington V[a] (ms; 1861-63; black)

WASHINGTON / Va. (31; 1861; black)

Ms	Paid 5	150.
	10 [due]*	150.

Waskey's Mills

Waskey's Mills Va (ms; 1861-63; black)

Ms	Paid / 5 cts	150.

Waterford

PAID 5

A

WATERFORD / VA (32; 1861; black)

A	PAID 5	300.

Waynesboro

PAID 5

A B

10 PAID

C

Waynesboro Va (ms; 1864-65; black)

WAYNESBORO / Va. (30; 1861-64; black, blue)

A	PAID 5*	200.
B	5 PAID (blue) [altered 3 PAID]	300.
C	PAID 10 (blue)*	300.

Wellville

Wellville Va (ms; 1861-62; black)

Ms	Paid 5*	150.

West Point

West Pt. Va (ms; 1861; black)

West Point Va (ms; 1861; black)

Ms	Paid 5	150.
	Paid 10*	150.

West View

West View Va (ms; 186-; black)

Ms	Due 10c	100.

White House

White House Va (ms; 1861-64; black)

Ms	Paid 10 cts*	150.

White Sulphur Springs [West Virginia]

A

White Sulphur Springs Va (ms; 1861-63; black)
WHITE SULPHUR SPRINGS / Va (35; 1861-62; black, brown)

A	PAID [no rate]	500.
	Same, 5 (ms)*	500.
	Same (brown), Way (ms)	1,000.
B	DUE 5 [not illustrated]*	500.
Ms	Paid 5*	300.
	Paid 10*	300.
	Due 5*	300.

Whitlock

Whitlock (ms; 1861; black)
WHITLOCK / VA (26; 1863; brown)

Ms	Paid 5*	150.

Wicomico Church

Wicomico Ch Va (ms; 1861; black)
Wicomico Church Va (ms; 1861; black)

Ms	Paid 5*	150.

Wilcox's Wharf

Wilcox's Wharf (ms; 1861; black)

Ms	Paid 5¢	150.

Williamsburg

A

B

C

D

E

WILLIAMSBURG / VA (26 DC YD; 1861-62; black)

A	PAID [no rate]*	200.
B	PAID 5	200.
	Same, revalued 10 (type F)*	300.
C	PAID 10*	200.
D	5 [due]*	200.
E	10 [due]	200.

Winchester

A B C

D

F G

H J K

Winchester Va (ms; 1862-64; black)
WINCHESTER / VA. (26 DC YD; 1861-63; black,)
WINCHESTER / Va. (33; 1861-65; black, red)

A	PAID [no rate]*	100.
B	PAID 5	100.
	Same (red)*	200.
	Same, revalued 10 (Type J)	200.
	Same (red), revalued 10 (Type J)*	300.
C	PAID 5*	100.
D	PAID 10	100.
	Same, PAID struck twice	100.
	Same, revalued PAID 5 (Type B)	200.
	Same (red)	300.
E	DUE 5 [not illustrated]*	100.
F	Due 10	100.
G	Due 10	100.
	Same (blue)*	300.
	Same (blue), struck twice	300.
	Same (blue), changed to Paid 10 (ms)*	500.
H	DUE 10	100.
I	Due, 20 (circle) [not illustrated]*	300.
J	10 [due]	100.
	Same, Due (ms)*	100.
K	PAID 10	200.
Ms	Paid 5 cts*	100.
	Due / 5 (pencil)	100.
	Due 10	100.
	Due 20 cts	100.

Woodstock

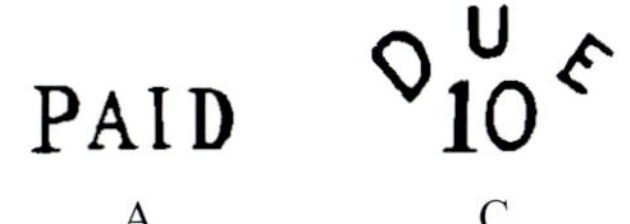

A C

Woodstock Va (ms; 1864; black)
WOODSTOCK / Va. (33; 1861-64; black)

A	PAID, 5 cts (ms)	200.
B	PAID (arc) / 5 (circle) [not illustrated]*	200.
C	DUE 10*	200.
Ms	Paid 5*	150.
	Paid 10	150.

Woodville

Woodville Va (ms; 1861-63; black)

Ms	Paid 5*	150.
Pk	no rate	150.

Wylliesburgh

Wylliesburg Va (ms; 1861-65; black)

Ms	Paid 10 c	150.
	Paid / 10	150.

Wytheville

A  B  C

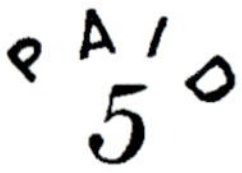

D 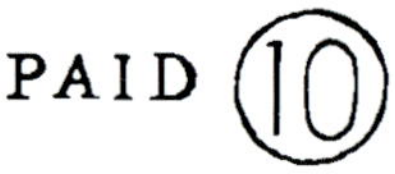 E

F  H

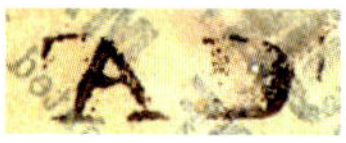

I

WYTHEVILLE / V^{a} (32; 1861-64; black)
WYTHEVILLE / V^{A} (32; 1861-64; black)
WYTHEVILLE / VA (26 DC; 186-; black)

A	PAID [no rate]	200.
B	PAID [no rate]	200.
C	PAID 5*	200.
D	PAID 5	200.
E	PAID 10*	200.
F	PAID 10*	200.
G	PAID 10 (bold 10) [not illustrated]	200.
H	5 (bold), Paid (ms)	200.
I	AD	500.

Yatesville

Yatesville Va (ms; 1861; black)

Ms	Paid 5	150.

Yorktown

A 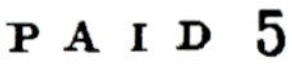 B

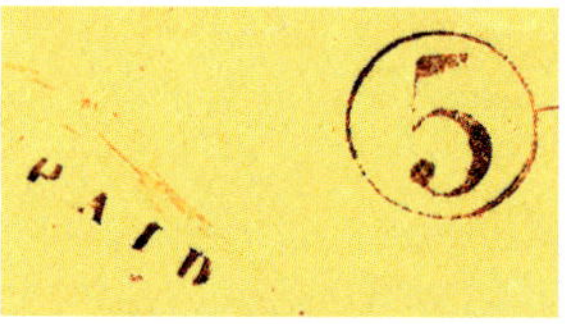

C  D 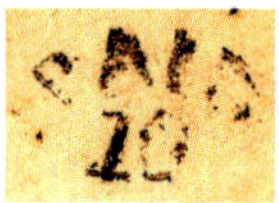 E

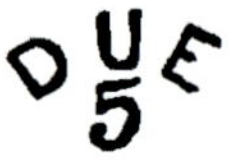

F 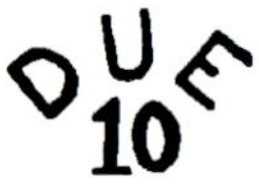 G  H

YORKTOWN / Va (30; 1861-62; black)

A	PAID, 10 (ms)	175.
B	PAID 5*	175.
C	PAID 5	175.
	Same, struck twice*	300.
D	PAID 5	175.
E	PAID 10	175.
F	DUE 5	175.
G	DUE 10	175.
H	5 [due]*	175.
	Same, [due], struck twice*	200.
Ms	Due 5*	150.
	Due 10*	150.
	5 [due]*	150.
	10 [due]	150.

Arizona Territory

United States Pre-Territory and Territory Periods

New Mexico: New Mexico consisted of a land area claimed by the United States as part of its settlement of the Mexican War in August 1845. Mexico officially ceded the land area to the United States under the terms of the Treaty of Guadalupe-Hidalgo signed on February 2, 1848. The United States proclaimed the area as a territory on September 9, 1850. Additional land was added to New Mexico Territory as part of the Gadsen Purchase in 1853. New Mexico Territory was comprised of present day Arizona, New Mexico and parts of present day Colorado and Nevada.

Arizona: Eager to become a territory, settlers in southern New Mexico Territory held a convention in April 1860 and adopted a constitution for a provisional territorial government for the area south of the 34th parallel. The US Congress refused to recognize this action due to the small population of the proposed territory. Arizona wasn't officially proclaimed a territory of the United States until February 24, 1863.

Independent Period

Arizona: The Mesilla Convention voted to secede on March 16, 1861. This ordinance was ratified by convention on March 23rd and by popular vote on April 8, 1861. In late July, Confederate forces under Lt. Col. John R. Baylor advanced into southern New Mexico Territory and occupied the town of Mesilla. On August 1st, Baylor proclaimed all of New Mexico Territory south of the 34th parallel to be the Confederate Territory of Arizona. President Davis approved an act to organize the Territory of Arizona on February 14, 1862.

New Mexico: The Territory of New Mexico never seceded from the United States and never entered the Confederate States as a territory or as a state. The only Confederate relationship for the towns in New Mexico Territory consisted of mail sent by military courier in those land areas where Confederate troops occupied Union territory.

Note: See the section "Independent State and Confederate Use of US Postage" for more information on the secession of Arizona.

Confederate Post Office in the Seceded Arizona Territory

The United States post offices in Arizona Territory became inoperative with the cessation of service by the Butterfield Overland mail and the San Antonio & San Diego Mail Line in August 1861. Prior to the interruption of those routes US postage rates appear to have remained in force. On September 25, 1861, the Confederate Postmaster General appointed William D. Skillman as postmaster at Mesilla. The Confederate Post Office Department also entered into a contract with George H. Giddings for the carriage of mail, effective November 1, 1861, over CSA Route 8076 (1) twice weekly between San Antonio and Mesilla, and (2) weekly between El Paso and Mesilla, and (3) fortnightly between Mesilla and San Diego. In spite of "N.M." in the various canceling devices, these are Arizona markings, as there was no seceded New Mexico Territory.

Confederate Territory of Arizona

Following congressional action, President Davis proclaimed Arizona as a territory of the Confederate States. After the Battle of Peralta on April 15, 1862 and the capitulation of Socorro on April 21, Confederate troops began abandoning Arizona and heading through Mesilla to El Paso and San Antonio, Texas. The Post Office Department canceled the mail contract for Route 8076, retroactive to June 30, 1862. Mail was carried up to one week prior to cancellation of the contract. In all, only 17 mail trips were completed under the contract. The last Confederate troops left Arizona Territory as of July 8, 1862.

The only operating Confederate post office in the Confederate Territory of Arizona was Mesilla. Postmaster Skillman appropriated the old Mesilla, N.M. canceling device from the Union post office and used it in his new Confederate Arizona Territory post office. In spite of "N.M" in the canceling device, this is an Arizona marking, as there was no Confederate New Mexico Territory.

Postal Markings

Independent Period

(March 16, 1861 – February 13,1862)

Arizona

ARIZONA / N.M. (29; 1861; black) —
3¢ 1857

Note: There is one recorded example postmarked MA[R] 27 [1861]

Fort Buchanan

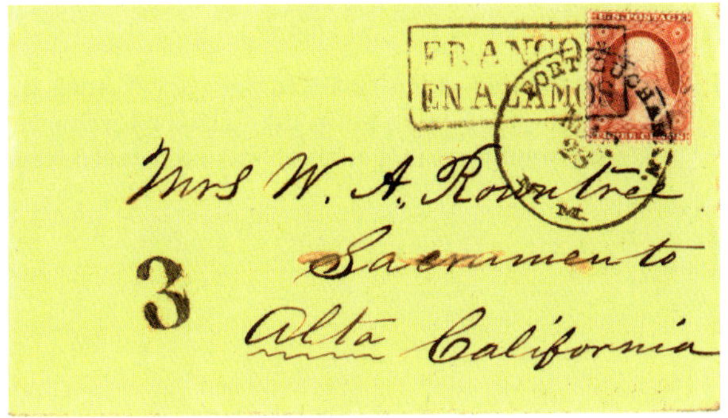

FORT BUCHANAN / N.M. (35; 1861; black) —
3¢ 1857

Note: There is one recorded example postmarked MAR 23 [1861].

Mesilla

MESILLA / N.M. (26; 1861-62; black)

Ms	Due 10	*17,000.*
Ms	Due 10c	*17,000.*

Tubac

TUBAC (ms; 1861; black) —
3¢ 1857

Note: There is one recorded example manuscript postmarked Apr. 4th 1861.

Confederate Territory Period

(February 14, 1862 – July 8, 1862)

Mesilla

MESILLA / N.M. (26; 1862; black)

Ms	Paid 10	*20,000.*
	Due 10	*20,000.*

Mesilla cover postmarked January 5, 1862 during the Independent Period while the Confederate Post Office operated in the Arizona Territory. In spite of "N.M." in the canceling device, this is an Arizona marking, as there was no seceded New Mexico Territory.

INDIAN NATIONS

The region of the United States west of the Mississippi River, sometimes referred to as "Indian Territory" or "Indian Country" was part of the Louisiana Purchase acquisition made by the United States from France in 1803. The area referred to comprised most of present day Oklahoma.

Indian Territory was officially organized by Act of Congress on June 30, 1834 as part of the forced resettlement of Native Americans in the southeast. Although the region is referred to as a "territory," the Indian Territory never achieved formal territorial status. Rather, the Indian Territory was loosely organized around the Five Civilized Nations of Native Americans - the Cherokees, Choctaws, Chickasaws, Creeks, and Seminoles - which owned all the land in common. The Five Nations governed the internal affairs of the region using its own police force and its own court system. In addition, the Department of Indian Affairs in Washington, DC asserted limited jurisdiction over the region, regulating trade with the Five Nations and seeking to "maintain peace" on the frontier. The United States Post Office Department provided sporadic and unreliable postal service within and through the region.

The Five Nations, which were sovereign tribal nations and not part of the United States, did not have to, nor could they, secede from the United States in order to develop a relationship with the Confederate States. The Five Nations or any tribe therein could, however, affiliate with the CSA in some capacity acceptable to it and to the CSA. The Five Nations achieved this through several agreements entered into between the individual tribes and the Confederacy. The Five Nations sent Messrs. Elias Cornelius Boudinot [Cherokee], Robert McDonald Jones [Choctaw] and Samuel Benton Callahan [Creek & Seminole] to the CSA as the territorial representatives of the Five Nations. The tribal nations also entered into individual treaties with the CSA. These treaties were: (1) Articles of Confederation, dated July 1, 1861, among the Muscogee/Creek, Seminoles, Choctaws, Chickasaws and the CSA; (2) Declaration of Causes, dated October 28, 1861, between the Cherokee Nation and the CSA; and, (3) Resolutions of the Choctaw Nation, dated February 7, 1861.

CSA MAIL SERVICE IN THE INDIAN NATIONS

With the outbreak of the Civil War and in particular the secession of the state of Arkansas, United States mail service and private mail service (such as Butterfield's Overland Mail) ceased operations in the Indian Nations. The CSA Post Office Department took over the eleven mail routes that had been in effect since 1858 and attempted to service the routes. To this end, it converted the pre-War contract designations for the routes (e.g., Route 7901) to new CSA designations (e.g., Route 373) and continued to use the same interim and terminal geographic points for each route so that the only change from the pre-War period with respect to these mail routes was the change of route numbers. Mail service in the Indian Nations under the CSA, like that provided by its predecessor, remained sporadic and not well established. As a result, some mail had to be handled by tribal or military couriers in order for it to reach its final destination.

The following routes are listed in *Indian Territory Mail* by G. Signorelli and T. Caldwell (privately published in 1966): USPOD Route 7901 became CSA Route 373 [Evansville, Arkansas to Fort Gibson, Arkansas]; USPOD Route 7903 became CSA Route 374 [Tahlequah, Arkansas to Grand Saline, Arkansas]; USPOD Route 7904 became CSA Route 375 [Kidron, Arkansas to Webber Falls, Arkansas]; USPOD Route 7905 became CSA Route 376 [Fort Smith, Arkansas to Kidron, Arkansas]; USPOD Route 7908 became CSA Route 378 [Fort Smith, Arkansas to Doaksville, Arkansas]; USPOD Route 7911 became CSA Route 381 [Fort Smith, Arkansas to Gainsville, Texas]; USPOD Route 7948 became CSA Route 406 [Fort Gibson, Arkansas to Fort Washita, Arkansas]; USPOD Route 7949 became CSA Route 407 [Fort Washita, Arkansas to Fort Arbuckle, Arkansas]; USPOD Route 7952 became CSA Route 409 and CSA Route 410 [Paraclifta, Arkansas to Doaksville Thule, Arkansas; and, Doaksville, Arkansas to Fort Washita, Arkansas, respectively]; USPOD Route 8734 became CSA Route 165 [Clarksville, Texas to Doaksville, Arkansas]; and, USPOD Route 8750 became CSA Route 179 [Fort Washita, Arkansas to McKinney, Texas].

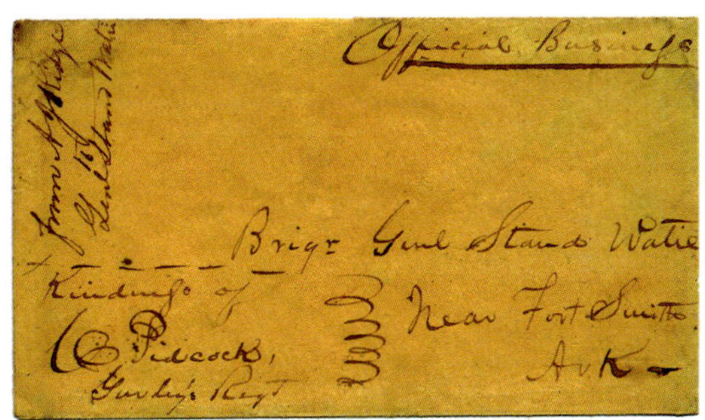

BOGGY DEPOT, CHOCTAW NATION

Boggy Depot CN (ms; 186-; black)

Ms	No paid or rate marking	5,000.

CHOCTAW AGENCY, CHOCTAW NATION

Choctaw Agency (ms; 1864; black)

Ms	Paid 10 cts	5,000.

FORT WASHITA, CHICKASAW NATION

FORT WASHITA / ARK. (33; 1862; black)

	Paid 10c	5,000.

No postmark

Ms	Paid 5 cts	5,000.

General issue

Ms	Fort Washita, C.N.	5,000.

Lukfahtah, Choctaw Nation

Luk fah tah C. N. (ms; 1862; black)

Ms Paid 5 9,000.

Other Uses

There are other recorded uses to and from towns and camps in the Indian Nations as well as military uses. These are listed below as a matter of record.

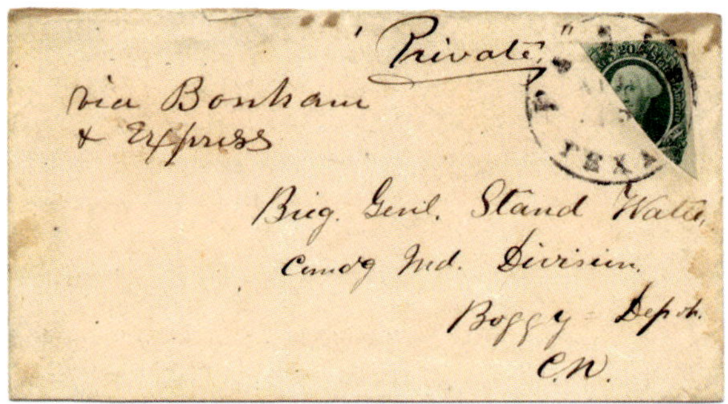

Boggy Depot, Choctaw Nation

Cover addressed to Boggy Depot with pen canceled 10¢ blue (2) – no postmark

Cover addressed to Boggy Depot with 20¢ green (13) bisect tied by Paris, Texas postmark

Cover endorsed "Express" addressed to Brig. Genl. Stand Watie at Boggy Depot (no indication carried in Confederate mails)

Camp Brown, Cherokee Nation

Cover endorsed "Official Business" addressed to Camp Brown (no indication carried in Confederate mails)

Camp Leflore, Choctaw Nation

Folded letter datelined Camp Leflore and carried outside the mail to Texas where it was posted

Camp on Verdegris, Cherokee Nation

Cover endorsed "Official" and addressed to Camp on Verdign's [*sic*] (no indication carried in Confederate mails)

Camp Porter, Creek Nation

Cover endorsed "Official" and addressed to Camp Porter (no indication carried in Confederate mails)

Doaksville, Choctaw Nation

Doaksville C. N. 1863 manuscript postmark on cover with a pair 5¢ blue (7) to Texas

Cover addressed to Doaksville with New Orleans postmark and pair 5¢ New Orleans provisionals on reverse

Cover addressed to Doaksville with Waxahachie, Texas postmark and handstamped PAID / 10

Cover forwarded to Doaksville with Bonham, Texas postmark and handstamped 10

Cover forwarded to Doaksville with Waxahachie, Texas postmark and "Express" endorsement – no rate marking

Eagletown, Choctaw Nation

Cover addressed to Eagletown with Sherman, Texas postmark and handstamped PAID 10 marking

Cover addressed to Eagletown with Pine Bluff, Arkansas postmark and handstamped 10 / DUE

Fort Gibson, Cherokee Nation

Cover with two copies 5¢ green (1) on Post Office Department form addressed to Fort Gibson

Cover endorsed "Official" and "Express" addressed to Fort Gibson (no indication carried in Confederate mails)

Fort Towson, Indian Territory

Cover endorsed "S. S. Scott, Cmdg Ind Affairs" and addressed to Fort Towson (no indication carried in Confederate mails)

Tahlequah, Cherokee Nation

Cover endorsed "Official" addressed to Tahlequah (no indication carried in Confederate mails)

Webbers Falls, Cherokee Nation

Cover with pen canceled 5¢ green (1) addressed to Webbers Falls

Cover endorsed "Official" addressed to "Col. John Drew CSA, Comdg. Cherokee Reg, Webbers Falls C N"

Cover endorsed "Official Business" addressed to "Col. John Drew C.SA. / Commanding Regt C.N. / Webbers Falls, C.N.", pencil docketing "Pegg / April 4, 1862"

Military Dispatch Carried Outside the Mail

Cover with manuscript Crockett, Texas postmark addressed to "Gano's Brigade, Indian Territory"

Cover with uncanceled pair of 5¢ blue (7) addressed to "Genl. Stello's, Head Quarters, I. Nation."

Cover endorsed "O. B." addressed to "Brig. Genl. Stand Wati[e], Care of Brig Genl J. H. Cooper, Comdg Div, in the field, Indian Territory"

Semi-official cover with imprint of "Hd. Quarters Northern Division of Louisiana" addressed to "General Stand Watie, Principal Chief of the Cherokee Nation"

Cover endorsed "Official Business" addressed to "Brig. Genl. Stand Watie, Near Fort Smith, Ark."

Postmasters' Provisionals

Shortly after the Southern States began to secede from the Union, there were complaints that in reprisal the US Post Office Department was closing Southern post offices and not filling requisitions for new supplies of stamps. Covers with handstamped paid and rates are evidence that at least some post offices did run out of postage stamps. To meet the demand for stamps, some postmasters went one step further and provided either stamps of local manufacture or handstamped envelopes for use by postal customers as postal stationery as early as mid-February 1861. All such stamps and postal stationery which were prepared in advance of use are known as postmasters' provisionals.

3¢ 1861 Postmasters' Provisionals

When the new Confederate government was established in early February 1861, there was no Post Office Department. It was not until February 21, 1861 that the Post Office Department was established. This was followed by the appointment of John H. Reagan as Postmaster General on March 6. Quickly thereafter the organization of the Confederate Post Office Department began in earnest.

In the meantime, the US continued to provide postal service in the seceded states: US postage rates were in effect, postmasters were still under oath to the US Government and mail contractors operated under the control of the US Post Office Department. An Act of the Confederate Congress on 15 March acknowledged the operation of the postal service by the US. It also conferred certain powers on the Postmaster General if the US service was discontinued before the Confederate Post Office Department was prepared to assume control. In late March Postmaster General Reagan also confirmed the continued operation of the postal service by the US Post Office Department in circulars to mail contractors, postmasters and other postal employees. He directed that they continue their contracts, performance of duty and obligations to the US Government.

On May 13, 1861 Postmaster General Reagan issued a proclamation notifying all mail contractors, postmasters and other postal employees that the Confederate Post Office Department would assume complete control of the postal service in the Confederate States on June 1, 1861.

From the time the Confederate States were established in early February until the end of May, there were sporadic shortages of the US postage stamps at some Southern post offices. Stamps were necessary because US law required the prepayment of letters by stamps. To overcome these shortages, a few postmasters prepared their own stamps or handstamped envelopes for sale to their customers. Although not authorized, these provisional stamps and postal stationery were accepted as postage when mailed from their town of origin.

The convention for numbering these provisionals is based on a number comprised of four character groups. The first group is the letter "A" designating the 3¢ provisionals. The second group is the first three letters of the town name. The third group is the state abbreviation and the last group is the type: "A" for adhesive and "E" for entire. This is followed by a sequence number. Thus, the number A-MAD-FL-A01 is the number for the first listed adhesive from Madison, Florida.

Scott Catalogue numbers are listed in parentheses after the *Confederate States of America Catalog* and *Handbook of Stamps and Postal History* (CSA Catalog) numbers in the listings. Stated values are CSA Catalog values and not Scott Catalogue values.

The absence of a listing for a specific marking or type of cover in this catalog does not imply scarcity or high value.

Warnings about fakes or forgeries follow the listings of some provisionals. The absence of such a warning does not imply there are no fakes or forgeries of other provisionals. The warnings highlight those that are considered the most dangerous. Other fakes and forgeries exist.

Fort Valley, Georgia

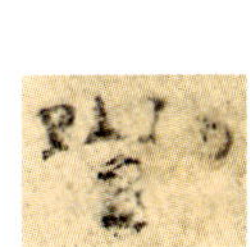

A

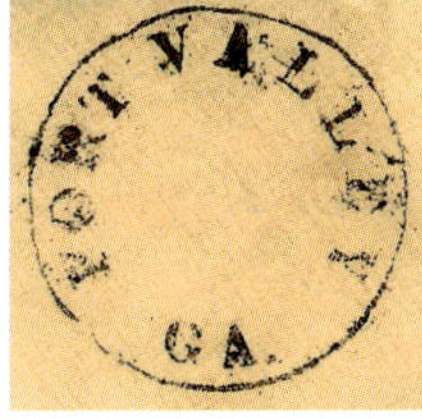

Control

Entire (Handstamped)

A-FTV-GA-E01

A 3¢ black NR —

The Fort Valley Georgia provisional was prepared by handstamping envelopes with a "PAID / 3" marking. An undated office postmark was struck on the envelope front as a control.

The only recorded example is used on a damaged cover addressed to New Orleans April 12 [1861].

See also, "Confederate Postmasters' Provisionals" section.

HILLSBORO , NORTH CAROLINA

A

Adhesive

A-HIL-NC-A01 (1AX1)
A 3¢ bluish black NR NR

On Cover

A-HIL-NC-A01 (1AX1)
A 3¢ bluish black —

The Hillsboro, North Carolina provisional was prepared by handstamping "PAID" on bluish white paper. The size of the paper is unknown, but it is possible several strikes were made on one piece of paper. These were then cut apart for use. The rate was determined by the date of use.

The only recorded example is postmarked May 27, 1861 to Raleigh, NC.

See also, "Confederate Postmasters' Provisionals" section.

JACKSON, MISSISSIPPI

A

Entire (Handstamped)

A-JAC-MS-E01 (2AXU1)
A 3¢ black NR 4,000.

The Jackson, Mississippi provisionals were prepared by handstamping envelopes with a circular marking containing "PAID", the rate "3" and "Cts.".

The only recorded example is postmarked April 27 [1861] to Marion, Mississippi and bears an 1861 year-dated patriotic seal.

See also, "Confederate Postmasters' Provisionals" section.

MADISON COURT HOUSE, FLORIDA

A *a*

Adhesive

A-MAD-FL-A01 (3AX1)
A 3¢ gold on bluish NR *20,000.*
a. "CNETS" error (3AX1a) NR *25,000.*

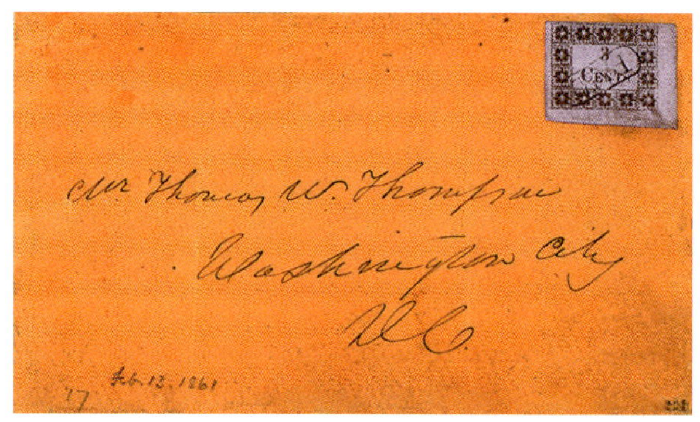

On Cover
A 3¢ gold on bluish (3AX1) *60,000.*

Postmaster Samuel J. Perry had the Madison stamps printed at the office of his eldest son, William, the editor and publisher of *The Southern Messenger.* They were printed on pale blue wove foolscap paper. During the printing process, a yellow bronze dust was blown on the ink before it was dry, which gave the frames and stars a metallic gold appearance.

In the US National Archives, there is a letter on file from Postmaster Perry to US Postmaster General Montgomery Blair that states Perry also made 1¢ stamps and that examples of both the 1¢ and 3¢ were enclosed to the USPOD therewith. Those stamps are no longer in the Archives with that letter.

Cancellations used were a black town postmark, oblong PAID, pen slash and manuscript "Paid in Money."

There is one recorded example of the A01 used on cover with the original clipped letterhead dated February 13, [1861].

There is one recorded example of the A01a (CNETS error).

Warning: There are forgeries of the Madison provisional in various colors and rates, none similar to the genuine stamp.

See also, "Confederate Postmasters' Provisionals" section.

Nashville, Tennessee

A

a

Adhesive

A-NAS-TN-A01 (4AX1)

A 3¢ carmine	300.	NA
a. Horizontal strip of 5 showing all positions	2,000.	NA

Nashville postmaster William D. McNish prepared a 3¢ provisional stamp with his name and initials, a large value 3 and the name of the town. However, this stamp was never valid for postage as a Confederate stamp. Tennessee did not secede from the Union until June 8, 1861. Thus any use of the stamp before this date would have been as part of the United States. Any use after this date would have been invalid as Confederate postage. In spite of its historical background, this stamp has continued to be considered a Confederate 3¢ provisional.

Warning: Dangerous forgeries exist.

See also, "Confederate Postmasters' Provisionals" section.

Selma, Alabama

A

Entire (Handstamped)

A-SEL-AL-E01 (5AXU1)

A 3¢ black	—	NR

The Selma, Alabama provisional was prepared by handstamping envelopes with a dateless office integral rate and paid marking.

The only recorded example is unused on a cover posted with a 10¢ engraved general issue (12-KB) postmarked Selma, Ala. Feb 23 to Perry, Georgia.

See also, "Confederate Postmasters' Provisionals" section.

Tuscumbia, Alabama

A

Entires

A-TUS-AL-E01 (6AUX1)

A 3¢ red	*12,500.*	—

The Tuscumbia, Alabama provisionals were prepared by handstamping envelopes with an integral office PAID marking with a 3 rate marking substituted for the date logos.

Most examples are unused under US 3¢ 1857 stamps.

Warning: Dangerous forgeries exist.

See also, "Confederate Postmasters' Provisionals" section.

Confederate Postmasters' Provisionals

When the Confederacy took control of the mail system on June 1, 1861, there were no Confederate postage stamps available. To meet the demand for this convenience, some postmasters prepared substitutes in the form of stamps, printed envelopes and handstamped envelopes. Today these are commonly referred to as postmasters' provisionals. The difference between the handstamped provisional envelopes and the handstamped and manuscript rate markings used by the vast majority of postmasters was that all provisionals were prepared in advance of use.

The nature of adhesives and printed envelopes poses no problem in meeting the test that they were prepared in advance of use. However, handstamped provisional envelopes can pose a problem because many were prepared using stampless marking devices. Fortunately many postmasters who prepared these provisionals incorporated a security feature or control in their markings. These controls include a second dated or undated postmark, different colored markings, special markings, and even the postmaster's initials.

For those provisionals that did not incorporate such a security feature, identification is more difficult. The existence of a postally unused example or use under a postally used general issue is normally considered *prima facie* evidence that the marking was applied in advance. In other cases the determination is not so clear.

Some of the listed handstamped provisionals are only a fancy handstamp or a combined paid and rate marking. Many of these were probably listed as provisionals in earlier catalogs based on these characteristics. Many of such markings would not meet the standards applied to more recently discovered provisionals. Most of these legacy markings have been retained as provisionals because there is insufficient evidence to either prove or disprove their provisional status.

Another group of markings accepted as provisionals are postmarks with integral rate and paid markings. Today our knowledge of such markings and their use reveals that some were also used as stampless markings. In such cases it is usually not possible to differentiate between a provisional and a stampless use.

Some covers with handstamped rate and paid markings or postmarks with integral rate and paid markings have manuscript "charge box" markings. Such markings are associated with stampless uses and are evidence the specific cover is not provisional in nature.

There is little question whether an adhesive provisional is used or unused. The same is not true of printed or handstamped provisional entires. If there are no postal markings on the envelope and it is unaddressed, it is considered unused. If there are no postal markings and the envelope is addressed, it is more difficult. Notations such as "courtesy of" or "politeness of" are evidence the entire was carried outside the mails. In other cases a relatively large number of addressed entires without a postmark are considered evidence that they were actually carried in the mails. These instances are noted in the listings for such towns.

In previous catalogs the printed entires were identified by the color of the envelopes. This identification by envelope color was also a characteristic of early catalog listings of handstamped provisionals. It wasn't until the 1959 edition of the *Dietz Confederate States Catalog and Handbook* that envelope color was discontinued. Most printed entires exist in more colors and shades than currently listed in catalogs. In other instances the same envelope has been described as different colors by different authorities. For these reasons the printed entires are listed by type without regard to envelope color.

Several new features are included in the provisional listings. These include the earliest recorded dates of use, recorded uses from another town and whether a provisional is unique.

The earliest recorded dates of use are included for the major catalog numbers when they can be determined. If a sub catalog number has an earlier recorded date of use than the major number it is also included. Information in italics has not been confirmed. When available the destination post office is included with the date to aid in identification. These dates are the earliest dates the editors could verify. Earlier uses may exist.

For the 5¢ provisionals, it is rather easy to determine the year of use because the 5¢ rate was in effect for only a year and a month. The 10¢ provisionals pose a more difficult problem because the rate was in effect throughout the Confederate period. Unless the postmark contains a year date, there is year dated docketing, an original enclosure or information about the addressee that can be year dated, there is no way to determine the year of use.

Most provisionals were prepared and used in the period before and right after the distribution of postage stamps by the Confederate Post Office Department in late October 1861. But this is not always the case. Many of the Texas provisionals were not prepared and used until communications across the Mississippi River were disrupted in 1863. There are other anomalies such as Griffin, Georgia which used provisionals for a very short period in late May and early June 1862.

Recorded uses of provisionals that entered the mail from other towns are included with the town of use, the date of use and whether the provisional was accepted as postage.

When there is only one recorded example of a specific provisional, it is so noted. Such information is based on the best information available to the editors. Other examples may exist.

The convention for numbering the provisionals is based on a number comprised of three character groups. The first group is the first three letters of the town name. The second group is the state abbreviation and the last group is the type: "A" for adhesive and "E" for entire. This is followed by a sequence number. Thus, the number ATH-GA-A01 is the number for the first listed adhesive from Athens, Georgia. In some cases it was not possible to use the first three letters of a town name due to duplication within a state. In these cases a different town abbreviation is used.

There are apparent gaps in catalog sub numbers for some on-cover adhesive varieties. This is done to avoid using the same catalog number assigned to an off-cover variety that may be completely different.

Scott Catalogue numbers are listed in parentheses after the *Confederate States of America Catalog* and *Handbook of Stamps and Postal History* (CSA Catalog) numbers in the listings. Stated values are CSA Catalog values and not Scott Catalogue values.

In the notes following each town listing, references to the provisionals are abbreviated for clarity. In descriptions of provisionals, the Type letter, e.g., A, is used. In the notes addressing dates of use and uses from other towns, only the last character group in the catalog number is used, e.g., E02. In cautionary and warning notes, the full catalog number is used.

This catalog does not include uses such as express covers or uses on advertising or college covers. Such uses normally sell at a premium. This catalog does not separately list and price adhesives that are cut to shape or used on a piece. Nor does the catalog separately list and price entires as cut squares or cut to shape. All such uses normally sell at a discount.

The absence of a listing for a specific marking or type of cover in this catalog does not imply unusual scarcity or high value.

Warnings about fakes or forgeries follow the listings of some provisionals. The absence of such a warning does not imply there are no fakes or forgeries of other provisionals. The warnings highlight those that are considered the most dangerous. Other fakes and forgeries exist.

Aberdeen, Mississippi

A

Entire (Handstamped)

ABE-MS-E01 (1XU1)
  A 5¢ black — NR *6,000.*
    a. Revalued "10" (ms) (1XU1*a*) — NR *10,000.*

The Aberdeen, Mississippi provisional was prepared by handstamping envelopes with an undated prewar postmark in which the date logos were replaced by a large "5" marking. A separate "PAID" marking was struck to the left of the rated postmark.

Earliest recorded date of use is September 13, [1861] to Macon, Miss.

Abingdon, Virginia

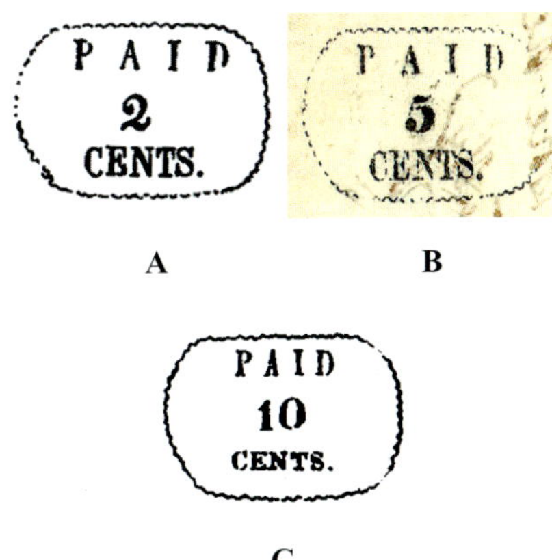

A B

C

Entires (Handstamped)

ABI-VA-E01 (2XU1)
  A 2¢ black — NR *12,500.*
    a. Revalued "5" (ms) — NR *15,000.*
ABI-VA-E02 (2XU2)
  B 5¢ black — NR 1,000.
ABI-VA-E03 (2XU3)
  C 10¢ black — NR *1,000.*
    a. Under a postally used general issue — *1,500.*

The Abingdon, Virginia provisionals were prepared by handstamping envelopes with a typeset device that included "PAID", "CENTS.' and the rate inside a fancy border.

Earliest recorded dates of use:
- E01 – December 13, 1861 on drop letter (only recorded example)
- E01a – July 21, 1861 to Jonesboro, East Tenn. (only recorded example)
- E02 – July 8, 1861 to *Kingston, Tenn.*
- E03 – None recorded
- E03a – Under 10¢ engraved general issue tied by manuscript Abingdon postmark dated March 7 to Dublin,Va. (only recorded example)

Caution: There is one recorded example of E02 with a "charge box" marking and one used on a folded letter. This indicates the provisional marking may also have been used as a stampless marking. Stampless uses are not easily distinguished from provisional uses. Each example must be considered on its own merits.

Albany, Georgia

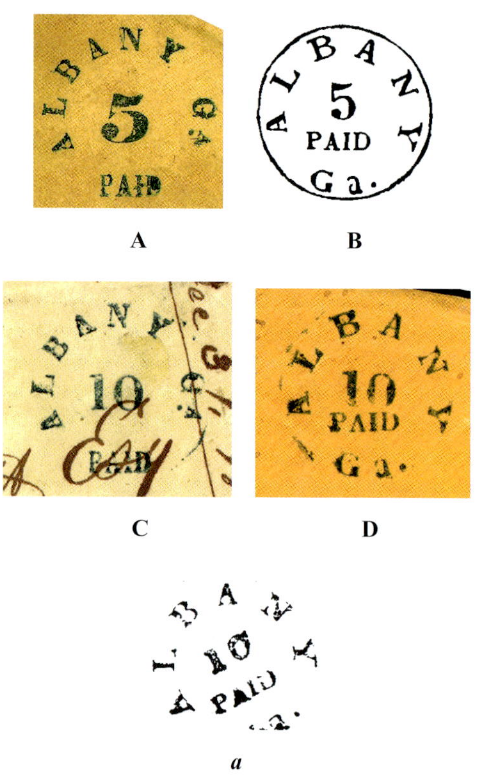

Entires (Handstamped)

ALB-GA-E01 (3XU1)

A	5¢ greenish-blue	NR	750.
	a. Revalued "10" (Type *a*) (3XU2*a*)	NR	*2,000.*
	b. Under a postally used general issue		*1,000.*

ALB-GA-E02 (3XU5)

B	5¢ greenish-blue*	NR	NR

ALB-GA-E03 (3XU2)

C	10¢ greenish-blue	NR	1,500.

ALB-GA-E04 (3XU6)

D	10¢ greenish-blue	NR	1,500.

The Type A and C Albany, Georgia provisionals were prepared by handstamping envelopes with an undated prewar postmark with integral "PAID" marking in which the date logos were replaced with "5" or "10" rate markings.

The Type B and D markings were prepared from another undated prewar postmark in which the date logos were replaced by "PAID" and "5" or "10" rate markings.

The Type *a* marking is similar to the Type D marking but has a smaller "10". The lower left part of the marking was struck off cover. The only recorded use of this marking is to revalue a single example of E01.

Earliest recorded dates of use:
E01 – June 15, 1861 to Elberton, Ga.
E02 – None recorded
E03 – January 1, [1863] to Newton, Ga. (only recorded example)
E04 – September 17, 1861 to Richmond, Va. (only recorded example)

Anderson Court House, South Carolina

A

B C

Entires (Handstamped)

AND-SC-E01 (4XU3)

A	PAID, black	500.	1,500.

AND-SC-E02 (4XU1)

B	5¢ black	NR	1,500.

AND-SC-E03 (4XU2)

C	10¢ black (value in manuscript)	NR	1,500.

The Anderson Court House, South Carolina provisionals were prepared by handstamping the undated office postmark on envelopes. Separately "PAID" and "5" markings were struck in the center of the undated postmark. For the 10¢ value "PAID" was struck in the center of the postmark and "10" added in manuscript.

Earliest recorded dates of use:
E01 – Unknown
E02 – October 2, [1861] to Richmond, Va.
E03 – Unknown

Note: Recorded uses of E01 indicate it was used on both drop letters and regular letters. As a result it is not known what rate it actually represented.

[–]	symbol used in place of value to mean insufficient information to assign a price
NR	used in place of value when no examples have been recorded
IH	institutional holding

Athens, Georgia

A

B

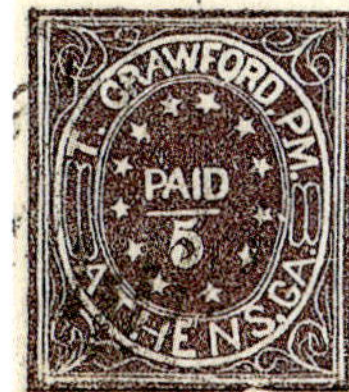

C

Red Type B showing recut scrolls in spandrels

a

b

Adhesives

ATH-GA-A01 (5X1)

A 5¢ purple on *white*	NR	1,000.

ATH-GA-A02 (5X1)

B 5¢ purple on *white*	NR	1,000.

ATH-GA-A03

C 5¢ purple pair on *white* (A + B) or (B + A)	NR	2,500.
a. Vertical pair (*tête-bêche*) (A + B) (5X1*a*)	NR	*10,000.*

ATH-GA-A04 (5X2)

A 5¢ red on *white*	NR	4,500.

ATH-GA-A05 (5X2)

B 5¢ red on *white*	NR	4,500.

On Cover

ATH-GA-A01 (5X1)

A 5¢ purple on *white*	1,500.

ATH-GA-A02 (5X1)

B 5¢ purple on *white*	1,500.
a. Used with Type A	*3,500.*
b. With "PAID" (Type *a*)	—
c. With "PAID 5" (Type *b*)	—
d. With "PAID" (Type *a*) and "PAID 5" Type *b*)	—

ATH-GA-A03 (5X1)

C 5¢ purple on *white* horizontal pair (A + B) or (B + A)	5,000.
a. Vertical pair (*tête-bêche*) (5X1*a*)	*20,000.*
b. Strip of four (B + A + B + A)	*50,000.*

ATH-GA-A04 (5X2)

A 5¢ red on *white*	*10,000.*

ATH-GA-A05 (5X2)

B 5¢ red on *white*	*10,000.*

The Athens adhesive provisionals were printed on white wove paper from a form consisting of two similar but distinctively different woodcut designs (A and B). This results in all pairs showing both types. All recorded vertical pairs are *tête-bêche* and show both types. In the Type A design the letter "T" in "T. CRAWFORD" is at the 10 o'clock position. In the Type B design the letter "T" is a the 9 o'clock position.

The first printing was in purple. A second printing was in red. Both types were recut prior to the second printing. The recutting is most noticeable in the colorless scrolls in the four spandrels. The scrolls are much wider in the red printing than those in the purple printing.

Earliest recorded dates of use:
- A01 – September 28, [1861] to Macon, Ga.
- A02 – October 3, [1861] to Marion, Ala.
- A03 – October 4, [1861] to Richmond, Va.
- A04 – March 12, [1862] to Macon, Ga.
- A05 – March 27, [1862] on half cover without address

Warning: Dangerous forgeries of A01 and A02 exist.

D

Entire (Handstamped)

ATH-GA-E01

D 10¢ black	NR	*2,500.*

The Type D marking is the same as that used on stampless envelopes. A single recorded example contains a handwritten note under the envelope flap, "Andrew had these envelopes stamped & I am obliged to use them or loose [*sic*] the postage." This is considered proof this envelope was prepared in advance of use. The envelope is postmarked September 9, [1861] to Richmond, Va.

Atlanta, Georgia

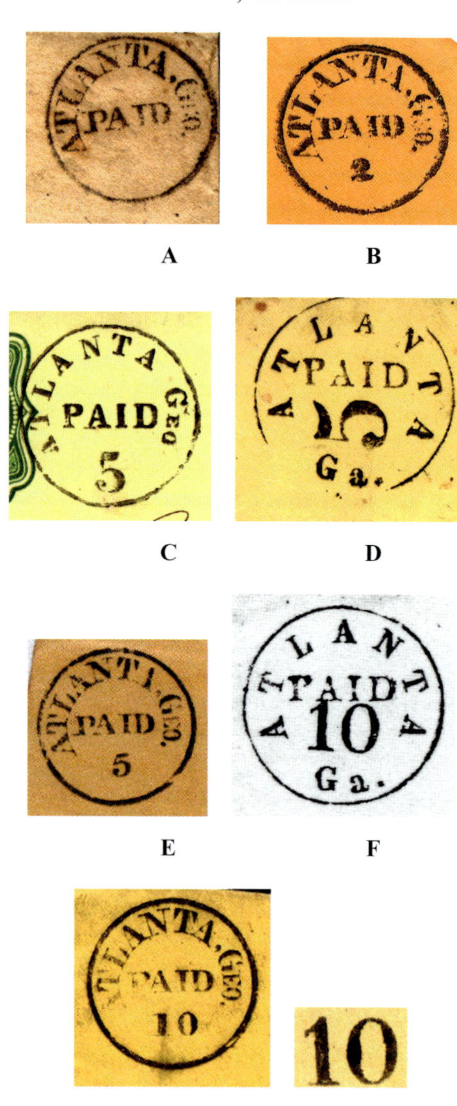

A B C D E F G *a*

Entires (Handstamped)

ATL-GA-E01			
A PAID, black		NR	*1,000.*
ATL-GA-E02 (6XU4)			
B 2¢ black		NR	3,500.
ATL-GA-E03 (6XU2)			
C 5¢ black		500.	750.
a. Revalued "10" (Type *a*) (6XU2*a*)		NR	1,500.
b. Under a postally used general issue			1,000.
ATL-GA-E04 (6XU1)			
C 5¢ red		NR	*2,500.*
ATL-GA-E05 (6XU8)			
D 5¢ black		NR	*2,500.*
ATL-GA-E06 (6XU5)			
E 5¢ black		NR	1,000.
a. Revalued "10" (Type *a*) (6XU5*a*)		NR	*1,500.*
b. Under a postally used general issue			*1,500.*
ATL-GA-E07 (6XU9)			
F 10¢ black		NR	750.
ATL-GA-E08 (6XU6)			
G 10¢ black		500.	750.
a. Under a postally used general issue			1,000.

The Atlanta, Georgia Types A, B, E and G provisionals were prepared by handstamping envelopes with a marking that resembles a postmark. "PAID" and "2," "5," or "10" rate markings were inserted in the center of the device to complete the marking. A single circular device was used and the rate values were changed as needed. The Type A marking has no rate value.

The Type A marking was probably used for drop letters and circulars.

The Type C marking was prepared by handstamping envelopes with an undated prewar postmark with integral "5" in which the date logos were replaced by a "PAID" marking.

Types D and F markings were prepared by handstamping envelopes with the undated office postmark and then striking "PAID" and "5" or "10" markings inside the postmark.

Earliest recorded dates of use are:

E01 – Unknown (only recorded example on corner card without a postmark).
E02 – Unknown
E03 – June 3, 1861 to Macon, Ga.
E04 – July 15, 1861 to Penfield, Ga. (only recorded example)
E05 – June 15, 1861 to Monticello, Ga. (only recorded example)
E06 – August 20, 1861 to Valley Town, N.C. (On express cover with Louisville, Ky. Adams Express marking dated August 2, 1861)
E07 – July 9, 1861 (address faded)
E08 – July 18, 1861 to Richmond, Va.

Caution: There is a recorded use of E03 on a forwarded envelope and a recorded use of E08 with a "charge box" marking and another on a forwarded envelope. There are no recorded stampless "PAID 5" and only a very small number of "PAID 10" stampless covers from Atlanta. This is evidence the E03 and E08 provisional markings were also used as stampless markings. Stampless uses are not easily distinguished from provisional uses. Each example must be considered on its own merits.

Warning: Dangerous forgeries of E03 exist.

Austin, Mississippi

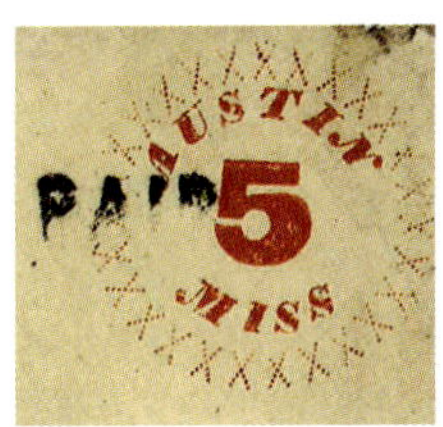

A

Entire (Printed)

AUS-MS-E01 (8XU1)
A 5¢ red with black "PAID" NR *70,000.*

The Austin, Mississippi provisional was prepared by printing envelopes with a typeset device with a bold "5" rate in the center. Separately a black "PAID" marking was struck to the side.

The only recorded example is postmarked December 2, 1861 to Wood Lawn, Tenn.

Austin, Texas

A

Adhesives

AUS-TX-A01 (9X1)
A 10¢ black on *white* NR NR
AUS-TX-A02
A 10¢ black on *buff* NR NR

On Cover

AUS-TX-A01 (9X1)
A 10¢ black on *white* 5,000.
AUS-TX-A02
A 10¢ black on *buff* 5,000.

The Austin, Texas adhesive provisionals were prepared by removing the date logos from the office postmark and replacing them with "PAID" and "10" markings. This device was used to handstamp sheets of lightly ruled paper. Individual stamps were cut apart for use as stamps.

There are four recorded covers with Austin adhesives. Two are tied by the town postmark, two are not.

Earliest recorded dates of use:
A01 – Illegible postmark to Bexar, Tex. (only recorded example)
A02 – August 23, 1862 to San Antonio, Tex.

B C

Entires (Handstamped)

AUS-TX-E01
B 5¢ black NR NR
a. Revalued "10" (ms) NR 1,000.
b. Revalued "10" (Type C) NR 1,000.
AUS-TX-E02 (9XU1)
C 10¢ black NR 1,500.

The Type B envelopes were prepared by handstamping envelopes with the same "PAID" and "5" rate markings used as stampless markings.

The Type C envelope was prepared by handstamping envelopes with the same rated marking used to prepare the adhesives.

Earliest recorded dates of use:
E01 – None recorded
E01a – June [1861] to Petersburg, Va. (only recorded example)
E02 – July 11, 1862 to Lampasas Springs, Tex.

Caution: Provisional uses of E01 are not easily distinguished from stampless uses. There is one recorded example E02 with a "charge box" marking. This indicates the provisional marking may also have been used as a stampless marking. Stampless uses are not easily distinguished from provisional uses. Each example must be considered on its own merits.

Autaugaville, Alabama

A B

Entires (Handstamped)

AUT-AL-E01 (10XU1)
A 5¢ blue-black NR *20,000.*

AUT-AL-E02 (10XU2)

B 5¢ black	NR	*15,000.*

The Autaugaville, Alabama provisionals were prepared by handstamping envelopes with two different rated devices.

The Type A device was a brass handstamp similar in design to the Athens, Georgia provisional. The Type B device was specially prepared and features the name of the postmaster around a star that includes the letters "P A I D" in the points of the star and a "5" in the center.

In the 1940s it was reported the Type A device and other Autaugaville handstamps were passed on to the grandson of the Confederate postmaster. However, The Type B device was not among them.

Earliest recorded dates of use:
- E01 – November 21, [1861] to Benton, Ala.
- E02 – October 8, [1861] to Lowndesboro, Ala. (only recorded example)

Caution: The only example of E02 is on a cover with a "charge box" marking. This is an indication this marking may have been used as a stampless marking.

Barnwell Court House, South Carolina

A

Entire (Handstamped)

BAR-SC-E01 (123XU1)

A 5¢ black	NR	2,000.

The Barnwell Court House, South Carolina provisional was prepared by handstamping envelopes with an undated prewar postmark. Separately a "5" marking was struck inside the postmark and a boxed "PAID" marking outside the postmark.

Recorded uses of the Barnwell provisional envelope do not bear postmarks.

[*Italic*]	value typeface indicating the item is difficult to price accurately
[*Italic*]	date or location indicates unconfirmed information
NR	used in place of value when no examples have been recorded

Baton Rouge, Louisiana

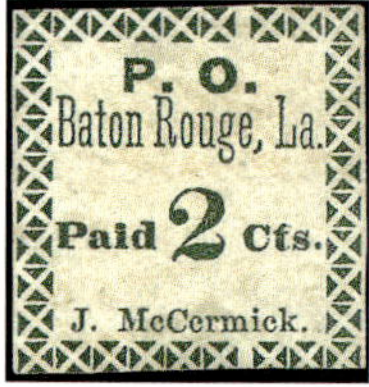

A

B

C

D

McCcrmick error

Maltese Cross Border Type B

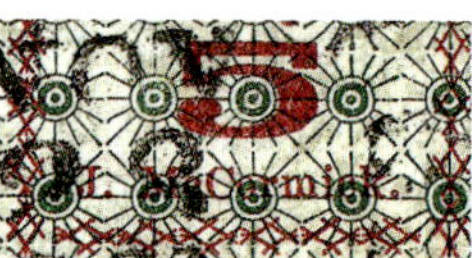

Crisscross Border Type C

Detail of Crisscross Border Piece

Adhesives

BAT-LA-A01 (11X1)		
A 2¢ green on white	*7,500.*	*5,000.*
a. "McCcrmick" error (11X1*a*)	*20,000.*	*10,000.*
BAT-LA-A02 (11X2)		
B 5¢ green and carmine on *white*	2,000.	1,250.
a. "McCcrmick" error (11X2*a*)	NR	*3,000.*
b. Pair	NR	3,000.
c. Strip of three	NR	5,000.
d. Strip of five	NR	*20,000.*
BAT-LA-A03 (11X3)		
C 5¢ green and carmine on *white*	3,500.	3,000.
a. "McCcrmick" error (11X3*a*)	NR	*5,000.*
BAT-LA-A04 (11X4)		
D 10¢ blue on *white*	NR	*12,500.*

On Cover

BAT-LA-A01 (11X1)	
A 2¢ green on *white*	*25,000.*
a. "McCcrmick" error (11X1*a*)	*30,000.*
BAT-LA-A02 (11X2)	
B 5¢ green and carmine on *white*	5,000.
a. "McCcrmick" error (11X2*a*)	*15,000.*
b. Pair*	*7,500.*
e. Mailed from another town	*10,000.*

BAT-LA-A03 (11X3)
  C 5¢ green and carmine on *white* 7,500.
BAT-LA-A04 (11X4)
  D 10¢ blue on *white* *75,000.*

The Baton Rouge, Louisiana provisionals were printed at the offices of the *Cornet and Gazette*, a local newspaper. There were ten subjects in a typeset form arranged (5 x 2). The Maltese cross border and central design of Types A, B and D are the same. Only the value lines are different. The words "Paid" and "Cts." were omitted on Type B due to the size of the numeral "5."

The central design of Type C is the same as that used for Type B. The Maltese cross border was replaced by a crisscross border. The change in the border resulted in the Type C stamp being slightly larger than the other types.

There are recorded uses of the 5¢ Type B stamp as early as August 1861. The earliest recorded use of the 5¢ Type C is in late November 1861. This indicates that the Type C was a second printing of the 5¢ stamp.

The "McCcrmick error" is found on position 7, (second stamp on second row). This error has been found on the 2¢ and both 5¢ adhesives. It has not been found on the 10¢ adhesive.

Earliest recorded dates of use:
- A01 – August 5, 1861 on drop letter
- A02 – July 25, 1861 to Evergreen, La.
- A03 – November 28, 1861 off cover
- A04 – October 3, 1861 off cover

Recorded examples that entered the mail at another town:
- A02 – Used from New Orleans (postmarked December 15, 1861 – accepted as postage)
- A02 – Used from New Orleans (postmarked January 31, 1862 – accepted as postage)

Warning: Dangerous forgeries of Type A02 and A04 exist.

Beaumont, Texas

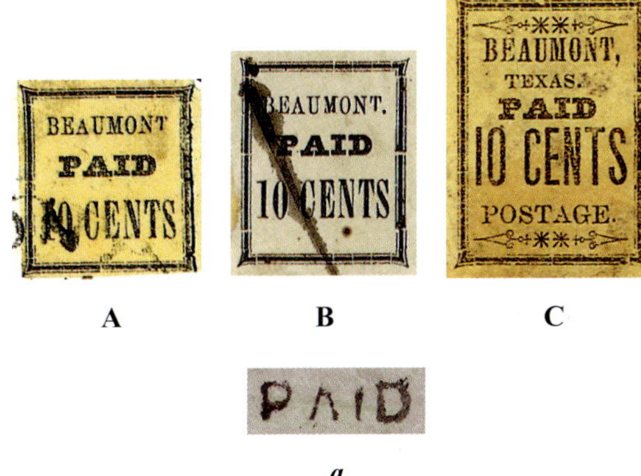

A B C

a

Adhesives

BEA-TX-A01 (12X1)
  A 10¢ black on *yellow** NR NR
BEA-TX-A02 (12X2)
  B 10¢ black on *pink* NR *10,000.*
BEA-TX-A03 (12X3)
  C 10¢ black on *yellow* NR NR

On Cover

BEA-TX-A01 (12X1)
  A 10¢ black on *yellow* *45,000.*
    a. With "PAID" (Type *a*)
BEA-TX-A02 (12X2)
  B 10¢ black on *pink* *20,000.*
BEA-TX-A03 (12XU3)
  C 10¢ black on *yellow* *75,000.*

The Beaumont Texas provisionals were typeset and printed on colored paper from three different typeset forms. Four positions of the Type B adhesive have been plated indicating a form of at least four settings (2 x 2). The Type A adhesive may have a similar number of settings. There is insufficient information on which to theorize the size of the Type C form.

The Type B adhesive is slightly taller than the Type A.

There are approximately 18 recorded examples of all the Beaumont provisionals used on cover. All bear postmarks with month dates of April to July. Those few covers with year dates are dated 1864. Based on this, it is assumed all the Beaumont provisionals were used in the spring and summer of 1864.

Earliest recorded dates of use:
- A01 – April 9, [1864] to San Augustine, Tex.
- A02 – June 18, [1864] to Houston, Tex.
- A03 – Undated postmark to Liberty, Tex. (only recorded example)

Bluffton, South Carolina

A

Entire (Handstamped)

BLU-SC-E01 (124XU1)
  A 5¢ black NR *5,000.*

The Bluffton, South Carolina provisional was prepared by handstamping envelopes with an undated prewar postmark.

Separately "PAID" and "5" markings were struck in the center of the postmark.

The only recorded example is postmarked October 8, [1861] to Charleston, [S.C.].

Bridgeville, Alabama

A

Tracing

Adhesives

BRI-AL-A01 (13X1)		
A 5¢ black on *white*, with red-ruled squares	NR	NR

On Cover

BRI-AL-A01 (13X1)	
A 5¢ black on *white*, with red-ruled squares	NR
a. Pair	*30,000.*

The Bridgeville, Alabama provisional was prepared by handstamping "PAID" over a circular "5" rate marking on paper with red-ruled squares.

The only recorded example is postmarked July 31, [1862] to Columbia, S.C.

Camden, South Carolina

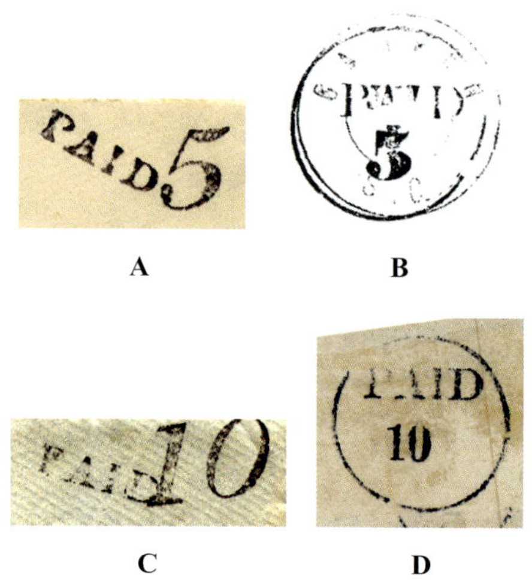

A B

C D

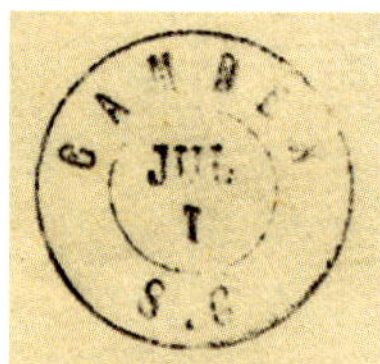

Control

Entires (Handstamped)

CAM-SC-E01		
A 5¢ black	NR	NA
a. Mailed from another town		1,500.
CAM-SC-E02 (125XU1)		
B 5¢ black (with control)	NR	1,500.
CAM-SC-E03		
C 10¢ black	NR	NA
a. Under a postally used general issue		1,500.
CAM-SC-E04 (125XU2)		
D 10¢ black	500.	NA
a. Under a postally used general issue		2,000.

The Camden, South Carolina Type A and C provisionals were prepared by handstamping envelopes with "PAID" and "5" or "10" rate markings.

The Type B provisional was prepared by handstamping envelopes with a "PAID" and "5" rate marking. In addition the envelope was struck with a dated postmark as a control.

The Type D provisional was prepared by handstamping envelopes with a circled "PAID / 10" marking.

Earliest recorded dates of use:

- E01 – None recorded
- E02 – July 15, 1861 to Charleston, S.C. (only recorded example)
- E03 – Unknown
- E03a – Under 10¢ blue lithograph postmarked February 11, [1862] to Collinsburgh, La.
- E04 – Unknown

Recorded example that entered the mail from another town:

- E01 – Used from Columbia, S.C. (postmarked November 15, [1861] – not accepted as postage)

Note: The E01, E03 and E04 markings were also used as stampless markings. They are considered provisionals only when unused, under a postally used general issue, or mailed from another town.

[–]	symbol used in place of value to mean insufficient information to assign a price
NR	used in place of value when no examples have been recorded

Canton, Mississippi

A

Entire (Handstamped)

CAN-MS-E01 (14XU1)

A 5¢ black		1,000.	2,750.
	a. Struck twice (10¢)	NR	—
	b. Revalued "10" (ms)* (14XU1*a*)	NR	5,000.
	c. Under a postally used general issue		3,500.

The Canton, Mississippi provisional was prepared by handstamping envelopes with a design that features a solid star with "PAID 5" between the points of the star. The negative "P" in the center of the star stands for the last name of the postmaster, William Priestley.

Earliest recorded dates of use:
E01 – July 2, [1861] to New Orleans
E01a – June 5, 1861 to Naylor's Landing, Yazoo River, [Miss.]

Recorded example that entered the mail at another town:
E01 – Used from Livingston, Miss. (postmarked September 23, [1861] – not accepted as postage)

Carolina City, North Carolina

A Control

Entire (Handstamped)

CAR-NC-E01 (118XU1)
A 5¢ black NR *5,000.*

The Carolina City, North Carolina provisional was prepared by handstamping envelopes with a circular "Paid / 5" marking. A typeset straightline "Carolina City, N. C" marking was struck as a control.

Earliest recorded date of use is October 7, [1861] to Amity Hill, N.C. and Sandy Grove, N.C. (two different covers).

Cartersville, Georgia

A

Entire (Handstamped)

CAR-GA-E01 (126XU1)
A PAID [5¢], red NR *2,000.*

The Cartersville, Georgia provisional marking was prepared by handstamping envelopes with the undated office postmark. Separately a "PAID" marking was struck inside the postmark. No rate was indicated but all recorded uses imply a five-cent rate.

Earliest date of use is June [1861] to Athens, Tenn.

Chapel Hill, North Carolina

A

Entire (Handstamaped)

CHA-NC-E01 (15XU1)
A 5¢ black NR *4,000.*

The Chapel Hill, North Carolina provisional was prepared by handstamping envelopes with the undated office postmark in which the date logos were replaced by a small "5". Separately a "PAID" marking was struck beside or partially inside the postmark.

Earliest recorded date of use is September 19, [1861] to Huntsville, N.C.

Note: There is one recorded example of a stampless cover with handstamped "PAID" and manuscript "5" markings. To the right of these markings is the provisional marking without the "PAID" marking. "Aug 2" in manuscript is written over the "5" of the provisional marking. This is considered a postmark and not a provisional use.

Charleston, South Carolina

A

Adhesive

CHA-SC-A01 (16X1)

A 5¢ blue on *white*		1,000.	750.
	a. Pair	2,500.	1,750.

On Cover

CHA-SC-A01 (16X1)

A 5¢ blue on *white*		2,000.
	a. Pair	5,000.
	b. Two singles	3,000.
	c. Used to pay forwarding postage	*2,500.*
	d. Used with a general issue	*3,000.*
	e. Mailed from another town	*3,000.*
	f. Used on overpaid drop letter*	*2,500.*

The Charleston, South Carolina adhesive was lithographed in blue on white wove paper by Evans & Cogswell Company of Charleston. The design of the central oval is similar to that of the 5¢ typographed envelopes that were issued earlier.

A transfer stone consisting of 15 subjects (5 x 3) was laid on the printing stone six times. The printed sheets consisted of 90 stamps (10 x 9) and sold for $5.00. The surcharge was to pay for printing costs.

The adhesives were placed on sale on September 4, 1861 and withdrawn on December 6 with the arrival of the first stamps from the Confederate Post Office Department. The provisional stamp continued to be used into early 1862. In mid-June the remaining provisional stamps were placed on sale again, apparently due to a shortage of regular postage stamps. It is estimated about 25,000 stamps were printed. All unsold stamps were either destroyed when the rate changed on July 1, 1862 or when the post office relocated on August 26, 1863.

Earliest recorded date of use is September 4, 1861 to Columbia, S.C.

Recorded examples that entered the mail at other towns:
- A01 – Used from Tudor Hall, Va. (postmarked November 9, [1861] – not accepted as postage)
- A01 – Used from Tudor Hall, Va. (postmarked November 19, [1861] – not accepted as postage)
- A01 – Used from Wideman's, S.C. (postmarked November 19, [1861] – accepted as postage)
- A01 – Unconfirmed use from Pocotaligo, S.C. (postmarked Nov 18, [1861] – not accepted as postage)

Warning: Dangerous forgeries of A01 exist.

B

C

Entires (Printed)

CHA-SC-E01 (16XU1-16XU5)

B 5¢ blue		—	4,000.
	a. With added "PAID / 5" (Type D)*	NR	NR
	b. Mailed from another town		—

CHA-SC-E02 (16XU6)

C 10¢ blue	NR	60,000.

The 5¢ typographed entires were printed by Evans & Cogswell Company of Charleston on envelopes of various colors. The envelopes were placed on sale on August 15, 1861.

Earliest recorded dates of use:
- E01 – August 16, 1861 to Laurens, S.C.
- E02 – July 11, [1862] to Anderson C.H., S.C. (only recorded example)

Recorded examples that entered the mails at other towns:
- E01 – Used from Adams Run, S.C. (postmarked September 5, [1861] – questionable if accepted as postage)
- E01 – Used from Walterborough, S.C. (postmarked September 19, [1861] – not accepted as postage)

Warning: Dangerous forgeries of E01 exist.

D

Entire (Handstamped)

CHA-SC-E07

D 5¢ black		NR	NR
	a. Mailed from another town		*1,000.*

The Type D marking was prepared by handstamping envelopes with a "PAID 5" rate marking.

Notes: The only recorded example of E07 as a provisional was used from Augusta, Georgia under a general issue stamp. This was erroneously listed as an Augusta, Georgia provisional in the past.

The E07 marking was also used as a stampless marking. It is considered a provisional only when unused, under a postally used general issue, or mailed from another town.

Charlotte, North Carolina

A

Entire (Handstamped)

CHR-NC-E01 (146XU1)

A	5¢ blue	NA	NA
	a. Under a postally used general issue		*1,500.*

The Charlotte, North Carolina provisional was prepared by handstamping envelopes with "PAID" and "5" markings.

The only recorded example is under a general issue post-marked May 26, [1862] from Wilmington, N.C.

Note: This marking was also used as a stampless marking. It is considered a provisional only when unused, under a postally used general issue, or mailed from another town.

Charlottesville, Virginia

A B

Control

Entires (Handstamped)

CHA-VA-E01 (127XU1)			
A	5¢ blue (with control)	NR	*1,000.*
CHA-VA-E02 (127XU2)			
B	10¢ blue (with control)	NR	*1,000.*

The Charlottesville, Virginia provisional was prepared by handstamping envelopes with "PAID" and "5" or "10" rate markings. The postmaster, Wm. M. Keblinger, then wrote his initials in the upper right corner of the envelope as a control.

Earliest recorded dates of use:
- E01 – *October 1861* to Richmond, Va.
- E02 – *September 3, 1861* to Newberry, S.C.

Chattanooga, Tennessee

A B

a

Entires (Handstamped)

CHA-TN-E01			
A	2¢ black	NR	NR
	a. Revalued 5 (Type *a*) (17XU3)	NR	*4,000.*
CHA-TN-E02 (17XU2)			
B	5¢ black	NR	2,500.

The Chattanooga, Tennessee provisionals were prepared by handstamping envelopes with a prewar undated postmark in which the date logos were replaced by "PAID" and "2" or "5" rate markings.

Earliest recorded dates of use:
- E01 – None recorded
- E01a – October 13, 1861 to Athens, E. Tenn. (only recorded example)
- E02 – July 9, 1861

Christiansburg, Virginia

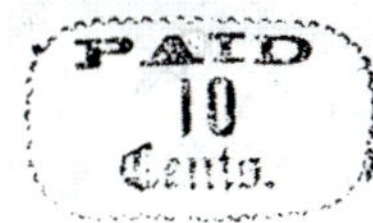

A B

Emtires (Handstamped)

CHR-VA-E01 (99XU1)		
A 5¢ black*	NR	NR
CHR-VA-E02 (99XU2)		
A 5¢ blue (shades)	NR	1,000.
CHR-VA-E03 (99XU4)		
A 5¢ green	NR	3,500.
CHR-VA-E04 (99XU5)		
B 10¢ blue	NR	3,500.

The Christiansburg, Virginia provisionals were prepared by handstamping envelopes with a typeset device that included the paid rate inside a fancy border.

Earliest recorded dates of use:

E01 – *August 24, [1861] to Bick Lick, Va.*

E02 – *July 18, [1861] to Wytheville, Va.*

E03 – June 18, [1861] to Dublin, Va. (only recorded example)

E04 – December 2 to Blacksburg, Va.

Caution: The lack of any recorded stampless markings from Christiansburg is evidence these markings were also used as stampless markings. Stampless uses cannot be readily distinguished from provisional uses. Each example must be considered on its own merits.

Warning: A fake use of E01 as an adhesive exists.

CLARKSVILLE, TEXAS

A

Entire (Handstamped)

CLA-TX-E01		
A 10¢ black	NR	NR
a. Under a postally used general issue		—

The Clarksville, Texas provisional was prepared by handstamping envelopes with a circular "PAID / 10" marking.

The only recorded example is under a pair of 5¢ typographs postmarked June 18, [1861] to Jefferson, Tex.

Note: This marking was also used as a stampless marking. It is considered a provisional only when unused, under a postally used general issue, or mailed from another town.

COLAPARCHEE, GEORGIA

A Control

Entire (Handstamped)

COE-GA-E01 (119XU1)		
A 5¢ black (with control)	NR	NR
a. Under a postally used general issue		2,500.

The Colaparchee, Georgia provisional was prepared by handstamping envelopes with a circular "PAID" marking in which a manuscript "5" was added. An undated office postmark was struck on the envelope front as a control.

Earliest recorded date of use is from Savannah, Ga. (postmarked April 13, [1862] – not accepted as postage). This and the only other recorded example were mailed back to Colaparchee from Savannah.

COLUMBIA, SOUTH CAROLINA

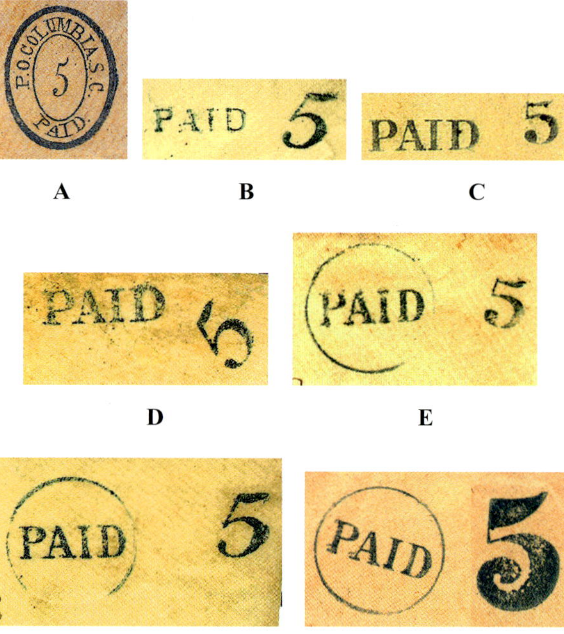

A B C

D E

F G

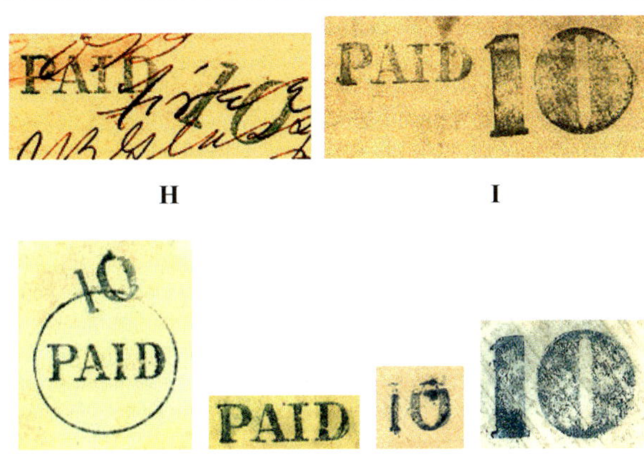

H I

J *a* *b* *c*

Oval Control **Circle Control**

Entires (Handstamped)

COL-SC-E01 (18XU1)		
A 5¢ blue (no control)	750.	1,250.
a. With added "PAID" (Type *a*)	NR	1,250.
b. (18XU3) Revalued "PAID 10" (Types a and *b*)	NR	2,000.
c. Revalued "PAID 10" Types *a* and *b*) plus "10" (Type *c*)	NR	—
d. Used with general issue	NR	*4,000.*
COL-SC-E02		
B 5¢ blue (oval control on reverse)	NR	750.
COL-SC-E03 (18XU4)		
C 5¢ blue (oval control on front)	NR	2,000.
COL-SC-E04 (18XU4*a*)		
C 5¢ blue (oval control on reverse)	NR	500.
a. Mailed from another town	NR	750.
COL-SC-E05		
D 5¢ blue (oval control on reverse)	NR	750.
COL-SC-E06		
D 5¢ blue (round control on reverse)	NR	1,000.
COL-SC-E07 (18XU4)		
E 5¢ blue (oval control on front)	NR	*2,500.*
COL-SC-E08		
F 5¢ blue (oval control on reverse)	NR	500.
a. Mailed from another town	NR	*750.*
COL-SC-E09		
F 5¢ blue (round control on reverse)	NR	750.
COL-SC-E10		
G 5¢ blue (oval control on reverse)	NR	750.
a. 5¢ blue (no control)	—	NA
b. 5¢ blue (no control), mailed from another town		1,000.
COL-SC-E11		
H 10¢ blue (oval control on reverse) marked "POB" and "Free" (ms)	NR	*1,000.*
COL-SC-E12		
I 10¢ blue (oval control on reverse)	NR	1,000.
COL-SC-E13		
J 10¢ blue (oval control on reverse)	NR	1,000.

The Columbia, South Carolina Type A provisional was prepared by handstamping an oval rated design on envelopes of various colors.

All other types were prepared by handstamping envelopes with a variety of "PAID" and "5" or "10" rate markings. An oval or circular control in the form of a seal with "S C" in the center was then struck on the front or reverse of the envelope. No control was struck on the E10b entire.

Earliest recorded dates of use:

E01 – June 23, [1861]
E01a – *September 16, [1861] to Longmire's Store, N.C.*
E01b – *December 19, [1861] to Tappahannock, Va.*
E01c – *January 1, [1862] to Charleston, S.C.*
E02 – June 24, [1861] to Unionville, S.C.
E03 – September 4, [1861] to Hopkins Turn Out, S.C.
E04 – Unknown
E04a – August 27, 1861 (used from Monticello, S.C.)
E05 – July 20, [1861] to Tudor Hall, Va.
E06 – *July 19, [1861] to Spartanburg, S.C.*
E07 – *August 26, [1861] to Yonguesville, S.C.*
E08 – June 27, [1861] to Richmond, Va.
E09 – *July 14, [1861] to Charleston, S.C.*
E10 – *July 1, [1861] to Berzelia, Ga.*
E11 – July 24, [1861] to Maysville, S.C.
E12 – August 27, [1861] to Memphis, Tenn.
E13 – July 12, [1861] to Fairfax C.H., Va.

Recorded examples that entered the mail at other towns:

E04 – Used from Monticello, S.C. (postmarked August 27, 1861 – accepted as postage)
E08 – Used from Richmond, Virginia (no postmark [drop letter] – not accepted as postage)
E10 – Used from Chattanooga, Tennessee (postmarked – , 1861 – not accepted as postage)

Note: The E10b entire without a control marking was also used as a stampless marking. It is considered a provisional only when unused, under a postally used general issue, or mailed from another town.

Warning: Dangerous forgeries of E01 exist.

[*Italic*]	value typeface indicating the item is difficult to price accurately
[*Italic*]	date or location indicates unconfirmed information
NR	used in place of value when no examples have been recorded

Columbia, Tennessee

A

Entire (Handstamped)

COL-TN-E01 (113XU1)

A	5¢ red	NR	*7,500.*

The Columbia, Tennessee provisional was prepared by handstamping envelopes with an undated prewar postmark in which the date logos were replaced by "PAID" and "5" markings.

The only recorded example is postmarked October 19, [1861] to Ashwood, Tenn.

Columbus, Georgia

A B

a *b* *c*

Entires (Handstamped)

COL-GA-E01 (19XU1)

A	5¢ blue	500.	750.
	a. With added "PAID 10" (Type *b*)	NR	1,000.
	b. With "DUE 5" (Type *c*)		*1,250.*
	c. Under a postally used general issue		*1,250.*

COL-GA-E02 (19XU2)

B	10¢ red	NR	2,000.
	a. With added "PAID 5" (Type *a)*		*2,000.*

The Columbus, Georgia provisionals were prepared by handstamping envelopes with an undated prewar postmark in which the date logos were replaced by "PAID" and "5" or "10" rate markings. The 5¢ marking was struck in blue and the 10¢ marking in red.

Earliest recorded dates of use:
- E01 – June 10, [1861] to Pensacola, Fla.
- E02 – August 6, [1861] to Richmond, Va.

Warning: There are faked uses of E01 and E02.

Courtland, Alabama

A

Entire (Handstamped)

COU-AL-E01 (103XU1)

A	5¢ red	*10,000.*	NR

The Courtland, Alabama provisional was prepared by handstamping envelopes with a woodcut design in which a "5" rate marking was inserted.

The only recorded example is addressed to Athens, Ala. but has no postmark.

Cuthbert, Georgia

A

Entire (Handstamped)

CUT-GA-E01

A	10¢ black	NR	NR
	a. Under a postally used general issue		*1,000.*

The Cuthbert, Georgia provisional was prepared by handstamping envelopes with "PAID" and "10" markings.

The only recorded example is used under a 10¢ engraved general issue tied by an indistinct Cuthbert postmark.

Note: This marking was also used as a stampless marking. It is considered a provisional only when unused, under a postally used general issue, or mailed from another town.

Dalton, Georgia

A

B C

Entires (Handstamped)

DAL-GA-E01 (20XU1*a*)

A	PAID [5¢] black	NR	750.

DAL-GA-E02 (20XU1)

B	5¢ black	NR	750.
	a. Revalued "10" (ms) (20XU1*b*)	NR	1,000.
	b. Revalued "20" (ms) (20XU1*c*)	NR	1,250.

DAL-GA-E03 (20XU2)

C	10¢ black	NR	1,500.

The Dalton, Georgia provisionals were prepared by handstamping envelopes with the office postmark in which the date logos were replaced by "PAID" and "5" or "10" rate markings.

The only recorded use of E01 was to pay the letter rate for a distance of less than 500 miles.

Earliest recorded dates of use:
- E01 – June 6, 1861 to Jonesboro, East Tenn. (only recorded example)
- E02 – June 22, 1861 to Fleetwood Academy, Va.
- E03 – July 17, 1862 to McKinley, Ala.

Caution: There are several recorded examples of Type B and C envelopes with "charge box" markings. This and the scarcity of stampless markings from Dalton is evidence the provisional marking was also used as a stampless marking. Stampless uses are not easily distinguished from provisional uses. Each example must be considered on its own merits.

Danville, Virginia

A

Adhesives

Wove paper

DAN-VA-A01 (21X1)

A	5¢ red on *white*	NR	*2,500.*
	a. Cut to shape	NR	*2,000.*

Laid paper

DAN-VA-A02 (21X2)

A	5¢ red on *white*	NR	*7,500.*

On Cover

Wove paper

DAN-VA-A01 (21X1)

A	5¢ red on *white*	5,000.
	a. Cut to shape	4,000.

Laid paper

DAN-VA-A02 (21X2)

A	5¢ red on *white*	NR

The Danville, Virginia adhesive provisionals were typeset and printed in the office of the *Democratic Appeal*, a local newspaper owned by postmaster William D. Coleman. The layout and size of the form is unknown.

Coleman was appointed postmaster in 1860 and resigned his office in March 1861. He was reappointed as postmaster in September 1861.

Many of the Danville adhesive provisionals were cut to follow the general outline of the design.

Earliest recorded dates of use:
- A01 – October 3, 1861 to South Boston, Va.
- A02 – Unknown – off cover (only recorded example)

Warning: Dangerous forgeries of Type A exist.

B

Entire (Printed)

DAN-VA-E01 (21XU1-21XU3)

B	5¢ black	NR	*10,000.*
	a. Imprint on right	*7,500.*	NR
	b. Used as drop letter		—
	c. Under a postally used general issue		NR

The Type B provisional was prepared by printing a typeset design on envelopes of various colors. The basic design is a stock shoe dealer's cut in which type was set to complete the design and the rate. The "SOUTHERN" portion of the imprint exists in various states from a near straight line to a distinct curve. Most imprints are on the left side of the envelope. There is one recorded example with the imprint on the right side.

Postmaster Payne was appointed postmaster on March 12, 1861 and continued as the Confederate postmaster until he was replaced by William D. Coleman in September 1861.

Earliest recorded date of use is July 10, [1861]

Warning: Dangerous forgeries exist.

10¢ Red Entire

A red 10¢ envelope similar to Type B exists (see illustration above). Most recorded examples are either unused or used with the stamps removed. There are two recorded examples with partial postmarks where part of the envelope was torn off. There is no conclusive evidence this envelope was used as a provisional during the Confederate period.

PAID 5

C **D**

PAID 5 PAID 10

E **F**

PAID 10

G

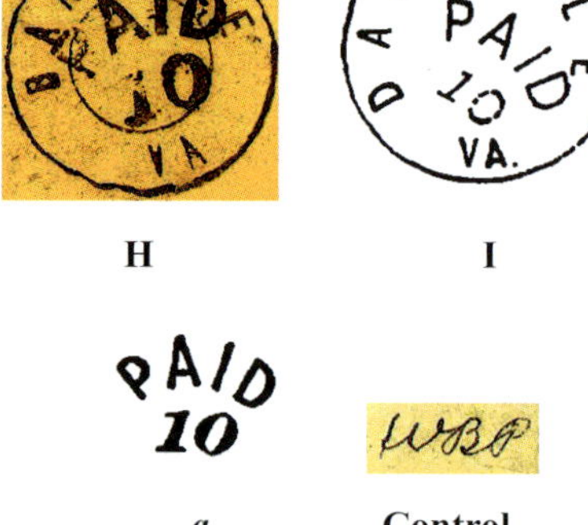

H **I**

PAID 10

a **Control**

Entires (Handstamped)

DAN-VA-E02			
C 5¢ black (with control)		NR	750.
DAN-VA-E03			
D 5¢ black (with control)		NR	*1,000.*
DAN-VA-E04 (21XU3A)			
E 5¢ black (with control)		NR	750.
a. 5¢ Under a postally used general issue (no control)			1,000.
DAN-VA-E05			
F 10¢ black (with control)		NR	750.
DAN-VA-E06 (21XU7)			
G 10¢ black (with control)		NR	750.
DAN-VA-E07 (21XU4)			
H 10¢ black		NR	750.
DAN-VA-E08 (21XU6)			
I 10¢ black		1,000.	NR
a. With added "PAID 10" (Type H) and "PAID 10" (Type *a*)		1,250.	NR

The Type C, E, F and G provisionals were prepared by handstamping envelopes with various "PAID" and "5" or "10" rate markings. Postmaster W. B. Payne added his initials as a control.

The Type D provisional was prepared by handstamping envelopes with an ornate typeset device with "PAID / 5 / Cents" in the center.

The Type H provisional was prepared by handstamping envelopes with an undated double circle office postmark and striking a "PAID / 10" marking in the center. The "PAID /

10" marking was larger than the inner circle of the postmark and overlaps part of the postmark.

The Type I provisional was prepared by handstamping envelopes with an undated circle postmark and striking a "PAID / 10" marking in the center.

Earliest recorded dates of use:

- E02 – June 29, [1861] to Leatherwood, Va. (only recorded example)
- E03 – August 23, [1861] to Henry, C.H., Va. (only recorded example)
- E04 – July 15, [1861] to Boonville, N.C.
- E05 – October 2, [1861] (only recorded example)
- E06 – September 10, [1861] to Atlanta, Ga.
- E07 – December 14, [1861] to Union Furnace, Va.
- E08 – None recorded

Note: The Type E marking is recorded with and without the control. Without the control it is considered a stampless marking unless it is unused, under a postally used general issue, or mailed from another town.

DEMOPOLIS, ALABAMA

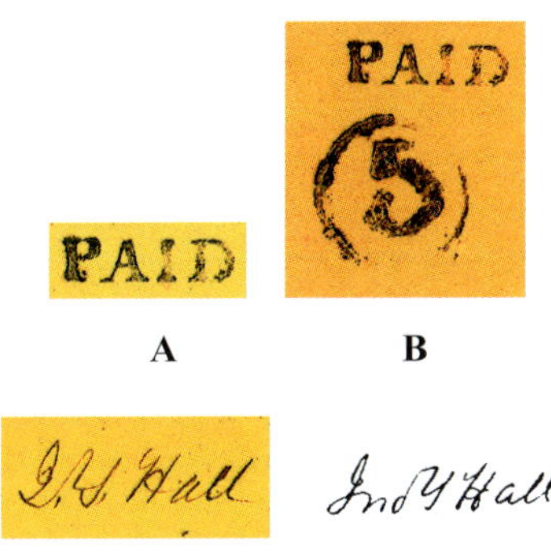

A **B**

Control A **Control B**

Entires (Handstamped)

DEM-AL-E01 (22XU3)		
A PAID black + 5 cts (ms) (with Control A)	NR	3,000.
DEM-AL-E02 (22XU2)		
B 5¢ black with Control A	NR	3,000.
a. Same, with Control B	NR	3,000.

The Demopolis, Alabama provisional was prepared by handstamping envelopes with a "PAID" marking. Some envelopes had the rate added in manuscript and others had the rate added by handstamping a circled "5" rate marking. Both types were then signed by the postmaster, Jno. Y. Hall, as a control. The control is found in two different forms.

Earliest recorded dates of use:

- E01 – November 2-, [1861] to Tuscaloosa, Ala. (only recorded example)
- E02 – December 5, [1861] to Lauderdale Springs, Ala.

EATONTON, GEORGIA

A

B **C**

Entires (Handstamped)

EAT-GA-E01 (23XU1)		
A 5¢ black	NR	1,500.
a. Revalued "10" (ms)	NR	1,750.
EAT-GA-E02 (23XU2)		
B 10¢ black ("5"struck twice)	NR	2,000.
EAT-GA-E03		
C 10¢ black	—	NA

The Type A provisionals were prepared by handstamping envelopes with an undated office postmark with the date logos replaced by a small "5" marking.

The Type B marking was prepared in the same manner as the Type A marking but a separate large "5" rate marking was struck twice to the side of the rate marking.

The Type C marking was prepared by handstamping envelopes with "PAID" and circled "10" markings.

Earliest recorded dates of use:

- E01 – August 28, [1861] to Mill Way P O, S.C.
- E02 – June 18, [1861] to Portsmouth, Va.
- E03 – To Milledgeville, Ga. (only recorded example on unpostmarked cover endorsed "Goodness of / Lieut J B Fair.")

Note: The Type C marking was also used as a stampless marking. It is considered a provisional only when unused, under a postally used general issue, or mailed from another town.

> NA used in place of a listing value when no examples are known to exist

Emory, Virginia

A

B

a

b

Adhesives

EMO-VA-A01 (24X1)
A 5¢ blue, "PAID" above rate NR NR
EMO-VA-A02 (24X1)
B 5¢ blue, "PAID" below rate NR NR

On Cover

EMO-VA-A01 (24X1)
A 5¢ blue, "PAID" above rate *15,000.*
a. With second "PAID" (Type *a*) on adhesive and "PAID 5" (Type *b*) *15,000.*
b. With "PAID 5" (Type *b*) *25,000.*
EMO-VA-A02 (24X1)
B 5¢ blue, "PAID" below rate *15,000.*
a. With "PAID 5" (Type *b*) *20,000.*

The Emory, Virginia adhesive provisional was prepared by handstamping "PAID" and "5" on the margin selvage of sheets of the U.S. 1¢ 1857 issue. One example is recorded with a partial plate number. All copies are imperforate on one or two sides and perforated 15 on the other sides. The "PAID" marking was struck both above and below the rate marking.

The postmark normally does not tie the stamp. Either a handstamped or manuscript postmark was used on adhesive provisional covers.

Earliest recorded dates of use:
A01 – July 22, 1861 to Castle Craig, Va.
A02 – June 24, 1861 to *Wytheville, Va.*

C

D

Entires (Handstamped)

EMO-VA-E01 (24XU1)
C 5¢ blue NR 1,000.
EMO-VA-E02 (24XU2)
D 10¢ blue NR NR
a. Under postally used US stamp NA *7,500.*

The Type C handstamped envelopes were prepared by handstamping envelopes with a woodcut design that included "PAID", "5" and the town name. The Type D envelopes were prepared by handstamping envelopes with a woodcut design that included the town name and the rate "10". Separately a "PAID" marking was struck to the side.

Earliest recorded dates of use:
E01 – Apr 16, [1862] to Marion, Va.
E02 – Under a US 3¢ stamp postmarked May 26, [1865] (only recorded example)

Fincastle, Virginia

A

Entire (Printed)

FIN-VA-E01 (104XU1)
A 10¢ black NR —

The Fincastle, Virginia provisional was typeset and printed in the upper right corner of envelopes.

The only recorded example is postmarked March 21 to Bonsacks, Va.

Forsyth, Georgia

A

B

Entire (Handstamped)

FOR-GA-E01 (120XU1)
A 10¢ black NR NR
a. Under a postally used general issue 1,500.
FOR-GA-E02 (120XU2)
B 10¢ black NR NR
a. Under a postally used general issue 1,000.

The Type A and B Forsyth, Georgia provisionals were prepared as woodcuts and handstamped on envelopes.

Earliest recorded dates of use:

E01 – Under a general issue stamp (since removed) to Milledgeville, Ga. (only recorded example)

E02 – Under a rouletted general issue stamp postmarked Mar --, [1865] to Barnesville, Ga. (only recorded example)

Fort Valley, Georgia

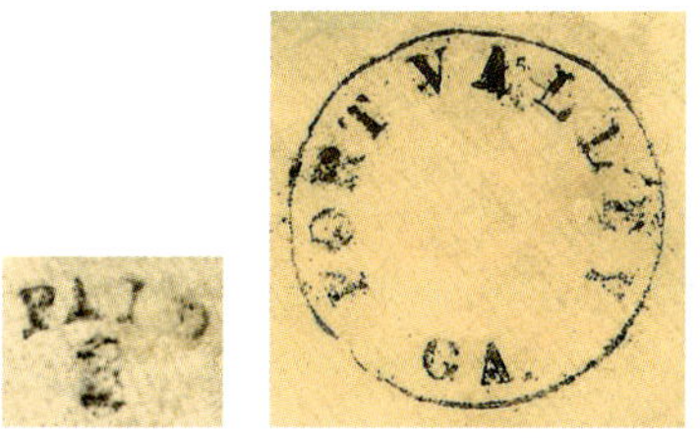

A Control *a*

Entires (Handstamped)

FTV-GA-E01
A 3¢ black
a. Revalued "5" (Type *a*) NR —

The Fort Valley Georgia provisional was prepared by handstamping envelopes with a "PAID / 3" marking and revaluing the marking with a handstamp "5" marking. An undated office postmark was struck on the envelope front as a control.

The only recorded example is a revalued cover addressed to Eufaula, Ala. with a July 6, 1861 enclosure.

See also, "3¢1861 Postmasters' Provisionals" Section.

Franklin, North Carolina

A

Entire (Printed)

FRA-NC-E01 (25XU1)
A 5¢ blue NR —

The Type A Franklin, North Carolina provisional was typeset and printed in the upper right corner of envelopes.

The only recorded example is postmarked January 21, [1862] to Waynesville, N.C.

Fraziersville, South Carolina

A

Entire (Handstamped)

FRA-SC-E01 (128XU1)
A 5¢ black NR *3,500.*

The Fraziersville, South Carolina provisional was prepared by handstamping envelopes with an office postmark in which the date logos were replaced with a "PAID" marking and a manuscript "5" rate.

The only recorded example is postmarked February 13, [1862] to Glymphville, S.C.

Fredericksburg, Virginia

A B

Adhesives

FRE-VA-A01 (26X1)		
A 5¢ blue on *thin bluish*	750.	1,000.
a. Pair	1,500.	NR
b. Block of four	3,000.	NR
FRE-VA-A02 (26X2)		
B 10¢ red (shades) on *thin bluish*	1,500.	NR

On Cover

FRE-VA-A01 (26X1)	
A 5¢ blue on *thin bluish*	5,000.
a. Pair	*12,500.*
c. Under a postally used general issue	5,000.

The Fredericksburg, Virginia adhesives were typeset and printed on thin bluish paper. The printer was probably Jesse White, a local printer, who also printed local currency notes.

The printing form consisted of ten subjects in two horizontal rows of five. For the 5¢ stamps, two impressions of the printing form were made on each printed sheet.

The same printing form was used to print the ten-cent adhesive by substituting "10" for the "5" in each of the ten subjects.

The Fredericksburg provisional stamps were placed on sale in early September 1861 and were used through mid November 1861.

Earliest recorded dates of use:

- A01 – September 12, [1861] to Richmond, Va.
- A02 – No used copy recorded

Warning: Dangerous forgeries of A02 with fake cancellations exist.

Gainesville, Alabama

A

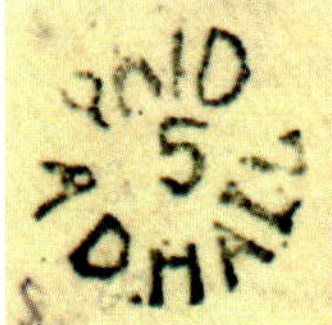

B

C

Entires (Handstamped)

GAI-AL-E01 (27XU1)			
A 5¢ black		NR	3,500.
a. Under a postally used general issue			4,000.
GAI-AL-E02			
B 5¢ black		NR	*5,000.*
GAI-AL-E03 (27XU2)			
C 10¢ black		NR	3,750.

The Gainesville, Alabama provisionals were prepared by handstamping envelopes with woodcut markings that include "PAID / 5" or "PAID / 10" and the postmasters name, A. D. Hall.

Earliest recorded dates of use:

- E01 – November 12, [1861] to Lauderdale Station, Miss.
- E02 – December 25, [1861] on partial envelope (only recorded example)
- E03 – Unknown

Galveston, Texas

A

B

C

D

E

F

Entires (Handstamped)

GAL-TX-E01 (98XU1)		
A 5¢ black	1,000.	2,000.
GAL-TX-E02		
B 5¢ black	NR	1,000.
GAL-TX-E03 (98XU5)		
C 5¢ black	NR	1,000.
GAL-TX-E04 (98XU2)		
D 10¢ black	NR	1,250.
GAL-TX-E05 (98XU3)		
E 10¢ black	NR	1,500.

GAL-TX-E06 (98XU4)

F 20¢ black NR 3,000.

The Type A and D Galveston, Texas provisionals were prepared by handstamping an ornate typeset design on envelopes and then striking a "5" or "10" rate marking either inside the design or to the side.

The Type B provisional was prepared by handstamping envelopes with an office postmark in which the date logos were replaced by "PAID" and "5" markings.

The Type C provisional was prepared by handstamping envelopes with the undated office double circle postmark and then handstamping "5" inside the postmark and "PAID" to the side.

The Type E and F provisionals were prepared by handstamping envelopes with an undated "3 PAID" integral postmark with the "3" removed. Separately a "10" or "20" rate marking was struck inside the postmark.

Earliest recorded dates of use:

- E01 – June 6, [1861] to Yorkville, S.C.
- E02 – — 31, 1861 to New Orleans (only recorded example)
- E03 – October 8, 1861 to Columbia, [*Tex.*]
- E04 – October 15, 1861 to Chapel Hill, [*Tex.*]
- E05 – Unknown
- E06 – August 18 to Shreveport, La. (only recorded example)

Caution: There is one recorded example of the Type E envelope with a manuscript "charge box" marking. This is evidence the marking may also have been used as a stampless marking. Stampless uses are not easily distinguished from provisional uses. Each example must be considered on its own merits.

Gaston, North Carolina

A

Entire (Handstamped)

GAS-NC-E01 (129XU1)

A 5¢ black NR *5,000.*

The Gaston, North Carolina provisional was prepared by handstamping envelopes with an undated office postmark in which the date logos were replaced with "PAID" and "5" markings.

The only recorded example is postmarked November 26, [1861] to Merry Hill, N.C.

Georgetown, South Carolina

A B

Control

Entires (Handstamped)

GEO-SC-E01 (28XU1)

A 5¢ black (with control) NR 750.

a. Under a postally used general issue *1,000.*

GEO-SC-E02 (28XU2)

B 5¢ black (with control) NR 1,250.

The Type A Georgetown, South Carolina provisional was prepared by handstamping a "PAID / 5" marking on envelopes. An undated office postmark was struck as a control on the reverse of the envelope.

The Type B provisional was prepared by handstamping envelopes with separate "PAID" and "5" markings. An undated office postmark was struck as a control on the reverse of the envelope.

Earliest recorded dates of use:

- E01 – September 26, 1861 to *Flat Rock, N.C.*
- E02 – June 20, 1861 to Scuppernong, N.C.

Note: The Type A and B markings were also used as stampless markings. Provisional uses must have the control marking.

[—]	symbol used in place of value to mean insufficient information to assign a price
NA	not applicable
[*Italic*]	value typeface indicating the item is difficult to price accurately
[*Italic*]	date or location indicates unconfirmed information
NR	used in place of value when no examples have been recorded

GOLIAD, TEXAS

A

B

C

D

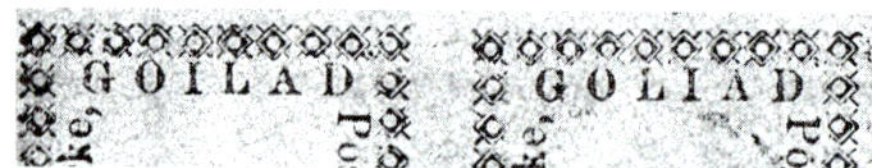

"GOILAD" error (left stamp)

Adhesives

GOL-TX-A01 (29X1)
- **A** 5¢ black on *white* — NR — *12,500.*

GOL-TX-A02 (29X2)
- **A** 5¢ black on *gray* — NR — *10,000.*

GOL-TX-A03 (29X3)
- **A** 5¢ black on *rose* — NR — *10,000.*

GOL-TX-A04 (29X6)
- **B** 5¢ black on *gray* — NR — *10,000.*
  - **a.** Pair *se-tenant*, one with "GOILAD" error (29X6*a*) — NR — *25,000.*

GOL-TX-A05 (29X8)
- **B** 5¢ black on *dark blue* — NR — NR

GOL-TX-A06 (29X4)
- **C** 10¢ black on *white* — *20,000.* — *15,000.*

GOL-TX-A07 (29X5)
- **C** 10¢ black on *rose* — NR — *10,000.*

GOL-TX-A08 (29X7)
- **D** 10¢ black on *gray* — NR — *10,000.*
  - **a.** "GOILAD" error (29X7*a*) — NR — *20,000.*
  - **b.** Ornamental printing on reverse — NR — NR

GOL-TX-A09 (29X9)
- **D** 10¢ black on *dark blue* — NR — 15,000.

On Cover

GOL-TX-A02 (29X2)
- **A** 5¢ black on *gray* — IH

GOL-TX-A03 (29X3)
- **A** 5¢ black on *rose* — *40,000.*

GOL-TX-A05 (29X8)
- **B** 5¢ black on *dark blue* — *10,000.*

GOL-TX-A07 (29X5)
- **C** 10¢ black on *rose* — *15,000.*

GOL-TX-A08 (29X7)
- **D** 10¢ black on *gray* — *25,000.*
  - **a.** "GOILAD" error (29X7*a*) — *30,000.*
  - **b.** Ornamental printing on reverse — *30,000.*

The Goliad, Texas adhesives were typeset and printed by Rev. A. M. Cox, owner of *The Messenger*, the local newspaper. The stamps were printed on three different colored papers. Some examples also have a blue wash that was applied after printing. The gray shade of paper is known with ornamental printing on the reverse. The papers vary in thickness with the gray colored paper the thinnest.

There are two distinct settings. The first has "Goliad" in italic type inside the border at the top. In the second setting, "GOLIAD" is spelled using Roman capitals and "J. A. Clarke," added along the left side and "Post Master." along the right side.

One of the positions in the second setting has two letters in "GOLIAD" transposed, producing the "GOILAD" error. This error occurs on both values indicating the settings were the same for both values with only the value changed. The layout and size of the printed sheet is not known.

All used examples of the Type A and C adhesives except one is canceled with manuscript "Clarke / P M" in red or black ink. All used examples of the Type B and D adhesives are canceled by a postmark, paid marking or pen stroke.

Earliest recorded dates of use:
- A01 – None recorded
- A02 – Unknown (Tapling Collection – only recorded example)
- A03 – No postmark to Austin City, Tex. – only recorded example)
- A04 – None recorded
- A05 – February to Columbia, Tex. (only recorded example)
- A06 – None recorded
- A07 – Unknown
- A08 – *October 1863* to Corpus Christie, Tex.

GONZALES, TEXAS

A

Adhesives

GON-TX-A01 (30X1)
- **A** [5¢] gold on *dark blue* — NA — NR

GON-TX-A02 (30X3)
- **A** [5¢] or [10¢] gold on *black* — NA — NR

GON-TX-A03 (30X2)

A [10¢] gold on *garnet* (shades)	NA	NR

On Cover

GON-TX-A01 (30X1)	
A [5¢] gold on *dark blue*	NR
a. Pair on cover	—
GON-TX-A02 (30X3)	
A [5¢] or [10¢] gold on *black*	—
GON-TX-A03 (30X2)	
A [10¢] gold on *garnet* (shades)	*12,500.*

The Gonzales, Texas provisional was an advertising label of the firm of Coleman & Law. The postmaster, John V. Law, was co-owner of the firm.

The labels were lithographed in multiples or sheets of unknown size. The inscription reads "Coleman & Law, Booksellers and Druggists, Gonzales, Texas". There is no value indicated.

In addition to being used as provisional stamps, the label has been found affixed to the inside of books and may have been affixed to medicine bottles.

All recorded uses of the A01 label were precanceled with the double circle town postmark. None of recorded examples of the other labels bear precancels.

All uses are on covers postmarked with the Gonzales double circle postmark. With the exception of one cover, the labels are not tied by the postmark. In most cases the stamps were pen canceled.

Over the years one or more examples have been described as gold on crimson and gold on garnet. All such examples are listed as gold on garnet.

An examination of available illustrations and descriptions shows that each cover bearing a Gonzales label also has a manuscript "Paid 5", "Paid 10" or handstamped "PAID" marking. Three covers with pairs of the gold on dark blue label are marked "Paid 10". This is clear evidence that, at the time of use, these labels represented 5¢ in postage. There is also a cover with a single gold on black label that is marked "Paid 5". In this case the label represented 5¢ in postage. Other uses of the gold on black or gold on garnet labels are on covers marked "Paid 10" or handstamped "PAID" indicating the label represented 10¢ in postage.

Earliest recorded dates of use:

A01 – Unknown

A02 – 5¢ value *December 1861* to Victoria, Tex. 10¢ value

A03 – *July 1864* to San Antonio, Tex.

Caution. Unused examples of the Gonzales labels cannot be authenticated. Off cover examples of the Gonzales labels cannot be authenticated as being postally used unless they have a legible handstamped postmark.

Warning. Dangerous fake uses of these labels exist. All examples should be authenticated.

GREENSBOROUGH, ALABAMA

A B C D *a* *b*

Entires (Handstamped)

GRE-AL-E01 (31XU1)		
A 5¢ black	NR	3,000.
a. With added "PAID 5" (Type *a*)	NR	—
GRE-AL-E02		
B 5¢ black*	NR	NR
a. Revalued "10" (Type *b*)	NR	—
GRE-AL-E03 (31XU2)		
C 10¢ black	NR	—
GRE-AL-E04 (31XU3)		
D 10¢ black	NR	5,000.

The Type A and C Greensborough, Alabama provisionals were prepared by handstamping envelopes with an undated prewar double circle office postmark. The postmark was then over struck with "PAID" and "5" or "10" rate markings.

The Type B and D provisionals were prepared in a similar manner using an undated circular postmark. These types were over struck with the same "PAID" and "5" or "10" rate markings.

The only recorded example of E01a was reportedly lost in the mails in 1899.

Earliest recorded dates of use:

- E01 – August 8, [1861] to Marion, Ala.
- E02 – None recorded
- E02a – December 18, [1861] to Richmond, Va.
- E03 – Unknown
- E04 – March 30 to Asheville, N.C. (only recorded example)

Greensboro, North Carolina

A   *a*

Entire (Handstamped)

GRE-NC-E01 (32XU1)

A	10¢ red	NR	1,000.
	a. Rerated "DUE 10" (Type *a*)	NR	1,500.

The Greensboro, North Carolina provisional was prepared by handstamping envelopes with an office postmark in which the date logos were replaced by "PAID" and "10" markings.

Earliest recorded date of use is unknown.

Caution: There are several recorded examples of the Type A envelope with a manuscript "charge box" notation. This is evidence the provisional marking was also used as a stampless marking. Stampless uses are not easily distinguished from provisional uses. Each example must be considered on its own merits.

Greenville, Alabama

A   B

Adhesives

GRV-AL-A01 (33X1)			
A 5¢ blue and red on *pinkish* glazed paper		*20,000.*	NR
GRV-AL-A02 (33X2)			
B 10¢ red and blue on *pinkish* glazed paper		NR	NR

On Cover

GRV-AL-A01 (33X1)	
A 5¢ blue and red on *pinkish* glazed paper	*35,000.*
GRV-AL-A02 (33X2)	
B 10¢ red and blue on *pinkish* glazed paper	—

The Greenville, Alabama adhesive provisionals were typeset and printed in red and blue on white glazed paper with a pink tone by the Greenville postmaster, Benjamin F. Porter. The size of a sheet is unknown.

The five-cent value (Type A) has a blue border with red rate and town name. The ten-cent value (Type B) has a red border with blue rate and town name.

The stamps are not tied on any of the recorded covers.

Earliest recorded dates of use:

- A01 – October19, [1861] to Pensacola, Fla.
- A02 – Unknown

Caution: Dangerous forgeries of A01 and A02 are known to exist. Most are on cover and are tied by a fake postmark.

Greenville, Tennessee

A

Entire (Handstamped)

GRV-TN-E01 (144XU1)

A	5¢ black	NR	NR
	a. Under a postally used general issue		—

The Greenville, Tennessee provisional was prepared by handstamping envelopes with an undated prewar postmark and then handstamping "PAID" and "5" inside the postmark.

The only recorded use is under a general issue stamp (since removed).

Greenville Court House, South Carolina

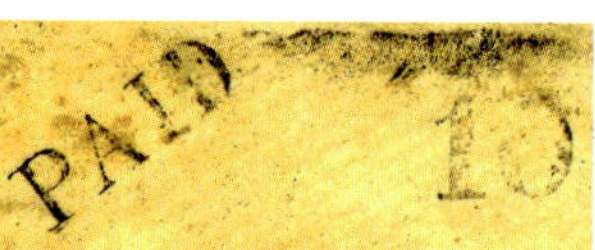

A   B

Control A

Control B

Control C

Entires (Handstamped)

GRV-SC-E01 (34XU1)

A	5¢ black (with control on reverse)	NR	1,500.

GRV-SC-E02 (34XU2)

B	10¢ black (with control on reverse)	NR	1,500.
	a. Revalued "20" (ms) (34XU2*a*)	NR	2,000.
	b. Under a postally used general issue		2,000.

The Greenville Court House, South Carolina provisionals were prepared by handstamping envelopes with "PAID" and "5" and "10" rate markings. One of three different postmarks was applied to the reverse of envelopes as a control. When dated the control must be dated the same as or prior to the date of the postmark on the face of the cover.

Earliest recorded dates of use:
E01 – June 11, [1861] to Pickens C.H., S.C.
E02 – December [1861] to Manassas Junction, Va.

Greenwood Depot, Virginia

A

Adhesive

Laid paper

GRW-VA-A01 (35X1)

A	10¢ black on *gray-blue*	NR	NR

On Cover

Laid paper

GRW-VA-A01 (35X1)

A	10¢ black on *gray-blue*	*20,000.*

The Greenwood, Virginia provisionals were prepared by handstamping "PAID" on gray-blue laid paper. The postmaster, James Bruce, then wrote "Ten Cents" above the "PAID" and signed his name below. Individual stamps were cut apart for use.

There are six recorded examples of the Greenwood Depot provisional used on cover. All are addressed to "Rev. Paul Whitehead, Macfarlands P.O, Va. Five have legible dates from July to October. Based on the year docketing on some covers, all are assumed to have been used in 1862.

Earliest recorded date of use is July 31, [1862] to Macfarland's, Va.

Griffin, Georgia

A

B

Entires (Handstamped)

GRI-GA-E01 (102XU1)

A	5¢ black	NR	2,000.

GRI-GA-E02 (102XU2)

B	10¢ black	NR	4,000.

The Griffin, Georgia provisionals were prepared by handstamping envelopes with the office postmark in which the date logos were replaced with "PAID" and "5" or "10" rate markings.

Earliest recorded dates of use:
E01 – May 31, [1862]
E02 – July 25 on a partial envelope (only recorded example)

Grove Hill, Alabama

A

Adhesive

GRO-AL-A01 (36X1)

A	5¢ black on *white*	NR	NR

On Cover

GRO-AL-A01 (36X1)

A	5¢ black on *white*	—

The Grove Hill, Alabama provisional was engraved on wood and handstamped on white wove paper.

Earliest recorded date of use is September 10, [1861] to Jackson, Ala.

There are two recorded examples (postmarked September 10 and October 26). On the earliest dated cover, the stamp is pen canceled; on the second cover the stamp is tied by the postmark.

Hallettsville, Texas

A

Adhesive

HAL-TX-A01 (37X1)

A	10¢ black on *gray-blue*	NR	NR

On Cover

HAL-TX-A01 (37X1)

A	10¢ black on *gray-blue*	—

The Hallettsville, Texas provisional was prepared by handstamping the postmark in which the date logos were replaced by a "10 / PAID" marking on gray-ruled paper. The markings were inverted when placed in the postmark. Individual stamps were cut apart for use.

The only recorded example is postmarked August 21 to Austin, Tex.

[—]	symbol used in place of value to mean insufficient information to assign a price
NR	used in place of value when no examples have been recorded
IH	institutional holding

Hamburgh, South Carolina

A

Entire (Handstamped)

HAM-SC-E01 (112XU1)

A	5¢ black	NR	3,000.

The Hamburgh, South Carolina provisional was prepared by handstamping envelopes with an undated office postmark in which the date logos were replaced with a "5" rate marking. Separately a "PAID" marking was struck outside the postmark.

Earliest recorded date of use is July 20, [1861] to Atlanta, Ga.

There is one recorded example of a Hamburgh provisional entire being forwarded from Charleston, S.C. with a Charleston adhesive provisional. The Hamburgh entire is postmarked December 5, [1861] and the Charleston forwarding provisional is postmarked December 7, 1861.

Harrisburgh, Texas

A B

Entires (Handstamped)

HAR-TX-E01 (130XU1)

A	5¢ black	—	NR

HAR-TEX-E02 (130XU2)

B	10¢ black	NR	—

The Harrisburgh, Texas provisionals were prepared by handstamping envelopes with an undated office postmark. Separately a boxed "PAID" marking and a "5" or "10" rate marking were struck inside the postmark.

Earliest recorded dates of use:

E01 – None recorded (unused copy is only recorded example)

E02 – October 28, [1863] to Houston, Tex. (cover front – only recorded example)

Helena, Texas

A

B

Adhesives

HEL-TX-A01 (38X1)
A 5¢ black on *buff* *12,500.* *10,000.*
HEL-TX-A02 (38X2)
B 10¢ black on *bluish-gray* NR *10,000.*

The Helena, Texas provisionals were typeset and printed on buff and bluish-gray wove paper.

The design is very similar to the Goliad, Texas Type A and C provisionals but there are differences in the number of ornaments in the border. It has been reported that one example of the Helena provisional is printed on paper with ornamental printing on the reverse. The same printing is found on the reverse of a Goliad provisional. The fact that some provisionals of both towns are on the same reused paper is strong evidence that both were printed by Rev. A. M. Cox of Goliad, Texas, who also printed the Goliad provisionals.

The layout and size of the printed sheet is unknown. All recorded copies are faulty or repaired. There are no recorded examples on cover.

Hillsboro, North Carolina

A

Adhesive

HIL-NC-A01 (39X1)
A 5¢ black with added "5" NR NR

On Cover

HIL-NC-A01 (39X1)
A 5¢ black with added "5" —

The Hillsboro, North Carolina provisional was prepared by handstamping "PAID" on white paper. The size of the paper is unknown, but it is possible several strikes were made on one piece of paper. These were then cut apart for use. *See also,* "3¢ 1861 Postmasters' Provisionals" section.

The only recorded example is postmarked June 7, [1861] to Suffolk, Va.

There is one recorded example of a manuscript "Paid 10" marking on a cover with an undated double circle control (see illustration above) and a postmark dated December 29. The two markings are in different shades of blue ink. The status of this cover as a provisional has not been determined.

Hollandale, Texas

A

Entire (Handstamped)

HOL-TX-E01 (132XU1)
A 5¢ black NR —

The Hollandale, Texas provisional was prepared by handstamping envelopes with an office postmark in which the date logos were replaced by a large "5" rate marking.

Earliest recorded date of use is September 7, [1861] to Columbia, Tex. (only recorded example). The right quarter of the provisional marking was torn off when the envelope was opened.

Houston, Texas

A

B

PAID

a

Entires (Handstamped)

HOU-TX-E01 (40XU1)		
A 5¢ red	NR	750.
a. Revalued "10" (ms) (40XU1*a*)	NR	1,250.
b. Revalued "PAID 10" (Type B) (40XU4)	500.	1,500.
c. Mailed from another town		1,000.
d. Under a postally used general issue		1,250.
HOU-TX-E02 (40XU2)		
B 10¢ red	500.	1,250.
a. Struck twice (40XU5)	NR	1,500.
b. Under a postally used general issue		1,750.
HOU-TX-E03 (40XU3)		
B 10¢ black	NR	NR
a. With added "PAID" (Type *a)*		2,000.
b. Under a postally used general issue		2,500.

The Houston, Texas provisionals were prepared by handstamping envelopes with an office postmark in which the date logos were replaced with "PAID" and "5" or "10" rate markings.

Earliest recorded dates of use:

E01 – July 3, 1861 to Anderson, Tex.
E01a – June 10, 1861 to Appomattox, Va. (only recorded example)
E02 – June 15, 1861 to *Boonville*
E02a – Unknown to New Braunfels, Tex. (only recorded example)
E03 – None recorded
E03a – October 10 to Oakland, [*Tex.*] (only recorded example)

Recorded examples that entered the mail at other towns:

E01 – Used from Little Rock Ark. to Kaufman, Tex. (postmarked May – unknown if accepted as postage)
E02 – Used from Navasota, Tex. to Shreveport, La. (illegible postmark on pair of 5¢ blue typographs – not accepted as postage)
E03 – Used from Navasota, Tex. to [Shreveport, La.] (illegible postmark on 20¢ green – not accepted as postage)

Caution: There is one recorded example of E01 on an express cover from the United States in August 1861. This is not considered a provisional use of the marking and is evidence the marking was also used as a stampless marking. Stampless uses are not easily distinguished from provisional uses. Each example must be considered on its own merits.

Huntsville, Texas

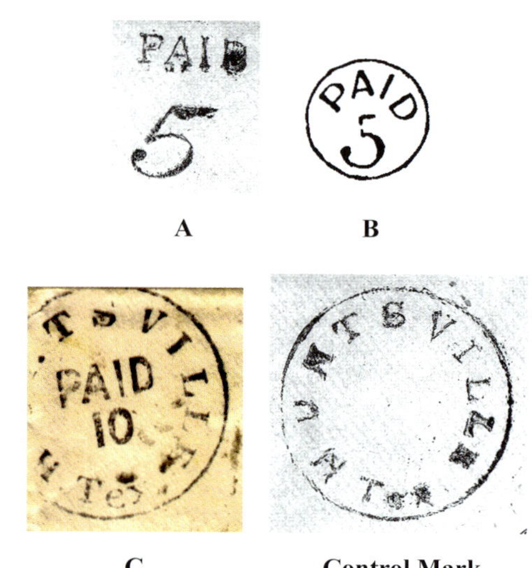

A B C Control Mark

Entires (Handstamped)

HUN-TX-E01 (92XU1)		
A 5¢ black (with control)	NR	5,000.
HUN-TX-E02		
B 5¢ black	NR	5,000.
HUN-TX-E03		
C 10¢ black	NR	7,500.

The Huntsville, Texas Type A provisional was prepared by handstamping envelopes with "PAID" and "5" rate markings. Separately an undated office postmark was struck as a control.

The Type B provisional was prepared by handstamping envelopes with a circular "PAID / 5" marking inside the undated office postmark.

The Type C provisional was prepared by handstamping envelopes with the office postmark in which the date logos were replaced by "PAID / 10" markings.

Earliest recorded dates of use:

E01 – February 17, [1862] to Montgomery, Tex. (only recorded example)
E02 – Unknown to Crockett, Tex. (postmark partially removed and replaced – only recorded example)
E03 – August 17 to San Antonio, Tex. (only recorded example)

[–] symbol used in place of value to mean insufficient information to assign a price
NR used in place of value when no examples have been recorded
IH institutional holding
NA used inplace of alisting value when no examples

Independence, Texas

A

B

Adhesives

IND-TX-A01 (41X1)		
A 10¢ black *on buff*	NR	NR
IND-TX-A02 (41X3)		
B 10¢ black *on buff*	NR	NR
a. Without manuscript "Pd"	NR	NR

On Cover

IND-TX-A01 (41X1)	
A 10¢ black *on buff*	*25,000.*
IND-TX-A02 (41X3)	
B 10¢ black *on buff*	*25,000.*
a. Without manuscript "Pd"	*10,000.*

The Independence, Texas Type A and B provisionals were prepared by handstamping buff paper with an undated office postmark. Separately either a large or small "10" marking was handstamped inside the postmark.

Most examples were cut to shape, but there is one example of A02 cut square.

The Type A has been reported on dull rose paper, but this has not been verified. It may actually be the stamp listed on buff paper.

There is one recorded example of A02 that does not appear to have the "Pd" over the rate possibly due to fading.

Earliest recorded dates of use:

A01 – July 31, [*1862*] to Houston, Tex. (only recorded example)

A02 – November 24, [*1864*] to Shreveport, La.

A02a – April 29 to Sandy Point, Tex. (only recorded example)

Isabella, Georgia

A

Entire (Handstamped)

ISA-GA-E01 (133XU1)		
A 5¢ (ms) black	NR	—

The Isabella, Georgia provisional was prepared by handstamping envelopes with the undated office postmark. Separately "5¢" was added in manuscript inside the postmark.

The only recorded example is postmarked October 25, [1861] to Macon, Ga.

Iuka, Mississippi

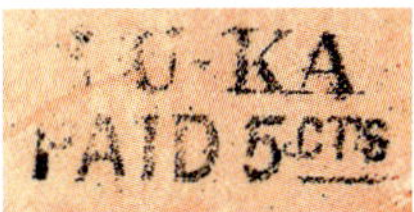

A

Entire (Handstamped)

IUK-MS-E01 (42XU1)		
A 5¢ black	NR	1,500.

The Iuka, Mississippi provisional was prepared by handstamping envelopes with an "I-U-KA / PAID 5$^{\underline{\text{CTS}}}$" marking.

Earliest recorded date of use is September 26, 1861 to Warrenton, Miss.

Warning: Dangerous forgeries of this marking exist.

Jackson, Mississippi

A

B

C

a

Entires (Handstamped)

JAC-MS-E01		
A 3¢ black		
a. Revalued "5" (Type B)	NR	2,500.
b. Revalued "10" (Type C)	NR	3,000.
c. Revalued "5" (Type *a*), then revalued "10" (Type C)	NR	*5,000.*

JAC-MS-E02 (43XU1)

B	5¢ black	—	750.
	a. Revalued "10" (Type C) (43XU1*a*)	NR	2,500.
	b. Revalued "15" by adding "1" (ms)	NR	*2,500.*

JAC-MS-E03 (43XU2)

C	10¢ black	—	2,500.
	a. Revalued "5" (Type B) (43XU4)	NR	3,000.

The Jackson, Mississippi provisionals were prepared by handstamping envelopes with circular markings containing "PAID" and the rate "3", "5" or "10" and "CENTS". *See also,* "3¢ 1861 Postmasters' Provisionals" section.

There is a large variety of the Jackson provisional markings including revalued and double struck markings. There may be types other than those listed above.

Earliest recorded dates of use:

E01 – NA
E01b – June 3, [1861] to Spotsylvania C.H., Va. (only recorded example)
E02 – June 5, [1861] to *New Orleans, La.*
E03 – July 16, [1861] Richmond, Va.
E03a – June 16, [1862] to Warrenton, Miss (only recorded example)

Caution: There is one recorded example of JAC-MS-E02 with a "charge box" marking. This and the scarcity of stampless markings from Jackson are evidence the provisional marking was also used as a stampless marking. Stampless uses cannot be readily distinguished from provisional uses. Each example must be considered on its own merits.

See *also*, "3¢1861 Postmasters' Provisionals" Section.

Jacksonville, Alabama

A

Entire (Handstamped)

JAC-AL-E01 (110XU1)

A	5¢ black	—	2,500.

The Jacksonville, Alabama provisional was prepared by handstamping envelopes with a typeset marking containing "PAID / 5 / W T A." The initials are a mystery because they are not the initials of the two Jacksonville postmasters appointed through November 1861.

Earliest recorded date of use is February 11, 1862 to Cedar Bluff, Ala.

Unused examples are addressed but have no postmark.

Jacksonville, Florida

A Control

Entire (Handstamped)

JAC-FL-E01 (134XU1)

A	5¢ black (control on reverse)	NR	—

The Jacksonville, Florida provisional was prepared by handstamping envelopes with separate "PAID" and "5" markings. Separately the undated office postmark was struck as a control on the reverse.

The only recorded example is postmarked November 8, [1861] to Tampa, Fla.

Jetersville, Virginia

A

Adhesive

Laid paper

JET-VA-A01 (44X1)

A	5¢ black on *white*	NR	NR

On Cover

Laid paper

JET-VA-A01 (44X1)

A	5¢ black on *white*	NR
	a. Vertical pair	—

The Jetersville, Virginia provisional was prepared by handstamping a small "5" on white laid paper. To the right side of the "5" the postmaster, A. H. Atwood, added his initials in manuscript.

Earliest recorded date of use is July 25, [1861] to Waterproof, La. (only recorded example).

Jonesboro, Tennessee

A

Entire (Handstamped)

JON-TN-E01 (45XU1)
  A 5¢ black NR 5,000.
JON-TN-E02 (45XU2)
  A 5¢ dark blue NR 5,000.

The Jonesboro, Tennessee provisionals were prepared by impressing a circular brass seal inscribed "J. E. Williams. / PAID *5* / Jonesboro. T." on envelopes. Williams was the postmaster at Jonesboro.

Earliest recorded dates of use:
  E01 – *December 24, [1861] to Rutledge, Tenn.*
  E02 – October 7, [1861] to Cumberland Ford, Ky.

Note: Addressed covers bearing these provisional markings but no postmark are considered postally used.

Kingston, Georgia

A

B C D

Entires (Handstamped)

KIN-GA-E01 (46XU4)
  A 5¢ black NR *12,500.*
KIN-GA-E02 (46XU2)
  B 5¢ black NR 2,500.
KIN-GA-E03 (46XU1)
  C 5¢ black NR 1,500.
KIN-GA-E04 (46XU5)
  D 5¢ black NR 750.

The Type A Kingston, Georgia provisional was prepared by printing or handstamping a three-line typeset design that includes the town name, state and full date on the left side and the rate on the right.

The Type B provisional was prepared by handstamping envelopes with a typeset device that included "PAID / 5 / CENTS' with a small "C" to the left of the "5" and a small "S" to the right of the "5".

The Type C provisional was prepared by handstamping envelopes with a typeset device similar to the Type B design but which used larger fonts without the "C" and "S."

The Type D provisional was prepared by handstamping envelopes with an office postmark in which the date logos were replaced with "PAID / 5 / CENTS."

Earliest recorded dates of use:
  E01 – June 13, 1861 to Cedar Town, Ga. (only recorded example)
  E02 – June 19, [1861] to Floyd Springs, Ga.
  E03 – September 4, [1861] to Lynchburg, Va.
  E04 – September 2, [1861] to Lynchburg, Va.

Notes: The only recorded example of E01 has a charge box marking. This is evidence this marking may have been used as a stampless marking.

There is a stampless marking very similar to the Type B marking in size and format. The most significant difference is the stampless marking does not have the letters "C' and "S" on either side of the "5".

Caution: There is one recorded example of the Type C envelope and several of the Type D envelopes with "charge box" markings. This is evidence these provisional markings were also used as a stampless markings. Stampless uses cannot be readily distinguished from provisional uses. Each example must be considered on its own merits.

Knoxville, Tennessee

A B

Detail of Last Printing

Adhesives

Laid paper

KNO-TN-A01 (47X1)		
A 5¢ brick red on *grayish*	1,000.	750.
a. Pair	3,000.	2,000.
b. Vertical strip of three	5,000.	NR
KNO-TN-A02 (47X2)		
A 5¢ carmine on *grayish*	NR	1,500.
a. Horizontal strip of three	—	NR
KNO-TN-A03		
A 5¢ red on *grayish*	—	—
KNO-TN-A04 (47X3)		
B 10¢ green on *grayish*	NR	NR

On Cover

Laid paper

KNO-TN-A01 (47X1)	
A 5¢ brick red on *grayish*	3,500.
a. Pair	7,500.
KNO-TN-A02 (47X2)	
A 5¢ carmine on *grayish*	5,000.
KNO-TN-A04 (47X3)	
B 10¢ green on *grayish*	*60,000.*

The designs for the 5¢ and 10¢ Knoxville provisionals were engraved on wood and reproduced as stereotypes or electrotypes from which a plate of multiple subjects was prepared. The layout and size of printed sheets is unknown. It is believed the printing plate was prepared using six subjects prepared from the original die. A vertical strip of three with large margins top and bottom suggests that the sheet consisted of three horizontal rows. Printings using the original plate for the 5¢ value were made in brick red and carmine.

A limited last printing of the 5¢ value (A03) was made using new subjects prepared from the original die. The printing form for the last printing contained three subjects with 5 mm margins between the subjects. Stamps from the last printing can be identified by the "O" of "CHARLTON" being open at the top and a colorless line through the star above the "E" of "KNOXVILLE". None is recorded used.

The design of the Knoxville adhesives is nearly identical to the Nashville adhesives. The Nashville engraver, Dan Adams, is suspected of engraving the stamps for both towns.

Knoxville used a variety of cancellations on the adhesives. These include pen cancels, the Type F handstamped provisional marking and several postmarks. Many of the postmarks are poorly struck, making the date illegible.

Earliest recorded dates of use:

- A01 – Stamp tied by E06 marking on cover with October 28, 1861 answered docketing to Nashville, Tenn.
- A02 – Stamp tied by E06 marking on cover with October 23, 1861 Richmond, Va. postmark
- A03 – Unknown
- A04 – Illegible postmark to Ashland, Va. (only recorded example)

Caution: After the war additional prints were made from new subjects prepared from the original die. They were printed on both fine laid paper and wove paper in red, brown and black.

Warning: Dangerous forgeries exist.

C

D

Entires (Printed)

KNO-TN-E01 (47XU1 and 47XU2)		
C 5¢ blue	NR	2,500.
KNO-TN-E02 (47XU3 and 47XU4))		
D 10¢ red	NR	—

The Knoxville printed envelopes were press printed on white and orange colored envelopes of various sizes. The circular design is composed of printer's type within brass rule circles with a stock cut of an eagle in the center.

All recorded examples of the full envelope are addressed but bear no postmark. All are considered postally used.

The only recorded example of E02 is cut to shape.

Warning: Dangerous forgeries exist.

[—]	symbol used in place of value to mean insufficient information to assign a price
NR	used in place of value when no examples have been recorded

E

F

Entires (Handstamped)

KNO-TN-E03 (47XU5)

E 5¢ black	NR	1,000.
a. (47XU5*a*) 5¢ revalued 10	NR	2,000.

KNO-TN-E04 (47XU5)

F 5¢ black	NR	1,000.

The Knoxville handstamped envelopes were prepared by handstamping envelopes with the office postmark in which the date logos were replaced with "PAID" and "5" rate markings. The Type E marking has "PAID" above the "5" and the Type F marking has the "PAID" below the "5."

Most covers bearing the Type E and F markings do not bear postmarks but are considered postally used.

Earliest recorded dates of use:
- E03 – July 30, 1861 (receipt docketing) to Kingsport, East Tenn.
- E04 – September 14, 1861 (receipt docketing) to Kingston, Tenn.

LaGrange, Texas

A

B

C

Entires (Handstamped)

LAG-TX-E01 (48XU1)

A 5¢ black	NR	2,000.

LAG-TX-E02 (48XU2)

B 10¢ black	NR	2,500.

LAG-TX-E03

C 10¢ black	NR	2,500.

The LaGrange, Texas provisionals were prepared by handstamping envelopes with a prewar office postmark in which the date logos were replaced with "PAID" and "5" or "10" rate markings. The Type A and B markings have "PAID" above the rate and the Type C marking has "PAID" below the rate.

Earliest recorded dates of use:
- E01 – August 20, 1861 to Houston, Tex.
- E02 – Unknown
- E03 – Unknown

Note: The earliest recorded use of E01 is on a twice used folded letter. The second use was in 1865.

Caution: There are recorded examples of the Type A, B and C envelopes with "charge box" markings. This indicates the provisional marking may also have been used as a stampless marking. Stampless uses cannot be readily distinguished from provisional uses. Each example must be considered on its own merits.

Lake City, Florida

A

Control A

Control B

Entire (Handstamped)

LAK-FL-E01 (96XU1)

A 10¢ black (with Control A on reverse)	NR	5,000.
a. With Control B on reverse	NR	5,000.
b. Mailed from another town		—

The Lake City, Florida provisional was prepared by handstamping envelopes with a "PAID 10" marking. Separately an undated postmark or a typeset device containing the postmaster's name, "E. R. Ives," was struck as a control on the upper back flap of envelopes.

The recorded Lake City provisionals represent two different correspondences. One correspondence is docketed 1864. It is assumed the other correspondence was mailed during the same period.

Earliest recorded dates of use:
E01 – Apr 18, [1864] to Sparta, Ga.
E01a – April 27, [1864] to Sparta, Ga.

Recorded example that entered the mail at another town:
E01 – Under general issue tied by Charleston, S.C. (postmark dated May 7 – not accepted as postage)

Laurens Court House, South Carolina

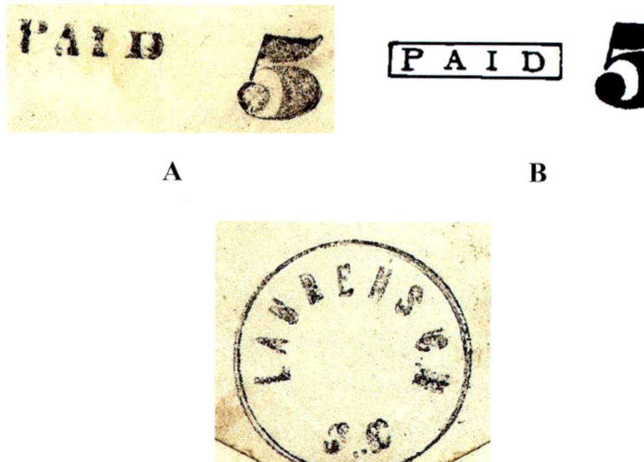

A B

Control

Entires (Handstamped)

LAU-SC-E01 (116XU2)
A 5¢ black (with control) NR 1,500.
LAU-SC-E02 (116XU1)
B 5¢ black (with control) NR 1,500.

The Laurens Court House, South Carolina provisionals were prepared by handstamping envelopes with either of two types of "PAID" markings and a "5" marking. Separately an undated office postmark was struck as a control on the reverse.

Earliest recorded dates of use:
E01 – June 8, [1861] to Rome, Ga.
E02 – July 4, [1861] to Cassville, Ga. (only recorded example)

Lenoir, North Carolina

A

Adhesive

LEN-NC-A01 (49X1)
A 5¢ blue on *white*, orange-ruled paper 7,500. 5,000.

On Cover

LEN-NC-A01 (49X1)
A 5¢ blue on *white*, orange-ruled paper *12,500.*
a. On partially ruled paper *12,500.*

The Lenoir, North Carolina adhesive provisional was engraved in wood and handstamped in blue on white wove paper with orange cross-ruling. The horizontal lines are widely spaced and bold. The vertical lines are closely spaced with every fifth line bolder. Depending on where in a sheet a stamp was printed, it could have three or four horizontal lines and 20 or 21 vertical lines.

On cover examples are recorded tied by the office postmark, a paid marking, pen canceled with an "X" or uncanceled.

A diary entry by G. W. F. Harper, assistant postmaster at Lenoir, states he made the woodcut for the stamp on September 19, 1861.

Earliest recorded date of use is September 21, [1861] to Newbern, N.C. and Richmond, Va. (two covers).

B C

Entires (Handstamped)

LEN-NC-E01 (49XU1)
B 5¢ blue (on piece) NR —
a. Struck twice (10¢) (49XU2) NR *20,000.*
LEN-NC-E02 (49XU3)
C 5¢ blue NR 2,500.
a. Marking in black and blue NR 2,500.

The Type B provisionals were prepared by handstamping envelopes with the same woodcut used to prepare the Type A adhesive provisional.

The Type C provisionals were prepared by handstamping envelopes with an office postmark in which the date logos were replaced with "PAID" and "5" markings.

On E02a there are two strikes of the marking, one superimposed on the other. The markings have traces of black and blue ink indicating the office was changing ink color. All markings are faint.

Earliest recorded dates of use:
- E01 – None recorded on cover
- E01a – November 11, to Knoxville, Tenn. (only recorded example)
- E02 – September 18, [1861] to Fort Defiance, N.C.
- E02a – Illegible postmark to Fayetteville, N.C. (only recorded example)

Lexington, Mississippi

A

B

Entires (Handstamped)

LEX-MS-E01 (50XU1)			
A 5¢ black		NR	3,000.
	a. Under a postally used general issue		3,500.
LEX-MS-E02 (50XU2)			
B 10¢ black		NR	NR
	a. Under a postally used general issue		4,500.

The Lexington, Mississippi provisionals were prepared by handstamping envelopes with an office postmark in which the date logos were replaced with "PAID," and "5" or "10" rate markings and the initials "E. H., P. M." The initials were those of the postmaster, Erastus Haskins.

Earliest recorded dates of use:
- E01 – October 3, [1861] to Jackson, Miss.
- E01a – Under 5¢ typograph to Jackson, Miss. (only recorded example)
- E02 – None recorded
- E02a – Under general issue (since removed) to Watkinsville, Ga. (only recorded example)

[*italic*]	value typeface indicating the item is difficult to price accurately
NR	used in place of value when no examples have been recorded

Lexington, Virginia

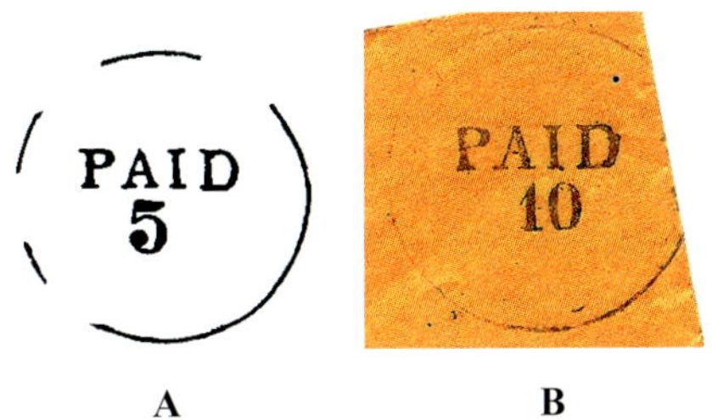

A B

Entire (Handstamped)

LEX-VA-E01 (135XU1)		
A 5¢ blue	500.	NA
LEX-VA-E02 (135XU2)		
B 10¢ blue	500.	NA

The Lexington, Virginia provisionals were prepared by handstamping envelopes with circular "PAID / 5" and "PAID / 10" rate markings. On many examples there is no sign of the circle or only a partial circle

Caution: These same markings were used as stampless markings. Consequently these are considered provisionals only when unused, under a postally used general issue, or mailed from another town.

Liberty, Virginia

A

Adhesive

LIB-VA-A01 (74X1)			
A 5¢ black on *white*		NR	NR

On Cover

LIB-VA-A01 (74X1)			
A 5¢ black on *white*		NR	*35,000.*
	a. Mailed from another town		*40,000.*

The Liberty, Virginia provisional was typeset and printed on white laid paper. The layout and size of the sheet is unknown but two different settings are known. Individual stamps were cut apart for use.

No uses of the adhesive are tied to the cover.

Earliest recorded date of use is July 7, [1861] to Raleigh, N. C.

Recorded example that entered the mail at another town:
E01 – Used from Salem, Va. (postmarked Dec 6, [1861] – undetermined if accepted as postage)

LIMESTONE SPRINGS, SOUTH CAROLINA

A

B

Adhesives

LIM-SC-A01
A 5¢ black on *light green* NR NR
LIM-SC-A02
B 5¢ black on *white* (121X2) NR NR
LIM-SC-A03
B 5¢ black on *light blue* (121X1) NR NR

On Cover

LIM-SC-A01
A 5¢ black on *light green* *10,000.*
LIM-SC-A02
B 5¢ black on *white* (121X2) NR
a. Two singles *25,000.*
LIM-SC-A03
B 5¢ black on *light blue* (121X1) *10,000.*
a. Two singles *20,000.*

The Limestone, South Carolina provisionals were prepared by handstamping a "5" rate marking on white or tinted paper. Type A was cut using a circular die. The Type B stamps were cut into irregular rectangular pieces.

All recorded examples of these adhesives are uncanceled on covers without postmarks.

Note: Those adhesives listed as light green and light blue may actually be the same color.

LIVINGSTON, ALABAMA

A

Adhesive

LIV-AL-A01 (51X1)
A 5¢ blue on *white* NR *12,500.*

On Cover

LIV-AL-A01 (51X1)
A 5¢ blue on *white* *150,000.*
a. Pair —

The Livingston, Alabama provisional was lithographed on white wove paper.

Some believe that there are similarities in the design of the Livingston and Mobile adhesive provisionals and this indicates they were prepared by the same firm. There is no conclusive evidence to support this theory.

The layout and size of the sheet is unknown. However, the existence of a pair is proof there were multiple subjects on the lithographic stone.

Earliest recorded dates of use:
A01 – November 15, [1861] to Hollow Square, and Marion Ala. (two covers)
A01a – November 12, [1861] to Manassas Junction, Va. (only recorded example)

LYNCHBURG, VIRGINIA

A

Short transfer

Adhesive

LYN-VA-A01 (52X1)
A 5¢ blue (shades) on *white* 1,500. 1,000.
a. Pair NR NR
b. Short transfer on bottom 1,750. 1,250.

On Cover

LYN-VA-A01 (52X1)
A 5¢ blue (shades) on *white* 5,000.
a. Pair 20,000.

The Lynchburg, Virginia provisional design was engraved in wood and electrotypes made to produce a multiple subject form. The stamp was printed on white wove paper in several shades of blue.

Earliest recorded dates of use:
A01 – August 15, [1861] to Petersburg, Va.
A01a – August 28, [1861] to Florence, Ala.

Warning: Private printings and forgeries are known to exist.

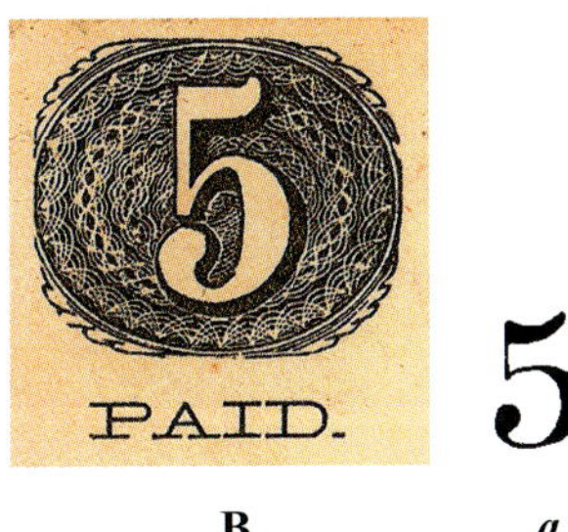

5

B *a*

Entires (Printed)

LYN-VA-E01 (52XU1-XU4)		
B 5¢ black	500.	2,500.
a. With added "5" (Type *a*)	NR	—

The envelope design is a stock electrotype with lathe-work background and a large "5." Below the design the word "PAID" was set in printer's type. The setting was printed on envelopes of varied colors and sizes.

The design was normally printed in the upper left corner. There is one recorded patriotic envelope with the design printed in the upper right corner (no postmark).

Earliest recorded date of use is June 4, 1861 to Lovington, Va.

Warning: Private printings and forgeries are known to exist.

Macon, Georgia

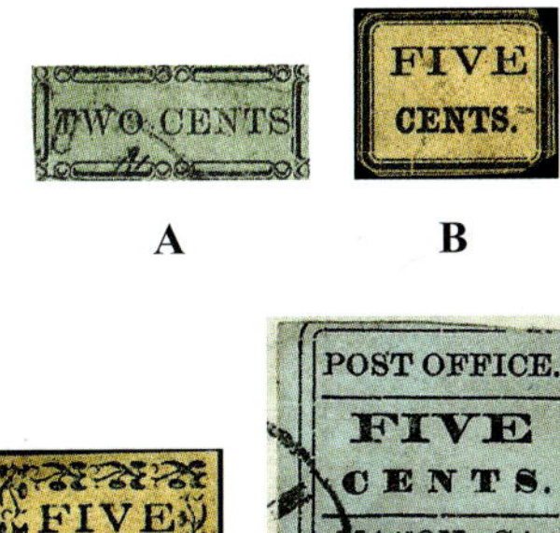

A **B** **C** **D**

Adhesives

Wove paper

MAC-GA-A01 (53X5)		
A 2¢ black on *light gray-green*	NR	NR
MAC-GA-A02 (53X4)		
B 5¢ black on *yellow*	2,000.	1,500.
MAC-GA-A03 (53X3)		
C 5¢ black on *yellow*	2,000.	NR
MAC-GA-A04 (53X1)		
D 5¢ black on *blue-green / gray-green*	NR	750.
a. Comma after "OFFICE"	NR	1,000.
b. Pair	NR	NR

Laid paper

MAC-GA-A05 (53X7)		
B 5¢ black on *yellow**	—	NR
MAC-GA-A06 (53X6)		
C 5¢ black on *yellow**	5,000.	NR
MAC-GA-A07 (53X8)		
D 5¢ black on *blue-green / gray-green**	NR	NR

On Cover

Wove paper

MAC-GA-A01 (53X5)	
A 2¢ black on *gray-green*	*40,000.*
MAC-GA-A02 (53X4)	
B 5¢ black on *yellow*	5,000.
a. Vertical pair	IH
b. Vertical pair *tête-bêche* (53X4*a*)	—
c. Mailed from another town	—
MAC-GA-A03 (53X3)	
C 5¢ black on *yellow*	*7,500.*
a. Pair	*10,000.*
MAC-GA-A04 (53X1)	
D 5¢ black on *blue-green / gray-green*	4,000.
a. Comma after "OFFICE"	*5.000.*
b. Pair	*10,000.*

Laid paper

MAC-GA-A05 (53X7)	
B 5¢ black on *yellow**	—
MAC-GA-A06 (53X6)	
C 5¢ black on *yellow**	—
MAC-GA-A07 (53X8)	
D 5¢ black on *blue-green / gray-green**	—

The Macon, Georgia adhesive provisionals were typeset from printer's type and printed on wove paper tinted yellow, blue-green or green-blue. Some examples are said to be on tinted laid papers.

It is speculated there were ten subjects (5 x 2) in the printing form for each stamp. Differences in each setting can be identified by the differences in type and border piece spacing.

Recent plating efforts confirmed ten subjects (5 x 2) in the printing form for MAC-GA-A03 and MAC-GA-A06. There is some evidence that a sheet consisted of more than one pane.

The existence of *tête-bêche* pairs of the Type B stamp indicate that the form for this stamp was printed on one side of a sheet of paper and the paper turned and printed on the other side. This method of printing may have been used for the Type A, B and C adhesives as well. There is no evidence the Type D adhesive, which is a larger size, was printed using this method.

There is conflicting information on covers with adhesive provisionals on laid paper. In some instances the same cover is described as having an adhesive on both regular and laid paper. Reported examples on cover are listed but have not been confirmed.

Earliest recorded dates of use:
- A01 – Unknown
- A02 – June 7, [1861] to Milledgeville, Ga.
- A03 – June 21, [1861] to Marietta, Ga.
- A04 – September 18, [1861] to Cedar Springs, Ga.
- A05 – Unknown
- A06 – Unknown
- A07 – Unknown

Recorded examples that entered the mail at another town:
- A02 – Used from Henderson, Ga. (postmarked August 7, [1861] – questionable if accepted as postage)

Caution: Whether some or all the Macon adhesives were printed on laid paper is questionable. The issue is further complicated by extremely dangerous forgeries on laid paper. Copies said to be on laid paper should be authenticated.

Warning: There are dangerous forgeries of Type D.

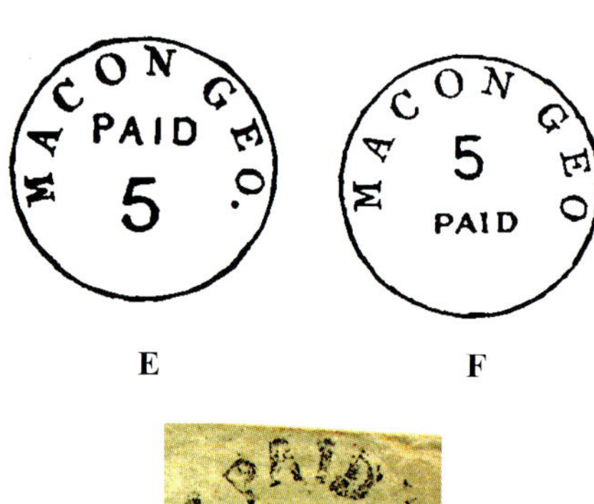

E F

G

Entires (Handstamped)

MAC-GA-E01 (53XU1)

E	5¢ black	NR	750.

MAC-GA-E02 (53XU1)

F	5¢ black	NR	750.

MAC-GA-E03

G	10¢ black	250.	NA

The Type E and F handstamped Macon provisional envelopes were prepared by handstamping envelopes with a prewar office postmark in which the date logos were replaced by "PAID" and "5" markings.

The Type G handstamped provisional envelopes were prepared by handstamping envelopes with a "PAID / 10" rate marking.

Earliest recorded dates of use:
- E01 – August 16, [1861] to Augusta, Ga.
- E02 – October 29, [1861]
- E03 – Provisional only when unused

Caution: There are several recorded examples of the Type E and F provisional envelopes with penciled "5" markings apparently applied by the postal clerk at the time of mailing. This is considered evidence the provisional markings were also used as stampless markings. Stampless uses cannot be readily distinguished from provisional uses. Each example must be considered on its own merits.

Type G marking was also used as a stampless marking. It is considered a provisional only when unused, under a postally used general issue, or mailed from another town.

Madison, Georgia

A

Entire (Handstamped)

MAD-GA-E01 (136XU1)

A	5¢ red	NA	NA
	a. Under a postally used general issue		750.
	b. Mailed from another town		750.

The Madison, Georgia provisional was prepared by handstamping envelopes with "PAID" and "5" rate markings.

Earliest recorded dates of use:
- E01 – Provisional only when unused
- E01b – Under general issue postmarked Washington, Ga. August 22, 1861 (only recorded example)

Recorded example that entered the mail at another town:
- E01b – Used from Washington, Ga. (postmarked Aug 22, 1861 – not accepted as postage)

Note: The Type A marking was also used as a stampless marking. It is considered a provisional only when unused, under a postally used general issue, or mailed from another town.

Madison Court House, Florida

A

Entire (Printed)

MAD-FL-E01 (137XU1)
A 5¢ black NR *30,000.*

The Madison, Florida provisional was typeset and printed on envelopes. *See also,* "3¢ 1861 Postmasters' Provisionals" section.

The only recorded example is postmarked September 2, [1861] to Green Hill, Ala.

Marietta, Georgia

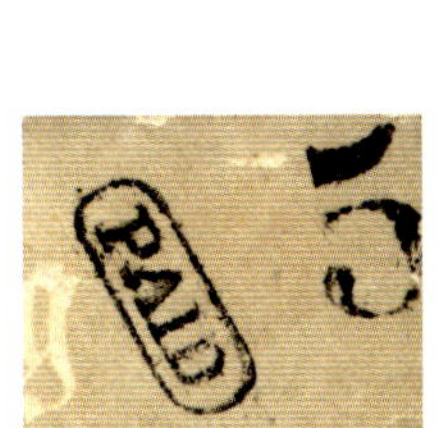

A Control

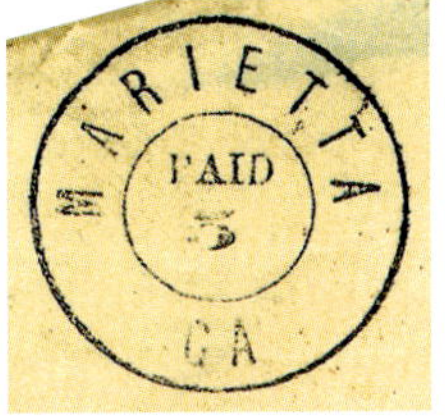

B *a* *b*

Entires (Handstamped)

MAR-GA-E01 (54XU4)
A 5¢ black (with control) NR 1,000.
MAR-GA-E02 (54XU1)
B 5¢ black NR 750.
a. Revalued "10" (Type *b*) (54XU1*a*) NR 1,000.
b. Revalued "PAID 10" (Type *a* and *b*) NR —

The Type A Marietta, Georgia provisional was prepared by handstamping envelopes with "PAID" and "5" rate markings. Separately an undated double circle postmark was struck as a control on the cover front.

The Type B provisional was prepared by handstamping envelopes with the double circle office postmark in which the date logos were replaced with "PAID" and "5" markings. There is no control associated with this type.

Earliest recorded dates of use:
E01 – July 2, [1861] to Augusta, Ga.
E02 – July 25, [1861] to Athen[s], Ga.

Caution: There are two recorded examples of E02 with "charge box" markings. This indicates the marking may have also been used as a stampless marking. Stampless uses cannot be readily distinguished from provisional uses. Each example must be considered on its own merits.

Marion, Virginia

A B

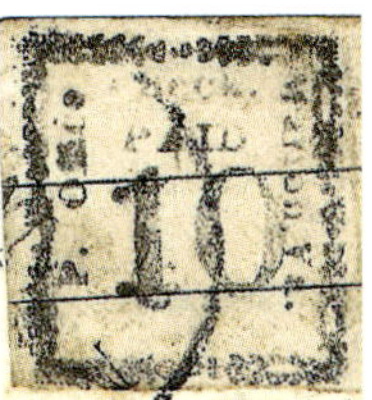

10¢ with horizontal lines

Adhesives

Wove paper

MAR-VA-A01 (55X1)
A 5¢ black on *white* NR 5,000.
MAR-VA-A02 (55X2)
B 10¢ black on *white* — NR
a. With two printed black horizontal lines (front and black) NR NR

Laid paper

MAR-VA-A03 (55X3)
A 5¢ black on *bluish* — *10,000.*

On Cover

Wove paper

MAR-VA-A01 (55X1)
A 5¢ black on *white* *12,500.*

MAR-VA-A02 (55X2)

B	10¢ black on *white*	*15,000.*
	a. With two printed black horizontal lines (front and black)	*10,000.*

The Marion, Virginia provisionals were typeset and printed on heavy white wove and bluish laid paper. Only the frame and inscriptions were printed. The rates were handstamped in the center as needed.

Earliest recorded dates of use:
A01 – June 7, [1861] to Rural Retreat, Virginia
A02 – September 24, [1861] to Emory, Virginia
A03 – Unknown

Note: There is one recorded example of A02a with two printed black horizontal lines across the stamp (front and back). The meaning of these lines is unknown.

Warning: Reprints were made from the original typeset form to which a numeral was added. These "printed" numerals are smaller than those on the authentic provisionals.

Mar's Bluff, South Carolina

A

Entire (Handstamped)

MAR-SC-E01 (145XU1)

A	5¢ black	NR	NA
	a. Mailed from another town		1,000.

The Mar's Bluff, South Carolina provisional was prepared by handstamping envelopes with "PAID" and "5" markings.

The only recorded example was used from Florence, S.C. on July 30, [1861] (not accepted as postage).

Note: This marking was also used as a stampless marking. It is considered a provisional only when unused, under a postally used general issue, or mailed from another town.

[—]	symbol used in place of value to mean insufficient information to assign a price
NA	not applicable
[*Italic*]	value typeface indicating the item is difficult to price accurately
[*Italic*]	date or location indicates unconfirmed information
NR	used in place of value when no examples have been recorded

Memphis, Tennessee

A

B

a

Cracked plate

Partial Print

Adhesives

MEM-TN-A01 (56X1)

A	2¢ blue (shades) on *white* pelure paper	150.	1,000.
	a. Cracked plate	500.	NR
	b. Partial print	500.	NR
	c. Pair	300.	NR
	d. Block of four	750.	NR

MEM-TN-A02 (56X2)

B	5¢ red on *white* (shades)	250.	250.
	a. On pelure paper* (56X2*c*)	NR	NR
	b. Pair	500.	—
	c. Horizontal pair, *tête-bêche* (56X2*a*)	NR	NR
	d. Vertical pair, *tête-bêche* (head-to-head) (56X2*a*)	NR	NR
	e. Vertical pair, *tête-bêche* (foot-to-foot) (56X2*a*)	NR	NR
	f. Pair, one sideways (56X2*b*)	2,500.	NR
	g. Block of four	1,500.	NR

On Cover

MEM-TN-A01 (56X1)

A	2¢ blue (shades) on *white* pelure paper	7,500.

MEM-TN-A02 (56X2)

B	5¢ red on *white* (shades)	1,500.
	b. Pair	3,000.
	c. Horizontal pair, *tête-bêche* (56X2*a*)	7,500.
	d. Vertical pair, *tête-bêche* (head-to-head) (56X2*a*)	7,500.

e. Vertical pair tête-bêche (foot-to-foot) (56X2*a*) —
h. Strip of four 7,500.
i. With "DUE 5" marking 2,000.

The Memphis, Tennessee provisional adhesive designs were engraved on wood and reproduced as stereotypes from which a plate of multiple subjects was prepared.

The printing of the adhesives and envelopes was done in the office of the Memphis *Avalanche,* owned by M. C. Galloway, who was also the Memphis postmaster.

The 2¢ stamp was printed on pelure paper in panes of 50, arranged in ten horizontal rows of five subjects. An existing full pane reveals that five positions sustained irreparable damage such that only about two thirds of the design printed (positions 5, 10, 15, 20 and 50).

The 5¢ stamp was printed on white wove paper. The size of the stamp pane is unknown, but it is believed it contained 50 or 52 subjects.

At least three different printings were made of both values. The multiple printings account for the various shades.

Earliest recorded dates of use:
A01 – August 20, 1861 on piece
A02 – July 8, 1861 to Facility, Tenn.

Note: It has been reported that some of the 2¢ stamps were printed on white wove paper but this has not been confirmed. The 5¢ red is reported to have been printed on thin or pelure paper. This has not been confirmed and any copies said to be on pelure paper should be authenticated.

Warning: There are dangerous forgeries of Types A01 and A02.

C

Entire (Printed)

MEM-TN-E01 (56XU1-56XU4))

C	5¢ red	NR	2,500.
	a. Used with A02		5,000.
	b. Used with a general issue		5,000.
	c. Mailed from another town		5,000.
	d. With "DUE 5" marking (Type a)		3,000.

The Memphis printed envelopes were printed from an electrotype of the same woodcut used for the 5¢ adhesive. It was printed in the upper right corner on envelopes of various colors.

Earliest recorded dates of use:
E01 – July 4, 1861 to Kingsport, Tenn.
E01a – June 20, [1861] to Havana, Ala.

Recorded examples that entered the mail at another town:
E01 – Used from Chattanooga, Tenn. (postmarked August 27, not accepted as postage)
E01 – Used from Tullahoma, Tenn. (postmarked November 16, not accepted as postage)

MICANOPY, FLORIDA

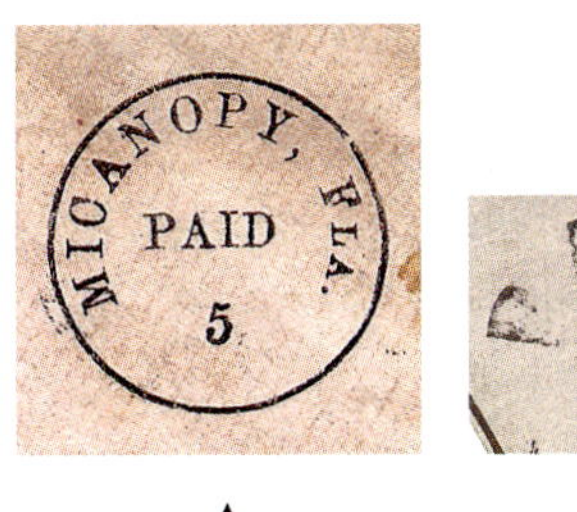

A *a*

Entire (Handstamped)

MIC-FL-E01 (105XU1)

A	5¢ black	NR	*10,000.*
	a. With "PAID 5" (Type *a*)		—

The Micanopy, Florida provisional was prepared by handstamping envelopes with a circular postmark in which the date logos were replaced with "PAID" and "5" markings.

Earliest recorded dates of use:
E01 – April 21, [1862] to Clay County, Ga.
E01a – April 12, [1862] to Augusta, Ga.

MILLEDGEVILLE, GEORGIA

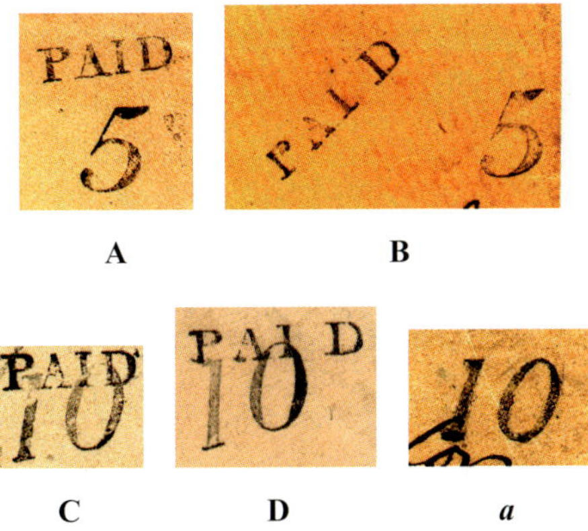

A B

C D *a*

Controls

E **F**

Entires (Handstamped)

MIL-GA-E01 (57XU1)			
A 5¢ black (with control)	NR	500.
a. Under a postally used general issue		500.
MIL-GA-E02 (57XU1*a*)		
B 5¢ black (with control)	NR	500.
a. Revalued 10 (Type *a*) (57XU1*b*)	NR	1,250.
b. Under a postally used general issue		750.
MIL-GA-E03 (57XU4)		
C 10¢ black (with control)	NR	750.
a. Under a postally used general issue		1,000.
MIL-GA-E04 (57XU4*a*)		
D 10¢ black (with control)	NR	750.
MIL-GA-E05 (57XU5)		
E 10¢ black	250.	500.
MIL-GA-E06 (57XU5*a*)		
F 10¢ black	NR	750.

The Type A, B, C and D Milledgeville, Georgia provisionals were prepared by handstamping envelopes with "PAID" and "5" or "10" rate markings. Separately an undated office postmark was struck as a control.

There are two types of the "PAID" marking. One has regular spacing (Types A and C) and one has extra space between the "I" and "D" (Types B and D).

Two different undated office postmarks were used as controls. One measures 33 mm in diameter and the other 30 mm. There is one recorded example of the 30 mm control.

The Type E and F provisionals were prepared by handstamping envelopes with the 30 mm postmark in which the date logos were replaced with "PAID" and "10" markings. On Type E the "10" is thin and tall. On Type F the "10" is shorter and more widely spaced.

Earliest recorded uses:

E01 – July 4, [1861] to Crawfordville, Ga.
E02 – July 17, [1861] to Crawfordville, Ga.
E02a – December 5, [1861] to Richmond, Va. (only recorded example)
E03 – November 17, [*1864*] to Americus, Ga.
E04 – Unknown
E05 – April 12, [*1865*] to Lincolnton, Ga.
E06 – November 18, [*1864*] to Madison, Ga.

Caution: There is one recorded example of the Type E and F envelopes with a "charge box" marking. This indicates the marking may have also been used as a stampless marking. Stampless uses cannot be readily distinguished from provisional uses. Each example must be considered on its own merits.

MILTON, NORTH CAROLINA

A **Control**

Entire (Handstamped)

MIL-NC-E01 (138XU1)		
A 5¢ black (ms rate)	NR	2,000.

The Milton, North Carolina provisional was prepared by handstamping envelopes with a "PAID" marking and a manuscript "5" rate. Separately a marking bearing the name "N. B. PATTON" was struck as a control. The name is that of the postmaster.

Earliest recorded date of use is October 16, [1861] to Black Walnut, Va.

MOBILE, ALABAMA

A **B**

Line through "O" of "POST"

Adhesives

MOB-AL-A01 (58X1)		
A 2¢ black on *white*	2,000.	1,000.
a. With plate imprint	—	NR
b. Pair	NR	2,500.
MOB-AL-A02 (58X2)		
B 5¢ blue on *white*	250.	250.
a. With plate imprint	—	—
b. Vertical line through "O" of "POST"	NR	—
c. Pair	NR	500.
d. Strip of three	NR	NR
e. Strip of four	NR	NR

On Cover

MOB-AL-A01 (58X1)	
A 2¢ black on *white*	10,000.
b. Pair	*15,000.*
MOB-AL-A02 (58X2)	
B 5¢ blue on *white*	1,500.
a. With plate imprint	—
b. Vertical line through "O" of "POST"	—
c. Pair	2,500.
d. Strip of three	*5,000*
e. Strip of four	*15,000*
f. Mailed from another town	*4,000*

The Mobile, Alabama provisionals were lithographed on white wove paper. The same design was used for both denominations by changing the numeral in the center star.

The number of subjects on the printing stone is unknown. Work on plating MOB-AL-A02 indicates there was more than one pane on the printed sheet.

The existence of pairs and strips of three with the vertical line through the "O" of "POST" on each stamp is evidence this is not a plate scratch. Rather the scratch was imparted to the master die or transfer stone prior to the completion of the actual printing stone.

There is a recorded example of a near vertical line through the "O" of "OFFICE" on A02. It has not been determined if this is a plate variety or a transient printing variety.

Earliest recorded dates of use:
- A01 – August 5, 1861 to Rock Mills, Ala.
- A02 – July 14, 1861 to Wilsonville, Ala.

Recorded examples that entered the mail at another town:
- A02 – Used from Claiborne, Ala. (postmarked January – accepted as postage)
- A02 – Used from Montgomery, Ala. (postmarked — 25, 1861 – accepted as postage)

Note: There is one recorded example of A02c (block of four on cover). The right side of the right stamps and the right side of the cover are reconstructed.

Montgomery, Alabama

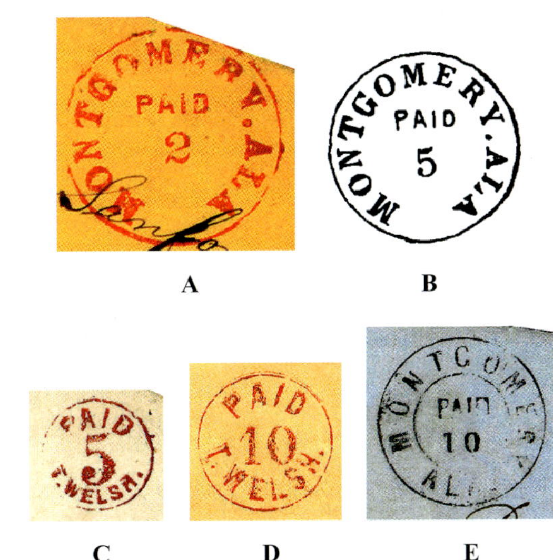

A B C D E

Entires (Handstamped)

MON-AL-E01 (59XU7)		
A 2¢ red	NR	2,500.
MON-AL-E02 (59XU7A)		
A 2¢ blue	NR	3,000.
MON-AL-E03 (59XU8)		
B 5¢ black	NR	2,500.
MON-AL-E04 (59XU1)		
C 5¢ red	NR	1,000.
a. Revalued "10" (Type D) (59XU1*a*)	NR	2,000.
MON-AL-E05 (59XU2)		
C 5¢ blue	—	1,000.
a. Under a postally used general issue		—
MON-AL-E06 (59XU3)		
D 10¢ red	NR	1,000.
a. Revalued "5" by red Type C marking	NR	2,000.
MON-AL-E07 (59XU4)		
D 10¢ blue	NR	1,000.
MON-AL-E08 (59XU9)		
E 10¢ black	—	2,000.
a. Mailed from another town		—

The Type A and B Montgomery, Alabama provisionals were prepared by handstamping envelopes with an office postmark in which the date logos were replaced with "PAID" and "2" or "5" rate markings.

The Type C and D provisionals were prepared by handstamping envelopes with specially prepared rate devices that included the name of the postmaster, T. Welsh.

The Type E provisional was prepared by handstamping envelopes with a double circle office postmark in which the date logos were replaced with "PAID" and "10" markings.

Earliest recorded dates of use:

- E01 – Unknown
- E02 – Unknown
- E03 – June 3, 1861 to Greenville, S.C.
- E04 – June 4, 1861 to Ft. Morgan, Ala.
- E05 – October 1, 1861 to Demopolis, Ala.
- E06 – June 16, 1861
- E07 – October 3, 1861 to Red Oak Grove and Museville, Va. (two covers)
- E08 – Unknown

Recorded example that entered the mail at another town:

- E08 – Used under general issue from Grenada, Miss. (postmarked April 6 on reverse – not accepted as postage)

Caution: The existence of E01, E04 and E07 with "charge box" markings, E08 on a folded letter and the lack of any recorded "PAID 5" or "PAID 10" handstamped markings are evidence these markings were also used as stampless markings. Stampless uses are not easily distinguished from provisional uses. Each example must be considered on its own merits.

Mount Lebanon, Louisiana

A

Adhesive

MOU-LA-A01 (60X1)

A	5¢ red brown on *white*	NR	NR

On Cover

MOU-LA-A01 (60X1)

A	5¢ red brown on *white*	*250,000.*

The Mount Lebanon, Louisiana provisional was impressed on white wove paper from an engraved woodcut. The engraving included a border of ruled lines and a center circle. Using italic printers type, "Mt Lebanon La" was punched in the wood. Similarly the rate "5" was also punched into the wood. This resulted in the letters and rate being reversed on the printed stamp.

The one recorded example of this stamp shows portions of several adjoining stamps indicating the printing form contained multiple subjects. The stamp is pen canceled and the envelope is not postmarked.

Nashville, Tennessee

A B

Type B with "TENM" variety

Type B with white spot in lower right corner

Adhesives

Ribbed paper

NAS-TN-A01 (61X2)			
A 5¢ carmine (shades)		1,000.	750.
	a. Pair	NR	—
	b. Vertical *tête-bêche* pair (61X2*a*)	NR	NR
NAS-TN-A02 (61X3)			
A 5¢ brick red (shades)		1,000.	500.
	a. Pair	NR	1,250.
	b. Vertical *tête-bêche* pair	—	NR
NAS-TN-A03 (61X5)			
A 5¢ violet brown (shades)		750.	500.
	a. Pair	—	NR
	b. Vertical *tête-bêche* pair (61X5*a*)	NR	4,000.
	c. Block of four	—	NR
NAS-TN-A04 (61X4)			
A 5¢ gray (shades)		1,250.	1,000.
NAS-TN-A05 (61X6)			
B 10¢ green		NR	2,500.
	a. TENM variety	—	—
	b. White spot	NR	—

On Cover

Ribbed Paper

NAS-TN-A01 (61X2)		
A 5¢ carmine		3,500.
	a. Pair	5,000.
	b. Vertical *tête-bêche* pair (61X2*a*)	*17,500.*

NAS-TN-A02 (61X3)
- **A** 5¢ brick red (shades) — 3,000.
  - **a**. Pair — 4,000.

NAS-TN-A03 (61X5)
- **A** 5¢ violet brown (shades) — 4,000.
  - **a**. Pair — 7,500.
  - **b**. Vertical pair, *tête-bêche** (61X5*a*) — NR

NAS-TN-A04 (61X4)
- **A** 5¢ gray (shades) — 5,000.
  - **a**. Pair — 7,500.
  - **b**. Strip of five — —

NAS-TN-A05 (61X6)
- **B** 10¢ green — *20,000.*
  - **a**. "TENM" variety — —
  - **b**. White spot — —
  - **d**. Used with NAS-TN-A01 — *85,000.*
  - **e**. Mailed from another town* — —

The Nashville, Tennessee adhesive provisionals were engraved on wood and reproduced as stereotypes from which a plate of multiple subjects was prepared. The layout and size of printed sheets is unknown. Printing was on gray-blue ribbed paper. Examples are found on both horizontal and vertical ribbed paper. *See also,* "3¢ 1861 Postmasters' Provisionals" section.

The stamps were engraved by Dan Adams, an engraver in Nashville, and are said to have been printed at the office of the *Nashville Gazette*.

The existence of pairs tête-bêche is an indication the printing form had a small number of subjects and the stamps were printed along one side of a sheet and the sheet turned and printed on the other side.

The design of the two stamps is nearly identical to the Knoxville adhesives. This is a strong indication that the same person engraved the designs for both towns.

Earliest recorded dates of use:
- A01 – August 9, 1861 to Athens and Pulaski, Tenn. (two covers)
- A02 – July 28, 1861 to Athens, Tenn.
- A03 – July 28, 1861 to Paris, Tenn.
- A04 – October 30, [1861] to Macon, Miss.
- A04a – October 23, 1861 to Army of the Potomac, Va.
- A05 – July 27, 1861 on piece

Recorded example that entered the mail at another town:
- A05 – Used from *Huntersville,* [*West*] *Virginia* (postmarked *November 16, 1861* – questionable if accepted as postage)

Note: The 10¢ green provisional has two major plate varieties. The first is the "TENM" variety which is found on all examples from one position. The second is the "white spot" variety which is found on some but not all stamps with the "TENM" variety. Apprently this variety resulted from damage or deterioration of the plate after printing began.

Warning: Dangerous forgeries of the 5¢ adhesive exist.

10

C *a*

Entires (Handstamped)

NAS-TN-E01 (61XU1)

C	5¢ blue	NR	750.
	a. Revalued "10" by Type *a* (61XU2)	NR	3,500.

The Type C handstamped provisional was prepared by handstamping envelopes with a 32 mm office postmark in which the date logos were replaced by "PAID / 5" markings.

Earliest recorded dates of use:
- E01 – July 2, 1861 to Planters, Ark.
- E01a – July 2, 1861 to Austin Tex.

Caution: There are two recorded examples of the Type C marking on envelopes with a manuscript "5" rate marking. These markings are evidence the provisional marking was also used as a stampless marking. Stampless uses cannot be readily distinguished from provisional uses. Each example must be considered on its own merits.

New Orleans

A B

Adhesives

NEW-LA-A01 (62X1)

A	2¢ blue (shades) on *white*	200.	750.
	a. With plate imprint	—	—
	b. Printed on both sides (62X1*a*)	NR	NR
	c. Pair	400.	2,000.
	d. Block of four	2,000.	NR

NEW-LA-A02 (62X2)

A	2¢ red (shades) on *white*	200.	1,500.
	a. Pair	400.	NR
	b. Block of four	1,000.	NR

NEW-LA-A03 (62X3)		
B 5¢ brown (shades) on *white*	250.	150.
a. With plate imprint	—	—
b. With inverted plate imprint	NR	—
c. Printed on both sides (62X3*a*)	NR	2,500.
d. Pair	—	300.
e. Block of four	1,000.	NR
f. Strip of three	NR	NR
g. Strip of four	NR	NR
h. Strip of five	NR	—

NEW-LA-A04 (62X3*b*)		
B 5¢ ocher (shades) on *white*	NR	500.
a. With plate imprint	NR	—
b. Pair	NR	—

NEW-LA-A05 (62X4)		
B 5¢ red brown (shades) on *bluish*	300.	200.
a. With plate imprint	—	—
b. Printed on both sides (62X4*a*)	NR	3,000.
c. Pair	750.	500.
d. Block of four	NR	2,500.

NEW-LA-A06 (62X5)		
B 5¢ yellow brown on *off white*	200.	250.
a. With plate imprint	—	NR
b. With partial second plate imprint	—	NR
c. Pair	400.	500.
d. Block of four	1,000.	NR

NEW-LA-A07 (62X6)		
B 5¢ red (shades) on *white*	—	*7,500.*

NEW-LA-A08 (62X7)		
B 5¢ red on *bluish*	NR	*12,500.*

On Cover

NEW-LA-A01 (62X1)	
A 2¢ blue (shades) on *white*	3,500.
a. With plate imprint	—
b. Printed on both sides (62X1*a*)	*10,000.*
c. Pair	*12,500.*
e. Strip of five	—

NEW-LA-A02 (62X2)	
A 2¢ red (shades) on *white*	*20,000.*

NEW-LA-A03 (62X3)	
B 5¢ brown (shades) on *white*	500.
d. Pair	750.
e. Block of four	*5,000.*
f. Strip of three	*2,500.*
g. Strip of four	*3,500.*
h. Strip of five	*5,000.*
i. Mailed from another town	3,000.

NEW-LA-A04 (62X3*b*)	
B 5¢ ocher (shades) on *white*	2,000.
a. With plate imprint	—
b. Pair	4,000.

NEW-LA-A05 (62X4)	
B 5¢ red brown (shades) on *bluish*	500.
a. With plate imprint	—
b. Printed on both sides (62X4*a*)	*7,500.*
c. Pair	1,000.
e. Used with a general issue	*15,000.*
f. Mailed from another town	7,500.

NEW-LA-A06 (62X5)	
B 5¢ yellow brown on *off white*	750.
a. With plate imprint	—
b. Pair	1,500.

The New Orleans, Louisiana adhesive provisionals were engraved on wood and reproduced as stereotypes or electrotypes from which a plate of multiple subjects was prepared. Both stamps were printed in panes of 40 subjects (8 x 5). There were two printings of the two-cent stamps and three of the five-cent stamps. The printings are easily identified by type:

2¢ Adhesive
First printing: 2¢ red on *white* (A02)
Second printing: 2¢ blue on *white (*A01)
5¢ Adhesive
First printing: 5¢ brown and ocher on *white* (A03 and A04)
Second printing: 5¢ red brown on *bluish* (A05)
Third printing: 5¢ yellow brown on *off white* (A06)

Evidence indicates the 2¢ red (A02) was printed before the 2¢ blue (A01) but was not placed on sale until much later.

Earliest recorded dates of use:
A01 – July 14, [1861] to Charleston, S.C.
A02 – January 6, [1862] to Benton, Ark.
A03 – June 16, [1861] to Memphis, Tenn.
A03e – June 12, [1861] to Jefferson, Tex.
A04 – June 18, [1861] to Vicksburg, Miss.
A04b – June 16, [1861] off cover
A05 – August 27, [1861] to Vacherie, La.
A05a – August 21, [1861] off cover
A06 – December 3, [1861] to Natchez and Vicksburg, Miss. (two covers)
A07 – None recorded
A08 – December 4, [1861] off cover

Recorded examples that entered the mail at another town:
A03 – Used from Grand Gulf, Miss. (postmarked June 18, [1861] – accepted as postage)
A03– Used from Grand Gulf, Miss. (postmarked June 21, [1861] on piece – undetermined if accepted as postage)
A03 – Used from St. Francisville, La. (postmarked June 27, [1861] – accepted as postage)
A03 – Used from Baton Rouge, La. (postmarked Ju- 2, [1861] on piece – undetermined if accepted as postage).
A03 – Used from St. Joseph, La. (postmarked August 3, [1861] – accepted as postage)
A03 – Tied by Natchez, Miss. "STEAM" marking (accepted as postage)
A05 – Used from Shieldsborough, Miss. (postmarked October 10, [1861] – accepted as postage)

Warning: Dangerous forgeries of Type A and B exist.

C D

J.L. RIDDELL, P.M.

Control

Entires (Handstamped)

NEW-LA-E01 (62XU1)
C 5¢ black (with control) NR 3,500.
NEW-LA-E02 (62XU2)
D 10¢ black (with control) NR *10,000.*

The Type C and D markings were prepared by handstamping envelopes with specially prepared rate markings. All recorded examples were also struck with a separate marking with the name of the postmaster, J. L. Riddell. Whether this marking was used as control is not clear.

The E01 marking was also used to cancel provisional adhesives.

Earliest recorded dates of use:
E01 – August 15, 1861 to Natchez, [Miss.]
E02 – August 31, 1861 to Natchez, [Miss.]

Note: Previously a PAID 2 marking similar in design to the Type C and D markings was listed as a provisional. No evidence could be found to support its continued listing as a provisional. The provisional status of the Type C marking is also in question, as this marking and the control are found on covers with New Orleans adhesive provisionals. The absence of New Orleans stampless paid and rate markings is further evidence the Type C and Type D markings were used as both provisional and stampless markings.

New Smyrna, Florida

A

Adhesive

NEW-FL-A01 (63X1)
A 5¢ black on *white,* with blue-ruled lines NR NR

On Cover

NEW-FL-A01 (63X1)
A 5¢ black on *white,* with blue-ruled lines NR
a. Revalued "10" *50,000.*

The New Smyrna, Florida provisional was prepared by handstamping a circular "5" rate marking on white blue ruled paper.

The only recorded example is postmarked February 10 on a patriotic flag envelope to Castania Grove, N.C.

Norfolk, Virginia

A B

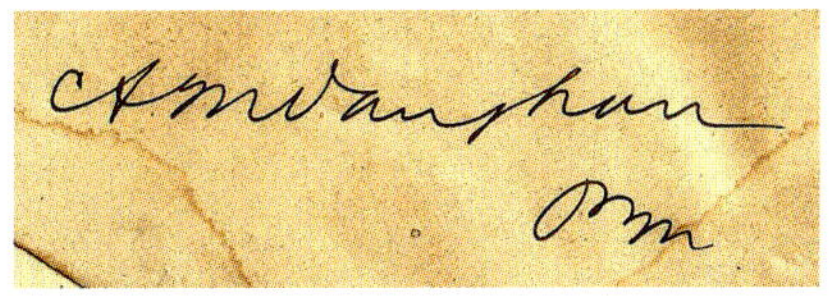

Control

Entires (Handstamped)

NOR-VA-E01 (139XU1)
A 5¢ blue (control on reverse) 1,000. 1,500.
NOR-VA-E02 (139XU2)
B 10¢ blue (control on reverse) NR 1,750.

The Norfolk, Virginia provisionals ware prepared by handstamping envelopes with "PAID" and "5" or "10" rate markings. Separately the postmaster, Augustus M. Vaughan, signed his name on the reverse as a control.

Earliest recorded dates of use:
E01 – *October 11, 1861 to Scuppernong, North Carolina*
E02 – October 2, 1861 to Mobile, Alabama

Oakway, South Carolina

A

Adhesive

OAK-SC-A01 (115X1)
A 5¢ black on *white* NR NR

On Cover

OAK-SC-A01 (115X1)

A	5¢ black on *white*	*50,000.*

The Oakway, South Carolina provisional was prepared by handstamping white paper with a circled "5" woodcut.

Earliest recorded date of use is September 18, 1861 to Pickens C.H., S.C.

There are two recorded examples. In both cases the adhesives were cut to shape before use. One of the recorded examples is tied by a manuscript "Paid" marking and the other is not tied.

Oxford, North Carolina

A

Entire (Handstamped)

OXF-NC-E01

B	10¢ black	NR	NA
	a. Under a postally used general issue		1,000.

The Oxford, North Carolina provisional was prepared by handstamping envelopes with a "PAID / 10" marking. The circle was notched to produce a segmented circle.

Earliest recorded date of use is February 7, [1865] under a 10¢ engraved general issue tied by an Oxford, N.C. postmark to Sassafras Fork, N.C.

Note: This marking was also used as a stampless marking. It is considered a provisional only when unused, under a postally used general issue, or mailed from another town.

Patterson, North Carolina

A **B**

Control

Entires (Handstamped)

PAT-NC-E01

A	5¢ black with control	750.	NA

PAT-NC-E02

B	10¢ black with control	NR	—

The Patterson, North Carolina provisionals were prepared by handstamping envelopes with ornate "PAID 5" and "PAID 10" markings and the undated postmark as a control.

The ornate paid markings were also used to cancel stamps on letters mailed from Patterson.

Earliest recorded dates of use:
- E01 – None recorded
- E02 – No postmark to Oaks, N.C. (only recorded example)

Note: These markings were also used as stampless markings. They are considered provisionals only when unused, under a postally used general issue, or mailed from another town.

Pensacola, Florida

A

Entire (Handstamped)

PEN-FL-E01 (106XU1)

A	5¢ black	NR	—
	a. Revalued "10" (ms) (106XU1*a*)	NR	—

The Pensacola, Florida provisional was prepared by handstamping envelopes with a rated woodcut marking. The woodcut features a star with "PAID 5" between the points of the star. In the center is the letter "H." The significance of the letter "H" is unknown.

Earliest recorded dates of use is July 24, [1861] to Jackson, Miss.

Petersburg, Virginia

A

Adhesive

PET-VA-A01 (65X1)

A 5¢ red on *white*	1,750.	750.
a. Pair	NR	2,000.
b. Block of four	—	NR

On Cover

PET-VA-A01 (65X1)

A 5¢ red on *white*	2,000.
a. Pair	*10,000.*
c. Used with a general issue	*50,000.*

The Petersburg, Virginia provisionals were typeset and printed on thick white wove paper by A. F. Crutchfield & Co., publishers of the Petersburg *Daily Express*.

The printing form consisted of ten separate settings arranged in two rows of five stamps each. The design featured the town name and the name of the postmaster, William E. Bass. Individual positions are easily identified by minor typographical variations in the inscriptions and border pieces.

Some examples show a colorless line through one or more letters in "BURG" of "PETERSBURG." On other examples the letter "e" in "Office" appears as a "c". These are the result of wear or physical deterioration in one or more of the settings in the printing form.

Earliest recorded date of use is September 24, [1861] to New Orleans, La.

Warning: A dangerous forgery of the Petersburg adhesive exists.

Pittsylvania Court House, Virginia

A

CENTS. CENT S.

Normal **Extra Space**

Adhesives

Wove paper

PIT-VA-A01 (66X1)

A 5¢ red on *white*	7,500.	NR
a. Extra space between "T" and "S"	NR.	5,000.

Laid paper

PIT-VA-A02 (66X2)

A 5¢ red on *white*	NR	NR
a. Extra space between "T" and "S"	NR	NR

On Cover

Wove paper

PIT-VA-A01 (66X1)

A 5¢ red on *white*	*40,000.*
a. Extra space between "T" and "S"	NR

Laid paper

PIT-VA-A02 (66X2)

A 5¢ red on *white*	*45,000.*
a. Extra space between "T" and "S"	—

The Pittsylvania Court House, Virginia provisionals were typeset and printed on white wove and laid paper. Printing was done in the job-office of the Danville *Democratic Appeal* owned by W. D. Coleman, the postmaster at Danville, Virginia.

The Pittsylvania adhesive was prepared from the same settings used to prepare the Danville adhesive. The only change was to replace the name of the Danville postmaster with that of the Pittsylvania postmaster, J. P. Johnson. In the process of changing the name, the line "5 CENTS." was reset in one position creating a variety with extra space between the "T" and "S" of "CENTS."

There is one recorded example of the extra space between the "T" and "S" variety on cover in the Tapling Collection at the British Museum. It is not known if this example is on wove or laid paper.

Examples are known cut square, cut octagonally and cut to shape.

Earliest recorded dates of use:
A01 – September 25, [1861] to Danville, Va.
A02 – October 9, [1861] to Richmond, Va.

There is one recorded example of A01 unused. The uncanceled stamp was steamed off a cover leaving the original gum intact.

Warning: There are dangerous forgeries of this stamp.

Plains of Dura, Georgia

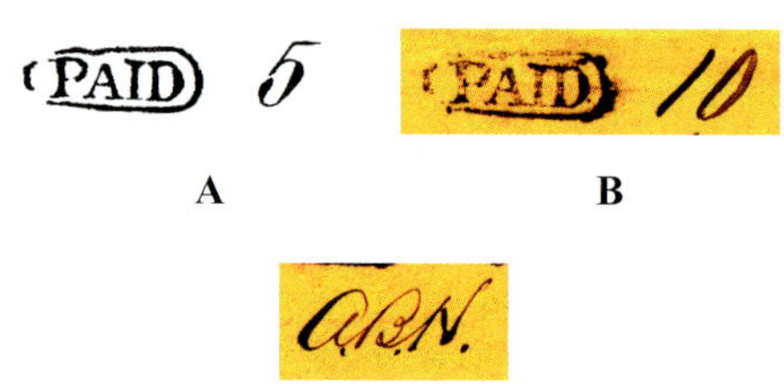

A B

Control

Entires (Handstamped)

PLA-GA-E01 (140XU1)		
A 5¢ black	NR	2,500.
PLA-GA-E02 (140XU2)		
B 10¢ black	NR	2,500.

The Plains of Dura, Georgia provisionals were prepared by handstamping envelopes with a "PAID" marking. Separately a "5" or "10" rate was applied in ink. The initials of the postmaster, Athern B. Hawkes, were applied as a control.

Earliest recorded dates of use:
- E01 – August 2, [1861] to Athens, Ga. (only recorded example)
- E02 – August 15 to Richmond, Va. (only recorded example)

Pleasant Shade, Virginia

A

Adhesives

PLE-VA-A01 (67X1)		
A 5¢ blue on *white*	5,000.	*10,000.*
a. Pair	—	NR
b. Block of six	—	NR

On Cover

PLE-VA-A01 (67X1)	
A 5¢ blue on *white*	*30,000.*
a. Pair	—

The Pleasant Shade, Virginia provisional was printed on white wove paper by A. F. Crutchfield & Co. of Petersburg, Virginia. Five of the ten settings used for the Petersburg provisional were used for the Pleasant Shade provisional. The town name and postmaster's name were removed and replaced by Pleasant Shade and the name of the postmaster, Robert E. Davis.

The new form consisted of five settings arranged horizontally in a different sequence from those in the Petersburg form. The existence of a vertical pair and block of six indicate multiple impressions of the form were made on a single sheet.

Earliest recorded dates of use:
- A01 – December 22, [1861] to Staunton, Va. (Tapling Collection)
- A01a – November 24, [1861 to Petersburg, Va.

Plum Creek, Texas

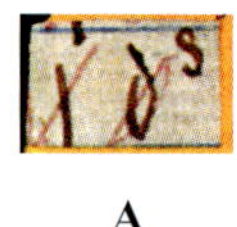

A

Adhesive

PLU-TX-A01		
A 10¢ black on *white* with ruled lines	NR	NR
PLU-TX-A02 (141X1)		
A 10¢ black on *bluish* with ruled lines	NR	NR

On Cover

PLU-TX-A01		
A 10¢ black on *white* with ruled lines	NR	—
PLU-TX-A02 (141X1)		
A 10¢ black on *bluish* with ruled lines	NR	—

The Plum Creek, Texas provisional was prepared by writing "10" in ink on white and bluish paper with ruled lines. As needed each "10" marking was cut from the sheet. The adhesives are found in both a rectangular and parallelogram form.

Earliest recorded date of use:
- A01 – July 9 to Corpus Christi, Tex (only recorded example)
- A02 – July 19, 1864 to Gonzales, Tex. (only recorded example)

Note: The two recorded examples are on covers that have manuscript "Paid 10" markings. One also has a handstamped "10" marking. The origin of this marking is unknown.

Port Gibson, Mississippi

A Control

Entire (Handstamped)

POR-MS-E01 (142XU1)

A	5¢ black (with control)	NR	1,000.

The Port Gibson, Mississippi provisional was prepared by handstamping envelopes with a "PAID 5" marking to which the postmaster, William T. Morris, added his signature as a control.

Earliest recorded date of use is January 6, 1862 to Oakland College, Miss.

Port Lavaca, Texas

A

Adhesive

On Cover

POR-TX-A01 (107X1)

A	10¢ black on *white*	NR	—

The Port Lavaca, Texas provisional was typeset from a stock "cut" of a steam ship with the rate and town name added in printer's type. The setting was printed or handstamped on a sheet of paper. Individual stamps were cut from the sheet for use.

The only recorded example is postmarked January 19 to Prairie Lea, Tex. The postmark does not tie the stamp nor is it canceled in any manner.

Quincy, Florida

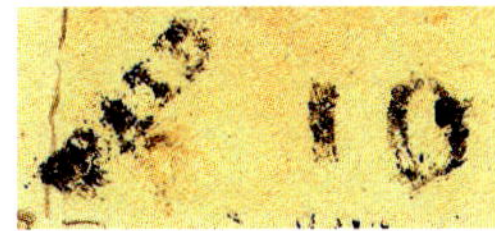

A

Entire (Handstamped)

QUI-FL-E01

A	10¢ black	NR	NR
	a. Under a postally used general issue		—

The Quincy, Florida provisional was prepared by handstamping "PAID" and "10" markings on envelopes. The only recorded example is under a pair of 5¢ typographs postmarked March 10 to Athens, Ga.

Note: This marking was also used as a stampless marking. It is considered a provisional only when unused, under a postally used general issue, or mailed from another town.

Raleigh, North Carolina

A *a*

Entires (Handstamped)

RAL-NC-E01 (68XU2)			
A	5¢ blue	NR	2,500.
RAL-NC-E02 (68XU1)			
A	5¢ red	NR	500.
	a. With additional PAID (Type *a*)	NR	500.
	b. Struck twice with additional PAID (Type *a*)	NR	750.

The Raleigh, North Carolina provisional was prepared by handstamping envelopes with a prewar integral "5" postmark which had the rim removed and "PAID" inserted in place of the date logo.

Earliest recorded dates of use:
- E01 – June 4, 1861 to Maple Springs and Camp Hall, N.C. (two covers)
- E02 – June 11, 1861 to Leicester, N.C.

Caution: There is a recorded example of E02 with a "charge box" marking and one on a folded letter. This indicates the provisional marking may have also been used as a stampless marking. Stampless uses cannot be readily distinguished from provisional uses. Each example must be considered on its own merits.

Rheatown, Tennessee

A

Adhesives

RHE-TN-A01 (69X1)

A	5¢ red on *white*	2,500.	5,000.
	a. Pair (*b* + *c*)	7,500.	NR

On Cover

RHE-TN-A01 (69X1)

A	5¢ red on *white*	*35,000.*

The Rheatown, Tennessee provisional was typeset and printed on white wove paper in a form of three settings. The three settings can be identified by the different patterns of the top border pieces and differences in the border pieces surrounding the value panel.

In the first setting (*a*), the direction of the top border pieces reverse above the "E" of "PENCE". Additionally, the outside border piece to the right of "D" in "PAID" is missing the curved line on the right side. In the second setting (*b*), the right-most top border piece is inverted with the base up. Additionally, the inside border piece to the left of "P" in "PAID" is inverted. In the third setting (*c*), the direction of the top border pieces reverse between the "N" and "C" of "PENCE". Additionally, the border piece over the "D" of "PAID" is missing the bottom curved line.

The central design of the Rheatown settings (value panel and border) were also used to print the Tellico Plains, Tennessee provisionals. The only difference is settings *a* and *c* were reversed in the Tellico Plains printing form. The plating characteristics in the border pieces are illustrated under the Tellico Plains provisionals.

The use of the same value panel and border settings in the Rheatown and Tellico Plains provisionals is evidence the same printer prepared and printed both. It is believed the Rheatown provisionals were printed first as the earliest recorded date of use is from this town.

The only recorded pair is from settings *b* + *c* with a wide right margin. There is a recorded single from setting *a* with a wide left margin indicating it was the left stamp in the printing form.

The stamps were canceled either by the town postmark or a pen cancel.

The August 20, 1870 issue of the *American Journal of Philately* contains a letter from former Confederate postmaster, David Pence. In the letter Pence states he used the provisional stamps from "about August, 1861, to Midsummer in 1862, until Confederate stamps were distributed for general use."

Note: The price for A01 on cover is for a stamp tied by the town postmark. Stamps with manuscript cancels sell for less.

Warning: A dangerous forgery exists.

RICHMOND, TEXAS

A

B

10

a

Entires (Handstamped)

RIC-TX-E01 (70XU1)

A	5¢ red	NR	1,500.
	a. Revalued "10" (Type *a*) (70XU1*a*)	NR	3,500.

RIC-TX-E02 (70XU2)

B	10¢ red	NR	2,000.
	a. Revalued "15" (ms) (70XU2*a*)	NR	4,000.

The Richmond, Texas provisionals were prepared by handstamping envelopes with an office postmark in which the date logos were replaced with "PAID / 5" and "PAID / 10" markings.

Earliest recorded dates of use:

E01 – July 10, [1861] to New Orleans, La.
E02 – Unknown
E02a – December 17, [1861] to Texana, Tex. (only recorded example)

Caution: The lack of any recorded "Paid 5" markings from Richmond is evidence the Type A marking was also used as a stampless marking. There is one recorded example of E02 with a "charge box" marking. This indicates this provisional marking may have also been used as a stampless marking. Stampless uses cannot be readily distinguished from provisional uses. Each example must be considered on its own merits.

RINGGOLD, GEORGIA

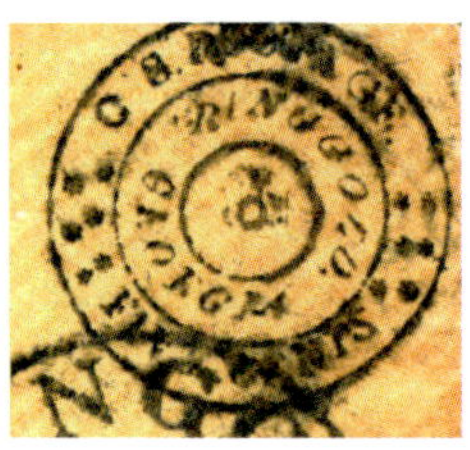

A

Entire (Handstamped)

RIN-GA-E01 (71XU1)

A	5¢ blue-black	NR	5,000.

The Ringgold, Georgia provisional was typeset in three concentric rings. The outer ring contains "C. S. POSTAGE" and "FIVE CENTS". The middle ring contains the name of the town and state. In the center circle is an indistinguishable design. The setting was handstamped on envelopes.

Earliest recorded date of use is August 15, 1861 to Augusta, Ga.

Caution: There is one recorded example of E01 with a "charge box" marking and another example on a folded letter. This indicates this provisional marking may have also been used as a stampless marking. Stampless uses cannot be readily distinguished from provisional uses. Each example must be considered on its own merits.

RUTHERFORDTON, NORTH CAROLINA

A

Adhesive

On Cover

RUT-NC-A01 (72X1)
 A 5¢ black on *white* —

The Rutherfordton, North Carolina provisional was prepared by handstamping an undated office postmark on white paper. Separately "Paid / 5 cts" was added in manuscript at the center of postmark. These were then cut apart in rough circles to use as stamps.

The only recorded example is postmarked December 27, 1861 to Longmire's Store, S.C. The manuscript postmark (date only) does not tie the stamp to the cover.

SALEM, NORTH CAROLINA

A

B

C

PAID 5 **PAID 10**

a *b*

Entires (Handstamped)

SAL-NC-E01 (73XU1)		
A 5¢ (ms) black	NR	2,000.
a. With additional "PAID 5" (Type *a)*	NR	2,500.
SAL-NC-E02 (73XU3)		
B 5¢ black	NR	1,500.
a. Obliterated and revalued "PAID 10" (Type *b*) ("PAID" struck twice) (73XU3*a*)	NR	2,500.
b. Under a postally used general issue		2,500.
SAL-NC-E03 (73XU2)		
C 10¢ black	NR	2,500.

The Salem, North Carolina provisionals were prepared by handstamping envelopes with a specially prepared brass device that included the name of the postmaster, O. A. Keehln. Separately "PAID" and "5" were struck within the device. On others the rates "Paid 5" and "Paid 10" were applied in manuscript.

Earliest recorded dates of use:
E01 – August 22, [1861]
E01a – July 15, [1861] to Clemmonsville, N.C.
E02 – November 27, [1861] to Raleigh, N.C.
E02a – November 19, [1861] to Patterson, N.C.
E03 – September 27, [1861] to New Orleans, La. (only recorded example)

Warning: Postwar reprints prepared by O. A. Keehln are quite common and difficult to distinguish from authentic markings.

[—]	symbol used in place of value to mean insufficient information to assign a price
NA	not applicable
[*Italic*]	value typeface indicating the item is difficult to price accurately
[*Italic*]	date or location indicates unconfirmed information
NR	used in place of value when no examples have been recorded

Salisbury, North Carolina

A

Entire (Printed)

SAY-NC-E01 (75XU1)
A 5¢ black NR *5,000.*

The Salisbury, North Carolina provisional was typeset from a stock cut of an eagle with the town name and rate added in printer's type. Apparently the name of the postmaster was also included at the bottom, but that portion of the stamp is torn off the only surviving copy. It was printed in the upper left corner of envelopes.

The only recorded example is postmarked September 1 to Clover Depot, Va. The stamp is on a heavily stained light green envelope that was badly damaged when opened. There is a handstamped "PAID" marking on the envelope in addition to the town postmark.

San Antonio, Texas

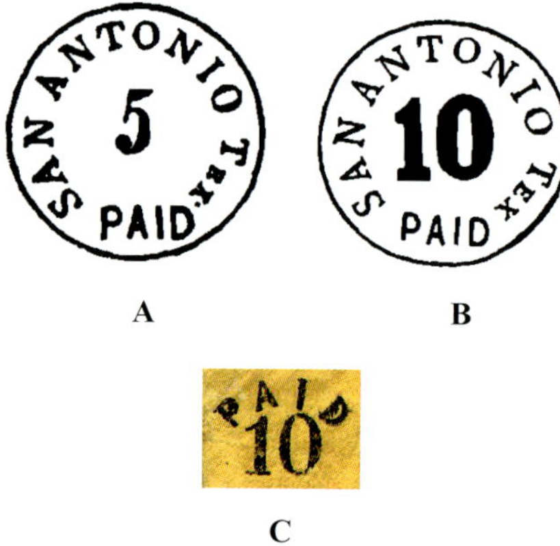

A B

C

Entires (Handstamped)

SAN-TX-E01 (76XU1A)
A 5¢ black NR —
SAN-TX-E02 (76XU2)
B 10¢ black* NR NA
SAN-TX-E03 (76XU1)
C 10¢ black 500. NA

The Type A and B San Antonio, Texas provisionals were prepared by handstamping envelopes with an integral "PAID" prewar office postmark with the date logos replaced with "5" or "10" rate markings.

The Type C provisional was prepared by handstamping envelopes with a "PAID / 10" marking.

Earliest recorded dates of use:
E01 – — 14 To Oakland, Tex. (only recorded example)
E02 – None recorded
E03 – Only recorded use is postwar

There is a recorded example of the E02 marking in red cut to shape and affixed to a cover addressed to Alleyton, Tex. The cover has a green San Antonio, Tex. postmark dated October 28. The status of this cover as a provisional is undetermined.

Note: The Type C marking was also used as a stampless marking. Consequently these markings are considered provisionals only when postally unused, used under a general issue stamp or used from another town.

Caution: There is one recorded example of E02 on an envelope with a "charge box" marking. This indicates the provisional marking may have also been used as a stampless marking. Stampless uses cannot be readily distinguished from provisional uses. Each example must be considered on its own merits.

Sandersville, Georgia

A

Entire (Handstamped)

SAN-GA-E01
A 10¢ blue NR NR
a. Under a postally used general issue 500.

The Sandersville, Georgia provisional was prepared by handstamping envelopes with "PAID" and "10" markings.

The only recorded example is postmarked February 2 to Atlanta, Ga.

Note: This marking was also used as a stampless marking. It is considered a provisional only when unused, under a postally used general issue, or mailed from another town.

Savannah, Georgia

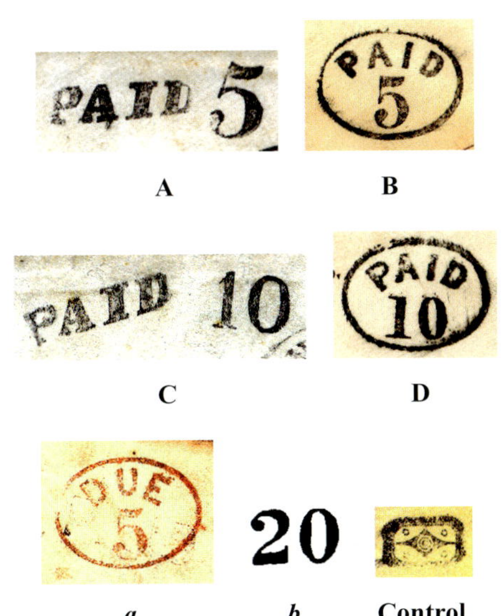

A B

C D

a *b* Control

Entires (Handstamped)

SAV-GA-E01 (101XU2)		
A 5¢ black (with control)	NR	500.
a. Revalued "20" (Type *b*) (101XU2*a*)	NR	1,500.
b. With "DUE / 5" (Type *a*)		750.
SAV-GA-E02 (101XU1)		
B 5¢ black (with control)	NR	500.
a. Revalued "10" (Type D) (101XU1*a*)	NR	1,000.
b. With "DUE / 5" (Type *a*)		750.
c. Mailed from another town		1,000.
SAV-GA-E03 (101XU4)		
C 10¢ black (with control)	NR	750.
a. Under a postally used general issue		1,000.
SAV-GA-E04 (101XU3)		
D 10¢ black (with control)	250.	750.

The Type A and C Savannah, Georgia provisionals were prepared by handstamping envelopes with "PAID" and "5" or "10" rate markings. Separately a rosette marking was applied as a control.

The Type B and D provisionals were prepared by handstamping envelopes with specially prepared oval "PAID / 5" and "PAID / 10" markings. Separately the rosette marking was applied as a control.

Earliest recorded dates of use:
E01 – June 3, 1861 to Sparta, Ga.
E02 – July 17, 1861 to Barnsville C.H., S.C.
E03 – June 1, 1861 to Staunton, Va.
E04 – October 10, 1861 to Richmond, Va.

Recorded example that entered the mail at another town:
E02 – Used from Milledgeville, Ga. (postmarked August 4, [1861] - not accepted as postage)

Selma, Alabama

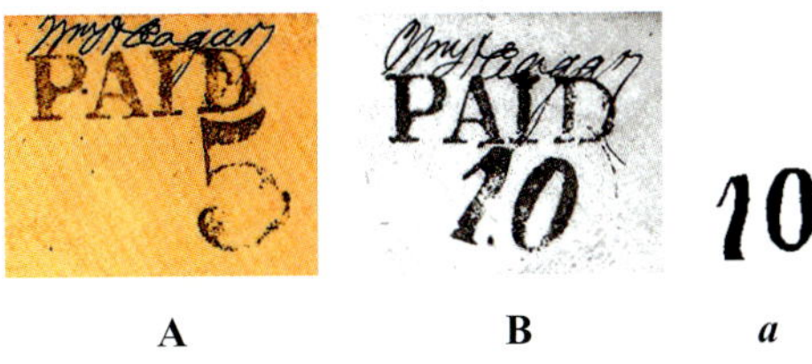

A B *a*

Entires (Handstamped)

SEL-AL-E01 (77XU1)		
A 5¢ black (with "Wm H Eagar" signature control)	750.	1,000.
a. Revalued "10" (Type *a*) (77XU1*a*)	NR	—
SEL-AL-E02 (77XU2)		
B 10¢ black (with "Wm H Eagar" signature control	1,500.	NR
a. With "W H E" initials control*	NR	NR

The Selma, Alabama handstamped provisionals were prepared by handstamping envelopes with "PAID" and "5" or "10" rate markings. As a control the Selma postmaster, William H. Eager, signed his name above the markings as "Wm H Eagar" or wrote his initials as "W H E". *See also,* "3¢ 1861 Postmasters' Provisionals" section.

Some addressed uses do not bear the Selma postmark but are considered postally used.

The only recorded example of E01a is under a 5¢ general issue tied by a target cancel on an envelope with a Selma January [1862] postmark.

Earliest recorded dates of use:
E01 – June 4, [1861] to Marion, Ala.
E02 – No postmark to New Orleans, La. (only recorded example)

Sparta, Georgia

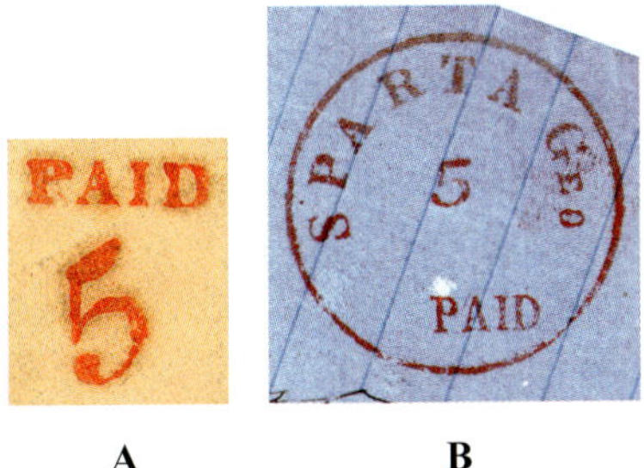

A B

C

Entires (Handstamped)

SPA-GA-E01		
A 5¢ red	500.	NR
SPA-GA-E02 (93XU1)		
B 5¢ red	NR	1,500.
SPA-GA-E03 (93XU2)		
C 10¢ red	NR	2,000.

The Type A Sparta, Georgia provisional was prepared by handstamping envelopes with "PAID" and "5" markings.

The Type B and C provisionals were prepared by handstamping envelopes with a prewar integral "3 PAID" office postmark from which the "3" was removed and the date logos replaced with either a "5" or "10" rate marking.

Earliest recorded dates of use:
- E01 – None recorded
- E02 – December 16, [1861] to Waynesville, Ga.
- E03 – January 28, [1862] to Richmond, Va. (only recorded example)

Note: The Type A marking was also used as a stampless marking. It is considered a provisional only when unused, under a postally used general issue, or mailed from another town.

Caution: There are two recorded examples of Type C on folded letters and one example on an envelope with a "charge box" marking. This is evidence the provisional marking was also used as a stampless marking. Most stampless uses are indistinguishable from provisional uses. Each example must be considered on its own merits.

Spartanburg, South Carolina

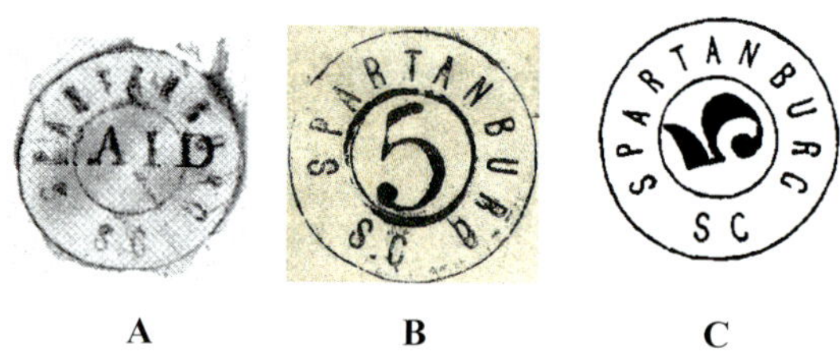

A B C

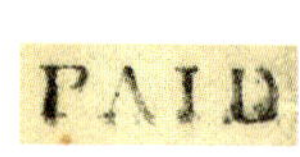

a *b* *c*

Adhesives

SPA-SC-A01 (78X1*a*)		
A PAID black on *white**	NR	NR
SPA-SC-A02 (78X1)		
B 5¢ black *on white*	NR	*7,500.*
SPA-SC-A03 (78X2)		
C 5¢ black *on bluish*	NR	NR
SPA-SC-A04 (78X3)		
C 5¢ black *on brown*	NR	NR

On Cover

SPA-SC-A01 (78X1)	
A PAID black *on white**	NR
a. Revalued "5" with "PAID" (Type *a*) and "5" (Type *b*)	*20,000.*
SPA-SC-A02 (78X1)	
B 5¢ black on *white*	*20,000.*
a. Pair with additional "PAID" (Type *a*) and "10" (Type *c*) (78X1a)	*25,000.*
SPA-SC-A03 (78X2)	
C 5¢ black *on bluish*	—
SPA-SC-A04 (78X3)	
C 5¢ black *on brown*	—

The Type A Spartanburg, South Carolina adhesive provisional was prepared by handstamping white paper with an undated double circle office postmark. Instead of a rate, "PAID" was struck inside the postmark. This was apparently meant for drop letters or circulars.

The Type B and C provisionals were prepared by handstamping white, bluish and brown paper with an undated double circle office postmark. To complete the Type B marking, a thin circled "5" was struck inside the postmark. To complete the Type C marking, a bold "5" was struck inside the postmark.

It is reported that some of the Type B and C provisionals are on white and bluish paper with ruled lines. These are unconfirmed because auction descriptions of stamps supposed to have the ruled lines are conflicting.

Most of the adhesives were cut to shape. Only two or three examples are recorded cut square.

Earliest recorded dates of use:
- A01 – None recorded
- A01a – July 5, 1861 to Lea Noir (Lenoir), N.C. (only recorded example)
- A02 – June 18, 1861 to Richmond, Va.
- A03 – September 2, 1861 to Tudor Hall, Va. (only recorded example)

A04 – —— 22, 1862 to Mount Tabor, S.C. (only recorded example)

Warning: There are dangerous forgeries of A02.

D

Control

d

Entire (Handstamped)

SPA-SC-E01 (78XU1)

D	10¢ black with control on reverse	NR	*4,000.*
	a. Struck over "5" (Type *d*)	NR	*5,000.*

The Type C provisional was prepared by handstamping envelopes with "PAID" and "10" markings. The undated double circle town postmark was struck on the reverse as a control.

Earliest recorded dates of use:
E01 – November 4, 1861 to Tudor Hall, Va.
E01a – October 30, 1861 to Tudor Hall, Va. (only recorded example)

Statesville, North Carolina

A

a

Entire (Handstamped)

STA-NC-E01 (79XU1)

A	5¢ black	NR	1,000.
	a. Revalued "10" (Type *a*) (79XU1*a*)	NR	2,500.
	b. Revalued "10" (ms) with "Way" (ms)		—

The Statesville, North Carolina provisional was prepared by handstamping envelopes with a boxed "PAID / ◂ 5 ▸" marking.

Some strikes of the provisional marking show black dashes in the lower left and lower right corners of the marking as in the illustration of the marking above

Earliest recorded dates of use:
E01 – September [1861] to *Raleigh, N.C.*
E01a – December 30, [1861] to Gainesville, Fla.
E01b – No postmark to Davidson College, N.C. (only recorded example)

Caution: There is one recorded example E01 on a folded letter. This is an indication the provisional marking may have also been used as a stampless marking. Stampless uses cannot be readily distinguished from provisional uses. Each example must be considered on its own merits.

Warning: Facsimiles of this marking exist and many are on paper from the war period.

Sumter, South Carolina

A

B

a

Entires

SUM-SC-E01 (80XU1)

A	5¢ black	NR	NA
	a. Revalued "10" (Type a) (80XU1a)		—
	b. Mailed from another town		1,000.
	c. Under a postally used general issue		2,000.

SUM-SC-E02 (80XU2)

B	10¢ black	NR	NA
	a. Under a postally used general issue		*3,000.*

The Sumter, South Carolina provisionals were prepared by handstamping envelopes with a "PAID" and "5" or "10" rate markings.

The year date in the Sumter postmark was not changed from 1861.

Earliest recorded dates of use:
E01 – Unknown
E02 – Unknown

Recorded example that entered the mail at another town:
E01 – Used from Columbia, S.C. (postmarked October 2, [1861] – not accepted as postage)

Note: There is an envelope with the E02 marking rerated "2" in manuscript and used as a drop letter. There are several different theories regarding the nature of this use. Some believe it is a provisional, others a stampless use. It is listed as a stampless use in this catalog.

The Type A and B markings were also used as stampless markings. They are considered provisionals only when unused, under a postally used general issue, or mailed from another town.

Talbotton, Georgia

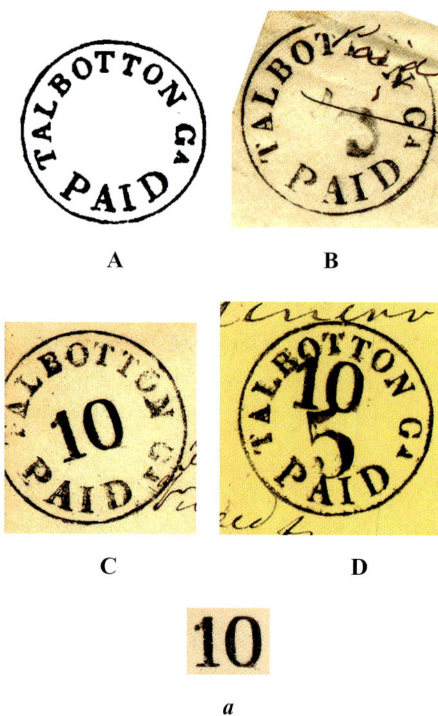

A B

C D

a

Entires

TAL-GA-E01		
A PAID	NR	NR
a. Under a postally used general issue		1,000.
TAL-GA-E02 (94XU1)		
B 5¢ black	NR	1,000.
a. Revalued "10" (Type *a*) (94XU1*a*)	NR	1,500.
TAL-GA-E03 (94XU2)		
C 10¢ black	NR	1,500.
TAL-GA-E04		
D 15¢ black (5 +10)	NR	2,500.

The Talbotton, Georgia provisionals were prepared by handstamping envelopes with an undated prewar integral "PAID" office postmark. Separately "5" or "10" rate markings were applied in the center of the postmark. Type A has no rate marking and was probably used for drop letters and circulars.

The Type D marking is not a revalued provisional. The careful placement of the rate markings to indicate 15¢ is consistent with the use on a triple rate legal envelope.

Earliest recorded dates of use:

- E01 – April 21, 1862 with 5¢ green general issue (only recorded example)
- E02 – July 19, 1861 to Macon, Ga.
- E03 – February 14, 1862 to Richmond, Va.
- E04 – July 18, 1861 to Marion County, Ga. (only recorded example)

Caution: There are several recorded examples of Type C with "charge box" markings. This is evidence the provisional marking was also used as a stampless marking. Stampless uses cannot be readily distinguished from provisional uses. Each example must be considered on its own merits.

Talladega, Alabama

A B

Entires

TAL-AL-E01 (143XU1)		
A 5¢ black*	NR	NA
TAL-AL-E02 (143XU2)		
B 10¢ black	—	NA

The Talladega, Alabama provisionals were prepared by handstamping envelopes with a "PAID" marking with the letters "IE" over it and a "5" or "10" rate marking to the right. The letters "IE" were the initials of the postmaster, Isaac Estell.

Caution: There is conflicting evidence regarding these markings. Some evidence indicates they were prepared as provisionals with the initials "I E" added as a control. Other evidence such as a "charge box" markings indicate stampless uses. As a result these are considered provisionals only when unused, under a postally used general issue, or mailed from another town.

Tellico Plains, Tennessee

A B

C

Adhesives (on laid paper)

TEL-TN-A01 (81X1)		
A 5¢ red on *white*	2,000.	NR
a. Comma after "JOHNSON"	2,000.	2,500.
TEL-TN-A02 (81X2)		
B 10¢ red on *white*	2,000.	NR
a. 5¢ + 10¢ (*b* + *c*) pair, *se-tenant* (81X2)	7,500.	NR
TEL-TN-A03		
C 5¢ + 5¢ + 10¢ (*a* + *b* + *c*) red strip of three on *white, se-tenant*	*10,000.*	NR

On Cover

TEL-TN-A01 (81X1)	
A 5¢ red	*40,000.*

The Tellico Plains, Tennessee provisionals were typeset and printed on white laid paper in a form of three settings. The complete form of the three settings is 5¢ + 5¢ + 10¢ (settings *a* + *b* + *c*). The three settings are identified by the value and punctuation following "JOHNSON".

The settings are illustrated and described below:

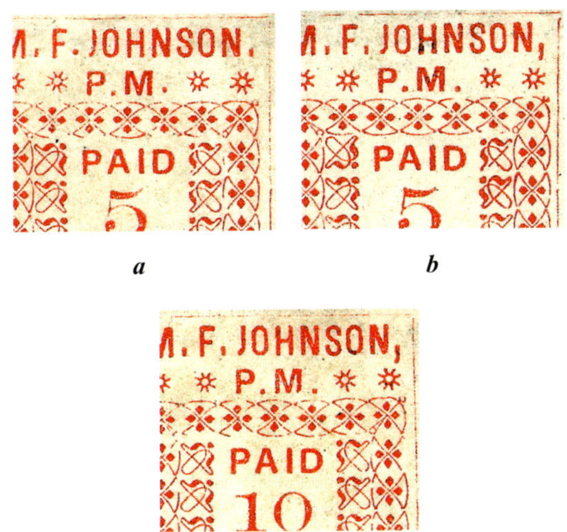

a *b*

c

In the first setting (*a*), the value is "5" and the word "JOHNSON" is followed by a period. Additionally, the border piece over the "D" of "PAID" is missing the bottom curved line. In the second setting (*b*), the value is "5" and the word "JOHNSON" is followed by a comma. Additionally the border piece to the left of the "P" in "PAID" is pointed upward. In the third setting (*c*), the value is "10" and the word "JOHNSON" is followed by a comma. Additionally, the outside border piece to the right of "D" in "PAID" is missing the curved line on the right side.

The central design of the settings (value panel and border) of the Tellico Plains provisionals are the same as those used for the Rheatown, Tennessee provisionals. The only difference is that, in the printing form, settings *a* and *c* are reversed from those in the Rheatown printing form.

Earliest recorded date of use is December 10, 1861 to Knoxville, Tenn. The cover has no postmark, only a manuscript date that ties the stamp.

Thomasville, Georgia

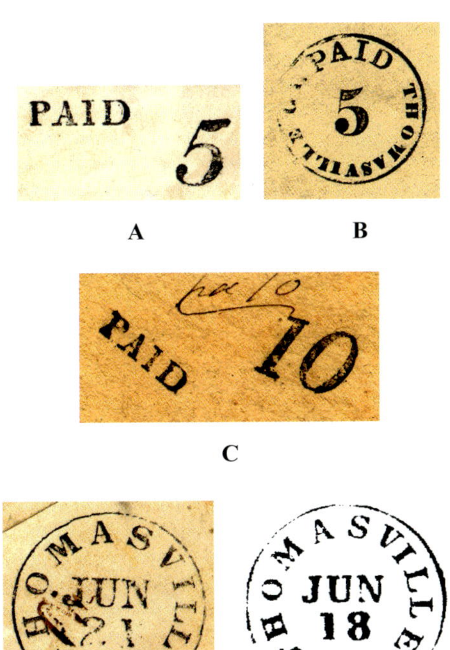

A B

C

Control Control

Entires

THO-GA-E01 (82XU1)		
A 5¢ black (with control)	NR	750.
a. Without control	250.	NA
THO-GA-E02 (82XU2)		
B 5¢ black	NR	1,000.
THO-GA-E03		
C 10¢ black (without control)	250.	NA

The Type A and C Thomasville, Georgia provisionals were prepared by handstamping envelopes with "PAID" and "5" or "10" rate markings. A dated office postmark was struck on the reverse as a control. The control must be dated on or before the date of the postmark.

The Type B provisional was prepared by handstamping envelopes with a marking that resembles a postmark with an integral "PAID" and a "5" in the center.

The two controls look very much alike but there are differences in both size and form. In Control A the "E" of "THOMASVILLE" is much closer to the "a" of "Ga" than in Control B.

Earliest recorded dates of use:
- E01 – June 21, [1861] to Quitman, Ga.
- E02 – July 24, 1861 to Griffin, Ga.
- E03 – No postmark to Richmond, Va. (only recorded example)

Note: The Type A and C markings (without controls) were also used as stampless markings. They are considered provisionals only when unused, under a postally used general issue, or mailed from another town.

Caution: There is one recorded example of the Type B marking used as a forwarding marking and one recorded example on a cover with a "charge box" marking. This indicates the provisional marking may have also been used as a stampless marking. Stampless uses cannot be readily distinguished from provisional uses. Each example must be considered on its own merits.

Tullahoma, Tennessee

A

Control

Entire

TUL-AL-E01 (111XU1)

A 10¢ black (with control)	NR	*3,500.*

The Tullahoma, Tennessee provisional was prepared by handstamping envelopes with a "PAID / 10" marking. An undated office postmark was struck on the front or reverse as a control.

Earliest recorded date of use is March 28, 1863 to Walton Co, Fla.

Caution: There are dangerous fakes of the Tullahoma postmark.

Tuscumbia, Alabama

A

B

Entires

TUS-AL-E01 (84XU2)		
A 5¢ red	NR	*5,000.*
TUS-AL-E02 (84XU1)		
A 5¢ black	—	*3,500.*
TUS-AL-E03 (84XU3)		
B 10¢ black	NR	*5,000.*

The Tuscumbia, Alabama provisionals were prepared by handstamping envelopes with a prewar office integral "PAID" postmark in which the date logos were replaced with "5" or "10" rate markings. *See also,* "3¢ 1861 Postmasters' Provisionals" section.

Earliest recorded dates of use:
- E01 – June 12, [1861] to Florence, Ala. (only recorded example)
- E02 – September 14, [1861] to New Orleans, La.
- E03 – September 13, [1861] to Richmond, Va. (only recorded example)

Note: There is one recorded example of E02 postmarked October 20, 1862 with the signature "Jno M Powers, PM" across the marking. The significance of the signature is unknown and the 1862 year date in the postmark is questionable.

Caution: The lack of recorded stampless rate markings from Tuscumbia is evidence the provisional markings were also used as stampless markings. Stampless uses cannot be readily distinguished from provisional uses. Each example must be considered on its own merits.

Uniontown, Alabama

A

B

C

Adhesives

Laid paper

UNI-AL-A01 (86X1)		
A 2¢ dark blue on *gray blue*	NR	NR
UNI-AL-A02		
A 2¢ dark blue on *white*	NR	NR
a. (86X2) Sheet of four	*50,000.*	NR
UNI-AL-A03 (86X3)		
B 5¢ green on *gray blue*	5,000.	4,000.
a. Pair	—	NR
UNI-AL-A04 (86X4)		
B 5¢ dark green on *white*	NR	NR
UNI-AL-A05 (86X5)		
C 10¢ red on *gray blue*	NR	NR
a. On paper with stationer's embossed crest	NR	NR

On Cover

Laid paper

UNI-AL-A01 (86X1)	
A 2¢ dark blue *on gray blue*	*20,000.*
UNI-AL-A03 (86X3)	
B 5¢ green *on gray blue*	*10,000.*
UNI-AL-A04 (86X4)	
B 5¢ dark green *on white*	7,500.
a. Pair	*20,000.*
b. On paper with stationer's embossed crest	—
UNI-AL-A05 (86X5)	
C 10¢ red *on gray blue*	*30,000.*
a. On paper with stationer's embossed crest	—

The Uniontown, Alabama provisionals were typeset and printed on white and gray-blue laid paper. Stamps exist on both horizontally and vertically laid paper. The same settings were used to print all values with only the numeral changed.

The printing form consisted of four settings (2 x 2) as evidenced by a block of four of A02 with very wide margins. There is one recorded example from position 4 with extremely wide margins indicating that at least one setting was used to print individual stamps.

The primary means of identifying the four positions is by the corner pieces in each setting and the dashes that appear before, between or after "C S A".

Position 1: There are four lozenge corner pieces set at 45 degree angles to the corners. There are dashes **between** each letter (C-S-A).

Position 2: There are fancy border pieces in the upper corners and figure "8" border pieces in the bottom corners. There are dashes **between** each letter (C-S-A).

The setting for position 2 is unique in that the border pieces between "CSA" and "POSTAGE" are figure "8" pieces. In all other positions they are lattice border pieces.

Position 3: There are four lozenge corner pieces. The upper corner lozenges point down to the left and the bottom corner lozenges point down to the right. There are dashes **before, between** and **after** each letter (-C-S-A-).

Position 4: There are four lozenge corner pieces set at 45 degree angles to the corners. There are dashes **between** each letter and **after** the last letter (C-S-A-).

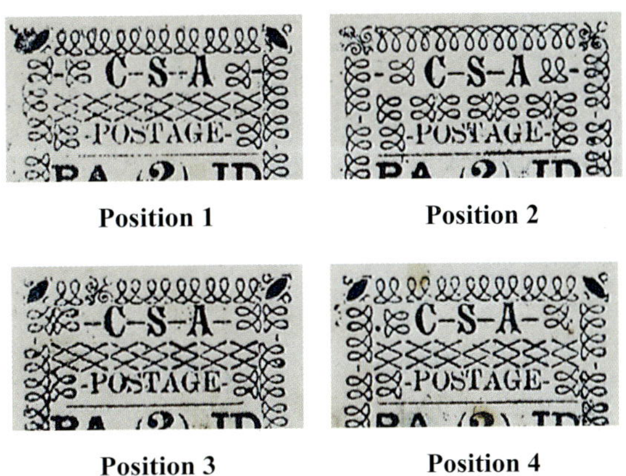

Position 1 **Position 2**

Position 3 **Position 4**

The majority of covers with Uniontown provisionals bear illegible postmarks.

The earliest recorded dates of use:
- A01 – None recorded
- A02 – 1862
- A03 – September 6, [1861] to Marion, Ala.
- A04 – January [1862] to Montgomery, Ala.
- A05 – September 22, [1861] to Port Royal, Va.

UNIONVILLE, SOUTH CAROLINA

A

Adhesive

UNI-SC-A01 (87X1)		
A 5¢ black on *grayish*	NR	NR

On Cover

UNI-SC-A01 (87X1)		
A 5¢ black on *grayish*	NR	*15,000.*
a. Pair	NR	*30,000.*

The Unionville, South Carolina provisional was prepared by handstamping "PAID" and "5" on grayish paper that was first ruled in blue ink to form frame lines.

Earliest recorded date of use is June 11, [1861] to Mt. Tabor, [S.C.] based on a letter insert.

Valdosta, Georgia

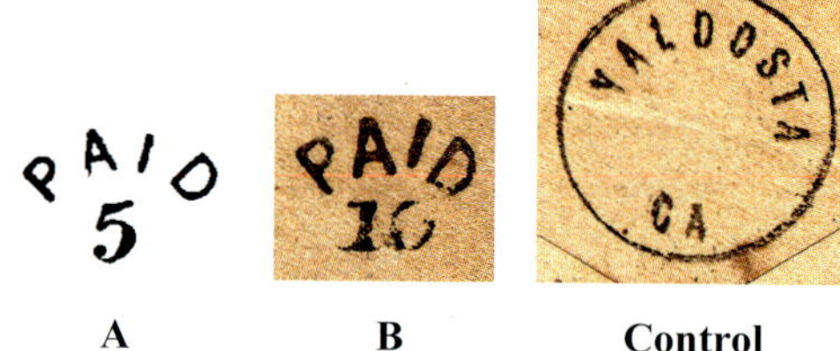

A B Control

Entires (Handstamped)

VAL-GA-E01 (110XU2)
A 5¢ black struck twice (control on front) NR 1,500.
VAL-GA-E02 (110XU1)
B 10¢ black (control on reverse) NR 1,500.

The Valdosta, Georgia provisionals were prepared by handstamping envelopes with either a "PAID / 5" or "PAID / 10" marking. Separately an undated office postmark was applied as a control.

Earliest recorded dates of use:
E01 – March 3, [1865] (from docketing) to Aiken, S.C. (only recorded example)
E02 – August 18, 1864 to Grahamville, S.C. (only recorded example)

Velasco, Texas

A

Entire (Handstamped)

VEL-TX-E01
A 10¢ black — NA

The Velasco, Texas provisional was prepared by handstamping envelopes with a circled "PAID 10" marking.

There is one recorded example. It has the notation "Politeness / M A Lawkin Esqr." and no postmark, indicating it was carried outside the mails.

Note: This marking was also used as a stampless marking. It is considered a provisional only when unused, under a postally used general issue, or mailed from another town.

Victoria, Texas

A B C

a *b*

Adhesives

VIC-TX-A01 (88X1)
A 5¢ red-brown on *green* glazed paper *17,500.* NR
VIC-TX-A02 (88X2)
B 10¢ red-brown on *green* glazed paper *15,000.* NR
VIC-TX-A03 (88X3)
C 10¢ red-brown on *green* glazed pelure paper *15,000.* *10,000.*

On Cover

VIC-TX-A02 (88X2)
B 10¢ red-brown on *green* glazed paper NR
a. With "PAID" (Type *a*) *100,000.*
b. With "PAID 10" (Type *b*) *100,000.*

The Victoria, Texas provisionals were typeset and printed on surface-colored green paper. The layout and size of the printing form is unknown. Several settings can be identified by minor variations in the spacing of the inscriptions.

Earliest recorded dates of use:
A01 – None recorded
A02 – March 30, [*1863*] to Brownsville, Tex.
A03 – October (off cover)

Warning: There are forgeries of A01.

Walterborough, South Carolina

A

Entire (Handstamped)

WAL-SC-E01 (108XU2)

A	10¢ carmine	NR	2,000.

The Walterborough, South Carolina provisional was prepared by handstamping envelopes with an ornate typeset rate marking.

Earliest recorded date of use is unknown.

Caution: There are two recorded examples of this provisional envelope with a "charge box" marking and at least one on a printed form. This is evidence the provisional marking was also used as a stampless marking. Most stampless uses cannot be distinguished from provisional uses. Each example must be considered on its own merits.

WARRENTON, GEORGIA

A

Entire (Handstamped)

WAR-GA-E01 (89XU1)

A	5¢ black	NR	1,000.
	a. Revalued "10" (ms) (89XU1*a*)	NR	1,500.

The Warrenton, Georgia provisional was prepared by handstamping envelopes with the office postmark in which the date logos were replaced by "PAID" and "5" markings.

Earliest recorded dates of use:
E01 – August 21, [1861] to *Berzilla, Ga.*
E01a – July 20, [1861] to Richmond, Va.

Warning: There are dangerous forgeries of E01.

WASHINGTON, GEORGIA

A

Control

Entire (Handstamped)

WAS-GA-E01 (117XU1)

A	10¢ black (control on reverse)	NR	1,000.

The Washington, Georgia provisional was prepared by handstamping envelopes with "PAID" and "10" markings. Separately the undated office postmark was struck on the reverse as a control.

The Washington postmark deteriorated rapidly after June 1861 resulting in strikes that may show little or no date. Such strikes are not control marks. The control mark is only on the reverse of envelopes.

Earliest recorded date of use is August 19, 1861 to Charlottesville, Va.

Note: The image of the control illustrated above was taken from a cover with a resealed flap. The control is actually circular.

WEATHERFORD, TEXAS

A

Entire (Handstamped)

WEA-TX-E01 (109XU1)

A	5¢ black*	NR	NR
	a. Struck twice (10¢) (109XU2)	NR	*10,000.*

The Weatherford, Texas provisional was engraved in wood with printer's type inserted in the four corners spelling out the word "P-A-I-D". This device was then used to handstamp envelopes.

Earliest recorded dates of use:
E01 – None recorded
E01a – June 21, [1861] to Batesville, Ga. (only recorded example)

WINNSBOROUGH, SOUTH CAROLINA

A

B

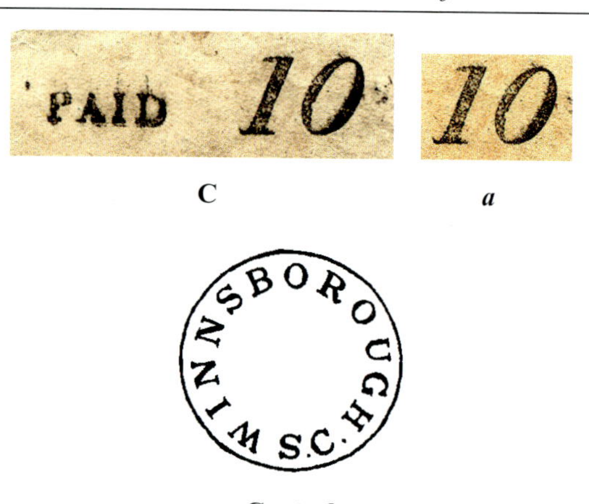

C a

Control

Entires (Handstamped)

WIN-SC-E01
  A 5¢ black NR 1,500.
WIN-SC-E02 (97XU1)
  B 5¢ black (with control) NR 1,500.
    a. Revalued "10" (Type a) NR 2,000.
WIN-SC-E03 (97XU2)
  C 10¢ black (with control) — 2,000.
    a. Under a postally used general issue 2,500.

The Winnsborough, South Carolina Type A provisional was prepared by handstamping envelopes with the office postmark in which the date logos were replaced by "PAID" and "5" markings. The Type B and C provisionals were prepared by handstamping "PAID" and "5" or "10" rate markings on envelopes with the undated office postmark struck on the reverse as a control.

A Winnsborough cover with a PAID marking but no rate and the undated office postmark struck on the reverse is reported but has not been verified.

Earliest recorded dates of use:
- E01 – August 1, [1861] to Mt. Holly, S.C.
- E02 – November 25, [1861] to Columbia, S.C.
- E02a – August 23, [1862] to Charleston, S.C. (only recorded example)
- E03 – December 7 to Savannah, Ga. (only recorded example)

Wytheville, Virginia

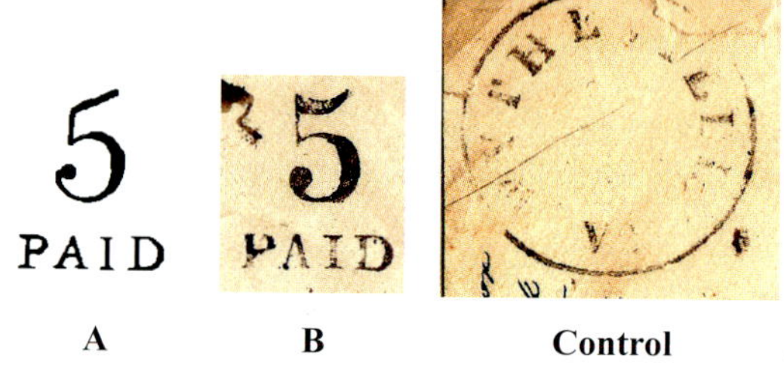

A B Control

Entires (Handstamped)

WYT-VA-E01
  A 5¢ black (with control) NR 750.
WYT-VA-E02 (114XU1)
  B 5¢ black (with control) NR 750.

The Wytheville, Virginia provisionals were prepared by handstamping "PAID" and "5" markings on envelopes. The undated office postmark was struck as a control on the front of the envelope.

Earliest recorded dates of use:
- E01 – June 11, [1861] to Salem, [Va]
- E02 – October 4, [1861] to Salem, Va.

Abbreviations and Symbols

Symbol	Definition	Placement
*	Unsupported item[1]	After item description
—	Not possible to value accurately	Price
Italic	Insufficient data to properly value	Price
Italic	Unconfirmed information	Date or location
IH	Institutional holding	Price
NA	Not applicable	Price
NR	None recorded	Price

[1] Item unsupported by an illustration. Listing based on a previous entry in a catalog listing Confederate items.

GENERAL ISSUES NUMBERING SYSTEM

The numbering system used in this catalog is an extension of the Dietz and Scott numbers. The first number is the traditional one. This is followed by letters and numbers to indicate a major variety. These varieties have long been recognized, but were never given a formal designation. The table that follows illustrates the new numbering system with the corresponding Scott number in parentheses.

GENERAL ISSUES

CSA	Scott	Description
1-AB	(1c)	5¢ green lithograph, Stone AB
1-1	(1)	5¢ green lithograph, Stone 1
1-2	(1)	5¢ green lithograph, Stone 2
1-2-M		5¢ green lithograph, Stone 2, misplaced transfers
2-H	(2b)	10¢ blue, Hoyer & Ludwig
2-P	(2)	10¢ blue, J. T. Paterson
2-Y	(2e)	10¢ blue, J. T. Paterson, Stone Y
3	(3)	2¢ green lithograph
4-2	(4)	5¢ blue lithograph, Stone 2
4-2-M		5¢ blue lithograph, Stone 2, misplaced transfer
4-3	(4)	5¢ blue lithograph, Stone 3
5	(5)	10¢ rose lithograph
5-S		10¢ rose lithograph, shifted transfers
6	(6)	5¢ typographed, De La Rue London
7-L	(7)	5¢ typographed, printed in Richmond on London paper
7-R	(7)	5¢ typographed, printed in Richmond on Local paper
8	(8)	2¢ engraved
9	(9)	10¢ engraved, TEN
10	(10)	10¢ engraved, Frame Line
11-AD	(11)	10¢ engraved Type I, Archer & Daly
12-AD	(12)	10¢ engraved Type II, Archer & Daly
11-KB	(11)	10¢ engraved Type I, Keatinge & Ball
12-KB	(12)	10¢ engraved Type II, Keatinge &Ball
13	(13)	20¢ engraved
14	(14)	1¢ typographed, De La Rue London, never issued

ADDITIONAL DESIGNATIONS

CSA - v	variety
CSA - i	imprint or inscriptions
CSA - w	printer's waste
CSA - M	misplaced transfers
CSA - S	shifted transfers

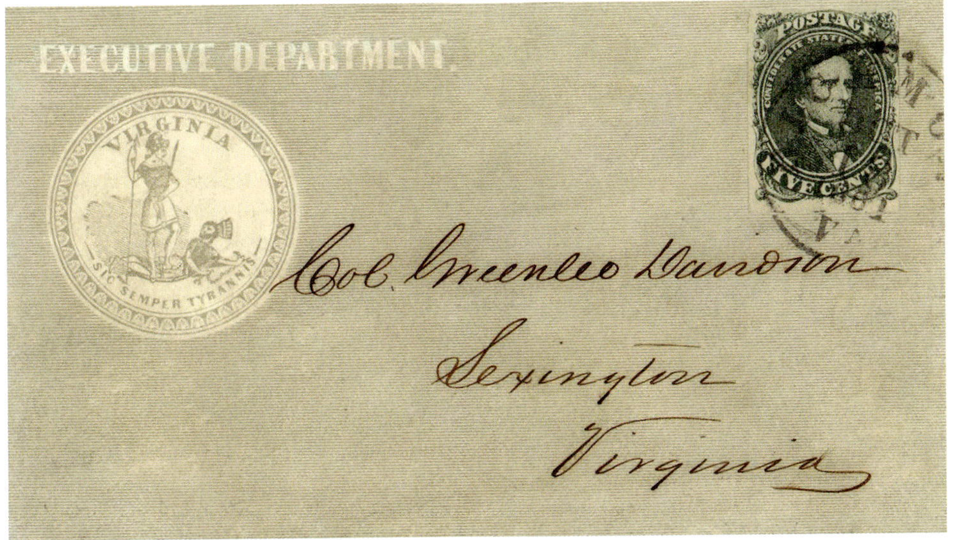

The *Richmond Daily Examiner* reported that the 5¢ general issue stamps were first sold on Wednesday, October 16, 1861. The first adhesive stamp issued by the Confederate States of America was the 5¢ Green from Stone AB. This example is on an Executive Department semi-official envelope used from Richmond, Virginia with an October 18, 1861 postmark.

General Issues

The Lithographed Issues

All of the lithographed general issues of the Confederate States were prepared using the same basic process and in the same format. It is not known how the master dies for the 2¢, 5¢ and 10¢ stamps were executed. They could have been drawn directly on a small lithographic stone or engraved on metal. Fifty impressions were printed from the master die with a special oily transfer ink. Each image was closely trimmed and mounted face up in five rows of ten subjects each on a ruled sheet of paper to facilitate alignment. The sheet was then placed face down and transferred or laid down on a lithographic stone to produce a transfer stone having fifty images.

Stamps could be printed directly from the 50 subject transfer stone. This was not economical due to the labor involved in printing and the small paper size. Instead, impressions were made from the transfer stone. Using the same procedure used to prepare the transfer stone, the four transfer units were laid down on the lithographic printing stone. The result was a printing stone of 200 subjects arranged in two panes of 100 subjects separated by a vertical gutter.

Each step in the preparation of a printing stone provided the chance for individual stamp images to receive distinctive flaws or imperfections. When finally laid down on the printing stone, these are known as plate variations and are constant on all stamps produced from the printing stone. These variations are the basis of plating a stamp produced by the lithographic process.

The variations can be designated by when or where they occur in the process of preparing the printing stone. Those that occur in the preparation of the transfer stone are known as transfer stone variations and can be plated to the transfer stone as constant varieties. Variations in individual stamps appear in the same position in each of the four transfer units that make up a sheet. Such a variety occurs once in 50 stamps. Those defects or variations that occur in the preparation of the printing stone from the transfer units will result in deviations that can be plated to a single position in a full sheet. Such a variety occurs once in 200 stamps for that printing stone.

Plating positions on a transfer stone are designated by numbering each stamp on the transfer stone starting at the upper left (1) and ending at the lower right (50). Each transfer unit may also be given a suffix designation based on its relative position on the stone: UL, LL, UR or LR and even to a specific printing stone when more than one is known from a transfer stone. A diagram of the transfer units making up a printing stone of 200 subjects is illustrated below.

Arrangement of a printing stone of 200 subjects showing the four transfer units and plating positions

Upper Left Transfer Unit (UL)										Upper Right Transfer Unit (UR)									
1	2	3	4	5	6	7	8	9	10	1	2	3	4	5	6	7	8	9	10
11	12	13	14	15	16	17	18	19	20	11	12	13	14	15	16	17	18	19	20
21	22	23	24	25	26	27	28	29	30	21	22	23	24	25	26	27	28	29	30
31	32	33	34	35	36	37	38	39	40	31	32	33	34	35	36	37	38	39	40
41	42	43	44	45	46	47	48	48	50	41	42	43	44	45	46	47	48	48	50
1	2	3	4	5	6	7	8	9	10	1	2	3	4	5	6	7	8	9	10
11	12	13	14	15	16	17	18	19	20	11	12	13	14	15	16	17	18	19	20
21	22	23	24	25	26	27	28	29	30	21	22	23	24	25	26	27	28	29	30
31	32	33	34	35	36	37	38	39	40	31	32	33	34	35	36	37	38	39	40
41	42	43	44	45	46	47	48	48	50	41	42	43	44	45	46	47	48	48	50
Lower Left Transfer Unit (LL) **Left Pane**										Lower Right Transfer Unit (LR) **Right Pane**									

Scott Catalogue numbers are listed in parentheses after the *Confederate States of America Catalog* and *Handbook of Stamps and Postal History* (CSA Catalog) numbers in the listings. Stated values are CSA Catalog values and not Scott Catalogue values.

Plating positions can also be designated based on numbering a full pane of 100 subjects by starting at the upper left (1) and ending at the lower right (100). Each position can be further identified to a pane by adding the suffix L or R.

Plate positions given for plate varieties are transfer stone positions and have no relative transfer stone position indicated. Plate positions for printing stone plate varieties include the appropriate transfer stone position or pane position designator.

More than one printing stone was prepared for the stamps numbered CSA 1-2, 2-H, 2-P and 4-2. The duplicate stones can be identified by differences in the alignment between the upper and lower transfer units and by the relative orientation of the left and right panes on a sheet. Some individual positions with unique characteristics are also identifiable. The use of multiple printing stones explains why a given variety may occur once in 50 examples, once in 200 examples or greater. When a variety occurs once in 50 examples, there is a direct link to the transfer stone. When more than one printing stone was used, the occurrence of printing stone varieties cannot be computed with certainty, because each printing stone was not necessarily used to produce the same number of stamps.

5¢ Green Lithograph

A single master engraving was used in the preparation of the 5¢ green stamps. It was used to prepare three different transfer stones designated Stone AB, Stone 1 and Stone 2. These transfer stones were then used to prepare printing stones bearing the same stone designations. The designation Stone AB is attributed to Edward S. Knapp, who in the 1920s was uncertain if there was one or two transfer or printing stones. It now appears that stamps from Stone AB were printed from one printing stone with two panes of 100 subjects each. There is one printer's imprint at the bottom of each pane under positions 45, 46 and 47 lower. This is the only 5¢ lithograph to have a printer's imprint.

Distinguishing the stamps from the three different stones is difficult, with plating the most reliable method of identification. Some of the general characteristics follow.

Stamps from Stone AB can be difficult to distinguish from Stone 1 and 2. The stamps usually have a distinctive dull olive green color, but this shade is also known from CSA 1-1 and 1-2. To be identified as a Stone AB print, a stamp must also have at least one of the following characteristics:

1) Used before October 23, 1861, the earliest established date for Stone 1
2) Extremely sharp and uniform image, although not a definitive characteristic
3) Hoyer & Ludwig imprint in the lower sheet margin
4) Stamp cannot be plated as Stone 1 or Stone 2
5) Stamp plated as Stone AB

Stamps from Stone 1 have a lighter or finer printed impression than those from Stone AB or Stone 2.

The print quality of stamps printed from Stone 2 varies, but most stamps have a heavier or thicker appearance than those from Stone AB or Stone 1.

CSA 1-AB
5¢ Green - Stone AB

Printer: Hoyer & Ludwig of Richmond, Virginia
Master engraving by: Charles Ludwig, on metal
Vignette: Jefferson Davis
Printing: Lithographed from a printing stone of 200 subjects consisting of two panes of 100
Plating: Incomplete
Imprint: HOYER & LUDWIG, RICHMOND, VA
Color: Dull green or olive green shades, but may also exist in a bright green shade
Paper: White wove paper of varying thickness
Gum: Clear to light cream
Separations: Issued imperforate
Printing estimate: 9,250,000 total for Stones AB, 1 and 2 in green
Earliest recorded use: Oct 16, 1861, also first day
Largest known multiples: Unused block of 4, unused imprint strip of 4, used block of 4, used strip of 10

Transfer Stone AB was laid down with great care, making plating difficult. The scarcity of large multiples and the precision used in laying down the plate are the reasons that plating is currently incomplete. Used copies of stamps from Stone AB are scarce and unused copies are rare, indicating printing from this stone was limited. As these were the first stamps, the supply was quickly exhausted thus the scarcity of unused examples.

The stamp was first sold at the Richmond, Virginia post office on October 16, 1861 as noted in the *Richmond Daily Examiner* of that date. This is also the date of the earliest recorded use.

Imprint strip, 1-AB-i1

Stamps

1-AB (1c)	olive green	900.	225.
1-ABa	bright olive green	NR	550.
	Pair	*3,500.*	800.
	Block of 4	*12,500.*	*4,000.*

Imprints

1-AB-i1	Printer's imprint, single stamp	2,250.	1,500.
	Printer's imprint, strip of four	*15,000.*	NR

White curl, left of head, 1-AB-v1

Varieties

1-AB-v1	White curl, left of head pos. 46L (1 of 200)	1,750.	1,000.

Covers

Single on cover	450.
Pair on cover	1,000.

Markings (as a percent, plus or minus, of the price)

	off cover	**on cover**
Blue town	+20%	+30%
Red town	+50%	+60%
October 1861 postmark	+100%	+250%
Grid or target	+20%	+30%
Paid or numeral	+30%	+200%
Kentucky town	+50%	+400%
Express company	+100%	+200%
Steam or Steamboat	+100%	+200%
Pen cancel	-75%	-20%

CSA 1-1
5¢ Green - Stone 1

Printer: Hoyer & Ludwig of Richmond, Virginia
Master engraving by: Charles Ludwig, on metal
Vignette: Jefferson Davis
Printing: Lithographed from more than one printing stone of 200 subjects, each consisting of two panes of 100
Plating: Complete as to the transfer stone positions
Imprint: None
Color: Many shades of green, but mainly lighter green shades
Paper: White wove paper of varying thickness
Gum: Clear to light yellow
Separations: Issued imperforate
Printing estimate: 9,250,000 total for Stones AB, 1 and 2 in green
Earliest recorded use: October 23, 1861
Largest known multiples: Unused pane of 100, block of 50, used strip of 10

A new transfer stone from the master engraving was laid down for Stone 1 (1-1). The transfer stone consists of 50 impressions from the master engraving, as with all of the lithographs. This stamp is the most common of the 5¢ green lithographs. Variations in each position are constant, but are quite minute, making plating somewhat difficult. This stamp is known with private separations. See the Perforated and Rouletted Stamps section for more details.

Stamps

1-1a (1*a*)	light green	250.	150.
1-1b (1*b*)	dark green	375.	225.
1-1c (1*c*)	olive green	350.	225.
1-1d	bright green	375.	225.
	Pair	750.	350.
	Pair with vertical gutter	*3,500.*	NR
	Block of 4	1,500.	2,500.

X in gutter, 1-1-i1

Imprints and Inscriptions

1-1-i1	X in gutter between pos. 30 and 21 and between 40 and 31 (Note: not always present) (1 in +200)	*1,800.*	*1,250.*

Cedilla C, 1-1-v1

Clipped upper right spandrel, 1-1-v2

Broken line over FI in oval, 1-1-v3

Parasite lower right scroll, 1-1-v4

Flaw on AT of States, 1-1-v5

Rocket flaw, 1-1-v6

White spot, transient, various, 1-1-v7

White shirt, transient, 1-1-v8

Varieties

1-1-v1	Cedilla C, pos. 22 (1 in 50)	350.	200.
1-1-v2	Clipped upper right spandrel, pos. 48 (1 in 50)	350.	200.
1-1-v3	Broken line over FI in oval, pos. 47 (1 in 50)	350.	200.
1-1-v4	Parasite over lower right scroll, pos. 1 (1 in 50)	350.	200.
1-1-v5	Flaw on AT of STATES pos. 38 (1 in 50)	350.	200.
1-1-v6	Rocket flaw, pos. 2, transient, 2 or 3 known	*1,250.*	*1,250.*
1-1-v7	White spot, transient, various forms and sizes	325.	200.
1-1-v8	White shirt, transient	325.	200.

Covers

Single	275.
Pair	500.
Government imprint, semi-official	750.
Patriotic	1,500.
Wallpaper	1,500.

Markings (as a percent, plus or minus, of the price)

	off cover	**on cover**
Blue town	+40%	+50%
Red town	+40%	+50%
Green town	+100%	+200%
October 1861 postmark	+100%	+250%
Grid or target	+20%	+30%
Paid or numeral	+30%	+250%
Arkansas town	+100%	+300%
Florida town	+150%	+300%
Kentucky town	+150%	+300%
Tennessee town	+50%	+100%
Texas town	+75%	+200%
West Virginia town	+200%	+500%
Express company	+200%	+500%
Railroad	+200%	+400%
Steam or Steamboat	+200%	+500%
Pen cancel	-75%	-20%

CSA 1-2
5¢ Green - Stone 2

Printer: Hoyer & Ludwig of Richmond, Virginia
Master engraving by: Charles Ludwig, on metal
Vignette: Jefferson Davis
Printing: Lithographed from more than one printing stone of 200 subjects, each consisting of two panes of 100
Plating: Complete as to the transfer stone positions
Imprint: None
Color: Numerous shades of green, but primarily darker shades
Paper: White wove paper of varying thickness
Gum: Clear to light yellow
Separations: Issued imperforate
Printing estimate: 9,250,000 total for all of Stones AB, 1 and 2 in green
Earliest recorded use: December 2, 1861
Largest known multiples: Unused block of 32

A new transfer stone was again laid down for Stone 2 (1-2) from the master engraving. It consists of 50 units, as with all of the lithographs. The basic plating for Stone 2, as printed in both green (1-2) and blue (4-2), is identical with respect to the transfer stone. There are some additional constant variet ies that occurred when the printing stones were laid down.

These constant transfer stone varieties are often more evident in the blue printings. A detailed plating of Stone 2 appeared in *The Confederate Philatelist* in an intermittent series of articles in Vol. 11, No. 8 through Vol. 13, No. 2, November 1966 – April 1968. The varieties listed are for positions 1 of 50 on the transfer stone.

See the section on Misplaced and Shifted Transfers for details on some of these varieties from Transfer Stone 2.

Typical horizontal separation between U & L transfer units, 1-2e

1-2 (1)	green	325.	175.
1-2a (1*a*)	light green	275.	175.
1-2b (1*b*)	dark green	350.	225.
1-2c	olive green	400.	225.
	Pair	600.	375.
	Block of 4	*1,750.*	*2,250.*
1-2d	Pair, vertical gutter between (used single known showing part of 20L & 11R)	NR	NR
1-2e	Pair, horizontal separation between upper and lower transfer unit positions (e.g., 41U-1L, etc.)	850.	600.

SA in gutter between panes, 1-2-il

Imprints and Inscriptions

1-2-i1	SA in gutter between pos. 50L and 41R (3 known)	NR	*3,000.*

Lines in shirt, 1-2-v2

Deep cut in bottom, 1-2-v4

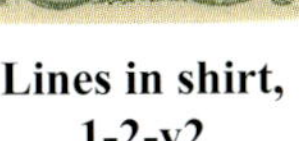

Lines in shirt, 1-2-v2

Deep cut in bottom, 1-2-v4

FIVE CENTS filled in pos. 48 shown, 1-2-v6

Varieties

1-2-v1	Spur, upper left scroll, pos. 21 (1 in 50) same as 4-2-v1	350.	200.
1-2-v2	Lines in shirt, pos. 5 (1 of 50) same as 4-2-v2	350.	200.
1-2-v3	Cut in right inner oval, pos. 10 (1 of 50) same as 4-2-v3	350.	200.
1-2-v4	Deep cut, pos. 44 (1 of + 200) Not the same as 4-2-v4		400.
1-2-v5	Goose neck, pos. 25, same as 4-2-v7	350.	200.
1-2-v6	FIVE CENTS filled in, constant, each varies per position, pos. 46L, 47L, 48L, 49L (each being 1 in +200)	*900.*	*1,000.*
1-2-M	Misplaced transfers, see separate section		

Covers

Single	275.
Pair	500.
Government imprint, semi-official	600.
Patriotic	1,250.
Wallpaper	1,450.

Markings (as a percent, plus or minus, of the price)

	off cover	on cover
Blue town	+20%	+30%
Red town	+50%	+50%
Green town	+100%	+150%
Orange town	+150%	+250%
December 1861 postmark	+100%	+200%
Grid or target	+20%	+30%
Paid or numeral	+30%	+200%
Arkansas town	+100%	+300%
Florida town	+150%	+350%
Kentucky town	+150%	+400%
Tennessee town	+50%	+100%
Texas town	+75%	+200%
West Virginia town	+200%	+500%
Express company	+250%	+500%
Railroad	+200%	+400%
Steam or Steamboat	+200%	+500%
Pen cancel	-75%	-20%

10¢ Blue Lithograph
Hoyer & Ludwig, J. T. Paterson & Stone Y

The 10¢ blue lithograph is in reality three distinctive stamps, three designs and at least two different contractors. Charles Ludwig of the printing firm of Hoyer & Ludwig in Richmond, Virginia prepared the original 10¢ master engraving from which three stamps ultimately evolved: Hoyer & Ludwig (2-H), Paterson (2-P), and Stone Y (2-Y). Two of the types are identified by the printers: Hoyer & Ludwig of Richmond, Virginia and J. T. Paterson & Co. of Augusta, Georgia.

The design of the 10¢ blue has a rectangular border instead of the irregular border on the 5¢ green stamp. Trimming single impressions to make up the transfer stone thus was much simpler and resulted in only a few small defects in the borders of some stamps. The resulting lack of distinguishing characteristics makes plating this stamp somewhat difficult.

The Hoyer & Ludwig transfer stone was prepared from the master die. It appears J. T. Paterson & Co. used an impression from one of the Hoyer & Ludwig stones, either the transfer stone or a printing stone, and slightly modified it. This image was then used to lay down their transfer stone. This may explain why even the best Paterson stamps are not as sharp as those printed by Hoyer & Ludwig. The image Paterson used has a number of small and distinctive changes, some apparently deliberate, thus making it a new stamp. More than one printing stone was made for both the 2-H and 2-P from the same transfer stones.

Stone Y (2-Y) is also considered a distinct stamp, as the design and printing details differ. The panes have no imprint, however, the image and sequence of known uses strongly suggest it was produced by J. T. Paterson & Co. The designation of Stone Y dates back to the 1920s, although there is no indication of why the "Y" was chosen over another designation.

[*italic*]	value typeface indicating the item is difficult to price accurately
NR	used in place of value when no examples have been recorded

Scott Catalogue numbers are listed in parentheses after the *Confederate States of America Catalog and Handbook of Stamps and Postal History* (CSA Catalog) numbers in the listings. Stated values are CSA Catalog values and not Scott Catalogue values.

CSA 2-H, 2-P & 2-Y
Details

The following characteristics distinguish a Hoyer & Ludwig print from a Paterson print and Stone Y.

Hoyer & Ludwig (2-H) and Paterson (2-P) Characteristics

A. A small dash completes the point of the lower portion of the upper left triangle in Paterson stamps. This characteristic does not exist on Hoyer & Ludwig stamps.

B. A strong horizontal line of color joining the "N" of "CONFEDERATE" to the outer curved line of the panel is common on Paterson stamps. Some postions on the Hoyer & Ludwig stone show an extremely fine line of dots in this area.

C. A break or near break in the curve over the "T" of "STATES" is common on the Hoyer & Ludwig stamps. This line is not broken on the Paterson stamps. This is a poor characteristic, as a number of positions on Hoyer prints show this break to be quite light.

D. There is a cross-bar in the "A" of "STATES" on Paterson stamps. This is not a constant characteristic and should not be seriously considered. There is no trace of the cross-bar on Hoyer & Ludwig prints.

E. Paterson prints show a ragged line around the "OF AMERICA" panel, particularly at the top of the lettering. On the Hoyer & Ludwig stamps there are, at most, a few dots.

Stone Y (2-Y) Characteristics

A. A small dash added to the point of the lower portion of the upper left triangle, is the classic Paterson distinguishing characteristic and is present on Stone Y.

B. The "N" of "CONFEDERATE" is not joined by a strong line to the outer curved line of the panel as on Paterson prints, though some Stone Y positions show an extremely faint line.

C. A break in the curve over the first "T" of "STATES" is present on Hoyer & Ludwig, but closed on Paterson; may be either open or closed on Stone Y.

D. The "A" of "STATES" usually does not show the cross-bar on either Stone Y or Hoyer & Ludwig prints, but it normally shows on Paterson prints.

E. The lines on the top of the panel "OF AMERICA", a major Paterson characteristic, is not present on Stone Y.

F. There is a small mark over the "OF" in "OF AMERICA" on Stone Y prints.

G. The classic Stone Y colorless flaw to the left of the head is usually present, but is not evident on many Stone Y prints.

H. A small > shaped mark slightly above and to the right of the mouth is not on Paterson or Hoyer & Ludwig prints, but present on some Stone Y prints.

I. A heavy mark above and somewhat to the right of Jefferson's eye differs from that on the Hoyer & Ludwig and Paterson prints, but is distinctive on some Stone Y prints.

J. The front lock of Jefferson's hair is incomplete on Stone Y prints. This is a major characteristic.

CSA 2-H
10¢ Blue - Hoyer & Ludwig

Printer: Hoyer & Ludwig of Richmond, Virginia
Master engraving by: Charles Ludwig, on metal
Vignette: Thomas Jefferson
Printing: Lithographed from more than one printing stone, each of 200 subjects consisting of two panes of 100
Plating: Plated to the transfer stone

Imprint: LITH. OF HOYER & LUDWIG, RICHMOND, VA.
Color: Shades of blue
Paper: White wove paper of varying thickness
Gum: Clear to light yellow or cream tone
Separations: Issued imperforate
Printing estimate: 1,403,000, based on incomplete records
Earliest recorded use: November 8, 1861
Largest known multiples: Unused block of 50, a pane of 100 was recorded in 1929, used strip of 7

A transfer stone was laid down for the 10¢ Hoyer (2-H) from the master engraving as 50 units, five rows of ten subjects, as with all of the lithographs. The basic plating for the 10¢ Hoyer, which was printed in both blue (2-H) and rose (5), is identical with respect to the transfer stone characteristics. There are additional constant varieties that occurred when the printing stones were laid down.

Recent findings indicate that there was more than one printing stone for 2-H, probably two. Each pane has a similar printer's imprint under positions 45L and 46L, "LITH. OF HOYER & LUDWIG, RICHMOND, VA."

This stamp is known with private separations. See the Perforated and Rouletted Stamps section for more details.

Stamps

2-H	blue	700.	250.
2-Ha (2b)	dark blue	700.	250.
2-Hb	light blue	800.	300.
	Pair	1,500.	1000.
	Block of 4	3,500.	*3,500.*

Lith. of Hoyer & Ludwig, Richmond Va., Type 1

Lith. of Hoyer & Ludwig, Richmond Va., Type 2

Imprints

2-H-i1	Type 1, G of LUDWIG vertically aligned between pos. 45 and 46 Lower Setting per single stamp*	1,850.	1,500.
2-H-i2	Type II, E of HOYER vertically aligned between pos. 45 and 46 Lower Setting per single stamp*	*5,500.*	NR

*Although the imprint appears under a pair of stamps, the price is for a single stamp with a partial imprint as most known copies are singles. A multiple with the full imprint would command a substantial premium.

Varieties listed as 1 of 50 are on the transfer stone and appear on 2-H and 5.

TEN appears as ZEN, pos. 4, 2-H-v1

GE of POSTAGE joined, pos. 10, 2-H-v2

White arrow, third spiked ornament on right, 2-H-v3

Period between TEN and CENTS, pos. 24, 2-H-v4

Shooting star, pos. 14, 2-H-v5

White Mouth, pos. 32, 2H-v6

Stamps touching, pos. 41-42 touching 1-2, 2-H-v7

Circular flaw, 2-H-v8

Varieties

2-H-v1	TEN appears as ZEN, pos. 4 (1 of 50) same as 5-v1	850.	275.
2-H-v2	GE of POSTAGE joined, pos. 10 (1 of 50) same as 5-v2	850.	275.
2-H-v3	White arrow, third spiked ornament at right, pos. 45 (1 of 50) same as 5-v3	850.	275.
2-H-v4	Period between TEN and CENTS, pos. 24 (1 of 50) same as 5-v4	850.	275.
2-H-v5	Shooting star, pos. 14 (1 of 50)	850.	275.
2-H-v6	White mouth, constant, not on all transfer units (1 of +200)	1,450.	1,000.
2-H-v7	Stamps touching, pos. 1- 2 and 41-42, block of 4	*9,500.*	NR
2-H-v8	Circular flaw, upper left star, pos. 11, similar to pos. 14	850.	275.

Covers

Single	450.
Pair	2,000.
Block of four	*5,500.*
Government imprint, semi-official	750.
Patriotic	2,500.
Wallpaper	1,500.

Markings (as a percent, plus or minus, of the price)

	off cover	**on cover**
Blue town	+20%	+30%
Red town	+50%	+50%
November 1861 postmark	+100%	+200%
Grid or target	+20%	+30%
Paid or numeral	+30%	+200%
Arkansas town	+100%	+300%
Florida town	+150%	+400%
Kentucky town	NR	+600%
Tennessee town	+50%	+100%
Texas town	+50%	+200%
West Virginia town	+200%	+600%
Straightline town	+200%	+600%
Express company	+200%	+800%
Railroad	+200%	+500%
Steam or Steamboat	+200%	+800%
Pen cancel	-75%	-20%

CSA 2-P
10¢ Blue - Paterson

Printer: J. T. Paterson Co. of Augusta, Georgia
Master engraving by: Charles Ludwig, on metal
Vignette: Thomas Jefferson
Printing: Lithographed from more than one printing stone of 200 subjects each consisting of two panes of 100
Plating: Complete as to the transfer stone positions
Imprint: J. T. Paterson & Co. Augusta Ga.
Color: Shades of light blue with a few examples in shades of dark blue
Paper: Porous white wove paper of varying thickness
Gum: Clear to a light yellow or cream tone
Separations: Issued imperforate
Printing estimate: 4,918,000
Earliest recorded use: July 25, 1862
Largest known multiples: Unused pane of 100, unused block of 50, used block of 6

The image used for the preparation of the 10¢ Paterson stamps is the same as that used by Hoyer & Ludwig, (2-H). It may have been taken from the master; more likely it was from an impression taken from either the transfer stone or a printing stone, as it does not show the detail expected from an impression from the original engraving. This image was changed slightly and can be distinguished from the Hoyer & Ludwig design.

The imprint of "J. T. Paterson & Co. Augusta Ga." appears at the bottom of each pane under positions 95 and 96. One recorded block does not show this imprint, indicating it either came from a new printing stone or the imprint was removed or later added.

Indigo, 2-Pc

Vertical gutter between panes, 2-Pd

Stamps

2-P (2)	blue	300.	250.
2-Pa (2*a*)	light blue	300.	250.
2-Pb (2*b*)	dark blue, various shades	NR	*1,000.*
2-Pc (2*c*)	indigo	NR	*4,250.*
	Pair	1,000.	700.
	Block of 4	2,500.	*4,500.*
2-Pd	Pair with vertical gutter (5 recorded)	*5,000.*	NR

Imprint J. T. Paterson & Co. Augusta Ga.

Imprints

2-P-i1	Single with imprint, pos. 45 and 46 Lower Settings (1 of +100)	1,250.	1,650.
2-P-i2	Block of 9 from imprint position, but no imprint	*9,000.*	NR

Star in O of POSTAGE, 2-P-v1

White pearls, varieties, transient, 2-P-v2

Varieties

2-P-v1	Star in O of POSTAGE, pos. 25 (1 of 50)	500.	275.
2-P-v2	White pearls surround vignette, various, transient	600.	300.

Printed on both sides, 2-P-w1 Ga.

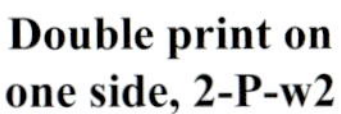

Double print on one side, 2-P-w2

Printed on both sides, two impressions on one, 2-P-w3

Printer's Waste

2-P-w1 (2*d*)	Stamp printed on both sides	NR	*2,000.*
2-P-w2	Double print on one side	NR	2,000.
2-P-w3	Double print on one side, single print on other	NR	2,000.
2-P-w4	Stamps and Currency printed on one side, currency on other, unique	*25,000.*	NR

Covers

Single	450.
Pair	1,000.
Government imprint, semi-official	750.
Patriotic	2,000.
Wallpaper	1,500.

Markings (as a percent, plus or minus, of the price)

	off cover	**on cover**
Blue town	+20%	+30%

Red town	+50%	+50%
Green town	+100%	+200%
Violet town	+100%	+200%
July 1862 postmark	+100%	+200%
Grid or target	+20%	+30%
Paid or numeral	+30%	+200%
Arkansas town	+100%	+300%
Florida town	+75%	+200%
Texas town	+50%	+200%
Tennessee town	+50%	+100%
West Virginia	+200%	+500%
Express company	+300%	+500%
Railroad	+200%	+500%
Steam or Steamboat	+200%	+500%
Pen cancel	-75%	-20%

CSA 2-Y
10¢ Blue - Stone Y

Printer: J. T. Paterson Co. of Augusta, Georgia
Master engraving by: Charles Ludwig, on metal
Vignette: Thomas Jefferson
Printing: Lithographed from a printing stone of 200 subjects consisting of two panes of 100
Plating: Incomplete
Imprint: None
Color: Shades of light blue
Paper: Thick porous white wove paper
Gum: Light yellow or cream tone
Separations: Issued imperforate
Printing estimate: not determined
Earliest recorded use: August 25, 1862
Largest known multiples: Unused block of 15 and used blocks of 8 and 6

The image for this stamp was probably taken from a well-used Paterson printing stone or perhaps a deteriorated transfer stone. For 2-Y a new transfer stone of 50 subjects having five rows of ten images was prepared. The image does not appear to have any intentional changes in the design. Some form of flaw to the left of the Jefferson's head is usually, though not always, present. A flaw in the front lock of Jefferson's hair appears more definitive than the classic head flaw. The details of these flaws are not constant in the various positions on the transfer stone.

The overall quality of the printing for this stamp is poor and the stamp appears crude, especially compared with Hoyer & Ludwig printings (2-H).

Stamps

2-Ya	light blue	1,100.	250.
2-Yb (2-e)	light greenish blue	1,500.	325.
	Pair	*4,000.*	1,200.
	Block of 4	*15,000.*	*7,500.*

Covers

Single	450.
Pair	2,500.
Patriotic	2,000.
Wallpaper	1,500.

Markings (as a percent, plus or minus, of the price)

	off cover	**on cover**
Blue town	+20%	+30%
Red town	+50%	+50%
Green town	+75%	+100%
Violet town	+75%	+100%
Grid or target	+20%	+30%
Arkansas town	+100%	+300%
Florida town	+150%	+400%
Tennessee town	+50%	+100%
Texas town	+50%	+200%
Straightline town	NR	NR
Pen cancel	-75%	-20%

CSA 3
2¢ Green

Five and ten cents stamps were printed and distributed in the fall of 1861 to meet the basic need for postage stamps. However, there was still a need for a 2¢ stamp to pay the drop letter rate and for newspapers, circulars, pamphlets and periodicals.

In the spring of 1862, a master die for the 2¢ green stamp (3) was prepared by Charles Ludwig of the firm of Hoyer & Ludwig in Richmond, Virginia.

The stamp is plated with respect to the transfer stone and in some cases to the panes on the printing stone.

Printer: Hoyer & Ludwig of Richmond, Virginia
Master engraving by: Charles Ludwig, on metal
Vignette: Andrew Jackson
Printing: Lithographed from a single printing stone of 200 subjects consisting of two panes of 100
Plating: Transfer stone plated
Imprint: None
Color: Shades of green
Paper: White wove paper of varying thickness
Gum: Clear to light yellow and cream
Separations: Issued imperforate
Printing estimate: 738,000, based on incomplete original records
Earliest recorded use: March 21, 1862.
Largest surviving multiples: Unused block of 24, used block of 10; a pane of 100 was known in the 1920s but since broken up

A transfer stone was laid down for the 2¢ green (3) from the master engraving as 50 units, five rows of ten subjects, as with all of the lithographs. There are additional constant varieties that occurred when the printing stone was laid down, thus some positions have a rarity of 1 of 50 and others 1 of 200.

Vertical gutter pair, 3e

Stamps

3 (3)	green	1,000.	750.
3a (*3a*)	bright yellow green	2,000.	2,000.
3b	light green	900.	600.
3c	dark green	1000.	850.
3d	dull yellow green	950.	800.
	Pair	2,250.	1,750.
	Block of 4	6,250.	7,500.
3e	Pair, with vertical gutter	4,750.	5,500.

Dash between stamps, 3-v1

Left top-knot. 3-v2

Right top-knot, 3-v3

Short transfers, 3-v4 and 3-v5

Spur, 3-v6

Streak of printer's ink, transient, 3-v8

Varieties

3-v1	Dash between pos. 4-5 (1 in 50), pair	2,500.	2,500.
3-v2	Left top-knot, pos. 31R (1 in 50)	1,250.	850.
3-v3	Right top-knot, pos. 30L (1 in 50)	1,250.	850.
3-v4	Short transfer, pos. 95L (1 in 200)	1,750.	1,250.
3-v5	Short transfer, pos. 96L (1 in 200)	1,500.	1,000.
3-v6	Spur, upper left, pos. 60L	1,250.	850.
3-v7	Blank area, transient flaw (many varieties)	1,250.	850.
3-v8	Streak of printer's ink, transient	1,050.	800.

Covers

Single, drop letter	2,750.
Single on single-sheet printed circular	3,500.
Single, newspaper use	*9.500.*
Single, booklet use	*12,000.*
Three stamps, one a bisect (5¢ rate)	*15,000.*
Strip of 5 to make 10¢ rate	7,500.
Wallpaper	4,250.

Markings (as a percent, plus or minus, of the price)

	off cover	on cover
Blue town	+20%	+30%
Red town	+50%	+50%
Grid or target	+20%	+30%
Arkansas town	+100%	+300%
Texas town	+200%	+300%
Express Company	+200%	+600%
Railroad	NR	NR
Pen cancel	-75%	-20%

5¢ Blue Lithograph

New printing stones were laid down for the printing of the 5¢ blue stamp. These are designated as Stone 2 (4-2) and Stone 3 (4-3). The designations start with Stone 2 because this stone was prepared from the same transfer stone used to prepare the 5¢ green Stone 2 and is the most common. Stone 3 can be difficult to distinguish from Stone 2.

CSA 4-2
5¢ Blue - Stone 2

Printer: Hoyer & Ludwig of Richmond, Virginia
Master engraving by: Charles Ludwig, on metal
Vignette: Jefferson Davis
Printing: Lithographed from at least three printing stones of 200 subjects each consisting of two panes of 100
Plating: Transfer stone plated
Imprint: No printers imprint
Color: Light to a dark blue
Paper: White wove paper of varying thickness
Gum: Clear to light and medium yellow
Separations: Issued imperforate
Printing estimate: 6,762,000 for Stones 2 and 3 based on incomplete records
Earliest recorded use: February 26, 1862
Largest known multiples: Unused part sheet of 197, used block of 4

The printing stones used for the blue Stone 2 stamps (4-2) were prepared from the same transfer stone as the green Stone 2 stamps (1-2). There is no indication that any blue Stone 2 stamps were printed from the same printing stone as the green. The printing stone arrangement is the same for both stamps; two panes of 100 consisting of two transfer stone units of 50 for a sheet of 200 stamps.

Plating of transfer Stone 2 is complete and is the same for both the 5¢ blue (4-2) and green stamps (1-2). The plating characteristics for each transfer stone position are more evident in the blue printing than the green printing. A detailed plating appeared in *The Confederate Philatelist* in an intermittent series of articles in Volume 11, No. 8 through Volume 13, No. 2, November 1966 – April 1968.

See the section on Misplaced and Shifted Transfers for details on some of these varieties from Transfer Stone 2.

Vertical Gutter between panes, 4-2d

At least two printing stones were used for 4-2, as established by the gutter spacing. However, at least one additional printing stone was used, as evidenced by the mysterious misplaced transfers on what is called Plate X. See the section on Misplaced and Shifted Transfers for details on this variety.

Stamps

4-2 (4)	blue	200.	125.
4-2a (4*a*)	dark blue	250.	140.
4-2b (4*b*)	milky blue	350.	175.
4-2c	light blue on thin hard paper	450.	350.
	Pair	400.	275.
	Block of 4	1,000.	*5,500.*
4-2d	Pair with vertical gutter, narrow or wide spacing (*e.g.*, pos. 10-1, 20-12, etc.)	1,000.	3,500.
4-2e	Pair having horizontal separation, upper and lower transfer positions such as 41-1, etc.	700.	NR

The varieties listed as 1 of 50 are on the transfer stone and also appear on the green printing, 1-2. The varieties listed as one in +200 are constant varieties, created when another printing stone was laid down. These varieties are not on the transfer stone. The + indicates at least two printing stones were used, but the relative quantity of stamps printed from each is not known. See the section on Misplaced and Shifted Transfers for other varieties.

Spur, upper left scroll, 4-2-v1

Lines in shirt, 4-2-v2

Cut in right inner oval, 4-2-v3

Major bottom clip, 4-2-v4

Minor bottom clip, 4-2-v5

Gooseneck, lower right, 4-2-v7

Large blob, upper right, 4-2-v8

Large white spots, transient, 4-2-v9

Varieties

4-2-v1	Spur, upper left scroll, pos. 21 (1 of 50) same as 1-2-v1	235.	175.
4-2-v2	Lines in shirt, pos. 5 (1 of 50) same as 1-2-v2	235.	175.
4-2-v3	Cut in right inner oval, pos. 10 (1 of 50) same as 1-2-v3	235.	175.
4-2-v4	Major clip, pos. 44R (1 of +200)	550.	*300.*
4-2-v5	Minor clip, pos. 43R (1 of +200)	450.	*250.*
4-2-v6	Lesser varieties of 4-2-v4 & v5, different positions	300.	225.
4-2-v7	Gooseneck, pos. 25 (1 of 50)	300.	225.
4-2-v8	Blob UR corner pos. 40 (1 of +400)	450.	300.
4-2-v9	Large white spots, various & transient	300.	225.
4-2-v10	Printer's ink smudge, transient	225.	150.
4-2-M	See Misplaced and Shifted Lithograph Transfers		

Cammann, 4-2-i1

Imprint and Inscriptions

4-2-i1	"Cammann"inscription, between pos. 31R and 40L (one recorded)	NR *15,000.*

Covers

Single on cover	300.
Pair on cover	550.
Government imprint, semi-official	750.
Patriotic cover	2,000.
Wallpaper cover	1,200.

Markings (as a percent, plus or minus, of the price)

	off cover	**on cover**
Blue town	+25%	+30%
Red town	+50%	+50%
February or March 1862 postmark	+100%	+200%
Fancy killer	+50%	+250%
Grid or target	+25%	+25%
Paid or numeral	+30%	+250%
Arkansas town	+40%	+300%
Florida town	+50%	+250%
Texas town	+40%	+200%
Straightline town	+100%	+200%
Express company	+150%	+600%
Steam or Steamboat	+200%	+400%
Pen cancel	-75%	-25%

[*italic*] value typeface indicating the item is difficult to price accurately

NR used in place of value when no examples have been recorded

CSA 4-3
5¢ Blue - Stone 3

Stone 3 (CSA 4-3) was prepared from a new transfer stone consisting of 50 positions, five rows of ten subjects, each taken from the 5¢ master die. In laying down this transfer stone, more care was taken in trimming the edges of the impressions from the master die than with the Stone 2 stamps. As a result, the various clips and cuts on the perimeter that are quite common for Stone 2 are seldom encountered with Stone 3.

With practice, most stamps printed from Stone 3 can be identified from the clarity of the impression and the shades of blue. Positive Stone 3 identification requires plating.

Printer: Hoyer & Ludwig of Richmond, Virginia
Master engraving by: Charles Ludwig, on metal
Vignette: Jefferson Davis
Printing: Lithographed from a printing stone of 200 subjects consisting of two panes of 100
Plating: Printing stone plated
Imprint: none
Color: Light milky to dark blue
Paper: White wove paper of varying thickness
Gum: Clear to light and medium yellow
Separations: Issued imperforate
Printing estimate: 6,762,000 for Stones 2 and 3, based on incomplete records
Earliest recorded use: April 10, 1862
Largest known multiples: Unused dark blue block of 40, unused milky blue block of 6, used milky blue block of 4, used strip of 7

Stamps

4-3	light blue	750.	175.
4-3a (4*a*)	dark blue	1,000.	200.
4-3b (4*b*)	milky blue	1,450.	225.
	Pair	1,800.	600.
	Block of 4	*9,000.*	*10,000.*
	Pair with vertical gutter	*6,000.*	*4,500.*
	Block of 4 with vertical gutter	*12,500.*	NR

CE of CENTS joined, 4-3-v1

Leaking N, 4-3v3

Clipped transfer, 4-3-v4

Varieties

4-3-v1	Top of CE of CENTS joined, pos. 33 (1 of 50)	850.	350.
4-3-v2	Flying bird, pos. 19 (1 of 50)	850.	350.
4-3-v3	Leaking N, pos. 1 (1 of 50)	1,000.	350.
4-3-v4	Clipped, pos. 21UR (1 of 200)	*2,500.*	NR

Covers

Single	300.
Pair	1,200.
Government imprint, semi-official	750.
Patriotic	2,000.
Wallpaper	1,200.

Markings (as a percent, plus or minus, of the price)

	off cover	on cover
Blue town	+30%	+30%
Red town	+30%	+50%
April 1862 postmark	+100%	+200%
Bar killer	+10%	+25%
Fancy killer	+50%	+150%
Paid or numeral	+30%	+250%
Express company	+150%	+500%
Steam or Steamboat	+150%	+300%
Pen cancel	-75%	-25%

CSA 5
10¢ Rose

This stamp was printed by Hoyer & Ludwig of Richmond, Virginia. The plating of the 10¢ rose is the same as for the 10¢ blue (2-H), as they originate from the same transfer stone. It is not known if the 10¢ rose (5) was printed from the same printing stone as the 10¢ blue (2-H); this can be determined as more vertical gutter multiples become available for study.

See Misplaced and Shifted Lithograph Transfers for details on some of these 10¢ rose stamps.

Printer: Hoyer & Ludwig of Richmond, Virginia
Master engraving by: Charles Ludwig, on metal
Vignette: Thomas Jefferson
Printing: Lithographed from a printing stone of 200 subjects with two panes of 100
Plating: Transfer stone plated
Imprint: LITH. OF HOYER & LUDWIG, RICHMOND, VA.
Color: Shades of rose to carmine
Paper: White wove paper of varying thickness
Gum: Clear to light yellow or cream tone
Separations: Issued imperforate
Printing estimate: 1,151,000 based on incomplete records
Earliest recorded use: March 10, 1862
Largest known multiples: unused block of 10, used block of 6

Stamps printed in a light salmon color are on a thin almost translucent paper. No private separations are recorded for this stamp. There are several replaced or shifted transfers on the printing stone. See Misplaced and Shifted Lithograph Transfers for a listing of these mysterious stamps.

Stamps

5 (5)	rose	1,300.	500.
5a	dull rose	1,400.	550.
5b	brown rose	1,600.	600.
5c	salmon	1,800.	700.
5d	carmine rose	2,250.	1,100.
5e (*5a*)	carmine	*5,000.*	2,250.
	Pair	3,500.	2,000.
	Gutter pair	NR	*4,000.*
	Block of 4	*12,000.*	*10,000.*

Scratched Stone, 5-v5

Varieties

5-v1	TEN appears as ZEN, pos. 4 (1 of 50), same as 2-H-v1	1,500.	550.
5-v2	GE of POSTAGE joined, pos. 10 (1 of 50), same as 2-H-v2	1,500.	550.
5-v3	White arrow, third spiked ornament on right, pos. 45 (1 of 50), same as 2-H-v3	1,500.	550.
5-v4	Shooting star position, pos. 14 (1 of 50), same as 2-H-v4	1,500.	550.
5-v5	Scratched stone (pos. 40, 39, 49 and 48) (each, 1 of 200)	1,850.	750.

Note: Shifted transfers, see Misplaced and Shifted Lithograph Transfers

Printer's imprint, 5-i1

Cammann inscription, 5-i2

C in gutter, 5-i3

Imprint and Inscriptions

5-i1	Imprint, on one stamp (1 of 100)	3,250.	1,750.
	Imprint, pair showing full imprint (1 of 100), imprint identical to 2-H-i1	8,500.	NR
5-i2	"Cammann" inscription showing most of the name, nearest pos. 50	NR	*12,500.*
5-i3	Most of top of "C" of "Cammann"showing, nearest pos. 41	NR	4,000.

Note: "Cammann" appears in the gutter between pos. 50 and 41

Covers

Single on cover	850.
Pair on cover	2,750.
Government imprint, semi-official	1,500.
Patriotic	3,000.
Wallpaper cover	2,500.

Markings (as a percent, plus or minus, of the price)

	off cover	**on cover**
Blue town	+30%	+30%
Red town	+50%	+50%
Green town	NR	NR
March 1862 postmark	+100%	+200%
Grid or target	+30%	+50%
Arkansas town	+50%	+100%
Florida town	+75%	+150%
Tennessee town	+30%	+50%
Texas town	+50%	+75%
Straightline town	+75%	0%
Express company	NR	+500%
Steam or Steamboat	NR	+500%
Pen cancel	-75%	-25%

Misplaced and Shifted Lithograph Transfers

CSA 1-2-M & 4-2-M Misplaced Transfers

A misplaced transfer is an image that is on a printing stone in a position that differs from that on the transfer stone. In the example that follows, a horizontal pair, both stamps are positions 3 on the transfer stone; at least one of these positions is a misplaced transfer on the printing stone, perhaps both are.

The misplaced transfers were first discovered in the 1920s by Edward S. Knapp and others. They were originally thought to be damaged positions that had been erased and replaced on the printing stones that were in stamp production. Although this is a viable explanation, it now appears that they were on new printing stones and were corrections made when the printing stones were initially laid down.

The known 5¢ misplaced transfers all originate with Transfer Stone 2. This was the last 5¢ transfer stone made and was used to produce more printing stones than any other for both the green and blue printings. The exact alignment of the transfer stone units on each printing stone proves there were multiple printing stones and that the green stamps were not printed from the same stones as the blue stamps. No specific blue or green misplaced transfer is known to exist in the other color.

Only one or two copies are known of most of the misplaced transfers. This is partly because they are rare, but also because they must be plated to prove their status as misplaced transfers. The rarity is substantiated by an extremely evident example, the famous Twin Scroll, position 1 in place of position 10UL. Only four examples of this variety are known; census numbers 1-2-m1 through m4 (see census table in this section). This variety is well illustrated in *The Postal Service of the Confederate States of America* by August Dietz, 1929, page 105, and later Dietz catalogs. To date, only 24 misplaced transfer stamps have been identified; 16 in green and 8 in blue as collectible items.

5¢ Green, Stone 2, positions 3 & 3, 1-2-M10

5¢ Green, Twin Scroll, position 1 over 10, UL pane, 1-2-M2

Twin Scroll, 5¢ green, position 1 placed over position 10, apparently was done to improve the vertical alignment of the setting. In laying down Transfer Stone 2 the top row, positions 1-10 are closer together than the remaining 4 rows. In order to properly align the stamps, position 10 was replaced on all 4 stone positions on one printing stone. The other three such replacements, upper right, lower left and lower right, are less evident and do not show the Twin Scroll. Probably for that reason only one example of the other replacements is recorded to date.

For the normal Transfer Stone 2, position 10 is evidently out of line with respect to the right vertical column of each pane. For one printing stone, the misplaced transfers are an evident attempt to improve the alignment. All four positions 10 are replaced. For the UL the replacement was position 1 and for the UR the replacement was position 35. The LL and LR were replaced with positions 3 and 25, but it is not known which is L and which is R.

An impossible position is a position that can not be in the same position that it is on the transfer stone, though there is only a single stamp to prove the possible location. As an example, a copy of position 5 would have stamps on three sides and could show a sheet margin on the top. If this position 5 had a sheet margin on the left, right or bottom side it could not be a normal stamp on the printing stone, rather it must be a misplaced transfer.

5¢ Blue, Impossible Positions, position 37 with a right sheet margin, 4-2-M7

The 5¢ blue, Stone 2, Plate X represents an especially interesting misplaced transfer. For one UR pane on the top row, position 10 was replaced by position 40 and for the second row positions 12 – 20 were replaced with 42 – 50. Two unused blocks, a used pair and a used single are known from Plate X. Other 5¢ blue misplaced transfers may also be from this plate.

Many of the misplaced transfers and shifted transfers are unique, their status is proven by the relation to other attached stamps in surviving multiples. Information provided in the census of known examples below is useful in helping validate other possible examples. The numbers are census numbers and not catalog numbers. In several cases there are two numbers for the same misplaced transfer, which represent different items in the census.

Over the years, auction catalogs have often described multiples coming from the joining of the upper and lower transfer units that show poor alignment and even cuts into the design as misplaced transfers. They are interesting and constant varieties, but they are not misplaced transfers. For example, a vertical pair that is position 44 over 4 is a normal combination for the separation between the upper and lower transfer stone units, despite the misalignment. The misplaced transfers are significant as they are both constant varieties and were deliberately made though we can only speculate on the reason.

5¢ Blue, Plate X, 4-2-M3

Misplaced Transfers, CSA 1-2-M & 4-2-M

Census Numbers	Name or Description	Transfer Stone Positions	Printing Stone Positions	Number of Stamps In unit	Notes
1-2-M1	Twin Scrolls	1	10 UL	1	Used; single; cds
1-2-M2	Twin Scrolls	1	10 UL	1	Unused; single
1-2-M3	Twin Scrolls & 11	1/11	10/20 UL	2	Fredericksburg, Va; Mar 27
1-2-M4	Twin Scrolls & 11	1/11	10/20 UL	32	Unused; block 32
1-2-M5	Impossible	9-35	9-10 UR	2	Norfolk, Va; Jan 7, 1862
1-2-M6	Duplicate Scrolls	21	?	1	Oxford, Miss; March 7, 1862
1-2-M7		35	10 top sheet	1	Montgomery, Ala; May 14, 1862
1-2-M8	Impossible	49-50/9-3	10 LL	4	Unused; block
1-2-M9	Impossible	9-25	9-10 LR	2	Monticello, Ga; Dec 31
1-2-M10	Twin Positions	3-3	?	2	Richmond, Va; Feb 25, 1862
1-2-M11	Impossible Margin	5	L sheet margin vertical	1	Wilmington, NC; Jan 26, 1862
1-2-M12	Impossible Vertical	7-2/17-12	misplaced	4	Warrington, Fla.; Feb 4
		20	20	1	Used; grid cancel
1-2-M13	Shadow Line	50	?	1	Unused; single
1-2-M14	Shadow Line	50	?	1	Fayetteville, NC; Apr 1862
1-2-M15	Impossible	19-41	?	2	Petersburg, Va.
1-2-M16	Impossible	13/30	?	2	Unused; vertical pair
4-2-M1	Printing Stone X	9-2	?	2	Richmond, Va; Jun 6, 1862
4-2-M2	Printing Stone X	9-2	?	2	Montgomery, Tex; Aug 1862
4-2-M3	Printing Stone X	3-9,40/46-50	3-10/16-20	13	Unused; block of 13
4-2-M4	Printing Stone X	2-5/42-45	2-5/12-15	8	Unused; block of 8
4-2-M5	Printing Stone X	2/42	2-12	2	used, pen cancel; off cover
4-2-M6	Printing Stone X	40	10	1	Georgetown, SC; Jun 18, 1862
4-2-M7	Impossible Margin	37	R sheet	1	New Orleans, La; Apr 26, 1862
4-2-M8	Impossible	19-48		2	Winchester, Va; Oct 9; off cover

CSA 5-S
Shifted Transfers

For the 10¢ rose lithograph, there is something even more intriguing than the Stone 2, 5¢ green and blue misplaced transfers. For lack of a better name, they have been referred to as replaced or shifted transfers. They were first discovered in the 1920s by Edward S. Knapp and today are as much of a mystery as then.

10¢ Rose, Shifted Transfer at the Bottom, 5-S-2

They are given catalog status as they are definitely constant varieties; up to six examples of some positions are known. The study is hampered by the lack of multiples and the general scarcity of the 10¢ rose. For the 10¢ rose shifted transfer, there is only one known multiple and 20 singles. They are mostly the replacement of the 4th vertical column, positions 4, 14, 24, 34, and 44 plus a partial replacement of the 2nd vertical column, positions 12 and 42.

These stamps all appear to be the same positions entered in the proper transfer stone position, however they show some doubling with slight shifting of lines. The original theory is that they were erased positions on the printing stone and re-entered as the same positions. Another theory is that they were on a new printing stone and, in laying down the stone, there was a wrinkle in the transfer paper that accounts for some doubling. They are significant, as they are definite constant varieties and not transient ones.

Shifted Transfers, 10¢ Rose, CSA 5-S

Census Numbers	Transfer Stone Positions	Printing Stone Positions	Number Recorded
5-S-1	4	4	5
5-S-2	14	14	6
5-S-3	24	24	1
5-S-4	34	34	2
5-S-5	44	44	5
5-S-6	12	22	1
5-S-7	42	42	1

General Issues

The Typographed Stamps

In October 1861 Major Benjamin F. Ficklin, an agent of the Confederate government, was dispatched to Europe to obtain stamps, steel dies and plates for printing stamps of several denominations. Ficklin arrived in England at the end of October and quickly made an agreement with the firm of Thomas De La Rue & Company, Ltd. in London for stamps, printing plates, paper, ink, and a small perforating machine. Although it was the intention of Postmaster General Reagan to obtain steel plates for intaglio printing, Ficklin actually obtained hardened copper plates for typographic printing.

Original 5¢ De La Rue Die, courtesy of the British Library

The De La Rue contract was initially for 1¢ and 5¢ stamps to supply the common 5¢ rate and the 1¢ drop circular rate. J.F. Jubert de la Ferté engraved master steel dies for both values. From the master die of the 5¢ value, 100 impressions were made in lead. These individual impressions were locked into a frame, 10 x 10 and covered with graphite. A copper electrotype copy was then made to form a pane of 100. To complete the process, the copper shell was ultimately treated chemically to harden the surface and minimize wear.

Four panes of 100 subjects were joined together to form a plate of 400, backed with lead. The plate was then mounted on a lapped flat cast iron base in preparation for printing. The same process was used for the 1¢ stamp. The De La Rue records indicate the 1¢ was also a plate of 400, but the archival sheet found at De La Rue is only a half sheet of two panes totaling 200 subjects.

Plating positions for the typographed stamps are given for the 100 subject pane. The upper left stamp is position 1, upper right is position 10, second row upper left is position 11, second row upper right is position 20, and thus systematically continues to the lower right position 100. The four panes that make up a full sheet of 400 are designated UL, UR, LL and LR as shown in the illustration below.

Plate of 400 with position designations for the panes of 100

UL	UR
LL	LR

The typographic printing process involves printing from the raised lines that form the surface of the plate. These elevated areas receive ink on their surface, which is transmitted to the paper by means of contact and pressure. The area below the contact surface of the plate receives no ink in this process and thus appears colorless on the printed sheet.

The workmanship at De La Rue was of the highest quality. Virtually everything is perfect: the individual images, the alignment between the stamps and panes, and the quality of the stamps printed. The 1¢ (14) and the 5¢ (6) are of excellent quality. For the 1¢ and 5¢ stamp there were four shipments of stamps and other printing items from De La Rue.

The first shipment of 5¢ stamps was invoiced on January 30, 1862 and left from Southampton aboard the Confederate blockade runner *Nashville*. This shipment consisted of 2,150,000 5¢ stamps, a printing plate for the 5¢ stamp and one small perforating machine. The shipment arrived in Richmond and is confirmed on page 10 of John H. Reagan's *Report of the Postmaster General to the President, February 28th, 1862*, which states "2,150,000 5¢ stamps have just been received from Europe."

The second shipment was invoiced on February 11, 1862 and sent by Fraser, Trenholm and Co. This shipment consisted of 5,400,000 5¢ stamps.

The third shipment was the famous "lost shipment." It was invoiced on February 20, 1862 and left London on March 1, 1862 aboard the blockade runner *Bermuda*. It arrived at St. George, Bermuda on March 19 or 20. It sailed from St. George on April 23 and was captured April 27 by the U.S. Navy Ship *Mercedita*. The shipment of 4,855,000 5¢ stamps and a second printing plate for the 5¢ stamp were seized. The stamps were destroyed by court order. The plate was acquired by the Franklin Institute, Philadelphia in March 1954; prints were privately made on the order of Philip H. Ward, Jr. The Franklin Institute sold the plate to the Smithsonian National Postal Museum in April 2011.

The last shipment for the 1¢ & 5¢ stamps was invoiced on March 15, 1862 and shipped *circa* March 24, 1862. This shipment consisted of 400,000 1¢ stamps, a printing plate for the 1¢ stamps, a third printing plate for the 5¢ stamp, and a Super Royal printing press for stamps. The disposition of this shipment upon arrival in the Confederacy is unknown. There is no indication of a 1¢ plate arriving in the Confederacy.

Three 5¢ plates were made; one, if not two, arrived in the Confederacy. Charles J. Phillips studied these stamps and provides a detailed analysis in August Dietz's 1929 book, *The Postal Service of the Confederate States of America* (pages 161-62 and 181). He indicates De La Rue printed from two plates, but the Confederacy from only one.

The De La Rue records indicate the paper sent to the Confederacy for stamp production measured 22 x 18.25 inches and was described as glazed. The blue ink was always described as fugitive, meaning the ink would run if washed with a solvent.

CSA 6
5¢ Blue - London Printing

The stamps printed in London (6) were well printed in one specific shade of blue on a distinctive thin surfaced paper of European origin. There are no true plate varieties, but there are a few extremely minute plate marks. The pane positions within the sheet can only be established by sheet margins.

Defective printings are rare. The details of the design are extremely sharp. It can be somewhat difficult to distinguish the London Printing (6) from the Richmond (local) printing on London paper (7-L). On the local printing, the ink is often poorly mixed and is not the exact shade of the London printing. The gum is more of a brownish or yellowish shade. The Richmond printings (7-R) are always inferior prints. They exist in many shades of blue, the paper is of a thicker and poorer quality, and the gum is always a brownish shade. They are scarcer than either numbers 6 or 7-L.

The printing plates consist of 4 panes of 100 subjects to produce a sheet of 400. Evidence indicates that De La Rue used two plates to print this stamp. This helps explain the sharpness of impressions.

The De La Rue stamp shipments to the Confederacy were cut into panes of 100 and packaged in large envelopes. As a result, no gutter multiples exist.

[–]	symbol used in place of value to mean insufficient information to assign a price
[*italic*]	value typeface indicating the item is difficult to price accurately
NR	used in place of value when no examples have been recorded

CSA 6

Printer: Thomas De La Rue & Co., Ltd.; London, England
Master engraving by: J. F. Jubert de la Ferté on steel
Vignette: Jefferson Davis
Printing: Typographed from an electrotype plate of 400 subjects consisting of four panes of 100 subjects; two plates were used
Plating: Incomplete
Imprint: None
Color: Light blue
Paper: Thin surfaced paper
Gum: Clear to white
Separations: Imperforate
Printing Invoiced: 12,405,000 5¢ stamps. Only 7,405,000 were received by the CSA; 4,855,000 on the *Bermuda* were captured and ordered destroyed by Federal court order. Slight discrepancy in numbers noted.
Earliest recorded use: April 16, 1862
Largest known multiples: Unused pane of 100 and used block of 14.

Unused stamps are priced with gum. Gum problems such as brown spots or cracks are considered defects.

Stamps

6 (6)	light blue	30.	40.
	Pair	60.	100.
	Block of 4	120.	500.

Dent in outer frame, 6-v1

Poor printing, 6-v2

Varieties

6-v1	Small dent in outer frame, pos. 10UR	150.	95.
6-v2	Poor printing, transient	200.	150.

Covers

Single on cover prior to July 1, 1862	160.
Single on cover, overpaid drop rate	325.
Pair on cover	120.
Government imprint, semi-official	375.
Patriotic	1,400.
Wallpaper	700.

Markings (value as a percent, plus or minus, of the price)

	off cover	on cover
Blue town	+20 %	+30 %
Red town	+50 %	+50 %
Green town	+100 %	+200 %
April 1863 postmark	+100 %	+300 %
Grid or target	+20 %	+20 %
Paid or numeral	+100 %	+300 %
Arkansas town	+100 %	+300 %
Florida town	+200 %	+500 %
Texas town	+75 %	+200 %
Straightline	+100 %	+200 %
Express	+200 %	+800 %
Railroad	+200 %	+400 %
Steamboat	+200 %	+1,000 %
Pen cancel	-50 %	—

CSA 7-L

5¢ Blue, Richmond Printings on London Paper

Plates made in London by De La Rue were sent to Richmond along with a quantity of paper and ink. The Richmond printings on London paper are inferior to those done in London as to the quality of the impression and the exact shade of ink. The London printings have the fine horizontal lines around the portrait nearly perfect, as to being sharp and clear. On the Richmond printings these lines and others normally show imperfections such as small droplets of ink. The Richmond gum is always inferior, a brownish color and poorly distributed. None the less, it is difficult to distinguish CSA 6 from early printings of CSA 7-L, especially if no gum is present or used on cover.

Plate varieties on the Richmond printings are limited to the "white tie", scratched plate varieties, and damage in the outer frame for subjects on the perimeter of each pane. This damage sometimes causes the ink to blend into the solid color background eliminating the outer frame line. Brass rules were added to the top of the plate to minimize wear. These print as light parallel lines, with one or two lines showing beyond the edge of the plate. To date, they are only noted on the stamps on London paper, but should also exist on local paper printings.

There are a number of interesting transient printing varieties resulting from the presence or absence of ink. Such varieties are especially apparent in the inscription panels where an ink spot or bubble could easily change the appearance of one letter to another.

Printed in Richmond on London Paper, CSA 7-L

Printer: Archer & Daly of Richmond, Virginia
Master engraving by: J. F. Jubert de la Ferté on steel
Vignette: Jefferson Davis
Printing: Typographed from an electrotype plate of 400 subjects consisting of four panes of 100 subjects
Plating: Incomplete
Imprint: None
Color: Blue
Paper: Thin surfaced paper from Thomas De La Rue & Co., Ltd.; London, England
Gum: Clear to white
Separations: Imperforate
Printing estimate: 36,250,000 for 7-L and 7-R based on incomplete records
Earliest recorded use: July 13, 1862
Largest known multiples: unused half sheet of 200, used block of 12, strip of 8

Unused stamps are priced with gum. Gum problems such as brown spots or cracks are considered defects.

Vertical gutter between panes

Stamps

7-L (7)	light blue (similar to London color)	20.	30.
7-La (7a)	blue	25.	40.
	Pair	40.	75.
	Block of 4	80.	275.
	Horizontal pair with vertical gutter	200.	NR

White tie, 7-L-v1

Brass rules, 7-L-v2

Dent in outer frame, 7-L-v3

One outer frame filled in with ink, 7-L-v4

Two outer frames filled in with ink, 7-L-v5

FIVE as FoIVE, various transient, 7-L-v7

Varieties

7-L-v1	White tie, pos. 30 UR (1 of 400)	200.	250.
7-L-v2	Brass rules, top sheet margin	125.	NR
	block of 10	950.	NR
7-L-v3	Small dent in outer frame, pos. 10 UR (1 of 400)	125.	95.
7-L-v4	Outer frame line filled in with ink on one side, various	35.	50.
7-L-v5	Outer frame lines filled in with ink on two sides, various	150.	100.
7-L-v6 (7b)	Printed on both sides	1,750.	850.
7-L-v7	Various transient printing varieties		

Covers

Single on cover, overpaid drop rate	250.
Pair on cover	140.
Government imprint, semi-official	400.
Patriotic	1,200.
Wallpaper	750.

Markings (value as a percent, plus or minus, of the price)

	off cover	on cover
Blue town	+20 %	+30 %
Red town	+50 %	+50 %
Green town	+70 %	+100 %
Brown town	+70 %	+100 %
August 1863 postmark	+100 %	+300 %
Grid or target	+20 %	+20 %
Paid or numeral	+100 %	+300 %
Arkansas town	+100 %	+300 %
Florida town	+200 %	+500 %
Texas town	+75 %	+200 %
Straightline	+100 %	+200 %
Express	+200 %	+800 %
Railroad	+200 %	+400 %
Pen cancel	-50 %	—

CSA 7-R
5¢ Blue, Richmond Printing on Local Paper

As the supply of paper and ink from London ran out, supplies from local sources were used. This resulted in deterioration in the quality of the printed stamps. While the ink varied considerably, most stamps are darker blue shades. The locally obtained paper was thicker and more porous. The combination of poor ink and paper led to increased plate wear and further deterioration in the quality of the printed impressions. The inferior gum was poorly distributed and varied from shades of yellow to brownish.

Plate varieties on the Richmond printings on local paper are limited to the "white tie" and damage in the outer frame for subjects on the perimeter of each pane. This damage sometimes causes the ink to blend into the solid color background eliminating the outer frame line. There are a number of interesting transient printing varieties resulting from the presence or absence of ink. Such varieties are especially apparent in the inscription panels where an ink spot or bubble could easily change the appearance of one letter to another. One such variety is 7-R-v7 in which the "FIVE" appears to be "FLVE".

CSA 7-R

Printer: Archer & Daly of Richmond, Virginia
Master engraving by: J. F. Jubert de la Ferté on steel
Vignette: Jefferson Davis
Printing: Typographed from an electrotype plate of 400 subjects consisting of four panes of 100 subjects
Plating: Incomplete
Imprint: None
Color: Dark blue shades
Paper: Thick porous paper
Gum: Yellow to brownish, poorly distributed
Separations: Imperforate
Printing estimate: 36,250,000 for 7-L and 7-R based on incomplete records
Earliest recorded use: Unknown
Largest known multiples: Unused pane of 100, used block of 20 and used strip of 10

Unused stamps are priced with gum. Gum problems such as brown spots or cracks are considered defects.

White tie, 7-R-v1

Outer frame line filled in one side, 7-R-v2

Outer frame line filled in two sides, 7-R-v3

Printed on both sides, 7-R-v5

FIVE as FLVE, variety transient, 7-R-v7, etc.

Bottom of upper stamp not printed, 7-R-v8

Stamps

7-R (7)	blue	45.	35.
7-Ra	light blue	35.	30.
7-Rb (7a)	dark blue	45.	40.
	Pair	90.	75.
	Block of 4	200.	500.
	Horizontal pair with vertical gutter pair	—	—

Varieties

7-R-v1	White tie, pos. 30 UR, see 7-L-v1	275.	150.
7-R-v2	Outer frame line filled in with ink on one side, various	65.	55.
7-R-v3	Outer frame lines filled in with ink on two sides, various	160.	150.
7-R-v4	Brass rules	NR	NR
7-R-v5 (7b)	Printed on both sides	2,750.	1,750.
7-R-v6	Scratched plate, various	75.	75.
7-R-v7	Various transient printing varieties: Pop-eye, blind eye, FIVE GENTS, and FIVE appearing as: FbVE, FPVE, FLVE, OFIVE		
7-R-v8	Transient printing variety, part not printed at bottom		

Covers

Single on cover, overpaid drop rate	275.

Pair on cover	175.
Government imprint, semi-official	550.
Patriotic	1,250.
Wallpaper	750.
Trans-Mississippi, 40¢	7,500.
Trans-Mississippi, 50¢ preferred rate*	*9,000.*

***Note:** There is no evidence this 50¢ rate was officially implemented. There are several covers recorded paying this rate. The only recorded 50¢ preferred rate with CSA 7-R is a rebacked cover front.

Markings (value as a percent, plus or minus, of the price)

	off cover	on cover
Blue town	+20 %	+30 %
Red town	+50 %	+50 %
Green town	+100 %	+200 %
Brown town	+100 %	+200 %
April 1863 postmark	+100 %	+300 %
Grid or target	+20 %	+20 %
Paid or numeral	+50 %	+200 %
Arkansas town	+100 %	+300 %
Florida town	+200 %	+500 %
Texas town	+75 %	+200 %
Straightline	+100 %	+200 %
Express	+200 %	+800 %
Railroad	+200 %	+400 %
Pen cancel	-50 %	—

CSA 14
1¢ Orange

This stamp was ordered from the firm of De La Rue in London, England. The De La Rue order entry is dated March 15, 1862 and shipped *circa* March 24, 1862. The stamps were never issued, even though there was a one-cent rate for drop circulars and effective July 1, 1863 for all circulars, pamphlets and periodicals not exceeding one ounce in weight. The stamps appeared on the Confederate Post Office stamp order form, indicating they were held in inventory at Richmond.

No example saw postal service in the Confederacy. One partial pane was fashioned into an envelope and sent through the U.S. mail in the mid 1860s.

The printing plate consisted of four panes of 100, resulting in a printed sheet of 400 stamps. Prior to shipment to the Confederacy, the sheets were cut into panes of 100. No gutter multiples are known except for the one half proof sheet of two horizontal panes that was retained in London by De La Rue. This half sheet has since been broken up and is now in collector hands. The color of these stamps is slightly different from the delivered stamps, perhaps because the ink differed or the sheet was never gummed. The master die and the printing plate are lost.

CSA 14

Printer: Thomas De La Rue & Co., Ltd.; London, England
Master engraving by: J. F. Jubert de la Ferté on steel
Vignette: John C. Calhoun
Printing: Typographed from an electrotype plate of 400 subjects consisting of four panes of 100 subjects
Plating: Incomplete
Imprint: None
Color: Orange to deep orange
Paper: Thin surfaced paper
Gum: Clear to white
Separations: Imperforate
Printing Invoiced: 400,000 stamps
Earliest recorded use: Never issued, no used CSA postal examples known
Largest known multiples: Unused pane of 100

Unused stamps are priced with gum. Gum problems such as brown spots or cracks are considered defects.

1¢ Deep Orange, CSA 14a

Stamps

14 (14)	orange	120.	NA
14a (14a)	deep orange	225.	NA
	Pair	250.	NA
	Block of 4	500.	NA

General Issues

The Engraved Issues

Beginning with the first advertisements for postage stamps in February, 1861, Confederate Postmaster General John H. Reagan sought engraved, intaglio printed stamps equal to those produced by the North. Initially, they could not be obtained and Reagan had to be satisfied with lithographed and then typographed stamps. These were a concern because they were subject to forgery and could result in a loss of revenue to the Post Office Department.

In the Fall of 1861, John Archer, an engraver previously employed by the American Bank Note Company, arrived in Richmond and set up a printing business. He formed a partnership with Joseph D. Daly, a local plasterer, in the spring of 1862 and together they founded the firm of Archer & Daly. Daly was a man of some means and political influence. As a result, he was able to obtain the contract to print the typographed stamps from the plates supplied by De La Rue of London. The firm continued to produce typographed stamps until they were able to supply engraved stamps in quantity.

John Archer engraved the first three designs, the TEN, 10¢ Frame Line, and 10¢ Type I stamps. Another engraver, Frederick W. Halpin, arrived in Richmond in early 1863 and joined Archer & Daly. He engraved the 2¢, 10¢ Type II, and 20¢ stamps. Four of the six stamps were released for sale in mid-April 1863, indicating production started at least a month before the release.

The appearance of the four different engraved stamps is so close in time that one can only speculate as to the actual production sequence. There is one undisputable fact: the 2¢, TEN, 10¢ Frame Line and 20¢ stamps all have numerous evident defects in the entry of the images onto the plate. The 10¢ Type I and II stamps have almost no such defects. From this it can be assumed that experience was gained in making the plates for the first four stamps and the techniques were perfected before the 10¢ Type I and II plates were made.

Both the TEN and the 10¢ Frame Line stamps were printed from copper plates. Both could be considered trials, the "Premiere Gravures" of the Confederacy. Due to rapid wear, the copper plates could not sustain the quantities needed for the Confederacy and a plate size of 100 subjects for the TEN and the Frame Line was too small for economic printing. It is evident these two stamps were produced in limited quantities and only in early 1863.

It is reasonable to assume that the Post Office Department and the printer reached an agreement to go ahead and initially produce stamps from these trial plates, as well as the 10¢ Types I and II plates, in an effort to build the inventory as quickly as possible. The typographed plate in use by Archer & Daly was deteriorating and the lithographed stamps still in production were considered less than satisfactory. The Department was in need of as many engraved 10¢ stamps as possible for initial distribution in April of 1863.

All of the 10¢ engraved stamps use a portrait of Jefferson Davis for the vignette, though design details vary. On the TEN stamp, the value is spelled out. The Frame Line has ruled lines that create a box or frame around each stamp. It is not known which came first, the TEN or the 10¢ Frame Line.

The vignette of the TEN suggests it came first and was rejected. Legend is that the vignette of Davis bore too much of a resemblance to President Lincoln. For whatever reason, a new vignette of Davis was created and adopted for use on both the 10¢ Frame Line and the 10¢ Type I. Later, Frederick Halpin adapted the same design when he engraved the master die for the 10¢ Type II.

A small perforating machine obtained from De La Rue in England was used for some trials of the 10¢ Type I and II stamps, however, the machine was not designed for the mass production of stamps and was only used for limited trials. The small quantity of perforated 10¢ stamps produced was distributed with other 10¢ stamps. These are the only officially perforated stamps issued by the Confederate Post Office Department. (See also, Perforated and Rouletted Stamps section for more details)

CSA 8 2¢ Brown Red

The 2¢ brown red stamp was engraved on steel by Frederick W. Halpin. It was then transferred onto a single steel plate of 200 subjects consisting of two panes of 100 arranged 10 by 10. There is no printer's imprint. The stamp was printed by Archer & Daly on white wove paper of varying thickness. The stamps range in color from brown red to rose. The gum is colorless. The stamps were issued imperforate.

Apparently there was some difficulty in preparing the printing plate, as the die was not uniformly impressed into the plate. This is most noticeable in the short transfers in which a line or two of the design are not present. There are also a number of double transfer varieties, usually in the words "POSTAGE" or "TWO CENTS". There are also a number of short transfers on the sides in which a line or two are not present. For the left pane, there are evident varieties on positions 37, 91 and 92 and for the right pane on positions 1, 5, 18, 36, 38, 50, 59 and 63 as well as others that are not quite as evident. There are a number of short transfers which are quite small, but still valid plate varieties. The lightly scribed grid that appears on some printings of the 20¢ does not appear on this stamp. This stamp can and should be plated, especially before the remaining panes are broken up.

Caution: The 2¢ brown red stamp was not commonly used for postage and quantities of unused stamps remained after the war. Used examples are much scarcer than unused ones. Examples exist on and off cover with forged cancellations. To be valued as a used stamp, on or off cover, the cancellation must be recognizable and proven authentic. A stamp or cover with a smudge of ink or dirt or an illegible marking is not valued as a used stamp.

Printer: Archer & Daly of Richmond, Virginia
Engraving by: Frederick Halpin on steel
Vignette: Andrew Jackson
Printing: Intaglio from a steel plate of 200 subjects arranged as two panes of 100
Plating: Incomplete, but possible
Imprint: None
Color: Brown red to rose
Paper: White wove paper of varied thickness
Gum: Colorless
Separations: Issued Imperforate
Printing estimate: 1,636,000 based on incomplete records
Earliest recorded use: April 21, 1863
Largest known multiples: Unused sheet of 200, used block of 12 and used strip of 10

Unused stamps are priced with gum. Gum problems such as brown spots or cracks are considered defects.

Gutter pair, 8

Stamps

8 (8)	brown red	70.	200.
8a (8a)	pale rose	90.	250.
	Pair	150.	600.
	Block of 4	325.	1,500.
	Horizontal pair with vertical gutter	300.	NR
	Block of 4, with vertical gutter	650.	NR

Double Transfer in POSTAGE, 8-v1

Double Transfer to right, 8-v2

Double Transfer in TWO CENTS, 8-v3

Short Transfer on right, 8-v4

Double Transfer in POSTAGE and TWO CENTS, 8-v5

Double Transfer in left "2", 8-v6

Varieties

8-v1	Double transfer in "POSTAGE", pos. 1R	250.	275.
8-v2	Short transfer to right, pos. 38R	200.	275.
8-v3	Double transfer in "TWO CENTS", pos. 36R	200.	275.
8-v4	Double transfer on right, pos. 91L	250.	275.
8-v5	Double transfer in "POSTAGE", "TWO CENTS", and entire subject out of line, pos. 92LP	350.	375.
8-v6	Double transfer in left "2", pos. 50R	250.	275.

Covers

Single, drop rate	1,250.
Other 2¢ rates	*3,000.*
Strip of five to pay 10¢ rate	5,000.
Government imprint, semi-official	*2,500.*
Wallpaper	2,500.

[–]	symbol used in place of value to mean insufficient information to assign a price
[*italic*]	value typeface indicating the item is difficult to price accurately

Markings (as a percent, plus or minus, of the price)

	off cover	on cover
Blue town	+30%	+30%
Red town	+50%	+50%
April, 1863	+100%	+300%
Grid or target	+20%	+20%
Paid or numeral	+100%	+200%
Arkansas town	+200%	+300%
Railroad	+200%	+300%
Pen cancel	-75%	-40%

CSA 9 10¢ Blue - TEN

This stamp is distinctive because the value is spelled out in letters instead of numerals, TEN. All other Confederate stamps have the value in numerals. The TEN stamp was engraved on steel by John Archer. It was then transferred onto a single copper plate of 100 subjects arranged 10 x 10. In his 1929 book, August Dietz speculated that the plate had 200 subjects; there is no evidence to support this. There is no printer's imprint. The stamp was printed by Archer & Daly on white wove paper of varying thickness. The stamps are blue, ranging in shades from a light to milky and gray blue. The gum ranges from colorless to a light yellow. The stamps were issued imperforate; no private separations are known.

The use of a copper plate indicates this issue was produced as a trial or experiment. The quantity printed was rather small and distribution was not widespread.

Printer: Archer & Daly of Richmond, Virginia
Engraving by: John Archer on steel
Vignette: Jefferson Davis
Printing: Intaglio from a copper plate of 100 subjects
Plating: Incomplete
Imprint: None
Color: Shades of blue, light blue, milky blue, and gray blue
Paper: White wove paper of varied thickness
Gum: Colorless to light yellow
Separations: Issued imperforate
Printing estimate: 500,000
Earliest recorded use: April 23, 1863

Largest known multiples: Unused block of 30, used block of 4 and used strip of 7

Unused stamps are priced without gum.

Stamps

9 (9)	blue	900.	550.
9a (9a)	milky blue	1,000.	650.
9b (9b)	gray blue	1,100.	750.
	Pair	2,000.	2,500.
	Block of 4	7,500.	NR

Short Transfer at bottom, 9-v2

Double Transfer TEN CENTS, 9-v3

Same position as 9-v3, but with Scratch on head, 9-v4

Small and large Bruise, 9-v5 & 9-v6

Varieties

9-v1	Short transfer at top	1,300.	850.
9-v2	Short transfer at bottom	*1,100.*	*850.*
9-v3	Double transfer, "TEN CENTS"and short transfer at bottom	*1,100.*	*800.*
9-v4	Same position as 9-v3, but with Scratch on head	*1,350.*	*800.*
9-v5	Damaged plate, small bruise	*1,350.*	*850.*
9-v6	Damaged plate, large bruise	*1.600.*	*850.*

Covers

Single	1,600.
Patriotic	3,500.
Wallpaper	2,500.
Trans-Mississippi, 40¢ rate	—

Markings (as a percent, plus or minus, of the price)

	off cover	on cover
Blue town	+20%	+30%
Red town	+50%	+50%
April 1863	+100%	+300%
Grid or target	+20%	+20%
Railroad	+200%	+200%
Pen cancel	-50%	-40%

CSA 10
10¢ Blue Frame Line

The distinctive feature of this stamp is the rectangular frame around each subject. These lines were engraved on the printing plate as a guide for aligning the die images as they were pressed into the plate. Because the frame lines are shared by adjacent stamps, a single stamp cut from a sheet may show only a portion of a single line or no lines at all.

There may be a break in the horizontal lines directly under the portrait of Jefferson Davis. The break appears in only 57 of the positions on the plate, while in 43 it has been repaired. The re-cut positions are: 19, 20, 23, 26 - 32, 37, 43-50, 55-60, 65, 67-70, 75, 76, 80, 88, 89, and 93-100. All 100 positions have been plated. Some varieties are listed below and appear to be permanent on the plate.

Frame Line strip of 3, CSA 10

Frame Line block of 4, CSA 10

The 10¢ Frame Line master die was engraved on steel by John Archer. It was then transferred onto a single copper plate of 100 subjects arranged 10 x 10. There was no imprint. The stamp was printed by Archer & Daly on white wove paper of varying thickness. The stamps are blue, with shades ranging from blue to milky blue and a greenish blue. The gum ranges from colorless to a light yellow. The stamps were issued imperforate.

The copper plate and the small number of subjects on the plate suggest this issue was produced as a trial or experiment. The quantity printed was rather small and distribution was limited.

Current research indicates the original engraved die used for the Frame Line was later used for the Type 1 engraved stamps
(11-AD and 11-KB). The break in the lines under the portrait that is evident in many Frame Line positions and is constant in all of the later Type 1 stamps, CSA 11.

Caution: Fraudulent examples of the 10¢ Frame Line have been made for many years by drawing in one or more lines on a 10¢ Type I or Type II stamp (CSA 11 and 12). The Type I is quite similar in design to the Frame Line, while the Type II is not.

Major Recut at bottom, 10-v1

Short Transfer at bottom, 10-v2

Short Transfer lower left, 10-v3

Recut at bottom, 10-v4

Short Transfer under N of CENTS, 10-v5 Break under portrait

Double Transfer in POSTAGE, 10-v6

Short Transfer under N of CENTS, 10-v7 No break under portrait

Short Transfer lower left, 10-v8

Scratch through "The", 10-v9

Printer: Archer & Daly of Richmond, Virginia
Engraving by: John Archer on steel
Vignette: Jefferson Davis
Printing: Intaglio from a copper plate of 100 subjects
Plating: Complete
Imprint: None
Color: Shades of blue, light blue, milky blue, and greenish blue
Paper: White wove paper of varied thickness
Gum: Colorless to light yellow
Separations: Issued imperforate

Printing estimate: 500,000
Earliest recorded use: April 19, 1863
Largest known multiples: Unused block of 4, unused strip of 7 and used strip of 6

Unused stamps are priced without gum.

Stamps

10 (10)	blue	5,000.	1,900.
10a (10a)	milky blue	5,000.	1,900.
10b (10b)	greenish blue	5,500.	2,000.
10c (10c)	dark blue	5,500.	2,000.
	Pair	15,000.	6,500.
	Strip of 4	*26,000.*	*13,500.*
	Block of 4, one known	*45,000.*	NR

Varieties

10-v1	Major re-cut at bottom, double transfer in POSTAGE, horizontal line under NT of CENTS, pos. 19	7,500.	3,000.
10-v2	Short transfer at bottom, pos. 22	6,500.	2,250.
10-v3	Short transfer lower left, pos. 47	6,500.	2,250.
10-v4	Recut at bottom, pos. 57	6,500.	2,250.
10-v5	Short transfer under "N" of CENTS, break under portrait, pos. 72	6,000.	2,125.
10-v6	Double transfer in POSTAGE, pos. 74	5,750.	1,950.
10-v7	Short transfer under N of CENTS, no break under portrait, pos. 76	5,750	1,950.
10-v8	Short transfer lower left, pos. 82	6,000.	2,000.
10-v9	Scratch through "The", short transfer LR, pos. 90	5,250.	1,800.
10-v10	Minor double transfers, various	5,500.	1,850.
10-v11	Minor short transfers, various, mostly at bottom	5,250.	1,750.

Covers

Single	3,500.
Pair	9,500.
Patriotic	8,500.
Wallpaper	*8,000.*

Markings (as a percent, plus or minus, of the price)

	off cover	**on cover**
Blue town	+20%	+30%
Red town	+50%	+50%
April, 1863 use	+100%	+200%
Straightline cancel	+100%	+200%
Pen cancel	-50%	-40%

10¢ Blue Archer & Daly – Types I & II

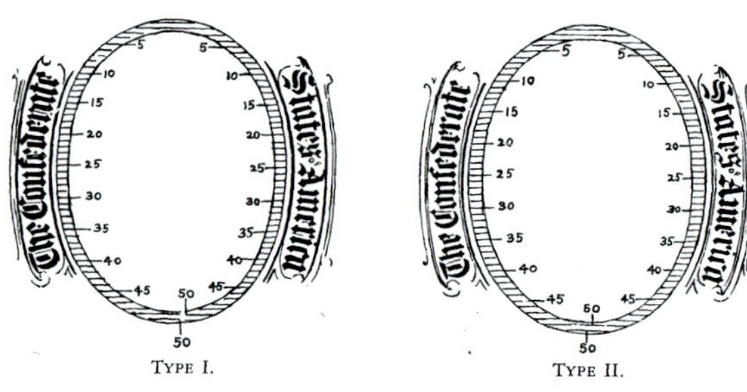

Type I. Type II.

The 10¢ 11-AD and 12-AD stamps, also referred to as Type I (11-AD) and Type II (12-AD), are quite similar, but while the designs appear almost identical, there are distinct differences between the two types; they are completely separate engravings. The major differences are:

Type I

- The horizontal lines under the portrait and above the "EN" of "CENTS" are broken
- The stamp does not have an added outer line following the contour of the stamp, as with Type II
- There are two incomplete horizontal lines in the oval frame below the "P" in "POSTAGE"
- The left-most scroll to the left of "P" in "POSTAGE" appears turned toward the viewer
- The letter "n" in "Confederate" appears as a "u"
- The top serif on the letter "A" in "America" is long

Type II

- The horizontal lines under the portrait and above the "EN" of "CENTS" are complete
- The stamp has an added outer line following the contour of the stamp, however, this line may only appear in part or may not appear at all depending on the printing
- There are no incomplete horizontal lines in the oval frame below the "P" in "POSTAGE"
- The left-most scroll to the left of "P" in "POSTAGE" appears flat
- The letter "n" in "Confederate" appears normal
- The top serif on the letter "A" of "AMERICA" has a short serif

Type I & II Portrait and Size Differences

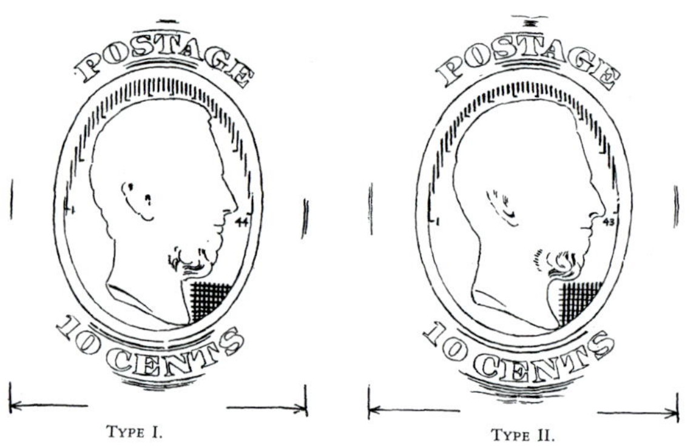

Type I. Type II.

The details of the portrait differ for the two types. For Type I, the beard under Jefferson Davis's chin is a bit crude with several sharp lines, as are the cheek lines, while they are more refined on Type II. There are 44 vertical background lines for Type I and 43 for Type II. The vertical and horizontal background lines for Type I are equal in thickness; for Type II, the vertical lines are thicker and the horizontal lines are thin.

Characteristics of AD printings vs. KB

The same plates used by Archer & Daly were later used by Keatinge & Ball to produce more Type I and Type II stamps. The Archer & Daly prints can be distinguished from Keatinge & Ball prints by the following characteristics:

- The AD printing is of a relatively high quality
- The cross-hatch lines behind the Davis portrait are clearly visible
- Stamp color is lighter than the dark blue KB normally used
- Colorless areas of stamps have no pigment cast
- The paper used is of a higher quality
- Clear gum

CSA 11-AD
10¢ Blue Archer & Daly – Type I

The 10¢ Type I master die was engraved on steel by John Archer. The original engraved die used for the Frame Line (10) was later used for the Type 1 engraved stamps (11-AD and 11-KB). It was then transferred onto two steel plates of 200 subjects each consisting of two panes of 100 arranged 10 by 10. The stamp was printed by Archer & Daly on white wove paper of varied thickness. The stamp color is blue with shades of light blue, milky blue, greenish blue, dark blue and green. The gum is colorless. The stamps were issued imperforate. A small quantity were perforated as a trial and distributed with other 10¢ stamps.

First imprint N° 2 only, 11-AD-ib

Full imprint with Daly scratched through, 11-AD-ie

11-AD-if, Left Pane

11-AD-if, Right Pane

Type 1, CSA 11, was printed from two plates numbered N° 1 and N° 2. Printer's imprints were placed at the bottom of each pane. For both plates, N° 1 and N° 2, the left pane has the plate number under position 96 and on the right pane it is under position 95. On the left pane, the imprint is to the left of the plate number and is under positions 91-95. On the right pane, the imprint is to the right of the plate number and is under positions 96-100. The first imprint was only the plate number, 11-AD-ia and ib. Later the full company name was added: "Archer & Daly, Bank Note Engravers, Richmond, Va.", 11-AD-ic and id. When Daly left the firm, his name was first lined out and then removed. Ultimately on plate N° 2 the Richmond, Va. removed.

The various forms of the imprint and the associated plate are listed below:

11-AD-ia *N° 1*
11-AD-ib *N° 2*
11-AD-ic
Archer & Daly, Bank Note Engravers, Richmond, Va. N° 1
11-AD-id
Archer & Daly, Bank Note Engravers, Richmond, Va. N° 2
11-AD-ie
Archer ~~& Daly~~, Bank Note Engravers, Richmond, Va. N° 2
11-AD-if
Archer Bank Note Engravers, Richmond, Va. N° 1
11-AD-ig
Archer Bank Note Engravers, Richmond, Va. N° 2
11-AD-ih
Archer Bank Note Engrave Richmond, Va. N° 1
11-AD-ii
Archer Bank Note Engravers N° 2

Printer: Archer & Daly of Richmond, Virginia
Engraving by: John Archer on steel
Vignette: Jefferson Davis
Printing: Intaglio from a steel plate of 200 subjects arranged as two panes of 100
Plating: Incomplete
Imprints: Described in text
Color: Shades of blue, light blue, milky blue, greenish blue and green
Paper: White wove paper of varied thickness
Gum: Colorless
Separations: Issued imperforate
Printing estimate: 47,611,000 for 11-AD and 12-AD, based on incomplete records
Earliest recorded use: April 21, 1863
Largest known multiples: Unused sheet of 200, plate 1; unused pane of 100, plate 2

Unused stamps are priced with gum. Gum problems such as brown spots or cracks are considered defects.

Gutter pair, 11-AD

Stamps

11-AD (11)	blue	15.	20.
11-ADa (11a)	milky blue	45.	50.
11-ADb (11b)	dark blue	25.	30.
11-ADc (11c)	greenish blue	30.	50.
11-ADd (11d)	green	125.	175.
	Pair	35.	70.
	Block of 4	65.	300.
	Horizontal pair with vertical gutter	150.	NR
	Block of 4, with vertical gutter	350.	NR

Imprints

11-AD-ia, b	Strip of 3 with plate number only	175.	NR
	Block of 6 with plate number only	400.	NR

11-AD-ic to -ii	Single with partial imprint	35.	80.
	Strip of 6 with full imprint	275.	NR
	Block of 12 with full imprint	550.	1,650.

Left Short Transfer, 11-AD-v1 and v2

Plate scratch, one of several, 11-AD-v5

Official perforations, 11-AD-v8

Varieties

11-AD-v1	Short transfer at left, plate 1, right pane, pos. 99	175.	120.
11-AD-v2	Short transfer at left, plate 1, right pane, pos.100	200.	150.
11-AD-v3	Short transfer at top, quite minor	60.	45.
11-AD-v4	Double transfer, quite small	60.	45.
11-AD-v5	Scratched plate, several varieties	60.	35.
11-AD-v6	Chilled plate, printing lacking	25.	30.
11-AD-v7	Overheated plate, printing filled in	25.	30.
11-AD-v8 (11e)	Officially perforated, gauge 12 ½	400.	400.

Covers

Single	120.
Pair	325.
Wallpaper	750.
Government imprint, semi-official	450.
Patriotic	1,000.
Trans-Mississippi, 40¢ rate	7,500.
Trans-Mississippi, 50¢ preferred rate*	8,500.
Officially perforated, 12 ½ gauge	800.

***Note:** There is no evidence this rate was officially implemented; there are several covers recorded paying a 50¢ Trans-Mississippi rate.

Markings (as a percent, plus or minus, of the price)

	off cover	**on cover**
Blue town	+20%	+30%
Red town	+50%	+50%
Green town	+75%	+200%
Brown town	+100%	+200%
Violet town	+100%	+200%
April 1863	+100%	+300%
March, April, May 1865	+75%	+200%
Grid or target	+25%	+25%
Paid or numeral	+100%	+300%
Arkansas town	+150%	+400%
Florida town	+100%	+300%
Tennessee town	+50%	+200%
Texas town	+75%	+200%
Express	+200%	+800%
Railroad	+200%	+600%
Steamboat	+200%	+1,000%
Pen cancel	-40%	—

CSA 12-AD
10¢ Blue Archer & Daly – Type II

The 10¢ Type II master die was engraved on steel by Frederick Halpin. It was then transferred onto two steel plates of 200 subjects each consisting of two panes of 100 arranged 10 by 10. The stamp was printed by Archer & Daly on white wove paper of varied thickness. The stamp color is blue with shades of light blue, milky blue, greenish blue and green. The gum is colorless.

Vertical gutter between panes

Type II, CSA 12, was printed from two plates, Nº 3 and 4. For plate Nº 3, the plate number for both the left and right panes are under position 95. For both panes, the inscriptions are to the right of the plate number and under positions 96 - 100.

For plate Nº 4, the plate number for both the left and right plates is under, but between, positions 95 and 96. For both panes, the inscriptions are to the left of the plate number and under positions 91 - 95.

The various forms of the imprint and the associated plate are listed below:

First imprint, 12-AD-ia

***Daly* removed, 12-AD-id**

Archer & Daly removed, 12-AD-if

12-AD-ia			*Nº 3.*
12-AD-ib			*Nº 4.*
12-AD-ic			
Archer & Daly,	*Bank Note Engravers,*	*Richmond, Va.*	*Nº 3.*
12-AD-id			
Archer	*Bank Note Engravers,*	*Richmond, Va.*	*Nº 3.*
12-AD-ie	*Bank Note Engrav*	*Richmond, Va.*	*Nº 3.*
12-AD-if	*Bank Note Engrav*	*Richmond, Va.*	*Nº 4.*

Printer: Archer & Daly of Richmond, Virginia
Master engraving by: Frederick Halpin on steel
Vignette: Jefferson Davis
Printing: Intaglio from a steel plate of 200 subjects arranged as two panes of 100
Plating: Incomplete
Imprints: Described in text
Color: Shades of blue, light blue, milky blue, greenish blue, dark blue and green
Paper: White wove paper of varied thickness
Gum: Colorless
Separations: Issued imperforate
Printing estimate: 47,611,000 for 11-AD and 12-AD, based on incomplete records
Earliest recorded use: May 1, 1863
Largest known multiples: Unused sheet of 200

Unused stamps are priced with gum. Gum problems such as brown spots or cracks are considered defects.

Stamps

12-AD (12)	blue	25.	35.
12-ADa (12a)	milky blue	50.	60.
12-ADb (12b)	light blue	35.	40.
12-ADc (12c)	greenish blue	35.	50.
12-ADd (12d)	dark blue	30.	40.
12-ADe (12e)	green	175.	150.
	Pair	50.	100.
	Block of 4	100.	300.
	Horizontal pair with vertical gutter	200.	NR
	Block of 4, with vertical gutter	400.	NR

Imprints

12-AD-ia,b	Strip of 3 with plate number only	200.	NR
	Block of 6 with plate number only	375.	NR
12-AD-ic to -if	Single with partial imprint	40.	80.
	Strip of 6 with full imprint	325.	NR
	Block of 12 with full imprint	650.	NR

[–]	symbol used in place of value to mean insufficient information to assign a price
[*italic*]	value typeface indicating the item is difficult to price accurately
NR	used in place of value when no examples have been recorded

Double Transfer at bottom, 12-AD-v1

Short Transfer at bottom, 12-AD-v2

Overheated plate, 12-AD-v3

Short Transfer at bottom, 12-AD-v4

Official perforations, 12-AD-v5

Varieties

12-AD-v1	Double transfer, in 10 CENTS, various, quite small	80.	75.
12-AD-v2	Short transfer, bottom, various	75.	65.
12-AD-v3	Chilled plate, printing lacking	35.	30.
12-AD-v4	Overheated plate, printing filled in	35.	30.
12-AD-v5 (12f)	Official perforations, gauge 12 ½	400.	400.

Covers

Single	150.
Pair	350.
Government imprint, semi-official	450.
Wallpaper	800.
Patriotic	1,000.
Trans-Mississippi, 40¢ rate	7,500.
Trans-Mississippi, 50¢ preferred rate*	8,500.
Officially perforated, gauge 12 ½	1,750.

***Note:** There is no evidence this rate was officially implemented; there are several covers recorded paying a 50¢ Trans-Mississippi rate.

Markings (as a percent, plus or minus, of the price)

	off cover	on cover
Blue town	+20%	+30%
Red town	+50%	+50%
Green town	+100%	+200%
Brown town	+100%	+200%
Violet town	+100%	+200%
April 1863	+100%	+300%
March, April, May 1865	+75%	+200%
Grid or target	+25%	+25%
Paid or numeral	+100%	+200%
Arkansas town	+150%	+400%
Florida town	+100%	+300%
Tennessee town	+50%	+200%
Texas town	+75%	+300%
Express	+200%	+800%
Railroad	+200%	+600%
Steamboat	+200%	+1,000%
Pen cancel	-40%	—

10¢ Blue Keatinge & Ball Types I & II

The 10¢ Type I and II Archer & Daly plates were sent to Columbia, South Carolina, and transferred to the firm of Keatinge & Ball for subsequent printing. The stamps Keatinge & Ball printed from these four plates are distinctive from the AD printings. The stamps produced by AD were definitely superior to those later made by KB as to the print quality, paper and gum. Type I stamps come from plates numbered 1 & 2, the Type II stamps come from plates numbered 3 & 4.

In most cases, a Keatinge & Ball print can be distinguished from an Archer & Daly print by the following characteristics:

- KB stamps are mostly a dark blue color
- The cross-hatch lines behind the portrait of Davis are normally filled in
- Colorless areas of the stamps have a pigmented cast from poor plate wiping instead of being clear
- The paper is poor quality and slightly thicker
- The gum is streaked and brownish

Caution: The early printings by Keatinge & Ball can be difficult to distinguish from Archer & Daly prints based solely on the quality of the printing and the color.

It appears that the last AD imprint with the Daly removed, was still on the Type II plate, when KB started printing. Later the KB imprints were added, but the existing AD plate numbers remained. The KB plate wiping is normally poorly done. In plate wiping, the plate is inked and the excess ink, that on the surface and not in the recessed engraved lines, is wiped off. When the wiping is poorly done, this surface will print with a slight pigmented cast and is not clear.

A Type II block, plate No. 4, with the remnants of the AD imprint showing only ***Bank Note Engrav Richmond, Va Nº 4***, has recently been discovered that is a KB printing.

The engraved 2¢ and 20¢ plates made by AD are thought to have been transferred to KB, but there is no indication that KB printed from them.

CSA 11-KB
10¢ Blue Keatinge & Ball – Type I

The Type I stamps printed by Keatinge & Ball were from the two plates, Nº 1 and Nº 2. The original plates were made by Archer & Daly and were subsequently transferred to Keatinge & Ball. The stamps were printed on thick paper of uneven quality. The color is usually deep blue and, less frequently, bright blue. The gum is uneven, streaked and dark. The stamps were issued imperforate.

The transfer of the plates from A & D to K & B involved changes in the imprints. Before or after the plates were transferred, the remaining portions of the Archer & Daly imprints except for the plate numbers were removed and those of Keatinge & Ball added. For the left pane, the imprint is to the left of the plate number, positions 90-96. For the right pane, it is to the right of the imprint, positions 96-100, *Keatinge & Ball, Bank Note Engravers, Columbia, S.C.* For CSA 12, plate 4, an example of the last A&D imprint has recently been found that is definitely a K&B printing, thus it is possible that this also exist for plates 1, 2 and 3.

Keatinge & Ball imprint, 11-KB-i1

11-KB-ia
Keatinge & Ball, Bank Note Engravers, Columbia, S.C. Nº 1
11-KB-ib
Keatinge & Ball, Bank Note Engravers, Columbia, S.C. Nº 2
Printer: Keatinge & Ball, Columbia, South Carolina
Master engraving by: John Archer on steel

Vignette: Jefferson Davis
Printing: Intaglio from a steel plate of 200 subjects arranged as two panes of 100
Plating: Incomplete
Imprints: Described in the text
Color: Shades of deep blue, bright blue
Paper: Thick and uneven
Gum: Brownish and streaked
Separations: Issued imperforate
Printing estimate: 15,125,000 for 11-KB and 12-KB based on incomplete records
Earliest recorded use: Not presently known
Largest known multiples: Unused sheet of 200, both plates; used block of 4 and used strip of 4

Unused stamps are priced with gum. Gum problems such as brown spots or cracks are considered defects.

Stamps			
11-KB (11)	blue	15.	20.
11-KBa	bright blue	50.	70.
11-KBb (11)	dark blue	20.	25.
	Pair	35.	100.
	Block of 4	70.	300.
	Horizontal pair, with vertical gutter	200.	NR
	Block of 4, with vertical gutter	450.	NR
Imprints			
11-KB-ia,b	Single with partial imprint	30.	125.
	Strip of 6 with full imprint	300.	NR
	Block of 12 with full imprint	475.	NR
Varieties			
11-KB-v1	Short transfer at left, plate 1, right pane, pos. 100	175	125.
11-KB-v2	Short transfer at left, plate 1, right pane, pos. 99	175.	125.
11-KB-v3	Short transfer at top, quite minor	50.	35.
11-KB-v4	Double transfer, quite small	50.	35.
11-KB-v5	Scratched plate, several varieties	50.	35.
11-KB-v6	Chilled plate, printing lacking	25.	25.
11-KB-v7	Overheated plate, printing filled in	20.	20.

Covers	
Single	150.
Government imprint, semi-official	450.
Patriotic	1,000.
Trans-Mississippi, 40¢ rate	7,500.
Wallpaper	800.

Markings (as a percent, plus or minus, of the price)

	off cover	on cover
Blue town	+50%	+50%
Red town	+75%	+75%
Violet town	+100%	+100%
March, April, May 1865	—	+200%
Grid or target	+20%	+40%
Paid or numeral	+100%	+300%
Arkansas town	+100%	+400%
Texas town	+75%	+300%
Railroad	+200%	+500%
Pen cancel	-40%	—

CSA 12-KB
10¢ Blue Keatinge & Ball – Type II

The Type II stamps printed by Keatinge & Ball were from the two plates, N° 3. and N° 4. The original plates were made by Archer & Daly and were subsequently transferred to Keatinge & Ball. The stamps were printed on thick paper of uneven quality. The color is usually deep blue and, less frequently, bright blue. The gum is uneven, streaked and dark. The stamps were issued imperforate.

The transfer of the plates to K & B involved changes in the imprints. Before or after the plates were transferred the remaining portions of the Archer & Daly imprints, except for the plate numbers, were removed and those of Keatinge & Ball added.

For plate 3, the plate number is under position 95 for both the left and right panes; the imprint, *Keatinge & Ball, Bank Note Engravers, Columbia, S.C.*, is to the right of the plate number, positions 96-100.

For plate 4, the plate number for both the left and right plates is under, but between, positions 95 and 96. For both panes, the inscriptions are to the left of the plate number and under positions 91 - 95.

A Type II block from plate 4 with the remnants of the Archer & Daly imprint showing Bank Note Engrave Richmond, Va. N° 4., exists that is a Keatinge & Ball printing, The block shows all traces of the "Daly" portion of the imprint removed. The block does not include that portion where the "Archer" imprint would be, so no conclusion can be drawn about the balance of the imprint. At least a portion of the last Archer & Daly imprint was still on the 10¢ Type II plate when Keatinge & Ball began printing from it. Later, the Keatinge & Ball imprint, *Keatinge & Ball Bank Note Engravers, Columbia, S.C.*, was added. The existing Archer & Daly plate numbers remained.

KB printing and imprint, Plate N° 3., 12-KB-ia

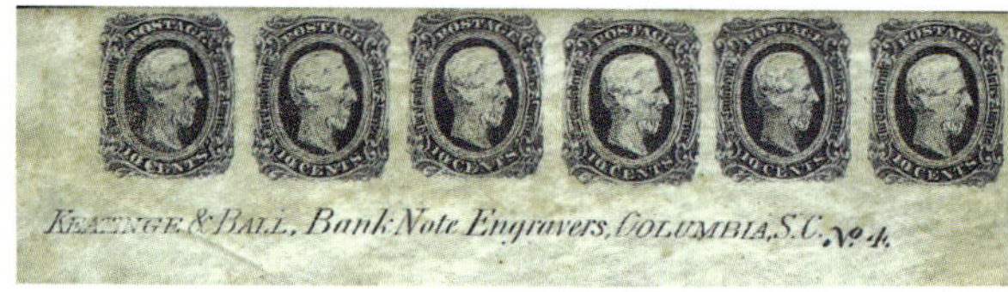

KB printing and imprint, Plate N° 4., 12-KB-ib

KB printing from plate having remnants of AD imprint, 12-KB-id

12-KB-ia
Keatinge & Ball, Bank Note Engravers, Columbia, S.C. N° 3.
12-KB-ib
Keatinge & Ball, Bank Note Engravers, Columbia, S.C. N° 4.
12-KB-ic *Bank Note Engrave Richmond, Va. N° 3.*
not recorded
12-KB-id *Bank Note Engrav Richmond, Va. N° 4.*
"e" lightly printed or absent

Printer: Keatinge & Ball, Columbia, South Carolina
Master engraving by: Frederick Halpin on steel
Vignette: Jefferson Davis
Printing: Intaglio from a steel plate of 200 subjects arranged as two panes of 100
Plating: Incomplete
Imprints: Described in the text
Color: Shades of deep blue, bright blue
Paper: Thick and uneven
Gum: Brownish and streaked
Separations: Issued imperforate
Printing estimate: 15,125,000 for KB-11 and KB-12 based on incomplete records
Earliest recorded use: Not presently known
Largest known multiples: Unused sheet of 200, used block of 14 and used strip of 4

Unused stamps are priced with gum. Gum problems such as brown spots or cracks are considered defects.

Stamps

12-KB	blue	25.	30.
12-KBa	bright blue	50.	70.
12-KBb (12)	dark blue	20.	25.
	Pair	50.	100.
	Block of 4	100.	350.
	Horizontal pair with vertical gutter	200.	NR
	Block of 4, with vertical gutter	450.	NR

Imprints

12-KB-ia,b	Single with partial imprint	50.	85.
	Strip of 6 with full KB imprint	300.	NR
	Block of 12 with full imprint	475.	NR
12-KB-ic,d	KB printing, strip of 6 with AD imprint	*750.*	NR
	Block of 12 with full imprint	*1250.*	NR

Varieties

12-KB-v1	Double transfer, minor	50.	60.
12-KB-v2	Short transfer, bottom, see 12-AD-v2	50.	60.
12-KB-v3	Chilled plate, printing lacking	50.	60.
12-KB-v4	Overheated plate, printing filled in	35.	45.

Covers

Single	120.
Government imprint, semi-official	500.
Patriotic	1,000.
Trans-Mississippi, 40¢ rate	7,500.
Wallpaper	850.

Markings (as a percent, plus or minus, of the price)

	off cover	**on cover**
Blue town	+50%	+50%
Red town	+75%	+100%
Violet town	+100%	+300%
March, April, May 1865	—	+200%
Grid or target	+20%	+40%
Arkansas town	+100%	+400%
Tennessee town	+50%	+300%
Texas town	+75%	+300%
Railroad	+200%	+500%
Pen cancel	-40%	—

[–]	symbol used in place of value to mean insufficient information to assign a price
[*italic*]	value typeface indicating the item is difficult to price accurately
NR	used in place of value when no examples have been recorded

CSA 13
20¢ Green

The 20¢ green stamp was engraved on steel by Frederick W. Halpin. It was then transferred onto a single steel plate of 200 subjects consisting of two panes of 100 arranged 10 by 10. The stamps were printed by Archer & Daly and the early printings bore their imprint; it was removed at some later date. The stamps were printed on white wove paper of varying thickness. The stamps range in color from bright green to a deep rich green. The gum is colorless.

This stamp shows a number of faint horizontal and vertical lines between many positions on the plate. These were evidently scored on the plate as an aid in positioning the transfer from the die. This concept is similar to the Frame Line (CSA 10), however, the lines are extremely light and began to disappear after the early printings. There is also a faint outer line completely surrounding the contour of the entire design which also began to disappear after the early printings. There are a number of random but constant fine colored dots over much of the plate; they are the result of imperfections in the steel. This stamp has only been partially plated.

Caution: The 20¢ green stamp was not commonly used for postage and quantities of unused stamps remained after the war. Used examples are much scarcer than unused ones. To be valued as a used stamp, on or off cover, the cancellation must be recognizable and proven authentic. An unrecognizable smudge of dirt, ink or other marking is not valued as a used stamp. Examples exist on and off cover with forged cancellations.

Printer: Archer & Daly of Richmond, Virginia
Engraving by: Frederick Halpin on steel
Vignette: George Washington
Printing: Intaglio from a steel plate of 200 subjects arranged as two panes of 100
Plating: Incomplete
Imprint: Archer & Daly, Richmond, Va., only on early printings
Color: Shades of green and yellowish green
Paper: White wove paper of varied thickness

Gum: Colorless
Separations: Issued imperforate
Printing estimate: 2,350,000 based on incomplete records
Earliest recorded use: June 1, 1863
Largest known multiples: Unused sheet of 200, used block of 14 and used strip of 5 on cover

Unused stamps are priced with gum. Gum problems such as brown spots or cracks are considered defects.

Deep Green, 13b

Stamps

13 (13)	green	40.	325.
13a (13a)	yellowish green	70.	500.
13b (13b)	deep green	70.	500.
13c (13c)	bluish green	100.	750.
13d	bright green	40.	325.
	Pair	90.	750.
	Block of 4	200.	2,500.
	Horizontal pair with vertical gutter	375.	NR
	Block of four with vertical gutter	825.	NR

Imprint Strip, 13-i

Imprints

13-i	Imprint, strip of 4	700.	NR
	Imprint, block of 8	1,850.	NR

Double Transfer in 20 and STATES, 13-v1

Double Transfer in 20, 13-v2

Double Transfer, end of UR corner, 13-v3

Double Transfer in STATES, 13-v4

Impression of "20" on forehead, 13-v5

Varieties

13-v1	Major double transfer in "20" and "STATES", pos. 24L (position is out of horizontal alignment)	200.	400.
13-v2	Minor double transfer, in "20", pos. 35R	125.	350.
13-v3	Double transfer in upper right corner, pos. 89R	125.	350.
13-v4	Double transfer in "STATES", pos. 65L	100.	425.
13-v5	"20" on forehead, printing freak	2,500.	NR
13-v6	Double transfers, minor, 24L, 41L, 10R, 15R, 25R, 35R and 89R	75.	300.

Covers

Single	1,200.
Pair	1,800.
Government imprint, semi-official	2,500.
Wallpaper	2,000.
Patriotic	3,500.
Trans-Mississippi, 40¢ rate	*10,000.*
Diagonal bisect used as 10¢ on cover	2,500.
Horizontal bisect used as 10¢ on cover	4,000.

Markings (as a percent, plus or minus, of the price)

	off cover	on cover
Blue town	+20%	+50%
Red town	+50%	+75%
Violet town	+100%	+150%
Grid or target	+20%	+20%
Arkansas town	+100%	+300%
Tennessee town	+100%	+300%
Texas town	+75%	+200%
Express	+200%	+600%
Railroad	+200%	+400%
Pen cancel	-75%	-40%

Essays and Proofs

Essays

An essay is a design for a stamp submitted to a government for approval. It may be in the form of a paste-up model, drawing, die proof or a sheet of stamps with the intention of getting a contract. The proposed design differs in some way from the issued stamp.

On March 27, 1861, the Post Office Department published a request for bids for stamps in the 2¢, 5¢, 10¢ and 20¢ denomination. These advertisements appeared in a number of Northern and Southern newspapers in early April 1861. Bids and samples of the proposed stamps were received from a number of companies including: Edmund Hoole, Mt. Vernon, NY; Butler & Carpenter, Philadelphia, Pa; George F. Nesbitt, New York; American Bank Note Co., New York; A. Hoen & Co., Baltimore; J.W. Hayes, Newark, N.J.; and Hoyer & Ludwig, Richmond, Va. From these requests, there are a number of essays of proposed stamps. The original proposals to print stamps are in the National Archives and are detailed in *The Postal Service of the Confederate States of America* by August Dietz. The surviving proofs and essays are attributed to the files of H. St. George Offutt, Chief of the Contract Bureau. They migrated to private hands in the late Nineteenth century.

E Essay for a CSA General Issue

Essays for General Issues

E-1

E-2

E-3

E-4

American Bank Note Company, New York

E-1	5¢ green and black, George Washington, paste-up and printed portions	3,750.
E-2	5¢ red and green, vignette of cotton, paste-up and printed portions	3,750.
E-3	10¢ red, engraved on India, mounted on card, Thomas Jefferson	3,000.
E-4	10¢ blue, engraved on India, mounted on card, Thomas Jefferson	3,000.

E-5 & 6

E-7

Manouvrier, New Orleans

E-5-6	E5 - E6 are on one card, unique 2¢ black wash drawing, plowing scene and 10¢ black wash drawing, steamboat and dock	8,000.
E-7	5¢ black, Liberty Head in circle, engraved and drawn design; previously attributed to Manouvrier, actual origin unknown	4,500.

E-8

E-9

E-10

A. Hoen & Co., Baltimore, Maryland

E-8	2¢ black, corn vignette, lithographed	2,250.
E-9	5¢ black, wheat vignette, lithographed	2,250.
E-10	10¢ black, cotton vignette, lithographed	2,250.

E-11

E-11a

E-12

Hoyer & Ludwig, Richmond, Virginia

E-11	10¢ blue, flag vignette, lithographed	450.
	Sheet of 14	*9,500.*
E-11a	10¢ dark blue, lithographed	950.
E-12	10¢ black, lithographed	1,500.

Proofs

Proofs are impressions taken from an officially approved design die, plate or stone.

DP	Die proof
DPP	Die proof progressive
TCD	Trial color die proof, printed in trial color
TCP	Trial color plate proof, printed in a trial color
PP	Plate proof, printed in the issued color
SO	Specimen overprint

1-AB-PP

1-AB-PP (1P5)	5¢ green lithograph, Stone AB	*2,750.*

2-H-PP

2-H-PP (2P5)	10¢ blue lithograph, Hoyer & Ludwig	*1,500.*

2-Y-TCP

2-Y-TCP (2TC5)	10¢ black lithograph, Stone Y, J. T. Paterson	*5,500.*

It is not known if the lithographed proofs were printed from the transfer stones or the printing stones, probably the transfer stones. The 10¢ can be plated to the transfer stone positions which are the same as the printing stone. The 5¢ can not be plated. It most likely came from Stone AB which has not yet been plated.

6-DPPaa

6-DPPab

6-DPPac

6-DPPaa	5¢ black on glazed card, cut to shape	*1,750.*
6-DPPab	5¢ black on glazed card, cut to shape	*1,750.*
6-DPPac	5¢ black on glazed card, cut to shape	*1,750.*

6-DPPba

6-DPPbb

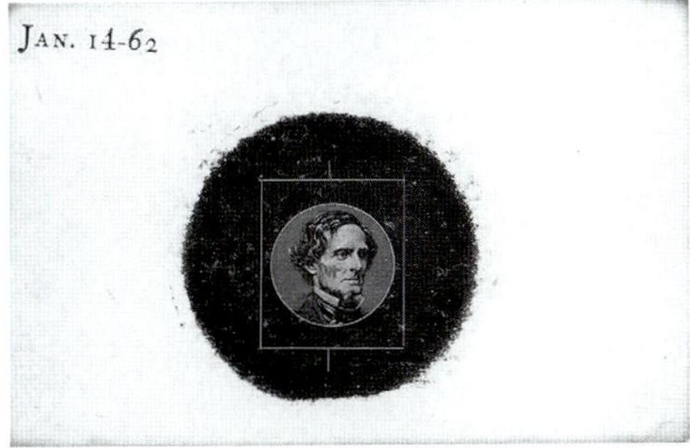

6-DPPbc

All De La Rue die proofs are on glazed cards measuring 93 x 61 mm, unless otherwise stated. At the time of production or later, some of these proofs were cut down in size and others were printed on cards of different size.

6-DPPba	5¢ black on full card, dated Jan 8-62	*1,750.*
6-DPPbb	5¢ black on full card, dated Jan 14-62	*1,750.*
6-DPPbc	5¢ black on full card, dated Jan 14-62 (minor differences)	*1,750.*

6-DPa

644/1

6-DPba, front of proof

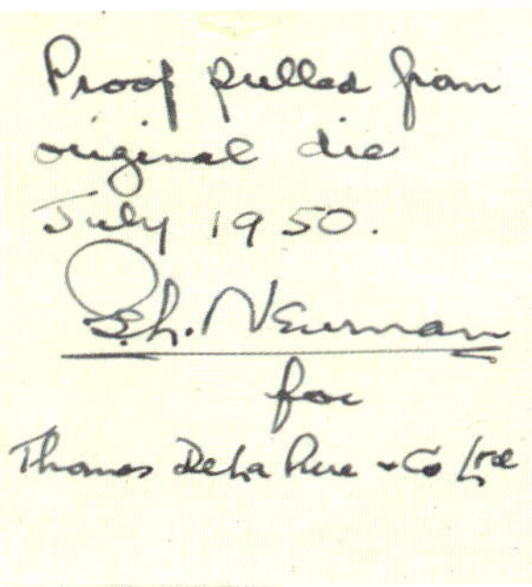

6-DPba, back of proof

6-DPa (6P1)	5¢ blue on full card	2,500.
6-DPb	5¢ blue on 57 x 61 mm card	
	a. manuscript inscriptions 644/1 inscribed, printed July 1950 for Thomas De La Rue & Co., Ltd.	1,250.
	b. manuscript inscription 644/3	1,000.

6-TCDda with Imprint

6-TCDa (6TC1)	5¢ pink on full card, no imprint	*2,500.*
6-TCDb (6TC1)	5¢ black on full card, no imprint	1,500.
6-TCDc (6TC1)	5¢ black on card 97 x 114 mm, no imprint	1,500.
6-TCDd (6TC1)	5¢ black on full card, with imprint	*2,750.*
	a. Oct 30, 1862, BEFORE STRIKING	
	b. Nov 28, 1864, pen notation 6322 and JL	
	c. Nov 28, 1864, pen notation 6324 and JL	
	d. Nov 28, 1864, vignette cut out and mounted on separate card	
6-TCDe (6TC1)	5¢ black on card 57 x 61 mm	
	a. printed inscription 219528	1,250.
	b. printed July 1950	1,250.
6-TCDf (6TC1)	5¢ black, cut to stamp size	850.
6-TCPg (6TC5)	5¢ black on wove paper	*1,250.*
6-TCPh (6TC5)	5¢ gray blue on wove paper	*1,000.*

Combination Die Proof, 6-DP & 14-DP

6&14-DP (6P, 14P 1)	5¢ blue & 1¢ orange die proofs on one card 120 x 90 mm	*8,500.*

De La Rue Plate Proof, Cross Gutter, 6-PPa

One sheet of 400 for the 5¢ was found framed at a De La Rue office in 1976. The company considered it a plate proof, never gummed, on stamp paper. The proof color is extremely close, if not identical, to the issued stamp. The paper has a distinctive yellow cast over the printing plate area and the stamps show an ink smudge in positions 99-100 LR, but otherwise are virtually perfect.

Horizontal and vertical gutter multiples of the issued stamp can only exist from the proof sheet as De La Rue cut the finished sheets into panes of 100 before sending to the Confederacy. The listed "specimen" overprint was also found at that time in an old De La Rue register of specimens.

6-PPa (6P5)	5¢ blue De La Rue plate proof on stamp paper	150.
	Pair	300.
	Pair, horizontal or vertical gutter, only known from the proof sheet	*1,200.*
	Cross-gutter block, unique	*9,500.*
6-PPb	5¢ black on wove paper	2,250.

SPECIMEN overprint CSA SO-6

6-SO	5¢ blue, De La Rue "SPECIMEN" overprint	—

Note: Other "SPECIMEN" overprints exist on the De La Rue stamps that may or may not be authentic.

Richmond Trial Color Plate Proof, 7-TCPb

7-TCPa (7TC5) 5¢ carmine on stamp paper *1,750.*
7-TCPb (7TC6) 5¢ carmine on thin card *1,750.*

Trial Color Die Proof, 8-TCDa

Trial Color Die Proof, 8-TCDb

8-TCDa (8TC1a) 2¢ blue die proof, showing outer rectangular frame lines *5,000.*
8-TCDb 2¢ black die proof, no outer rectangular frame lines showing, cut close *4.000.*

TEN Die Proof, 9-TCD

9-TCD (9TC1a) 10¢ black on wove paper *6,000.*
11-DPP 10¢ blue progressive die proof *5,000.*

Early State of the Die, 12-DPPa

12-DPPa 10¢ blue, early state on wove paper, outer lines crude, as are those for the hair and ear *4,500.*

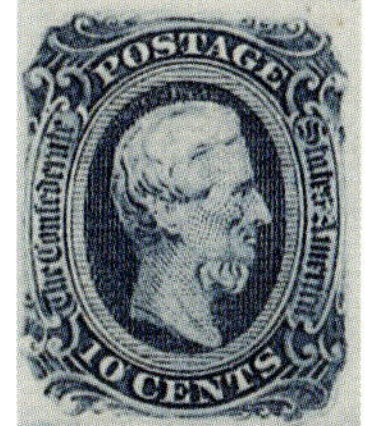

Late State of the Die, 12-DPPb

12- DPPb 10¢ blue progressive die proof (late state), several exist, each different *3,000.*

Plate Proof on Ribbed Paper in blue, 12-PP

12-PP (12P7) 10¢ blue plate proof on thick ribbed paper —

Note: status of this item has not been fully established

Progressive Die Proof in Green, 13-DPP

13-DPP (13P1a) 20¢ green on wove paper *4,500.*

Trial Color Die Proof, 13-TCD

13-TCD (13TC1a) 20¢ red brown on wove paper *4,500.*

Original Artist Sketch, 14-SK

14-SK	1¢ original artist sketch in pencil for the stamp, unique	*4,000.*

Note: a similar but different sketch exists.

Trial Color Die Proof, 14-TCDcc

14-DPPa	1¢ black, cut to size, significant portrait, engraved	*2,500.*
14-DPPb	1¢ black, cut to size, same, less detailed	*2,500.*
14-TCDa (14TC1)	1¢ on full card, no inscription	*3,000.*
14-TCDb	1¢ black on card, cut down to stamp size	*1,250.*
14-TCDc	1¢ black on full card with inscription	*4,500.*
	a. Mar. 6-62	
	b. June 17, 1863, pen notation 2684 and JL	
	c. June 17, 1863, pen notation 2685 and JL	
	d. July 31, 1863, J at right, pen notation 3399 and JL	

Die Proof, 14-DP

14-DP (14P1)	1¢ orange on full card 92 x 61 mm, with manuscript notation "J.C. Calhoun. Esq." back notation "Received from Major Ficklin agent for Confederate States, March 1862"	*4,500.*

CSA 14-PP

1¢ Plate Proof

One part sheet of 200 of the 1¢ was found framed at a De La Rue office in 1976. The company considered it a plate proof, never gummed, on stamp paper. The proof color is extremely close, if not identical, to the issued stamp. The paper has a distinctive yellow cast over the printing plate area. The listed "SPECIMEN" overprint was also found at that time in an old De La Rue register of specimens.

14-PP (14TC5)	1¢ orange De La Rue plate proof on stamp paper	250.
	Pair	500.
	Horizontal pair with vertical gutter between	*2,500.*

SPECIMEN overprint CSA SO-14

14-SO	1¢ orange De La Rue "SPECIMEN" overprint	—

Unofficial Printings

Unofficial printings of general issue stamps have been occasionally made from original CSA plates or plate fragments, but were not printed during the Civil War era.

Fakes of the authentic stamps and of the bogus issues have been around since the 1860s and these early fabrications are highly collected, but of relatively little value. In recent years, a number of images relating to Confederate stamps have been made. The Springfield Facsimiles, first printed in 1934, are of this category. They were created without the permission of August Dietz from drawings he made in the 1920s of Confederate stamps. Dietz made deliberate alterations to the drawings, which enables the identification of these facsimiles. With the evolution of computers and color printers, many such items have been made since the 1990s, some excellent quality but most poorly done. As they can be run off from a computer at little cost, they are of little value.

General Issues

5¢ De La Rue stamps printed from the plate captured on the *Bermuda,* 6-U-1a

This authentic De La Rue 5¢ plate was sent to the Confederacy in 1862 on the blockade runner *Bermuda*. It never reached the Confederacy, as it was captured by the U.S.S. *Mercedita* and became a prize of war. The plate was acquired by the Franklin Institute, Philadelphia in March 1954 from which prints were privately made on the order of Philip H. Ward, Jr. The Franklin Institute sold it to the Smithsonian National Postal Museum in April 2011.

Because the Ward private printings are from an authentic De La Rue plate, they can be deceptive if one is not familiar with the authentic stamps. The Ward printings in blue replicate three authentic stamps: CSA No. 6, 7L, and 7R. Both the blue and black Ward printings show quite consistent printing as to even ink distribution, but they are filled in and do not show the fine detail of any of the authentic stamps. The horizontal lines surrounding the portrait are almost completely filled. The shade of the ink is quite close to No. 6, but has a bit duller appearance. The Ward printing in black is not a problem, as only one authentic example is known, a plate proof, 6-PPb.

Ward, CSA 6-U-1a

CSA 6

CSA 7-L

CSA 7-R

6-U-1a	blue on thin wove paper	3.
	Pane of 100	150.
	Sheet of 400	600.
6-U-1b	black on thin wove paper	2.
	Pane of 100	100.
	Sheet of 400	400.

The De La Rue Altered Plates

Anticipating new postage rates, the Confederacy ordered plates in the 2¢ and 10¢ denomination from De La Rue in 1862. The 2¢ die was created by altering the denomination on a copy of the 1¢ die and the 10¢ by altering a copy of the 5¢ die. There is no evidence of any printings of these stamps in London or in the Confederacy, however, both plates arrived in the Confederacy. No trace of the 2¢ or the 10¢ die, contemporary die proof impressions, or stamps is known to exist. The 2¢ image is listed under U1 and the 10¢ under U2.

The De La Rue records on the altered plates are contained in a ledger titled *Thos. De La Rue & Co, 110 Bunhill Row, Day Book P*. The entry on page 143 is dated November 7, 1862 and lists the 10¢ mounted plate costing £100 plus 15s for packing - the standard charge for the period. The 2¢ plate lists the same for a total of £201, 10s. The entry appears to be a paid one, thus not a shipping one. There is a reported reference to the "Export Ledger 430", but this has not been found.

The 2¢ plate was found in 1926 and survived intact on its original steel mounting; it is now privately owned, the original mounting plate has since been removed. The original 10¢ plate of 400 was found in the 1880s and separated into four panes of 100. The steel mounting is lost. One pane of 100, known as the Sitter plate, is in mint condition; it is in private hands and only a few prints have been made for archival purposes. Another section of 100 is owned by the Chicago Historical Society and over the years only a few prints have been made. A third pane of 100 has been recently discovered and is in private hands. The fourth section was cut up in the 1880s into smaller sections: one of seventy and two of nine are known, with nothing known of the remaining 12 subjects.

The partial section of 70 (10 horizontal, 7 vertical) was used to make numerous private prints as early as the 1880s in various colors and papers. Of the two units of nine, one is in the Columbus Historical Society; it has been used for several printings and has been reproduced for others. The second unit of nine was at one time in Baltimore and has been used for only a few private printings. Over the years, many more stamps were created by copying the image. It is likely that over 200 variations exist printed from this original plate or by copying the image.

These listings for unofficial printings are intended to be an outline of what exists and not a definitive listing. It is the best available at this time.

Today, there are numerous images of these stamps being created and sold that have no relation to the original printing plates - especially the 10¢ altered plate. They are not listed in this catalog and have little value.

CSA U-1
2¢ Altered Plate

2¢ Altered Plate, Dietz 1926, U-1a

U-1a	deep green on ivory vellum, printed by August Dietz, 1926	
	Single stamp	3.
	Sheet of 400	400.

2¢ Altered Plate, Dietz 1955, U-1b

U-1b	green, 1955 sheet inscription "Commemorating the 69th Annual Convention of the American Philatelic Society, Norfolk, Virginia, September 21, 22, 23 & 24, 1955"	
	Single stamp	2.
	Sheet of 100	50.
U-1c	green, orange or brown, 1955, no sheet inscription	
	Single stamps	3.
	Sheet of 100	100.

Note: Also known with overprints, Dixipex II, 1959

[–]	symbol used in place of value to mean insufficient information to assign a price
[*italic*]	value typeface indicating the item is difficult to price accurately
IH	used in place of listing value when the item is held by an institution
NR	used in place of value when no examples have been recorded

CSA U-2
10¢ Altered Plate

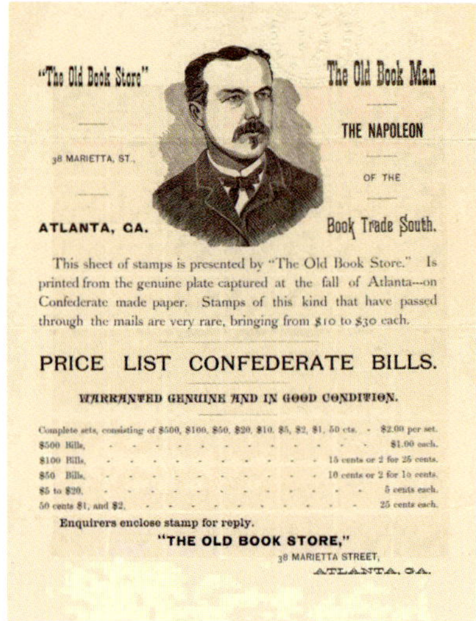

Old Book Store Atlanta flyer, advertising side, U-2-1a

Old Book Store Atlanta flyer, stamp side, U-2-1a

10¢ Altered Plate, 1886 printing, U-2-1b

10¢ Altered Plate, *circa* 1897 printing, U-2-1c

Atlanta section, of 70

U-2-1a	*Circa* 1880, Old Book Store, Atlanta, light gray, priced as a unit; image of 70 printed on one side and advertisement on the other.	*2,500.*
U-2-1b	1886, gray, soft paper, priced as a unit	*850.*
U-2-1c	*Circa* 1897, in green, red & blue, each priced as a unit	375.
U-2-1d	*Circa* 1920, black, Dietz, enameled stock, proof quality, priced as a unit	150.
U-2-1e	1936, imprint Third International Philatelic Exhibition, priced as a unit; image of 70 printed on one side and advertisement on the other	100.

Columbus, U-2-2a

Columbus, signed by Frank Baptist, U-2-2b

Columbus Section of 9

U-2-2a	Dietz 1918, black on card, inscription differs from below, priced as a unit	25.
U-2-2b	Dietz 1918, black on card, signed by Frank Baptist, priced as a unit	45.
U-2-2c	Dietz, *circa* 1926, Columbus Section, black, priced as a unit	35.
U-2-2d	1974 Columbus Philatelic Society printing, card, priced as a unit	25.
U-2-2e	1974, U-2-2d but without imprint	40.

Baltimore, U-2-3

Baltimore Section of 9

U-2-3a	Dietz, *circa* 1926, Baltimore Section, black	175.
U-2-3b	Dietz, *circa* 1926, Baltimore Section one side, Columbus the other, black	125.

Portion of Unknown Partial Pane, U-2-4

Unknown Section of 100

U-2-4	*Circa* 1900, black, poorly printed, only partial pane present but 10 high, from a unit of 100	—

Note: This may or may not be from the same plate as U-2-5a, b

Detail of Chicago Pane, U-2-5a

Detail of Chicago Pane, U-2-5b

Chicago Historical Society Section of 100

U-2-5a	*Circa* 1920-30, light blue, priced as pane of 100	*600.*
U-2-5b	*Circa* 1970, blue, priced as pane of 100	*300.*

Detail of Sitter Pane, U-2-6a

Sitter Section of 100

U-2-6a	*Circa* 1990, black on glazed card, proof quality	IH
U-2-6b	*Circa* 1990, green on glazed card, excellent quality	IH

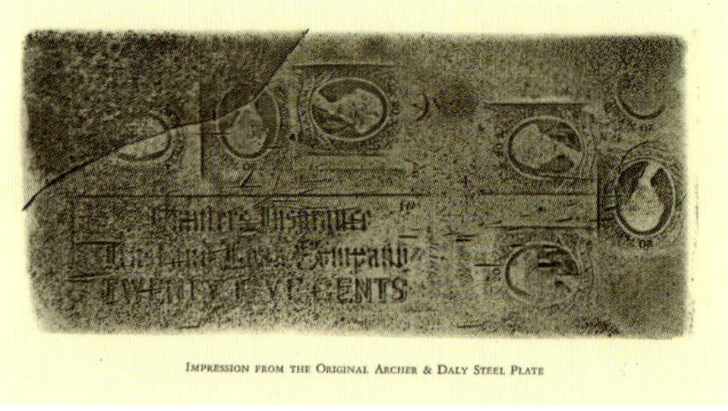

Print from an original CSA trial plate, U-T-1

Original trial die impression on a Confederate steel-plate consisting of one image of the 10¢ A&D type I, six images of the 20¢ Engraved, and part of a 20¢ note. From the poor condition of the plate, it is not certain if the impressions are proofs or die essays. Prints were made from the plate in black by August Dietz in the 1920s. The printing was about 100, of which 50 were inserted in the 1929 Deluxe edition of *The Postal Service of the Confederate States of America.*

U-T-1	black with greenish tinge on card, *circa* 1926 by August Dietz	175.

Note: The CSA altered plates, 2¢ and 10¢, have been especially subject to reproduction from new plates or computer files that have no relation to the originals. Our listings are only for stamps printed from the original CSA printing plates. The reproductions have no more relation to the prints from the original plates than a photograph of a stamp relating to the authentic stamp. Such images have little significance and only token value as they can be made at any time costing only the value of the paper and ink.

Perforated and Rouletted Stamps

Official Perforations

From the outset of planning operations, the Confederate States Post Office Department wanted to provide the public with perforated postage stamps. Initial advertisements for sealed bids to print and supply the Department with stamps included the requirement that bidders furnish stamps "perforated around their edges." In the end, influenced by factors not directly related to the production of stamps, the Department waived that requirement and awarded the printing contract to Hoyer & Ludwig, the Richmond firm whose bid did not include an agreement to supply perforated stamps.

The Department persisted in its desire to supply the public with perforated stamps. In January 1862, the Department ordered a perforating machine from Thomas De La Rue & Company, Ltd. in England. It is not clear from extant records when the machine arrived in Richmond. However, once the perforating device was in hand (sometime between early 1862 and the spring of 1863), the Department undertook trial runs using the machine to perforate a small quantity of the new steel plate printed adhesives (11-AD and 12-AD). This experiment proved to be unsatisfactory, because it took too long to perforate too few stamps. As a result, the Department gave up its attempt to perforate stamps as impractical and distributed the experimentally perforated stamps, along with regular imperforate stamps, to various post offices.

Officially Perforated Stamps

The characteristics of officially perforated stamps are readily observable and measurable. All officially perforated stamps have perforations which (1) measure 12½ gauge, (2) are irregular with respect to the quality of the perforations, usually have some blind perforations, and (3) occur only on the Archer & Daly printings (11-AD and 12-AD).

Perforations: 12½ gauge
11-AD; 12-AD
Earliest recorded use: July 13, 1863.

Note: 11-AD and 12-AD both were subjected to the perforation experiment and likely made their way into the public supply chain simultaneously. The earliest recorded date for an officially perforated stamp is an 11-AD.

Single	400.	400.
Pair	850.	850.
Strip of three	1,300.	—
Block of four	1,800.	2,500.
Vertical gutter block of four	3,000.	NR
Used on cover		800.
Used on cover tied by military field cancel		600.

The Post Office Department distributed the experimental, officially perforated stamps among ten states. The bulk of reported covers were used at post offices located in Alabama, Georgia and Mississippi. There are recorded uses of perforated stamps from the following post offices:

Alabama: Blakely, Cahaba, Demopolis, Eufaula, Mobile, Montgomery, Nicolson's Store, Opelika, Selma
Florida: Lake City
Georgia: Atlanta, Blowing Cave, Columbus, Grantville, Greensborough, Griffin, Macon, Marietta, Newnan, Savannah
Louisiana: Shreveport
Mississippi: Columbus, Crystal Springs, Macon, Marion, Okolona
North Carolina: Charlotte, Fayetteville, Raleigh, Summerville, Trenton
South Carolina: Greenville
Tennessee: Chattanooga
Texas: Navasota, Plantersville
Virginia: Fork Union, Gordonsville, Harrisonburg, Lynchburg, Orange C.H., Petersburg, Richmond

Privately Rouletted Stamps

Both before and after the Confederate Post Office Department experiment with perforated stamps, individual citizens or postmasters added separations to the imperforate stamps supplied by the Department. These privately rouletted stamps are believed to have been prepared at, or in the general vicinity of, at least four towns, using at least eight different stamps: 1-1, 2-H, 4, 6, 11-AD, 12-AD, 12-KB, and 13.

The term "privately rouletted" as used in Confederate philately includes stamps that technically were rouletted or perforated. The private roulettes are identified and referred to by the names of those towns or geographic areas from which most uses have been recorded.

Listing Criteria

To be listed in this section, private roulettes must meet three tests: (1) the separations must have been produced by some mechanical means (rather than, for example, by an individual wielding a knife or by someone tearing the stamps apart); (2) the separations must be measurable with reasonable accuracy and consistency; and (3) the separations must be repeatable in form. The intent of this three-pronged test is to eliminate from the listing any stamp having separations which are the singular product of an individual.

Stamps with private roulettes have been identified from the following locations:

Baton Rouge, Louisiana

Roulette: 20 gauge
1-1, 2-H
Earliest recorded use (Early Period): February 24, 1862
Earliest recorded use (Late Period): September 8, 1862

Two Periods of Use
Early Period and Late Period

Within the period February 24 through November 24, 1862, there are key dates relevant to the Baton Rouge roulettes. Early Period: prior to May 8, 1862 when the city fell to occupying Union forces. Late Period: after August 21, 1862 when the city was again occupied by Confederate forces. No roulettes used from Baton Rouge have been reported in the gap between these two periods. The latest recorded use of the Baton Rouge roulette prior to the Union occupation is April 29, 1862. The first use after the reoccupation of the city by the Confederate forces is September 8, 1862.

Because the single letter rate was increased from 5¢ (for under 500 miles) to 10¢ (irrespective of distance) as of July 1, 1862, all Baton Rouge roulette covers after the reoccupation of the city by Confederate forces bear two 5¢ stamps (as a pair or two singles) or a single 10¢ stamp for the single letter rate.

5¢ lithograph single	500	800.
10¢ lithograph single	NR	800.
5¢ lithograph used on cover		2,000.
5¢ lithograph pair or two singles used on cover		2,500.
10¢ lithograph used on cover		3,000.

In addition to Baton Rouge uses, covers with stamps having the Baton Rouge roulette have been reported from New Orleans, Plaquemine, Ponchatoula and St. Martinsville, Louisiana; Corinth and Jackson, Mississippi; and Tudor Hall, Virginia. It is believed that the stamps bearing these separations were carried by individuals to, and used at, these other towns.

Baton Rouge "Desk Find" covers: These covers consist of 75 preprinted, partially addressed envelopes, each originally bearing a single unused 5¢ (1-1) stamp separated with the Baton Rouge roulette. The covers were discovered in 1938 in a desk in New Orleans that was shipped there from Baton Rouge. The find was sold to the Weill Brothers of New Orleans who subsequently sold the covers to their clientele. The find originally was believed to consist of 50 covers, and was so reported in the philatelic press. However, Raymond H. Weill reportedly told one prominent postal historian that the find consisted of 75 covers. Each cover is pre-addressed to New Orleans, with space left on the envelope for the sender to write in the name and street address of the addressee. No used covers bearing stamps from or similar to the stamps that were part of the "Desk Find" have been reported. Off-cover, unused examples of the stamps without gum that reputedly have been removed from "Desk Find" covers have been reported, but it is impossible to distinguish such stamps from other, non-Desk Find Baton Rouge roulettes.

5¢ lithograph single unused on cover	500.	NR

Forsyth, Georgia

Sawtooth roulette: 8½ gauge
11-AD; 12-AD; 12-KB
Earliest recorded use: December 10, 1864

10¢ engraved single	600.	400.
10¢ engraved used on cover		800.

Some authors and auction catalog describers have asserted that there were three types of Forsyth separations: (1) sawtooth roulettes, (2) sewing machine perforations and, (3) serpentine roulettes. It appears, however, that there was only one type separation: sawtooth roulette.

None of the separations identified as being from towns located near Forsyth appear to match those from Forsyth, although they are similar in style to the Forsyth sawtooth roulette.

Oxford, North Carolina

Oxford Roulette

Oxford Coil

Roulette: 15 gauge
6, 11-AD or 11-KB; 12-AD or 12-KB; 13. It is not possible to determine from the sources if the10¢ engraved stamps are AD or KB printings.
Earliest recorded use: May 03, 1863

5¢ typograph pair	NR	NR
10¢ engraved single	NR	600.
20¢ engraved single	NR	750.
5¢ typograph pair on cover		1,250.
10¢ engraved used on cover		900.
Pair [or two 10¢ engraved singles] used on cover		1,250.
20¢ engraved used on cover		3,750.

Some of the Oxford privately separated stamps appear to have been cut into horizontal strips and rouletted vertically between the stamps, leaving the top and bottom of each stamp with a straight-edge. These stamps sometimes are referred to as the "Oxford Coils."

Migrating Oxford Roulette Uses: One example of the Oxford roulette on cover was reported used on August 1, 1863 at Henderson, North Carolina. Because the roulettes are identical to those originating at Oxford and the shade of the stamp (11-AD) is identical to known Oxford uses, it is believed that the stamp on this cover is likely an Oxford roulette that had been carried the forty miles to Henderson by an individual.

Harrisonburg, Virginia

Roulette: 17 gauge
11-AD, 12-AD
Earliest recorded use: August 26, 1863

10¢ engraved used on cover	750.
10¢ engraved double roulette variety used on cover	1,500.

The best known separation type originating in Virginia's Shenandoah Valley was the Harrisonburg roulette. Harrisonburg separations used at other Shenandoah Valley towns have been identified from Bentivoglio, Bridgewater, Charlottesville, Crawfordville, Howardsville, Lexington, Martinsville, Mount Crawford, and Port Republic.

There is one authentic example reported with a 12½ gauge on a folded letter front with a Harrisonburg postmark tying the stamp. It is possible that this item was carried to Harrisonburg from some other nearby location in the Shenandoah Valley.

Shenandoah Valley

There is evidence that privately separated stamps were created at or in the vicinity of some Shenandoah Valley towns located near military camps, as a convenience to troops in the field. These stamps were used on covers which appear to have originated in or were addressed to postal addresses also located in the Shenandoah Valley, including Harrisonburg. All these stamps were cancelled using military field target cancels, but without identifying town postmarks. All have a roulette gauge that measures 12 rather than the Harrisonburg 17 gauge. In the past, these covers were attributed to Harrisonburg, although none bears a Harrisonburg post office town postmark or other indicia of origin.

Roulette: 12 gauge
Confirmed towns of use: None
Origin of use: Unidentified military field office
Possible origin of separation: Army of Northern Virginia
11-AD or 11-KB; 12-AD or 12-KB. (It is not possible to determine from the sources if the stamps are AD or KB printings.)
Earliest recorded use: Late 1864

10¢ engraved single	NR	500.
10¢ engraved used on cover		750.

Other Private Separations: Genuine Private Separations from Unidentified Locations of Manufacture: There are covers bearing stamps with other private separations which can be identified with respect to their post offices of mailing, but for which there are too few examples known (in most cases only one cover reported) to determine the places where separations were manufactured and applied to the stamps. Covers have been reported with such privately separated stamps mailed at the following towns: Shuqualak, Mississippi; Ashboro, North Carolina; Navasota, Texas; Martinsville and Tudor Hall, Virginia.

Caution: Privately separated stamps which are not on cover should be viewed with skepticism unless they can be favorably compared to known authentic specimens, on or off cover, and which have received certificates of authenticity from a recognized certification organization with a specialized knowledge of Confederate material.

[—] symbol used in place of value to mean insufficient information to assign a price

NR – used in place of value when no examples have been recorded

Harrisonburg roulette (double roulette at top and right) used on cover.

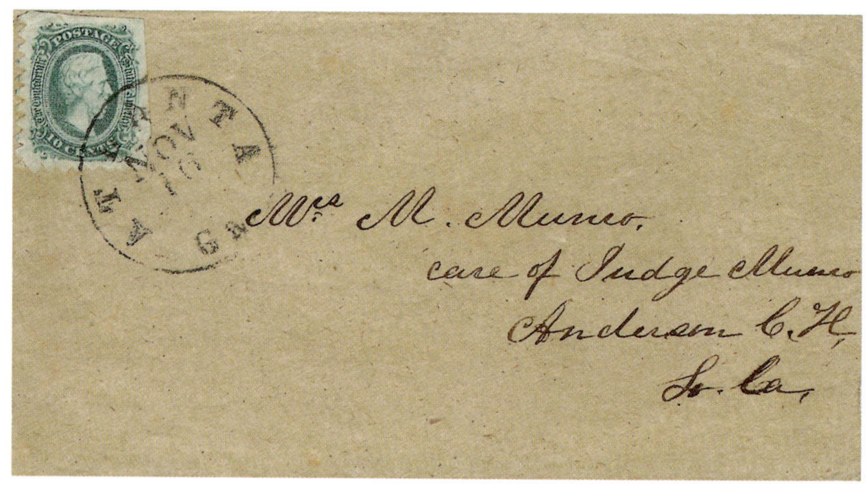

Sawtooth roulette attributed to Forsyth, Georgia but used on cover from Atlanta, Georgia.

Fakes and Facsimiles

Even as the Civil War raged, publishers and stamp dealers in the North created, collected and traded in Confederate stamps. Initially, the stamps were genuine Confederate stamps. As the popularity of stamp collecting surged in the late 1860s and supplies of genuine stamps dwindled, facsimiles were created to satisfy collectors' demand for specimens to fill their stamp albums. Today we treat these stamps as if they were originally created as fakes intended to deceive collectors, but generally that was not the case.

A similar situation occurred in Europe in the middle to late 1860s. Catalogers and dealers, such as Dr. John Gray, Mount Brown, Thomas Dalston, J. M. Stourton, E. L. Pemberton, T. Lewes, Stafford Smith, and J-B Moens acquired examples of Confederate stamps (some genuine, some not) from dealers in the United States and listed them in their mostly unillustrated catalogs and sold the listed items to collectors and other dealers as genuine Confederate stamps.

For the modern day collector of Confederate fakes, distinguishing the genuine stamp from the fake usually presents no problem, as shown by the first pair of stamps that follow. Sometimes, however, the differences between the genuine stamp and the fake are more difficult to distinguish, as shown by the second pair of stamps.

Genuine CSA 1

Fake

Genuine CSA 1

Fake

Who Were the Fakers?

United States. In the United States, the best known creators of Confederate fakes (stamps, postmarks and covers) were J. W. Scott, Samuel C. Upham, James A. Petrie, S. Allan Taylor, George Hall, Tatham Stamp Company, and John A. Fox.

J. Walter Scott

J. W. Scott (New York City) was a prominent nineteenth century and early twentieth century stamp auctioneer, catalog and album publisher, stamp dealer, and philatelic author who created Confederate facsimiles to use as illustrations in his stamp catalogs. He also printed the stamps and assembled them into packets which he sold to collectors as facsimile space fillers. His facsimiles were crude woodcuts and are not easily mistaken for the genuine item.

Two types of J. W. Scott fakes of CSA 1

Genuine NEW-LA-A01

Scott NEW-LA-A01

Another faked stamp frequently encountered, believed to have been made by J. W. Scott, is the so-called "New York Counterfeit" of CSA 6. This can be distinguished from the genuine because the fake's color is greenish-blue rather than blue, and the cross-bars of the "F" and "E" of "FIVE" on the fake are shorter than on the genuine stamp.

Genuine CSA 6

Scott
"New York Counterfeit"

Samuel C. Upham

Samuel C. Upham (Philadelphia) was a stationer and publisher who is well known for the patriotic covers he created as well as for the fake Confederate currency and stamps he produced. Beginning in 1862, he advertised and sold his facsimiles to collectors and stamp dealers alike.

Samuel Upham fakes of CSA 1 and CSA 5

Genuine MEM-TN-A01 Upham MEM-TN-A01

George Hall

George Hall is an obscure figure among fakers, but he produced one identifiable Confederate fake – that of CSA 1, which is known in green and red. This fake is crude and cannot be mistaken for the genuine stamp.

George Hall fake of CSA 1

James A. Petrie

Dr. James A. Petrie began his career as early as 1865 as a creator and seller of Confederate reprints made from genuine plates he acquired. Petrie also created fakes of postmasters' provisionals which he based on genuine examples of stamps he had acquired, but for which he had no genuine plates. Petrie also produced reprints and fakes of covers bearing imprinted postmasters' provisionals. He sold his stamps and covers as if they were genuine. Petrie was known to have sold fakes to the eminent collectors Ferrari and Tapling, as well as others.

S. Allan Taylor

S. Allan Taylor began his career in 1863 as one of the most prolific creators of Confederate fakes. Taylor's replications of the general issue stamps attempted to resemble the genuine items, probably because he had access to genuine stamps. Taylor's postmasters' provisional products, however, rarely resembled the genuine item or were crude imitations or outright fantasies that he printed on different color papers. The quality of Taylors' products varied from the garish to the sublime. All known Taylor fakes are found as singles; there are no pairs, strips or blocks recorded.

Genuine CSA 5 Taylor

Taylor Charleston Fantasies

The Springfield Fakes

Tatham Stamp Company (Springfield, Massachusetts) created a series of facsimiles originally offered in the mid-1930s in packets of twelve stamps consisting of the regular issues excluding CSA 7 and 12. Later they were issued in packets of fourteen stamps which included CSA 7 and 12. The Tatham stamps, known as "Springfields", closely resemble the designs of their genuine counterparts, having been copied from card dies created by August Dietz for his 1929 book, *The Postal Service of the Confederate States of America.* The original Dietz drawings were copyrighted, and the use of these drawings was done without permission.

The Springfields can be distinguished from their genuine counterparts based on the color of the paper (cream or brownish) and the rough quality of the printing. The Springfields were sold as singles, blocks of four, and sheets of twenty-five stamps. Although originally made available as loose stamps in packets, they eventually were offered as part of booklets called Tasco Educational booklets in 1941.

Genuine CSA 1

Springfield

When first issued, the Springfields did not show any indication that they were facsimiles. After the first printing, all Springfields were marked either "Facsimile' or "Facsimilie" (sic) on the back.

John A. Fox

John A. Fox was a twentieth century stamp dealer who created fake covers. His products have been well documented in the literature and can usually be identified by the handwriting used for the address panels and by the postmarks he created. Fox typically used genuine envelopes and genuine Confederate stamps, and then married them with his fake postmarks. Fox's products generally have high eye appeal.

John A. Fox fake cover: Genuine unused patriotic cover and genuine pair of CSA 6; fake address panel and fake postmark.

Europe. In Europe, most of the early publishers did not illustrate their catalogs. One of the first to do so, however, and one of the influential players in the field of fakes, was J-B Moens of Belgium.

Jean-Baptiste Philippe Constant Moens

In preparing his catalogs, starting in 1864, J-B Moens used Confederate images prepared from facsimile stamps created by Samuel C. Upham of Philadelphia. Moens' advertisements misrepresented the illustrations in his catalogs as accurate representations of the genuine stamps. Subsequently, other dealers created their own fake stamps based on the illustrations in Moens' catalogs. These fabrications are generally described as stamps that are "after Moens" (meaning, copied from Moens).

The Modern Swiss Fakes

A frequently encountered series of fakes that are often confused with Springfields and genuine stamps are those that were produced in Switzerland in the 1970s. These appear genuine to the untrained eye, but are stamped on the back to indicate they are facsimiles. These can be distinguished from the Springfields because the Swiss fakes used Scott's post-1940 numbering system for marking the backs, while the Springfields used Scott's pre-1940 numbering system.

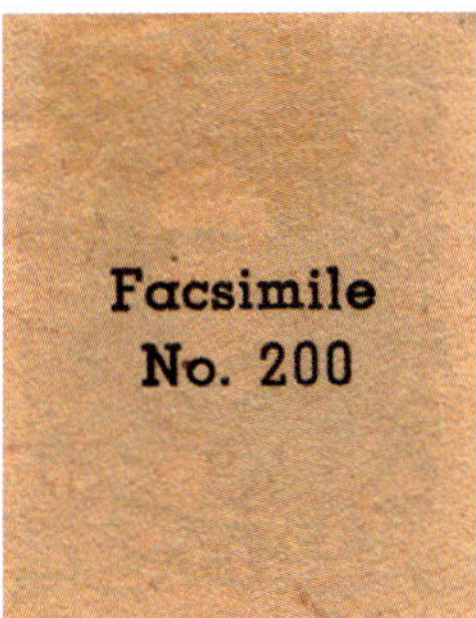

Springfield

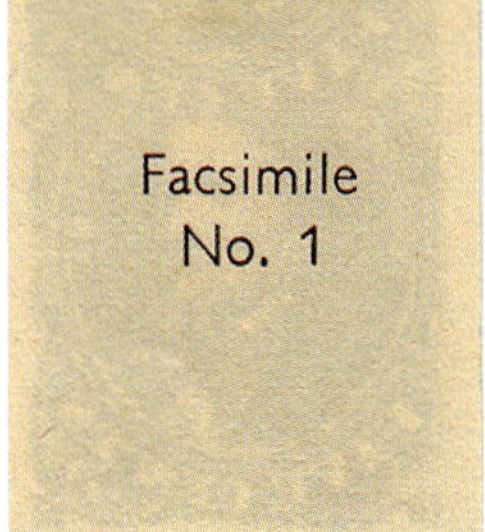

Modern Swiss Fake

Jean de Sperati

Jean de Sperati was the most skilled faker whose products are the most difficult to distinguish from the genuine. He created forgeries of CSA 5 and CSA 9. He also made fake postmarks he applied to his creations and to genuine Confederate stamps.

Sperati's fake of CSA 5 is fairly easy to recognize. The "T" of "TEN" usually has two red dots in the vertical bar; the "1" of the bottom left side "10" is flawed at its bottom; and, the "1" of the top right side "10" is malformed and resembles a "3".

Genuine CSA 5

Sperati

There are three types of Sperati CSA 9 (Types A, B and C). There are several points that distinguish a Sperati forgery from a genuine CSA 9. The easiest ways to identify a Sperati 9 are (1) the connection of the top bar of the "T" and "E" in the "TEN" (Types A and B) and (2) the white spot that appears in the blue area just to the right of the word "POSTAGE" (Types A, B and C).

Genuine CSA 9

Sperati Type A

Sperati Type B

Sperati Type C

The Birmingham Fakes

Another dangerous product from Europe was the group of CSA 1, 3, and 4 created in Birmingham, England by an unidentified faker. These were well crafted fakes that often pass as genuine. The fake CSA 1 and 4 were created in green, red and blue. The distinguishing feature of the Birmingham CSA 1 and 4 is that the fake was better designed than the genuine stamp, and corrects some of the genuine stamp's design flaws. The most obvious correction was made to the scroll at the lower right corner. On the authentic stamp, this scroll is flat. On the Birmingham fake, this scroll is rounded to match the scroll at lower left.

The Birmingham imitation of CSA 3 lacks the periods after the letters "C", "S" and "A" that are present on the genuine stamp. The fake CSA 3 was printed in yellow-green.

Genuine CSA 1

Birmingham

Genuine CSA 3

Birmingham

Erasmo Oneglia

A third major European forger, but one who created only one type Confederate forgery, was Erasmo Oneglia. He created an engraved CSA 8 that is close to the genuine stamp yet easily distinguishable from it. Oneglia created all his fakes, including his one Confederate fake, to sell to collectors as genuine stamps. On the Oneglia Confederate fake, the portrait was poorly done, especially in the eyes and mouth, and the ornamentation to the left of the word "TWO" appears as three round pearls rather than as one solid piece with one pearl in its center as on the genuine stamp.

Genuine CSA 8

Oneglia

Other Fakes and Fakers

In addition to the fakes of the general issue stamps, several fakers created (1) fakes of postmasters' provisional-stamps,

(2) outright fantasies which purported to be genuine postmasters' provisional stamps, and (3) fake postmarks which they applied to some of their fakes or applied to genuine Confederate stamps.

Like John A. Fox, Sperati was notorious for creating fake postmarks which he applied to his imitation stamps as well as to genuine Confederate stamps. Several of Sperati's postmarks represent no danger of being mistaken for the genuine since they were variations on New York Post Office foreign mail handstamps applied to genuine Confederate stamps or were the faked postmarks of other northern cities. Some Sperati postmarks, however, purport to be from Confederate post offices and cities. The following town postmarks are recorded as being created and used by Sperati: Charleston, S.C.; Chattanooga, TN; Cincinnati, OH; Detroit, MI; Middle Bury, VA; Mobile, AL; New Orleans, LA; New York, NY; and Richmond, VA.

Fake Perforations

Another type fake often encountered are fake perforations applied to genuine Confederate stamps. These often can be identified because they (1) are the wrong gauge - not the 12½ found on the genuine experimental perforated stamps, (2) were applied to the wrong stamps (CSA 6 or 7, and 8 or 13) or (3) are flawless perforations, unlike the genuine perforations, which frequently include blind perforations (perforations not fully removed).

Genuine Perforations

Incorrect Gauge 14

Wrong Stamp

Wrong Stamp

Wrong Stamp

A genuine unused patriotic envelope to which a genuine unused CSA 3 has been added and tied with a fake Jackson, Mississippi postmark. The added address and postmark are attributed to John Fox.

CASH PAID FOR OLD CONFEDERATE

POSTAGE STAMPS

5c Green, 5c Blue.
Pay 5c each.

2c Rose.
40c each, used.
4c each, unused.

WE want to buy in quantities, all Stamps issued by the Confederate Government during the Civil War of 1861-65, and for which we pay good prices. We also buy the Local or City issues; these stamps were issued by the postmasters in 1861 and are of the most value. Prices sent on application.

These stamps can be found in old trunks, desks, secretaries, garrets, etc., in most of the old houses in the South, and we want Boys and Girls in all parts of the South to look up these stamps and send them to us and we will pay good Cash prices for them.

2c Green,
Pay 35c each.

1c Orange,
3c each.

☞*All stamps must be on Original Envelopes if possible. No torn or mutilated stamps taken.*

AGENTS WANTED ALL OVER THE SOUTH.

Good Commissions Paid.

20c Green,
50c each, if used.
3c each, if unused.

5c Blue,
75c per 100.

WE ALSO BUY . . . OLD UNITED STATES STAMPS. .

10c Blue,
75c each.

10c, Red, 50c.
10c, Blue, 15c.

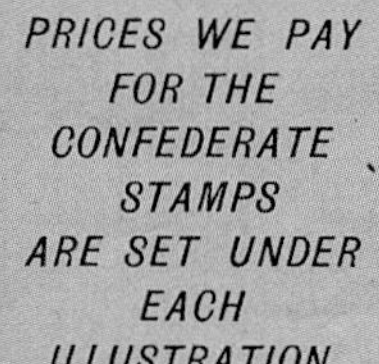

PRICES WE PAY FOR THE CONFEDERATE STAMPS ARE SET UNDER EACH ILLUSTRATION.

10c Blue,
60c per 100, used.

Address all communications to

STANDARD STAMP CO.,

N. B. REFERENCES FURNISHED IF DESIRED.

925 LA SALLE STREET, ST. LOUIS, MO.

A flyer advertising for the purchase of Confederate stamps ca. 1890 from the Standard Stamp Co. of St. Louis. Most of the illustrations appear to have been copied from the J.W. Scott facsimiles.

Color Cancels

Postmarks in colors other than black are uncommon. Of the color cancels known, the most common colors are blue and red. Other colors are quite scarce. Less than 250 Confederate post offices used color cancels and nearly half of these were blue cancels. Cancels listed with an asterisk (*) have not been seen by the editors of this edition, but have not been absolutely eliminated as possible as they were listed in prior catalogs.

When determining the color of postal markings, consideration must be given to multiple facts about the cover. Just because a marking looks green doesn't mean green ink was used to produce it. Many inks have changed over time and the paper color under the ink can cause the ink to look different than its original color. Blue ink on a yellow or orange envelope looks green. Brown markings, in some cases, are oxidized red ink or the result of both red and black ink being used by the same canceller and not true brown ink. There are definite and distinct examples of rare colors genuinely used on Confederate covers – striking examples of genuine green, red and yellow postmarks are true collector gems and bring substantial premiums.

The following list of towns known to have used colored inks includes only cities where the color was used on the postmark cancel. Previous listings also included colors used on rate markings. The editors limited this listing to postmark cancels to ensure it accurately reflects postmark uses.

The presence of the town name in the color lists will help verify the use of a color postmark at a given post office. Unlisted towns do not necessarily indicate a more scarce marking than those listed. It merely indicates the editors have not previously seen examples.

Blue Markings

Abingdon, VA
Adairsville, GA
Albany, GA
Arcadia, LA
Ashboro, NC
Auburn, AL
Balcony Falls, VA
Barnesville, GA
Blairsville, GA*
Bolivar, TN
Bowling Green, KY
Bowling Green, VA
Brownsville, NC
Caldwell, TX
Camp Stockton, TX
Cassville, GA
Catlett, VA
Chambers C.H., AL
Charlotte C.H., VA
Charlotte, NC
Charlotte, TN
Chester C.H., SC
Christiansburg, VA
Clarksville, GA
Clarksville, TN
Clarksville, VA
Clinton, MS
Codville Depot, VA*
Collierstown, VA
Colliersville, TN
Columbia, SC
Concord, NC
Corinth, MS
Cotile, LA
Courtland, AL
Covington, GA
Covington, TN
Cross Keys, AL
Culloden, GA
Culverton, GA
Danville, VA
Decatur, GA*
Dublin, GA*
Drakes Branch, VA
Dublin, VA
Ellaville, GA
Emory, VA
Enfield, NC
Etowah, GA
Fancy Hill, VA
Fayette, MS
Fillmore, LA
Fort Valley, GA
Forestville, NC
Franklin Depot, VA
Glade Springs Depot, VA
Graham, NC
Graham's Turn Out, SC*
Greensborough, NC
Greenwood, MS
Greenwood, SC
Greenville, MS
Havana, AL
Hempstead, TX
Hillsboro, NC
Howardsville, VA
Huntsville, AL
Jeffress' Store, VA
Jonesboro, TN
Jonesville, VA
Kenanville, NC
Lawrenceville, VA
Lebanon, VA
La Grange, GA*
Lenoir, NC
Lexington, VA
Louisville, GA
Louisa C.H., VA
Luray, VA
Lynchburg, VA
Lynnville, TN
Manassas, GA
Marion C.H., SC
Martindale, NC
Milledgeville, GA
Milliken's Bend, LA
Monroe, GA
Montgomery, AL
Montgomery Springs, VA*
Moorefield, VA*
Morgantown, NC
Mount Pleasant, NC
Nashville, TN
Natural Bridge, VA*
Newbern, NC
Newton Factory, GA*
Norfolk, VA
North Mt. Pleasant, MS
Opelika, AL
Open Pond, AL*
Oso, TX
Oxford, GA
Paris, TX
Pattonsburg, VA
Pendleton, SC
Petersburg, VA
Pleasant Shade, VA
Portsmouth, VA
Raleigh, NC
Rehoboth, AL
Renwick, GA
Richmond, TX
Richmond, VA
Ringgold, GA
Roswell, GA
Salem, VA*
Saltville, VA
San Antonio, TX
Sandersville, GA
South Florence, AL
St. Joseph, LA
St. Matthews, SC
Stone Mountain, GA
Sulphur Springs, TX
Talladega, AL*
Taylorsville, NC
Troup Factory, GA
Tuskegee, AL
Tye River Warehouse, VA
University of Virginia, VA
Vaiden, MS
Villula, AL
Wadesborough, NC
Watkinsville, GA
Waynesboro, VA
Wentworth, NC
Winchester, VA*
Wetumpka, AL
Winchester, TN

Red Markings

Abbeville C.H., SC
Abingdon, VA
Adairsville, GA
Alexandria, LA
Autaugaville, AL
Beaumont, TX
Blacks & Whites, VA
Bolton's Depot, MS
Brick Store, GA

Buck Eye, GA
Buckingham C.H., VA
Buena Vista, GA
Caldwell, TX
Camden, AL
Camden, SC
Cartersville, GA
Centreville, TX
Cheneyville, LA
Chester C.H., SC
Christiansburg, VA
Churchland, VA
Clarksville, VA
Clinton, AL
Cobham, VA
Columbia, NC
Cotton Gin Port, MS*
Crawfordville, MS
Cumberland, VA
Curdsville, VA
Danville, VA
Decatur, GA
Dover, GA
Dunns Rock, NC
Edgard, LA
Egypt, MS
Elkville, NC
Emory, VA*
Evergreen, LA
Fairfield, VA*
Floyd C.H., VA*
Gaston, AL
Gaston, NC
Glenn Springs, SC
Grantville, GA
Grantville, VA
Greensborough, GA
Greensborough, NC
Hamburg, SC
Hamilton, MS
Hamptonville, NC
Harrellsville, NC
Hempstead, TX
Hermitage, LA
Hertford, NC
Honey Grove, TX
Huntsville, AL
Kingsport, TN
Kosciusko, MS
Jefferson, TX*
Lavaca, AL
Lexington, GA
Lincolnton, NC
Linton, GA
Lone Star, TX
Lynchburg, VA
Madison, GA
Madison, NC
Marion, AL
Mebanesville, NC
Middleton, MS
Milliken's Bend, LA
Monroe, NC
Monroeville, AL
Monterey, AL
Morton, MS
Mount Meigs, AL
Mount Mourne, NC
New Albany, MS*
New London, VA
New Orleans, LA
Newberry, SC
Opelika, AL
Oso, TX
Petersburg, VA
Philomath, GA
Pittsylvania C.H., VA
Plymouth, NC
Point Coupee, LA
Pomaria, SC
Ponchatoula, LA
Raleigh, NC
Raysville, GA*
Red House, VA
Red River Landing, LA
Robertsville, SC*
Russellville, AL*
San Antonio, TX
San Augustine, TX
Savannah, GA
Smithfield, VA
Social Circle, GA
Sparta, GA
Spring Hill, TX
Taylorsville, VA
Terry, MS
Tunnel Hill, GA
Victoria, TX
Walterborough, SC
Washington, MS*
Waynesboro, VA*
Warsaw, NC
Waterloo, LA
Wedowee, AL
Winchester, TN
Winchester, VA*
Whitesville, GA
Woodville, GA
Yanceyville, NC

Brown Markings

Amherst C.H., VA
Amite City, LA
Arnaudville, LA
Belleview, TX
Black Mingo, SC
Black Walnut, VA*
Blackville, SC*
Brashear City, LA
Brownsburg, VA
Burnt Ordinary, VA
Cady's Tunnel, VA
Campbellton, MS
Charleston, TN
Charlotte C.H., VA
Charlotte, TN
Chester C.H., SC
Chewalla, TN
Christiansburg, VA
Chunenugge, AL
Clarksville, GA
Cobham, VA
Columbia Mills, GA
Crawfordsville, GA*
Culloden, GA
Dahlonega, GA*
Decatur, GA
Durham, NC
Fairfield, VA
Falmouth, VA*
Fayetteville, VA
Fort Mill, SC
Franklinton, NC
Frog Level, SC
Hatchechubbee, AL
Hollow Square, AL
Jefferson, AL
Johnsonville, SC
Laurel Hill, LA
Liberty Hill, SC
Lisbon, VA
Lynchburg, VA
Madison, AR*
Madison, NC
Marion Station, MS
Matagorda, TX
Midlothian, VA
Millican, TX
Milton, NC
Mossing Ford, VA
Opelika, AL
Orange C. H., VA*
Osyka, MS
Palmyra, VA
P. Hill (Pleasant Hill), NC
Riceboro, GA
Rock Fish, VA
Russellville, AL*
Quitman, GA
Scuppernong, NC
Siloam, MS*
Standardsville, VA
Stony Point, VA*
Syracauga, AL
Tappahannock, VA
Tompkinsville, AL
Triune, TN
Victoria, TX*
Vienna, GA
Villula, AL
Waukeenah, FL
Water Valley, MS*
Whitlock, VA

Green Markings

Castroville, TX
Centre Point, AL
Chester C.H., SC
Clarksville, VA
Durham, NC
Green Cut, GA
Greensborough, GA
Hicksford, VA
Lynchburg, VA
Monroe, GA
Monticello, GA
Ninety Six, SC
Princeton, AR
Renwick, GA
Roswell, GA
Saltville, VA
San Antonio, TX
Summers, VA*
Wedowee, AL

Orange Markings

Blacks & Whites, VA*
Clinton, AL*
Geneva, GA*
Kosciusko, MS
Lexington, GA*
Madison, GA
Orange C.H., VA
Raleigh, NC
Smithfield, VA
Taylorsville, VA*
Victoria, TX

Red-Brown Markings

Kingston, GA
Linton, GA*
Walterborough, SC

Violet Markings

Augusta, GA
Filmore, LA
Lynchburg, VA
Madison, AR*
Pendleton, SC
Roswell, GA
Whitesville, NC

Magenta Markings

Stony Point, VA

Ocher Markings

Union Point, GA

Atypical and Straightline Cancels

Atypical cancels are the result of a local postmaster designing and making his own separate handstamp device, usually a woodcut. Such markings had the intended purpose of canceling stamps. These types of handstamps are not common on Confederate stamps, as the majority of the Confederate postmasters simply used the postmark itself to cancel the stamps.

Which cancellations to include as atypical is somewhat subjective. Ordinary grids and targets are not included, as they were commonly used. Some were left over from the pre-Confederate period and others were issued by the Confederate Post Office Department for use on military field mail and can be found in the "Confederate Army Camp Markings" section.

For example, the postmaster at Canton, Mississippi used many very distinctive and different grid cancels. Covers with these markings are fairly numerous, and for the purposes of this catalog are not listed or priced separately. Also, "PAID," "5" or "10" handstamps used on stampless covers were sometimes used to cancel general issue stamps. These were standard rating devices and are not considered atypical.

The editors fully acknowledge that there are other cancellations that could perhaps be listed, but the following were chosen as the most distinctive and prominent. Illustrations show the cancels as they actually appear. Values are for clear strikes on the most common stamps in very fine condition. Incomplete or poor strikes sell for considerably less.

AC-01

AC-02

		off cover	on cover
AC-01	Abingdon, Va.		
	Flower	350.	800.
AC-02	Camden, Miss.		
	Cross	NR	*1,000.*

AC-03

AC-04

		off cover	on cover
AC-03	Canton, Miss.		
	Circle of diamonds	*350.*	*1,000.*
AC-04	Caseyville, Miss.		
	Negative star	*750.*	*1,500.*

AC-05

AC-06

		off cover	on cover
AC-05	Faison Depot, N.C.		
	Double circle of wedges	*750.*	*1,500*
AC-06	Greensborough, Ga.		
	Array of small rectangles	NR	*1,000.*

AC-07

AC-08

		off cover	on cover
AC-07	Harrisonburg, Va.		
	Circle of wedges	NR	*2,500.*
AC-08	Lyons, Tex.		
	Boxed target	NR	*1,500.*

AC-09

AC-10

		off cover	on cover
AC-09	Mount Crawford, Va.		
	Crossroads	250.	800.
AC-10	New Iberia, La.		
	Box of squares	NR	*1,000.*

AC-11

AC-12

		off cover	on cover
AC-11	Patterson, N.C.		
	"PAID 10 C" inside a circle	250.	750.

		off cover	on cover
AC-12	Ridgeway N.C. Circle of fancy wedges	NR	*1,500.*

AC-13

AC-14

AC-13	Rodney, Miss. Circle of squares	NR	*1,000.*
AC-14	Salem, N.C. Cross hatch	NR	*1,000.*

AC-15A

AC-15B

AC-15C

AC-15A	Tuscaloosa, Ala. Large 8-pointed star with bulls-eye center	350.	800.
AC-15B	Tuscaloosa, Ala. Smaller 8-pointed star with a central target	NR	*1,500.*
AC-15C	Tuscaloosa, Ala. Cross	375.	*1,000.*

Straightline Town Postmarks

Postmasters were required to mark letters they received with the name of their post office, the abbreviated name of the state or territory and the day of the month. Postmasters implemented these requirements in various ways. The straightline handstamp postmarks were the easiest to manufacture locally, as they could be made utilizing printer's type or simply carving the marking on the end grain of a block of fine-grained wood. A carved wooden handstamp would be subjected to a harsh blow each time it was used, which resulted in alteration of the device over time.

SL-01

SL-01	Bath Alum [Va] (32x5; black)	1,500.	NR

SL-02

		off cover	on cover
SL-02	BIG SHANTY [Ga] / month, day (26x10; black)	350.	1,000.

SL-03A

SL-03B

SL-03A	Goodson [Va] / Sept (28x14; black)	*750.*	*2,000.*
SL-03B	Goodson [Va] / Oct (28x13; black)	500.	1,500.

SL-03C

SL-03C	Goodson [Va] with month removed (28x6; black)	350.	1,000.

HARDEMAN TEX.

SL-04

SL-05

SL-04	HARDEMAN TEX. (30x3; black)	NR	1,500.
SL-05	HARRINGTON N.C. (22x2; black)	NR	*2,000.*

SL-06A

		off cover	on cover
SL-06A	HATCHECHUBBEE / ALA. (40x3; black)	*500.*	1,500.

SL-06B

		off cover	on cover
SL-06B	HATCHECHUBBEE [Ala] (40x3; black)	NR	*2,000.*

SL-07A

SL-07B

		off cover	on cover
SL-07A	JACKSON [Miss] with ball on "J" intact (35x8; black)	500.	1,500.
SL-07B	JACKSON [Miss] with ball on "J" missing (35x8; black)	350.	1,000.

SL-07C

		off cover	on cover
SL-07C	JACKSON MISS (31x3; black)	500.	1,500.

SL-08

		off cover	on cover
SL-08	KERNERSVILLE / N.C. (41x9; black)	NR	*2,000.*

SL-09

		off cover	on cover
SL-09	Martindale, N.C. (42x3; black)	NR	—

SL-10

		off cover	on cover
SL-10	Montpelier, Va (55x5; black)	750.	NR

SL-11

SL-12

		off cover	on cover
SL-11	RAVENS NEST, VA. / month, day, and year (25x6; black)	750.	NR
SL-12	SEVENMILE FORD VA (37x3; black)	NR	—

SL-13

SL-14

		off cover	on cover
SL-13	Tawboro', N.C. (27x3; black)	NR	—
SL-14	TUPELO MIS (23x3; black)	*500.*	1,500.

SL-15

		off cover	on cover
SL-15	TYNER [Tenn] / month and day (vertical) (23x5; black)	NR	2,500.

Goodson [Va] straightline with month removed, SL-03C

Tuscaloosa Ala star AC-15A on forwarded cover

Confederate Army Camp Markings

The Confederate military generally used local civilian post offices to process their mails during the war. In some cases, military mail monopolized the civilian postmaster's attentions. Thus, post offices such as Tudor Hall, Traveler's Repose, Accokeek, and Jamestown, Virginia; Cumberland Gap, and Chickamauga, Tennessee; Bowling Green and Columbus, Kentucky; and Pollard, Alabama are known mostly for their army-origin mail. These were not official army post offices. In a few cases, civilian offices were opened at personal, rather than official, initiative to specifically serve a nearby body of troops. Camp Shenandoah, Virginia and Zollicoffer's Brigade, Kentucky are notable examples. These essentially civilian post offices are listed with their respective states.

It was not until 1863 that the Confederate Post Office Department established official post offices for the two principal Confederate armies: one for the Army of Northern Virginia and another for the Army of Tennessee. Evidence also exists that the Army of the Valley had an official post office in 1864. These army post offices traveled with their respective armies and processed their mail.

The Army of Tennessee post office employed a name postmark; the corresponding offices for the Army of Northern Virginia and Army of the Valley did not. Both offices used anonymous killers and rate markings on outgoing mail. Many of these devices were obtained from civilian offices where they lay unused. Some appear to have been made specifically for the purpose.

A summary of the evolution of Confederate army postal service can be found in *The 2001 Congress Book*, "Evolution of Confederate Army Mail Service during the War for Southern Independence," by Stefan Jaronski (pp. 73-110). The current catalog listings supersede the 2001 article. The prices in this section are only for uses on cover. Off-cover prices are not listed. Values are for the most common stamp issues.

Army of Northern Virginia

John L. Eubank, a former artillery battery commander with Lee's army in Virginia, was appointed postmaster of the Army of Northern Virginia in mid-August 1863. His appointment was not officially announced until December of that year. He and a handful of military clerks detached from units initially operated at Orange Court House, Virginia simultaneously with that town's post office, and just a few hundred yards away. He later moved with the army and served its troops until the very end of hostilities in Virginia. From the summer of 1864 until April 1865, Eubank operated out of the Richmond Post Office Building.

Stamped, prepaid mail from the Army of Northern Virginia typically bears one of a series of handstamped grids or a "bulls-eye" target. A series of rate markings were used on soldiers' due mail. No specific name postmark for the Army of Northern Virginia exists, unlike the case with the Army of Tennessee. Strikes of the grid cancellers are often partial or blurry and thus can be difficult to identify as to type.

Army of Northern Virginia Postal Markings

Grids and Targets on prepaid mail

ANV-01

ANV-02

ANV-03

ANV-01	Grid (7 bars spaced 2 mm; enclosed circle; 21; 1864-65; black)	125.
ANV-02	Grid (7 bars; enclosed circle; 18; 1864; black)	100.
ANV-03	Grid (7 bars spaced 3 mm; enclosed circle; 20; 1865; black)	150.

ANV-04

ANV-05

ANV-06

ANV-04	Grid (8 bars; enclosed circle; 20; 1864; black)	150.
ANV-05	Grid (6 bars; unenclosed; 17; 1863; black)	200.
ANV-06	Grid (7 bars; unenclosed; 21; 1864; black)	200.

ANV-07

ANV-08

ANV-09

ANV-07	Grid (7 bars; unenclosed; 20; 1864; black)	125.
ANV-08	Grid (9 bars; unenclosed; 17; 1863; black)	175.
ANV-09	Grid (8 bars; unenclosed oval; 15x20; 1864; black)	200.

ANV-10

ANV-11

ANV-12

ANV-10 Grid (9 bars; unenclosed, slightly elliptical; 20; 1864-65; black) 200.
ANV-11 Grid (10 bars; unenclosed; 18; 1864-65; black) 175.
ANV-12 Grid (11 bars; unenclosed; 22; 1864; black) 150.

ANV-13

ANV-13 Target (4 rings; large center; 20; 1863-65; black) 100.

Due Rate Markings

ANV-14

ANV-15

ANV-16

ANV-14 DUE 10 (middle bar of "E" missing; 17x15; 1863; black) 175.
ANV-15 DUE 10 (18x16; 1863-64; black) 175.
ANV-16 10 (enclosed in circle; 19; 1864; black) 125.

ANV-17

ANV-18

ANV-19

ANV-17 DUE 10 (straight cap "1"; 21x6; 1863-64; black) 125.
ANV-18 DUE 10 (slanted cap "1"; 21x7; 1864-65; black) 125.
ANV-19 10 (enclosed in DLC; 18; 1864; black) 75.

ANV-20

ANV-20 10 (Petersburg Type L; 186-; blue, red, black) 200.

Army of Tennessee

Harvey T. Phillips, the former postmaster of Chattanooga, initially became the unofficial postmaster of the Army of Tennessee, on his own initiative, upon the evacuation of Chattanooga on September 6, 1863. His actions were recognized as temporary by the Confederate Post Office Department on October 9, 1863. The Army of Tennessee post office was officially established on December 14, 1863.

Postmaster Phillips initially used the "Chattanooga Ten." postmark from September 8, 1863 until January 23, 1864. Military use of this postmark on prepaid mail can be recognized from the date and postage stamp. During the fall of 1863, Phillips operated from a railroad car behind Confederate lines, nearby and simultaneously with the civilian post office of Chickamauga, Tennessee. The semi-circle CHICKAMAUGA postmark is of civilian, not military, origin. Engraved 10¢ issues postmarked "Chattanooga, Ten." after September 6 through January are Military mail.

Phillips then moved to Dalton, Georgia, operating simultaneously with that office through the winter of 1863-64, and subsequently moved with the army during its defense of Georgia, the invasion of Tennessee in 1864, and the defense of the Carolinas in the final months of the war. Engraved 10¢ issues postmarked "Chattanooga, Ten." after September 6 through January are military mail.

A three-line typeset ARMY of TENN device was used from mid-January to mid-April 1864. Several variants of this marking exist – either multiple devices or different states of repair of one device. Towards the end of their use, the letters became increasingly clogged or worn and the strikes degenerated to illegibility. Two anonymous grid cancels were subsequently used by Phillips and his staff. The first of these is very similar to one marking of the Army of Northern Virginia (Type ANV-2). Only an enclosure, a notation on the envelope, or knowledge of the sender and his unit can reveal the cover's true origin. Some of the markings are quite common; others are very scarce. While strikes of the two grid cancellers are generally clearer than those of the Army of Northern Virginia, they can still be difficult to type. On soldier due mail, the location of the soldier's unit can be matched against the postmark date to determine the true nature of the marking.

Army of Tennessee Markings

ATN-01

ATN-01 CHATTANOOGA Ten. (33; Sep 8, 1863 – Jan 23, 1864; black) 150.
Same, DUE 10 [ATN-5] 175.

ATN-02a

ATN-02b

ATN-02c

ATN-02 ARMY of TENN (14x12; 1864; black)

a. Spacing between lines is 3 and 1 mm; "A" tilted to right and in line with edge of "E" 500.
   Same, DUE 10 [ATN-5] 750.
b. Spacing between lines is 3 and 1 mm, "A" not tilted, in line with stem of "T" 500.
c. Spacing between lines is 2 and 1 mm, "A" tilted and in line with stem of "T" 750.

Grids and Targets on prepaid mail

ATN-03

ATN-04

ATN-03 Grid (7 bars; enclosed circle; 18; 1864; black) 175.
ATN-04 Grid (7 bars; enclosed circle; 20; 1865; black) 175.

Due Rate Markings

ATN-05

ATN-06

ATN-05 DUE 10 (20x14; 1864; black) 75.
ATN-06 DUE / 10 (20x14; 1864; black) 175.

ATN-7

ATN-8

ATN-07 10 (italic, 17x11; 1864; black) 175.
ATN-08 10 (9x12; 1864; black) 200.
ATN-09 Ms Due 10 (1864) 125.

Anonymous Rate Markings Associated with Army of Tennessee

ATN-10 (Augusta, Ga.)

ATN-11 (Grifin, Ga.)

ATN-10 10 (Augusta, Ga. type J; 1865; violet) 300.
ATN-11 10 (Griffin, Ga. type F; 1864; black) 175.

Note: probably applied by respective civilian post offices to army mail deposited with them.

Army of the Valley

In 1864, General Jubal Early's 2nd Corps of the Army of Northern Virginia was split off from the Army of Northern Virginia to counter threats from Federal forces in the Shenandoah Valley and, ultimately, to invade Maryland to the suburbs of Washington, D.C. that summer. This body of troops was called the Army of the Valley. It operated until October 1864, at which time most of the troops were transferred to the defense of Richmond and Petersburg. A post office was established to handle mail to and from the Army of the Valley, but the identity of the postmaster remains unknown. A manuscript due marking has been identified in association with the office, but no marking on prepaid mail has been clearly characterized. The true origin of the due marking can only be derived from knowledge about the sender's army service record and association of his unit with Early's forces in the Shenandoah Valley, contents or notations on the envelope. Only a few covers are known.

Army of the Valley Postal Markings

AV-01 Ms Due 10 (1864; black) 200.

> Listing descriptions include the number of bars in a target or grid, whether enclosed, the diameter or size of the marking in millimeters and the period of use.

Confederate Generals' Mail

During the war, a large number of officers held the rank of general in the Confederate army or state militias. Only those with the rank of general conferred by the Confederate government are included in this section. These include 426 generals and one admiral nominated by President Davis and confirmed by the Senate. Of these, 124 have been recorded as sending mail. There are examples of mail sent to approximately 50 generals for whom there are no recorded examples of mail sent by them.

Under the provisions of the Act of July 29, 1861 general officers, like all other soldiers, were allowed to send letters and other matter authorized by law without prepayment of postage. The postage was to be collected from the recipient.

General Robert E. Lee endorsed almost all his envelopes in the top right hand corner "R. E. Lee, Gen'l." Such uses, mostly hand-carried, are known as "field letters." Other generals also endorsed their letters in a like manner. The reason or purpose of the endorsement is unknown. Fewer than twenty postally used war-time envelopes with the "R. E. Lee, Gen'l" endorsement have been recorded.

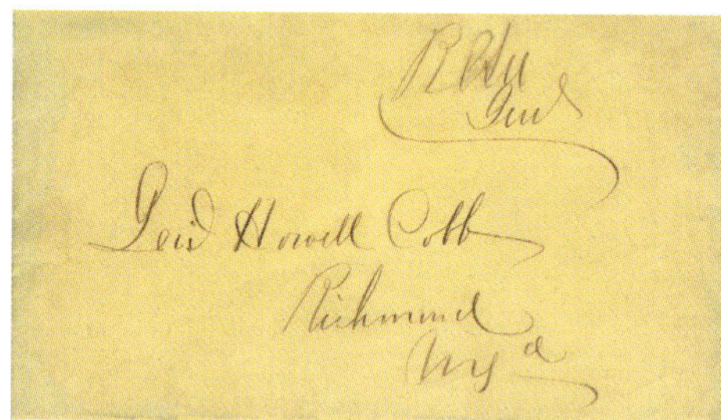

Envelope with autograph: "R.E. Lee / Gen'l"	7,500.
Same, on cover with Confederate handstamped paid or canceled Confederate stamp	*17,500.*

Mail is recorded from the following generals:

Alexander, E.P.
Allen, H.W.
Anderson, G.B.
Anderson, (J.) P.
Anderson, J.R.
Barry, J.P
Beauregard, P.G.T.
Bee, H.P.
Bell, T.H.
Benning, H.L.
Bonham, M.L.
Bragg, B.
Brevard, T.W.
Brown, W.M.
Bryan, G.
Cabell, W.L.
Capers, E.
Chesnut, J., Jr.
Chilton, R.H.
Clark, J.B.
Clayton, H.D.
Cobb, H.
Cobb, T.R.R.
Cocke, P. St.G.
Conner, J.
Corse, M.D.
Davis, W.G.M.
Deas, Z.
DeLagnel, J.A.
Dunovant, J.
Elliot, S. Jr.
Ewell, R.S.
Ferguson, S.W.
Forney, W.H.
Frazer, J.W.
French, S.G.
Garnett, R.B.
Gary, M.W.
Gatlin, Richard C.
Gibson, R.L.
Gilmer, J.F.
Girardy, V.J.B
Gist, S.R.
Goggin, J.M.
Gordon, G.W.
Gorgas, J.
Gregg, M.
Griffith, R.
Grimes, B.
Hagood, J.
Hampton, W.
Hardee, W.J.
Hays, H.T.
Hebert, P.O.
Higgins, E.
Hill, D.H.
Hindman, T.C.
Imboden, J.D.
Jackson, J.K.
Jackson, T.J.
Jenkins, M.
Johnson, A.R.
Johnson, B.T.
Johnson, E.
Johnston, J.E.
Jones, W.E.
Kennedy, J.D.
Kirkland, W.W.
Lawton, A.R.
Lee, E.G.
Lee, F.
Lee, R.E.
Lee, S.D.
Leventhorpe, C.
Lily, R.D.
Longstreet, J.
Marshall, H.
McGowan, S.
McLaws, L.
Mahone, W.
Morgan, J.H.
Northrop, L.B.
Page, R.L.
Paxton, E.F.
Payne, W.H.F.
Pegram, J.
Pender, W.D.
Pettigrew, J.J.
Polk, L.E.
Posey, C.
Preston, W.
Rains, J.E.
Ramseur, S.D.
Randolph, G.W.
Ransom, R., Jr.
Ripley, R.S.
Rodes, R.E.
Rosser, T.L.
Ruggles, D.
Sanders, J.C.C.
Semmes, P.J.
Semmes, R.
Shelley, C.M.
Sibley, H.H.
Slaughter, J.E.
Smith, E.K.
Sorrel, G.M.
Steuart, G.H.
Stevens, C.H.
Stovall, M.A.
Stuart, J.E.B.
Taliaferro, W.B.
Taylor, R.
Terry, W.
Toombs, R.A.
Tracy, E.D.
Trapier, J.H.
Trimble, I.R.
Vaughn, A.J., Jr.
Walker, Leroy P.
Walker, W.H.T.
Waterhouse, R.
Wise, H.A.
Wright, A.R.
Wright, M.K
York, Z.
Young, P.M.B.
Young, William H.

Official Imprints

The franking privilege, as authorized under United States law, was abolished by an Act of the Confederate Congress on February 23, 1861. In its place, Congress authorized designated officials of the Post Office Department to send free of postage all mail relating exclusively to their official duties or to the business of the Department. Subsequent acts of May 13, 1861 and May 23, 1864 added several more officials to the list authorized to send mail free of postage. The new "official mail" was effective on June 1, 1861 with the takeover of the postal operations in the South by the Confederate Post Office Department.

About the same time, Confederate postal officials had a variety of official envelopes prepared with imprints of the various bureaus and offices of the Department. Many were overprinted on seized stocks of Nesbitt and Star Die envelopes remaining in Southern post offices. Others were printed on commercial envelopes. These were the only official envelopes of the Confederacy that could be carried in the mail free of postage when properly endorsed by an authorized official of the Department.

The official imprints of the Confederate Post Office Department can be divided into two groups: those used by the Post Office Department in Richmond, Virginia and those used by the Trans-Mississippi Agency in Marshall, Texas. Uses from the Department in Richmond are known throughout the war. Uses from the Trans-Mississippi Agency date from May 1864 when the "official Mail" privilege was extended to the Agent for the Trans-Mississippi Department and the Auditor of that agency.

The Confederate Congress authorized the following franking privileges effective the dates listed below:

Effective June 1, 1861
- Postmaster General and chief clerks
- Auditor of the Treasury for the Post Office Department
- Chief of Appointment Bureau
- Chief of Contract Bureau
- Chief of Finance Bureau

Effective May 23, 1864
- Agent for the Trans-Mississippi Agency
- Auditor of the Trans-Mississippi Department

Prices in the section are for used covers in very fine condition. A used envelope must bear the signature of an authorized official and should bear a postmark and normally a "FREE" marking. Superb examples sell for more. Those in less than very fine condition sell for less. Unused examples sell for significantly less

In all instances the valuation is for the most common type of US envelope. Scarcer varieties of envelopes command a premium. The absence of a specific imprint or combination with envelopes does not imply scarcity or high value.

Definition of terms:

1853-55 Envelope: US Nesbitt issue without regard to size or paper color

1860-61 Envelope: US "Star Die" Nesbitt issue without regard to size or paper color

Commercial Envelope: Plain manufactured envelope without regard to size or paper color.

Editorial Note: Prior catalog editions utilized black and white ink tracings prepared many decades ago. These are not exact renderings of the imprints, only close representations. For example, tracings may show "Official Business" or other wording in a location which may not be as it actually appears on the envelopes. Or a state seal may exist on the envelope but is not noted in the old listings. The quality of the tracings is often poor, although many have been digitally enhanced. Where available, color images of actual imprints have replaced old tracings. When color images are used, imprints should be assumed to be at the upper right unless noted otherwise. Due to the variety of sources and image resolutions, the exact size of the images relative to each other may vary. There is no distinction made in the size of the envelopes, whether standard or legal size. Imprints often are known on both sizes.

Official Envelopes
Post Office Department

Confederate States of America,
POST OFFICE DEPARTMENT.

POD-01 Without signature (see note below)
- **a.** Commercial envelope 750.

Confederate States of America,
Post Office Department.

POD-02 Without signature (see note below)
- **a.** Commercial envelope* 750.

Confederate States of America,
POST OFFICE DEPARTMENT.

POD-03 Without signature (see note below)
- **a.** Commercial envelope 750.

Note: Used with postage paid by stamps prior to the takeover of the postal system on June 1, 1861 and implementation of the official free mail. Earliest recorded use is March 26, 1861 at Montgomery, Alabama. These were not actual official envelopes but, as forerunners of the Post Office Department franked envelopes, they are listed here as a matter of record.

Postmaster General

CONFEDERATE STATES OF AMERICA,
POST OFFICE DEPARTMENT,
OFFICIAL BUSINESS,
John H Reagan
POSTMASTER GENERAL.

PMG-01 John H. Reagan signature
- **a.** Commercial envelope *2,500.*

Note: Imprinted envelopes without signature but hand-addressed by John H. Reagan are known.

Imprinted envelopes with signature of H. St. Geo. Offutt as Acting Postmaster General are also known.

Appointment Bureau

Confederate States of America,
POST OFFICE DEPARTMENT,
OFFICIAL BUSINESS.
CHIEF OF THE APPOINTMENT BUREAU.

APP-01 B.N. Clements signature; "P" of "POST" under "St" of "States"; "O" of "OFFICIAL" under "FF" of "OFFICE"
- **a.** 3¢ 1860-61 envelope 500.
- **b.** Commercial envelope 450.

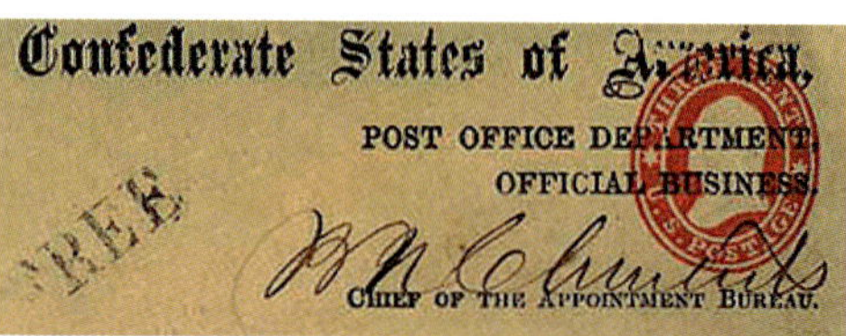

APP-02 B.N. Clements signature; "P" of "POST" under "St" of "States"; "O" of "OFFICIAL" under second "F" of "OFFICE"
- **a.** 3¢ 1860-61 envelope 500.
- **b.** Commercial envelope 450.

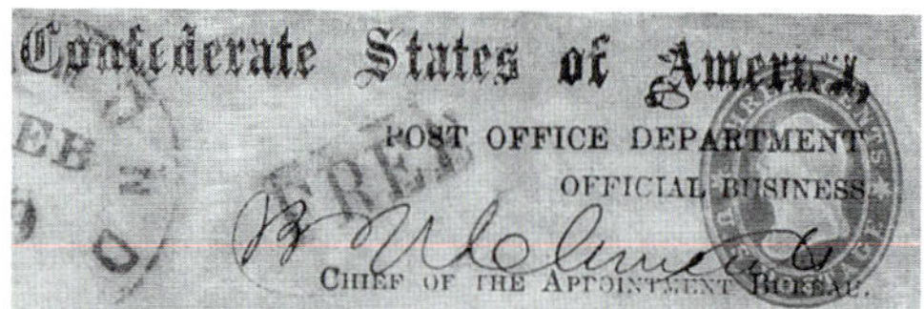

APP-03 B.N. Clements signature; "P" of "POST" under "St" of "States"; "O" of "OFFICIAL" under "IC" of "OFFICE"; "A" of "APPOINTMENT" under "FI" of "OFFICE"
- **a.** 3¢ 1860-61 envelope 500.

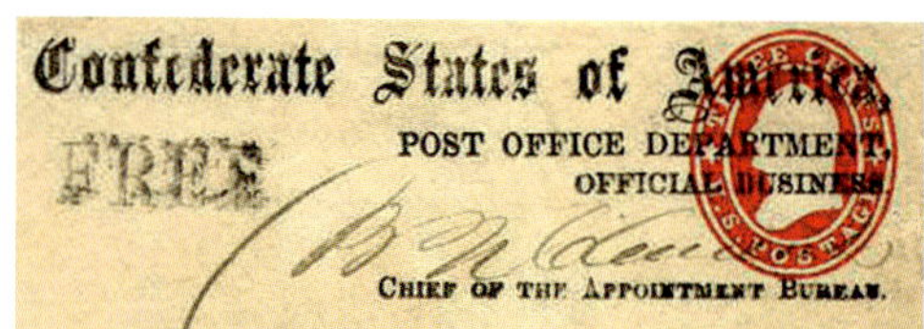

APP-04 B. N. Clements signature; "P" of "POST" under "St" of "States"; "O" of OFFICIAL" under "IC" of "OFFICE"; "A" of "APPOINTMENT" under "C" of "OFFICE"
- **a.** 3¢ 1853-55 envelope 500.
- **b.** 6¢ 1853-55 envelope* —
- **c.** 10¢ 1853-55 envelope 1,000.
- **d.** 3¢ 1860-61 envelope 500.
  Same, envelope inverted 750.
- **e.** Commercial envelope 450.

Confederate States of America,
POST OFFICE DEPARTMENT.
OFFICIAL BUSINESS
Appt.
CHIEF OF THE BUREAU

APP-05 B. N. Clements signature on FIN-04 with "Appt." (ms) over "FINANCE"
- **a.** 3¢ 1860-61 envelope 500.

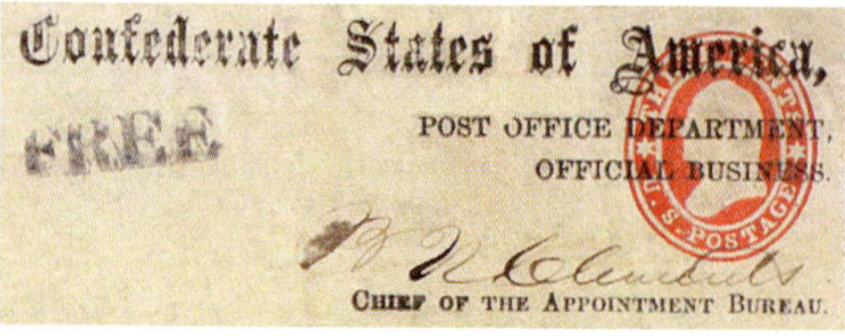

APP-06 B.N. Clements signature; "P" of "POST" under "at" of "States"
- **a.** 3¢ 1860-61 envelope 500.
- **b.** Commercial envelope 450.

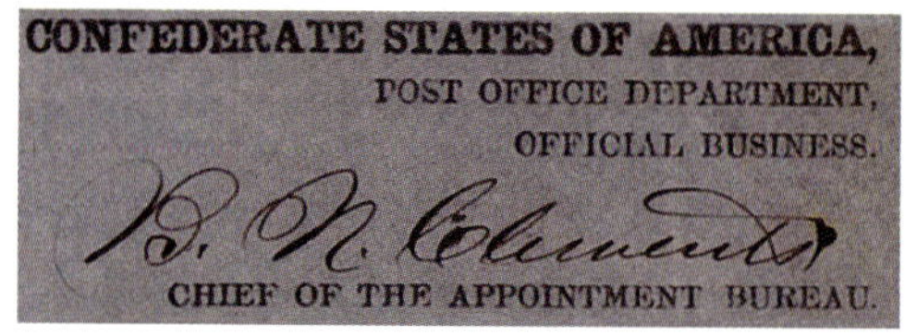

APP-07 B.N. Clements signature; "PO" of "POST" under "S" of "STATES"
- **a.** Commercial envelope 500.

In all instances, the valuation is for the most common type of US envelope. Scarcer varieties of envelopes command a premium. The absence of a specific imprint or combination with other envelopes does not imply scarcity or high value.

CONFEDERATE STATES OF AMERICA,
POST OFFICE DEPARTMENT.
OFFICIAL BUSINESS.
CHIEF OF THE APPOINTMENT BUREAU

APP-08 B.N. Clements signature; "P" of "POST" under "AT" of "STATES"

- **a.** 3¢ 1853-55 envelope 500.
- **b.** 6¢ 1853-55 envelope* —
- **c.** 3¢ 1860-61 envelope 500.
- **d.** Commercial envelope 450.

Note: See also, FIN-09.

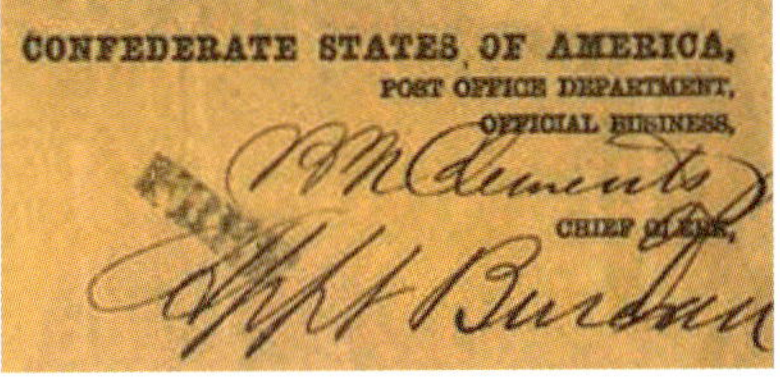

APP-09 B. N. Clements signature on CLK-08 with "of" (ms) over "CLERK" and "Appt Bureau" (ms) below.

- **a.** Commercial envelope 500.

Auditor's Office

AUD-01 B. Baker signature

- **a.** Commercial envelope 500.

AUD-02 B. Baker signature; "P" of "POST" under "fe" of "Confederate"

- **a.** Commercial envelope 500.

AUD-03 B. Baker signature; "P" of "POST" under "te" of "Confederate"

- **a.** 3¢ 1860-61 envelope 450.
- **b.** Commercial envelope 450.

Note: Image taken from private use of official envelope.

AUD-04 B. Baker signature

- **a.** Commercial envelope 600.

FREE.
OFFICIAL BUSINESS.
CONFEDERATE STATES OF AMERICA,
GENERAL POST OFFICE DEPARTMENT.
AUDITOR'S OFFICE.
Auditor.

AUD-05 H. C. Richardson signature; "Acting" (ms)

- **a.** Commercial envelope 450.

CONFEDERATE STATES OF AMERICA,
GENERAL POST OFFICE DEPARTMENT,
AUDITOR'S OFFICE.

AUD-06 W.W. Lester signature; "G" of "GENERAL" under "T" of "CONFEDERATE"

- **a.** Commercial envelope 450.

AUD-07 B. Baker signature on imprinted envelope like AUD-06

- **a.** Unknown type of envelope* —

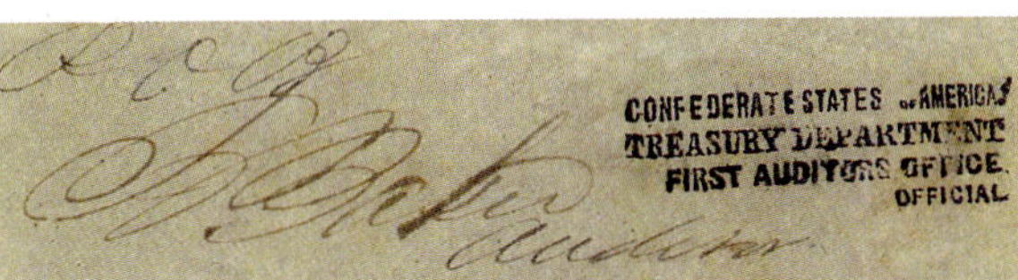

AUD-08 B. Baker signature with "POB" and "Auditor" (ms)

- **a.** Commercial envelope 500.

AUD-09 H. St. Geo. Offutt signature; "Acting" (ms)

- **a.** Commercial envelope 450.

[–]	symbol used in place of value to mean insufficient information to assign a price
[*italic*]	value typeface indicating the item is difficult to price accurately

AUD-10 J. W. Robertson signature; "Acting" (ms)
- **a.** Commercial envelope 450.

AUD-11 B. Baker signature
- **a.** Commercial envelope 450.
- **b.** Same, handstamped signature 400.

AUD-12 B. Baker signature
- **a.** Commercial envelope 450.
- **b.** Same, handstamped signature 400.

AUD-13 B. Baker Signature; printed "Postmaster," at center of envelope
- **a.** Commercial envelope 450.

AUD-14 J. W. Robertson signature; "Acting" (ms); printed "Postmaster," at center of envelope
- **a.** Commercial envelope 450.

AUD-15 I. W. M. Harris signature on imprinted envelope like AUD-14
- **a.** Unknown type of envelope* —

Contract Bureau

CON-01 H. St. Geo. Offutt signature; "P" of "POST" under "St" of "States"; "O" of "OFFICIAL" under "FF" of "OFFICE"
- **a.** Commercial envelope 450.

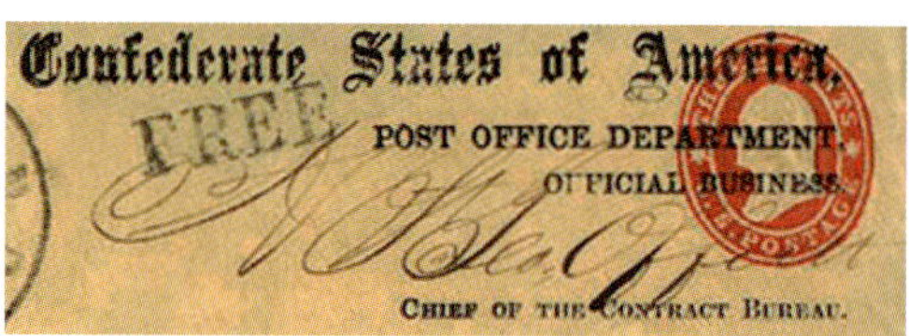

CON-02 H. St. Geo. Offutt signature; "P" of "POST" under "St" of "States"; "O" of OFFICIAL" under "IC" of "OFFICE"
- **a.** 3¢ 1853-55 envelope 500.
- **b.** 10¢ 1853-55 envelope* —
- **c.** 3¢ 1860-61 envelope 500.

CON-03 St. Geo Offutt signature on APP-01 or APP-02 with "Contract" (ms) over "APPOINTMENT"
- **a.** 6¢ 1853-55 envelope* —
- **b.** 3¢ 1860-61 envelope 500.
- **c.** Commercial envelope 450.

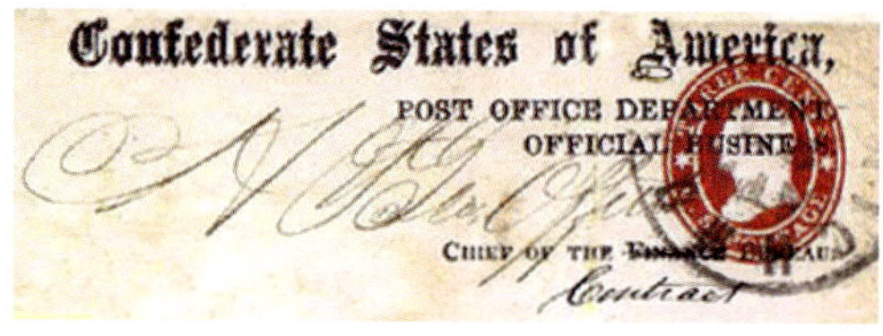

CON-04 H. St. Geo. Offutt signature on FIN-05 with "Contract" (ms) over "FINANCE"
- **a.** 3¢ 1860-61 envelope 600.

> Prices in the section are for used covers in very fine condition. A used envelope must bear the signature of an authorized official and should bear a postmark and normally a "FREE" marking. Superb examples sell for more. Those in less than very fine condition sell for less.

CON-05 H. St. Geo. Offutt signature; "P" of "POST" under "at" of "States"

a. Commercial envelope 450.

CON-06 H. St. Geo. Offutt signature; "P" of "POST" under second "t" of "States"

a.	3¢ 1853-55 envelope	500.
	Same, "CO" of "CONTRACT" missing	600.
b.	10¢ 1853-55 envelope	1,000.
c.	3¢ 1860-61 envelope	500.
d.	Commercial envelope	450.

Note: See also, CLK-02

Finance Bureau

FIN-01 Jno. L. Harrell signature on POD-01 with "Official Business" and "Chief of Finance Bureau" (ms)

a.	3¢ 1860-61 envelope	500.
b.	Commercial envelope	450.

FIN-02 Jno. L. Harrell signature; "P" of "POST" under "St" of "States"; "O" of "OFFICIAL" under "FF" of "OFFICE"

a.	3¢ 1853-55 envelope	500.
b.	3¢ 1860-61 envelope	500.
c.	Commercial envelope	450.

FIN-03 Jno. L. Harrell signature; "P" of "POST" under "St" of "States"; "O" of "OFFICIAL" under "IC" of "OFFICE"

a.	3¢ 1853-55 envelope	500.
b.	10¢ 1853-55 envelope	1,000.
c.	3c 1860-61 envelope	500.

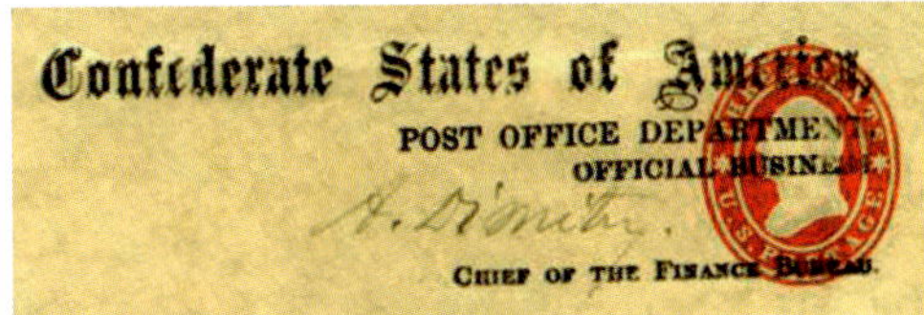

FIN-04 A. Dimitry signature; "P" of "POST" under "St" of "States"; "O" of "OFFICIAL" under "IC" of "OFFICE"

a.	3¢ 1853-55 envelope	500.
b.	3¢ 1860-61 envelope	500.

Note: Above imprint reported with fourth line slightly larger [not illustrated]. See also, APP-05

FIN-05 J. L. Lancaster signature on imprinted envelope like FIN-04

a. Unknown type of envelope* —

FIN-06 Jno. L. Harrell signature; "P" of "POST" under "at" of "States"

a.	3¢ 1853-55 envelope	500.
b.	10¢ 1853-55 envelope*	—
c.	3¢ 1860-61 envelope	500.
d.	Commercial envelope	450.

Note: Above imprint reported with fourth line slightly larger [not illustrated]

> In all instances, the valuation is for the most common type of US envelope. Scarcer varieties of envelopes command a premium. The absence of a specific imprint or combination with other envelopes does not imply scarcity or high value.

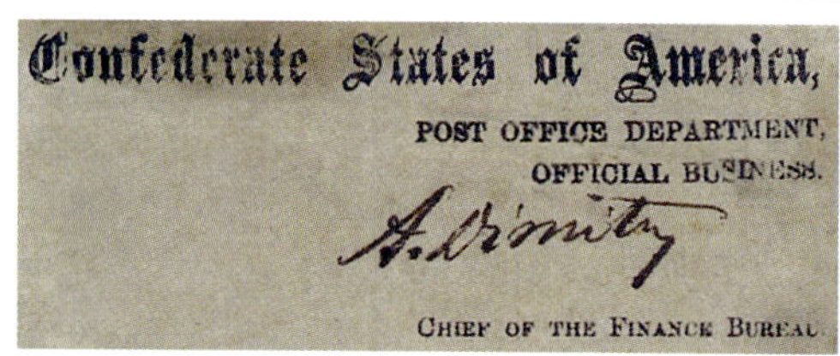

FIN-07 A. Dimitry signature; "P" of "POST" under "at" of "States"

- **a.** 3¢ 1860-61 envelope 500.
- **b.** Commercial envelope 450.

Note: See also, CLK-07

CONFEDERATE STATES OF AMERICA,
POST OFFICE DEPARTMENT.
OFFICIAL BUSINESS.
CHIEF OF THE FINANCE BUREAU.

FIN-08 Jno. L. Harrell signature

- **a.** 3¢ 1860-61 envelope 500.
- **b.** Commercial envelope 450.

Note: See also, DLO-03.

FIN-09 Jno. L. Harrell signature on APP-08 with "Finance" (ms) under "APPOINTMENT" [not illustrated]

- **a.** Commercial envelope 450.

Third Auditor's Office

THR-01 A. Moïse, Jr. signature; "P" of "POST" under "St" of "States"

- **a.** Commercial envelope 450.

THR-02 I. W. Harris signature; "P" of "POST" under "ta" of "States"

- **a.** Commercial envelope 450.

Chief Clerk

Confederate States of America,
POST OFFICE DEPARTMENT
OFFICIAL BUSINESS
CHIEF OF THE APPOINTMENT BUREAU.

CLK-01 B. Fuller signature on APP-02 with "Clerk" (ms) under "OF THE APPOINTMENT"

- **a.** 3¢ 1853-55 envelope 500.

Confederate States of America,
POST OFFICE DEPARTMENT,
OFFICIAL BUSINESS.
Clk. P.O.D.

CLK-02 B. Fuller signature on CON-06 with "Clk. P.O.D." (ms) over "OF THE CONTRACT BUREAU"

- **a.** 3¢ 1860-61 envelope 500.

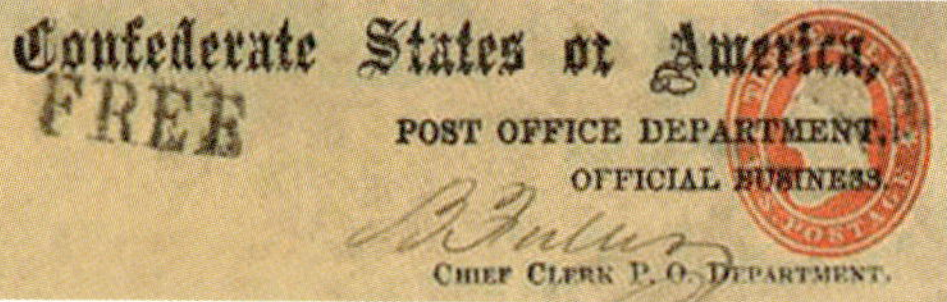

CLK-03 B. Fuller signature; "P" of "POST" under "St" of "States"

- **a.** 3¢ 1853-55 envelope 500.
- **b.** 3¢ 1860-61 envelope 500.
- **c.** Commercial envelope 450.

CLK-04 John B.A. Dimitry signature; "Act." Or "Act'g" (ms)

- **a.** 3¢ 1853-55 envelope 500.
- **b.** 3¢ 1860-61 envelope 500.

CLK-05 B. Fuller signature; "P" of "POST" under "at" of "States" [not illustrated]*

- **a.** 3¢ 1860-61 envelope 500.

Confederate States of America,
POST OFFICE DEPARTMENT.
OFFICIAL BUSINESS.
W.D. Miller
CHIEF CLERK

CLK-06 W.D. Miller signature
a. 3¢ 1860-61 envelope 500.

CLK-07 B. Fuller signature on FIN-07 with "Clerk" or "Clerk P.O.D." (ms) over "OF THE FINANCE BUREAU" [not illustrated]*
a. 3¢ 1853-55 envelope 500.
b. 3¢ 1860-61 envelope 500.

CLK-08 Only recorded as altered for use by the Appointment Bureau. See APP-09 for illustration.

J.G. Griswold
Act'g CHIEF CLERK P. O. DEPARTMENT.

CLK-09 J.G. Griswold signature; "Act'g" (ms)
a. 3¢ 1860-61 envelope 500.

Note: Illustration is of partial imprint

Trans–Mississippi Agency

The Trans-Mississippi Department was provided with official stationery, all of which are signed by Jas. H. Starr.

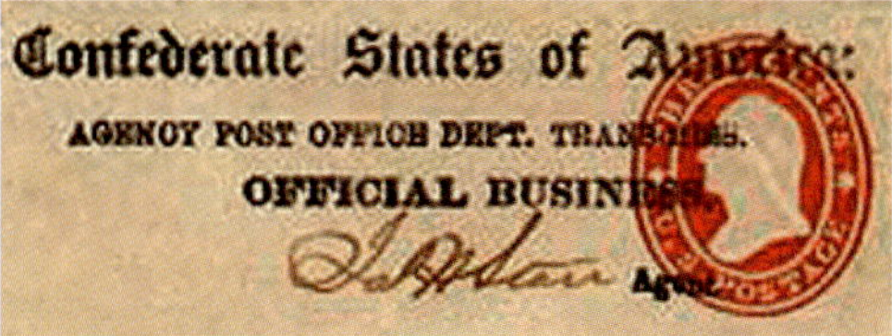

TRN-01 Jas H. Starr signature
a. 3¢ 1860-61 envelope 750.

TRN-02 Jas. H. Starr signature; colon or comma after "America"
a. 3¢ 1860-61 envelope 750.

TRN-03 Jas. H. Starr signature; colon or comma after "America"
a. 3¢ 1860-61 envelope 750.
b. Commercial envelope 750.

TRN-04 Jas. H. Starr signature
a. 3¢ 1860-61 envelope 750.

Confederate States of America.
AGENCY TRANS-MISS. P.O. DEP'T.
OFFICIAL BUSINESS.
J.H. Starr Agent.

TRN-05 Jas. H. Starr signature; boxed label
a. Commercial envelope *1,000.*

Dead Letter Office

Confederate States of America,
POST OFFICE DEPARTMENT,
DEAD LETTER OFFICE,
OFFICIAL BUSINESS.
A. Dimitry
CHIEF OF THE FINANCE BUREAU.

DLO-01 A. Dimitry signature; "P" of "POST" under "St" of "States"
a. Commercial envelope 750.

Prices in the section are for used covers in very fine condition. A used envelope must bear the signature of an authorized official and should bear a postmark and normally a "FREE" marking. Superb examples sell for more. Those in less than very fine condition sell for less.

DLO-02 Jno. F. Harrell signature; "P" of "POST" under second "t" of "States"

- **a.** 3¢ 1860-61 envelope 750.
- **b.** Commercial envelope 750.

CONFEDERATE STATES OF AMERICA,
POST OFFICE DEPARTMENT,
OFFICIAL BUSINESS.
CHIEF OF THE FINANCE BUREAU.
Dead Letter Office

DLO-03 Jno. F. Harrell signature on FIN-08 with "Dead Letter Office" (ms)

- **a.** Commercial envelope 750.

FIN-03 – Chief of the Finance Bureau Official envelope with Jno. L. Harrell signature

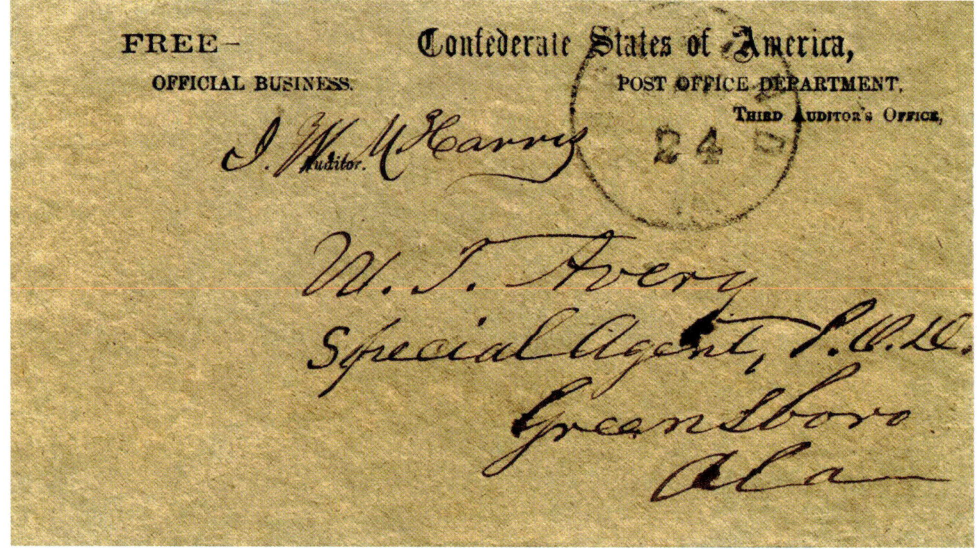

THR-02 – Third Auditor's Office Official envelope with I. W. Harris signature

Semi-Official Imprints

In addition to the official imprints of the Confederate Post Office Department, other departments of the Confederate Government prepared envelopes with their own imprints for official business. Individual states of the Confederacy also prepared envelopes with the imprints of their various government branches. These are considered semi-official in nature, as they required the payment of postage for transmission through the mails.

Although most Confederate semi-official imprints include the branch of government, it is not always easy to determine to which Department they belong. This is further confused by state semi-official imprints prepared by branches of state governments that mirrored the same branches of the Confederate Government. Some of these imprints bear no indication of either Confederate or state origin. The editors have made every effort to list the semi-official imprints under the proper department, bureau, service, district, division or army of the Confederate and state governments.

Prices in this section are for used covers in very fine condition. Those in less than very fine condition sell for less. A used envelope typically bears a handstamped rate or an adhesive postage stamp, but some examples are known carried outside of the mail system. Prices listed are for the most common postal use. Scarcer stamps, rare postmarks, or connections to historic figures and events all command higher prices.

Editor's Note: Prior catalog editions utilized black and white ink tracings prepared many decades ago. These are not exact renderings of the imprints, only close representations. For example, tracings may show "Official Business" or other wording in a location which may not be as it actually appears on the envelopes. Or a state seal may exist on the envelope but is not noted in the old listings. The quality of the tracings is often poor, although many have been digitally enhanced. Where available, color images of actual imprints have replaced old tracings. When color images are used, imprints should be assumed to be at the upper right unless noted otherwise. Due to the variety of sources and image resolutions, the exact size of the images relative to each other may vary. There is no distinction made in the size of the envelopes, whether standard or legal size. Imprints often are known on both sizes.

Confederate Government Imprints

Confederate Government semi-official imprints include those of the Executive, State, Treasury, Justice, Navy and War Departments and the Patent Office. The majority of imprints are for Departments, Bureaus, Services, Districts, Divisions and Armies under the War Department.

Military unit imprints previously listed for units below the regimental level have been deleted. It was determined these were not for the purpose of sending official business. Rather, they represent private stationery prepared by or for individuals within the units.

If a particular imprint cannot be found in this section, look under "State Imprints."

Executive Department

President's Office

Confederate States of America,
PRESIDENT'S OFFICE.
(Official Business.)

ED-01 "P" of "PRESIDENT'S" under first "e" of "Confederate" 1,000.

Note: Imprint reported with second line slightly larger

ED-02 "P" or "PRESIDENT'S" under "ra" of "Confederate" 1,000.

Executive Department

Confederate States of America,
EXECUTIVE DEPARTMENT,
(Official Business.)

ED-03 "E" of "EXECUTIVE" under second "e" of "Confederate" 750.

Confederate States of America.
EXECUTIVE DEPARTMENT
(Official Business.)

ED-04 "E" of "EXECUTIVE" under "er" of "Confederate" 750.

CONFEDERATE STATES OF AMERICA,
Executive Department,
OFFICIAL BUSINESS.

ED-05 "E" of "Executive" under "A" of "CONFEDERATE" 750.

CONFEDERATE STATES OF AMERICA,
Executive Department,
OFFICIAL BUSINESS.

ED-06 "E" of "Executive" under "S" of "STATES" 750.

Department of Justice

Department of Justice

Confederate States of America,
DEPARTMENT OF JUSTICE.

JD-01 500.

CONFEDERATE STATES OF AMERICA,
DEPARTMENT OF JUSTICE.

JD-02 500.

Confederate States of America,
DEPARTMENT OF JUSTICE.

JD-03 500.

Other Offices

Confederate
Office ~~United~~ States Attorney,
For ~~Southern~~ District of Mississippi.

JD-04 "Confederate" (ms) over "United" and "Southern" deleted (ms) 750.

CONFEDERATE STATES
Court House.
OFFICIAL BUSINESS.

JD-05 500.

Department of State

Department of State

Confederate States of America,
DEPARTMENT OF STATE.

DS-01 "D" of "DEPARTMENT" under "fe" of "Confederate" 750.

Confederate States of America,
DEPARTMENT OF STATE.

DS-02 "D" of "DEPARTMENT" under "d" of "Confederate" 750.

Confederate States of America,
DEPARTMENT OF STATE.

DS-03 "D" of "DEPARTMENT" under "r" of "Confederate" 750.

CONFEDERATE STATES OF AMERICA,
DEPARTMENT OF STATE.

DS-04 "D" of "DEPARTMENT" under "D" of "CONFEDERATE" 750.

CONFEDERATE STATES OF AMERICA,
DEPARTMENT OF STATE.

DS-05 "D" of "DEPARTMENT" under "R" of "CONFEDERATE" 750.

Navy Department

Navy Department

Confederate States of America,
NAVY DEPARTMENT.

ND-01 750.

Confederate States,
NAVY DEPARTMENT.

ND-02 750.

Confederate States of America,
NAVY DEPARTMENT.
OFFICIAL BUSINESS.

ND-03 Two bottom lines closely spaced 750.

Confederate States of Americ
NAVY DEPARTMENT.
OFFICIAL BUSINESS.

ND-04 Two bottom lines widely spaced 750.

Confederate States of America,
NAVY DEPARTMENT.
[OFFICIAL BUSINESS.]

ND-05 750.

Confederate States,
NAVY DEPARTMENT,
OFFICIAL BUSINESS.

ND-06 750.

> Due to the variety of sources of scans and image resolution, the exact size of the images relative to each other may vary.

Confederate States,
Navy Department.

ND-07 750.

Confederate States,
Navy Department.
OFFICIAL BUSINESS.

ND-08 750.

CONFEDERATE STATES,
NAVY DEPARTMENT
OFFICIAL BUSINESS.

ND-09 750.

CONFEDERATE STATES,
NAVY DEPARTMENT,
Official Business.

ND-10 750.

Confederate States of America
NAVY DEPARTMENT.
OFFICIAL BUSINESS.

ND-11 1,000.

Office of Orders and Details

Confederate ... America,
OFFICE ... AIL,
NAV... NT.

ND-12 750.

Confederate States of America,
Office of Orders and Detail,
NAVY DEPARTMENT.

ND-13 750.

Confederate States of America,
Office of Orders and Detail,
NAVY DEPARTMENT.

ND-14 750.

Confederate States,
Navy Department,
Office of Orders and Details.
OFFICIAL BUSINESS.

ND-15 750.

CONFEDERATE STATES,
NAVY DEPARTMENT.
OFFICE OF ORDERS AND DETAIL.
Official Business.

ND-16 "N" of "NAVY" under "F" of "CONFEDERATE" 1,000.

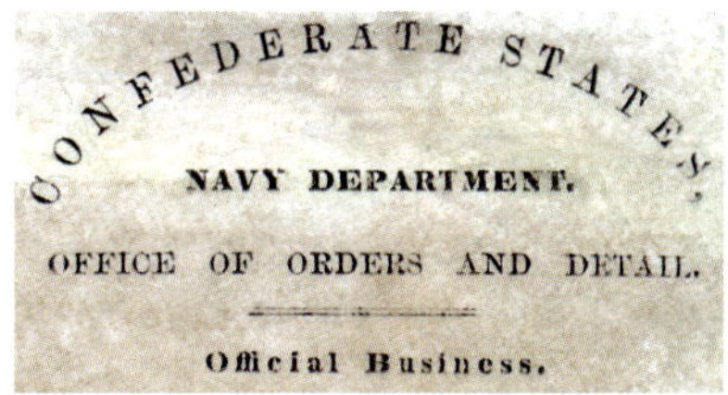

ND-17 "N" of "NAVY" under first "E" of "CONFEDERATE" 1,000.

Office of Ordnance and Hydrography

C. S. NAVY DEPARTMENT,
Office of Ordnance and Hydrography.

ND-18 "H" of "Hydrography" under "P" of "DEPARTMENT" 750.

C. S. NAVY DEPARTMENT,
Office of Ordnance and Hydrography.

ND-19 "H" of "Hydrography" under "PA" of "DEPARTMENT" 750.

Black and white tracings from previous catalogs are not exact renderings of the imprints. Tracings may show "Official Business" or other wording in a location which may not be as it actually appears on the envelopes.

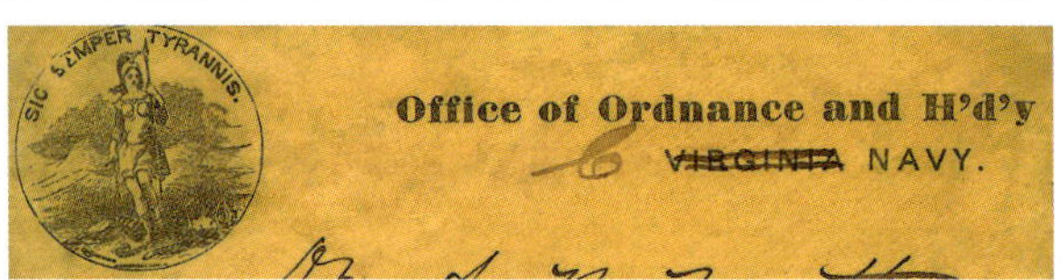

ND-20 "VIRGINIA" lined out and replaced by "C" or "CS" (ms) 1,000.

Note: See also, State Imprints S-VA-21 for Virginia use of this envelope

Office of Provision and Clothing

Confederate States, Navy Department,
OFFICE OF PROVISION AND CLOTHING.

ND-21 750.

Naval Stations and Yards

C. S. NAVY AGENT
Augusta Ga

ND-22 "Augusta Ga" (ms) under imprint 750.

C. S. NAVY AGENT,
AUGUSTA GEORGIA.
[OFFICIAL BUSINESS]

ND-23 1000.

C. S. NAVAL STATION,
Savannah, Ga.,
Commandant's Office.
[Official.]

ND-24 1,000.

Naval Commandant's Office,
Wilmington, N. C.

ND-25 1,000.

Naval Commandant's Office,
CHARLESTON, S. C
OFFICIAL BUSINESS.

ND-26 1,000.

Constructor's Office,
PEE DEE NAVY YARD.

ND-27 Mar's Bluff Navy Yard, South Carolina 1,000.

Commandant's Office,
NAVAL STATION,
Marion C. H., S. C.

ND-28 1,000.

Paymaster's Office,
NAVAL STATION,
Marion C. H., S. C.

ND-29 1,000.

River Defense Service

C. S. River Defence Service.
Gun-Boat Genl Bragg

ND-30 With gun-boat name added in ms 1,500.
a. Used from hospital (no gun-boat name) 1,000.

Treasury Department

Treasury Department

Treasury Department, C.S.A.

TD-01 350.

Confederate States of America,
TREASURY DEPARTMENT.

TD-02 350.

Confederate States of America,
TREASURY DEPARTMENT.

TD-03 Second line extends beyond "America," 350.

Confederate States of America,
TREASURY DEPARTMENT.

TD-04 "T" of "TREASURY" under "ed" of "Confederate" 350.

Note: Above imprint reported with second line slightly larger

Confederate States of America,
TREASURY DEPARTMENT.

TD-05 "T" of "TREASURY" under "d" of "Confederate" 350.

Note: Above imprint reported with second line slightly larger

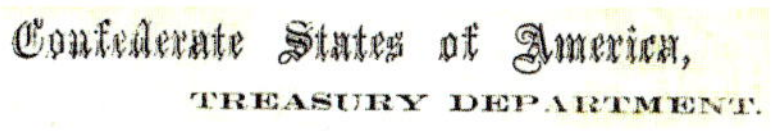

Confederate States of America,
TREASURY DEPARTMENT.

TD-06 "T" of "TREASURY" under "a" of "Confederate" 350.

Confederate States of America,
TREASURY DEPARTMENT.

TD-07 "T" of "TREASURY" under "n" of "Confederate"; second line sans serif 350.

Confederate States of America,
TREASURY DEPARTMENT,

TD-08 "T" of "TREASURY" under first "e" of "Confederate", second line sans serif 350.

Confederate States of America,
Treasury Department.

TD-09 "T" of "Treasury" under first "e" of "Confederate", second line upper and lower case 350.

Confederate States of America,
TREASURY DEPARTMENT.

TD-10 350.

Confederate States of America,
TREASURY DEPARTMENT.

TD-11 400.

Office of the Commissioner of Taxes

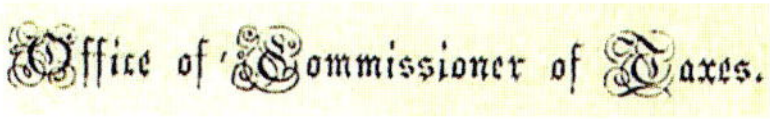

Office of Commissioner of Taxes.

TD-12 350.

Office of the Commissioner of Taxes.

TD-13 350.

a. Same, with embossed seal of "De la Rue & Co. London" under back flap 400.

Office of Commissioner of Taxes.
OFFICIAL BUSINESS.

TD-14 350.

Office of the Commissioner of Taxes.
OFFICIAL BUSINESS.

TD-15 350.

Register's Office

Confederate States of America,
TREASURY DEPARTMENT,
REGISTER'S OFFICE.

TD-16 400.

Confederate States of America,
Treasury Department,
REGISTER'S OFFICE.

TD-17 400.

Confederate States of America,
Treasury Department,
REGISTER'S OFFICE.

TD-18 400.

Treasurer's Office

Confederate States of America,
TREASURER'S OFFICE.

TD-19 350.

Confederate States of America,
Treasurer's Office.

TD-20 "T" of "Treasurer's" under "a" of "Confederate" 350.

Confederate States of America,
Treasurer's Office.

TD-21 "T" of "Treasurer's" under third "e" of "Confederate" 350.

Confederate States of America,
TREASURER'S, OFFICE

TD-22 "T" of "TREASURER'S" under "S" of "States" 350.

CONFEDERATE STATES OF AMERICA,
TREASURER'S OFFICE.

TD-23 350.

Treasury Department, C. S. A.
TREASURER'S OFFICE.

TD-24 Letters of "TREASURER'S OFFICE" close-spaced 350.

Treasury Department, C. S. A.
TREASURER'S OFFICE.

TD-25 Letters of "TREASURER'S OFFICE" open-spaced 350.

Confederate States of America,
Treasury Department,
TREASURER'S OFFICE.

TD-26 350.

Trans-Mississippi Agency

Confederate States of America.
TREASURY AGENCY, TRANS-MISS. DEPT.,
OFFICIAL BUSINESS

TD-27 750.

War Tax Office

WAR TAX OFFICE
COLUMBIA, S. C.

TD-28 Imprint at top left 400.

War Tax Office,
COLUMBIA, S. C.

TD-29 Imprint at top left 400.

First Auditor's Office

Confederate States of America,
TREASURY DEPARTMENT,
First Auditor's Office.

TD-30 350.

Confederate States of America,
TREASURY DEPARTMENT,
FIRST AUDITOR'S OFFICE.

TD-31 350.

CONFEDERATE STATES OF AMERICA,
TREASURY DEPARTMENT,
FIRST AUDITOR'S OFFICE.

TD-32 350.

CONFEDERATE STATES OF AMERICA
TREASURY DEPARTMENT
FIRST AUDITORS OFFICE
OFFICIAL

TD-33 350.

Second Auditor's Office

Confederate States of America,
TREASURY DEPARTMENT.
2. Auditors office

TD-34 "2. Auditor's office" (ms) added as third line 350.

Treasury Department C. S. A.,
SECOND AUDITOR'S OFFICE.
(Official Business.)

TD-35 350.

Treasury Department C. S. A.,
SECOND AUDITOR'S OFFICE.
(Official Business.)

TD-36 "S" of "SECOND" under "as" of "Treasury" 350.

Treasury Department C. S. A.,
SECOND AUDITOR'S OFFICE.
(Official Business.)

TD-37 "S" of "SECOND" under "r" of "Treasury" 350.

Office of Supervising Special Agent
OF TREASURY DEPARTMENT,

TD-38 350.

Other Offices

Office of Supervising Special Agent
OF TREASURY DEPARTMENT,
MOBILE.

TD-39 500.

Assistant Treasurer's Office,
CHARLESTON, S. C.

TD-40 500.

ASSISTANT TREASURER'S OFFICE, OFFICIAL BUSINESS.
CHARLESTON, S. C.

TD-41 500.

Assistant Treasurer's Office,
COLUMBIA, S. C.
Official Business.

TD-42 500.

War Department

War Department

Confederate States of America,
WAR DEPARTMENT.

WD-01 "W" of "WAR" under space between "Confederate" and "States" 400.

Confederate States of America
WAR DEPARTMENT.

WD-02 "W" of "WAR" under "ta" of "States" 400.

Confederate States of America
WAR DEPARTMENT.

WD-03 400.

Confederate States of America,
WAR DEPARTMENT.

WD-04 400.

CONFEDERATE STATES OF AMERICA.
War Department.

WD-05 400.

CONFEDERATE STATES OF AMERICA,
WAR DEPARTMENT.

WD-06 400.

Confederate States of America,
WAR DEPARTMENT,
OFFICIAL BUSINESS.

WD-07 "W" of "WAR" under "S" of "States" 400.

Confederate States of America,
WAR DEPARTMENT,
OFFICIAL BUSINESS.

WD-08 "W" of "WAR" under first "t" of "States"; "O" of "OFFICIAL" under first "E" of "DEPARTMENT" 400.

Confederate States of America,
WAR DEPARTMENT,
OFFICIAL BUSINESS.

WD-09 "W" of "WAR" under first "t" of "States"; "O" of "OFFICIAL" under "A" of "DEPARTMENT" 400.

Adjutant and Inspector General's Department

Adjutant General's Office

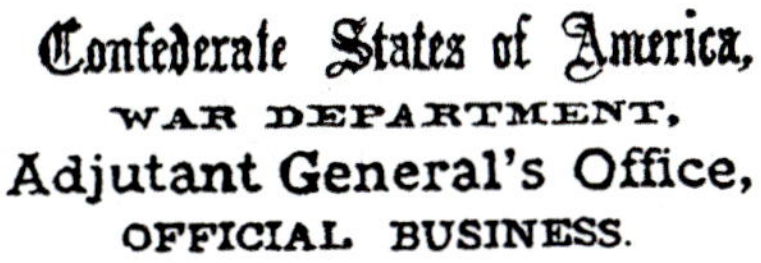

Confederate States of America,
WAR DEPARTMENT,
Adjutant General's Office,
OFFICIAL BUSINESS.

WD-AG-01 400.

Adjutant General's Office,
OFFICIAL BUSINESS.

WD-AG-02 400.

ADJUTANT GENERAL'S OFFICE.
OFFICIAL BUSINESS.

WD-AG-03 400.

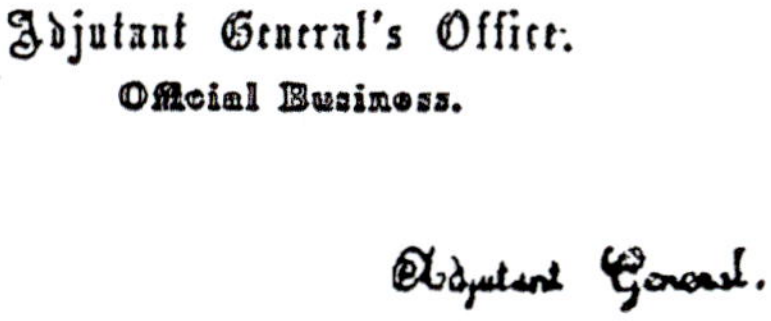

Adjutant General's Office.
Official Business.

Adjutant General.

WD-AG-04 400.

Adjutant and Inspector General's Office

Adjutant & Inspector General's Office
OFFICIAL BUSINESS

WD-AG-05 400.

Confederate States of America,
ADJUTANT AND INSPECTOR GENERAL'S OFFICE.
OFFICIAL BUSINESS.

WD-AG-06 "O" of "OFFICIAL" under "EC" of "INSPECTOR" 400.

Confederate States of America,
ADJUTANT AND INSPECTOR GENERAL'S OFFICE.
OFFICIAL BUSINESS

WD-AG-07 "O" of "OFFICIAL" under space between "INSPECTOR" and "GENERAL" 400.

WD-AG-08 400.

WD-AG-09 400.

Roll of Honor

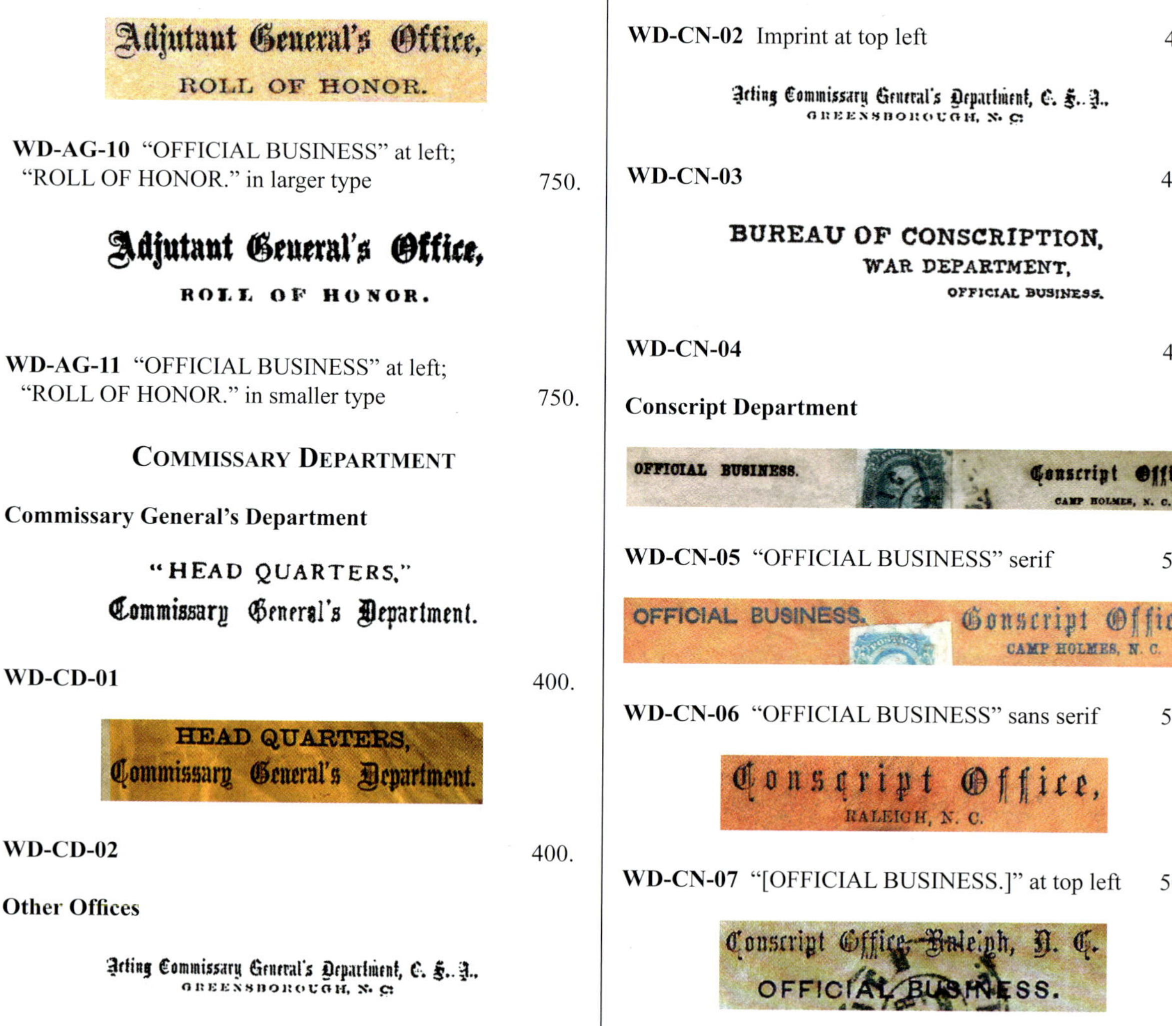

WD-AG-10 "OFFICIAL BUSINESS" at left; "ROLL OF HONOR." in larger type 750.

WD-AG-11 "OFFICIAL BUSINESS" at left; "ROLL OF HONOR." in smaller type 750.

Commissary Department

Commissary General's Department

WD-CD-01 400.

WD-CD-02 400.

Other Offices

WD-CD-03 500.

WD-CD-04 500.

Bureau of Conscription

Bureau of Conscription

WD-CN-01 400.

WD-CN-02 Imprint at top left 400.

WD-CN-03 400.

WD-CN-04 400.

Conscript Department

WD-CN-05 "OFFICIAL BUSINESS" serif 500.

WD-CN-06 "OFFICIAL BUSINESS" sans serif 500.

WD-CN-07 "[OFFICIAL BUSINESS.]" at top left 500.

WD-CN-08 500.

WD-CN-09 Period after "Department" 500.

Head-quarters, Conscript Department,
COLUMBIA, S. C.
OFFICIAL BUSINESS.

WD-CN-10 Comma after “Head-quarters” and “Department” 500.

Note: Some envelopes known with pre-printed address

Headquarters,
Conscript Department.
COLUMBIA, S. C.
OFFICIAL BUSINESS.

WD-CN-11 “C” of “COLUMBIA” under “ns” of “Conscript” 500.

Headquarters,
Conscript Department.
COLUMBIA, S. C.
OFFICIAL BUSINESS.

WD-CN-12 “C” of “COLUMBIA” under “sc” of “Conscript” 500.

Office of Com'd'nt Conscripts, Tenn.
ON OFFICIAL BUSINESS.

WD-CN-13 750.

Head Quarters Conscript Service,

WD-CN-14 (Texas) 750.

Enrolling Offices

WD-CN-15 500.

Chief Enrolling Office,
Seventh Congressional District, Wadesboro', N
Official Business.

WD-CN-16 500.

Chief Enrolling Office,
SEVENTH DISTRICT, WADESBOROUGH, NORTH CAROLINA
OFFICIAL BUSINESS.

WD-CN-17 500.

HEADQUARTERS POST COMMAND, AND
CHIEF ENROLLING OFFICE, FIFTH CONG'L DIST. SO. CA
(OFFICIAL BUSINESS.)

WD-CN-18 500.

Camps of Instruction

Head Quarters Camp of Instruction
RALEIGH, N. C.

WD-CN-19 500.
a. Same, “OFFICIAL BUSINESS” at left 500.

Camp of Instruction,
NEAR RALEIGH, N. C.

WD-CN-20 “OFFICIAL BUSINESS.” at left 500.

HEADQUARTERS,
CAMP OF INSTRUCTION,
COLUMBIA, S. C.
OFFICIAL BUSINESS.

WD-CN-21 500.

CONFEDERATE STATES OF AMERICA.
Head Quarters—Forces at Staunton, Va.,

WD-CN-22 500.

Bureau of Engineers

Engineer Bureau

Confederate States of America
War Department,
Engineer Bureau.

WD-EN-01 500.

Confederate States of America,
WAR DEPARTMENT,
ENGINEER BUREAU.
OFFICIAL BUSINESS.

WD-EN-02 500.

Confederate States of America,
WAR DEPARTMENT,
ENGINEER BUREAU.
OFFICIAL BUSINESS.

WD-EN-03 500.

Due to the variety of sources of scans and image resolution, the exact size of the images relative to each other may vary.

Other Offices

Pay Office Engineer Department, C. S.
No. 14, Law Building, Franklin Street
Official Business.

WD-EN-04 500.

WD-EN-05 Depot Engineer's Supplies, ATLANTA, GA.; OFFICIAL BUSINESS on three lines [not illustrated] 500.

C. S.
Depot Engineer's Supplies,
MACON, GA.
OFFICIAL BUSINESS.

WD-EN-06 Imprint at top left 500.

C. S.
DEPOT ENGINEER'S SUPPLIES.
MACON, GA.
OFFICIAL BUSINESS.

WD-EN-07 Imprint at top left 500.

Bureau of Indian Affairs

Confederate States of America,
War Department, Office of Indian Affairs

WD-IA-01 1,500.

Medical Department

Surgeon General's Office

Confederate States of America.
SURGEON GENL'S OFFICE.

WD-MD-01 400.

Confederate States of America,
SURGEON GENERAL'S OFFICE.

WD-MD-02 "S" of "SURGEON" under "ra" of "Confederate" 400.

Confederate States of America,
SURGEON GENERAL'S OFFICE.

WD-MD-03 "S" of "SURGEON" under "t" of "Confederate" 400.

Confederate States of America,
WAR DEPARTMENT,
SURGEON GENERAL'S OFFICE.

WD-MD-04 400.

Confederate States of America.
SURGEON GENERAL'S OFFICE.
OFFICIAL BUSINESS.

WD-MD-05 "S" of "SURGEON" under "de" of "Confederate"; "O" of "OFFICIAL" under "ER" of "GENERAL'S" 400.

Confederate States of America.
SURGEON GENERAL'S OFFICE.
OFFICIAL BUSINESS.

WD-MD-06 "S" of "SURGEON" under "de" of "Confederate"; "O" of "OFFICIAL" under "L" of "GENERAL'S" 400.

Confederate States of America,
SURGEON GENERAL'S OFFICE.
OFFICIAL BUSINESS.

WD-MD-07 "S" of "SURGEON" under "ra" of "Confederate" 400.

CONFEDERATE STATES OF AMERICA.
SURGEON GENERAL'S OFFICE.

WD-MD-08 "S" of "SURGEON" under first "E" of "CONFEDERATE" 400.

Note: Image taken from private use of semi-official envelope

CONFEDERATE STATES OF AMERICA,
SURGEON GENERAL'S OFFICE.
OFFICIAL BUSINESS.

WD-MD-09 "S" of "SURGEON" under "AT" of "CONFEDERATE" 400.

CONFEDERATE STATES OF AMERICA,
SURGEON GENERAL'S OFFICE,
OFFICIAL BUSINESS

WD-MD-10 "S" of "SURGEON" under space between "CONFEDERATE" and "STATES" 400.

Other Surgeon General's Offices

Surgeon General's Office.–Shreveport, La.
Official Business.

WD-MD-11 600.

WD-MD-12 "OFFICIAL BUSINESS." at top left 500.

Trans-Mississippi Department

WD-MD-13 600.

Conscript Service

WD-MD-14 500.

Note: Imprint reduced at right on only image available

Medical Directors

WD-MD-15 500.

WD-MD-16 "G" of "GENERAL" under "D" of "Director's"; "O" of "OFFICIAL" under "L" of "GENERAL" 500.

WD-MD-17 "G" of "GENERAL" under "D" of "Director's"; "O" of "OFFICIAL" under "H" of "HOSPITALS" 500.

WD-MD-18 "G" of "GENERAL" under "Di" of "Director's" 500.

WD-MD-19 "PRINTED CIRCULAR" imprint at top left 500.

WD-MD-20 500.

WD-MD-21 "R" of "RICHMOND" under "D" of "Director's" 500.

WD-MD-22 "R" of "RICHMOND" under "ir" of Director's" 500.

Note: Image taken from private use of semi-official envelope

Medical Purveyors

WD-MD-23 500.

WD-MD-24 500.

WD-MD-25 500.

OFFICIAL.
Medical Purveyor's Office, Knoxville, Tenn.

WD-MD-26 600.

Confederate States of America,
Medical Purveyor's Office, Richmond, Va.
OFFICIAL BUSINESS.

WD-MD-27 400.

Hospital Inspectors

CONFEDERATE STATES OF AMERICA,
Office Inspector of Hospitals,
OFFICIAL BUSINESS.

WD-MD-28 500.

General Hospitals

Confederate States Army.
GUYTON GENERAL HOSPITAL,
GUYTON, GA.

WD-MD-29 "OFFICIAL BUSINESS." at top left 500.

GENERAL MILITARY HOSPITAL (No. 2.)
WILSON, N. C.

WD-MD-30 500.

Note: Image taken from private use of semi-official envelope

TEXAS GENERAL HOSPITAL.
OFFICIAL BUSINESS.

WD-MD-31 750.

Official Business.
General Hospital, C. S. A., No. 1,
Post at Lynchburg, Va.

WD-MD-32 "Charge Box 25." imprint at top left 500.

Nitre and Mining Bureau

Nitre and Mining Bureau

WAR DEPARTMENT, C. S. A.
NITRE AND MINING BUREAU.

WD-NM-01 Imprint at left with "OFFICIAL BUSINESS." imprint at right 500.

C. S. NITRE AND MINING BUREAU.
OFFICIAL BUSINESS.

WD-NM-02 "O" of "OFFICIAL" under "I" of "MINING"; imprint at left 500.

C. S. NITRE AND MINING BUREAU.
OFFICIAL BUSINESS.

WD-NM-03 "O" of "OFFICIAL" under "NG" of "MINING"; imprint at left 500.

CONFEDERATE STATES OF AMERICA,
WAR DEPARTMENT,
NITRE AND MINING BUREAU,
OFFICIAL BUSINESS.

WD-NM-04 "W" of "WAR" under "T" of "CONFEDERATE" 500.

CONFEDERATE STATES OF AMERICA,
WAR DEPARTMENT,
NITRE AND MINING BUREAU.
OFFICIAL BUSINESS.

WD-NM-05 "W" of "WAR" under "TE" of "CONFEDERATE"; "D" of "DEPARTMENT" under "A" of "STATES"; imprint at left 500.

CONFEDERATE STATES OF AMERICA,
WAR DEPARTMENT,
NITRE AND MINING BUREAU.
OFFICIAL

WD-NM-06 "W" of "WAR" under "E" of "CONFEDERATE" 500.

CONFEDERATE STATES OF AMERICA,
WAR DEPARTMENT,
NITRE AND MINING BUREAU.
OFFICIAL BUSINESS

WD-NM-07 "W" of "WAR" under last letter and space after "CONFEDERATE"; "D" of "DEPARTMENT" under second "T" of "STATES" 500.

CONFEDERATE STATES OF AMERICA,
WAR DEPARTMENT,
NITRE BUREAU,
OFFICIAL BUSINESS

WD-NM-08 "W" of "WAR" under space before and first letter of "STATES" 500.

NFEDERATE STATES OF AMERICA,
WAR DEPARTMENT,
NITRE BUREAU,
OFFICIAL BUSINESS.

WD-NM-09 "W" of "WAR" under "TA" of "STATES" 500.

Nitre and Mining Service

C. S. NITRE AND MINING SERVICE,
Official Business.

WD-NM-10 Imprint at top left 500.

C. S. NITRE AND MINING SERVICE.
OFFICIAL BUSINESS.

WD-NM-11 Imprint at top left 500.

C. S. NITRE AND MINING SERVICE.
OFFICIAL BUSINESS.

WD-NM-12 "O" of "OFFICIAL" under "NG" of "MINING" 500.

CONFEDERATE STATES OF AMERICA,
NITRE AND MINING SERVICE,
OFFICIAL BUSINESS.

WD-NM-13 "N" of "NITRE" under first "S" of "STATES" 500.

CONFEDERATE STATES OF AMERICA,
NITRE AND MINING SERVICE.
OFFICIAL BUSINESS.

WD-NM-14 "N" of "NITRE" under first "T" of "STATES"; imprint at left 500.

C. S. NITRE AND MINING SERVICE,
DISBURSING OFFICE.
OFFICIAL BUSINESS.

WD-NM-15 750.

Ordnance Bureau

Ordnance Bureau

Ordnance Bureau

WD-OD-01 350.

ORDNANCE BUREAU.

WD-OD-02 350.

Ordnance Office

Confederate States of America,
ORDNANCE OFFICE,
WAR DEPARTMENT.

WD-OD-03 400.

Confederate States of America,
WAR DEPARTMENT,
ORDNANCE OFFICE,
OFFICIAL BUSINESS.

WD-OD-04 400.

Confederate States of America,
WAR DEPRATMENT,
ORDNANCE OFFICE,
OFFICIAL BUSINESS.

WD-OD-05 "DEPARTMENT" misspelled 400.

Armories and Arsenals

MOUNT VERNON ARSENAL
OFFICIAL BUSINESS

WD-OD-06 (Alabama) 500.

ATLANTA ARSENAL
official business

WD-OD-07 500.

AUGUSTA ARSENAL,
Official Business.

WD-OD-08 500.

AUGUSTA ARSENAL,
OFFICIAL BUSINESS.

WD-OD-09 500.

Note: Image taken from private use of semi-official envelope

CONFEDERATE STATES ARMORY,
MACON, GA.
OFFICIAL BUSINESS.

WD-OD-10 500.

Confederate States Armory,
HOLLY SPRINGS, MISS.
OFFICIAL BUSINESS

WD-OD-11 750.

Black and white tracings from previous catalogs are not exact renderings of the imprints. Tracings may show "Official Business" or other wording in a location which may not be as it actually appears on the envelopes.

Confederate States Armory,
ASHEVILLE, N. C.
OFFICIAL BUSINESS.

WD-OD-12 500.

CONFEDERATE STATES OF AMERICA,
ORDNANCE DEPARTMENT,
Fayetteville Arsenal and Armory.

WD-OD-13 500.

CHARLESTON ARSENAL.
OFFICIAL BUSINESS.

WD-OD-14 Imprint at top left 500.

TEXAS ARSENAL, SAN ANTONIO.
OFFICIAL BUSINESS.

WD-OD-15 750.

Confederate States Armory,
RICHMOND, VA.
OFFICIAL BUSINESS.

WD-OD-16 500.

C. S. Arsenal,
RICHMOND, VA.
Official Business.

WD-OD-17 500.

Laboratories

CONFEDERATE STATES OF AMERICA,
LABORATORY DEPARTMENT.
OFFICIAL BUSINESS.

WD-OD-18 500.

C. S. Central Laboratory. (Ord.)
MACON, GA.
OFFICIAL BUSINESS.

WD-OD-19 500.

C. S. Central Laboratory, (Ordn.)
MACON, GA.
[OFFICIAL BUSINESS.]

WD-OD-20 Wavy line under second line 500.

C. S. Central Laboratory, (Ordn.)
MACON, GA.
[OFFICIAL BUSINESS.]

WD-OD-21 Straight line under second line 500.

Bureau of Prisoner Exchange

Office Commissioner for Exchange,
Fortress Monroe.
VA

WD-PE-01 1,500.

Quartermaster Department

Quartermaster Department

Quartermaster's Department.

WD-QM-01 350.

Confederate States of America
Quartermaster's Department,

WD-QM-02 400.

CONFEDERATE STATES OF AMERICA.
Quartermaster's Department.

WD-QM-03 400.

OFFICIAL BUSINESS.
QUARTERMASTER'S DEPARTMENT.

WD-QM-04 400.

Confederate States of America,
Quartermaster's Department,
[Official Business.]

WD-QM-05 400.

Confederate States of America,
Quartermaster's Department.
[Official Business.]

WD-QM-06 400.

Confederate States of America.
Quartermaster's Department.
Official Business.

WD-QM-07 400.

Quartermaster General's Office

Confederate States of America,
QUARTER MASTER GENERAL'S OFFICE.
(Official Business.)

WD-QM-08 400.

Confederate States of America,
Quarter Master General's Office.
(Official Business.)

WD-QM-09 400.

CONFEDERATE STATES OF AMERICA.
Quartermaster General's Office.
OFFICIAL BUSINESS.

WD-QM-10 400.

Other Quartermaster Offices

Office Assistant Quartermaster.
OFFICIAL BUSINESS.

WD-QM-11 400.

Confederate States of America,
ASSISTANT QUARTER MASTER'S DEPARTMENT.
OFFICIAL BUSINESS.

WD-QM-12 400.

Controlling Quartermaster's Office, Ala.
OFFICIAL BUSINESS.

WD-QM-13 500.

OFFICIAL.
Quartermaster's Department,
Selma, Ala.

WD-QM-14 500.

QUARTERMASTERS DEPT
S. Hillyer
Maj & Qm
C.S.A.
SELMA, ALA.

WD-QM-15 500.

OFFICIAL BUSINESS.
Charge Box
POST QUARTER-MASTER'S OFFICE
Lake City, Florida,

WD-QM-16 750.

WD-QM-17 500.

Note: Image taken from private use of semi-official envelope

OFFICIAL.
Q. M. DEPARTMENT,
COLUMBUS, GA.

WD-QM-18 400.

WD-QM-19 (Columbus, Georgia) 500.

WD-QM-20 (Georgia, town unknown) 400.

OFFICIAL BUSINESS
FROM
G. M. FOGG, JR., CAPT. A. Q. M.,
Brookhaven, Miss.

WD-QM-21 500.

OFFICIAL BUSINESS. { A. Q. M. Department,
MERIDIAN, MISSISSIPPI,
S. F PENNINGTON,
Post and Depot Q. M. }

WD-QM-22 500.

Quartermaster's Office C. S. A.
RALEIGH, N. C.

WD-QM-23 "R" of "RALEIGH" under "m" of "Quartermaster; "OFFICIAL BUSINESS." at left 500.

a. Same, "OFFICIAL BUSINESS." on third line 500.

Quartermaster's Office, C. S. A.
RALEIGH, N. C.
OFFICIAL BUSINESS.

WD-QM-24 "R" of "RALEIGH" under "a" of "Quartermaster's" 400.

OFFICIAL BUSINESS.
Quartermaster's Office, C. S. A.
RALEIGH, N. C.

WD-QM-25 400.

OFFICIAL BUSINESS.
Post Quartermaster's Office, C. S. A.
RALEIGH, N. C.

WD-QM-26 Imprint at top left 400.

OFFICIAL BUSINESS.
Post Quarter Master's
TRANSPORTATION DEPARTMENT
RALEIGH, N. C.

WD-QM-27 500.

Confederate States of America,
OFFICE ASST. QUARTERMASTER.

WD-QM-28 (Hardeeville, South Carolina) 400.

WD-QM-29 500.

> There is no distinction made in the size of the envelopes, whether standard or legal size. Imprints often are known on both sizes.

QUARTERMASTER'S OFFICE,
CAMP PICKENS (Manassas.)

WD-QM-30 400.

Quartermaster's Department,
Staunton, Virginia.

WD-QM-31 400.

Quartermaster's Office,
STAUNTON, VA.

WD-QM-32 Imprint at top left 400.

Locomotive Shops

WD-QM-33 Imprint at top left 750.

OFFICIAL BUSINESS.
C. S. LOCOMOTIVE SHOPS,
RALEIGH, N. C.

WD-QM-34 Imprint at top left 750.

Note: Image taken from private use of semi-official envelope

Signal Bureau

Signal Bureau

WD-SB-01 Imprint at top left 750.

WAR DEPARTMENT
SIGNAL BUREAU.
OFFICIAL BUSINESS

WD-SB-02 750.

WAR DEPARTMENT
SIGNAL BUREAU
OFFICIAL BUSINESS

WD-SB-03 750.

Signal Office

WD-SB-04 750.

Subsistence Department

Subsistence Department

Subsistence Department, C.S.

WD-SD-01 350.

WD-SD-02 350.

Confederate States of America,
SUBSISTENCE DEPARTMENT.

WD-SD-03 "S" of "SUBSISTENCE" under "r" of "Confederate" 350.

Confederate States of America,
SUBSISTENCE DEPARTMENT.

WD-SD-04 "S" of "SUBSISTENCE" under "a" of "Confederate" 350.

CONFEDERATE STATES OF AMERICA,
SUBSISTENCE DEPARTMENT.

WD-SD-05 350.

SUBSISTENCE DEPARTMENT,
C. S. A.
OFFICIAL BUSINESS.

WD-SD-06 350.

Subsistence Bureau

Confederate States of America,
SUBSISTENCE BUREAU.

WD-SD-07 350.

Field Offices

Subsistence Department, C.S.
GREENSBOROUGH, N. C.

WD-SD-08 400.

Subsistence Department,
Greensboro, N. C.

WD-SD-09 400.

Subsistence Department, C. S. A.
OFFICIAL BUSINESS.

WD-SD-10 400.

Confederate States of America,
SUBSISTENCE DEPARTMENT.
OFFICE OF CHIEF COMMISSARY OF VIRGINIA.

WD-SD-11 400.

[OFFICIAL.] CONFEDERATE STATES OF AMERICA,
SUBSISTENCE DEPARTMENT,
OFFICE OF CHIEF COMMISSARY OF VIRGINIA.

WD-SD-12 400.

CONFEDERATE STATES OF AMERICA,
SUBSISTENCE DEPARTMENT.
OFFICE OF CHIEF COMMISSARY OF VIRGINIA.

WD-SD-13 "[OFFICIAL.]" at top left 400.

Military Departments

Department No. 1

Confederate States of America,
HEAD QUARTERS, DEPT. No 1,
OFFICIAL BUSINESS.

WD-ZA-01 500.

Confederate States of America,
HEAD QUARTERS, DEPT. No. 1.
OFFICIAL BUSINESS.

WD-ZA-02 500.

Confederate States of America.
HEADQUARTERS DEPARTMENT No. 1.
OFFICIAL BUSINESS.

WD-ZA-03 500.

Department of Alabama, Mississippi and East Louisiana

INSPECTOR GENERAL'S OFFICE,
DEPARTMENT OF
Alabama, Mississippi & East Louisiana.
OFFICIAL BUSINESS.

WD-ZA-04 750.

INSPECTOR GENERAL'S
OFFICE,
DEPARTMENT OF ALABAMA,
MISSISSIPPI and EAST LOUISIANA.
OFFICIAL BUSINESS.

WD-ZA-05 750.

OFFICIAL BUSINESS. { CHIEF Q. M. OFFICE.
Dept. Ala., Miss. and East La.,
JNO. W. YOUNG,
Major & Chief Q. M.

WD-ZA-06 750.

Department of Appomattox

Head Quarters---Department of Appomattox
OFFICIAL BUSINESS.

WD-ZA-07 600.

Note: See also, WD-ZA-11, Department of Norfolk for similar imprint

WD-ZA-08 600.

Department of the Cumberland

HEAD QUARTERS CHIEF OF CAVALRY,
DEPARTMENT OF THE CUMBERLAND
OFFICIAL BUSINESS

WD-ZA-09 750.

a. Same but with periods added at end of second and third lines 500.

Department of East Tennessee

Chief Pay M. W. Office, Dep't E. T.
OFFICIAL BUSINESS.

WD-ZA-10 750.

Department of Norfolk

Head Quarters---Department of Norfolk,
OFFICIAL BUSINESS.

WD-ZA-11 500.

Note: See also, WD-ZA-07, Department of Appomattox for use of this imprint by that Department

Department of North Carolina

Head Quarters Dep't North Carolina,
OFFICIAL BUSINESS.

WD-ZA-12 500.

Head Quarters, Department of N. C.
(OFFICIAL BUSINESS.)

WD-ZA-13 500.

Note: Image taken from private use of semi-official envelope

Head Quarters Dept. N. C.,
OFFICIAL BUSINESS.

WD-ZA-14 500.

Department of North Carolina and Southern Virginia

CONFEDERATE STATES,
Head-Quarters Department N. Carolina and Southern Va.
OFFICIAL BUSINESS.

WD-ZA-15 Imprint at top center 500.

Department of Northern Virginia

HEAD QUARTERS,
DEPT. NORTHERN VA.

WD-ZA-16 500.

HEAD QRS. DEPARTMENT
NORTHERN VA.

WD-ZA-17 500.

Department of South Carolina

Quartermaster's Office, C. S. Army,
Military Department of South Carolina.
Official Business.

WD-ZA-18 500.

Note: The position of "Official Business." may be different from that shown

Quartermaster's Office, C. S. Army,
Military Department of South Carolina.

WD-ZA-19 500.

Department of South Carolina and Georgia

CONFEDERATE STATES.
Department of South Carolina and Georgia
OFFICIAL BUSINESS.

WD-ZA-20 Imprint at top center 500.

CONFEDERATE STATES.
Head Quarters, Department of South Carolina and Georgia
OFFICIAL BUSINESS.

WD-ZA-21 Imprint at top center 500.

CONFEDERATE STATES.
Office of Chief Quartermaster
Military Department of So. Ca. and Ga.

WD-ZA-22 "OFFICIAL BUSINESS." at top left 750.

Department of South Carolina, Georgia and Florida

CONFEDERATE STATES.
Head Quarters, Department of South Carolina, Georgia and Florida.
OFFICIAL BUSINESS.

WD-ZA-23 Imprint at top center 750.

CONFEDERATE STATES.
Head Quarters, Department of So. Ca., Ga. and Fla.
OFFICIAL BUSINESS.

WD-ZA-24 Imprint at top center 750.

HEAD QUARTERS, 1st MILITARY DISTRICT,
Department of South Carolina, Georgia and Florida.
OFFICIAL BUSINESS.

WD-ZA-25 Imprint at top center 750.

HEAD QUARTERS, 1st MILITARY DIST.
Department of South Carolina, Georgia and Florida,
OFFICIAL BUSINESS

WD-ZA-26 750.

HEAD QUARTERS, 2ND AND 6TH MILITARY DISTRICTS.
Department of South Carolina, Georgia and Florida.
OFFICIAL BUSINESS.

WD-ZA-27 Imprint at top center 750.

Trans-Mississippi Department

Head Quarters Department of Trans-Mississippi
OFFICIAL BUSINESS.

WD-ZA-28 750.

Head Quarters, Trans-Miss. Department
OFFICIAL BUSINESS.

WD-ZA-29 750.

Head Quarters, Trans-Mississippi Dep't.
OFFICIAL BUSINESS

WD-ZA-30 750.

Head Quarters, Engineer Department.
Department of Trans-Mississippi
OFFICIAL BUSINESS.

WD-ZA-31 750.

Note: The position of "OFFICIAL BUSINESS." may be different from that shown

INSPECTOR GENERAL'S OFFICE,
Trans-Mississippi Department.
Official Business.

WD-ZA-32 750.

Note: The position of "Official Business." may be different from that shown

Western Department

Headquarters Western Department,
OFFICIAL BUSINESS.

WD-ZA-33 600.

Military Districts

District of Florida

Military District of Georgia,
OFFICE OF CHIEF COMMISSARY.

WD-ZB-01 750.

District of Georgia

[OFFICIAL.] Military District of Georgia,
OFFICE OF ASSISTANT COMMISSARY.

WD-ZB-02 "OFFICIAL BUSINESS." at top left 500.

Military District of Georgia,
OFFICE OF CHIEF COMMISSARY.

WD-ZB-03 "[OFFICIAL.]" at top left 500.

[OFFICIAL.] Military District of Georgia,
OFFICE OF ASSISTANT COMMISSARY.

WD-ZB-04 500.

Note: The position of "[OFFICIAL.]" may be different from that shown

CONFEDERATE STATES.
Head Quarters Military District of Georgia,
ORDNANCE OFFICE,
OFFICIAL BUSINESS.

WD-ZB-05 Imprint at top center 500.

District of Western Louisiana

HEADQUARTERS,
DISTRICT WESTESN LOUISIANA.

WD-ZB-06 750.

HEADQUARTERS,
DISTRICT WESTERN LOUISIANA.

WD-ZB-07 750.

Office Adjutant and Inspector General,
District Western Louisiana.

WD-ZB-08 "OFFICIAL BUSINESS." at top left 500.

Office Adjutant and Inspector General,
District Western Louisiana.

WD-ZB-09 500.

INSPECTOR GENERAL'S OFFICE,
DISTRICT WESTERN LOUISIANA.

WD-ZB-10 500.

If a particular imprint cannot be found in this section, look under "State Imprints."

District of South Carolina

HEAD QUARTERS 4TH SUB-DISTRICT,
District of South Carolina,
OFFICIAL BUSINESS.

WD-ZB-11 500.

District of Texas, New Mexico and Arizona

Head Quarters, Dist. of Texas, New Mexico and Arizona,
OFFICIAL BUSINESS.

WD-ZB-12 2,000.

Confederate States of America.
Head Quarters, District Texas, New Mexico and Arizona.
OFFICIAL BUSINESS

WD-ZB-13 2,000.

Artillery Head Quarters,
District of Texas, New Mexico and Arizona.

WD-ZB-14 "OFFICIAL BUSINESS." at top left 2,000.

Head Quarters, Bureau of State Troops,
Dist. of Texas, New Mexico & Arizona.
OFFICIAL BUSINESS

WD-ZB-15 2,000.

HEAD QRS. RESERVE CORPS.
District of Texas, New Mexico and Arizona.
OFFICIAL BUSINESS

WD-ZB-16 2,000.

Sub District of Texas

Head Quarters, Northern Sub-District of Texas.
(OFFICIAL BUSINESS.)

WD-ZB-17 750.

District of the Gulf

Hd. Qrs. Dist. of the Gulf,
MOBILE, ALABAMA
[Official Business.]

WD-ZB-18 750.

District of Pamlico

Quarter-master's Department, District of Pamlico.
OFFICIAL BUSINESS.

WD-ZB-19 750.

Military Divisions

Headquarters Middle Military Division,
OFFICIAL BUSINESS.

WD-ZC-01 750.

Headquarters Middle Military Division.
OFFICIAL BUSINESS.

WD-ZC-02 750.

Army Headquarters

Confederate Armies

Head Quarters Armies Confederate States,
OFFICIAL.

WD-ZD-01 500.

Army of Northern Virginia

Head Quarters Cavalry Corps,
ARMY OF NORTHERN VIRGINIA.

WD-ZD-02 "A" of "ARMY" under "ua" of "Quarters" 500.

Head Quarters Cavalry Corps,
ARMY OF NORTH RN VIRGINIA.

WD-ZD-03 "A" of "ARMY" under "ar" of "Quarters" 500.

Head Quarters Lee's Brigade,
2nd. Division Cavalry, A. N. Va.
1864.

WD-ZD-04 500.

Army of the Potomac

HEAD QUARTERS,
ARMY OF POTOMAC, C. S. A.

WD-ZD-05 500.

Head Quarters, 1st. Corps, Army of the Potomac.
——ON OFFICIAL BUSINESS.——

WD-ZD-06 Imprint at top center 500.

Head Quarters, 1st. Corps, Army of the Potomac.
——ON OFFICIAL BUSINESS

WD-ZD-07 No dash after "BUSINESS" 500.

HEAD QUARTERS,
1st CORPS, ARMY OF THE POTOMAC
—OFFICIAL BUSINESS.—

WD-ZD-08 500.

HEAD QUARTERS, 2nd Corps,
ARMY OF THE POTOMAC, C. S. A.

WD-ZD-09 500.

Head Quarters Cavalry Brigade,
ARMY OF THE POTOMAC.

WD-ZD-10 500.

Headquarters Cavalry Brigade,
ARMY OF THE POTOMAC.
Officer Commanding Co.........................
....Brigade,
....

WD-ZD-11 500.

Army of Mississippi

Army of Mississippi
(OFFICIAL BUSINESS.)

WD-ZD-12 Imprint at top left 500.

HEAD QUARTERS,
Army of the Mississippi,
—OFFICIAL BUSINESS.—

WD-ZD-13 "H" of "HEAD" above space between "Army" and "of"; imprint at top center 500.

HEAD QUARTERS,
Army of the Mississippi,
—OFFICIAL BUSINESS.—

WD-ZD-14 "H" of "HEAD" above "o" of "of"; imprint at top center 500.

Head-Quarters, Army of Mississippi,
ADJUTANT & INSPECTOR GENERAL'S OFFICE.
OFFICIAL BUSINESS.

WD-ZD-15 Second line serif 500.

Head-Quarters Army of Mississippi,
ADJUTANT AND INSPECTOR-GENERAL'S OFFICE.
OFFICIAL BUSINESS

WD-ZD-16 Second line sans serif; imprint at top left 500.

Army of Tennessee

Head-Quarters, Army of Tenn.
OFFICIAL BUSINESS.

WD-ZD-17 500.

Headquarters Army Tennessee, OFFICE CHIEF OF STAFF.
OFFICIAL BUSINESS

WD-ZD-18 500.

TD-20 – Confederate States of America, Treasurer's Office.

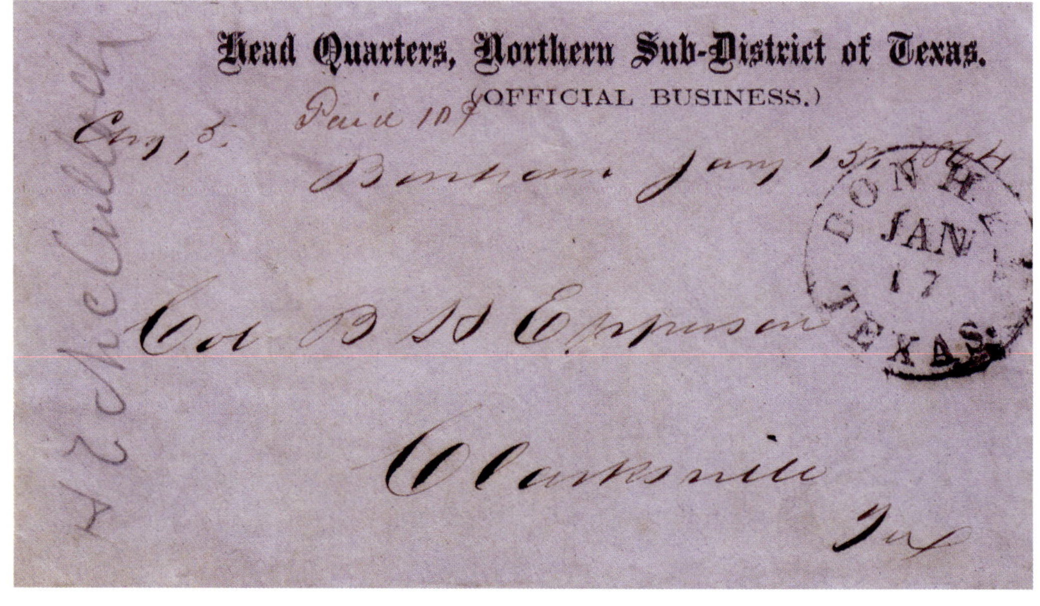

WD-ZB-17 – Head Quarters, Northern Sub-District of Texas.

State Imprints

Various branches of state governments prepared envelopes with the imprint of their respective offices for official business. Most imprints included the state name in the imprint. Other imprints included only the name of the organization or the name of the organization and a town. Some states, most notably North Carolina, established government agencies to support their troops. This was in addition to the support provided by the Confederate Government agencies of the same names. Many of these imprints bear no indication of the government of origin. Every effort was made to properly identify the government associated with such imprints.

If a particular imprint cannot be found under "State Imprints," look under "Semi-Official Imprints."

Alabama

Executive Department

Executive Department of Ala.
OFFICIAL BUSINESS

S-AL-01 500.

Quartermaster Department

Office Quartermaster Gen'l of Ala.
OFFICIAL BUSINESS.

S-AL-02 400.

Quartermaster's Department of Alabama,
OFFICIAL BUSINESS

S-AL-03 400.

Florida

Executive Department

Executive Department,
TALLAHASSEE, FLORIDA.

S-FL-01 Second line serif letters 1,000.

Executive Department.
TALLAHASSEE, FLORIDA.

S-FL-02 "T" of "TALLAHASSEE" under "cu" of "Executive" 1,000.

Executive Department,
TALLAHASSEE, FLORIDA.

S-FL-03 "T" of "TALLAHASSEE" under "ut" of "Executive" 1,000.

State Department

State Department
TALLAHASSEE, FLORIDA.

S-FL-04 1,000.

Georgia

Executive Department

EXECUTIVE
DEPARTMENT.
GEORGIA.

S-GA-01 500.

S-GA-02 500.

Adjutant and Inspector General's Office

Official Business. STATE OF GEORGIA.
Adjutant and Inspector General's Office.

S-GA-03 "G" of "General's" under "O" of "OF" 400.

OFFICIAL BUSINESS. STATE OF GEORGIA.
Adjutant and Inspector General's Office.

S-GA-04 "G" of "General's" under "O" of "GEORGIA" 400.

STATE OF GEORGIA
Adjutant and Inspector General's Office.
OFFICIAL BUSINESS

S-GA-05 400.

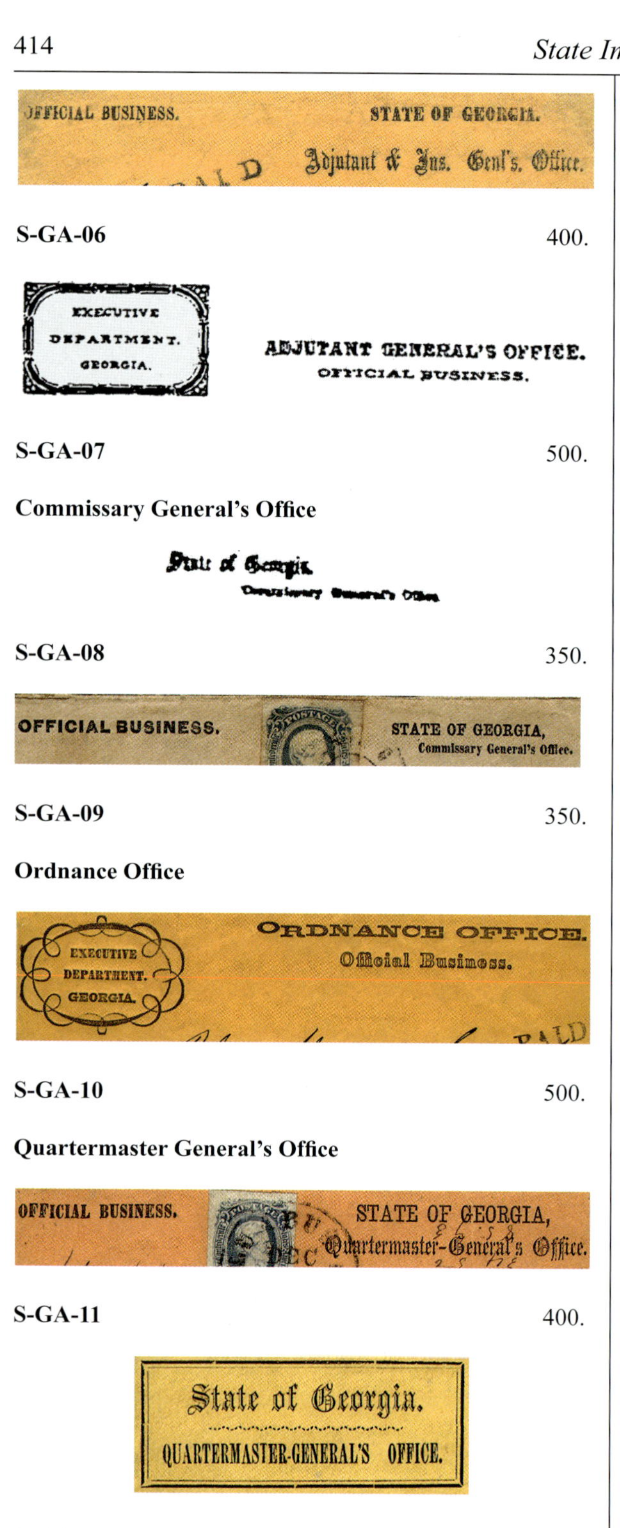

S-GA-06 400.

S-GA-07 500.

Commissary General's Office

S-GA-08 350.

S-GA-09 350.

Ordnance Office

S-GA-10 500.

Quartermaster General's Office

S-GA-11 400.

S-GA-12 400.

S-GA-13 400.

S-GA-14 400.

S-GA-15 400.

S-GA-16 400.

Georgia State Guard

S-GA-17 "G" of "GUARD" under "T" of "QUARTERS" 400.

S-GA-18 "G" of "GUARD" under "E" of "QUARTERS" 400.

LOUISIANA

Executive Office

S-LA-01 750.

S-LA-02 750.

Note: Illustration may be of partial imprint

S-LA-03 750.

There is no distinction made in the size of the envelopes, whether standard or legal size. Imprints often are known on both sizes.

Mississippi

Adjutant and Inspector General's Office

HEAD-QUARTERS, STATE MISSISSIPPI,
ADJUTANT AND INSPECTOR GENERAL'S OFFICE.
OFFICIAL BUSINESS.

S-MS-01 500.

Note: The position of "OFFICIAL BUSINESS" may be different from that shown

Head-Quarters, State of Mississippi,
ADJUTANT AND INSPECTOR-GENERAL'S OFFICE,
OFFICIAL BUSINESS.

S-MS-02 500.

Note: The position of "OFFICIAL BUSINESS" may be different from that shown

---

North Carolina

Executive Department

State of North Carolina,
EXECUTIVE DEPARTMENT.

S-NC-01 "E" of "EXECUTIVE" under "a" of "State" 500.

State of North Carolina,
EXECUTIVE DEPARTMENT

S-NC-02 "E" of "EXECUTIVE" under "e" of "State" 500.

State of North Carolina,
EXECUTIVE DEPARTMENT.

S-NC-03 "E" of "EXECUTIVE" under space between "State" and "of" 500.

State of North-Carolina,
EXECUTIVE DEPARTMENT.

S-NC-04 "E" of "EXECUTIVE" under "e" of "State"; hyphen between "North" and "Carolina" 500.

> Black and white tracings from previous catalogs are not exact renderings of the imprints. Tracings may show "Official Business" or other wording in a location which may not be as it actually appears on the envelopes.

State of North-Carolina,
EXECUTIVE DEPARTMENT.

S-NC-05 "E" of "EXECUTIVE" under space between "State" and "of"; hyphen between "North" and "Carolina" 500.

S-NC-06 500.

Adjutant General's Office

Adjutant General's Office,
OFFICIAL BUSINESS.

S-NC-07 400.

OFFICIAL BUSINESS. Adjutant General's Office
RALEIGH, N. C.

S-NC-08 "R" of "RALEIGH" under "u" of "Adjutant" 400.

OFFICIAL BUSINESS. Adjutant General's Office,
RALEIGH, N. C.

S-NC-09 "R" of "RALEIGH" under "ta" of "Adjutant" 400.

OFFICIAL BUSINESS. Adjutant General's Office,
RALEIGH, N. C.

S-NC-10 "R" of "RALEIGH" under "a" of "Adjutant" 400.

Adjutant General's Office,
RALEIGH, N. C.

S-NC-11 "R" of "RALEIGH" under "an" of "Adjutant" 400.

S-NC-12 "R" of "RALEIGH" under "n" of "Adjutant" 400.

S-NC-13 "R" of "RALEIGH" under "n" of "Adjutant"; no "O" in "OFFICIAL" 400.

S-NC-14 "R" of "RALEIGH" under "n" of "Adjutant"; "OFFICIAL BUSINESS" sans serif 400.

S-NC-15 400.

OFFICIAL BUSINESS. Adjutant General's Office, RALEIGH, N. C.

S-NC-16 400.

Medical Department

STATE OF NORTH CAROLINA,
Medical Department---Official Business.

S-NC-17 500.

Ordnance Department

Ordnance Department, N. C.
OFFICIAL BUSINESS.

S-NC-18 400.

Note: The position of "OFFICIAL BUSINESS" may be different from that shown

Official Business. Ordnance Department, RALEIGH, N. C.

S-NC-19 400.

Ordnance Department, RALEIGH, N. C. Official Business.

S-NC-20 400.

ORDNANCE DEPARTMENT,
RALEIGH, N. C.

S-NC-21 400.

Ordnance Department,
RALEIGH, N C
OFFICIAL BUSINESS

S-NC-22 400.

Note: The position of "OFFICIAL BUSINESS" may be different from that shown

Ordnance Department
RALEIGH, N. C.
OFFICIAL BUSINESS.

S-NC-23 400.

Quartermaster Department

OFFICIAL BUSINESS. Quarter Master's Department, RALEIGH, N. C.

S-NC-24 400.

Note: Image taken from private use of semi-official envelope

OFFICIAL BUSINESS. Quartermaster's Department, RALEIGH, N. C.

S-NC-25 400.

OFFICIAL BUSINESS.
Quartermaster's Department,
RALEIGH, N. C.

S-NC-26 400.

OFFICIAL BUSINESS
Quartermaster's Department,
RALEIGH, N. C.

S-NC-27 400.

OFFICIAL BUSINESS.
Quartermaster's Department,
RALEIGH, N. C.

S-NC-28 400.

OFFICIAL BUSINESS.
Quartermaster's Department.
RALEIGH, N. C.

S-NC-29 Imprint in top left corner 400.

Note: Some envelopes known with full or partial pre-printed addresses

Due to the variety of sources of scans and image resolution, the exact size of the images relative to each other may vary.

OFFICIAL BUSINESS.
Office of Chief Quartermaster,
RALEIGH, N. C.

S-NC-30 400.

Quarter-Master's Department,
Greensborough, N C.

S-NC-31 400.

QUARTER MASTERS DEPARTMENT.
GREENSBOROUGH. N. C.

S-NC-32 400.

Quartermaster's Department.
SALISBURY, N. C.
OFFICIAL BUSINESS.

S-NC-33 400.

S-NC-34 500.

Subsistence Department

Subsistence Department,
RALEIGH, N. C.

S-NC-35 400.

S-NC-36 400.

North Carolina Reserve

Headquarters Reserve, N C
OFFICIAL BUSINESS

S-NC-37 400.

If a particular imprint cannot be found in this section, look under "State Imprints."

Head Quarters Reserve N. C.
ADJUTANT GENERAL'S OFFICE.
OFFICIAL BUSINESS.

S-NC-38 400.

South Carolina

Executive Department

EXECUTIVE DEPARTMENT.

S-SC-01 500.

State of South Carolina.
EXECUTIVE DEPARTMENT.

S-SC-02 "E" of "EXECUTIVE" under "at" of "State"; imprint at top center. 500.

State of South Carolina,
EXECUTIVE DEPARTMENT.

S-SC-03 "E" of "EXECUTIVE" under "te" of "State"; imprint at top center. 500.

State of South Carolina,
EXECUTIVE DEPARTMENT.

S-SC-04 "E" of "EXECUTIVE" under "e" of "State" 500.

State of South Carolina,
EXECUTIVE DEPARTMENT.

S-SC-05 500.

State of South Carolina,
EXECUTIVE DEPARTMENT.

S-SC-06 500.

STATE OF SOUTH CAROLINA,
Executive Council Chamber.

S-SC-07 500.

S-SC-08 600.

Treasury Department

STATE OF SOUTH CAROLINA
TREASURY DEPARTMENT.

S-SC-09 600.

Adjutant and Inspector General's Office

State of South Carolina,
Adjutant and Inspector General's Office.
OFFICIAL BUSINESS.

S-SC-10 400.

STATE OF SOUTH CAROLINA.
Adjutant and Inspector General's Office.
OFFICIAL BUSINESS.

S-SC-11 400.

STATE OF SOUTH CAROLINA,
HEAD QUARTERS,
Adjutant and Inspector General's Office.

S-SC-12 400.

HEAD QUARTERS.
Adjutant & Inspector General's Office.
OFFICIAL BUSINESS.

S-SC-13 400.

Surgeon General's Department

SURGEON GENERAL'S DEPARTMENT,
STATE OF SOUTH CAROLINA.

S-SC-14 500.

State Headquarters

State of South Carolina,
HEAD QUARTERS.

S-SC-15 "S" of "QUARTERS" under "o" of "Carolina" 400.

State of South Carolina,
HEAD QUARTERS.

S-SC-16 "S" of "QUARTERS" under "a" of "Carolina" 400.

STATE OF SOUTH CAROLINA,
HEAD QUARTERS.

S-SC-17 400.

HEADQUARTERS.
COLUMBIA, S. C.
OFFICIAL BUSINESS.

S-SC-18 400.

STATE OF SOUTH CAROLINA
HEAD QUARTERS

S-SC-19 600.

State of South Carolina.
HEAD QUARTERS.

S-SC-20 600.

POST HEADQUARTERS,
COLUMBIA, S. C.
OFFICIAL BUSINESS.

S-SC-21 400.

Headquarters Reserve Forces

Head-quarters Reserve Forces,
COLUMBIA, S. C.
OFFICIAL BUSINESS.

S-SC-22 400.

Tennessee

S-TN-01 Illuminated envelope; imprint at left 750.

Texas

Department of State

S-TX-01 Illuminated envelope 1,000.

Adjutant and Inspector General's Office

STATE OF TEXAS,
Adjutant and Inspector General's Office.
Official Business.

S-TX-02 750.

Comptroller's Office

Comptroller's Office.

To Esq.,
Assessor and Collector County,
TEXAS

S-TX-03 750.

Texas Reserve Corps

Head Quarters, Reserve Corps, State of Texas.
OFFICIAL BUSINESS.

S-TX-04 750.

Virginia

Executive Department

STATE OF VIRGINIA,
EXECUTIVE DEPARTMENT.

S-VA-01 Imprint at lower left 500.

Commonwealth of Virginia.
Executive Department.
(OFFICIAL BUSINESS.)

S-VA-02 500.

S-VA-03 Illuminated envelope; imprint at left 750.

Treasury Office

S-VA-04 Imprint at left 600.

Auditors

S-VA-05 Illuminated envelope; imprint at left "(Office of the Auditor of Public Accounts)" 750.

S-VA-06 Illuminated envelope; imprint at left "(Office of the Second Auditor)" 750.

S-VA-07 Illuminated envelope; imprint on back flap 600.

Black and white tracings from previous catalogs are not exact renderings of the imprints. Tracings may show "Official Business" or other wording in a location which may not be as it actually appears on the envelopes.

Board of Public Works

S-VA-08 600.

S-VA-09 Illuminated envelope; imprint at left "(Office of the Board of Public Works)" 750.

State Printing Office

STATE PRINTING OFFICE,
RICHMOND, VA.

S-VA-10 400.

Adjutant General's Office

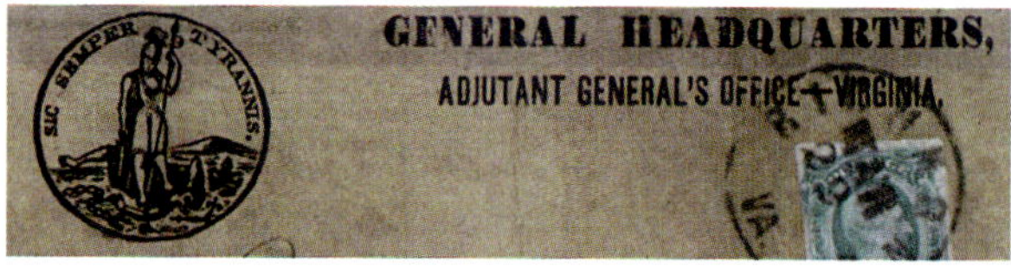

S-VA-11 500.

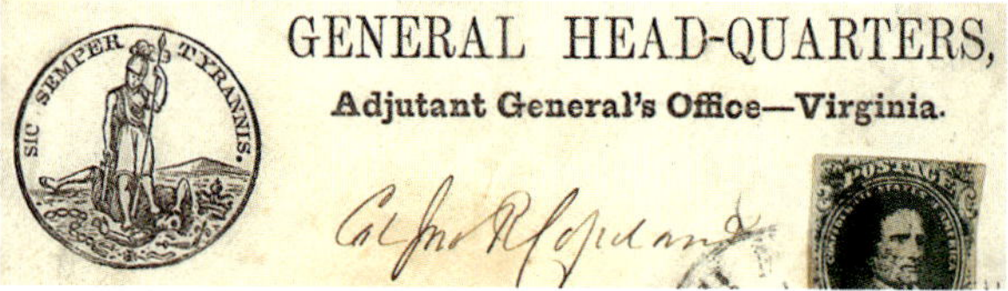

S-VA-12 500.

Ordnance Department

S-VA-13 500.

ORDNANCE DEPARTMENT,
State of Virginia.

S-VA-14 400.

Ordinance Department
OF VIRGINIA.

S-VA-15 400.

Surgeon General's Department

S-VA-16 500.

Virginia Forces

Head-Quarters of the Virginia Forces.

S-VA-17 Virginia state seal at left with "SO BE IT EVER TO TYRANTS" below seal 500.

S-VA-18 400.

Inspector General's Office,
VIRGINIA FORCES.

S-VA-19 500.

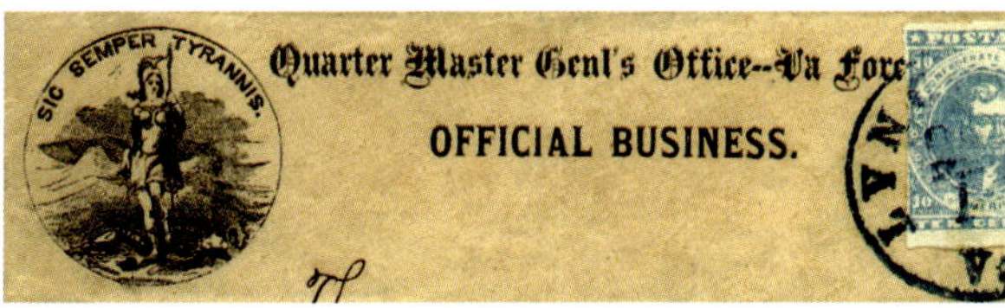

S-VA-20 500.

Virginia Navy

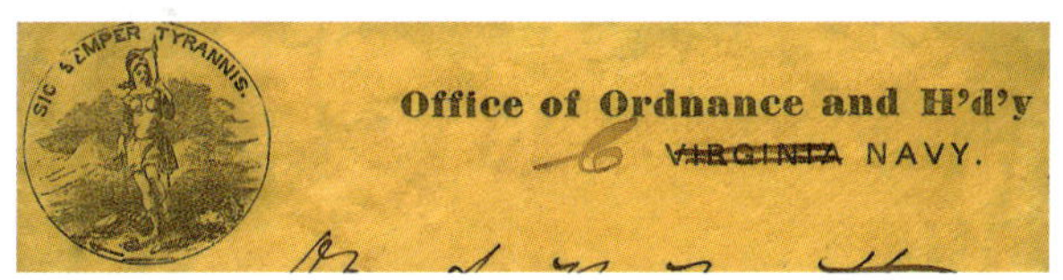

S-VA-21 Illustration is from Confederate use of Virginia envelope 500.

Note: See also, Semi-Official Imprints section ND-20 for CSA use of this envelope

Virginia Volunteers

Quartermaster's Office,
VIRGINIA VOLUNTEERS,
STAUNTON, VA.

S-VA-22 *750.*

S-NC-16 - Adjutant General's Office, Raleigh, N.C.

S-SC-12 - State of South Carolina, Head Quarters, Adjutant and Inspector General's Office

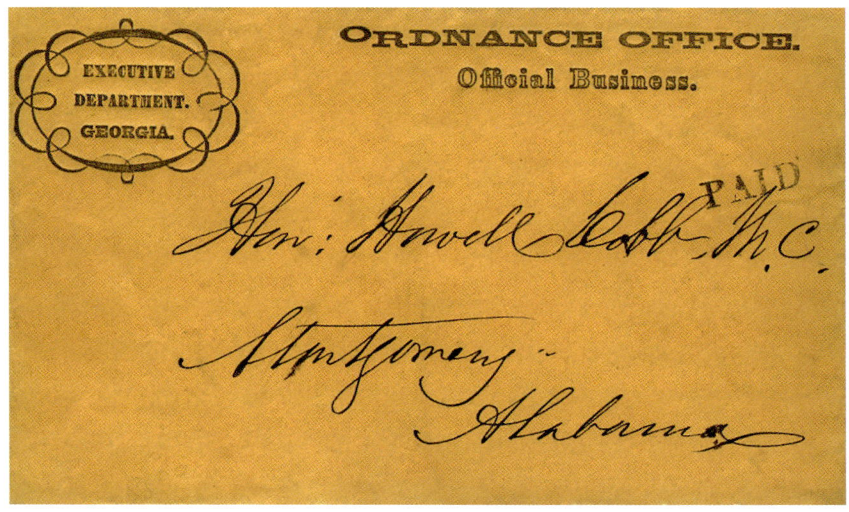

S-GA-10 – Executive Department, Georgia. Ordnance Office.

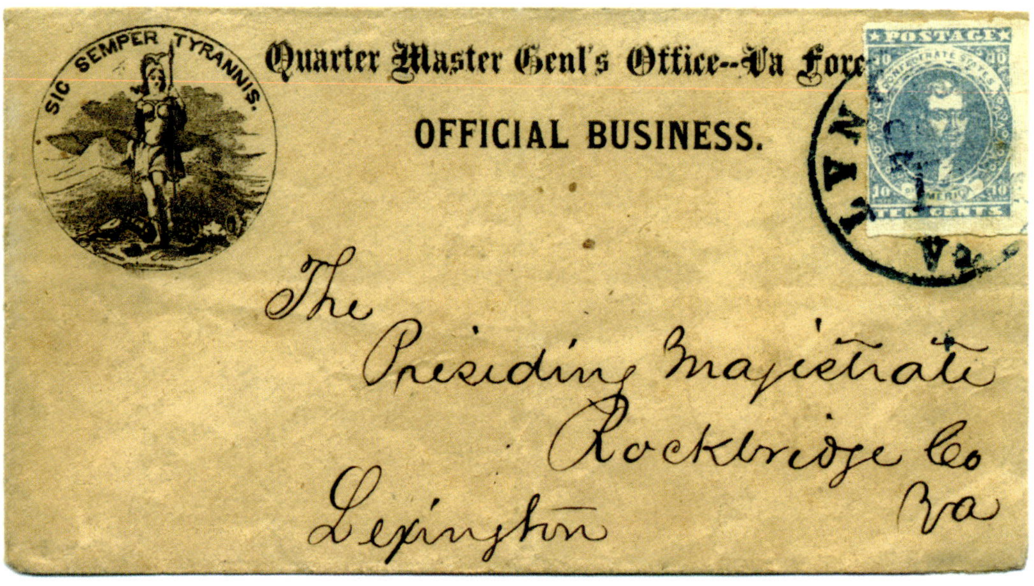

S-VA-20 – Quarter Master Genl's Office--Va Forces

Confederate Patriotic Covers

Introduction

At the outset of any war, there is always an outpouring of patriotic fervor on both sides that at times can be quite intense. In 1861, a phenomenon developed that had not been seen before to any great extent in this country -- the appearance of the patriotic cover. Even before the war began, the North had developed the art of the illustrated cover to a fine degree by producing colorful design covers for Presidential campaigns. The onset of the war itself opened the floodgates for the production of all sorts of patriotic covers from the Northern printers such that many thousands were printed and immediately became popular with the Northern letter-writing public. There are literally thousands of different Northern designs of Civil War period patriotic covers showing flags, eagles and various other patriotic symbols as well as covers with cartoon and caricature designs scorning and ridiculing the South for slavery and the Southern way of life. So besides showing patriotic zeal, these covers could also display emotions and feelings of disdain, derision, and even outright hatred. Northern patriotic covers are rarely seen postally used prior to the firing on Fort Sumter.

But things were just a bit different in the South. The South did not have the overall printing capability of the North, so such a huge volume of patriotic cover material simply could not be produced at the level that is seen from the Union side. But once war was imminent, the people of the South wanted to show their patriotic fervor. Southern printers began to turn out patriotic covers with the new "Stars and Bars" flag. Even Northern printers got into the act and printed covers with Confederate flag designs and sold them to the South in the early months of the Confederacy before cross border trade was halted. Therefore, some CSA patriotic covers may show the imprint of a Northern printer. The use of Southern patriotic covers can be found beginning in the early Spring of 1861 and actually predate the Union patriotic covers.

The majority of the Confederate patriotic covers show the "Stars and Bars" in quite a number of flag design variations with the star count numbering from 7 to 13 depending on when the cover was printed with a star added when each state was admitted to the Confederacy. Others show what is termed the "Jefferson Davis Medallion" while still others show soldiers, dragoons, cannons, tents, and other military and miscellaneous themes. Many are in full color while others are in black or in a blue, red, brown, purple or gold mono-color. Often a patriotic verse, slogan, motto, or military unit designation of some type will be included on the cover as well as the imprint of the printer.

The majority of Confederate patriotic covers were used relatively early in the war. The earlier Confederate patriotic covers were generally of high quality. As the war progressed into 1863 and paper and envelope shortages started to take hold, the few locally printed Confederate patriotic covers tended to show a lower quality with poorer quality paper and printing. The postal use of such covers began to fade from the scene as envelopes became increasingly scarce. Few Confederate patriotic covers were used after 1863.

In order for a Confederate patriotic design to be listed in this catalog, at least one known example showing Confederate postal use must be verified. Only Confederate patriotic designs on complete original covers which were genuinely postally used in the Confederate period are listed. The one exception to this rule is the few designs found only on Confederate used lettersheets and not as yet known on a matching envelope.

As opposed to the many thousands of Union designs, less than 200 different Confederate designs are known and recorded showing period postal use. Unused Confederate themed patriotic covers are not listed except for a small group of designs not known postally used but believed to be of Southern manufacture (see appendix). A number of Southern themed envelopes were also printed as souvenirs shortly after the war and later in conjunction with United Confederate Veterans reunions. Such examples are beyond the scope of this catalog and are not listed.

Occasionally a Confederate cover can be found with a hand-drawn patriotic design of a flag or a cannon or some other symbol either in simple pen and ink or as a more elaborate design in color. These are very desirable items, but they are in and of themselves individually unique and are not cataloged or valued.

The collector is advised that this is an area which contains a number of fraudulent covers. There exist genuine unused patriotic envelopes which have been transformed by adding a genuine Confederate stamp with a counterfeit postmark and a hand written address. Likewise, genuine period patriotic covers addressed and hand carried outside the postal system are known to which a genuine stamp has been added and tied by a counterfeit postmark. Detecting such covers can at times be very difficult, thus formal certification of a patriotic cover may be considered if there is any doubt as to authenticity.

Explanatory Notes

Illustrations—Where possible, the illustrations of the patriotic designs are taken directly from the covers themselves. Where this is not possible due to scarcity of the covers or due to the current whereabouts of such covers being unknown, illustrations are then taken from secondary sources. Many minor variations exist as a result of different printers using similar designs. Where constant minor varieties are known to exist, this is so noted in the listing. For continuity, the same design number designations as were used in previous catalogs have been retained. Variations of certain designs that were in the past included as a single major catalog entry have been broken out into separate minor numbers. New major designs not appearing in the previous catalogs have been given new numbers in continuity with the established numbers.

Verses, Slogans, Imprints—The verses, slogans, and imprints known to be associated with some Confederate patriotic designs are alphabetically listed separately for easier reference. Designs that are known to exist with these added embellishments are so noted in the listing with the number designation of the verse, slogan or imprint corresponding to the alphabetical listing. It should be noted that some of these designs also exist with no verse, slogan, or imprint. Therefore, many designs may exist either with or without the listed embellishments. Separate advertising imprints can be found on certain Confederate patriotic covers and are often unique to and specifically applied on behalf of an individual company. Patriotic covers with added separate advertising are most desirable but cannot be individually cataloged.

Patriotic Lettersheets—A significant number of the designs found on patriotic covers also have a matching patriotic lettersheet. When a matching lettersheet design is known, it is so noted in the listing with "LS" after the description. Not all the designs have matching lettersheets and, conversely, there are some designs that are known only on a lettersheet and have no known corresponding design on an envelope.

Valuation—The valuations given in this listing are for stampless postally used covers in very fine condition. The actual use of the cover with U.S. stamps, Confederate provisional or general issue stamps, a matching lettersheet, added individual advertising, and numerous other factors may greatly increase the basic valuation. Conversely, covers in a poorer condition will generally sell for less. Where not enough information is known to make a proper and precise value judgment, the estimated dollar value appears in italics. Genuine period Confederate patriotic covers that were hand carried outside the Confederate postal system are quite collectible. These covers will have a period hand written address with perhaps the name of the person carrying the cover also included, but no postal markings. Such hand carried covers are not listed or valued in this catalog but will generally sell for considerably less than their postally used counterpart. Similarly, period Confederate patriotic design envelopes also exist in unused condition. These, too, generally sell for far less than their postally used counterparts.

Verses

A great many Confederate patriotic covers and lettersheets have, along with the flag or other design, a printed verse of one or more stanzas with the purpose of further instilling a feeling of patriotic fervor. These verses are certainly full of zeal for the cause as many are quite martial and defiant in tone. In some instances, the same patriotic designs may exist with or without a verse. In this catalog, the verses have been rearranged and renumbered in order alphabetically by the first word of the first line for easier referencing.

1. Above us our banner waving...
2. Advance the flag in Dixie...
3. All ye Sons of the South, who are ready to fight...
4. Arise, arise each Southern man...
5. Bright banner of freedom with pride I unfurl (unfold) thee...
6. Come every Texas lady...
7. Dear banner with thee I return...
8. Death to each marauding band...
9. Death to the invaders of our land...
10. Far better to perish with honor...
11. Farewell, dear friends oh farewell...
12. Flag of the South! Aye fling its folds...
13. Gather round your Country's flag...
14. Hark! how, on Northern blasts elate...
15. Hear the Northern thunders mutter...
16. How the South's great heart rejoices...
17. Hurrah for the Stars and Bars of Secession!...
18. If on earth we meet no more...
19. In Dixie's land we take our stand...
20. Land of the South! The fairest land...
21. Let Beauregard's dauntless breast...
22. March to the battle field...
23. May brave Jeff Davis dauntless breast...
24. May these Northern fanatics who abuse their Southern neighbors...
25. Men of the South arise, arise...
26. Men of the South, free born race...
27. No reconstruction with the vile North, never...
28. Now round this gallant leader...
29. Oh long shall these tri-colors wave...
30. On, on to the rescue, the vandals are coming...
31. Our banner's up, and there will stand...
32 Our country's flag we will defend…
33. Our Father's faith let us keep till death...
34. Our flag shall proudly stream...
35. Rise each valiant warrior-knight...
36. Southrons on! No stain ever rested...
37. Stand by that flag, men of the South...
38. Stand by your cannon cheerily rolls the drum...
39. Stand firmly by your cannon...
40. Stand firmly by your cannon hark the tempest and the gun...
41. Swear upon your Country's altar...
42. The fight at Manassas was glorious and great...
43. The tempest of war may o'shadow our land...
44. The tyrant has sworn we all shall be slaves...
45. To arms! to arms! quick be ready...
46. To arms! to arms! Ye (Southern) brave(s)...
47. Under this flag and DAVIS command...
48. United and firm, independent and free...
49. We will face the foe upon the field...
50. We'll show no quarter to the traitorous North...
51. We're the sons of sires that baffled...
52. What is a letter? Let affection tell...
53. When the tempest of war overshadows our land...
54. Who for Justice, Truth and Law...
55. With our front in the field, swearing never to yield...
56. With the cannons flash and the cannons crash...

Slogans, Mottoes, and Phrases
Military Unit Designations

This section includes all words or phrases with a patriotic theme as well as military unit designations that appear on Confederate patriotic covers that are not part of the actual design itself. These slogans, etc., are many and varied. These items have been numbered alphabetically according to the first letter in the word or phrase for easy referencing.

1. 7th Mississippi Volunteers, Company "C," Amite Rifles, - Capt B. F. Jones
2. Baldwin Blues, 4th Reg. Ga. Vol.
3. BARTOW
4. Bartow Artillery (C. S. A.)
4a. Beauregard Rifles
5. Berry Infantry, Rome, Geo.
6. Brown Rebels, 18th Regiment, Confederate Troops
6a. Camp Brown, Union City, Tenn
6b. Camp C. C. Dahlgren, 3rd Miss. Brigade
7. Camp of Instruction, Brookhaven, Miss. Leake Co. Rovers, Capt. Campbell
8. Camp McDonald
9. Camp Stephens 5th Geo. Reg.
10. Camp Stephens, Griffin, Ga.
11. Camp Stephens, Upson Guards, Pensacola, Fla.
12. Capt Cropp's Company, 1st Florida Regiment
13. Capt. Drapers Company, 7th Reg. Alabama Vol.
13a Capt. Gaston's Company, 7th Reg Alabama Vol.
13b Capt. Gee's Company, 1st Florida Regiment
14. Capt. Powell's Company, 1st Florida Regiment
14a Capt. Spraberry's Company, Geo Battalion
15. Cap't. Frierson's Company, 3d Florida Regiment
16. Cap't. Meyer's Company, 1st Florida Regiment
17. C. C.
18. Chipola Rifles, Capt. H. Hyer Baker, Georgia Battery, 5th Geo. Reg..
19. Co. A., lst Reg. Fla. Vols.
20. Columbus Rifles
21. Company A, 7th Alabama Regiment
22. Company D, 7th Alabama Regiment
23. Company K, 7th Alabama Regiment
24. Confederate States of America
25. Confederate States of America Headquarters Forces, Staunton, Va.
26. Crescent Rifles, Co. H., 7th Reg. La. Volunteers
27. C. S. A. (Old English script letters)
27a. Davis Infantry Com. K. 7th Regiment Ga. Vols.
28. Davis Invincibles (Capt. S. D. Irvin)
29. Death to the Invaders
30. Deo Juvante Vicunius
31. Dulce et decorum est pro patria mori
32. Echols Guards, 8th Reg. Ga. Vols.
33. Fast Colors warranted not to run
34. Forest City Foundry, Savannah, Ga.
35. Forti Et Fideli Nil Difficile
36. Fredonia Hards, Capt. H. J. Jones, etc. (boxed)
37. From Cap't Johnson's Comp'y, Talladega Rifles, Talladega Battery
38. From Capt. Posey's Com'y Red Eagles, Fort Barancas
39. From Capt. Stubbe's Comp'y. Guards, Sunny South
40. From 'Our Boys,' Company A, Tenth Regiment, Mississippi Volunteers,
42. Gaines Invincibles
43. Georgia Battery, Griffin Light Guard, Pensacola, Fla. (two similar versions)
44. Give 'em fits, Bragg
45. God and our rights
46. Grenada Rifles
47. Hamilton Guards
48. Headquarters Chatham Artillery
49. Headquarters Forces at Staunton, Va.
50. Henry Grays
51. Houston, Texas
52. I go to illustrate Georgia. Bartow
53. Lawrence Rifles
54. Let her bang ye heroes, Victory is Ours
55. Let Us Alone
56. Liberty or Death
57. McRae Rough & Readys - Cobbs Reg. Ga. Vol. Commanded by Capt. McRae
58. Millions for Defense
59. Natchez Rifles (Capt. A. V. Davis)
60. Our New Flag
61. Pettus Guards. Always Ready
62. Prarie Guards, 1st Florida Regiment
63. Remember Bethel, Sumter and Manassas (two similar)
64. Rome Light Guards, 8th Reg. Ga. Vol.
65. Run Yank or Die
66. Sardis Volunteers
67. "Semper Paratus," Quitman Light Artillery of Natchez.Capt. R. T. English
68. Shuberta Rifles, Fortune favors the Brave
69. So be it ever to tyrants
70. Spring Place Volunteers
71. They've killed me boys but never give up the field! BARTOW (three versions)
72. Victory or Death. Madison Rifles, Company I, Tenth Regiment, Mississippi
73. Volunteers, C.S.A. (boxed)
74. Walton Infantry
74a. Warrington, Flor. (boxed)
75. Washington Artillery
76. We Ask no Quarters
77. We'll Persevere

Imprints

Found on some Confederate patriotic covers in smaller printed letters is the name of the printer or the seller of the envelope with or without the name of the city or town in which it was printed. These are known as the "Printer's Imprint." These imprints are listed and numbered alphabetically.

1. 10 Camp St., N.O.
2. Allen's Book Store, Galveston & Houston
3. Childs, N. O.
4. Copyright claimed, HM & TWC Box 417, Nashville, Tenn.

4a. E. J. Purse, Book, Job and Color Printer, Savannah, Ga.
5. (Engraved & Printed by) T. S. Reynolds, Atlanta, Ga
6. For Sale by Alpheus Boiling, Yorktown, Va. (Cobbs Legion) (Camp near Richmond, Va.)
7. Forsgard & Norton, Booksellers & Stationers, Houston, Texas
8. Gary Music and Printing, Richmond
9. GEO. ELLIS, OPPOSITE, POST-OFFICE, N. O.
10. Hammond, N.O.
11. H. Phill & Co. (Griffin, Ga.)
12. Jas. L. Gow, Printer, Augusta, Ga., Patent Applied for
13. Jas. McPherson & Co., Booksellers and Stationers, Whitehall Street, Atlanta, Ga.
14. J. K. SUTTERLEY, Bookseller, under the St. Charles Hotel, N. O.
15. L. (E.) Pradat, Gothic Store
16. Manufactured by Lowenburg & Bro. (Beaufort, N.C.).
17. Manufactured (Man'td) by W. & J. Bonitz, Goldsboro, N.C.
17a Nash, Print
17b New Orleans Exchange Depot, Corner White Street
18. New Orleans Mirror Print
19. Parrott, Alexandria
20. Published by A. Dapremont, N. O.
21. R. Barton, Bayou Sara
22. R. C. Hite, Printer, 43 Jefferson St., Memphis, Tenn.
23. R. Coburn, Bookseller, N.O.
24. Rea's Rotary Press Print, New Orleans
25. R. H. Richards, Bookseller & Dealer in Music and Musical Instruments, Lagrange, Geo.
26. Saunders, Clark & Jones, Prs., Patent Applied for
27. Sold at Green & Co.'s Book Store, Nashville, Tenn.
28. Sold by C. H. Nobles & Co./Pensacola
29. Sold by G. Ellis, Post Ofrice News Depot, N.O.
30. Sold by Geo. T. Baldwin
31. (Sold by) J. W. Randolph, Richmond (Richm'd)
32. Sold by Starke & Cardoza, Richmond
33. Sold only by (made) by Vickery & Co. Norfolk
34. T. Fitzwilliam, Stationer, 76 Camp St., N. O.
35. The Mercury, Charleston, So. Ca.
36. West & Johnston, Richm'd.
37. Whitaker-Wilmington

CSA National Flag

The vast majority of designs seen on Confederate patriotic covers are flags. The first national flag known as the "Stars and Bars" in variation from seven stars to thirteen stars predominates. But the second national flag known as the "Stainless Banner" or the "Jackson Flag" can also be found. The third national flag was adopted near the very end of the Confederacy and does not make an appearance on any known Confederate period patriotic cover. Most of the patriotic flag designs are found in red, white, and blue multi-color while a few others are in simple black.

Seven Star Flags

The seven star "Stars and Bars" was the official national flag beginning with its adoption on March 4, 1861, and ending with the admission of Virginia. The stars represented the states of South Carolina, Mississippi, Florida, Alabama, Georgia, Louisiana and Texas.

F7-1A

F7-1B

Overall Stars and Bars with the name of the President and Vice President in the red bars and a flagstaff at the left. Two major varieties.

F7-1A	Names in negative white letters with larger lettering. Minor varieties.	3,500.
F7-1B	Names in outlined white letters with smaller lettering.	4,000.

F7-2A

F7-2B

Overall plain Stars and Bars. Two major varieties with regard to the flagstaff. Minor varieties with regard to partial, complete or no white border around the flag. Minor varieties with regard to the size of the stars and the bars.

F7-2A	No flagstaff at left. (Imprint:12, 26)	3,500.
F7-2B	Flagstaff at left. (Imprint: 12, 26)	4,500.

F7-3

F7-4

F7-3	Overall plain Stars and Bars design with no flagstaff. The stripes appear as woven cloth with horizontal laid lines. Minor varieties.	4,000.
F7-4	Extended flag, spearhead on the flagstaff. Minor Varieties as to size of the flag. (LS) (Imprint: 17) (Slogan: 20, 51)	1,000.

[*]	symbol used after an item description to mean an unsupported listing
[–]	symbol used in place of value to mean insufficient information to assign a price
[*italic*]	value typeface indicating the item is difficult to price accurately

F7-5A

F7-5B

Waving flag, curled end, stars in a circle. Three major varieties and other very minor varieties as to size and shading.

F7-5A Large stars with a ball on the flagstaff, (LS) (Imprint: 12, 27) 1,500.

F7-5B Large stars very sharply defined with a ball on the flagstaff. Flag is slightly more extended and with markedly less curl at the end. 5,000.

F7-5C

F7-6

F7-5C Small stars with a liberty cap on the flagstaff. (LS) (Imprint: 12, 27) 2,500.

F7-6 Extended waving flag, spearhead on the flagstaff, stars in a circle. (Imprint: 20, 24) 4,000.

F7-7A

F7-7B

Extended flag, two ropes, ball on flagstaff, stars in a circle. Two major size varieties.

F7-7A Small Flag with stars not well defined. 1,500.

F7-7B Larger flag with well defined stars. (LS) 1,500.

F7-8

F7-9

F7-8 Very small extended flag, one long rope, long flagstaff, stars in a circle. (Verse: 42) (Imprint: 7) 3,500.

F7-9 Extended flag with "Southern Rights" banner at the top as part of the design, stars in a circle. (Slogan: 55) (Imprint: 9, 15, 37) 2,500.

F7-10

F7-11

F7-10 Very long horizontally extended flag, ball on flagstaff, stars in a circle. (LS) (Slogan: 34) (Imprint 4a) 3,500.

F7-11 Large waving flag, ball on flagstaff, wavy curl at end of flag, stars in a circle. One cover recorded in prior catalogs with design in color, but its current existence cannot be verified.* —

F7-12A

F7-12B

Flag strongly sloping to the right, liberty cap on flagstaff, stars in a circle. Two major varieties. Minor variations in the cap and shading.

F7-12A Star at upper left is outside the circle. 2,500.

F7-12B All seven stars in a circle. 2,500.

F7-13

F7-14

F7-13 Long waving flag, spearhead on flagstaff, stars in a circle of six with the seventh star in the center. 3,000.

F7-14 Lightly waving flag, spearhead on flagstaff, "Steamer Vicksburg / B. Holmes, Master" (above the flag) and "Leave New Orleans Tuesday at 3 P. M. / Vicksburg Saturday at 6 A. M." (below the flag) printed as part of the design. 7,500.

Note: Although technically an advertising cover, this has traditionally been listed as a patriotic design in previous catalogs.

F7-15 F7-16

F7-15 Waving Flag, spearhead on flagstaff, "Steamer GENL Quitman/J. M. White, Master (above the flag) and "Leaves New Orleans Thursday 5 P. M./Greenville Sunday 8 A. P. (below the flag) printed as part of the design. 5,000.

Note: Although technically an advertising cover, this has traditionally been listed as a patriotic design in previous catalogs.

F7-16 Large waving flag, tassels, ball on flagstaff, six-pointed stars in a circle. 2,500.

F7-17 F7-18

F7-17 Sloping waving flag, long tassels, liberty cap on flagstaff, six-pointed stars in a circle. Black. (Slogan: 5) 5,000.

F7-18 Extended flag, three loops joining the flag, small ball on flagstaff, sharp five pointed stars in a circle. (LS) 1,000.

F7-19 F7-20

F7-19 Extended flag, liberty cap on flagstaff, large sharp five-pointed stars in a circle. (Imprint: 12) 3,500.

F7-20 Large waving flag, small ball on flagstaff, "C. S. A." below the flag in red. Old English script as part of the design, stars in a circle. 4,500.

F7-21 F7-22

F7-21 Small waving flag, small ball on flagstaff, small stars in a circle. Poorly printed blurred design. (Verse: 32) 2,000.

F7-22 Waving flag, long tassels, ball on flagstaff, small six-pointed stars in a circle. 7,500.

F7-23 F7-24

F7-23 Large waving flag, small ball on flagstaff, stars in a circle. Found printed only on the reverse of the envelope. Design in color. 7,500.

F7-24 Waving flag on sloping staff, liberty cap on flagstaff, large sharp five-pointed stars in a circle, "Our President, Jeff Davis" (above the flag) and "Vice President Alex H. Stephens" (below the flag) printed as part of the design. Black. 4,000.

F7-25 F7-26

F7-25 Waving flag extending far from flagstaff, spearhead on flagstaff, stars in a circle. One cover recorded in prior catalogs with design in color, but its current existence cannot be verified. —

F7-26 Extended flag, ball on flagstaff, stars in a circle, streamer extending down the left side of the staff "Southern Literary Messenger" and a pennant below the flag "Union of the South" printed as part of the design. Red. 7,500.

F7-27

F7-28

F7-27 Very small extended flag, small ball on the flagstaff, stars in a circle. 7,500.

F7-28 Waving flag with sloping staff, two ropes, large sharp five-pointed stars in a circle. Known only on used lettersheets. Not known on a cover. (LS) 1,000.

F7-29

F7-30

F7-29 Long extended flag, two ropes, small spearhead on the flagstaff, stars in a circle. 3,000.

F7-30 Small waving flag, two crossed tassels, spearhead on flagstaff, stars in a circle. 5,000.

F7-31

F7-31 Small slightly waving flag, one free rope away from the flagstaff, spearhead on flagstaff, stars in a circle. 5,000.

Eight Star Flags

The eight star "Stars and Bars" was the official national flag beginning with the admission of Virginia to the Confederacy and ending with the admission of Arkansas.

F8-1

F8-2

F8-1 Waving flag with slightly sloping staff, stars in a circle. Although once believed to exist postally used in two major varieties (spear or liberty cap), this major design has not been seen in many years. No examples of this design in either major subtype with CSA postal use can be currently verified. Design in color. —

F8-2 Waving flag, curled end. Same design as F7-5A with the eighth star added inside the circle of seven star. Design in color. 5,000.

F8-3

F8-4

F8-3 Long narrow waving flag, large liberty cap on flagstaff, stars in a circle. 5,000.

F8-4 Long extended flag, large ball on flagstaff. Somewhat crudely printed. 5,000.

F8-5

F8-6

F8-5 Small extended flag, two ropes, ball on flagstaff. Same design as F7-7A with the eighth star added in the center of the circle of seven. 1,500.

F8-6 Flag strongly sloping to the right, liberty cap on flagstaff. Same design as F7-12A with the eighth star added in the center of the circle of seven. 2,500.

F8-7

F8-8

F8-7 Flag waving around the staff, large liberty cap on flagstaff, stars in a circle of seven with the eighth star in the center. (Verse: 4) 3,500.

F8-8 Sloping waving flag, long tassels, liberty cap on flagstaff. Same design as F7-17 with the eighth star added in the center of the circle of seven. The center star may be the result of a printing flaw and not purposely added by the printer. Design in color. No example of this design can be currently verified. —

F8-9

F8-10

F8-9 Extended waving flag, spearhead on flagstaff. Same design as F7-6 with the eighth star added in the center of the circle of seven. (Imprint: 20) 3,000.

F8-10 Waving flag, curled end. Same design as F7-5C but with a large six-pointed star added in the center of the circle of seven five-pointed stars. *10,000.*

F8-11

F8-12

F8-11 Extended flag, spearhead on flagstaff. Same design as F7-4 with the eighth star added in the center of the circle of seven. Minor varieties. 3,000.

F8-12 Large waving flag, two tassels, ball on flagstaff, stars in a circle of seven with the eighth star in the center. Design in color. 5,000.

F8-13

F8-14

F8-13 Waving flag, spearhead on flagstaff. Stars in a circle of six with one star in the center and the eighth star at the lower right. (Imprint: 9) 3,500.

F8-14 Blue square canton only with a circle of seven stars and the eighth star in the center. 5,000.

F8-15

F8-16

F8-15 Blue octagonal canton with a circle of seven stars and a very large eighth star in the center. *10,000.*

F8-16 Waving flag, small curl at the end, liberty cap on flagstaff, stars in a circle. *10,000.*

F8-17

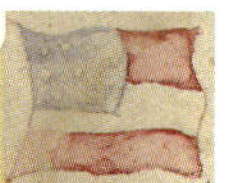

F8-18

F8-17 Overall Stars and Bars with the name of the President and Vice President in the red bars. Same design as F7-1A with an eighth star scratched into the center of the circle of seven. Most likely altered by hand and not a constant printing variety. 5,000.

F8-18 Blurred stenciled flag design with an extended flag, stars in a circle of seven with an eighth star in the center. 2,500.

F8-19

F8-19 Long extended flag, small spearhead on flagstaff, seven small stars in a circle and one large star in the center. 3,500.

Nine Star Flags

The nine star "Stars and Bars" was the official national flag beginning with the admission of Arkansas to the Confederacy and ending with the admission of North Carolina.

> [*italic*] value typeface indicating the item is difficult to price accurately

F9-1

F9-1 Waving flag, curled end, liberty cap on flagstaff. Stars in a circle. *10,000.*

F9-2A

F9-2B

Extended flag, plain flagstaff, stars in a circle of eight with the ninth star in the center.

F9-2A Small Stars. (LS) (Slogan: 48) 4,000.
F9-2B Large Stars. (LS) 4,000.

F9-3

F9-3 Large extended flag, tassels, ball on flagstaff, stars in a circle of seven with the eighth star in the middle and the ninth star at the lower right. (LS) (Verse: 46) *10,000.*

Ten Star Flags

The ten star "Stars and Bars" was the official national flag beginning with the admission of North Carolina to the Confederacy and ending with the admission of Tennessee.

F10-1

F10-2

F10-1 Overall Stars and Bars with the name of the President and Vice President in the red bars. Same design as F7-1A with three added stars — one star in the middle of the circle of seven and extra stars at top left and bottom left. 5,000.

F10-2 Extended flag, ball on flagstaff, five-pointed stars in a circle. May appear on the back flap with a horizontal staff. (LS) (Verse: 46) 1,000.

F10-3

F10-4

F10-3 Extended flag, ball on flagstaff, six-pointed stars in a circle. May appear on the back flap with a horizontal flagstaff. (LS) (Slogan: 57) 1,000.

F10-4 Small extended flag, two ropes, ball on flagstaff. Same design as F8-5 with two added stars at upper left and lower left. 1,500.

F10-5

F10-6

F10-5 Extended flag with long tassels, ball on flagstaff, loose rope hanging free, stars arranged in a circle of seven with added star in the center and two added stars at the left. (Verse: 2, 46) 5,000.

F10-6 Extended flag, small spearhead on the flagstaff, two tassels extending horizontally over the flag, stars arranged in a circle of nine with a large tenth star in the center. 3,500.

F10-7

F10-8

F10-7 Waving flag, curl on the end of the flag, liberty cap on flagstaff. Same design as F9-1 with the tenth star and a "T" for Tennessee (apparently the printer was unaware that North Carolina has already seceded) added in the center of the circle of nine. Design in color. (LS) (Verse: 12) 5,000.

F10-8 Small strongly waving flag, no rope, large spearhead on flagstaff, stars in a circle of seven with two stars inside the circle. Design in color. 4,000.

F10-9

F10-10

F10-9 Long waving flag, spearhead on the flagstaff, stars in a circle of six with four additional stars inside the circle. (Imprint: 14) 3,500.

F10-10 White "Jackson" flag with the upper left canton in the battle flag arrangement with the ten stars in a cross. (LS) (Verse: 10) 5,000.

F10-11

F10-12

F10-11 Extended flag, ball on flagstaff, blank streamer extending above the flag, stars in a circle of seven with three additional stars within the circle. Black. (LS) (Verse: 5, 37) (Imprint: 17) 1,000.

F10-12 Waving flag to the left, liberty cap on a severely sloping flagstaff, banner under the flag "Union of the South." Black. (Slogan: 25, 49) 5,000.

F10-13

F10-14

F10-13 Flag waving around the staff, large liberty cap on the flagstaff. Same design as F8-7 with two additional stars within the circle of seven. 3,500.

F10-14 Large waving flag, two tassels, ball on the flagstaff. Similar design to F8-12 with two added stars at upper left and lower right. (Slogan: 53) 5,000.

F10-15

F10-16

F10-15 Waving flag, liberty cap on flagstaff, curled end. Similar design to F8-10 with two added stars at upper and lower left. 7,500.

F10-16 Waving flag, spearhead on the flagstaff, stars in a circle. (Verse: 46) (Imprint: 33) 5,000.

F10-17

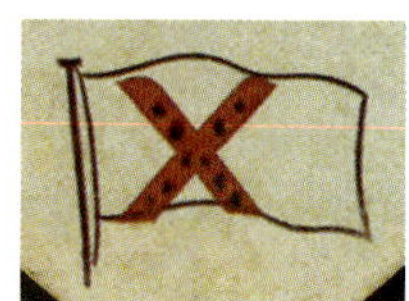
F10-18

F10-17 Extended flag, ball on flagstaff, stars in a circle of seven with three added stars inside the circle as a triangle. 5,000.

F10-18 Very small white flag with ten gold stars within crossed red stripes. Known only printed on the back flap. 5,000.

F10-19

F10-20

F10-19 Extended waving flag, spearhead on the flagstaff. Same design as F8-9 with two additional stars added at upper left and lower right. (Imprint: 21) 7,500.

F10-20 Stenciled flag design with an extended flag but the ten stars not well defined and in a haphazard arrangement. Short flag, ball on flagstaff. 2,500.

F10-21

F10-21 Stenciled flag design with an extended flag but the ten stars not well defined and in a haphazard arrangement. Extended flag with long flagstaff, one rope and a halyard, spearhead on flagstaff. 2,500.

Eleven Star Flags

The eleven star "Stars and Bars" was the official national flag beginning with the admission of Tennessee to the Confederacy and ending with the admission of Missouri.

F11-1

F11-2

F11-1 Extended flag, ball on flagstaff, stars in a circle. (LS) 1,500.

F11-2 Waving flag, ball on flagstaff, strongly curled at the end, stars in a circle. (Imprint: 27) 3,500.

F11-3

F11-4

F11-3 Waving flag flush on flagstaff, tassels over the top, liberty cap on flagstaff, stars in a circle. (LS) (Imprint: 23) 3,500.

F11-4 Extended flag, spearhead on flagstaff, hanging tassels, stars in a circle. Minor varieties as to size of the flag. (Verse: 5, 50) (Slogan: 42) 3,000.

F11-5

F11-6

F11-5 Large extended waving flag, spearhead on flagstaff, stars in a circle. Some examples have a missing star due to a printing flaw. (LS) (Verse: 46) (Slogan: 27, 36, 40, 67) (Imprint: 5, 22, 23, 27, 33, 34) 1,500.

F11-6 Extended flag, plain flagstaff, stars in a circle of seven with four added stars in the center in the shape of a crescent. Same design as F7-18 with the added crescent four star formation. 3,500.

F11-7

F11-8

F11-7 Extended waving flag, liberty cap on flagstaff, curl at the end, stars in a circle of seven with one in the middle and added stars at left upper, left lower, and right lower corners. (LS) (Verse: 46) 5,000.

F11-8 Extended flag, liberty cap on flagstaff, curl at the end. Same design as F10-7 with the eleventh star added at the lower left. "T" for Tennessee at the center of the circle. (Verse: 12, 46) 3,500.

F11-9

F11-9 Extended large flag to the left with a hand holding the flagstaff, stars in a circle. Large flag and large hand. (LS) (Slogan: 3, 21, 22, 33) 1,500.

F11-10A F11-10B

Extended flag to the left with a long slanted flagstaff, stars in a circle. Two major varieties.

F11-10A Small flag with a hand holding the flagstaff. (LS) (Slogan: 52, 71) 2,500.

F11-10B Somewhat larger flag with a slightly different wave and no hand holding the flagstaff. (Slogan: 52) 3,500.

F11-11 F11-12

F11-11 Waving flag, spearhead on flagstaff, stars in a circle of six with five stars added in the center as a cross. Found either on the front of the cover or on the backflap. (Slogan: 14) (Imprint: 7) 3,500.

F11-12 Waving flag, small spearhead on flagstaff, star pattern very irregular. (Verse: 29) (Slogan: 47, 58) 5,000.

F11-13 F11-14

F11-13 Waving flag, large spearhead on flagstaff. Same design as F10-8 with eleventh star added at upper right. 3,500.

F11-14 Flag waving around the staff, large liberty cap on flagstaff. Same design as F10-13 with eleventh star added at upper right. 3,500.

F11-15 F11-16

F11-15 Extended flag, spearhead on flagstaff, stars in a circle of ten with one in the center. 2,500.

F11-16 Waving flag, tassels, spearhead on flagstaff, stars in a circle of ten with one in the center. Examples in color have been noted in the past but are not currently confirmed. Minor varieties. Black. (Verse: 5, 13, 17, 30, 36, 40, 45, 46, 56) (Slogan: 24) (Imprint: 6, 31) 750.

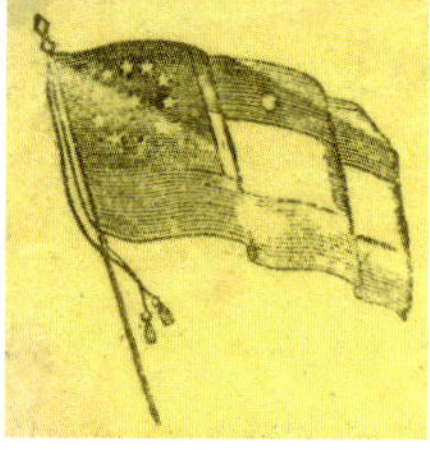

F11-17 F11-18

F11-17 Waving flag, tassels cross the staff, small spearhead on flagstaff, stars in a circle of ten with one in the center. Black. (LS) (Verse: 1, 5, 30, 46) (Imprint: 6, 31, 36) 1,500.

F11-18 Waving flag, large spearhead on flagstaff, stars in an irregular circle. Variations as to the slope of the flagstaff. (Imprint: 15) 3,500.

F11-19 F11-20

F11-19 Extended flag, tassel, ball on flagstaff, loose rope hanging free, stars in a circle of seven with one in the center and one in upper left, lower left, and lower right corners. (Verse: 46) (Slogan: 4a, 20, 68) 3,500.

F11-20 Waving flag to the left, two tassels, stars in an oval. *10,000.*

F11-21

F11-22

F11-21 Extended flag, two tassels, ball on flagstaff, halyard attached to short staff, stars in three columns. *10,000.*

F11-22 Waving flag, two tassels, spearhead on flagstaff, stars in a circle of ten with one in the center. *10,000.*

F11-23

F11-24

F11-23 Waving flag with curled end, spearhead on flagstaff, stars in a skewed circle of ten with seven stars in the top half of the circle and three stars in the bottom half and one in the middle. *10,000.*

F11-24 Flag waving to the left, tassels, streamer with "Leon Rifles" printed as part of the design, stars in the Southern Cross pattern. (Slogan: 19) (Imprint: 3) *10,000.*

F11-25

F11-26

F11-25 Waving flag, spearhead on flagstaff, stars in a circle of seven with one in the middle and added stars at left upper, left lower, and right lower corners. (Slogan: 1) (Imprint: 15) 5,000.

F11-26 Same design as F10-3 with an apparent eleventh star added at the right. Added apparent star may not have been intentional but simply a printing error. (Slogan: 26a) 2,500.

F11-27

F11-28

F11-27 Flag sloping to the right, ball on flagstaff, stars in a circle of ten with one in the center. 5,000.

F11-28 Stencil flag extended, plain flagstaff, stars in a circle of seven with four in the center. 3,500.

F11-29

F11-29 Waving flag with curled end, acorn on flagstaff, stars in a circle of ten with a larger star in the center. 5,000.

Twelve Star Flags

The twelve star "Stars and Bars" was the official national flag beginning with the admission of Missouri to the Confederacy and ending with the admission of Kentucky.

F12-1

F12-2

F12-1 Overall plain Stars and Bars with no flagstaff, stars in a circle of eight with four additional stars inside the circle. *10,000.*

F12-2 Extended flag, spearhead on flagstaff, stars in a circle. May or may not have a missing star at the upper right. 2,500.

F12-3

F12-4

F12-3 Small waving flag, short rope extending to the left, stars in a circle of eleven with one in the center. Minor varieties. 2,000.

F12-4 Large waving flag, tassels, ball on flagstaff. Same design as F8-10 but with added stars in each of the four corners. (LS) (Verse: 38, 41, 47, 54) (Slogan: 61) 2,500.

F12-5

F12-6

F12-5 Large waving flag, curl at end, ball on flagstaff, stars in a circle of eleven with one in the center and "M" for Missouri. (Verse: 12) (Slogan: 59) 3,500.

F12-6 Extended flag, tassels, ball on flagstaff, loose rope hanging free, stars in a circle of seven with one in the center and one in each of the four corners. (Verse: 46) 3,500.

Thirteen Star Flags

The thirteen star "Stars and Bars" was the official flag beginning with the admission of Kentucky to the Confederacy and ending with the adoption of the Second National Flag on May 1, 1863. The second national flag, known as the "Stainless Banner" or the "Jackson Flag," was the official flag until the adoption of the third national flag on March 4, 1865. Very few examples of the second national flag are found on patriotic covers, and none of the third national flag as it was adopted only within weeks of the end of the war.

F13-1

F13-2

F13-1 Waving flag flush on flagstaff, tassels over the top, liberty cap on flagstaff. Same design as F11-3 with two stars added inside the circle of eleven. Full color and also blue only. (Verse: 6) (Imprint 2, 28) 3,000.

F13-2 Extended flag, ball on flagstaff, stars in a circle of six inside a circle of seven. Blue. (Slogan: 77) 2,500.

F13-3

F13-3 Extended flag, stars in crossed blue stripes on a red field rectangular battle flag. (Verse: 6, 30) (Imprint: 2, 28) 3,000.

F13-4A

F13-4B

Second national flag "White Jackson Flag," stars in crossed dark blue stripes on canton. Two major types.

F13-4A Large flag with stars on a shaded field. Blue and white. 3,500.

F13-4B Smaller narrower flag with stars on an unshaded field. Blue and white. 4,500.

F13-5A

F13-5B

Second national flag, tassels, spearhead on flagstaff, stars in crossed black stripes on the canton with field shaded in black or red. Large white area of the flag heavily shaded in black. Two major types.

F13-5A Black background in the canton. Black. (Verse: 27) (Slogan: 60) 3,500.

F13-5B Red background in the canton. Black and red. (Verse: 27) (Slogan: 60) 3,500.

F13-6

F13-6 Small extended and very narrow flag (Stars and Bars), stenciled, stars in a haphazard column arrangement. Black. (Verse: 51) 2,500.

State Flags, Seals, Emblems

Confederate patriotic covers with state flags, seals, or emblems have been recorded from five states.

Georgia

FG-1

FG-2

FG-1 Flag with "SAV./VOL./GUARDS" as part of the design. Known only used with Savannah, Ga Paid/5 Handstamp with control mark. Black. 5,000.

FG-2 Georgia State Seal with "Banks County Guards" printed in the circle as part of the design. Black. 5,000.

Mississippi

FM-1

FM-2

FM-1 Mississippi Confederate State Seal with "Mississippi" above and "Jan 9, 1861" below. Black. (Imprint: 10) 3,500.

FM-2 Cotton Bale with "JAN. 9TH/1861/ MISSISSIPPI./IS KING" printed as part of the design. Black. 7,500.

FM-3

FM-3 "MISSISSIPPI" above a solid five pointed star. Black. 3,500.

South Carolina

FSC-1

FSC-2

FSC-1 Extended Palmetto State Flag with thin staff and flag attached to rope. Both small and large flags with no design difference except for the size. Blue. (Imprint: 35, 37) 3,500.

FSC-2 Extended Palmetto State Flag with sailor nailing the flag to the mast and a streamer above "SOUTHERN INDEPENDENCE" printed as part of the design. Black. (Verse: 13, 30, 45) (Slogan: 24) 3,500.

FSC-3A

FSC-3B

Extended Palmetto State Flag with thick staff and no rope. Data are for all varieties together.

FSC-3A Large flag with seven attachments to the flagstaff. Blue. (LS) (Imprint: 35) 3,500.

FSC-3B Flag with three attachments to the flagstaff. Both small and large flags with no design difference except for the size. Blue. (LS) (Imprint: 35) 3,500.

FSC-4

FSC-5

FSC-4 Palmetto State Flag flying to the left. Design in blue. 5,000.

FSC-5 Palmetto tree. Black. 5,000.

Texas

FTX-1

FTX-1 Texas State Flag. (LS) *10,000.*

[*]	symbol used after an item description to mean an unsupported listing
[–]	symbol used in place of value to mean insufficient information to assign a price
[*italic*]	value typeface indicating the item is difficult to price accurately

Virginia

There are a great many designs incorporating the Virginia State Seal printed on the cover. The vast majority of these covers are State Semi-Official Imprinted covers intended for government use. Only the following two designs qualify as patriotic covers.

FV-1

FV-2

FV-1	Virginia State Seal with "Virginia" above. Black. (Slogan: 56)	5,000.
FV-2	Medallion from the Virginia State Seal. Black. (Slogan: 69)	3,500.

Cannon

Cannons are a popular theme found on many Confederate patriotic covers. Most designs are a single color with black being the most common. A few examples are known in a combination of two or more colors and these command a premium. Cannon designs are assigned major numbers based upon design differences only and not for different colors.

CN-1A

CN-1B

CN-1C

Cannon firing left, large Stars and Bars flag with tassels. Three major varieties based on number of stars in the flag, and several minor varieties. Designs are found in four different colors and can be either monochromatic or with two or more colors. Data are for all three major varieties together. Valuation given is for black only which is the one most commonly seen. The addition of color will increase the basic valuation. Red, blue, purple, black. (LS) (Verse: 3, 13, 16, 21, 23, 28, 31, 38, 39, 45, 56) (Slogan: 24, 30, 31, 35, 44, 54, 63, 65) (Imprint: 6, 30, 32)

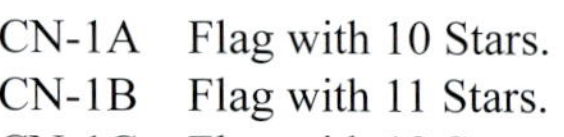

CN-1A	Flag with 10 Stars.	750.
CN-1B	Flag with 11 Stars.	750.
CN-1C	Flag with 12 Stars.	750.

CN-2

CN-3

CN-2	Cannon firing left, smaller Stars and Bars flag with eleven stars and no tassels. Flag in red, white, and blue; Cannon in blue; Smoke in red. Same design exists entirely in blue with only a single cover recorded. Valuation is for the multi-color design. (Verse: 35, 38, 39) (Slogan: 6b, 63) (Imprint: 14, 25, 29, 30)	3,500.
CN-3	Cannon firing on an angle to the left, smaller elongated Stars and Bars with twelve stars and two tassels. Design exists entirely in black, blue, or red. Valuation is for the black design which is the one most commonly seen. (LS) (Verse: 5, 33, 39, 46) (Slogan: 24, 45) (Imprint: 8, 17, 29, 31)	1,500.

CN-4

CN-5

CN-4	Cannon facing right and not firing, small Stars and Bars flag with eleven stars on a long flagstaff. Flag in red, white, and blue; Cannon in blue. (Slogan: 4, 11, 27, 43, 71) (Imprint: 11)	2,000.
CN-5	Large Cannon firing left with no flag. Black. (Verse: 30)	5,000.

CN-6

CN-7

CN-6 Cannon firing left, Stars and Bars flag with eleven stars. Similar in design to CN-1 but distinct differences in the cannon size, the smoke, the flag, and no tassels on the flagstaff. Black (Slogan: 65) (Imprint: 17a) 5,000.

CN-7 Cannon firing left, Stars and Bars flag with eleven stars. Very different appearance of the cannon, background, flag, and smoke. Blue. (Verse: 39) 5,000.

Tents and Flags

One of the more popular military patriotic themes is the Tents and Flags design with the "Stars and Bars" prominently displayed over a military tent.

TF-1

TF-2

TF-1 Large tent with 11-Star Stars and Bars flying to the left. Stars in a circle and a tassel on the staff (minor varieties). Tent in blue and flag in red, white, and blue. This design is seen with a large number of different military slogans. (Verse: 18) (Slogan: 2, 8, 9, 10, 11, 12, 13, 13a, 13b, 14, 14a, 15, 16, 18, 19, 27a, 28, 32, 37, 38, 39, 43, 62, 64, 66, 70, 74) (Imprint: 5) 1,250.

TF-2 Tent with soldier in front. Flag flying to the right. Tent and scene in blue with flag in full color. (Slogan: 10) (Imprint: 11) 7,500.

TF-3

TF-4

TF-3 Tent with soldier in front. Flag flying to the right. Larger more elaborate scene than TF-2 with a tree added. Tent and scene in blue with flag in full color. (Slogan: 10) (Imprint: 11) 5,000.

TF-4 Camp scene with standing soldier next to flag and tents in the background. Flag in full color with eleven stars arranged as a circle of ten and one in the center. 5,000.

TF-5

TF-6

TF-5 Stars and Bars (11 Stars) cross draped with the Louisiana "Pelican Regime" flag in full color with a tent in the background and "B." (Slogan: 26) 5,000.

TF-6 Circular Medallion with camp scene, flag, and standing soldier with tents in the background. "THE SOUTH" along the top rim and eleven stars along the bottom rim. Gray-Black. 5,000.

Soldiers

Displaying a martial patriotic theme are covers depicting soldiers either mounted or standing and with either a saber or a musket. In two designs, the soldier also holds a flag.

SM-1

SM-2

SM-1 Single Large Mounted Dragoon with raised saber. Black. (Verse: 5, 13, 21, 23, 36, 45, 52) (Slogan: 35, 63 (Imprint: 6) 1,000.

SM-2 Two Small Mounted Dragoons side by side. Same design as SM-1 but significantly smaller and doubled. Black. (Verse: 24) (Imprint: 17) 1,500.

SN-1

SN-2

SN-1 Two soldiers standing side by side at attention each with shouldered musket. Black. (Verse: 25) (Imprint: 17) 2,000.

SN-2 Single soldier standing with musket at port arms. Black. (Verse: 34) (Imprint: 17) 2,500.

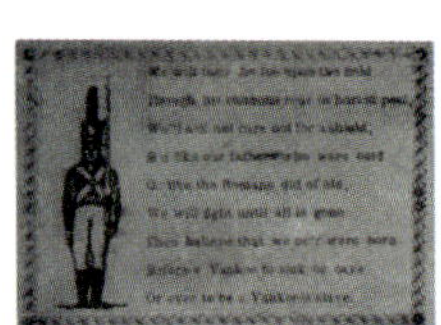

SN-3

SN-4

SN-3 Single soldier standing at attention with shouldered musket and inside an ornamental border with verse. Black. (Verse: 49) 5,000.

SN-4 Oval framed scene with a soldier holding a saber in one hand and an 11-Star Stars and Bars in the other hand. "FOR LAND & LIFE / CHILDREN AND WIFE" printed as part of the design. The design is monochromatic but known in four different colors. The valuation is for black. Designs in one of the other three colors will increase the basic valuation. Black, green, yellow, blue. 3,000.

SN-5

SN-5 Similar design to SN-4 but without the oval frame and in multi-color, somewhat different background, and the Stars and Bars has 12 Stars. "MY COUNTRY'S FREEDOM" and "VICTORY OR DEATH" printed as part of the design. (Imprint: 1) 5,000.

Jefferson Davis Medallions

The circular medallion style portrait of Jefferson Davis is one of the most popular of the Confederate patriotic designs. These designs range from the simple portrait to very elaborate designs with flags and allegorical scenes.

Jefferson Davis Portrait Circular Medallion "CONFEDERATE STATES OF AMERICA" (above) and "JEFF. DAVIS. / OUR FIRST PRESIDENT." (below). Flanked by crossed flags with an elaborate allegorical scene and a sunburst with stars as a background. Major varieties based on the number of stars in the flags and the sunburst. Found in mono-color in any of the colors listed and also in combinations of two or more colors as well as full multi-color. Valuation is for the basic black design. The addition of one, two, or more colors will significantly increase the valuation. Black, purple, brown, red, blue, violet. (LS) (Verse: 2, 3, 4, 6a, 17, 19, 22, 25, 28, 31, 38, 43, 44, 46, 48, 56)

JD-1A

JD-1B

JD-1C

JD-1A Seven Stars in both flags and sunburst. 1,000.

JD-1B Seven Stars in both flags and ten stars in sunburst. 1,000.

JD-1C Eleven Stars in both flags and sunburst. 1,000.

JD-2

JD-3

JD-2 Same design as JD-1 but the elaborate allegorical scene used as background below the medallion has been omitted. Medallion in red with flags and sunburst in full color. Eleven stars in both flags and sunburst. 3,000.

JD-3 Medallion portrait with the flags and all background omitted. Mono-color only. Blue, purple. (LS) (Verse: 20, 25) (Imprint: 22) 3,500.

JD-4

JD-5

JD-4	Similar to JD-1 but with "RIGHT MAN IN THE RIGHT PLACE" (above) and both flags with just a single star and the right flag with a palmetto tree. Sunburst with eight stars. Black. (Verse: 43)	3,500.
JD-5	Similar to JD-4 but the left flag has eleven stars and the right flag has only a single star with stripes and no palmetto tree. Eight stars in the sunburst. Black.	3,500.

Patriotic Slogans and Inscriptions

This is a separate section consisting of five items that are printed as stand-alone designs with patriotic slogans and inscriptions either as a prominently printed design or enclosed in an elaborate border. The first two deal with free trade with the world, one with a long biblical quotation in an elaborate frame, one with a patriotic slogan in an intricate wreath design, and one with a large printed "C. S. A."

PS-1

PS-2

PS-1	"A SOUTHERN CONFEDERACY! / Free Trade With the World" printed in two straight lines at the upper left. Black. (Imprint: 18)	2,500.
PS-2	"SOUTHERN CONFEDERACY / FREE TRADE/ WITH ALL THE WORLD" printed in three lines as an oval design at the upper left. Black.	2,500.

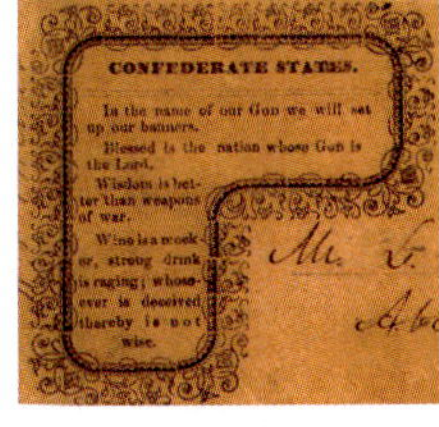

PS-3

PS-4

PS-3	Irregular angulated fancy border at the left enclosing "CONFEDERATE STATES" at the top followed by four biblical quotations all printed as part of the design. Black.	3,500.
PS-4	Elaborate floral wreath enclosing a patriotic verse as part of the design "Give this wreath to the brave, Who their country would save." Also known used in the North. Red and green.	3,500.

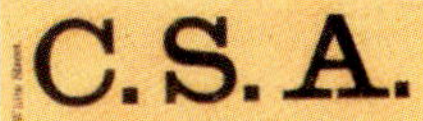

PS-5

PS-5	Printed "C. S. A." in large block letters at the upper left. (Imprint: 17b)	2,500.

Miscellaneous: Portraits, Scenes, Caricatures

MS-1

MS-2

MS-1	Oval Portrait of Gen P. G. T. Beauregard with eleven stars in the top part of the rim and "GEN'L G. T. BEAUREGARD, C. S. A." in the l ower rim. The design is monochromatic and is usually found in red or brown. Valuation is for a red or brown design. There is only one blue example known. Red, brown, blue. (Imprint: 18)	2,500.
MS-2	Allegorical River Scene with boat and mountains framed with cotton, sugar cane and tobacco plants. "CONFEDERATE STATES OF AMERICA" as part of the design. Blue, blue-green. (Verse: 8) (Slogan: 29)	3,000.

MS-3

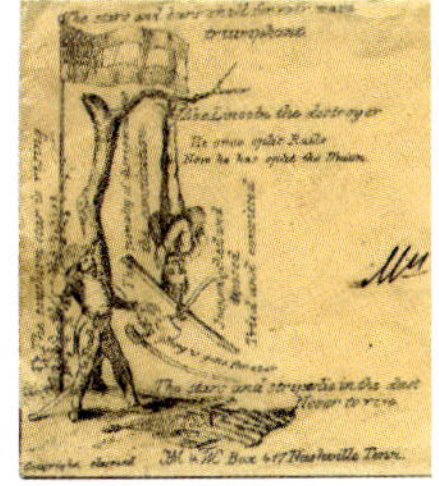

MS-4

MS-3	Very elaborate allegorical scene of CSA soldiers defending home, family, and country with the eleven star flag "OUR HOMES" (upper panel). Northerner pointing the way to a Negro slave carrying a bundle and flag, broken bust of Lincoln, and empty horn-of-plenty "PROTECTION"	

(lower panel). Full design in black with the Stars and Bars flag in full color. *15,000.*

MS-4 Hanging Lincoln — Very elaborate caricature of Lincoln hanging upside down from a tree and USA Gen Winfield Scott dropping his sword over the Stars and Stripes laying on the ground. Over the scene flies an eleven star Stars and Bars. Printed as part of the design are nine separate patriotic slogans. *15,000.*

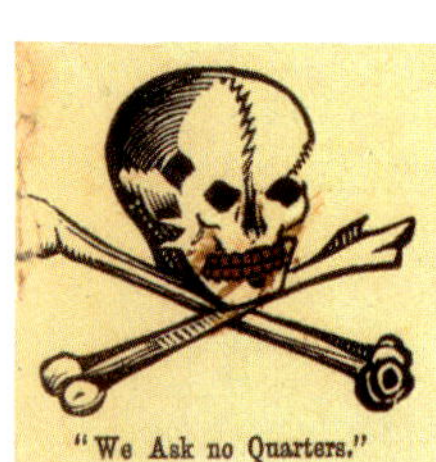

MS-5

MS-6

MS-5 Large Skull and Crossbones. Black. (Slogan: 76) 3,500.

MS-6 Allegorical design of a child seated on a globe holding the eleven star Stars and Bars and a snake. "ABOLITION" and "THE SUNNY SOUTH / OUR COUNTRY" printed as part of the design. 7,500.

Patriotic Stickers and Seals

Seven different adhesive Confederate patriotic stickers and seals have been recorded on postally used covers. The valuations given in the listings are for adhesives which are tied to a cover by a postmark or contemporary docketing. Untied stickers and seals on covers will sell for much less as they generally cannot be verified as original to the cover.

ST-1

ST-2

ST-3

ST-1 Seven star Stars and Bars in a circular frame over "SC" (Southern Confederacy) with "OUR FLAG" at the top. (Imprint: 20) 2,500.

ST-2 White flag with 10 gold stars in crossed red stripes circled by "CONFEDERATE STATES OF AMERICA" (upper) and "AIDE TOI DIEU TAIDERA" (lower). White flag, gold stars, red stripes, blue lettering. (LS) 3,500.

ST-3 Jefferson Davis Circular Medallion Portrait "THE RIGHT MAN IN THE RIGHT PLACE" (upper) and "OUR FIRST PRESIDENT" (lower). Brown. *5,000.*

ST-4

ST-5

ST-4 Sailor Nailing Flag to the Mast. Eleven Star Stars and Bars with a blue ornamental frame. 3,500.

ST-5 Allegorical scene with seven star Stars and Bars flying over a palmetto tree, cotton fields, and cotton bales. 7,500.

ST-6

ST-7

ST-6 White saltire battle flag design with twenty-five stars in crossed stripes. Die cut to shape. Black. 5,000.

ST-7 Stars and Bars Shield design with seven stars at the top over vertical bars. Die cut to shape. 2,000.

Appendix: Southern Designs Not Recorded Postally Used

This section shows a selection of patriotic designs with Southern themes that mostly by design appearance, content and style are believed to be Confederate in origin but for which no corresponding Confederate postal or lettersheet use has as yet been documented. No valuations are given for these items.

X-1

X-2

X-1 Overall Stars and Bars design with seven stars in a circle with the names of the President and Vice President in the red bars. Similar in style to F7-1A and F7-1B but with the names in large very fancy script lettering and no flagstaff. This design is known hand carried outside the postal system to New Jersey, but point of origin is unknown. No corresponding Confederate postal use has been documented.

X-2 Overall Stars and Bars with a seven star circle and a large eighth star in the center with "Va." "JEFF. DAVIS, President" (upper) and "A. H. STEVENS, Vice Pres." (lower). Very crudely printed with the bars apparently upside down and the Vice President's name misspelled. Believed to be a local printer's attempt to honor Virginia's admission to the CSA. Currently only one known unused cover.

X-3

X-4

X-3 Extended Stars and Bars with seven stars and very similar to F7-7B but with a distinctly different shape to the flag which makes it a separate design. Known only on poor quality unused covers indicating Southern origin but not known postally used.

X-4 Stars and Bars with stars arranged in a circle of seven with three additional stars in the center in a triangle pattern. Spearhead on flagstaff. General design of the flag is consistent with other known CSA designs and is similar to F10-17. There are a number of known unused covers with this design, but this pattern of ten stars with the spearhead on the flagstaff is not known postally used. Unused examples have been used to create known fraudulent covers.

X-5

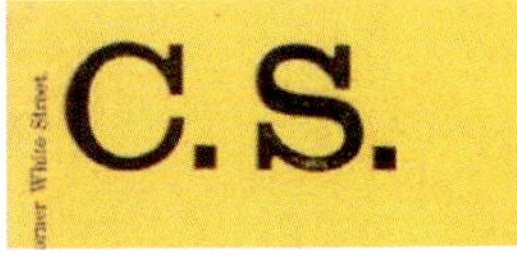

X-6

X-5 Stars and Bars with stars arranged as a circle of seven. There are no known postally used examples of this design, but the somewhat crude printing and the poor quality of the paper of the known unused cover strongly suggest that the design is Southern in origin.

X-6 This "C. S." slogan unused cover is essentially the same design as PS-5 but without the "A." It also has the same New Orleans imprint confirming that it is indeed Southern in origin. But no postally used examples have as yet been identified. Black. (Imprint: 17b)

X-7

X-8

X-7 Small waving Stars and Bars with nine stars arranged as a half circle left arc of eight stars with the ninth in the middle. An unusual design.

X-8 Small extended flag, large spearhead on flagstaff, seven stars in a circle. Very similar to other seven star designs but with no known examples showing authenticated postal use. Unused examples have been used to create fraudulent covers.

Addendum

Confirmed listings received after section layout complete.

Slogan 23a: Confederate Guards, Zebulon, Pike County, Georgia

F7-32

F7-32 Flag waving around the staff, large liberty cap on flagstaff, stars in a circle of seven. 2,000.

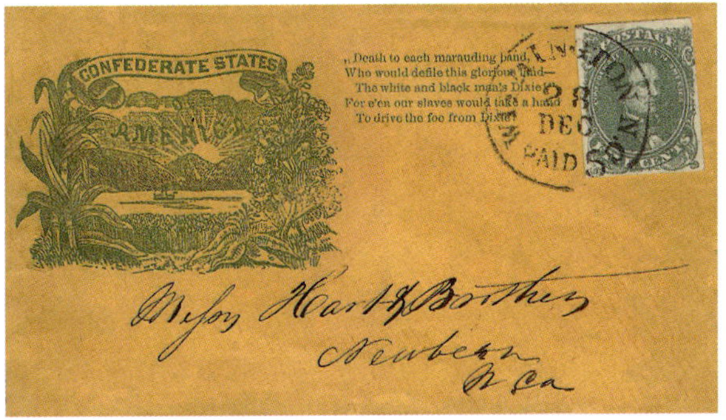

Allegorical River Scene, type MS-2

Overall Stars and Bars, type F7-1A

Hanging Lincoln, type MS-4

Advertising Covers

Advertising covers were used to promote the interests of various businesses, professions and trades. They range from simple imprints to fancy cameo designs and elaborate all-over lithographed designs. Northern printers dominated the market for intricately printed and cameo style envelopes prior to the war. The outbreak of hostilities eliminated Northern printers as the principal source of supply.

Supplies on hand at the beginning of the war were used until exhausted. Initially Southern printers filled orders for new supplies. But as the South shifted to a war-driven economy, the demand for advertising covers fell drastically. Although advertising covers were used throughout the war, most uses are concentrated in the first two years.

Design Types and Pricing

Design, size, color and attractiveness affect the market value of advertising covers. Bright colors, elaborate illustrated designs, historically important content and popular merchant categories command premiums.

A general pricing guide by design type follows. Prices are for covers in very fine condition with common stamps. Covers with scarcer stamps or extravagant designs command higher prices. Covers with defects sell for significantly less.

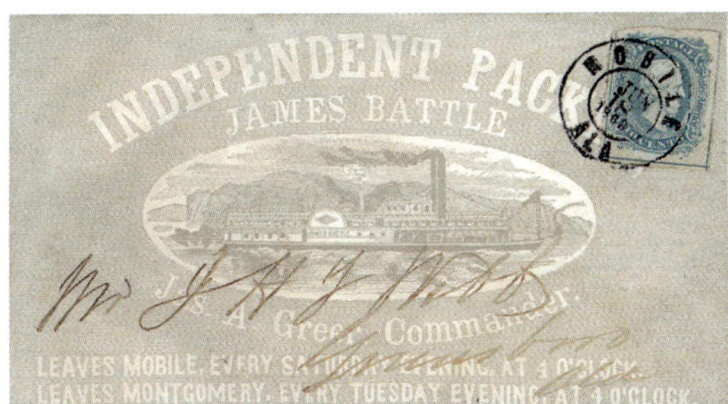

A – All-Over (the design fills the entire face of the envelope)

Simple design, not illustrated	500-750.
Average design, small illustration	750-1,000.
Fancy design, large illustration	1,000-2,500.

C – Cameo (a printed design in which the background is in color and primary image and lettering are colorless)

Small	350-500.
Medium	500-750.
Large	750-1,500.

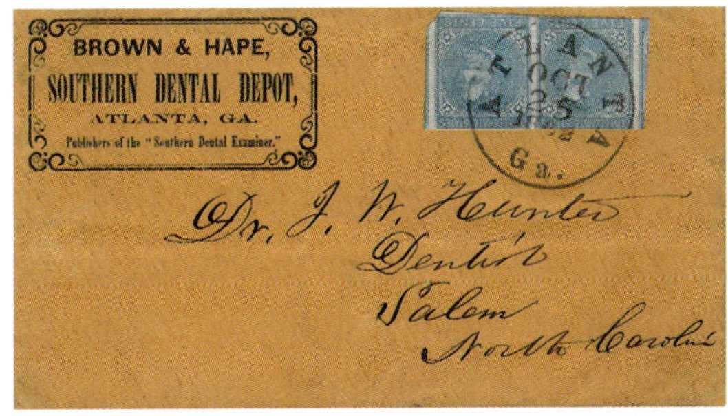

I – Imprint (any printed text or design) 350-500.

E – Embossed (similar to cameo, but colorless) 150-350.

H – Handstamped (similar to imprint, but applied by handstamping) 150-350.

S – Stenciled (similar to handstamped, but applied with a stencil) 150-350.

Listings

A complete census of all known designs is beyond the scope of this catalog. Only a sampling of the most commonly encountered designs is listed. The listings are arranged by state and within a state alphabetically by business name. Information for each entry includes the town, business and design type.

Alabama

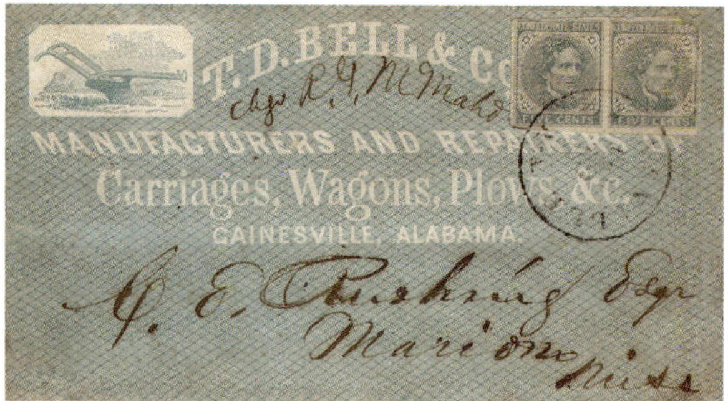

Battle House Drug Store (Mobile; druggist; A)
Central Bank of Alabama (Montgomery; bank; C)
Commercial Bank of Alabama (Selma; bank; I)
Daniel Pratt (Prattville; cotton gin; A)
Dickinson & Kilpatrick (Grove Hill; attorney; C)
Gary Magard & Co. (Mobile; commission merchant; C)
James Battle Independent Packet (Mobile; packet boat; A)
McPherson & Co. (Fort Deposit; dry goods; I)
Montgomery & McCarthy (Mobile; commission merchant; C)
T. D. Bell & Co. (Gainesville; carriage manufacturer; A)
Warrior Works, Leach & Avery (Tuscaloosa; plow manufacturer; C)
Wm. H. Ross & Co. (Mobile; grocer; A, C)

Arkansas

C. P. King (Helena; dry goods; I)
The True Southron (Pine Bluff; newspaper; I)

Florida

Florida House (St. Augustine; hotel; I)
Judson House (Jacksonville; hotel; C)

Georgia

Adams Express Company (Augusta; express company; A)
Adams Southern Express (Atlanta; express company; I)
Compton & Callaway (Milledgeville; grocer; C)
Fears & Swanson (Macon; grocer; C)
Greer & Lake (Macon; grocer; A)
Hand, Williams & Graves (Augusta; grocer; C)
Isaacs & Brother (Macon; confectionery; C)
J. A. Ansley & Co. (Augusta; commission merchant; C)
Jno. C. Whitner (West Point; gold dealer; A, E)
Lanier House (Macon; hotel; C)
M. P. Stovall (Augusta; commission merchant; E)
Planters Hotel (Augusta; hotel; I)
R. H. Richards (LaGrange; bookseller; patriotic I)
Robertson, Leslie & Co. (Troupe Factory; dry goods; A)
Salmons & Simmons (Atlanta; fancy goods; C)
Screben House (Savannah; hotel; A)
Southern Confederacy (Atlanta; newspaper; I)
The Constitutionalist (Augusta; newspaper; I)
W. A. Huff (Macon; grocer; C)
Wm. H. Goodrich (Augusta; grocer; C)

Louisiana

American Tract Society (New Orleans; books; A)
City Hotel (New Orleans; hotel; E)
Copes & Phelps (New Orleans; commission merchant; I)
Duncan, Payne & Co. (New Orleans; factor; I)
Goodrich & Co. (New Orleans; grocer; A)
L. W. Lyons & Co. (New Orleans; clothier; I)
George A. Pike, Office Of (Baton Rouge; printer; I)
Payne & Harrison (New Orleans; factor; E)
Pinckard, Steele & Co. (New Orleans; grocer; I)
Thos. H. Pitts (Shreveport; notary; I)

Mississippi

Bowman House (Jackson; hotel; A)
Carroll County Manufacturing (Carrollton; manufacturing; I)
Columbus Life Insurance Co. (Columbus; insurance; S)
Crutcher & Co. (Vicksburg; commission merchant; I)
Dew Drop, Vicksburg & Greensburg (Vicksburg; packet boat; A)
Steamer Vicksburg (Vicksburg; packet boat; I)
William McCutchen & Co. (Vicksburg; commission merchant; C)

North Carolina

Bank of Lexington (Lexington; bank; C)
J. G. Williams & Co. (Raleigh; bank; E)
J. W. Patton (Ashville; dry goods; C)
Raleigh & Gaston RR Co. (Raleigh; railroad; I)
Salem Mutual Insurance Co. (Salem; insurance; A)
Scott & Scott (Greensborough; attorney; I)
Thos. Carter's Garden & Nursery (Raleigh; nursery; I)

South Carolina

Adams Southern Express (Columbia; express company; I)
Bank of Charleston (Charleston; bank; I)
Chambers, Barnes & Co. (Charleston; commission merchant; A)
Charleston Hotel (Charleston; hotel; A)
D. F. Fleming & Co. (Charleston; boots and shoes; E)
Dunham, Taft & Co. (Charleston; boots and shoes; E)
Evans & Cogswell (Charleston & Columbia; printers; I)
Force & Mitchell (Charleston; boots and shoes; I)
Geo. W. Williams (Charleston; grocer; C)
Hamilton & Smith's Grocery (Charleston; grocer; I)
Hand, Williams & Farrow (Charleston; commission merchant; I)

Hayden & Whildon (Charleston; importers; E)
Henry Cobia & Co. (Charleston; commission merchant; E)
Hutson Lee (Charleston; broker & auctioneer; A, I)
J. N. Robeson (Charleston; commission merchant; I)
James M. Allen (Greenville; monuments; I)
Killian & Wings (Columbia; building supply; C)
McCarter & Dawson (Columbia; publisher; C)
O'Hear, Roper & Stoney (Charleston; commission merchant; I)
Reeder & DeSaussure (Charleston; grocer; E)
S. Townsend (Charleston; books; C, I)
Southern Mutual Life Insurance Co. (Columbia; insurance; I)
Sunday School Board (Greenville; books; I)
United States Hotel (Columbia; hotel; C)
Williams, Birnie & Co. (Charleston; grocer; C)

Tennessee

A. H. Hise (Memphis; hides & flour; E)
Branch Planter's Bank (Memphis; bank; I)
Cole & Dyer (Memphis; tobacco merchant; A)
Ewin Pendleton & Co. (Nashville; druggist; C)
Exchange & Deposit Bank (Knoxville; bank; I)
Gayoso House (Memphis; hotel; C)
John W. Crisp & Co. (Memphis; slave broker; I)
Lewis & Glass (Clarksville; country produce; C)
Memphis & Charleston Railroad Office (Memphis; railroad; H)
Morgan & Co. (Nashville; dry goods; I)
Stratton, McDavitt & Co. (Memphis; commission merchant; E)
Terrass Brothers (Nashville; grocer; A)
The Adams Express Company (Nashville; express company; I)
Worsham House (Memphis; hotel; C)

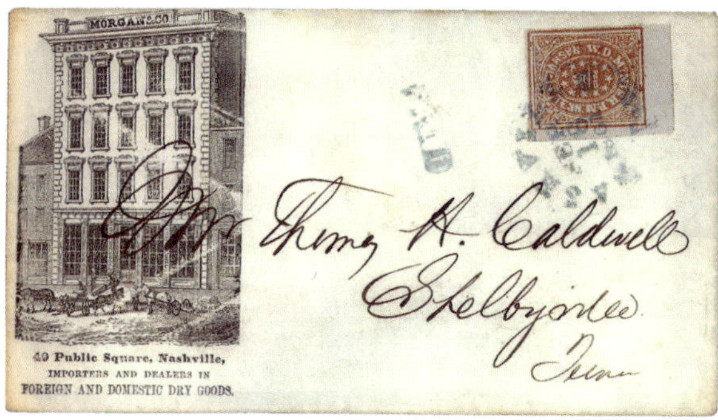

Texas

Ballinger & Jack (Houston; attorney; C)
H. Journeay (Galveston; building supply; C)
John H. Gooch (Palestine; attorney; A)
Leland's Rancho (Helena; ranch and farmer; I)
Peel, Dumble & Co. (Galveston / Houston; grocer; A)
Simmons & Bradley (Fairfield; attorney; I)

Virginia

Atlantic Hotel (Norfolk; hotel; A)
Bank of the Commonwealth (Richmond; bank; I)
Britton, Todd & Co. (Petersburg; commission merchant; C)
Brownley, Green & Co. (Petersburg; commission merchant; C)
Chas. S. Dawson (Richmond; druggist; A)

Chiles H. Ferrell (Halifax CH; attorney; I)
Citizens Savings Bank (Lynchburg; bank; I)
Davis, Dupree & Co. (Richmond; slave dealer; C)
Drummond & Parker (Petersburg; boots and shoes; A)
Evangelical Tract Society (Petersburg; newspaper; I)
Franklin Davis Nurseryman (Staunton; nursery; A, C)
Greenlee Davidson (Lexington; attorney; A)
Green's Mansion House (Alexandria; hotel; I)
Harvey, Armistead & Williams (Richmond; commission merchant; A, C)
Insurance Company State of Virginia (Richmond; insurance; A)
James River & Kanawha Company (Richmond; canal operating company; C)
Jno. R. Patterson & Co. (Petersburg; commission merchant; C)
John & George Gibson (Richmond; carpenter; A)
Lancaster House (Goodson; hotel; C)
Lynchburg Fire & Hose Insurance Co. (Lynchburg; insurance; I)
M. A. & C. A. Santos (Norfolk; druggist; C)
Martin, Tannahill & Co. (Petersburg; commission merchant; C)
McCorkle, Son & Co. (Lynchburg; commission merchant; I)
Newton's Atlantic Hotel (Norfolk; hotel; A)
Old Dominion Insurance (Richmond; insurance; A)
Peebles, Plummer & Co. (Petersburg; commission merchant; C)
R & P RR Co. (Richmond; railroad; I)
R. A. Young & Bro. (Petersburg; commission merchant; A, C)
R. H. Dibrell (Richmond; commission merchant; C)
Richmond & Petersburg RR Co. (Richmond; railroad; C)
Richmond Christian Advocate (Richmond; newspaper; C)
Rowland & Brothers (Norfolk; commission merchant; I)
S. R. Sullivan (Charlottesville; carriage dealer; C)
Samuel Ayres & Son (Richmond; commission merchant; C)
Spotswood Hotel (Richmond; hotel; A)
Spotts & Harvey (Richmond; commission merchant; A)
Taylor & Peebles (Petersburg; commission merchant; C)
Thos. Branch & Sons (Petersburg; commission merchant; I)
Tredegar Iron Works (Richmond; foundry; I, E)
Tyler & Son (Richmond; commission merchant; C)
W. D. Thompkins & Bro. (Richmond; commission merchant; E)
West & Johnson (Richmond; printer; I)

College Covers

College covers are another area of collecting interest. These covers are a subtype of advertising covers that have all-over designs, corner card designs or imprints relating to an educational institution. Some are institutions that today we call secondary schools.

Southern college covers were printed in both the North and South prior to the war. With the outbreak of hostilities, the northern printers were unable to fill any new orders. Southern printers continued to provide limited quantities based on the availability of envelopes. In spite of the limited number of college covers available, they were used throughout the Confederate period.

Included are college covers that are known to have been used during the three Confederate time periods: Independent State, Confederate State Use and Confederate. Other designs may exist, but they have yet to be identified by the editors. Some designs that were previously included have been omitted, as either their use during the Confederate time periods has not been verified or, in some cases, the institution was not founded until after the war.

The following are the basic design types:

All-Over or **"Illuminated"** (the design fills the entire face of the envelope)
Cameo (a printed design in which the background is in color and primary image and lettering are colorless)
Imprint (any printed text or design)
Embossed (similar to cameo, but colorless)
Handstamped (similar to imprint, but applied by hand stamping)

Institutions are listed alphabetically by state. Most of the all-over and cameo designs are known in different colors, but are not listed separately.

Alabama

AL-01

AL-01 Female Collegiate Institute, Athens (printed vertically at left) 1,000.

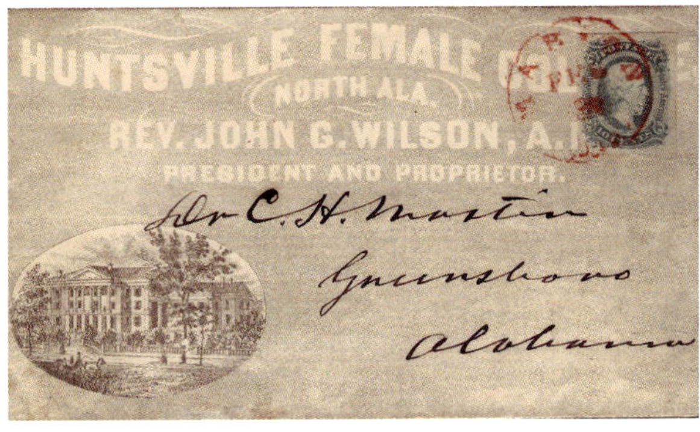

AL-02

AL-02 Huntsville Female College, Huntsville 1,250.

AL-03

AL-03 Marion Female Seminary, Marion 750.

AL-04

AL-04 Southern University, Greensboro 1,250.

AL-05 AL-06

AL-05 Tuskaloosa Female College, Tuskaloosa (Tuscaloosa) 750.
AL-06 Union Female College, Eufaula —

AL-07

AL-07a University of Alabama, Tuscaloosa (with Tuscaloosa) 1,000.

AL-07b

AL-07b University of Alabama, Tuscaloosa (without Tuscaloosa) 1,000.

Georgia

GA-01

GA-01 Atlanta Medical College, Atlanta —

GA-01

GA-03

GA-02 Carrollton Female Institute, Carrollton 750.
GA-03 Cassville Female College, Cassville 750.

GA-04

GA-04 College Temple, Newnan (all-over) 1,000.

GA-05

GA-05 Eatonton Female Academy, Eatonton 2,500.

GA-06

GA-06 Georgia Military Institute, Marietta (back flap)* 1,000.

GA-07a

GA-07a Griffin Female College, Griffin 4,500.

GA-07b

GA-07b Griffin Female College, Griffin 750.

GA-08

GA-09

GA-08 Lucy Cobb Institute, Athens 750.
GA-09 Marshall College, Griffin 750.

GA-10

GA-11

GA-10 Martin Institute, Jefferson 500.
GA-11 Medical College of Georgia, Augusta 750.

GA-12

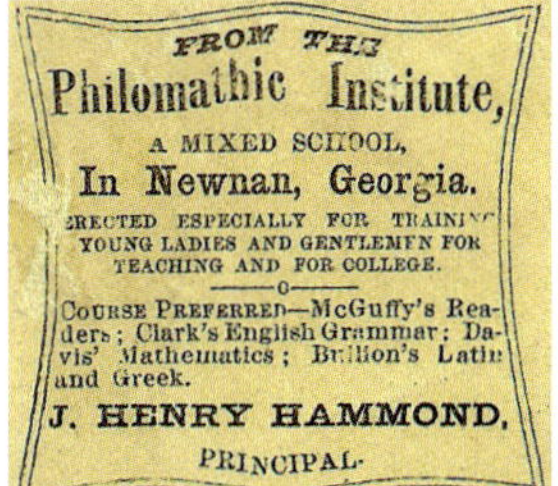

FROM THE
Philomathic Institute,
A MIXED SCHOOL,
In Newnan, Georgia.
ERECTED ESPECIALLY FOR TRAINING YOUNG LADIES AND GENTLEMEN FOR TEACHING AND FOR COLLEGE.
COURSE PREFERRED—McGuffy's Readers; Clark's English Grammar; Davis' Mathematics; Bullion's Latin and Greek.
J. HENRY HAMMOND,
PRINCIPAL.

GA-13

GA-12 Mercer University, Penfield 750.
GA-13 Philomathic Institute, Newnan 750.

GA-14a

GA-14a Synodical Female College, Griffin 4,500.

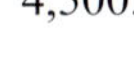

GA-14b

GA-14b Synodical Female College, Griffin 750.

GA-15a

GA-15b

GA-15a University of Georgia, Athens 1,250.
GA-15b University of Georgia, Athens 1,000.

GA-16a

GA-16b

GA-16a Wesleyan Female College, Macon 1,000.
GA-16b Wesleyan Female College, Macon 750.

GA-16c

GA-16d

GA-16c Wesleyan Female College, Macon 750.
GA-16d Wesleyan Female College, Macon 750.

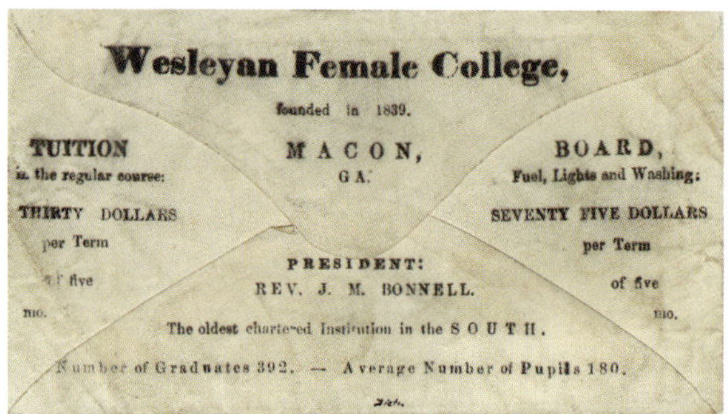

GA-16e

GA-16e Wesleyan Female College, Macon 750.

Kentucky

KY-01

KY-01 Bethel College, Russellville (printed vertically at left) 4,000.

Louisiana

LA-01

LA-01 Mt. Lebanon University, Mt. Lebanon —

> Basic design types:
>
> **All-Over** or "**Illuminated**" (the design fills the entire face of the envelope)
>
> **Cameo** (a printed design in which the background is in color and primary image and lettering are colorless)
>
> **Imprint** (any printed text or design)
>
> **Embossed** (similar to cameo, but colorless)
>
> **Handstamped** (similar to imprint, but applied by hand-stamping)

Mississippi

MS-01

MS-01 Brashear Female Academy, Port Gibson (all-over, color, printed vertically at left) 1,500.

MS-02

MS-02 Byhalia Female Institute, Byhalia 1,000.

MS-03

MS-03 Central Mississippi Female College, Lexington (printed vertically at left) 750.

MS-04

ODD FELLOWS' FEMALE COLLEGE,
Carrollton, Miss.
CHAS. P. McCROHAN, President.

MS-05

MS-04 Female Institute, Columbus 750.
MS-05 Odd Fellows' Female College, Carrollton 750.

MS-06

MS-06 Summerville Institute, Gholson 1,000.

MS-07

MS-07 Union Female College, Oxford 750.

MS-08

MS-08 University of Mississippi, Oxford (all-over, color) 1,500.

MS-09

MS-09 Yalobusha Baptist Female Institute, Carrollton 2,000.

North Carolina

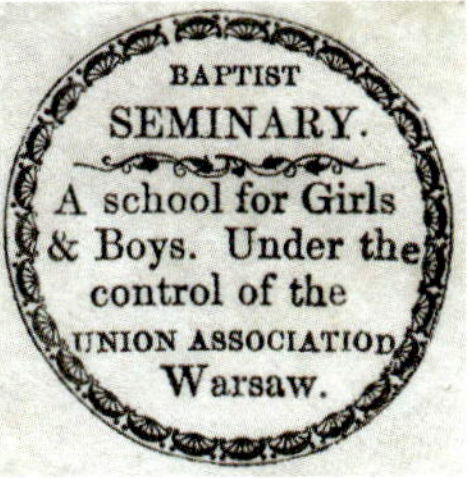

NC-01 NC-02

NC-01 Baptist Seminary, Warsaw 750.
NC-02 W. J. Bingham & Sons Select School, Oaks (embossed back flap) 500.

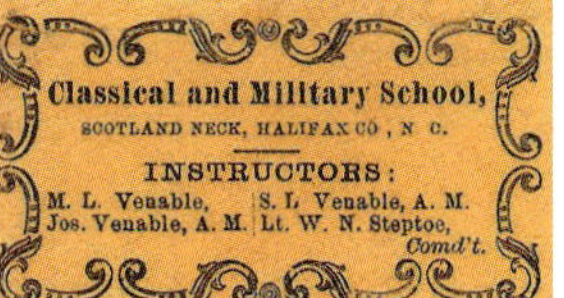

NC-03 NC-04

NC-03 Charlotte Female Institute, Charlotte 750.
NC-04 Classical and Military School, Scotland Neck —

NC-05

NC-05 Davenport Female College, Lenoir 750.

NC-06a

NC-06a Davidson College, Davidson College (all-over) 1,500.

NC-06b

NC-06b Davidson College, Davidson College (all-over) 1,500.

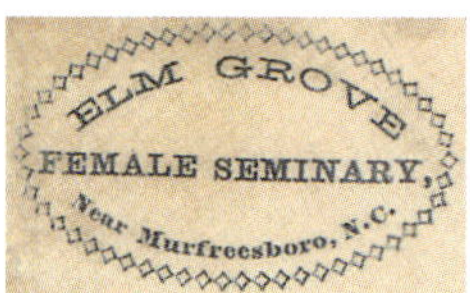

NC-07a

NC-07b

NC-07a Elm Grove Female Seminary, Near Murfreesborough 750.

NC-07b Elm Grove Female Seminary, Near Murfreesborough 750.

NC-08

NC-09

NC-08 Female Collegiate Institute, Warrenton 1,000.

NC-09 Greensborough Female College, Greensborough 750.

NC-10

NC-10 Hillsborough Military Academy, Hillsborough 1,000.

NC-11

NC-11 North Carolina College, Mt. Pleasant (all-over) 1,500.

NC-12

NC-12 Raleigh Female Seminary, Raleigh 750.

NC-13a

NC-13a Raleigh School for the Deaf & Dumb & the Blind, Raleigh (back) 1,250.

NC-13b

NC-13b Raleigh School for the Deaf, Raleigh 500.

NC-14a

NC-14a University of North Carolina, Chapel Hill 1,000.

Prices are for covers in very fine condition. Covers with scarcer stamps or extravagant designs command higher prices. Covers with defects sell for significantly less.

NC-14b

NC-14b University of North Carolina, Chapel Hill 1,000. 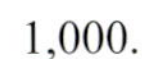

NC-15

NC-15 Wake Forest College, Wake Forest (all-over) 2,000.

NC-16a

NC-16a Wesleyan Female College, Murfreesborough 1,500.

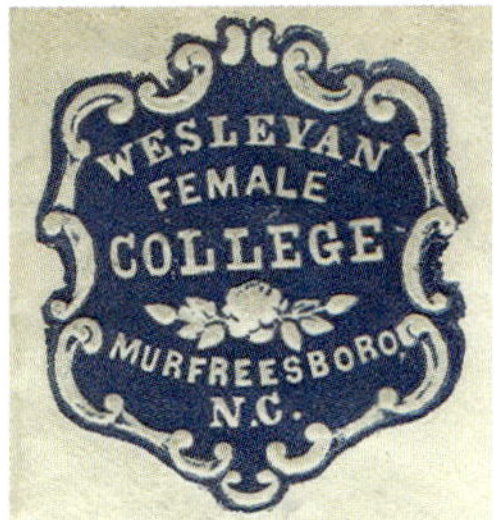

NC-16b

NC-16b Wesleyan Female College, Murfreesborough 750.

South Carolina

SC-01a

SC-01a Baptist Female College, Greenville 1,000.

SC-01b

SC-01b The Greenville Baptist Female College, Greenville (all-over) 1,500.

SC-02

SC-02 Barhamville, Columbia (on back flap) 500.

SC-03

SC-03 Columbia Female College, Columbia (all-over) 1,250.

Most of the allover and cameo designs are known in different colors, but are not listed separately.

SC-04

SC-04 Furman University, Greenville 1,500.

SC-05

SC-05 Masonic Female College, Cokesbury 1,000.

Tennessee

TN-01

TN-01 Aldehoff's Institute, Chattanooga 750.

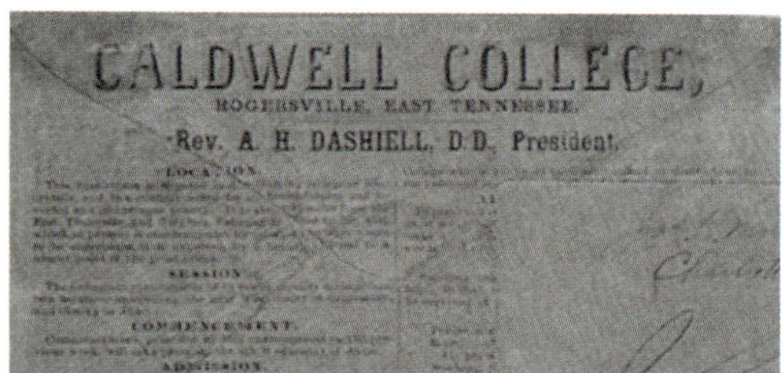

TN-02

TN-02 Caldwell College, Rogersville
(imprint on back) 1,000.

TN-03

TN-03 Cumberland University, Lebanon 1,500.

TN-04

TN-04 La Grange Synodical College,
La Grange (Phi Mu Society) 1,500.

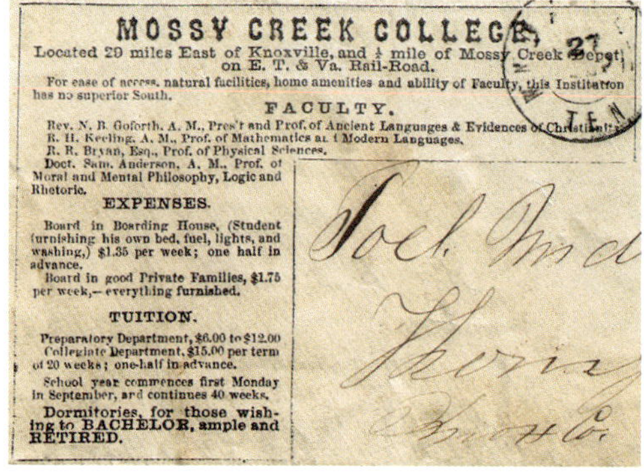

TN-05

TN5-05 Mossy Creek College, Mossy Creek 1,000.

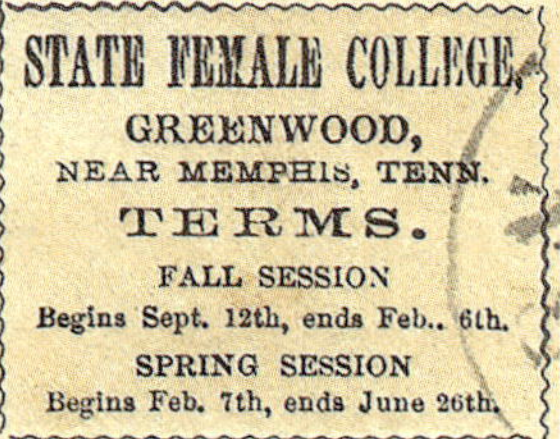

TN-06

TN-06 State Female College, Greenwood 750.

TN-07

TN-07 Tusculum College, Greenville (all-over, text imprint on back) 1,000.

TN-08

TN-08 University of East Tennessee, Knoxville (all-over) 1,500.

Texas

TX-01

TX-01 Larissa College, Larissa (black) —

Virginia

VA-01

VA-01 Brookhill School, Charlottesville (all-over, color) 1,000.

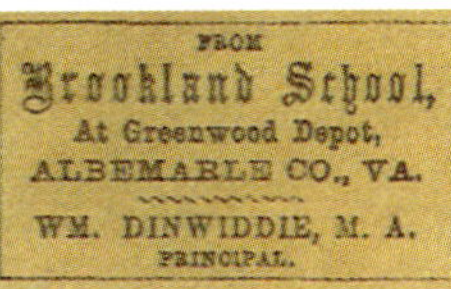

VA-02a

VA-02b

VA-02a Brookland School, Greenwood Depot 750.
VA-02b Brookland School, Greenwood Depot 500.

VA-03

VA-03 Buckingham Female Collegiate Institute, Gravel Hill (all-over) 1,250.

VA-04

VA-04 Chesapeake Female College, Hampton (color) —

VA-05

VA-06

VA-05 Collegiate Seminary for Young Ladies, Petersburg 500.
VA-06 Danville Female Academy, Danville

VA-07a

VA-07b

VA-07a Danville Female College, Danville 750.
VA-07b Danville Female College, Danville (black) 750.

VA-07c

VA-07c Danville Female College, Danville 750.

VA-07d

VA-07d Danville Female College, Danville 750.

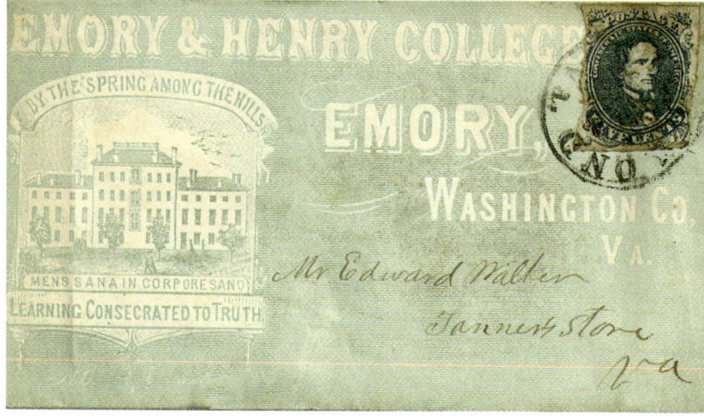

VA-08a

VA-08a Emory & Henry College, Emory (Hermesian Society imprint on back) 750.

VA-08b

VA-08b Emory & Henry College, Emory 1,250.

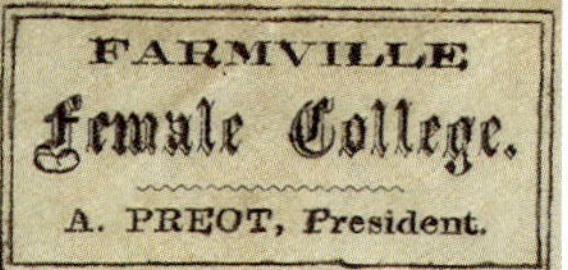

VA-09a

VA-09b

VA-09a Farmville Female College, Farmville 750.
VA-09b Farmville Female College, Farmville (black) 750.

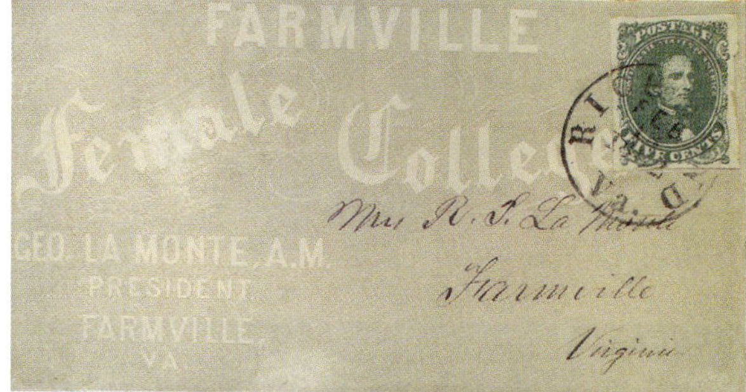

VA-09c

VA-09c Farmville Female College, Farmville 1,000.

VA-09d

VA-09d Farmville Female College, Farmville 1,000.

VA-09e

VA-09e Farmville Female College, Farmville 1,500.

VA-10

VA-10 Farmville Female Institute, Farmville 750.

VA-11

VA-11 Mount Laurel Academy, Mount Laurel 750.

VA-12

VA-12 Randolph Macon College, Boydton 750.

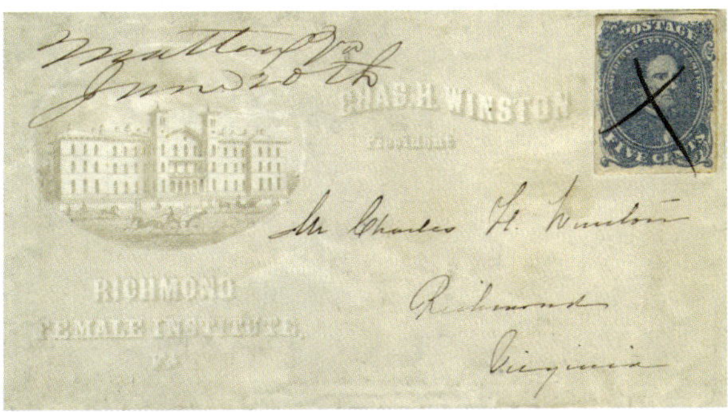

VA-13

VA-13 Richmond Female Institute, Richmond 750.

VA-14

VA-14a Roanoke College, Salem 1,250.

[*]	symbol used after an item description to mean an unsupported listing
[–]	symbol used in place of value to mean insufficient information to assign a price
[?]	symbol used to mean unknown measurement, date or color
[*italic*]	value typeface indicating the item is difficult to price accurately

VA-14a

VA-14b Roanoke College, Salem (Ciceronian Literary Society Seal) 1,000.

VA-14c

VA-14d

VA-14c Roanoke College, Salem 500.

VA-14d Roanoke College Demosthenean Society, Salem (all-over, color) —

VA-15

VA-15 Southern Waverley Institute, Richmond 750.

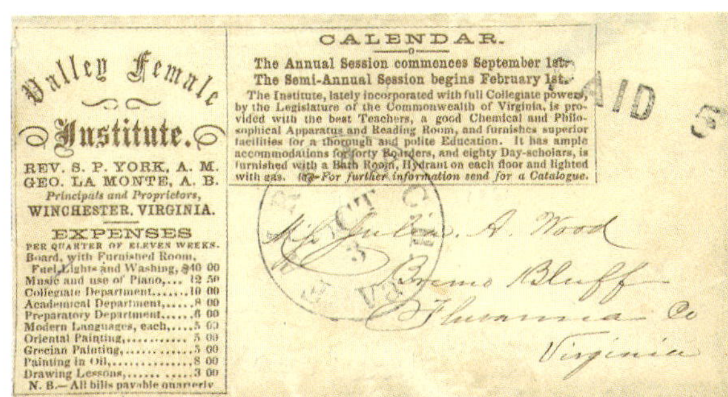

VA-16

VA-16 Union Female College, Danville 1,000.

VA-17a

VA-17a Valley Female Institute, Winchester 1,250.

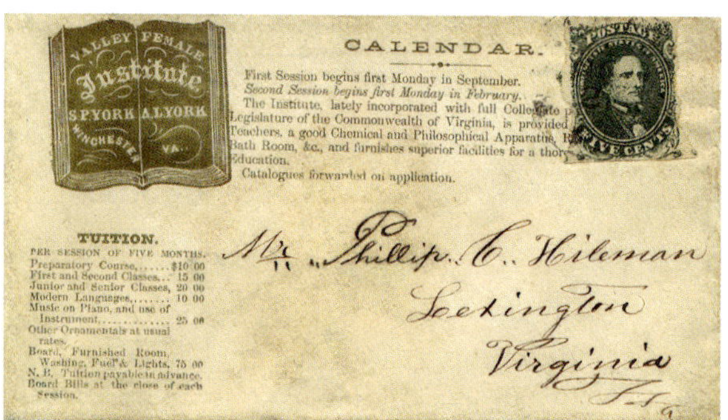

VA-17b

VA-17b Valley Female Institute, Winchester 1,250.

VA-18a

VA-18a Virginia Female Institute, Staunton 1,250.

VA-18b

VA-18b Virginia Female Institute, Staunton (back) 750.

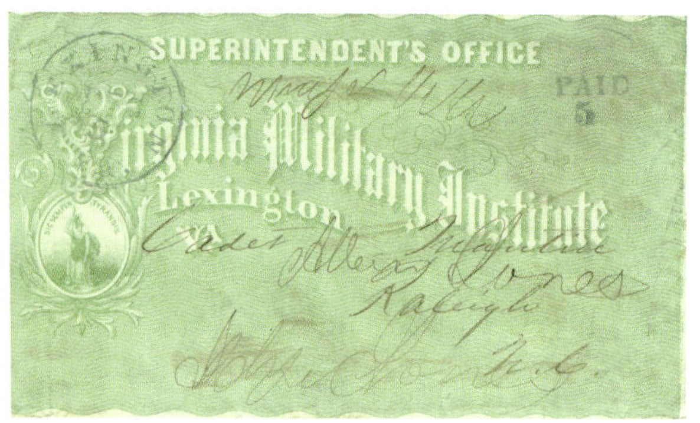

VA-19a

VA19a Virginia Military Institute, Lexington 1,250.

VA-19b

VA-19b Virginia Military Institute, Lexington with Sic Semper Tyrannis oval, no Superintendent's Office 1,250.

VA-19c Virginia Military Institute, Lexington no Sic Semper Tyrannis oval or Superintendent's Office [not illustrated] 1,250.

VA-19d

VA-19d Virginia Military Institute, Lexington 750.

VA-20

VA-20 Wytheville Female College, Wytheville 1,250.

VA-21

VA-21 Young Ladies Institute, Alexandria 750.

Way Mail

Way mail has been recognized as a category of mail since colonial times. It was addressed under the Constitutional postal system in the first United States postal statute (Section 15, Act of February 20, 1792), and was defined in Section 15 of the United States Act of May 8, 1794, as "... letters received by a post-rider or other mail carrier on his way between two post-offices ..." Beyond this formal definition, in practice, letters received at a post office too late to be bagged, but before the mail carrier departed, were also handled as way mail. Way mail was transported by whatever means the post rider or mail carrier happened to use to transport the mail — horse, stage coach, steamboat or railroad.

The Confederate Congress did not enact any laws specifically defining or regulating way mail. Confederate postmasters continued to follow the *United States Postal Laws and Regulations of 1859* which were adopted by an Act of the Confederate Congress on February 9, 1861.

Under the 1859 law and regulations, the post rider or mail carrier was required to deposit each way letter he received at the next post office to which he came. Each such letter was marked with the term "Way", and the mail carrier was paid a fee of 1¢ per letter, if he demanded such payment. This fee was then charged back to the addressee of the letter. In the case of loose letters carried by steamboats having a mail contract, the mail carrier or the captain of the contract vessel (if no mail carrier was aboard) was required to receive loose letters (as way letters) only if the letters were prepaid by stamps. Unpaid loose letters were treated as "ship" letters and rated differently from way mail.

The way marking applied to a way letter was both an origin marking and an accounting marking. As an origin marking, it indicated the post office where the letter entered the mail system when the carrier deposited the letter with the postmaster. As an accounting marking, it indicated that the way fee had been paid to the carrier and that the fee could be collected from the addressee.

The Way Mail listings are divided into the following periods: Independent State Uses, Confederate Use of US Postage and the Confederate period beginning 1 June 1861. Within each period, the way markings are listed first by those covers with postmarks and then those without postmarks. In the latter case, the marking is attributed to the town to which the cover is addressed.

Independent State Uses

Way Covers with Postmarks
(listed by town postmark)

New Orleans, Louisiana

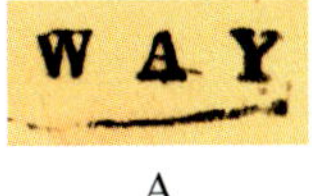

A

A	WAY	750.

CSA Use of US Postage

Way Covers with Postmarks
(listed by town postmark)

Alexandria, Virginia

Ms	Way	500.

Charleston, South Carolina

Ms	Way 1	1,000.

IH	used in place of listing value when the item is held by an institution
Ms	manuscript

New Orleans, Louisiana

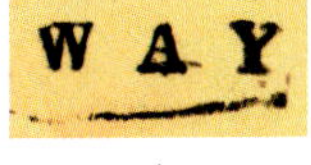

A

A	WAY	1,000.

Old Church, Virginia

Ms	Way 1	1,000.

Way Covers that Cannot be Attributed to a Specific Town

Westmoreland County, Virginia

Ms	Way 3	750.

Note: The addressee is believed to have resided in the vicinity of the post office located at Rice's Store, Virginia. This may be the point at which the letter entered the mails.

CSA Period beginning June 1, 1861

Way Covers with Postmarks
(listed by town postmark)

Ashboro, North Carolina

Ms	Way	750.

Beaumont, Texas

Ms Way 10 [handstamped "PAID" crossed out] 750.

Note: Cover cleaned and cross-out lines removed.

Brandy Station, Virginia

Ms Way 500.

Charleston, South Carolina

Ms Way 500.

Franklinton, North Carolina

Ms Way 750.

Macon, Georgia

Ms Way 750.

Natchez, Mississippi

Ms Way plus handstamped "STEAM" 2,000.

New Market, Virginia

Ms Way Paid 5 750.

Ninety-Six, South Carolina

Ms Way plus stampless "PAID / 5" (Type A) marking 750.

Richmond, Virginia

WAY

A

A WAY plus Richmond "DUE 10" (Type Q) 1,000.

Thomasville, North Carolina

Ms way paid 10 cts 750.

Vicksburg, Mississippi

Ms Way 5¢ 750.

Note: Confederate use is questionable.

White Sulphur Springs, [West] Virginia

Ms Way 500.
Way plus White Sulphur Springs stampless "PAID" (Type A) marking. 750.

Wilmington, North Carolina

A WAY [not illustrated] 1,000.

The way marking applied to a way letter was both an origin marking and an accounting marking. As an origin marking, it indicated the post office where the letter entered the mail system. As an accounting marking, it indicated that the way fee had been paid to the carrier.

Way Covers without Postmarks
(listed by addressed town)

Albertson's, North Carolina

A WAY [not illustrated] 500.

Note: The "WAY" marking may be that of Wilmington, North Carolina.

Blacks and Whites, Virginia

Ms Way 500.

Columbia, South Carolina

Ms Way 500.

Davidson College, North Carolina

Ms Way plus Statesville, NC provisional marking "PAID / 5" (STA-NC-H01) revalued "10" (pencil). 1,000.

Dysortville, North Carolina

Ms Way 500.

Fredericksburg, Virginia

Ms Way 500.

Kittrell [Kittrell's Springs], North Carolina

Ms Way 500.

Lynchburg, Virginia

Ms Way 500.

Petersburg, Virginia

Ms Way 500.

Richmond, Virginia

Ms Way plus blue Lexington, Virginia stampless "PAID / 5" (Type B) marking. 1,000.

Waynesboro, Georgia

Ms Way plus ms "GaRR" 1,500.

Wilkesborough, North Carolina

WAY

A

A WAY IH

Confederate Railroad Markings

Role of Railroads in Handling the Mails

In the decade preceding the formation of the Confederacy, railroads played a significant role in the movement of mail among post offices so that by 1860, wherever feasible, railroads gradually replaso that by 1860, railroads took over many mail routes previously operated by contractors with horses, stages and steamboats. Upon the formation of the Confederacy, as it had done with respect to other postal matters, the Confederate States' Post Office Department (CSPOD) desired to continue this practice and sought to engage the services of the railroads operating in the Confederate States.

As of November 1861, there were ninety-one railroads and branch lines operating in the Confederate States. Postmaster General John H. Reagan wished to enlist the services of these railroads in moving the mail, and sought to obtain their agreement to perform the same duties, in substantially the same manner, as they had performed them for the USPOD before 1860. However, because the CSPOD was financially impaired, Reagan knew that he would not be able to pay the railroads at the same level of compensation as they had been paid by the USPOD. He hoped that the railroads would agree to accept less compensation from the CSPOD as an act of patriotism. To achieve this, Reagan convened a convention of the railroad presidents on April 26, 1861 at Montgomery, Alabama to explain to them the weak financial condition of the CSPOD and to obtain their agreement to enter into contracts to carry the mail in return for reduced payments.

Of the ninety-one railroads Reagan invited to attend the convention, representatives of only thirty-five companies attended and, in the end, only fifteen railroads agreed to enter into contracts with the CSPOD. This situation continued into at least 1863. The objections of the attending railroads fell within two broad categories: (1) they could not or they would not perform the same services they had performed for the USPOD for less remuneration under the CSPOD plan, and/or (2) they refused to cede to the CSPOD any control over their day-to-day operations (as they would have had to do if they entered into contracts) with respect to scheduling and other operational matters. To work around this latter objection, several of the railroads represented at the convention offered to continue to carry the mails, but refused to formalize their relationship with the CSPOD by entering into written contracts. Reagan refused to accept this informal relationship and withheld payments to these railroads when they implemented this informal process on a local level.

Mail Handling by Railroads

The railroads that entered into contracts with the CSPOD carried three types of mail: mail contained in locked through bags; mail contained in locked local (or way) mail bags, and loose letters. All of this mail fell under the responsibilities of route agents.

Locked through bags contained mail received, sorted, rated and postmarked at a terminal post office for delivery by the route agent from the train to the terminal office. The bags were not opened by the route agent (who did not have a key to open their brass locks) and were not delivered by him to any interim post office. The route agent was merely the custodian of the through bags for the trip between terminal offices.

As a practical matter, there is no way for a collector to determine that the mail contained in the through bags traveled via railroad other than to know that this was the CSPOD method of transporting such mail. There were no distinguishing characteristics of such mail. The through bag letters entered the mails at the post office where they were deposited by the sender, received the postmark of the originating post office, and were rated and so marked at that originating post office. The letters then were processed via the normal distribution processes of the CSPOD until they eventually wound up in a locked through bag. Other than the circumstance of having been transported by train, nothing distinguished these letters from any other bagged mail moving between post offices, however transported. Accordingly, the route agents' markings listed in this section do not apply to through bag mail.

The railroads also carried local (or way) bag mail. These were pouches of mail made up at an interim post office (or by the route agent between terminal post offices) containing mail delivered to the route agent from post offices along the route. The letters in local bag mail were deemed to have entered the mails at the local post offices where they received the post offices' postmarks and were, if appropriate, also rated. The local pouches were secured by locks made of iron for which the route agent did have the key. The route agent received and processed the letters from the local post offices (as explained in the next section), sorted them according to their destinations, and then placed the mail in one or more other locked local bags according to their destinations. He thereafter delivered the letters from the local bags to representatives of local post offices along his route for further delivery or distribution by the local post offices. At the end of the trip, the route agent delivered the locked local bag and any mail it still contained to the terminal post office. Like through bag mail, letters received from local post offices and placed in the local bags did not receive the type of markings listed in this section of the catalog and cannot be distinguished from other bagged mail merely because they were carried on a train.

The third type of mail received by route agents was loose letters brought to the route agent at the train and given to him by the sender or the sender's representative. These letters were deemed to have entered the mails when the route agent received the letters and placed his route agent's handstamp on them (as if he were a clerk in a post office placing the post office's postmark on the letter). If the loose letter did not contain a postage stamp, the route agent would also place a due rating mark on the letter. The route agent thereafter would place the letter into the appropriate locked local mailbag for delivery to a post office or for further distribution. The marking placed on these letters by the route agent (collectively known as "route agents' markings") are listed in this section of the catalog.

Not all trains operating under a contract to carry the mails had a route agent aboard. Some trains, for example, carried only through letter bags. If a loose letter was given to a conductor or some other railroad employee, he was required to turn in the letter at the next post office on the train's route. For his trouble, he was paid 1¢ for each letter turned in if he required such payment. These letters were then marked "WAY", both to indicate that 1¢ had been paid to the person who delivered the letter to the post office (in the role of an accounting marking) and to indicate that the letter had entered the mails at the post office which applied the WAY marking (as an origin marking). For further discussion of this, see the section on WAY mail in this catalog.

Role of the Route Agent

The route agent was an employee of the CSPOD. As such, he took an oath to honestly perform his duties to the best of his ability. His oath was secured by a bond. The route agent rode trains having a contract to carry the mails. His first duty was to take charge of the mail entrusted to him on the railroad route between terminal stations to which he was assigned.

The route agent had exclusive custody of the mail entrusted to him, and he was required to maintain it safely while it was under his custody. He processed the mail contained in local bags given to him along his route. He also processed loose letters, as described above. Subject to one exception described below with respect to station agents, no one who was not a CSPOD employee was permitted to be in the presence of the mail once it had been turned over to the route agent. This restriction often was ignored by route agents who sometimes left the mail unattended or who permitted non-employees of the CSPOD to be in the presence of the mail. This was a frequent complaint of the CSPOD.

Route Agent's Marking

Each route agent placed his route agent's handstamp marking on loose mail given to him en route. The route agent's marking was tantamount to a post office's circle date stamp. It indicated that the letter had officially entered the mails. The marking consisted of the railroad's name or the names of the terminals or some combination of both, either spelled out in full or abbreviated. It was an official CSPOD marking.

Role of the Station Agent

A station agent was an employee of the railroad, not an employee of the CSPOD (merely by reason of his status as a station agent). He might also be an employee of the CSPOD, but this role would be independent of his role as station master. A station agent, among his other duties, would sell and cancel railroad trip tickets. There is limited evidence that he might also occasionally receive loose letters, although it is not clear if this practice was regular rather than haphazard or fortuitous, or if regular, whether that particular station agent was also a postmaster and acting in this latter capacity when he received mail. Occasionally, a station agent who received loose letters would place his handstamp (ticket canceling device) on the letter as if it were a route agent's marking. There is no reported evidence to indicate that such handstamps had any official CSPOD status when imprinted on mail, but it seems likely that such marked letters were treated as if they had officially entered the mails because such letters were thereafter carried in the mails without any other (or any official CSPOD) marking being placed on them.

Notwithstanding the foregoing, there is some evidence that station agents were sometimes formally sworn in as CSPOD representatives when there was no route agent present to take control of the mail that was in the station agent's possession. Thus, the *Instructions to the Special Agents of the Post Office Department of the Confederate States of America*, provided: "When there are no [route] agents on the route, notice closely who is charged with the custody of the mails; whether they are placed under lock, beyond the reach of any but duly authorized persons, and generally, whether proper provision is made for their safety in all respects. *Especially see that all persons employed by the railroad companies in the transfer or custody of the mails are qualified by oath as carriers* (italics added)." This might mean that station agents were sworn representatives of the CSPOD in cases where route agents were not present, in which event their markings would be tantamount to official CSPOD markings under such limited circumstances. More information is needed to determine the meaning and effect of the above language.

Criteria for Listing Markings

Listings for this section are limited to examples of markings originating from states after they formally seceded from the United States (see section on secession dates). Only handstamped railroad and station agent markings are included. Markings on covers that transmitted written communications are included with or without stamps and can include certain railroad business transmittals which were exempt from paying postage. For purposes of this listing, manuscript railroad markings and printed or handstamped corner cards are not included.

References: *Report of the Postmaster General*, Nov 27, 1861, p.14; Apr 29, 1861, p. 13; Nov 27, 1861, p. 14; Dec 7, 1863, pp. 10-11; and *Instructions to the Special Agents of the Post Office Department of the Confederate States of America* (1861), pp. 8-9.

[*]	symbol used after an item description to mean an unsupported listing
DC	double circle
YD	year date

Alabama & Tennessee River Railroad

Actual Tracing

ALA & TEN. RIV. / R. R. (34; 1861-62; black)

After secession	1,500.
General issue stamp	1,500.

Charlotte & South Carolina Railroad

C. & S. C. R. R. CO / CHARLOTTE, N. C. (34 x 25 YD; 1861-63; black)

No postal markings	1,000.

East Tennessee & Georgia Railroad

E. T. & G. R. R. R. S. RUSTON, AGT / * DALTON. * (34 DC YD; 1861; black)

No postal markings	1,000.

Memphis & Ohio Railroad

Actual Tracing

Memphis & Ohio R. R. / WITHE (34; 1862; black)

Paid 5cts (ms)	2,000.

Mississippi Central Railroad

HICKORY VALLEY / M. C. R. R. (34 YD; 1861; black)

Paid 5cts (ms)	1,500.
Paid 10 (ms)*	1,500.

WESTS / M. C. R. R. (34 YD; 1863; black)

General issue stamp	1,500.

Nashville & Chattanooga Railroad

ANDERSON / N. & C. R. R. (34 x 25 YD; 1863; black) [not illustrated]

DUE [no rate] [not illustrated]*	1,500.

DECHERD / N. & C. R. R. (35 x 26; 1862; black)*

General issue stamp*	1,500.

ESTELL SPRINGS / N. & C. R. R. (34 x 25 YD; 1862-63; black)

General issue stamp	1,500.
Due 10 (ms)	1,500.

SMYRNA / N. & C. R. R. (34 x 25 YD; 1862; black)

General issue stamp	1,500.

WARTRACE / N. & C. R. R. (34 x 25 YD; 1861-63; black)

After secession*	1,000.
General issue stamp	1,000.
PAID (oval box)	1,000.
PAID, 10 [not illustrated]*	1,000.
PAID 10 (arc)*	1,000.
DUE	1,000.
DUE, 10 (ms)*	1,000.
Paid 10 (ms)*	750.
Due 10 (ms)	500.

Virginia Central Railroad

VA. C. R. R. / AFTON (25; 1864; black)

General issue stamp	750.

One recorded example of Afton.

VA. C. R. R. / BUMPASS (25; 1861-64; black)

General issue stamp	750.
Paid 5 (ms)*	500.
Paid 10 (ms)*	500.
Due 10 (ms)*	500.

VA. C. R. R. / COBHAM (25; 1861-63; black)

General issue stamp	750.

VA. C. R. R. / FISHERVILLE (25; 1861-64; black, red)

General issue stamp	750.
General issue stamp (red)*	1,000.
PAID 5*	1,000.
10, Pd (ms)	500.
10, Due (ms)*	500.
Paid 5 (ms) (green)*	1,500.

VA. C. R. R. / JUNCTION (25; 1863; black)*

General issue stamp*	2,000.

VA. C. R. R. / KESWICK (25; 186-; black)

General issue stamp	2,000.

VA. C. R. R. / POND GAP (25; 186-; black)

General issue stamp	2,000.

VA. C. R. R. / SWOOPES (25; 186-; black)

General issue stamp	2,000.

Virginia & Tennessee Railroad

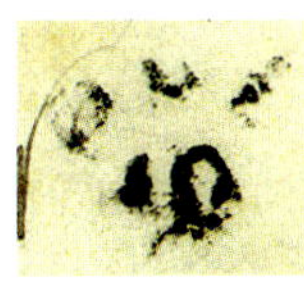

BRISTOL / V. & T. R. R. (30; 1862-63; black)

General issue stamp	750.
PAID [not illustrated]	1,000.
DUE 10	750.
Due 10 (ms)	750.

Western North Carolina Railroad

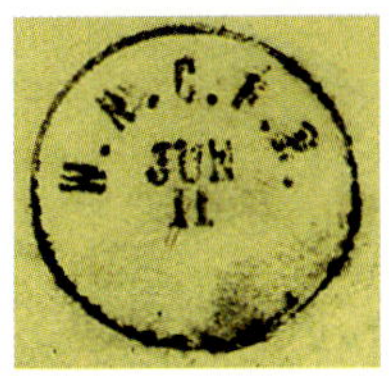

W. N. C. R. R. (25; 186-; black)

Paid 5cts (ms)	2,000.

One recorded example of Western North Carolina Railroad.

Nashville & Chattanooga Railroad / Wartrace

Virginia Central Railroad / Cobham

Nashville & Chattanooga Railroad / Estelle Springs

Virginia Central Railroad / Fisherville

Virginia Central Railroad / Bumpass

Inland Waterway Mail

No specific Confederate laws addressed inland waterway mail. Rather, inland waterway mail was governed by a statute passed by the Confederate Congress on February 9, 1861. This law provided that the laws of the United States that were in effect within the Confederate States on November 1, 1860, would remain in full force and effect in the Confederate States provided such laws did not conflict with the Confederate Constitution. By implication and practice, this also meant that these United States laws would apply to the extent that their provisions were not amended by the Confederate Congress. The applicable United States Post Office law governing the mails on November 1, 1860, was the Act of 1859 and the regulations promulgated under the Act. These were conveniently published in a single volume known as the 1859 Postal Laws and Regulations.

Inland waterway mail, strictly speaking, consisted of all letters, bills of lading, freight bills, and invoices transported by contract and non-contract vessels along the navigable lakes, bayous, inlets, harbors, rivers and their tributaries of the Confederacy. In practice, the phrase did not include such mail if the letters were carried in a locked mail bag aboard a vessel having a contract to carry the mail. Letters in locked mail bags received no special markings to indicate their waterway transport and cannot be distinguished from mail that was carried over land.

As used in this catalog, inland waterway mail means *loose* letters. These were letters handed to the master of a vessel or a route agent aboard a vessel.

There were two types of vessels or steamboats: *non-contract* (vessels that did not have a contract to carry mail) and *contract* (vessels that had a contract to carry to the mail). Contract vessels were further divided between those that had a route agent aboard and those that did not.

Types of Inland Waterway Mail

There were three types of inland waterway mail, each with different markings.

Prepaid Letters Carried by Non-Contract Vessels. Letters which were prepaid and were carried aboard a non-contract vessel were marked "STEAMBOAT", "STEAM" or some variation of this term. This was done by the post office clerk when the steamboat's master, in compliance with law, turned the letters in to the post office at the first port-of-arrival.

Prepaid Letters Carried by Contract Vessels. Loose letters that were prepaid and carried aboard a contract vessel were marked "WAY". This was done by the post office clerk at the port of arrival if the vessel did not have a government bonded route agent aboard. If there was a route agent aboard, the loose letters were marked by the route agent with his handstamp or manuscript route agent's marking.

Unpaid Letters. Letters that were not prepaid, whether carried aboard a contract vessel or a non-contract vessel, were marked and rated as ship mail. Although "SHIP" was the required marking by the 1859 Postal Laws and Regulations, there is no recorded example of a "SHIP" marking on Confederate inland waterway mail.

Postage Rates and Fees

The postage rates and fees charged, as well as the manner of handling loose letters carried aboard vessels, depended on whether or not such letters were prepaid and whether or not the vessels had a contract to carry the mails.

Letters Carried by a Non-Contract Vessel

A vessel that did not have a contract to carry the mail was officially referred to as a steamboat. This term did not refer to the actual maritime nature of the vessel. Rather, the term created a class of non-contract mail known as steamboat mail. The steamboat's captain, upon the arrival at a port having a post office, was required by the 1859 Postal Laws and Regulations to turn in to the postmaster all letters carried by the steamboat.

Prepaid Letter. If a letter turned in by the steamboat's captain was prepaid, the letter was charged the same postage as if the letter had been conveyed over land. The distance was measured from the place the letter was placed on board the steamboat to the destination post office. The postmaster paid the steamboat captain 2¢ for each letter and marked the letter with the accounting term, "STEAMBOAT", "STEAM" or an equivalent term. The addressee was not charged the 2¢ captain's fee for a prepaid letter.

Unpaid Letter. If a letter turned in by the steamboat's captain was not prepaid, the letter was charged as if it was a ship letter. If the letter was addressed to the port-of-entry, the charge was 6¢. If the letter was addressed to a destination beyond the port-of-entry, the charge was the ordinary land postage plus a 2¢ fee. The inland postage was calculated from the port-of-entry to the destination. The postmaster paid the vessel's captain the 2¢ fee for the letter and marked the letter with the accounting term "SHIP". The 2¢ captain's fee was separately charged to the addressee only if the letter was addressed beyond the port-of-entry. The 2¢ captain's fee was included in the 6¢ charge for letters addressed to the port-of-entry.

[—]	symbol used in place of value to mean insufficient information to assign a price
[*italic*]	value typeface indicating the item is difficult to price accurately

The above is an unpaid cover addressed to Natchez, MS, carried after June 1, 1861, aboard the vessel *Mary T.* A pencil notation on the front of the cover appears to indicate that it originated at Franklin (state unknown) on June 28, 1861. The cover entered the mails at Natchez, the office of destination, where the postmaster correctly rated the unpaid cover 6¢ as a ship letter addressed to the port-of-entry. The postmaster incorrectly marked the cover STEAM, rather than SHIP. The 2¢ paid to the vessel's captain was not charged to the addressee.

Letters Received by a Contract Vessel without a Route Agent Aboard

All loose letters received by a vessel's captain were to be turned in to the post office by the captain at the first port-of-call having a post office. The captain received a "Way" fee of 1¢ for each prepaid letter. This fee was not charged to the addressee. Letters were rated as follows:

Prepaid Letter. If a letter was prepaid, it was handled as if it had been mailed on land.

Unpaid Letter. If the letter was unpaid, the post office treated it as if it was a ship letter and the postage was 6¢ if addressed to the port-of-entry. If addressed beyond the port-of-entry the postage was the same as a letter sent by land from the port-of-entry to the destination plus 2¢.

Letters Received by a Contract Vessel with a Route Agent Aboard

A route agent aboard a contract vessel received loose letters directly from individuals or indirectly from the vessel's captain. The agent was required to deliver these letters to the post office at the next port-of-call. How these letters were handled depended on whether or not they were prepaid. The route agent received no fee for these letters. Letters were rated as follows:

Prepaid Letter. If a letter was prepaid, it was handled as if it had been mailed on land.

Unpaid Letter. If the letter was unpaid, the post office treated it as if it was a ship letter and the postage was 6¢ if addressed to the port-of-entry. If addressed beyond the port-of-entry the postage was the same as a letter sent by land from the port-of-entry to the destination plus 2¢.

The above is a cover carried aboard the mail contract vessel *Vicksburg* prior to June 1, 1861, when the mails of the Confederacy were still serviced by the United States Post Office Department. The cover was prepaid and was a loose letter given to the route agent aboard the *Vicksburg*, as indicated by the presence of the route agent's handstamp tying the United States postage stamps. The cover was a triple rate cover and was rated exactly as it would have been had it been placed aboard the vessel in a closed, locked mailbag, *i.e.*, rated for the distance from the post office of origin to the destination post office at Natchez.

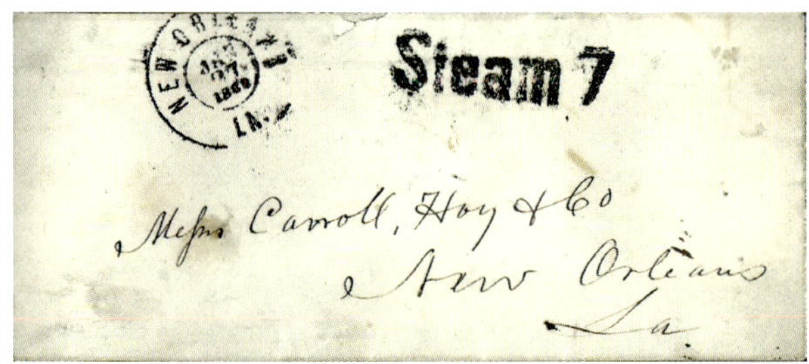

The above is an example of the anomalous way the New Orleans postmaster mishandled waterway covers that came into his post office. Because this loose letter was not prepaid, the New Orleans postmaster should have treated it as a ship letter addressed to the port-of-entry, and marked it SHIP 6. Instead, he marked this (and all similar recorded letters) STEAM and rated it 7¢ due (STEAM 7). Five cents was for a distance less than 500 miles and 2¢ for the captain's fee as if it was a ship letter addressed beyond the port-of-entry.

Steamboat, Steam and Rate Markings Used on Inland Waterway Mail

The terms "STEAM", "STEAMBOAT" and variations of these terms were official markings applied by postmasters at the post office receiving mail from non-contract vessels. The marking served two purposes. It was an accounting marking indicating that the steamboat's captain had been paid 2¢ for each letter he turned in to the postmaster. It also was an origin marking indicating that the letter officially entered the mails at the post office applying the marking. Very few post offices used handstamped "STEAM" or equivalent markings.

The steamboat, steam and rate markings used during the Independent State and Confederate periods are listed below:

Baton Rouge, Louisiana

A

A	STEAM (23 x 4; black)	500.

Cahaba, Alabama

A

A	STEAMBOAT (42 x 5; black)	1,000.

Mobile, Alabama

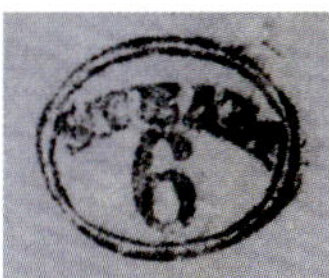

A B

A	STEAM / 6 (22 x 18; black)	—
B	STEAMBOAT (42 x 5; black)	750.

Montgomery, Alabama

A B

a

A	STEAMBOAT (37 x 4; black)	500.
	Same, with boxed "6" (Type *a*)	750.
B	STEAM BOAT (41 x 6; black, blue)	750.

Natchez, Mississippi

A *a*

A	STEAM (31 x 5; black)	1,500.
	Same, with "6" (Type *a*)	2,000.

New Orleans, Louisiana

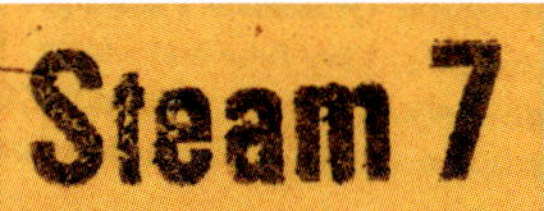

A B

C D

A	STEAM / 6 (20; black)	1,500.
B	Steam 7 (38 x 11 attached rate; black)	2,000.
C	STEAM (32 x 5; black)	1,250.
D	WAY (20 x 4, black)	1,500.

Note: The double circle postmark illustrated above is sometimes referred to as a wharf or riverside marking. There is no evidence to indicate that this marking was applied at the wharf rather than at the post office.

Savannah, Georgia

A

A	STEAM BOAT (38 x 5; black)	750.

Warning: Dangerous counterfeits of the Type A marking exist.

Handstamped Name-of-Boat Markings

Covers bearing handstamp markings showing the name of the vessel and other information about the packet boat are scarce. Because these markings were placed on loose letters by the packet boat's purser or some other crew member such markings are believed to indicate that the covers were actually carried by the named vessel. These markings are recorded on covers bearing stamps and postal waterway markings and also on covers without any postal markings or stamps.

The handstamped name-of-boat markings used during the Independent State and Confederate periods are listed below:

Alice Vivian (49 x 34, blue)

3¢ 1853-55 envelope with date docketing	2,000.
Operated on Alabama and Tombigbee Rivers	

B. L. Hodge (55 x 32, blue)
1¢ 1857-60 stamp with dated pmk 2,500.
Operated on Red River

Charmer (34 x 25, black)
3¢ 1860-61 envelope with dated pmk 1,250.
Operated on Mississippi and Yazoo Rivers

Cherokee (33; blue)
3¢ 1853-55 envelope with dated pmk —
Operated on Alabama and Mobile Rivers

Dr. Buffington (57 x 24, ultramarine)
3¢ 1860-61 envelope, no pmk —
Operated on Mississippi and Ouachita Rivers

Note: Use of this marking during the Independent State and Confederate periods is not confirmed.

Empire Parish (55 x 27, black, green)
5¢ green lithograph general issue 1,000.
5 cts Paid (ms) stampless 1,000.
Operated on Mississippi River

General Hodges (58 x 37, red, with and without clerk's name, "C.T. REEDER," at bottom)
3¢ 1860-61 envelope with dated pmk 1,500.
Operated on Mississippi and Red Rivers

General Quitman (47 x 26, ultramarine; red)
New Orleans 5¢ provisional —
Operated on Mississippi River

Golden Age (59 x 36, blue)
3¢ 1860-61 envelope with dated pmk 1,500.
Operated on Mississippi and Red Rivers

Grand Duke (35 YD, black)
3¢ 1857-60 stamp 1,250.
3¢ 1853-55 envelope 1,250.
3¢ 1860-61 envelope 1,250.
Operated on Mississippi and Red Rivers

J. F. Paragoud (38, black)
3¢ 1860-61 envelope, no pmk —
Operated on Mississippi and Ouachita Rivers

Note: Use of this marking during the Independent State and Confederate periods is not confirmed.

Julia Roane (60 x 35, red)
Unknown —
Operated on Mississippi and Arkansas Rivers

Note: Use of this marking during the Independent State and Confederate periods is not confirmed.

La Grande (34, red)
3¢ 1860-61 envelope with dated pmk 2,000.
Operated on Mississippi River

Mary E. Keene (54 x 31, red)
3¢ 1857-60 stamp on Confederate patriotic envelope —
New Orleans 5¢ provisional —
Operated on Mississippi River

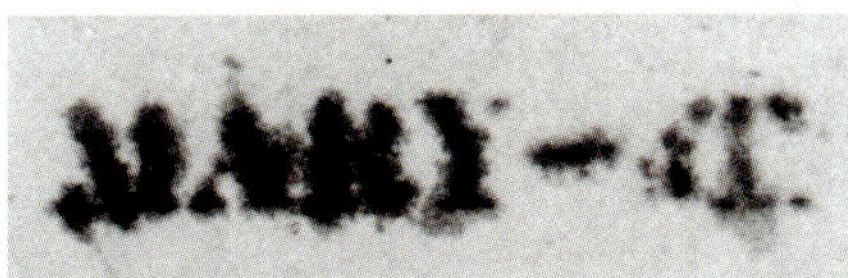

Mary T (50 x 8, black, red)
Unknown —
Operated on Mississippi River

Note: Use of this marking during the Independent State and Confederate periods is not confirmed.

M. Relf [*Milton Relf*] (46 x 22, red)
Use: 3¢ 1860-61 envelope, no pmk —
Operated on Mississippi River

Note: Use of this marking during the Independent State and Confederate periods is not confirmed.

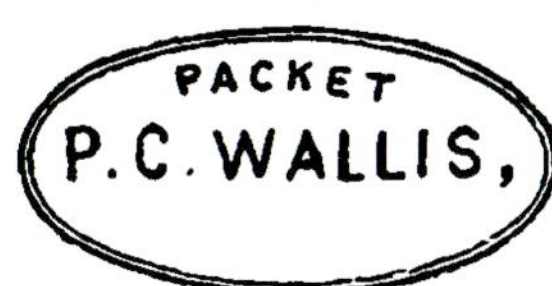

P. C. Wallis (47 x 22 black)
3¢ 1857-60 stamp with dated pmk 1,000.
Operated on Alabama River

Planter (43, black)
Unknown —
Operated on Mississippi River

Note: Use of this marking during the Independent State and Confederate periods is not confirmed.

Sallie Robinson (53 x 35, red)
New Orleans 5¢ provisional —
Operated on Mississippi River

Texas (54 x 35, blue)
New Orleans Steam 7 stampless 3,000.
Operated on Mississippi and Red Rivers

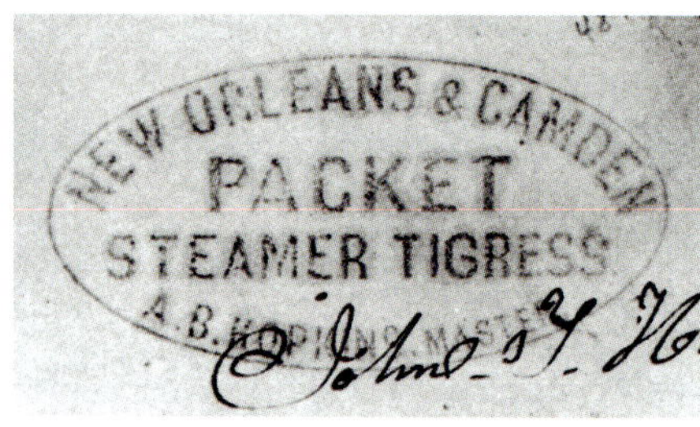

Tigress (63 x 33, red)
3¢ 1855-57 envelope with dated pmk 1,500.
Operated on Mississippi and Ouachita Rivers

Twilight (40 x 25, blue with changeable weekday)
5¢ general issue 1,000.
Operated on Mississippi and Ouachita Rivers

Vicksburg (48 x 24, blue)
3¢ 1857-60 stamp on envelope with date docket 2,500.
3¢ 1860-61 envelope with date docket 2,500.
Operated on Mississippi River

Wm. M. Morrison (50 x 36, black)
3¢ 1860-61 envelope with dated pmk 1,500.
Operated on Mississippi River

Manuscript Name-of-Boat Markings

In addition to the handstamp name-of-boat markings, collectors often encounter covers having the name of a packet boat written on them. These markings are often in the same hand and using the same ink as the cover's address. As such, they indicated the senders desire to have the named vessel carry the letters. Other evidence must be present on the cover to prove actual transport by the named vessel. In spite of the uncertainty regarding the transport of letters bearing manuscript name-of-boat markings, such covers are generally treated as if they were carried by the named vessel.

A manuscript name-of-boat marking, such as *Quitman* on the above cover, frequently is cited as evidence that the cover was carried by the named vessel. While it is true that the named vessel might have carried the cover, the written name, in and of itself, is not sufficient evidence of this. The written name is nothing other than an expression of the sender's desire that the cover be transported by the named vessel. Without other evidence independently demonstrating that the cover was carried by the named vessel, a vessel's name written on a cover might mean any one or more of the following: (1) that the cover was likely transported via water rather than over land; (2) that the sender wished the cover to be carried on the named vessel rather than on some other vessel; (3) that the cover was in fact transported by the named vessel.

Those vessels with manuscript name-of-boat markings from the Independent State and Confederate periods are listed below:

Acadia
Anna
Cherokee
Coquette
Dew Drop
Dolly Webb
Duke
Dixie
Empire Parrish
Fair Play
Fanny
Ferrand
General Hodges
General Quitman
Grand Duke
Iberville
Lafourche
Laurel Hill
Marengo
Mary T.
Peytona
Robt. E. Lee
Senator
St. Nicholas
Starlight
Texas
T.W. Roberts
Vicksburg
Warrior
Wm. Morrison

Those vessels with manuscript name-of-boat markings cited in literature but which have not been confirmed are listed below:

Beulah
Clipper
Creole
Emma Belle
Emma Graham
Era No. 4
Frolic

Printed Name-of-Boat Envelopes

Envelopes are known with printed corner cards or overall illustrations showing the name of a vessel. Use of these envelopes on board a steamboat can only be determined by the postal markings.

Printed name-of-boat envelopes used during the Independent Statehood and Confederate periods are listed below.

Name-of-Boat Marking (Printed Envelopes)

Dew Drop (All-over envelope)
5¢ green general issue 5,000.
PAID stampless 7,500.

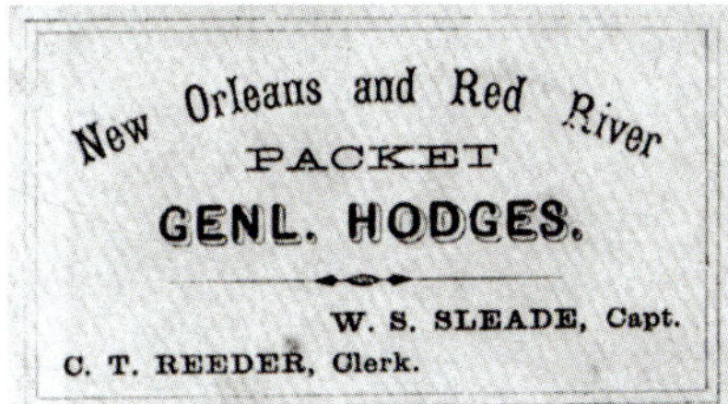

General Hodges (Printed corner card)
3¢ 1857-60 stamp with dated pmk 2,500.

General Quitman (Patriotic corner card)
3¢ 1857-60 stamp with dated pmk 5,000.

J. F. Pargoud (All-over envelope)
With patriotic sticker, no pmk —

Note: Use of this envelope in the Confederate period is not confirmed.

James Battle (All-over envelope)
10¢ blue Frame Line general issue *10,000.*
10¢ blue Archer & Daly general issue 4,500.

Judge Fletcher (Imprint cross top of envelope)
10¢ soldier's due letter 3,000.

Mary E. Keene (Printed corner card)
3¢ 1857-60 stamp with dated letter 2,500.

Planter (Printed corner card envelope)
10¢ blue Archer & Daly general issue 3,000.

Red Rover (All-over printed envelope)
10¢ blue Hoyer & Ludwig general issue 7,500.

St. Mary (Printed corner card)
PAID 5 stampless 3,000.

Vicksburg (Patriotic corner card)
3¢ 1857-60 stamp with dated pmk *10,000.*

Packet Boats

The phrase "packet boat" generally is used to describe any steam powered vessel which maintained regular schedules of sailing days, times and destinations. Some packet boats carried the mail under contracts with the Post Office Department.

The practice of the United States Post Office Department in awarding mail contracts before the Civil War required that packet boats be clean, safe and secure; and that they maintained regular and reliable sailing schedules as conditions of receiving mail contracts. These requirements likely were carried over when the Confederate Post Office Department took over the mails in the Confederate States on June 1, 1861.

The requirements that vessels be reliable, clean and safe to qualify for a mail contract was also an attractive inducement to potential passengers and to freight shippers. Accordingly, when a vessel met the government criteria and obtained a mail contract, the vessel's owner generally referred to his vessel as a mail packet boat in advertisements. Such notices carried special meaning to potential customers. If an advertisement for a packet boat does not mention having a mail contract, it is reasonable to assume that the vessel did not have a contract at that time.

Packet Boats with Verifiable Mail Contracts

Packet boats having verifiable mail contracts during the Independent State and Confederate periods, before the interdiction of the Mississippi River in late April 1862, are listed below:

Alamo
Dew Drop
Dixie
Dolly Webb
Ferd Kennett
General John A. Quitman
Grand Duke
Iberville
Lafourche
Louis d'Or
Mary E. Keene
Mary T.
Natchez
Percy
Pioneer
Roebuck
S. Mary
Starlight
T.W. Roberts
Vicksburg
Viola
Wm. M. Morrison

Packet Boats without Verifiable Mail Contracts

Those packet boats listed in earlier catalogs as having mail contracts during the Independent State and Confederate periods, but that have not been confirmed are listed below:

Acadia
Alice Vivian
Alonzo Child
Anna
B.L. Hodge
Beulah
C.E. Hillman
Charmer
Clara Dolson
Clipper
Comet
Creole
Diana
Doubloon
Dr. Buffington
Edward J. Gay
Emma Bett
Empire Parish
Era No. 4
Fair Play
Frolic
General G.L. Hodges
Golden Age
Grand Duke
J.F. Pargoud
James Battle
John Walsh
Judge Fletcher
Julia Roane
Laurel Hill
Le Grande
Lizzie Simmons
Louisville
M. Reif
Magenta
Magnolia
P.C. Wallis
Peytona
Planter
R.J. Lackland
Rapides
Red Rover
Republic
Sallie Robinson
Texas
Tigress
Twilight

Known Packet Boats without Reported Covers

Packet boats whose existence has been verified by advertisements, freight bills or other independent means, but for which no covers have been recorded are listed below:

Com. Farrand
Coquette
Countess
De Soto
Eleanor
Era No. 7
Henry J. King
Horizon
J.A. Cotton
Jeff Davis
J.M. Sharp
Junior
Lily
Little Rock
Moro
News Boy
Nina Simmes
Picayune No. 3
Queen of the West
Reindeer
Robert Fulton
St. Charles
Selma
Senator
Southern Republic
Southerner T.H. Judson
Sumter
Tahlequah
T.D. Hines
Victoria
Virginia
Warrior
W.B. Terry
W. Burton
Wm. S. Barry

Confederate Mail Carrier Services

Prior to the formation of the Confederate States, Charleston, South Carolina and New Orleans, Louisiana offered mail carrier services operated by the US Post Office Department. The services provided by the carriers were optional and included the following:

Local Delivery: From a pick up point to the addressee in the same city without actually entering the post office.

Post Office Delivery: Delivery from the local post office to the addressee.

Outbound Mail: From a pick up point to the local post office for entry into the mail system.

The carriers were employees of the Department, but were not paid a salary. Instead they were compensated only from the fees accrued by the services they provided. These carrier services continued after the takeover of the postal system by the Confederate Post Office Department on June 1, 1861 even though they were never specifically addressed in any Confederate postal legislation.

Charleston, South Carolina

Charleston's mail carrier service began operation in 1849 and utilized a variety of small labels. It was known as the "Penny Post" service and was operated by appointed carriers within the post office. By the time South Carolina seceded, the penny post labels were no longer used. The service continued after secession with envelopes simply marked "care of penny post", "penny post" or other similar notations.

The fees charged for the three services described above were 2¢ per letter. The carriers employed by the Charleston Post Office were John C. Beckman, Joseph G. Martin and John F. Steinbrenner, Jr.

The Charleston "Penny Post" is known to have continued until mid-1863, when the Union forces began shelling the city from Morris Island and the post office was relocated.

New Orleans, Louisiana

New Orleans' mail carrier service began operation in 1851 and utilized various handstamped markings. It was known as the "City Post" and by September 1854 it had adopted a circular canceller, with the notation **N.O.U.S. CITY POST** and a central month / day logo. According to newspaper notices, the carriers charged 1¢ for local delivery and 2¢ for post office delivery. There was no charge for outbound service.

New Orleans City Post marking

The New Orleans "City Post" service continued after Louisiana seceded, but was discontinued by April 1862 when Union forces occupied the city.

Note: Covers bearing postmaster provisionals or scarcer general issues command higher prices.

Charleston Penny Post local delivery

Charleston, South Carolina

CS-01	Local delivery	3,500.
CS-02	Post office delivery	2,500.
CS-03	Outbound mail	NR

New Orleans City Post post office delivery

New Orleans, Louisiana

CS-04	Local delivery	4,500.
CS-05	Post office delivery	3,500.
CS-06	Outbound mail	NR

Suspension of Mail across the Lines

On May 31, 1861 all mail service in the seceded states was suspended by the US Post Office Department. Letters for Southern post offices were forwarded to the US Dead Letter Office (DLO) in Washington, DC. Northbound mail from the South could no longer be forwarded because all the Southern postal routes had been suspended. On June 7, 1861 all postal communications between North and South were banned by the US Post Office Department.

Before the suspension of mail service, most mail was transported between the US and the Confederacy along two principal North-South postal routes: 1) in the East between Washington, D.C. and Richmond, Virginia and 2) in the West between Louisville, Kentucky and Nashville, Tennessee.

Tennessee did not secede until June 8, 1861 and even then there were divided loyalties in some sections of the state. As a result, some routes in the state remained open to both US and Confederate mail well into June.

Southbound Mail to the Confederacy via Washington, DC after May 23, 1861

US Dead Letter Office

May 28, 1861 letter sent from New York to Virginia with the small double-oval UDLO-01 marking. It was returned to the sender on June 4 with 3¢ postage due.

Southbound mail from the US to the eastern part of the Confederacy was carried over the Washington–Richmond route until Union forces occupied Alexandria, Virginia in late May. From this time on mail on this route was diverted to the US Dead Letter Office in Washington, DC. At the DLO, the letters were opened to ascertain the sender. Typically the sender's address was marked on the left front of the envelope, postmarked with the date of the letter's return to the sender, and marked 3¢ postage due. The earliest DLO postmarks were oval in shape. Beginning in late 1861 or early 1862, a circular DLO marking was used.

[–]	symbol used in place of value to mean insufficient information to assign a price
[*italic*]	value typeface indicating the item is difficult to price accurately

A

B

C

US Dead Letter Office

UDL-01	Double oval, small black (Type A)	2,500.
UDL-02	Single oval, large black (Type B)	2,500.
UDL-03	Circle, black (Type C)	3,500.

Mail from foreign countries that was diverted to the US DLO was sent back to the dispatching exchange office. In the case of the British mails, diverted mail was returned to the London Dead Letter Office, which applied one of two types of "Sent Back to England without a Reason for Non-Delivery" markings. An unframed variety was used from June until about August 1861. In September 1861, a framed version of this marking replaced the unframed variety and was used throughout 1862.

SENT BACK TO ENGLAND / WITHOUT A REASON / FOR NON-DELIVERY framed 3-line SBE-02 marking on cover mistakenly addressed to New Iberia Louisiana United States in the fall of 1862 while New Iberia was still under Confederate control.

A B

Sent Back to England

SBE-01	Unframed, red (Type A)	5,000.
SBE-02	Framed, red (Type B)	5,000.

Southbound Mail to the Confederacy via Louisville

May 31 to June 7, 1861

The May 31 discontinuance of mail service in the Southern States did not apply to Tennessee, as it had not yet seceded. As a result, mail continued to be sent to the Confederacy on the Louisville–Nashville route until both the Memphis and Nashville post offices were discontinued by the US Post Office Department in the first week of June. These letters usually show Confederate due markings in addition to the prepaid US postage.

June 4, 1861 letter sent from Nashville, Tennessee (still in the Union) to New Orleans. This letter was charged 10¢ Confederate postage due at New Orleans.

SB-01	US 3¢ franking with Due 5 or 10	2,500.

Southbound Mail to the Confederacy after June 7, 1861

Following the US closure of the Memphis and Nashville post offices, all southbound mail was diverted to the DLO. The DLO markings were used on diverted mails until about September 1861. In September, the first of the "Mails Suspended" markings replaced the DLO markings. The initial type was an oval marking which was used until the end of the war at the Washington, DC Dead Letter Office. Sometime in 1862, diverted covers from foreign countries began to receive these markings, so there was no further need for the "Sent Back to England" markings on British mails.

In 1865, a US straightline "mails suspended" marking came into use at Nashville. A smaller version of this marking without the upper framing line was also used at the end of the war.

Mails Suspended Markings

MAILS SUSPENDED handstamp marking MS-01 in blue on a cover with a Bahamas 6p Violet addressed to the Confederate States but posted after the fall of Charleston closed Nassau's last blockade running connection.

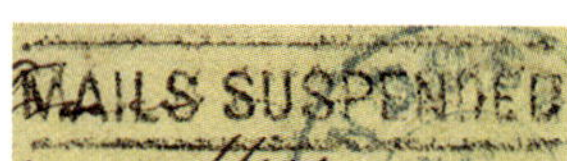

A B

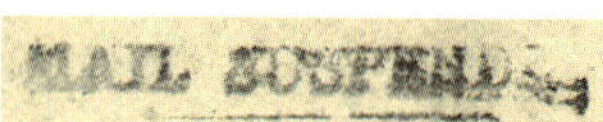

C

Mails Suspended

MS-01	Oval, black or blue (Type A)	2,500.
MS-02	Straightline, black (Type B)	1,000.
MS-03	Straightline, black (Type C)	1,000.

Northbound Mail from the Confederacy via Richmond

May 24-June 1, 1861

Northbound mail from the eastern Confederacy to the US was carried via Richmond and Washington until Union forces occupied Alexandria, Virginia in late May. Subsequently, northbound mail was diverted to the Confederate Dead Letter Office at Richmond from May 24 until June 1. There the letters were marked with a handstamped or manuscript marking.

Confederate Dead Letter Office

A

B

CDL-01 DLO, black oval (Type A) 5,000.
CDL-02 DLO, red manuscript (Type B) 7,500.

Northbound Mail from the Confederacy via Louisville

May 31-June 12, 1861

Postmaster General Montgomery Blair's order suspending mail service in the seceded states after May 31 did not prohibit the transportation of Southern letters in the US mails provided they reached a US post office. Although Tennessee had not yet seceded, it continued to receive mail from the Confederate States system and to transmit it to Louisville, Kentucky. Northbound mail from the western Confederacy was routed via Memphis or Nashville to Louisville from May 31 until operations at the Memphis and Nashville post offices were suspended by the US Post Office Department.

After the June 1, 1861 commencement of the Confederate postal service, letters to or from Tennessee may show both Confederate and US frankings. Following the discontinuance of Federal postal operations in Tennessee, this mail was often diverted to the DLO after having successfully passed through Nashville and Louisville. Such letters show DLO markings along with transit postmarks from the distributing post offices where they were diverted.

NB-01 10¢ CS and 3¢ US postage on northbound cover 3,000.

Secondary Railroad Mail Route between Kentucky and Tennessee

Even after the Nashville-Louisville postal route was suspended about June 12, the Paducah and Memphis Railroad postal route continued to link western Tennessee with western Kentucky. In an apparent oversight, this route between Union City, Tennessee and Paducah, Kentucky, was not suspended by the Union until August 30.

NB-02 Cover to Kentucky or Missouri with CS postage prepaid 2,500.

"Southern Letter Unpaid" Mail from the Confederacy

June 13-July 10, 1861

The US post office at Nashville was discontinued about June 12. However, mail continued to be forwarded north to Louisville. There, starting about June 13, all northbound mail was held. On June 24, the Louisville postmaster received instructions to "...forward letters from the South for the loyal states as unpaid after removing postage stamps but foreign letters on which pre-payment is compulsory must go to the Dead Letter Office." This caused the Louisville postmaster to prepare the "SOUTH^{N}. LETTER / UNPAID." marking to indicate that the US franking on these covers was invalid for postage. This mail was released from Louisville starting on June 25, typically with a Louisville "DUE 3" marking.

June 23, 1861 letter from North Carolina to Indiana, prepaid 10¢ CS and 3¢ US postage. It was marked "SOUTH^{N} LETTER UNPAID." and released from Louisville, Kentucky on July 6 with 3¢ due.

SLU-01 "South^{n}. Letter Unpaid.", blue, with CS and US franking *10,000.*
SLU-02 "South^{n}. Letter Unpaid.", blue, with CS postage paid by postmaster provisional *100,000.*
SLU-03 "South^{n}. Letter Unpaid.", blue, to Europe with postage prepaid with US stamps —

Letters addressed to Louisville for local delivery during this period did not receive the "SOUTH^{N} LETTER UNPAID" marking, but were rated for 3¢ postage due with a distinctive Louisville "DUE" marking.

SLU-04 Louisville large straightline DUE, blue, 3¢ postage due 2,500.

About July 10, 1861 Nashville stopped sending northbound mails to Louisville, thus ending these across the lines official mail routes.

Confederate Dead Letter Office CDL-01 marking on cover diverted after the mail route between Richmond and Washington, D.C. was terminated due to the Federal military occupation of Alexandria, Virginia on May 23, 1861.

SOUTH^{N}. LETTER UNPAID two-line SLU-02 marking on cover franked with a combination of New Orleans postmasters' provisionals and US 3¢ 1857 issue which was rejected by the Louisville post office.

Private Express Company Mail

At the beginning of 1861, the Adams Express Company held a virtual monopoly of the express business in what was to become the Confederate States. By April of 1861, the company realized that the Southern operations were in jeopardy and sold this portion of the company to a business group that incorporated as the Southern Express Company. Additional information on operations of express companies can be found in *Special Mail Routes of the American Civil War: A Guide to Across-the-Lines Postal History* by Steven C. Walske and Scott R. Trepel.

Private express company mail is divided into two different categories: Private across the lines express service and mail handled by express companies within the Confederate States.

Private express across the lines mail service includes mail handled by express companies that crossed the lines between Nashville, Tennessee and Louisville, Kentucky between June 1 and the end of the August 1861.

Mail handled by express companies within the Confederate States covers that mail received and delivered within the Confederate States between February 4, 1861 and the end of the war.

Across the Lines Express Service

The takeover of the mail system in the seceded states by the Confederate Post Office Department on June 1, 1861 caused an immediate disruption of mail service between North and South. In response, three private express companies began to provide across the lines express service.

The Southern Express Company was the largest. In April 1861 it purchased the Adams Express operations in the Southern States. The Southern Express continued to operate under the Adams name until late summer. For this reason it is referred to as Adams Express in this section.

In early June 1861, the American Letter Express Company was established to provide an express letter service using Louisville and Nashville as the termini between North and South.

Also in June, M. D. Whitesides announced a third across the line express service. This service operated between Franklin, Kentucky and Nashville, Tennessee.

On August 10, 1861 President Lincoln proclaimed that all commercial intercourse with the seceded states was to cease as of August 16. On August 26, Postmaster General Montgomery Blair extended that proclamation to include all correspondence, and the across the lines express business was terminated.

Northbound Private Express Mail

All express company instructions for northbound letters were basically the same. Letters properly addressed but without any postage affixed were to be enclosed in a plain envelope with the appropriate express fee. The outer envelope was then addressed to one of three express offices in Nashville. In the case of the Adams Express, letters could be dispatched at a local Adams Express office. In all cases, the Confederate postage was required to be paid from the place of mailing to Nashville.

All northbound mail was collected by the three different express companies at Nashville, Tennessee. The Adams and American Letter Expresses carried the mail across the lines to their respective offices in Louisville, Kentucky. There the proper US postage was affixed and in some cases the express company marking applied before the letters were placed in the US mails at Louisville. Express mail carried by Whitesides was carried across the lines from Nashville to Franklin, Kentucky where the correct postage was applied before the letters were placed in the US mails. There are no known Whitesides markings, only labels.

Southbound Private Express Mail

Instructions for southbound express letters stated each letter was to be placed in a US 3¢ stamped envelope. This envelope was to be placed in an outer envelope with the appropriate express fee and addressed to the Adams Express or American Letter Express office in Louisville, Kentucky. No southbound mail carried by the Whitesides Express has been identified.

All southbound mail was collected by the two express companies at Louisville, Kentucky. The mail was carried across the lines to their respective offices in Nashville, Tennessee. There the proper Confederate postage was affixed and in some cases the express company marking applied before each letter was placed in the Confederate mails at Nashville.

Adams Express

Adams Express Nashville oval

Adams Express Louisville marking

Adams Express large New York oval

The Adams Express fee for northbound mail was 25¢ for a letter of one half ounce or less. This rate, equivalent to "two bits," is frequently represented by "2/S", "25", "2/-", "R/W", "Paid Thro", or "2."

Note: Covers bearing Confederate adhesives provisionals, scarcer stamps, additional express markings, or addressed to foreign destinations command higher prices. Listings are for covers with Louisville express marking and postmark.

Adams Express Mail – Northbound

AEN-01	US franking and Louisville express marking, carried outside CS Mails	800.
	a. Same, with New York express marking instead of Louisville*	1,500.
AEN-02	US and CS frankings with Louisville express marking	1,500.
	a. Same, with Augusta express marking*	2,500.
	b. Same, with Charlotte, N.C. express marking	3,500.
	c. Same, with Knoxville express marking	3,500.
	d. Same, with Nashville express marking	2,500.

[*]	symbol used after an item description to mean an unsupported listing
[–]	symbol used in place of value to mean insufficient information to assign a price
[*italic*]	value typeface indicating the item is difficult to price accurately

THE ADAMS EXPRESS COMPANY,
S. A. JONES, AGENT,
LOUISVILLE, KY.,

Will forward letters to the Confederate States when the following directions are observed:

Enclose each letter in a U. S. GOVERNMENT ENVELOPE—an ordinary envelope with a stamp affixed **will not answer.** The Company will forward AND DELIVER at any point where it has an office, or will mail as near as possible to the point of address, paying Confederate postage, for a fee of 25 cents.

The rate here given is for letters not exceeding ½ oz. in weight; each ½ oz. being charged 3 cents by U. S. Government, and 25 cents by the Express Company.

Adams Express Label (Southbound)

The Adams express rate for southbound mail was 25¢ for a letter of one half ounce or less. This rate was not normally marked on southbound mail.

Adams Express markings of the Baltimore, Boston and Philadelphia offices are found on some southbound mail. A Louisville express marking reading "From the Adams Express Company, Louisville" was also used briefly in June 1861.

Adams Express Mail – Southbound

AES-01	US franking with the "From the Adams Express Company, Louisville" marking	—
AES-02	US and CS frankings with Louisville express marking	1,800.
	b. Same, with Augusta express marking	2,500.
	c. Same, with Nashville express marking	3,000.
	d. Same, with Knoxville express marking	2,500.
	e. Same, with Baltimore express marking	3,500.
	f. Same, with Boston express marking	3,500.
	g. Same, with Philadelphia express marking	3,500.
	h. Same, with New York express marking	2,000.
	i. Same, with large New York oval express marking	3,500.
	j. Same, with Indianapolis or Bardstown, Ky. express label*	4,000.
	k. Same, with Adams instruction label on reverse	2,500.

Warning: There are dangerous fakes of the large New York oval express marking.

American Letter Express

The American Letter Express fee for northbound mail was 15¢ for a letter of one half ounce or less. This fee was not marked on the letter.

Northbound express letters were marked with one of three different Louisville express markings, each of which had a different center: dated, "307 Green", and undated. Listings all bear one of these markings. A rarely-seen label requesting reimbursement of postage advanced was also used.

American Letter Express, Dated

American Letter Express, 307 Green

American Letter Express, Undated Small

Due the AMERICAN LETTER EXPRESS CO. 1f 60 cents (for postage advanced,) on this letter. Send the amount in money to the Company at Louisville, Ky.

American Letter Express Reimbursement Label

[IMPORTANT.]

To the People of the Confederate States.

THE AMERICAN

Letter Express Co.

(Chartered by an act of the Tennessee Legislature.)
Transmits Letters and Printed Matter to and from all points North and South.

DIRECTIONS:

(LETTERS GOING NORTH.)

Enclose and direct each letter to your correspondent as usual; put that letter in another envelope, and direct on this outside envelope to

American Letter Express Co.
NASHVILLE, TENN.

Enclosing 15 cents in money; this prepays all expenses to its destination.

The rates here given are for letters not exceeding half-ounce in weight: double, treble, &c. letters must have an additional amount enclosed in proportion to weight.

Do not use U. S. stamps or stamped envelopes—they are valueless when coming from the Confederate States.

PRINTED MATTER.

For single newspapers enclose the Company 10 cents.

Letters for Europe must have an additional amount enclosed, to enable the Company to prepay the international postage.

N. B. All letters accompanied with an insufficient amount to prepay to their destination are liable to be sent to the dead-letter office.

American Letter Express, Large Label (Northbound)

American Letter Express Mail – Northbound

ALN-01	US franking	3,000.
	a. Same, with undated Louisville express marking	3,000.
	b. Same, with Louisville "307 Green" marking	4,000.
	c. Same, with postage reimbursement label	*10,000.*
	d. Same with northbound instruction label on reverse	5,000.

The southbound rate for letters carried by the American Letter Express was 15¢ for delivery less than 500 miles from Nashville and 20¢ if more than 500 miles. The express rate was not always indicated on the letter.

Southbound express letters were marked with either of the Louisville markings described above or one of the Nashville markings as illustrated:

American Letter Express, Dated

American Letter Express, Jenkins and McGill

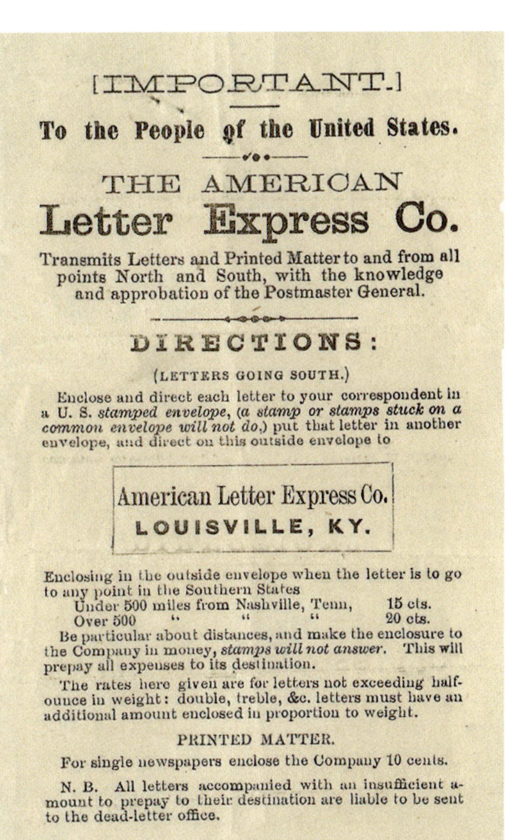

[IMPORTANT.]

To the People of the United States.

THE AMERICAN

Letter Express Co.

Transmits Letters and Printed Matter to and from all points North and South, with the knowledge and approbation of the Postmaster General.

DIRECTIONS:

(LETTERS GOING SOUTH.)

Enclose and direct each letter to your correspondent in a U. S. *stamped envelope*, (*a stamp or stamps stuck on a common envelope will not do*,) put that letter in another envelope, and direct on this outside envelope to

American Letter Express Co.
LOUISVILLE, KY.

Enclosing in the outside envelope when the letter is to go to any point in the Southern States
Under 500 miles from Nashville, Tenn, 15 cts.
Over 500 " " " 20 cts.

Be particular about distances, and make the enclosure to the Company in money, *stamps will not answer*. This will prepay all expenses to its destination.

The rates here given are for letters not exceeding half-ounce in weight: double, treble, &c. letters must have an additional amount enclosed in proportion to weight.

PRINTED MATTER.

For single newspapers enclose the Company 10 cents.

N. B. All letters accompanied with an insufficient amount to prepay to their destination are liable to be sent to the dead-letter office.

American Letter Express Label (Southbound)

"Letters Going North" label affixed to envelope addressed to the South. The label provided instructions for sending letters north.

American Letter Express – Southbound

ALS-01 US and Confederate frankings, with Nashville postmark 2,000.
- a. Same, with dated Louisville express marking 3,000.
- b. Same, with undated Louisville express marking 3,000.
- c. Same, with Louisville "307 Green" marking* 4,000.
- d. Same, with Nashville dated express marking 5,000.
- e. Same, with Nashville "Jenkins and McGill" express marking 6,000.
- f. Same, with manuscript "Pr Am Letter Express" marking 2,500.
- g. Same, with southbound American Letter Express instruction label on reverse 5,000.

Whitesides Express

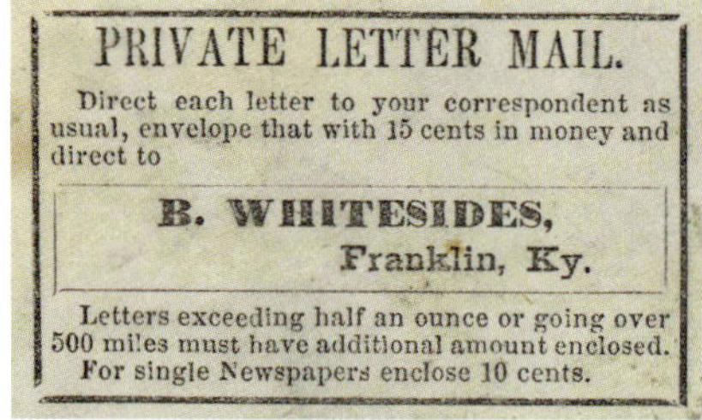

PRIVATE LETTER MAIL.

Direct each letter to your correspondent as usual, envelope that with 15 cents in money and direct to

B. WHITESIDES,
Franklin, Ky.

Letters exceeding half an ounce or going over 500 miles must have additional amount enclosed. For single Newspapers enclose 10 cents.

Whitesides Express Label

Whitesides Express Mail – Northbound

WEN-01 Three US 1¢ 1857-60 stamps and Franklin postmark with Whitesides label *20,000.*
- a. Same, on cover with Confederate PAID 10, US DUE 3 and Whitesides label *20,000.*

Whitesides Express label affixed to back of a cover to Otto, N.Y. of unknown origin in the Confederacy, delivered to Nashville and carried across the lines by Whitesides.

The Whitesides Express did not use markings. Instead letters had labels attached. There are only two recorded Whitesides Express covers. Both are northbound and both have labels affixed.

Private Express Companies

Before the formation of the Confederacy, several private express companies operated in the Southern States. Under the laws of the United States, they were authorized to carry letters contained in a stamped envelope available from the post office.

Under the Confederate Act of March 15, 1861, private express companies were authorized to carry all mailable matter provided the Confederate postage was paid. There was no restriction on how the postage was to be paid. In spite of this authorization, some express companies failed to pay the required postage. In an effort to eliminate this abuse, Postmaster General Reagan requested a change to the law. The Act of April 19, 1862 revoked the provisions of the Act of March 15, 1861 and reinstated the provisions contained in the US Postage Laws and Regulations of 1859. This effectively prevented express companies from carrying letters because the Confederate Post Office Department did not have the required stamped envelopes.

Although the Act of April 1862 effectively made it illegal for express companies to carry letters after May 31, 1862, it did not completely stop the practice as evidenced by covers with express markings used after this date.

Note: Prices are for covers bearing an express company marking. Uses with provisionals, general issues or unusual marking command higher prices.

Adams Express. This was the largest express company operating in the South prior to the formation of the Confederate States. In April 1861, offices in the Southern States were sold to the Southern Express. The express continued to operate under the Adams name until August 1861.

The only recorded example of the Adams Express Co., New Orleans, La. oval marking in green; used on a turned adversity cover.

A B

A	New Orleans, La., black	3,000.
B	Atlanta, Ga., black	2,500.
	Augusta, Ga., black*	2,500.
	Same, blue*	2,500.
	Charleston, S.C., blue	3,500.
	Charlotte, N.C., red	3,500.
	Chattanooga, Tenn., black	2,500.
	Knoxville, Tenn., black	2,500.
	Memphis, Tenn., red	2,500.
	Mobile, Ala., red*	3,500.
	Montgomery, Ala., black*	2,500.
	Nashville, Tenn., black	2,500.
	Same, blue*	2,500.
	New Orleans, La., black	3,500.
	Same, green	5,000.
	Vicksburg, Miss., red	3,500.

Southern Express. The largest private express operating in the Confederacy was the Southern Express Company. This company was established when offices of the Adams Express in the Southern States were purchased by Henry M. Plant, manager of the Southern Division of Adams Express, and several associates. The offices were purchased in April 1861, but the company did not begin operating under the Southern Express name until August. The Southern Express Company operated in all states of the Confederacy.

C

D E

C	Nashville, Tenn., blue	5,000.
D	Montgomery, Ala., blue	2,500.
E	Atlanta, Ga., black	2,500.
	Augusta, Ga., black	2,500.
	Same, blue	2,500.
	Chattanooga, Tenn., black	3,000.
	Knoxville, Tenn., black	2,500.
	Lynchburg, Va., black	2,500.
	Macon, Ga., black	2,500.
	Same, green	3,000.
	Manassas, Va., black	3,000.
	Memphis, Tenn., red	3,000.
	Montgomery, Ala., blue	2,500.
	Nashville, Tenn., black	3,000.
	Same, blue	3,000.
	New Orleans, La., black	3,000.
	Richmond, Va., black	2,500.
	Savannah, Ga., red	2,500.

Note: The Southern Express continued to operate in the South after the end of the war. Many of the Southern Express markings from the post war period are difficult to differentiate from Confederate uses.

Harnden's Express. This company merged with Adams Express in 1854, but some operations continued under the Harnden name. This name was dropped in all states by the start of the war except in some Georgia towns. By late 1861 the name was dropped when all the old Adams Express operations where changed to the Southern Express name.

F

F	Macon, Ga., black*	3,500.
	Same, red*	4,000.
	Same, green	4,500.
	Savannah, Ga., red	4,000.

Warning: There are dangerous fakes of the Macon Harnden's Express marking.

Pioneer Express. This express operated in Alabama, Kentucky, Mississippi and Tennessee. Known offices were located in Demopolis, Gainesville, and Selma, Ala.; Columbus, Corinth, and Grenada, Miss.; and Jackson and Memphis, Tenn. Although several recorded Confederate covers bear Pioneer Express markings, most markings are recorded from the post-war period.

G

G	Columbus, Miss. (double circle)*	3,000.
	Mobile, Ala., blue	3,000.

Costa's Foreign Mail Express. Antonio Costa conducted a post office-endorsed foreign mail express service out of New Orleans. Outbound mail was routed across Texas to Mexico were it was forwarded to Tampico for placement aboard ship. Inbound mail was to be directed via Tampico to the postmaster in Matamoros for forwarding on to New Orleans.

No recorded markings

South Western Express. This express was also established to provide mail service to "all parts of the world" by circumventing the Union blockade. Mail was routed from New Orleans through Texas to Mexico where agents placed the mail aboard a ship at Tampico. There is evidence this express had close ties with the Southern Express and may have actually been a branch of that company.

H

H	New Orleans, La., black	—

Early prisoner of war cover from a Union soldier captured at the Battle of First Manassas (Bull Run) and held at Ligon's Tobacco Warehouse in Richmond. Letter given to Adam's Express and carried to Louisville where it entered the US mails to Vermont.

Flag of Truce Mail and Censor Markings

There are two recognized types of flag of truce mail: prisoner of war and civilian. Both types were subject to censorship and usually, but not always, bear a manuscript or handstamped censor marking. Both types of flag of truce mail and associated censor markings are included in this section.

While not technically flag of truce mail, those letters from prisoners in parole camps are also included in this section.

Prisoner of War Flag of Truce Mail

As early as April 1861, both the North and South began to take military prisoners. At first these prisoners were paroled. After the Battle of Manassas (Bull Run) on July 21, 1861, both sides began to detain prisoners and were faced with the problems associated with holding and caring for them.

One of the major concerns of the prisoners was to communicate with their loved ones. They quickly found surreptitious methods to get letters across the lines. These were soon followed by both formal and informal flag of truce exchanges of mail.

Instructions were promulgated by individual Union military commanders in charge of exchange points, as they had control over all southbound flag of truce mail. The general instructions were that letters were limited to personal matters. The envelopes had to be endorsed by the prisoner and Confederate postage had to be prepaid. Letters were to be enclosed in an outer envelope and were to be addressed to the commander at the exchange point. Similar instructions were implemented by the Southern commanders for northbound flag of truce mail exchanges.

Adherence to the specific requirements was not always strictly enforced resulting in a wide variety of frankings and markings on prisoner of war mail.

The prison from which a letter was mailed can normally be determined by the postmark on the letter. If the letter was enclosed in an outer envelope, the prison of origin can only be determined by the letter contents, the censor markings or the service record of the prisoner.

Prisoner of war mail was exchanged throughout the war but the volume of such mail varied considerably. It generally reflected the policy regarding the exchange of prisoners. If prisoner exchanges were frequent and prison populations low, the volume of prisoner of war mail was relatively low. If the policy was to retain prisoners, the volume of prisoner of war mail increased. In general, letters addressed to prisons are much scarcer than letters from prisons. Mail from Confederate prisons is much rarer than mail from Union prisons.

Major Flag of Truce Exchange Points

Norfolk – Old Point Comfort

From September 1861 until May 1862, most southbound mail was directed to Fortress Monroe where it was exchanged under flag of truce with Confederate officials at Norfolk, Virginia. The letters were then placed in the Confederate mails at Norfolk. Northbound mail followed the reverse path, typically entering the US mails at Old Point Comfort, Virginia.

Petersburg – Old Point Comfort

After Federal troops occupied Norfolk on May 9, 1862, southbound mail entered the Confederate mails at Petersburg, Virginia. Northbound mail continued to be posted at Old Point Comfort and occasionally at Annapolis, Maryland and Washington, D. C.

Richmond – Old Point Comfort

Starting in July 1863 and until the end of the war, mail was exchanged at City Point, Virginia. Southbound mail entered the Confederate mails at Richmond or was carried by military courier to various prisons. Northbound mail entered the US mails at Old Point Comfort.

Charleston and Savannah – Port Royal

Flag of truce exchanges between US occupied Port Royal and Confederate Pocotaligo, South Carolina began about February 1864. Exchanges ended with the Federal capture of Pocotaligo on January 14, 1865.

Southbound mail entered the Confederate mails at Pocotaligo and Charleston, South Carolina and Augusta and Savannah, Georgia. Most northbound mail entered the US mails at Port Royal. Occasionally, US naval ships carried the mail directly from the exchange point to Philadelphia or New York where it entered the US mails.

Jackson – Vicksburg

Beginning in late 1864 through June 1865, mail was exchanged between Union-held Vicksburg, Mississippi and Confederate-held Jackson, Mississippi. Southbound mail entered the mail at Jackson or Clinton, Mississippi and northbound letters at Vicksburg.

Mobile – New Orleans

Beginning in the summer of 1863, prisoner mail was exchanged between Mobile, Alabama and New Orleans under the auspices of the Louisiana Relief Committee (see Covert Mail section). This exchange ended with the Federal capture of Mobile Bay on August 23, 1864. Southbound mail entered the Confederate mails at Mobile and northbound mail at New Orleans.

Shreveport – New Orleans

From July 1863 to the end of the war, mail was exchanged between Shreveport and New Orleans, Louisiana. Southbound mail entered the Confederate mails at Shreveport, Louisiana and northbound letters entered the US mails at New Orleans.

Galveston, Texas – US Blockading Squadron

From January 1863 until the end of the war, an exchange of mail took place between Galveston, Texas and the US West Gulf Blockading Squadron. There is no recorded southbound mail. Northbound mail was carried to several east coast ports where it entered the mails.

For more detailed information about prisons and their markings, see *Prisoners' Mail from the American Civil War* by Galen D. Harrison.

Censor Markings

There are two basic types of censor markings, those that were applied at prisons by prison staff and those applied by district provost marshals. Not all flag of truce mail bears a censor marking.

Most censor markings are manuscript. The few recorded handstamped markings are all from US prisons and provost marshal districts.

A list of all US and Confederate prisons with mail recorded to or from prisoners of war is included at the end of this section.

Note: The price of prisoner of war covers is influenced by a variety of factors. These include the route, the point of exchange, postal markings, frankings, censors' markings, the quantity of mail from a specific prison and historic connections to the writer or recipient. Prices in this section are for covers in very fine condition with the most common frankings.

Early Prisoner Mail Exchanges

Prior to the implementation of formal prisoner of war and mail exchanges about September 1861, prisoners resorted to various means to get letters home. Some were able to use the service of the Adams Express Company. Others had released prisoners smuggle letters for mailing at post offices in the North or for personal delivery. All recorded examples of prisoner of war mail from this period are from Union prisoners in Richmond.

PWE-01	Adams Express from US POW in Richmond	*20,000.*
PWE-02	Hand carried by returning US POW from Richmond	500.

Prisoner Mail with Manuscript Censor Markings

The following listings are for covers bearing postmarks from the towns where they entered the mail. Postmarks other than Old Point Comfort and Richmond command higher prices, as indicated by the subsequent listing of postmarks. These are not comprehensive listings. Postmarks that are not listed individually are encompassed by "other."

Northbound Mail

To US Prisons

PWM-01	US franking	500.

From US Prisons

PWM-02	US franking	300.

From CS Prisons

PWM-03	US franking	500.
PWM-04	CS handstamped and US frankings	1,500.
PWM-05	CS stamp(s) and US frankings	1,500.

Postmarks

Washington, D.C.	+100.
Annapolis, Md.	+200.
Boston, Mass.	+200.
Port Royal, S.C.	+200.
New Orleans, La.	+300.
New York, N.Y.	+300.
Philadelphia, Pa.	+300.
Vicksburg, Miss.	+300.
Other	+500.

Southbound Mail

To CS Prisons

PWM-06	CS handstamped franking	750.
PWM-07	CS stamp(s) franking	750.
PWM-08	US franking and CS handstamped franking	750.
PWM-09	US franking and CS stamp(s)	1,250.

From US Prisons

PWM-10	US franking and CS handstamped franking	750.
PWM-11	US franking and CS stamp(s)	1,250.
PWM-12	CS franking	500.

Postmarks

Norfolk, Va.	+100.
Charleston, S.C.	+200.
Savannah, Ga.	+200.
Jackson, Miss.	+300.
Mobile, Ala.	+300.
Petersburg, Va.	+300.
Shreveport, La.	+300.
Augusta, Ga.	+400.
Pocotaligo, S.C	+500.
Other	+500.

Prisoner Mail with Handstamped Censor Markings

The prices below reflect the added value of the censor marking on a prisoner of war cover.

Fort Delaware (Delaware City, Del.) – An oval handstamped examined marking was used from April to October 1864.

A

PWH-01	Type A (black)	+50.

Old Capitol Prison (Washington, D.C.) – Mail was examined at the Old Capitol Prison and at the Provost Marshal's Office. Five types of handstamped censor markings are recorded with several different signatures.

A

B

C

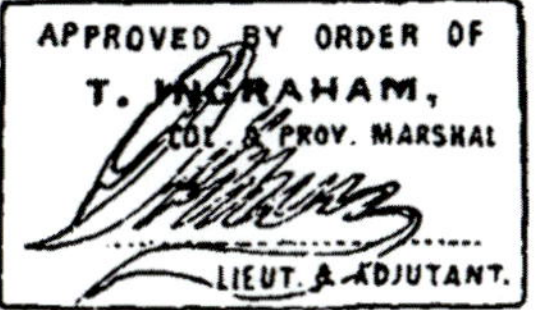

D

E

PWH-02	Type A (black)	+200.
PWH-03	Type B (black)	+750.
PWH-04	Type C (red)	+500.
PWH-05	Type D (red)	+500.
PWH-06	Type E (red)	+500.

Warning: Dangerous fakes of the Type A marking exist.

Camp Douglas (Chicago, Ill.) – Four different examined handstamps were used at Camp Douglas. The Type A marking was used from November 1863 to April 1864. Markings were in blue ink from November-December 1863 and in black ink after that. The Type B marking was used in the January-May 1865 period.

A

B

C

D

PWH-07	Type A (black)	+50.
	a. Same (blue)	+50.
PWH-08	Type B (black)	+100.
PWH-09	Type C (black)	+500.
PWH-10	Type D (black)	+500.

Rock Island Barracks (Rock Island, Ill.) – Three types of examined markings were used. The Type A was used from January-February 1864 and the Type B marking from February-April 1864. The Type C marking was used from May to July 1864 (black ink) and from August 1864 to February 1865 (blue ink).

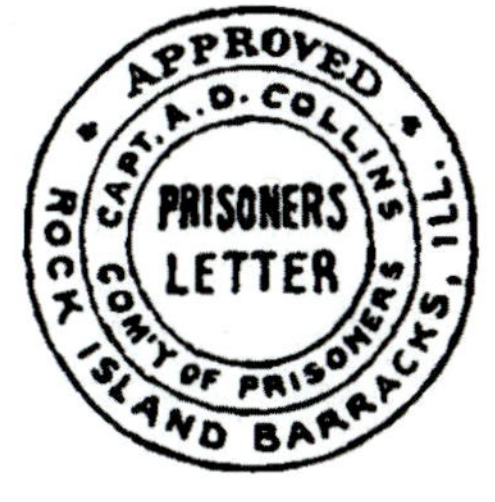

A

B

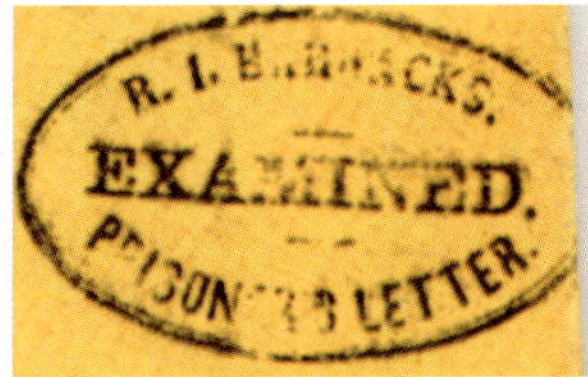

C

PWH-11	Type A (black)	+300.
PWH-12	Type B (black)	+300.
PWH-13	Type C (black)	+50.
	a. Same (blue)	+50.

Camp Morton (Indianapolis, Ind.) – Two types of examined markings were used at Camp Morton. There is a single recorded example of the Type A marking which was used in 1862. The Type B marking was used from August 1864 to February 1865.

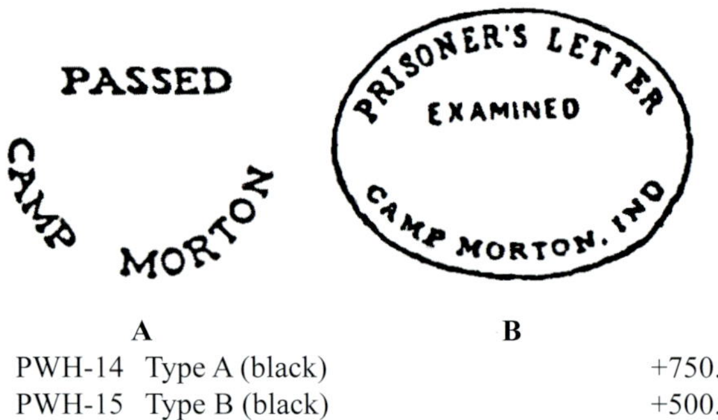

A B

PWH-14	Type A (black)	+750.
PWH-15	Type B (black)	+500.

Camp Hoffman (Point Lookout, Md.) – Three types handstamped markings were used. The Type A marking was used from October 1863 to April 1864, the Type B marking from July 1864 to March 1865 and the Type C marking from August to September 1864.

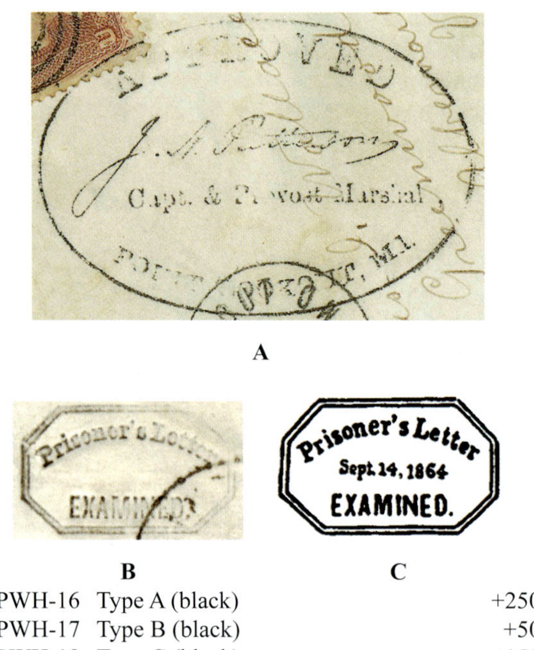

A

B C

PWH-16	Type A (black)	+250.
PWH-17	Type B (black)	+50.
PWH-18	Type C (black)	+150.

Elmira (Elmira, N.Y.) – The only censor marking used was an oval handstamp.

A

PWH-19	Type A (black)	+150.

District of North Carolina – There are two types of handstamps which mainly differ by the names of the examiner. Major Henry T. Lawson was provost marshal in the fall of 1864; Lieutenant Colonel Salter S. Poor replaced Lawson in October 1864.

A B

PWH-20	Type A (black)	+500.
PWH-21	Type A (black)	+500.

Camp Chase (Columbus, Ohio) – There are three varieties of the Camp Chase examined markings. The original marking was used by Lieutenant Colonel Poten beginning in January 1864. When Poten was replaced in March 1864, the handstamp was modified by the removal of "Poten" from the device. It was further modified in August 1864 by the removal of additional letters.

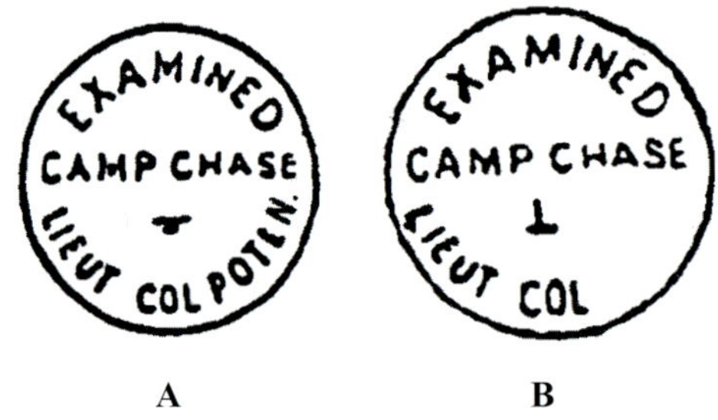

A B

[*]	symbol used after an item description to mean an unsupported listing
[–]	symbol used in place of value to mean insufficient information to assign a price
[*italic*]	value typeface indicating the item is difficult to price accurately

C

PWH-22	Type A (black)	+50.
PWH-23	Type B (black)	+50.
PWH-24	Type C (black)	+50.

Johnson's Island (Sandusky, Ohio) – Two types of handstamped censor markings were used at Johnson's Island.

A

B

PWH-25	Type A (black)	+50.
PWH-26	Type B (black)	+750.

US Hospital (Chester, Pa.) – The examiner at Chester Hospital used a blue signature handstamped under a manuscript "Examined & Approved" marking.

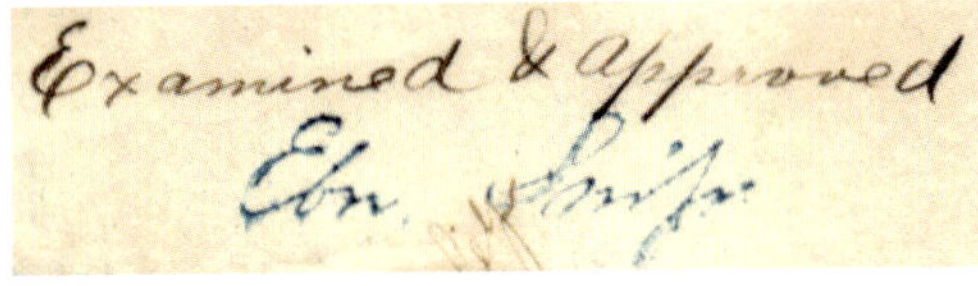

A

PWH-27	Type A (black)	+500.

District of Norfolk, Virginia – There were four different types of markings used. The first three were those of Charles M. Whelden. The first type has his name misspelled "Weelden." Horace T. Sanders replaced Whelden after August 1864.

A

B

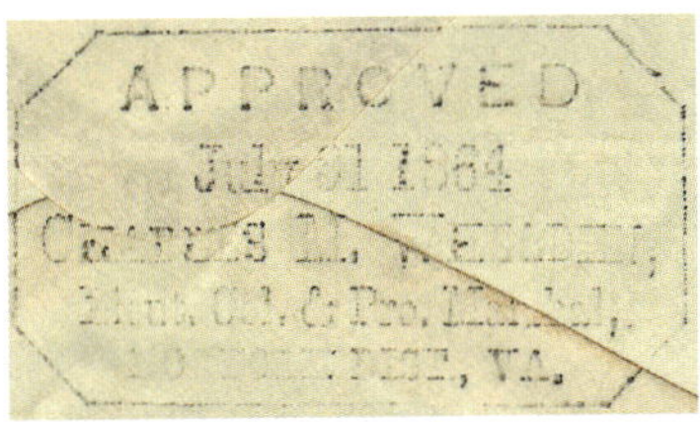

C

D

PWH-28	Type A (black)	+500.
PWH-29	Type B (black)	+500.
PWH-30	Type C (black)	+500.
PWH-31	Type D (black)	+500.

Parole Camp Mail

Frequently, captured soldiers would be "paroled" in the field. This meant they gave their word not to bear arms again until exchanged for a comparable number of paroled soldiers from the other side. Because of their status, they were held in special parole camps until exchanged. Union parolees were held in Union parole camps, and Confederate parolees in Confederate camps. There are very few recorded examples of prisoner mail from parole camps and none is recorded that crossed the lines. Detailed information on these camps can be found in *Prisoners' Mail from the American Civil War* by Galen D. Harrison.

A

Letters to or from Union parole camps can be identified by addresses, endorsements or letter contents. There is one recorded parole camp label.

No covers are recorded from Confederate parole camps.

Mail to or from Parole Camps (did not cross the lines)

PAR-01	US franking	300.
	a. Same, endorsed "Prisoner's Letter"	500.
	b. Same, with "Prisoner's Letter" label (Type A)	*5,000.*

Civilian Flag of Truce Mail

October 1864 northbound letter sent from Forkland, Alabama to Kentucky with CSA 11 and 3¢ US postage prepaid. It was endorsed via Richmond, and passed through Old Point Comfort on October 20.

The closure of across the lines express company operations at the end of August 1861 effectively stopped civilian correspondence between the North and South. When prisoner of war mail began to be exchanged between Old Point Comfort and Norfolk, Virginia in September 1861, it included some civilian flag of truce mail.

These mail exchanges were under the control of the military and were not intended for civilian mail. Any civilian mail that was exchanged was strictly at the discretion of the commanders of the flag of truce exchange points. In some cases, the commander refused to forward civilian flag of truce mail because of the extra burden it placed on censors and it was returned to the Dead Letter Office.

The same requirements for flag of truce mail that applied to prisoner of war mail also applied to civilian mail. Although these requirements were more strictly enforced for civilian mail, they were not always followed which resulted in a variety of frankings and markings.

In late January 1862, the Union Secretary of War, Simon Cameron, directed a halt to all exchanges of civilian flag of truce mail. This prohibition was affirmed by the new Union Secretary of War, Edwin Stanton, in May 1863.

In spite of the ban, some civilian flag of truce mail was exchanged throughout the war at the discretion of commanders at various flag of truce points.

Some civilian flag of truce covers were enclosed in an outer envelope while others were not. Those enclosed in an outer envelope show only US or Confederate franking. Others show franking of both sides. Not all flag of truce mail bears a censor marking.

Civilian flag of truce letters exchanged at the major points in Virginia bear postmarks from Old Point Comfort, Norfolk, Petersburg or Richmond, Virginia. In addition there were many other informal exchange points. These are rarer than mail exchanged at the major Virginia points and bring premiums.

District of East Tennessee provost marshal marking

Northbound Mail

CIV-01	US franking with manuscript censor marking	750.
CIV-02	CS handstamped and US frankings with manuscript censor marking	4,000.
CIV-03	CS stamp(s) and US frankings with manuscript censor markings	4,000.
	a. Same, with US Dead Letter Office handstamp marking	4,000.

Southbound Mail

CIV-04	CS handstamped franking with manuscript censor marking	750.
CIV-05	CS stamp(s) with manuscript censor markings	750.
	a. Same with East Tennessee Provost Marshal embossed censor marking	2,000.
CIV-06	US franking with manuscript censor marking	750.
CIV-07	US franking and CS handstamped franking with manuscript censor markings	1,250.
CIV-08	US franking and CS stamp(s) with manuscript censor markings	1,500.

Prisons with Recorded Uses

The following is a list of prisons with mail recorded to or from prisoners of war.

Confederate Prisons

Alabama

Cahaba (Castle Morgan)
Montgomery
Selma
Tuscaloosa

Georgia

Andersonville (Camp Sumter)
Atlanta

- Macon (Camp Oglethorpe)
- Madison
- Marietta (Old Military Prison)
- Savannah (Camp Davidson)

Louisiana
- Mansfield (temporary)
- Shreveport (Camp Boggs)

North Carolina
- Ashville (temporary)
- Plymouth (temporary)
- Salisbury
- Tarboro (temporary)

Pennsylvania
- Near Gettysburg (temporary)

South Carolina
- Charleston
  - City Jail
  - Fair Grounds (Race Course)
  - Marine Hospital
  - O'Connor House
  - Roper Hospital
  - Workhouse
- Columbia
  - Camp Asylum
  - Camp Sorghum
  - College Hospital
  - Richland Jail
- Florence
- Rickersville (1st SC Hospital)

Texas
- Hempstead (Camp Groce)
- Houston
- Tyler (Camp Ford)

Virginia
- Aiken's Landing (CSS *Shultz*)
- City Point (Camp Lewis)
- Danville
  - Buildings 1, 3, 4, 5, 6
  - Prison Hospital
- Frazier's Farm (temporary)
- Lynchburg
- Petersburg
- Richmond
  - Barrett's
  - Belle Isle
  - Castle Thunder
  - Castle Thunder Hospital (General Hospital #13)
  - Crew & Pemberton's (Crew & Conrad's)
  - General Hospital #1 (Alm's House)
  - General Hospital #21 (Gwathmey Factory Hospital or CS Military Prison Hospital)
  - Libby
  - Ligon's Tobacco Warehouse
  - Mayo's Warehouse
  - Scott's Tobacco Warehouse
  - Smith & McCurdy's Factory
  - Smith's Tobacco Warehouse
  - Taylor's Tobacco Warehouse
- Staunton
  - Staunton Hospital
  - Staunton Prison
- Tom's Brook (temporary)
- Winchester (temporary)

[West] Virginia
- Charlestown

Union Prisons

Arkansas
- Helena

Delaware
- Fort Delaware

District of Columbia
- Carroll Prison
- Lincoln General Hospital
- Old Capitol

Georgia
- Macon (House Arrest – temporary)
- Savannah (Fort Pulaski)

Illinois
- Alton
- Cairo
- Chicago (Camp Douglas)
- Rock Island
- Springfield (Camp Butler)

Indiana
- Indianapolis

Kentucky
- Louisville (Camp Boyd)
- Paducah

Louisiana
- New Orleans
  - Common Street (temporary)
  - Levee Cotton Press #4
  - Prytania Asylum
  - 21 Rampart Street

Maryland
- Antietam Field Hospital (temporary)
- Baltimore
  - Fort McHenry
  - West's Building Hospital
- Point Lookout (Camp Hoffman)
  - Hammond General Hospital

Massachusetts
- Boston (Fort Warren)

Mississippi
- Ship Island

Missouri
- Jefferson City (temporary)
- Saint Louis
  - Gratiot Street
  - Marine Hospital (temporary)
  - Myrtle Street
  - Schofield Barracks (temporary)

New York
  - Elmira
- New York City (Tombs)
- New York Harbor
  - Castle Williams (Governor's Island)
  - Fort Columbus (Governor's Island)

- Fort Hamilton (Brooklyn – political prisoners)
- Fort Woods (Bedloe's Island)
- Hart's Island
- Pelham (David's Island – Decamp General Hospital)

North Carolina
- Fort Fisher (temporary)

Ohio
- Cincinnati (McLean Barracks or Kemper Barracks)
- Columbus
  - Camp Chase
  - Ohio State Penitentiary
- Sandusky (Johnson's Island)

Pennsylvania
- Allegheny City Penitentiary (aka Western Penitentiary of Pennsylvania)
- Chester (Chester General Hospital – temporary)
- Germantown (Cuyler General Hospital – temporary)
- Gettysburg
  - Field Hospitals (temporary)
  - Letterman General Hospital (aka Camp Letterman)
- Harrisburg (Camp Curtin – temporary)

South Carolina
- Beaufort (US General Hospital)
- Hilton Head
- Morris Island Stockade

Tennessee
- Chattanooga (Department of the Cumberland)
- Fort Donelson (temporary)
- Knoxville Provost Marshal Prison
- Memphis Provost Marshal Prison
- Murfreesboro Army Hospital (temporary)
- Nashville Penitentiary (Tennessee State Penitentiary)

Virginia
- Appomattox Court House (temporary)
- City Point
  - Provost Marshal Prison (temporary)
- Fort Monroe
  - Casemate
  - Camp Hamilton
- Hampton (Chesapeake Hospital)
- Harrisonburg (temporary)
- Norfolk, House Arrest (temporary)
- Point of Rocks 18th Army Corps Hospital
- Winchester

West Virginia
- Kanawha Court House (temporary)
- Martinsburg (temporary)
- Wheeling (Athenaeum Prison – temporary)

Wisconsin
- Madison (Camp Randall)

US Ships
- US Steamer *Crescent*
- US Steamer *Dragoon*

For the most part, US Ships were used simply to deliver prisoners from one point to another. Only the *Crescent* and the *Dragoon* were used for a limited time as prison ships. Prisoner transport vessels can be identified by endorsements or contents.

Inner prisoner of war cover with Charleston, S.C. Sep. 2 [1864] postmark; sent from Lt. W. E. Johnson, one of the "Immortal 600", while aboard the USS *Crescent City.*

Federal Parole Camps and Temporary Sites

The following is a list of Federal parole camps from which mail to or from prisoner parolees are recorded. There are no Confederate parole camps with recorded mail.

District of Columbia
- Government Hospital for the Insane
- Parole Camp Jamison (temporary)

Florida
- Jacksonville (Parole Camp)

Illinois
- Chicago Parole Camp, Fair Grounds

Indiana
- Indianapolis Parole Camp

Maryland
- Annapolis
  - Camp Parole
  - College Green Barracks (General Hospital)
- Baltimore (Barnum's Hotel – temporary)

Mississippi
- Vicksburg Parole Camp

Missouri
- Saint Louis
  - Benton Barracks
  - Schofield Barracks

Ohio
- Columbus
  - Boarding House (183 Town Street)
  - Camp Chase (Parole Camp)
  - Neil House (Neal House – temporary)
- Sandusky (West House – temporary)

Virginia
- Alexandria (Camp Parole)
- Fort Monroe (Hygia Hotel – temporary)

Trans-Mississippi Mails

Union victories at New Orleans in April and Memphis in June 1862 effectively closed the Mississippi River to normal Confederate commerce. It also caused a major disruption of the Confederate mails across the river. In response to the failure of the Confederate Post Office Department to maintain a regular Trans-Mississippi mail, the Confederate Congress first authorized special mail agents to secure the mail. When this failed to achieve the desired result, Congress approved two premium services: a Preferred Mail Service and a Trans-Mississippi Express Mail. These two services are described in detail by Richard Krieger in *The Trans-Mississippi Mails after the Fall of Vicksburg* (1984).

Trans-Mississippi Preferred Mail Service

The Preferred Mail Service was approved by President Davis on April 16, 1863. This law authorized the Postmaster General to establish a "preferred" mail route to maintain communications across the Mississippi River, and to provide for "more speedy transmission of letters and dispatches." The rate for this route was set at 50¢ per half ounce. Research has found no evidence Postmaster Reagan took any action to implement this service. However, there are several recorded covers bearing 50¢ in postage and westbound Trans-Mississippi notations.

Westbound Trans-Mississippi cover bearing 50¢ in postage

Trans-Mississippi Express Mail Service

The "Trans-Mississippi Express Mail" was approved on May 1, 1863. This law authorized the Postmaster General to establish an express mail across the Mississippi River to secure greater speed than provided by the regular mail. Postmaster General Reagan set the rate at 40¢ per half ounce. This was a premium service and required prepayment of the express rate.

It took several months to establish the route and make arrangements for the necessary services. Trans-Mississippi Express mail is recorded as early as October 1863 and as late as April 1865.

Earliest recorded Express Mail cover sent from Petersburg, Virginia on October 26, 1863 to Shreveport, Louisiana

It was with great difficulty that the Trans-Mississippi mail got past Union patrols on the Mississippi River. There are less than 200 recorded express mail covers. Many are water stained, creased or soiled from rough handling while crossing the river. These covers generally bear the notations "Via Shreveport" or "Via Alexandria" if they originated west of the river, and "Via Meridian" or "Via Brandon" if they originated east of the river. West bound examples are more numerous than eastbound.

The Trans-Mississippi Express Mail was a premium service and required prepayment of the express rate. As such, soldier's letters that were sent postage due were not to be carried in this mail.

Note: Unusual markings and scarcer frankings sell for premium prices.

Westbound Trans-Mississippi Express Mail

TMW-01	Westbound with four A&D 10¢ stamps	4,500.
	a. Same, with strip of four A&D 10¢ stamps	6,500.
TMW-02	Westbound with four K&B 10¢ stamps	5,500.
TMW-03	Westbound with CSA 7-R in combination with other stamps	9,000.
TMW-04	Westbound with two 20¢ stamps	7,500.
TMW-05	Westbound with pair of 20¢ stamps	8,500.
TMW-06	Westbound with rate handstamped or in manuscript	5,000.
TMW-07	Westbound with double rate franking	*20,000.*
TMW-08	Westbound with rate paid by 50¢ in stamps	8,500

Eastbound Trans-Mississippi Express Mail

TME-01	Eastbound with four A&D 10¢ stamps	6,000.
	a. Same, with strip of four A&D 10¢ stamps	7,500.
TME-02	Eastbound with four K&B 10¢ stamps	7,000.
TME-03	Eastbound with CSA 7-R in combination with other stamps	*12,000.*

TME-04	Eastbound with two 20¢ stamps	*10,000.*
TME-05	Eastbound with pair of 20¢ stamps	*12,000.*
TME-06	Eastbound with rate handstamped or in manuscript	5,000.

10¢ Trans-Mississippi Rate

The establishment of the Trans-Mississippi Express Mail did not end regular mail service across the Mississippi. The 10¢ letter rate was still valid. Mail franked at this rate received lower priority handling so that the timely or actual delivery of such letters was uncertain.

TMW-09	Westbound Trans-Mississippi letter with a 10¢ franking	750.
TME-07	Eastbound Trans-Mississippi letter with a 10¢ franking	750.

Private Trans-Mississippi Expresses

The unreliability of the Trans-Mississippi mail service resulted in the creation of a number of private express services. These services endeavored to maintain communications across the Mississippi River. Some were started by businessmen, others by individuals, often ex-soldiers.

Many private express services have been identified through newspaper advertisements, records, or contents of soldiers' letters. Only those from which actual mail is known are listed. Information on the expresses not included here can be found in "Private Trans-Mississippi Mail Expresses during the War Between the States," Stefan T. Jaronski, *The Confederate Philatelist,* November 1987.

E. H. Cushing's Express

E. H. Cushing, editor of the *Houston Daily Telegraph*, began a private Trans-Mississippi express service designed to bring news to his newspaper and to facilitate letter communications with Texas troops serving in the east. The first notice of the service appeared in the *Houston Telegraph* in April 1862. The service was discontinued in September 1864 at the order of the Confederate Post Office Department.

Cushing attached four different types of advertising labels on the backs of some eastbound letters, and these are the most easily identified Cushing express letters.

The Type A label was used on eastbound mail in 1862 and 1863 and is on bluish or greenish paper. Surviving covers suggest that the bluish paper was used in 1862 and the greenish paper in 1863.

Forwarded by E. H. Cushing.

As we get no papers by mail now, our friends will confer a great favor by sending, or bringing us, all the papers they can get hold of, both Northern and Southern, addressed to Telegraph office, Houston, Texas.

A

The Type B Cushing label was used on eastbound mail in 1863 and early 1864, and is on white paper.

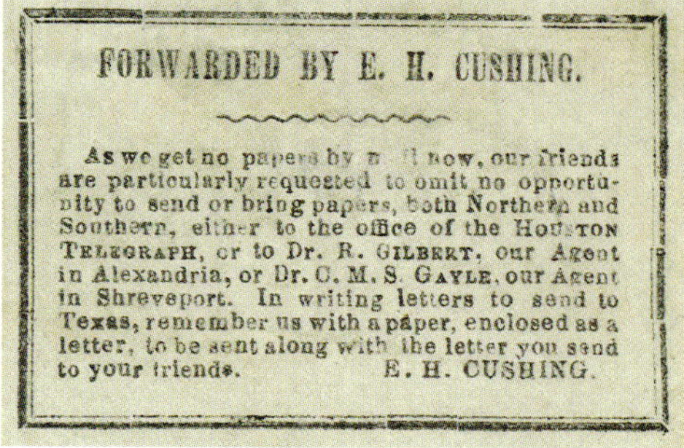

FORWARDED BY E. H. CUSHING.

As we get no papers by mail now, our friends are particularly requested to omit no opportunity to send or bring papers, both Northern and Southern, either to the office of the Houston Telegraph, or to Dr. R. Gilbert, our Agent in Alexandria, or Dr. C. M. S. Gayle, our Agent in Shreveport. In writing letters to send to Texas, remember us with a paper, enclosed as a letter, to be sent along with the letter you send to your friends. E. H. CUSHING.

B

The Type C Cushing labels were used on eastbound mail in 1864 and are on various colors of paper. There are four recorded sub-types, all with different 1864 Houston datelines, and containing different snippets of news from Texas. Known datelines are April 2, May 13, July 4, and August 17.

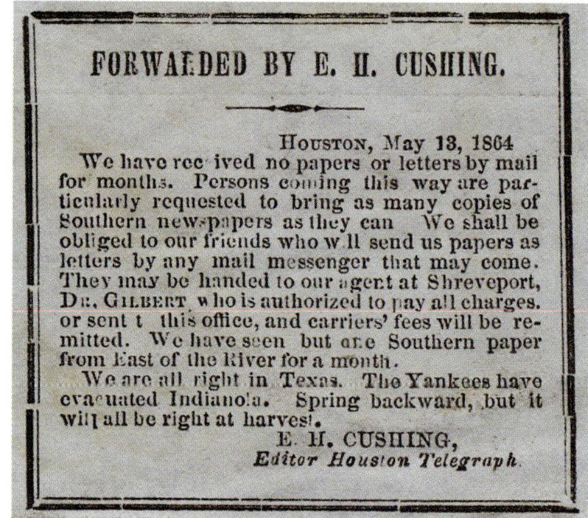

FORWARDED BY E. H. CUSHING.

Houston, May 13, 1864.

We have received no papers or letters by mail for months. Persons coming this way are particularly requested to bring as many copies of Southern newspapers as they can. We shall be obliged to our friends who will send us papers as letters by any mail messenger that may come. They may be handed to our agent at Shreveport, Dr. Gilbert, who is authorized to pay all charges, or sent to this office, and carriers' fees will be remitted. We have seen but one Southern paper from East of the River for a month.

We are all right in Texas. The Yankees have evacuated Indianola. Spring backward, but it will all be right at harvest.

E. H. CUSHING,
Editor Houston Telegraph.

C

The Type D Cushing label was used on eastbound mail in September 1864 and is on grayish paper. A label dated September 12 announced the end of the Cushing private mail service.

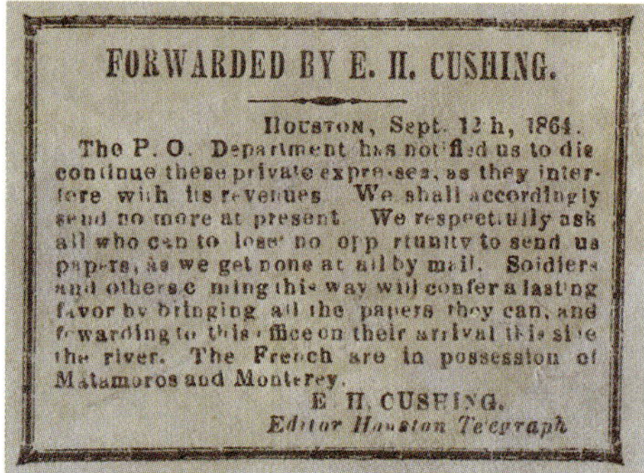

FORWARDED BY E. H. CUSHING.

Houston, Sept. 12th, 1864.

The P. O. Department has notified us to discontinue these private expresses, as they interfere with its revenues. We shall accordingly send no more at present. We respectfully ask all who can to lose no opportunity to send us papers, as we get none at all by mail. Soldiers and others coming this way will confer a lasting favor by bringing all the papers they can, and forwarding to this office on their arrival this side the river. The French are in possession of Matamoros and Monterey.

E. H. CUSHING.
Editor Houston Telegraph

D

TME-08 Cushing Type A label, attached to cover *10,000.*
TME-09 Cushing Type B label, attached to cover 5,000.
TME-10 Cushing Type C label, attached to cover 5,000.
TME-11 Cushing Type D label, attached to cover 7,500.

Westbound Cushing Express mails typically entered the Confederate postal system at Shreveport or Alexandria, Louisiana and show origination from Texas military units in the Army of Northern Virginia or the Army of Tennessee. The letters are known prepaid or with postage due. Because these letters have no labels, it is difficult to attribute them definitively to Cushing.

Arthur H. Edey's 5th Texas Regiment Express

The 5th Texas Regiment with the Army of Northern Virginia detailed Arthur Edey to carry mail from the regiment to families back home in Texas. He was assisted by W. U. Bayles, agent of the 5th Texas depot at Richmond, whose endorsements are known on several letters. Edey prepared typeset labels which read, "FORWARDED BY ARTHUR H. EDEY. *Agent, Fifth Reg't Texas Volunteers.*" These labels were normally affixed to back of envelopes. The earliest recorded use of an Edey label is on a cover docketed "From Richmond, Va. June 1862"; the latest recorded use of an Edey label is on a cover that arrived in Texas on October 24, 1862. All recorded examples were sent from east to west.

FORWARDED BY
ARTHUR H. EDEY, *Agent, Fifth Reg't Texas Volunteers.*

Arthur H. Edey's Express label

TMW-10 Edey label, attached to cover 7,500.
TMW-11 W. U. Bayles endorsement instead of Edey label 3,500.

Note: Labels affixed on the back of covers sell for less.

J. M. Barksdale's Express

J. M. Barksdale was a soldier in the 2nd Arkansas Mounted Rifles who was discharged for a disability in December 1862. By the summer of 1863, he was operating an express between Arkansas and Reynolds' Arkansas Brigade with the Army of Tennessee. He carried westbound letters to Washington, Arkansas, where they were placed in the Confederate mails. Return letters were to be sent to his attention at Washington. The charge was $1.00 per letter. No eastbound letters are recorded.

Envelopes carried by Barksdale Express can be identified by a $1.00 rate notation on the front and, on at least one cover, return mail instructions on back including the name "J. M. Barksdale."

J. M. Barksdale's Express, front of cover

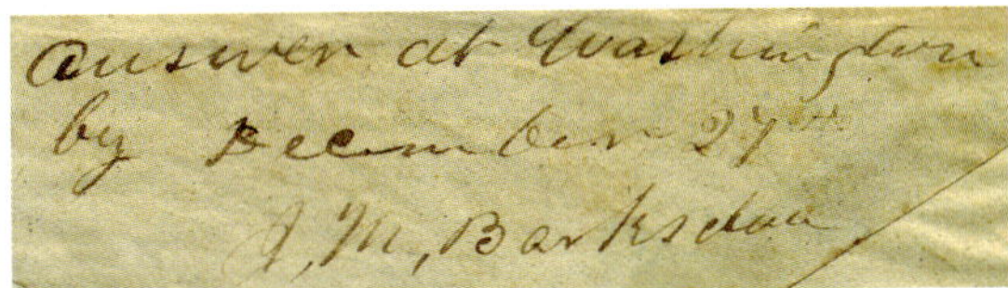

J. M. Barksdale's Express, endorsement on back

TMW-12 J.M. Barksdale endorsement on westbound Express letter 3,500.

Captain Bernos' Express

John Bernos was a Confederate Army Captain who, among his other duties, supervised the transmittal of military mail across the river. He also carried civilian mail, as evidenced by a notice in the November 27, 1863 edition of the Houston *Telegraph.* The notice gave the rate as $2.00 per letter with the Confederate postage prepaid by stamps.

Apparently Bernos operated the express in conjunction with Major S. B. French who both forwarded all the express letters in the Confederate mails on arrival in Richmond and collected mail for a westbound express.

There is only one recorded example of a Bernos Express cover. It is an eastbound cover identified by the endorsement "Kindness of Capt. Bernos" on the front. On the reverse is the notation "Forwarded by Major S. B. French, Richmond, Va., who will with pleasure forward any letter you may desire, to the Trans-Mississippi Department. Capt. Bernos will return in a few days."

[*italic*] value typeface indicating the item is difficult to price accurately

Captain Bernos Express, front of cover

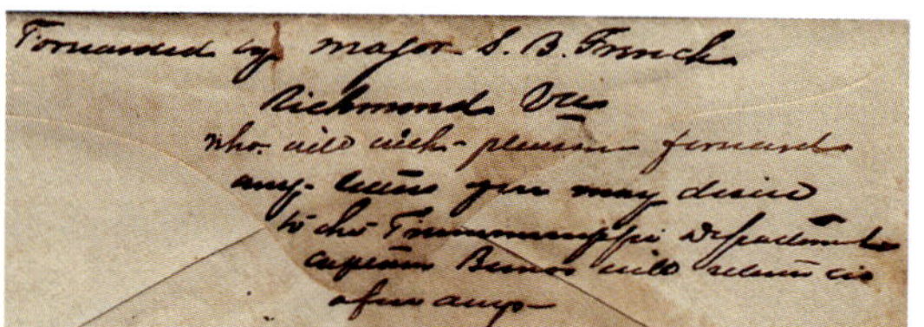

Captain Bernos Express, endorsement on back

TME-12 Captain Bernos endorsement on eastbound letter 3,500.

E. W. Black's Express

Elias W. Black was a soldier in the 4th Arkansas Regiment who was discharged for disability in June 1862. By the fall of 1863 he operated an express between Arkansas and McNair's Arkansas Brigade with the Army of Tennessee. He carried westbound letters to Washington, Arkansas, where they were place in the Confederate mails. Return letters were to be sent to his attention at Hampton, Arkansas. The charge was $1.00 per letter.

There is only one recorded example of a Black's Express cover. It is identified by a $1.00 rate notation on the front and return mail instructions on the back including the initials "E. W. B." It is westbound and postmarked October 21 at Washington, Arkansas.

E. W. Black's Express with endorsement

TMW-13 E.W. Black endorsement on westbound express letter 3,500.

I. W. Sturdivant's Express

I. W. Sturdivant operated an express between Marshall, Texas and the 7th Texas Infantry with the Army of Tennessee. He carried westbound letters to Marshall, Texas where they were placed in the Confederate mails. All recorded uses are westbound. The charge was $1.00 per letter.

Envelopes carried by Sturdivant's Express can be identified the by a "Per Mr. J W. Sturdivant" endorsement and a $1.00 rate notation on the front.

TMW-14 I. W. Sturdivant endorsement on westbound express letter 5,000.

Westbound cover from Natchitoches La. Sep. 17 [1862] with handstamped "10" and manuscript "Due", endorsed "S. S. Bryan, Texas Rangers C.S. Army" and carried west across the Mississippi with "*Favor of Mr. Lewis*" endorsement.

Courtesy Trans-Mississippi Service by Soldiers

Soldiers in one of the eastern armies could also send westbound letters with a furloughed soldier traveling across the Mississippi River. Families could send eastbound mail on the soldier's return trip. These envelopes are identified by endorsements.

TMW-15 Westbound with soldier's "care of" endorsement and CSA franking 750.

TME-13 Eastbound with soldier's "care of" endorsement and CSA franking 750.

Additional information on Trans-Mississippi Mails may be found in *Special Mail Routes of the American Civil War: A Guide to Across-the-Lines Postal History* by Steven C. Walske and Scott R. Trepel.

Blockade Run Mail

A blockade of Southern ports was proclaimed by President Lincoln on April 19, 1861. The Union Navy gradually implemented a blockade of all major Southern ports and eventually 3,500 miles of coastline. In response the owners of fast ships of shallow draft outfitted their vessels to run the blockade of Southern ports. These vessels operated primarily between the Southern ports of Charleston, Wilmington, Savannah, Mobile and ports in Bermuda, Nassau, and Cuba. The foreign ports served as trans-shipment ports where cargo was transferred from larger vessels to the smaller but faster blockade runners.

Blockade Run Mail Inbound to the Confederacy

Incoming mail to the Confederacy took two forms. The first was that sent to forwarders at the trans-shipment ports. There the letters were placed aboard a blockade runner for delivery to the post office at the port of entry as ship letters. The postage charge was 6¢, for delivery at the port of entry; for delivery beyond the port of entry it was the inland rate plus a 2¢ captain's fee. The 2¢ fee was not always assessed. These covers can be identified by the port of arrival postmark, a ship marking and the amount of postage due.

Other incoming letters were carried by passengers aboard the blockade runners. On arrival at the Southern port of entry, these letters were posted as ordinary letters. These can only be identified by their contents, endorsements or docketing.

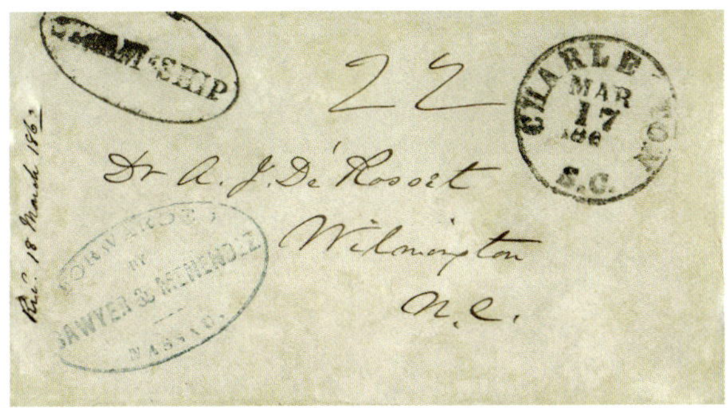

Blockade run cover forwarded by Sawyer & Menendez from Nassau to Charleston where it was marked "STEAM-SHIP" and rated for double-weight 22¢ postage due.

Blockade Run Mail Outbound from the Confederacy

Most outgoing blockade mail was directed to a forwarder at a Southern port. The forwarder would place the letters aboard a blockade runner and direct them to his agent at the foreign trans-shipment port. There the letters would be posted or forwarded to another forwarding agent before being placed in the mails. Outgoing letters handled in this manner are difficult to distinguish from regular letters posted at the same port. Blockade mail can only be identified by letter contents, endorsements, or docketing.

A few letters were sent through the Confederate mails to an individual at a Southern port of delivery for forwarding on a blockade runner. This mail is easily identified by the Confederate franking and the franking of the foreign port where the letter was posted.

The majority of outbound blockade run mail was posted to the Bahamas, Bermuda, New York, and Halifax. A number were forwarded under cover from Nassau, Bermuda or Havana to England, and entered the mails at Liverpool or London.

September 23, 1863 blockade run letter from Charleston, carried from Wilmington to Nassau where it was posted prepaid one shilling on October 24.

Forwarder Markings

Incoming blockade cover from Bermuda endorsed at lower left by Confederate agent Major Norman S. Walker.

Most blockade run mail, both inbound and outbound, was expedited by forwarders. Most forwarders did not mark the letters they handled. When they did, the markings generally take the form of handstamps, embossed cachets or manuscript endorsements. Forwarders or correspondents would occasionally endorse covers with the name of a particular blockade runner. Only a small number of blockade run letters have censor markings.

Prepaid blockade run letter carried from Nassau to Wilmington on January 5, 1865. The Nassau forwarder added his handstamp and endorsed it to the "*Wild Rover*".

Incoming Blockade Run Mail via Charleston

Markings on incoming blockade mail at Charleston, South Carolina typically include a circular dated postmark, a ship marking, and a manuscript indication of postage due. There are three recorded Charleston postmarks used on incoming blockade mail. Typically one of the following town postmarks was applied to letters as well as the ship marking.

Pmk A

Pmk B

Pmk C

Type A was used from May 1862 until January 1865, and suffered noticeable deterioration as the war progressed. Type B was used from July 1862 until December 1864. Type C is the least common, and was used from February 1863 to March 1864 period.

A

B

C

Three types of ship and rate markings were used. There are two recorded types of ship markings. The first is a straightline "SHIP" marking. All recorded examples were used in early August 1862. The second, and more common ship marking, is the oval "STEAM-SHIP". This marking was used throughout the war. The "6" rate marking was applied to letters for delivery at Charleston.

Covers franked with foreign postage, Confederate general issue stamps, ship name endorsements, forwarder handstamps, multiple rates, censor's examined markings or unusual uses command higher prices than those listed.

Incoming Blockade Run Mail via Charleston

BIB-01	"SHIP" (Type A, black) with manuscript 12¢	7,500.
BIB-02	"STEAM-SHIP" (Type B, black) with manuscript 12¢	4,000.
	a. Same, with manuscript "22" or "32"	5,000.
	b. Same, with Confederate franking	5,000.
BIB-03	"6" (Type C, black)	2,500.
BIB-04	Hand carried on ship	750.

Incoming Blockade Run Mail via Wilmington

Markings on incoming letters at Wilmington, North Carolina typically include a Wilmington circular dated postmark, a ship marking, and a manuscript indication of the postage due. There are three recorded postmarks used on incoming blockade run mail. Typically one of the following town postmarks was applied to letters as well as the ship marking.

Pmk A

Pmk B

Pmk C

The Type A postmark was used from January 1863 until January 1865. The Type B postmark was used from December 1862 until November 1863. The Type C postmark apparently replaced the Type B postmark and was used from October 1863 until May 1864.

S H I P

A

Wilmington used a single straightline "SHIP" marking. This marking is on virtually all incoming letters from December 1862 until February 1864. No ship markings appear on letters arriving at Wilmington after February 1864. All letters bear Wilmington postmarks.

Incoming Blockade Run Mail via Wilmington

BIB-05	"SHIP" (Type A, black), manuscript 12¢	4,000.
	a. Same, with manuscript "22" or "32"	5,000.
	b. Same, with Confederate franking	5,000.
BIB-06	Manuscript "6"	3,000.
BIB-07	Hand carried on ship	750.

Incoming Blockade Run Mail via Savannah

Savannah, Georgia was open to blockade running for only a limited time. There is one recorded incoming blockade letter from Savannah. It bears the Savannah postmark and an italic straightline "SHIP" marking.

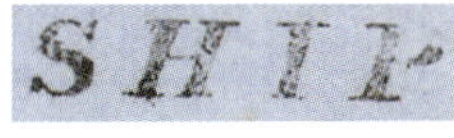

A

Incoming Blockade Run Mail via Savannah

BIB-08	"SHIP" (Type A, black) italic, with manuscript 7¢	7,500.

Incoming Blockade Run Mail via Mobile

Incoming letters to Mobile, Alabama were either carried in an outer envelope to a Mobile forwarder, who posted them with the correct Confederate postage, or they were carried in the blockade runner's mailbag. In the latter case, the mail was taken to the Mobile post office where it was postmarked and assessed postage as a ship letter. Mobile used a straightline "SHIP" marking on some blockade mail.

A

Incoming Blockade Run Mail via Mobile

BIB-09	Manuscript 12¢ and Mobile postmark	5,000.
	a. Same, with Confederate franking	7,500.
	b. Same, with straightline "SHIP" (Type A, black) marking	7,500.

Incoming Blockade Run Mail via New Orleans

Incoming mail was postmarked at New Orleans, Louisiana and marked with a straightline "STEAM" marking. Union forces anchored off New Orleans on April 25, 1862 ending all blockade running through that port.

STEAM

A

Incoming Blockade Run Mail via New Orleans

BIB-10	"STEAM" (Type A, black) with manuscript 10 and New Orleans postmark	5,000.

Incoming Blockade Run Mail via Galveston

All recorded incoming blockade letters at Galveston, Texas were carried in outer envelopes to Galveston, and posted in Houston with the proper Confederate postage. All recorded uses are between January 1864 and March 1865.

Incoming Blockade Run Mail via Galveston

BIB-11	Manuscript 10¢ or 20¢ and Houston postmark	5,000.
	a. Same, with Confederate stamp	7,500.

Outgoing Blockade Run Mail via Nassau

Blockade letters typically were marked with a red Nassau, Bahamas circular postmark and a manuscript indication of postage due or paid. Most of the prepaid letters were paid in cash, so there are few recorded covers franked with Bahamas postage stamps. Four different postmarks are recorded on outgoing blockade run mail:

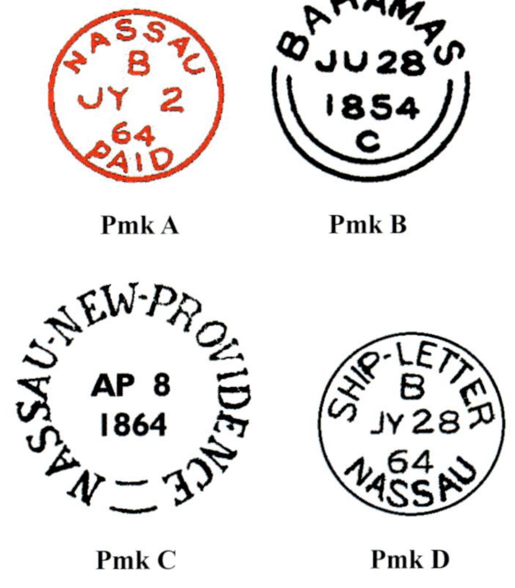

Pmk A Pmk B

Pmk C Pmk D

Two auxiliary markings were used at Nassau on outgoing blockade run mail:

A B

The Type A marking was used from February to October 1863. It was apparently replaced by the Type B marking in 1864. Type B, in red, was used on prepaid mail from November 1864 to February 1865.

Outgoing Blockade Run Mail via Nassau

BOB-01 Blockade letter with Nassau postmark 2,500.

Note: Some outgoing letters are known with censor or forwarder handstamps. Such uses command a premium.

Letters addressed to Nassau, Bahamas were rated as unpaid ship letters on arrival with 4p due. Some of these letters bear both Confederate postage and postmarks. These are the only recorded examples of outgoing blockade run mail that carry Confederate frankings and postmarks.

Letter sent from Raleigh, NC to Wilmington, NC where it was marked "ADVERTISED" and eventually forwarded by blockade runner to Nassau and then rated with four pence ship fee due.

Outgoing Blockade Run Mail via Bermuda

Although Bermuda was a very active blockade running port, little mail was processed by the Bermuda post office. Postal markings applied to outgoing letters via Bermuda typically include a circular dated postmark and a manuscript indication of postage due or paid. Most of the known letters were sent unpaid. The three principal types of Bermuda postmarks used on outgoing blockade run mail are illustrated below:

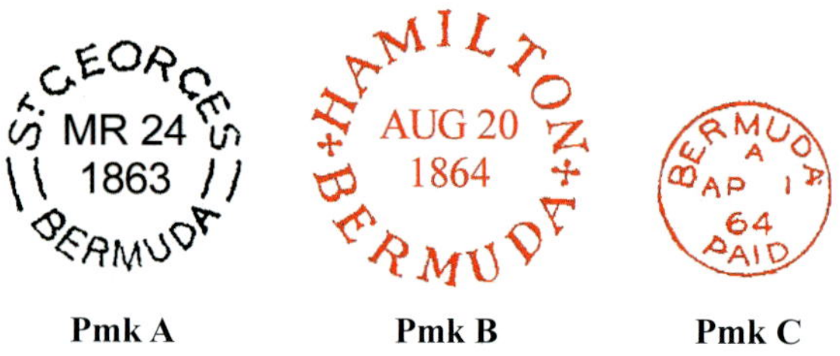

Pmk A Pmk B Pmk C

Two auxiliary markings were used at Bermuda on outgoing blockade run mail:

BERMUDA
SHIP LETTER

HAMILTON-BERMUDA
SHIP LETTER

A B

There is one recorded example of Type A used in October 1862. There is one recorded example of Type B used in July 1864.

Outgoing Blockade Run Mail via Bermuda

BOB-02 Blockade letter with Bermuda postmark 5,000.
a. Same, with Type A or B "SHIP LETTER" double straightline marking 7,500.

Outgoing Blockade Run Mail via Halifax

Very few outgoing blockade letters are recorded with Halifax, Nova Scotia transit postmarks. Most were carried on steamships running directly to Halifax from Wilmington in the August-December 1864 period. Some were carried through the blockade to Bermuda and then by steamship to Halifax.

Outgoing Blockade Run Mail via Halifax

BOB-03 Blockade letter with Halifax postmark 5,000.

Outgoing Blockade Run Mail via New York

Outgoing blockade run mail from New Orleans, Mobile and Galveston was either sent to forwarders in Havana, Cuba or in an outer envelope addressed to a New York forwarder. The typical postal marking on this type of mail is the New York "STEAMSHIP / 10" due marking seen on Havana to New York mail of this period. Mail addressed to New York forwarders was removed from the outer envelope and placed in the mail at that city or trans-shipped to a forwarder in England.

A

Outgoing Blockade Run Mail via New York

BOB-04 "STEAMSHIP / 10" (Type A, black) marking 2,500.

Outgoing Blockade Run Mail via Liverpool or London

Some mail was sent in outer envelopes to the care of forwarders in Liverpool or London. These forwarders either posted the inner letters in the British mails, or arranged to forward them to their destinations.

Blockade run letter sent from Savannah, Georgia to Rome, carried under cover via Charleston and Nassau to London, where a forwarder posted it prepaid with the 11d rate to the Roman States.

Outgoing Blockade Run Mail via Liverpool or London

BOB-05	Posted prepaid or with postage due in Liverpool or London	1,500.
BOB-06	With Liverpool ship postmark and postage due	2,500.

Blockade Run Prize Court Mail

Letter mailed from New York to Nassau and forwarded aboard the blockade runner *Defiance* to Savannah. Captured by the USS *Braziliera* on Sep. 7, 1862. Marked as evidence in Philadelphia Prize Court with magenta "84" at left and "No. 17. H. F." at right.

When Union naval forces captured a Confederate blockade runner, the value of the capture was shared among the crew of the capturing vessel. Mail carried on a captured ship was useful evidence in determining if the Confederacy was either the origin or intended destination. Accordingly, letters were often introduced into evidence at the prize court. Surviving prize court covers can be identified by the manuscript evidence dockets on them, typically in magenta ink. These markings are known from the New York and Philadelphia Prize Courts. The New York Prize Court commissioner was Henry H. Elliot, who marked evidence with the initials "HHE." The Philadelphia Prize Court commissioner was Henry Flanders, who marked evidence with the initials "HF."

Envelope sent from Pendleton, S.C. with PAID 5 that was introduced into evidence with the manuscript magenta docket "HHE" and case number "E 8"

Prize Court Mail

PC-01	Manuscript docketing "HHE"	3,500.
PC-02	Manuscript docketing "HF"	3,500.

Additional information on blockade run mail can be found in *Special Mail Routes of the American Civil War: A Guide to Across-the-Lines Postal History* by Steven C. Walske and Scott R. Trepel.

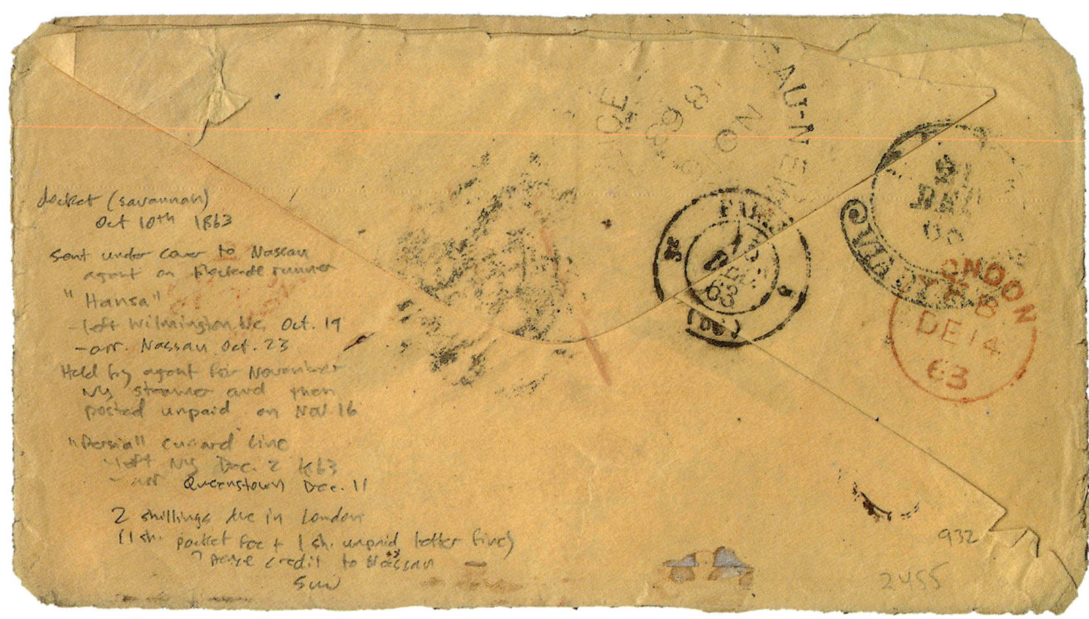

Letter sent from Savannah, Georgia to Rome, Italy via Charleston in care of two forwarders in Nassau, Bahamas and Queenstown, Ireland.

Covert Mail

Covert mail was that mail carried by individuals who slipped through enemy lines and placed letters in the postal system of the opposite side. In some cases, this was done covertly. In other cases, the mail was subject to examination by officials or self-appointed committees on the receiving side.

Three border regions which offered good opportunities for covert mail routes were:

1. The inland waterway consisting of Lake Ponchartrain and the Mississippi Sound between New Orleans and Mobile along the coasts of Louisiana, Mississippi and Alabama.
2. The upper Potomac River between Maryland and Northern Virginia.
3. The inland waterway consisting of the Chesapeake Bay and lower Potomac River between Maryland and Eastern Virginia.

Additionally, individuals occasionally received passes to cross the lines, and carried bootleg letters in their personal effects. Since these were also mailed on the opposite side, they are identified only by letter contents or by endorsements. These letters do not bear censor markings.

By their nature, most covert letters do not bear identifiable markings and entered the mails only after they crossed the lines. As such they have the same appearance as ordinary letters which originated at the place of mailing, and can be identified only by letter contents, endorsements, or censor markings. This section addresses only those covert mail operations from which mail is known.

Louisiana Relief Committee Mail

A pair of 5¢ blue lithographs tied on cover by a Mobile, Alabama double circle cancel bears the unmistakable "(La. Com.)" endorsement of the Louisiana Relief Committee.

On May 31, 1863 a group of expatriate New Orleans citizens in Mobile, Alabama organized a committee to alleviate the suffering of citizens who remained in occupied New Orleans. They arranged shipments of food and clothing to New Orleans and helped citizens leave New Orleans for the Confederacy. Included in the shipments were smuggled letters. Incoming letters from New Orleans were examined by the Provost Marshal at Mobile. The Union also used these trips to transmit prisoner of war mail to and from prisoners in New Orleans.

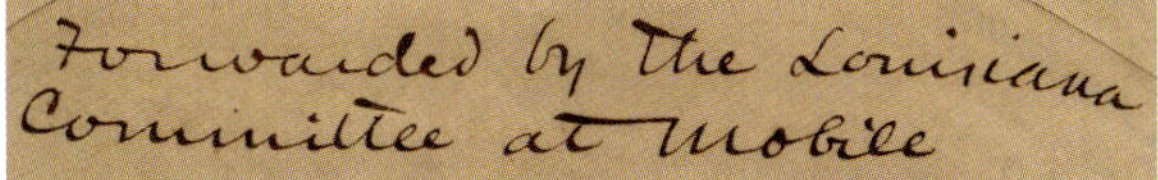

Louisiana Relief Committee endorsement to Mobile

Mail from New Orleans to the Confederacy is easily identified by the Louisiana Relief Committee manuscript endorsements. The most common endorsement is "Forwarded by the Louisiana Committee at Mobile", but other variants include "(La. Com.)" and "Mailed by La Relief Committee at Mobile."

Provost Marshal Jules Denis censored all incoming Relief Committee mail until he was replaced on June 24, 1864 by Colonel Thomas H. Taylor. No censor markings by Taylor are known. The Committee may have carried mail from Mobile to New Orleans, but none has been identified.

Southbound mail from New Orleans via Mobile and the "Louisiana Relief Committee"

Confederate franking and Louisiana Relief Committee endorsement 4,500.

Note: Covers franked with scarce general issue stamps or unusual uses command higher prices.

Other Mississippi Sound Mail Services

In addition to the well-known "Louisiana Relief Committee" mail, other clandestine services used the Mississippi Sound to carry mail. Because of their covert nature, little is known about who operated these, but a few surviving covers are evidence such operations did exist.

US Naval forces captured Ship Island in September 1861. After the capture of Ship Island and prior to the capture of New Orleans in April 1862, mail was smuggled from there to Ship Island for entry into the US mail.

Northbound Mississippi Sound Mail

Confederate New Orleans via Union controlled Ship Island, Mississippi 2,500.

J. B. Dutton Mail

Confederate raiders under the command of Major John Mosby terrorized the upper Potomac River area from January to June 1864. In response, the Union closed the river crossings from January 1864 to the end of the war. In the midst of this instability, J. B. Dutton established a private mail system between Waterford, Virginia and Point of Rocks, Maryland with the apparent tacit approval of the US provost marshal at the river crossing.

Virtually all of the recorded Dutton Mail covers were used from January 1864 to January 1865. Southbound mail was received by Dutton at Point of Rocks through the US mails. It was then hand carried across the Potomac River to the addressee in Virginia. This type of mail is identified by a straightline "J. B. DUTTON" handstamp, or by manuscript forwarded routing notations to Dutton or Point of Rocks. Northbound mail was apparently hand carried to Point of Rocks where it was placed in the US mails.

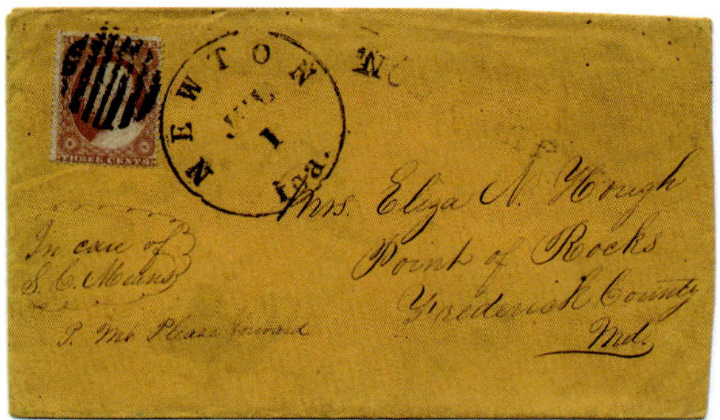

Letter from Newton, Iowa to Mrs. Eliza N. Hough at Point of Rocks, Maryland with inverted straightline cancel of J. B. Dutton. Note the manuscript endorsement "P. M. Please forward" (to Virginia where Mrs. Hough lived) at lower left.

"J. B. DUTTON." straightline marking

Southbound Dutton Mail

CM-1	US franking with "J.B. DUTTON." straightline marking	1,500.
	a. Same, with censor marking	2,000.
	b. Same, from Union Prison	2,000.
CM-2	US franking with manuscript endorsement to Dutton or Point of Rocks	1,000.

Only recorded Northbound Dutton Mail. Manuscript docketing "J. B. Dutton / Please forward."

Northbound Dutton Mail

CM-3	US franking from Point of Rocks, Md. with endorsement to Dutton	2,000.

Chesapeake Bay Mail

The Chesapeake Bay and Potomac River form a natural boundary between Virginia and Maryland. This boundary was patrolled by Union gunboats, but there were many opportunities for the clandestine exchange of mail between the North and South. In particular, Confederate sympathizers in Baltimore used this route to communicate with Richmond. There is significant evidence that an organized covert mail was operated along this route although few covers carried on this route have been identified.

This type of mail was posted in the receiving country's postal system after being smuggled, and can only be identified by contents, endorsements or docketing.

Chesapeake Bay Covert Mail

CM-4	Southbound via Baltimore and Richmond	1,000.
CM-5	Northbound via Richmond and Baltimore	1,000.

Mail Hand Carried Clandestinely Across the Lines

Some individuals covertly crossed the lines while others received passes to cross the lines. A few of these individuals smuggled letters and mailed them after they had crossed the lines.

These letters can only be identified by letter contents, endorsements or docketing.

Clandestine Across the Lines Mail

CM-6	Southbound cover	1,000.
CM-7	Northbound cover	1,000.

Glossary and Abbreviations

Across the Lines Mail – Mail carried across a border that separated the Confederate States from the United States. Across the lines mail also refers to mail that crossed the lines between the two military forces.

A&D – Archer & Daly.

Adhesive – A stamp. Also, substance applied to the back of stamps to facilitate attaching the stamps to letters. See also, Stamp; Gum.

Adversity Cover – An envelope fashioned from the backs of ledger sheets, printed circulars, fly-leafs in books, maps, rolls of wallpaper, or any other previously used piece of paper.

Advertised Cover – Cover that was not picked up by the addressee and which was included in a list of unclaimed letters advertised in a newspaper. Such covers are normally marked "advertised."

Advertising Cover – Envelope used as a form of advertising. These include embossed corner cards, fancy return address corner cards, illustrations of buildings or products, and all-over advertisements.

All Over Design – A design on an advertising cover, patriotic cover or college cover that fills the entire envelope front.

Altered Plate – A printing plate on which the value was deliberately altered. Commonly used to refer to the 2¢ and 10¢ De La Rue denominations created by altering the 1¢ and 5¢ dies; never put into use.

Archer & Daly – Engraver and printer of several general issue stamps.

Army Field Post Office – Temporary camp post offices, run by postmasters who traveled with the Confederate armies to provide postal services to the troops in the field. Army field post offices often used special postal markings on the mail they handled.

Arizona Territory – A self-proclaimed territory carved out of the New Mexico Territory that voted to secede from the United States on March 16, 1861. See also, New Mexico Territory.

Atypical Cancel – A cancel or postmark that is unlike normal canceling devices. Many comprise unusual designs generally pictorial or geometric in nature. Commonly referred to as a fancy cancel.

Authentication – See Expertizing.

Auxiliary Marking – Postal marking applied to covers to indicate that they received some special treatment or service. Markings include "Advertised," "Forwarded," "Way", etc.

Bagged Mail – Mail transported in locked mail bags carried by mail contractors or in the custody of route agents aboard trains or vessels having a contract to carry the mail.

Bisect – Stamp cut into two parts—vertically, horizontally or diagonally—with each half intended to pay all or part of the postage equal to one half the face value of the original stamp.

Blockade Cover / Mail – Mail that was successfully carried through the federal blockade, either incoming or outgoing.

Block – Four or more unsevered stamps in the form of a block versus a strip. See also, Multiple; Strip.

Bogus – Fabrication of a stamp, cancel, marking or other item of a design that never existed.

Burnish – Process of removing an unwanted entry from an engraved printing plate.

C – Circle.

Cameo – A printed design on an envelope in which the background is in color and the primary image and lettering are colorless.

Cancel – Postal marking applied to stamps to deface them and prevent reuse.

Carrier – See also, Carrier Service; Mail Carrier; Private Carrier.

Carrier Service – Mail pickup or delivery by representatives of a post office to and from the post office and businesses, residences and collection boxes. No official carrier service was operated by the Confederate Post Office Department.

CDS – Circular Date Stamp.

Changeling – Stamp on which the original color has changed as the result of a chemical reaction.

Chilled Plate – Stamp printed from an overly cool plate resulting in a lack of printing definition.

Cinderella – See Bogus.

Circular Date Stamp – Circular postmark which identifies the city, state, and normally the date of mailing.

Circular Rate – Postal rate for the transmittal of printed circulars and other printed matter. See also, Printed Matter.

Civilian Flag of Truce Mail – Flag of truce mail sent by a civilian rather than by a prisoner of war. See also, Flag of Truce Mail; Prisoner of War Mail.

College Cover – Cover imprinted with the name and generally the town of an educational institution. Imprints are usually in the form of a corner card or illustration of the institution. See also, Advertising Covers.

Combination Use – See Mixed Franking.

Confederate State Use of US Postage – Letters that entered the US mail in a state after it joined the Confederacy but prior to the assumption of postal operations by the Confederate Post Office Department.

Conjunctive Use – Combination of a postmasters' provisional stamp or envelope, used with a general issue stamp, handstamped paid or handstamped due marking to pay the required postage. See also, Mixed Franking.

Contract Vessel – A steam vessel having a contract with the Post Office Department to carry mail.

Control Mark – Handstamped marking placed on postmasters' provisional envelopes as a security measure to facilitate identification and to prevent counterfeiting. See also, Handstamped Provisional.

Corner Card – See Advertising Cover.

Counterfeit – A non-genuine specimen which mimics the genuine specimen, but was intended to be used by the counterfeiter as a substitution for the genuine specimen during the period of time when the genuine specimen was in legitimate use. No specimens are known to have been created in order to defraud the Confederate Post Office Department. See also, Facsimile; Fake; Forgery.

Cover – Postally used envelope, wrapper or folded letter sheet. See also, Entire; Envelope.

Covert Mail – Mail secretly transmitted to or from the Confederacy. Some Covert Mail was sanctioned by government agents but most was transmitted secretly without the knowledge of the government.

Cracked Plate – Printing plate that has a crack which shows on the printed stamps as a colored line.

Cross Border Mail – Mail, other than blockade mail, carried between the Confederacy and another country sharing a border with the Confederacy. The phrase is used in conjunction with mail to or from Mexico, Canada and the Maritime Provinces. See also, Across the Lines Mail; Through the Lines Mail.

CS – Confederate States.

CSA – Confederate States of America.

Date of Admission – Date on which a state was formally admitted as a member of the Confederate States of America.

Date of Secession – Date on which secession for a state was approved either in fact (*de facto*) without full compliance with all requirements of applicable law or was achieved strictly in compliance with the state's law (*de jure*). See also, *de facto*; *de jure*.

DC – Double Circle.

Dead Letter Office – Section or department of the US or Confederate Post Office Departments that received and processed undeliverable or prohibited mail.

de facto – Condition of secession in which not all of the legal preconditions to secession were fulfilled, but all of the relevant parties *acted as if* such conditions were met and secession was, therefore, accepted as achieved.

de jure – Condition of secession in which all of the material legal pre-conditions of secession were fulfilled.

De La Rue & Co. – British engraving and printing company located in London, England, which prepared the plates and printed CSA 6 and 14.

Delisted – Listing in a catalog that is consciously omitted from subsequent editions of that catalog. See also, Unlisted.

Demonetization – Process by the United States Post Office Department of declaring certain United States postage stamps and postal stationary envelopes worthless and invalid for postage.

Denomination – Face value of a stamp, representing the prepaid fee for services to be rendered by the Post Office Department.

Die – Original engraving of a stamp design on a lithographic stone or metal. The master die is replicated by various processes to prepare printing plates.

Die Proof – Printed impression made directly from the original or master die. See also, Plate Proof; Trial Color Proof.

DLC – Double [outer] Line Circle.

DLO – Dead Letter Office.

Docketing – Contemporary manuscript notation written on a cover by the recipient or someone acting on behalf of the recipient recording the receipt of the cover. Usually, docketing shows the date the cover was received or the date of the contents. Sometimes docketing also shows the name of the sender, the date the letter was answered or a summary of the contents.

Double Circle – A circular date stamp consisting of two concentric circles.

Double Impression – Stamp with one impression overlapping another resulting from a printing sheet being run through the press twice.

Double [outer] Line Circle – A circular date stamp with the rim comprised of two closely spaced concentric circles.

Double Transfer – Designates a doubling or duplication in some part of the design on an engraved stamp. Also called a re-entry.

Drop Letter – Letter deposited in a post office for delivery at the same office. See also, Overpaid Drop Letter.

Earliest Known Use – See Earliest Recorded Use.

Earliest Recorded Use – Earliest recorded date on which a stamp or envelope was used. Also referred to as earliest known use, earliest documented use or earliest reported use.

Electrotype – A process by which a design or group of designs is replicated by electroplating the mold of a relief engraving or typeset form.

Endorsement – Manuscript routing preference placed on a cover by the sender or a forwarder before or during transit.

Engraver – Skilled craftsperson who engraves a design.

Engraving – The process in which the design of a stamp is engraved or scratched in a lithographic stone or engraved in metal or wood. See also, Intaglio Printing.

Entire – Complete cover or envelope. See Cover; Envelope.

Envelope – Flat covering of paper used to enclose a letter, generally sealed with gum on the back flap. See also, Cover; Entire.

Essay – Official trial design for a proposed stamp which always differs from the stamp as issued.

Examined Marking – Handstamp or manuscript markings placed on a flag of truce cover to indicate it was censored. See also, Flag of Truce Mail; Prisoner of War Mail.

Expertizing – Process by which an authentication service renders an opinion on the genuineness of a stamp or cover.

Express Mail – Mail given special or expedited treatment by the Post Office Department in return for the payment of higher than normal postage. Also used to indicate mail carried by private mail carriers within the Confederacy. See also, Private Express Mail; Trans-Mississippi Express Mail.

Facsimile – Likeness or imitation of a genuine stamp sometimes marked to denote it is an imitation.

Fake – A likeness of an existing stamp, cancel, marking or other item made to defraud collectors.

Fancy Cancel – See Atypical Cancel.

Fantasy – A fabricated stamp, cancel, marking or other item of a design that never existed.

FL – Folded Letter.

Flag Design – A design on a patriotic cover showing a Confederate or state flag.

Flag of Truce Mail – Mail exchanged under a flag of truce between Confederate and Union military officials.

Folded Letter – Sheet of paper with a message written on one side, and folded in such a way that the name and address of the recipient could be written on the exposed blank side of the paper.

Forgery – A likeness of an existing stamp, cancel, marking or other item made to defraud collectors.

Forwarded Mail – A missent letter forwarded to the correct post office without additional postage charge. Also letters addressed to military members when they were officially ordered to a new location. See also, Missent Mail; Redirected Mail.

Franking – Mark or marking on a cover indicating that postage was paid or that the cover is entitled to be carried free of postage. A cover also is said to be franked if it bears a stamp.

Frame – Outer portion of a stamp design, which encloses the central portion (vignette) of the design. See also, Vignette.

Frame Line – A stamp with a single line frame around the design. Commonly used to refer to general issue stamp CSA 10.

Free Frank – Manuscript or handstamp marking on a letter indicating it was sent on official business of the Post Office Department and did not require the payment of postage.

Gauge – Measurement used to describe the number of separations in 2 mm. See also, Official Perforations; Perforations; Roulette; Separation.

General Issue Stamps – Stamps officially issued by the Confederate Post Office Department.

Grid – Cancellation or killer pattern composed of parallel lines. See also, Killer.

Guide Dots – Small dots used to facilitate the correct spacing and laying down of the transfer impressions on the plate.

Guide lines – Horizontal and vertical lines that extend wholly or partially across a plate to facilitate the correct spacing of the transfer die impressions on the plate.

Gum – Adhesive substance applied to the back of stamps to facilitate attaching them to a cover by moistening the adhesive substance.

Gutter – Space between one plate unit and the next in a pane or sheet. The term is generally applied to the wide space between panes.

H&L – Hoyer & Ludwig.

Handstamp Device – Hand-held device that is struck on an ink pad and then pressed on paper creating a postmark, cancel, or other making.

Handstamped Paid – One or more handstamps on a cover or wrapper indicating payment of postage. See also, Stampless Covers.

Handstamped Provisional – Envelope that was prepared in advance of sale by handstamping the rate and normally a control marking. See also, Control Marking.

Hoyer & Ludwig – Engraver and printer of several General Issue Stamps.

hsp – Handstamp.

Imperforate – Stamps with no means of separation other than cutting or tearing them apart. See also, Perforation; Roulette; Separation.

Imprint – A marginal inscription on a general issue or postmasters' provisional stamp. See also, Plate Imprint.

Imprinted Covers – Envelopes printed with the inscription of Confederate and individual state government departments for official business. See also, Official Imprints; Semi-Official Imprints; State Imprints.

Independent State Use of US Postage – Letters that entered the US mail while a state was an independent state. See Independent State Period.

Independent State Period – The period beginning on the date a state seceded from the United States through the day before the state was admitted to the Confederacy.

Indian Territory – Region west of the Mississippi River loosely organized around the Five Civilized Nations of Native Americans—the Cherokees, Choctaws, Chickasaws, Creeks, and Seminoles—which owned all the land in common.

Inland Waterway Mail – Mail carried by a vessel from a river landing or post office along an inland waterway to another post office along the vessel's route. See also, Name-of-Boat Marking; Packet; Steamboat.

Intaglio Printing – Printing from a plate where that portion of the design that will appear in color is recessed in the plate. Process used to print Confederate stamps beginning in 1863.

J. T. Paterson – See Paterson, J. T.

K&B – Keatinge & Ball.

Keatinge & Ball – Engraver and printer of several general issue stamps.

Killer – A handstamp device that makes re-use of a stamp impossible by defacing the stamp with printer's ink. See also, Cancel; Grid; Target.

Kiss prints – Partial duplication of a stamp design on a sheet caused when a sheet accidentally contacts the inked plate before or after printing the stamps.

Laid Paper – Paper which has horizontal and vertical narrow lines running through it. See also, Wove Paper.

Letter Carrier – Person who delivered mail between the post office, businesses, residences and collection boxes in Charleston and New Orleans.

Letter Press – See Typography.

Lithography – Printing from a stone plate. Process used to print the early general issues.

London Paper – Paper received by the Confederate Post Office Department from De La Rue & Co. and used to print general issue CSA 7-L in Richmond. See also, Richmond Print.

Loose Letter – A letter picked up by a vessel or train between post offices to be handed over to the postmaster at the next post office.

Louisiana Relief Committee at Mobile – Organization of citizens at Mobile, Alabama which fed and clothed refugees from New Orleans after they were expelled from the occupied city. The Louisiana Relief Committee at Mobile also smuggled mail to and from New Orleans after the Union occupation of the city.

Mail Carrier – An individual under contract who carried mail between post offices over post routes.

Mail Packet – Vessel having a contract with the Post Office Department to carry mail. See also, Packet.

Manuscript Cancel – A pen or pencil cancellation on a stamp or cover.

Margin Imprint – The printers' imprint in the margin of the printing plate. See also, Plate Imprint.

Master Die – The original die prepared by the engraver. See, Die.

Mint – A stamp in the same condition as it was sold at a post office. The original gum must be intact. See also, Original Gum.

Misplaced Transfer – Stamp image on a printing stone in a specific position that differs from the image in the same position on the transfer stone.

Missent Mail – Mail erroneously sent to the wrong post office that was forwarded to the correct post office without a further charge for postage. See also, Forwarded Mail; Redirected Mail.

Mixed Franking – Cover bearing two different stamp issues.

Money Letter – A letter marked with the amount of money it contains. This term is normally associated with letters carried by private express companies.

Mourning Cover – An envelope with a black border that signified mourning the death of a loved one.

ms – Manuscript.

Multiple – Two or more unseparated stamps. See also, Block; Pair; Strip.

Name-of-Boat Marking – Handstamped or manuscript marking containing the name of the boat, and sometimes the name of its captain or purser, applied to loose letters by the purser or captain of a vessel.

Nesbitt Envelopes – Series of postal stationery envelopes manufactured from 1853—1861 by the George F. Nesbitt & Company under contract with the United States Post Office.

Non-Contract Vessel – A vessel without a contract to carry mail but which was permitted to pick up loose letters along its route. See also, Inland Waterway Mail.

Official Imprints – Envelopes bearing imprints of the agencies, bureaus, and offices of the Confederate Post Office Department that were authorized to send official mail free of postage.

Official Perforations – Perforations applied on certain general issues on an experimental basis by the Confederate Post Office Department. See also, Gauge; Perforation; Separation.

Offset – Reversed impression on the back of a stamp resulting from the back of one sheet coming in contact with a still "wet" sheet during the printing process.

OG – Original Gum.

Original Gum – Gum on a stamp as issued by the Post Office Department. See also, Gum.

Overheated Plate – Stamp printed from overheated printing plate resulting in filled in designs.

Overpaid Drop Letter – Convenience overpayment of postage on a drop letter. See also, Drop Letter.

Packet – Term or phrase generally applied to vessels that maintained regular, published schedules over defined routes. The term does not imply the vessel had a mail contract. See also, Inland Waterway Mail; Mail Packet; Steamboat.

PAID – Marking applied to a cover to indicate that the sender had paid the postage.

Pair – Two unseparated adjacent Stamps. See also, Multiples.

Pane – A pane is the part of the printed sheet of stamps that is issued for sale at a post office. A pane may be an entire sheet, half or a quarter of an entire sheet depending on the size of the printing stone or plate. The most common arrangement for general issue stamps was two panes of 100 stamps each to make up the sheet.

Paper – See Laid Paper; Pelure Paper; Wove Paper.

Parole Camp – A camp, normally in a prisoner's home country, where paroled prisoners were held pending official exchange under the protocols for prisoner exchange.

Paterson, J. T. – Engraver and printer of some of the General Issue Stamps.

Patriotic Cover – Envelope bearing printed expression of patriotism in the form of flags, cannons, leaders, soldiers, and other wartime themes. See also, Patriotic Lettersheet.

Patriotic Lettersheet – Writing stationery bearing expressions of patriotism, often matching patriotic envelope designs and sold as sets. See also, Patriotic Covers.

Pen Cancel – See Manuscript Cancel.

Pelure Paper – A thin, hard, semi-transparent paper that is usually bluish or grayish in color.

Perforation – A series of holes (usually round) punched in the margins between stamps to facilitate separation from adjacent stamps. The resulting number of holes in two centimeters is called the "gauge" of that perforation. See also, Roulette; Separation.

pk – Postmark.

pl – Plate.

PL&R – Postal Laws & Regulations.

Plate – Removable part of a printing press from which stamps are printed. See also, Printing Plate.

Plate Imprint – Lettering in the sheet margin which normally contains the name and city of the printer of the stamps. A serial number assigned to the plate may also be present with or without other inscription.

Plate Proof – Trial printing, known as a strike, taken from a new printing plate for inspection purposes. This can be used to inspect for defects or to determine the best color for a stamp. See also, Die Proof; Proof; Trial Color Proof.

Plate Variety – Defect on a printing plate that is visible on a printed stamp from the same position. This is a constant variety appearing on every stamp after the plate received the defect.

Plating – Reconstructing a pane of stamps by determining the position of every stamp in the pane by its unique minor variations from the other stamps.

pmk – Postmark.

POD – Post Office Department.

pos – Position.

Position – The location of an individual stamp on a printing plate. See also, Plating.

Post Office Department – The department of the Confederate or US Government responsible for operation of the postal system.

Post Road – Route designated by Congress as an official route for the carriage of mail.

Post Route – The route over which mail is carried by contracted mail carriers from post office to post office.

Postage Due – Postage required to be paid by the recipient of mail for unpaid or underpaid postal charges.

Postal Laws and Regulations – Compilation of statutes and postal regulations that governed the operation of the US Post Office Department. The Confederate Post Office Department operated under the 1859 US PL&R to the extent that they did not conflict with any law passed by the Confederate Congress.

Postal Stationery – Envelope produced or prepared and sold by a local postmaster with the rate printed, handstamped or written in manuscript. Also, US government-issued envelopes bearing imprinted stamps. See also, Entire; Envelope; Nesbitt Envelopes; Star Die Envelopes.

Postmark – See Cancel; CDS.

Postmasters' Provisional – Locally prepared stamps and envelopes printed, handstamped or marked in manuscript with a value valid for postage. These were prepared in advance and sold by the postmaster for local use as postage stamps and postal stationery.

POW – Prisoner of War.

Preferred Mail – Special mail service authorized by an Act approved April 16, 1863 to carry letters and dispatches across the Mississippi River at the rate of 50¢ per half ounce. This service was never implemented.

Printed Matter – Printed handbills, circulars and pamphlets sent through the mail in unsealed envelopes or wrappers. Non-subscriber newspapers were also included in this class of mail.

Printed on Both Sides – A stamp with the same design printed all, or in part, on both sides.

Printing Plate – A plate used to print a sheet of stamps.

Printing Stone – A stone plate used to print a sheet of stamps by the lithographic process.

Printing Variety – Flaw in a stamp design, often caused by a transient bit of matter on the printing plate, which has not been identified as a constant plate variety. See also, Plate Variety.

Prisoner of War Mail – Mail to and from prisoners of war. See also, Examined Marking; Flag of Truce Mail; Provost Marshal.

Private Carrier – Non-government letter or mail carrier. Term often applied to individuals who operated Trans-Mississippi and covert mail services. See also, Letter Carrier; Mail Carrier; Covert Mail; Private Express Mail.

Private Express Mail – Mail carried by private express companies.

Private Separation – Any method of separation applied to stamps by private individuals. See also, Roulette.

Prize Court – A court having jurisdiction to determine if a merchant vessel or warship was lawfully seized in time of war. A prize court could authorize the destruction or sale of a lawfully captured ship and its cargo. In the latter event, the court also would order the distribution of proceeds to the crew of the seizing ship. See also, Prize Court Covers.

Prize Court Covers – Covers captured as part of the seizure of a ship as a lawful prize of war. Such covers were marked to indicate they were part of the inventory of a captured vessel and were used as evidence of the vessel's place of origin or destination.

Proof – Impression of a stamp printed directly from the die, plate or stone in advance of production, often in colors different than that of the production stamp. See also, Die Proof; Plate Proof; Trial Color Proof.

Provenance – Documented ownership history of an item.

Provisional Stamp – See Postmasters' Provisionals.

Provost Marshal – Officer that performed policing duties such as arrests, custody of prisoners, and examination of flag of truce mail. There were two types of provost marshals: those in military units and those assigned to a geographic district.

Railroad Cover – A letter handed to route agent or an employee of the railroad aboard a train for transmittal through the mail. See also, Loose Letters.

Railroad Marking – See Railroad Cover; Route Agent; Route Agent's Marking.

Redirected Mail – Mail forwarded by a post office at the request of the addressee. Redirected mail required payment of the postage to the new destination. Redirected Mail should not be confused with Missent Mail which did not require additional postage. See also, Forwarded Mail; Missent Mail.

Re-engraved – An alteration to a master die.

Re-entry – In intaglio printing the process re-entering the design of one or more stamps on the printing plate.

Relief Printing – See Typography.

Reprint – Stamp reprinted from the original printing plate or stone after the stamp is no longer valid for postage.

Ribbed Paper – Paper which was passed through ridged rollers giving it a ribbed effect.

Richmond Print – A stamp printed by Archer & Daly in Richmond from the 5¢ plates prepared by De La Rue & Co. (CSA 7-R).

Roulette – A piercing or slitting of the margins between stamps, without the removal of any paper, to facilitate their separation. See also, Sawtooth Roulette; Separation.

Route Agent – Employee of the Post Office Department who traveled with the mail aboard vessels or on railroads having contracts to carry the mail.

Route Agent's Marking – The handstamp or manuscript marking applied to letters received by a route agent for transmittal in the mail. Many route agent's markings look like postmarks but are different in that they include one or more terminals along the route agent's route rather than the name of the post office where the letter entered the mail.

Sawtooth Roulette – Roulettes that have the appearance of the teeth of a saw. See also, Roulette.

SC – Segmented Circle.

Scratched Plate – A scratch on a printing plate or stone that results in a plate variety on one or more stamps..

Secession – Process under which certain southern states attempted to withdraw from their compact with the United States. These states considered themselves to be independent states.

Segmented Circle – A marking in which the circle is broken by colorless gaps.

Se-tenant – Stamps that adjoin one another, but which have different designs or values.

Semi-Official Imprints – Imprinted envelopes prepared by Confederate and state governments for various departments. Semi-official envelopes required the prepayment of postage when placed in the mail. See also, State Imprints.

Separations – Perforations or roulettes applied to stamps to facilitate their separation. See also, Official Perforations; Perforation; Private Separation; Roulette.

SFL – Stampless folded letter.

Sheet – The complete impression from a printing plate or stone. See also, Panes.

Shift – Some part of the design of a stamp that is misaligned.

Shifted Transfer – A lithographic print showing a doubling or shifting of some lines.

Ship Mail – Loose letters, sometimes referred to as Ship Letters, given to the captain or purser of a vessel not having a contract to carry the mail. The term did not refer to the type of the vessel that carried the letter. See also, Post Roads; Steamboat Mail.

Short Transfer – The colorless portion of a printed stamp design caused by an incomplete impression of the design on the plate.

SL – Straightline.

Smuggled Mail – See Covert Mail.

Soldier's Mail – A category of mail created for members of the Confederate military that allowed them to send letters unpaid provided they were endorsed with the letter writer's name, rank and unit. Postage was to be collected from the recipient on delivery.

Soldier's Due Mail – See Soldier's Mail.

Soldier's Letter – See Soldier's Mail.

Southern Letter Unpaid – A marking applied to mail received at the Louisville, Kentucky post office from the Southern States as evidenced by affixed demonetized stamps. This marking was used from late June to mid July 1861.

Special Agent – An employee of the Post Office Department charged with inspecting and monitoring all aspects of postal operations and executing special tasks assigned by the Postmaster General.

Stamp Money – Small denomination currency issued by local postmasters and redeemable for postage at the issuing post office.

Stampless Covers – Folded letters and envelopes which have the postage paid or due indicated by handstamped or manuscript markings.

Stampless Folded Letter – See Folded Letter; Stampless Covers.

Star Die Envelopes – Series of postal stationary envelopes first manufactured in late 1860 by the George F. Nesbitt & Company under contract with the United States Post Office Department. The indicia on the envelopes have a small star in both sides of the oval design.

State Imprints – Envelopes prepared by various branches or departments of state governments showing imprints identifying those branches or departments. See also, Semi-Official Imprints.

Station Agent – An employee of a railroad company at a station. Some station agents were also employed as Route Agents. See also, Route Agent.

Steamboat – Steam powered vessel not having a contract to carry the mails, and which plied waters declared to be post roads. See also, Inland Waterway Post Roads.

Steamboat Mail – Generally used to refer to mail carried on a steamboat. Technically prepaid loose letters carried aboard a non-contract vessel. See also, Ship Mail; Inland Waterway; Post Roads.

Steamboat Marking – Notation placed on loose letters carried aboard steamboats. See also, Name-of-Boat Marking.

Stone – See Printing Stone; Transfer Stone.

Straightline Town Postmark – a postmark in the form of a straight line.

Strike – Postal marking, cancel, or auxiliary marking made on a cover by a handstamp device.

Strip – Three or more unseparated stamps joined vertically or horizontally in a row.

Target – Cancellation consisting of concentric circles.

T-E-N – Common manner of referring to general issue CSA 9.

Tête-bêche – Condition created in plate production or printing, in which one stamp is inverted in relation to the adjacent stamp.

Through the Lines Mail – Mail permitted to cross the lines from north to south or south to north under official sanction. The term includes flag of truce mail (both prisoner and civilian) and some covert mail. See also, Across the Lines Mail; Covert Mail; Flag of Truce Mail; Prisoner of War Mail.

Tied – Condition in which some part of a cancellation overlaps the stamp and the adjacent part of the cover to which it is affixed.

Transfer – Process by which a single image is transferred to a printing stone or printing plate. See also, Misplaced Transfer; Shifted Transfer.

Transfer Stone – Lithographic stone on which multiple images are laid down for transfer to the printing stone. See also, Lithography; Misplaced Transfer; Printing Stone; Transfer.

Trans-Mississippi Express Mail – A special mail service for mail directed across the Mississippi River via prescribed terminal post offices. This special class of mail required prepayment of a higher rate of postage than regular mail.

Transient Printing Variety – Printing variety that is not constant because it was caused by a temporary condition involving the printing plate or ink.

Trial Color Proof – Die proof or plate proof printed in a preproduction test to determine the production color of the stamp. See also, Die Proof; Plate Proof.

Turned Cover – Postally used envelope that was turned inside out and used again. See also, Adversity Cover.

Typeset – Stamps printed from moveable type fonts and designs used by printers.

Typograph(s) – CSA 6, 7 and 14 printed from plates manufactured by De La Rue & Co.

Typography – Printing from a plate where that portion of the design that will appear in color is raised above the rest of the design. Process used to print stamps from the De La Rue plates.

Unissued Stamp – Stamp officially prepared for postal use, but never issued, *e.g.*, CSA 14.

Unlisted – Stamp or other philatelic item not recorded by a catalog publisher or, if previously recorded, consciously not listed in the current edition of the catalog. See also, Delisted.

Unpaid Letter – A letter on which the postage was not prepaid.

Unused – Stamp that does not show any evidence of being used on a letter carried in the mail. See also, Mint; Original Gum.

Variety – A flaw or deviation from the normal design of a stamp. A variety can be in the form of a color variation or a flaw in the design. See also, Plate Variety; Printing Variety; Transient Printing Variety.

Verses – Printed lines of poetry sometimes found on patriotic covers. See Patriotic Cover.

Vignette – Central feature or design of a stamp, as distinct from the frame or framework.

Wallpaper Cover – Envelope fashioned from spare rolls of wallpaper. See also, Adversity Cover.

Watermark – Pattern or design impressed in paper during the manufacturing process.

Way Letter – Loose letter received along a mail route and turned in at the next post office on the route where it was marked "Way."

Way Marking – The word "Way" applied to a way letter by the clerk of a post office. See Way Letter.

Wove Paper – Paper used in the production of stamps which has no discernable pattern. See also, Laid Paper; Pelure Paper.

Wrapper – Sheet of paper used to wrap around a newspaper or other periodical to facilitate transmission through the mail. The wrapper contained the address and was sometimes postmarked.